IN RUSSIA

Islam
IN RUSSIA
THE POLITICS OF IDENTITY AND SECURITY

Foreword by Ambassador James F. Collins

SHIREEN T. HUNTER

The Center for Strategic and International Studies

with JEFFREY L. THOMAS and ALEXANDER MELIKISHVILI

M.E.Sharpe
Armonk, New York
London, England

Library of Congress Cataloging-in-Publication Data

Hunter, Shireen.
  Islam in Russia : the politics of identity and security / by Shireen
T. Hunter ; with Jeffrey L. Thomas and Alexander Melikishvili.
    p. cm.
  Includes bibliographical references and index.
  ISBN 0-7656-1282-8 (alk. paper) ; ISBN 0-7656-1283-6 (pbk. : alk. paper
  1. Islam—Russia (Federation) 2. Muslims—Russia (Federation) 3. Islam and politics—
Russia (Federation) 4. Muslims—Russia (Federation)—Political activity. 5. Russia
(Federation)—Politics and government. I. Thomas, Jeffrey L., 1964- II. Melikishvili,
Alexander. III. Title.

BP65.R8 H86 2003
947'.0088'2971—dc21   2003010364

Contents

Part II. Identity Politics in the Russian Federation: The Islamic Factor

List of Tables, Figures, and Maps

Tables

Figures

Maps

Foreword

From earliest times the Russian state, people, and culture have lived at a crossroads. Through more than a millennium of invasion and expansion, servitude and empire, Russia's people have met, confronted, absorbed, and repelled an unending stream of diverse civilizations. Each of these encounters has left its mark in shaping today's Russia and its multi-ethnic, multi-national, multi-confessional population as diverse as any in today's global society. It has also fostered and kept alive an abiding preoccupation among Russians with the question of Russian identity and just what it means to be a citizen of the Russian Federation. These questions have even greater immediacy and meaning today as Russia's diverse people wrestle with the consequences of the collapse of Soviet Communism and the subsequent search for direction and bearings in which the Russian nation finds itself engaged.

For centuries the majority of those who have addressed this matter have portrayed Russia as a land where the struggle for national and cultural identity has been between East and West. From the polemics of Slavophiles and Westernizers to today's debate over Russia's identity as European or Eurasian, the discourse has been dominated by attention to how Russia has dealt with Western influences and how relations with the Western world have shaped—or distorted—the Russian national destiny. Today that debate continues as Russia's new leaders decide whether Russia's future lies with Europe or whether Russian traditions, culture, and history set it uniquely apart and demand an alternative course.

In this debate, the role of Russia's significant Muslim minority and the place it occupies is most often nearly overlooked. Since September 11, however, events have brought the role of Islam in shaping our world to the forefront of our attention. It is, therefore, more than welcome that Dr. Shireen T. Hunter's present work directs our attention to the influence of Islamic cultures and societies over Russia's past, present, and future and offers a timely, comprehensive, thoughtful investigation of what role the people of Russia who have embraced Islam have played in molding today's Russia.

In this book, Dr. Hunter traces a long history of Islam's encounter with the society of Orthodox Russia. That history has, as Dr. Hunter challenges us to understand, remained a constant with which Russian leaders have had to deal no less than with the West, and no one can argue that events from the Mongol invasion to the Russian absorption of Central Asia to the retreat from Afghanistan have not had profound consequences for the Russian nation. Moreover, with a Muslim population today representing a substantial minority of Russia's citizens, the influences of this culture continue to have fundamental importance for the future of the Russian state.

Throughout this work Dr. Hunter provides thoughtful analysis of the way in which Russia's Muslim populations will challenge the nation's leaders to address the questions that arise from a past that has more often than not been characterized by tension between Muslim and non-Muslim Russia. She explores how the presence of this minority has significantly affected the nature of the society and political system of Russia in the past and the implications it holds for the future. She notes as well that how Russia has managed its relations with its own Muslim population has affected the relations the Russian nation has had with the Muslim world.

Religious revival has been a major feature of post Soviet Russia's transformation and Dr. Hunter calls attention to the potential strengths and weaknesses that have flowed from this development. In this connection, Dr. Hunter rightfully notes the importance of the Chechnya outcome for Russia's future. The reasons for the wars transcend simple religious struggle, but there is little doubt that underlying religious conflicts between the participants is a factor in the persistence of violence in the Northern Caucasus. And, post–September 11, it has become clear that some in the Islamic world have viewed the fight for Chechen independence as a front-line battle in a greater Islamic struggle against non-Islamic nations and peoples. Mercenaries from Afghanistan and other Islamic nations have fought alongside Chechen rebels in their belief that what was really at stake in the Northern Caucasus was a *jihad*. This reality, coupled with traditional suspicions among many Russians of Islamic-based cultures, has contributed to a condition that risks the hardening of a religious and cultural divide in Russia that can only undermine the longer term stability and civil society of a democratic Russia. Moreover, Dr. Hunter draws our attention to the fact that although fears that Chechnya violence could spread to destabilize other Islamic regions of Russia have not come to pass, religious-based differences retain the capacity to exacerbate tensions between Moscow and Russia's other Islamic regions and to complicate Russia's effort to establish a new basis for its relations with the Muslim world.

Dr. Hunter concludes her study by seeking to answer the fundamental question: whether Russia can transform itself into a pluralistic and democratic society. Many have sought to answer this question by focusing on the institutional difficulties inherent in moving from a totalitarian state to a democracy. While Muslims in Russia today enjoy more freedom than under the Soviet period, Islamic peoples and traditions, as the present work amply documents, remain at the margins of Russian political and economic life. Yet, few today can doubt that how Russia deals with its Muslim population will have the most profound ramifications not only for Russia's internal development, but also for the role Russia will be able to play internationally. Dr. Hunter's study is a remarkable addition to the broader subject of Russia's transformation. This work is path-breaking in its comprehensive discussion of an issue that deserves attention from not only scholars, but also those interested in understanding the factors that are shaping critical elements of Russia's internal and external policies. Dr. Hunter's work will become a valued resource for any student of contemporary Russia.

Ambassador James F. Collins
U.S. Ambassador to the
Russian Federation, 1997–2001

Preface

On 23 October 2002, a group of Chechen extremists, calling themselves the Riyadh as-Salihin (The Gardens of the Righteous), terrorized Moscow by holding almost 800 people hostage in the Dubrovka Theater for three days; the crisis ended on 26 October when the Russian Special Forces stormed the theater. The hostage takers represented a new and more extremist breed of those Chechen rebels who base their political ideology on Islam. However, although the political beliefs and the modus operandi of the hostage takers were different from those of the earlier generation of Chechen nationalists and Islamists, their demands were the same, namely, that Russia must withdraw its military forces from Chechnya and recognize the right of the Chechens to full self-determination.

The hostage-taking operation was the most dramatic manifestation of the problems that post-Soviet Russia has faced in its transition from a totalitarian, multiethnic empire to, it is hoped, a democratic and pluralist—albeit still multiethnic and multi-religious—society and polity. A central aspect of these problems has been the reopening of the debate about Russia's national identity and the unleashing of long-suppressed demands for self-determination, to varying degrees of intensity, on the part of non-Russian peoples, most notably the Muslims. Chechnya represents an extreme case where the drive for self-determination has led to violence and war, but more peaceful and less extreme demands for self-determination have also been widespread.

A varied and complex set of factors has been responsible for this phenomenon. Nevertheless, Islam, both as a religion and a culture, has been an important component of this complex set of factors. This is not surprising, since Islam constitutes an important part of the Russian Muslims' individual and collective identities.

The Muslims of Russia have a long history of both resisting Russian conquest, as in the case of Chechnya, and striving for self-determination and even outright independence whenever internal conditions in Russia have permitted. This was the case during the period of reform in 1905–7, on the eve of the October Revolution of 1917, and again between 1988 and 1991, at the time of Mikhail Gorbachev's reforms and the disintegration of the Soviet Union. In fact, interaction between

Russia and Islam spans nearly a millennium. This long experience has marked many aspects of the cultural and political development of both Russians and the Muslims of Russia, including their collective identities and their national and religious myths and symbols.

In the post-Soviet period, this interaction has continued and, in some respects, intensified. In particular, Islam's revival in Russia and the Muslims' drive for self-determination, coupled with their demands that Islam be recognized as an integral part of Russia's cultural and political landscape, have influenced many aspects of Russia's internal developments, from the formation of its new national identity to the shaping of its governmental and political system. These factors have also affected Russia's thinking on security and foreign policy issues and influenced the patterns of its external relations.

Since 1992, much valuable work on the status of Islam in post-Soviet Russia and its many implications for internal evolution and external relations has been done by Russian scholars, including Russian Muslims, as well as by Western scholars of Russia. However, there have not been many works that have brought together in one volume the multidimensional impact of Islam on post-Soviet Russia's internal development and on its external relations. It is hoped that this volume will help fill the gap and encourage more research on various aspects of this important issue.

This work was made possible by a generous grant from Carnegie Corporation of New York. I would therefore like to express my gratitude to the corporation for its support.

In preparing this study, I have greatly benefited from the excellent and extensive body of work produced by many generations of scholars of Russian history, politics, and society, including Russian Islam. I would like to acknowledge my deep sense of gratitude to all of them. I have especially benefited from the works of Alexandre Bennigsen, Marie Broxup, Alexei Malashenko, Wayne Allensworth, John Dunlop, and many others too numerous to list. I am also deeply grateful to all those officials, religious leaders, academics, and journalists in Moscow, Kazan, Ufa, and Rostov-on-Don who have given me the benefit of their knowledge and wisdom.

This work would not have been possible without the contributions of my two colleagues at the Center for Strategic and International Studies, Jeffrey L. Thomas and Alexander Melikishvili. Jeffrey Thomas did most of the research and writing on sections dealing with the impact of the Islamic factor on the evolution of Russia's political system, notably its federal structures. Alexander Melikishvili's help was invaluable in completion of the section dealing with the current status of Islam in Russia, especially its institutional infrastructure. I also owe a debt of gratitude to a string of young and talented interns who helped in research for the work. In particular, I would like to acknowledge the contributions of Susan Sypko, Alexander Sukin, Aziz Bakiev, Olena Nikolayenko, Koba Tsalani, and Maria Amelicheva. Notwithstanding all the help that I have received in preparing this volume, I alone am responsible for any errors of fact or judgment.

Shireen T. Hunter

Introduction

On the eve of the Soviet Union's disintegration in December 1991, the number of its Muslim citizens stood at about 50 million, just over a fifth of the total population of 280 million, making the USSR a middle-sized Muslim country.[1] The achievement of independence by the USSR's non-Russian republics in Central Asia, the South Caucasus, and the Baltic region, along with Moldova, Ukraine, and Belarus, dramatically altered the ethnic and religious landscape of the internationally recognized successor state to the Soviet Union, the Russian Federation. In the Soviet Union, ethnic Russians—excluding Belarussians and Ukrainians, who are ethnically close to Russians—constituted just over half of the population. Today, ethnic Russians are believed to constitute between 80 and 83 percent of the Russian Federation's population of 145 million.[2]

The Russian Federation is also a religiously more homogeneous country than was the Soviet Union. Because of definitional problems and the difficulties involved in the choice of criteria to determine confessional affiliation, including level of religious observance and cultural identification, it is hard to provide an accurate religious profile of Russia. Furthermore, for a variety of reasons, such as fear and expediency, people often hide their true religious beliefs and practices. Moreover, those who are not religiously observant—or even believers—may still belong culturally to a particular tradition. Thus, depending on which criteria are used, estimates of the number of followers of different religions, notably Muslims, vary widely.

The same problem, albeit to a lesser extent, arises in attempting to provide an estimate of the Russian Orthodox population. However, based on the cultural criteria that will be applied in this volume, because the level of religious observance within different communities tends to fluctuate, the Russian Federation, despite recent inroads made by various Christian sects and other less familiar religions, is an overwhelmingly Orthodox Christian country. Indeed, since the Soviet Union's disintegration, Orthodox Christianity has become a prominent feature of the Russian Federation's new social, cultural, and political landscape. This presence is reflected in the renovation of old churches, the building of new ones, and the greater political visibility of church leaders. The preamble of the 1997 Law on Freedom of Conscience and Religious Associations recognizes "the special contribution of Orthodoxy to the history of Russia and to the establishment and development of Russia's spirituality and culture." In November 2002, the Ministry of Education announced that a course in Orthodox civilization would be taught in Russian schools.[3]

All these trends indicate the reemergence of the historic symbiosis between the Russian state and the Orthodox Church. To be sure, the Orthodox Church today does not have the same influence that it did during the tsarist regime, although even then the interests of the church and the state did not always coincide.[4] Nevertheless, because the Orthodox Church is considered the depository of traditions, "people listen to it about what is right and wrong. It helps create the atmosphere within which politics are worked out."[5] Meanwhile, the view that Orthodox Christianity is one of the core components of Russian identity and nationalism has found new credence and adherents.[6]

Islam's Saliency

Despite the enhanced numerical and cultural importance of the Russian and Orthodox elements, the Russian Federation remains a multiethnic and multireligious entity.[7] This diversity is reflected in the Russian Federation's territorial and political structures. Some non-Russian peoples have their own republics with names that reflect their ethnic origin, such as Tatarstan, Bashkortostan, Ingushetia, and Chechnya. Within this diverse ethnic and religious context, Islam and Muslim peoples occupy a special place in terms of their actual and potential impact on many aspects of Russia's internal evolution, ranging from the nature of its post-Soviet national identity, the character of its nationalism, and its system of government to its worldview and the nature of its security and foreign policies.

This special significance of Islam derives from historic factors as well as from more recent developments. The large number of Muslims and the pattern of their geographical distribution within the Russian Federation, plus Islam's importance as an essential component of Russian Muslims' individual and collective identity and its significance for the social and political organization of Muslim societies, enhances its saliency. To these factors must be added the fact that Russia's neighbors to the south, both immediate and more distant, are predominantly Muslim. This reality means that Russia is vulnerable to developments within the Muslim world.

The Burden of the Past

The history of Russia's encounter with Islam spans a millennium. This long history of encounter between Russia and Islam and various Muslim peoples has significantly marked their respective collective consciousness, their national identities, and their store of national myths and symbols.

In Russia's case, this encounter has influenced many aspects of its national identity and its sense of its cultural uniqueness. It has given it a sense of mission and hence a messianic dimension to its national identity and the character of its interaction with the outside world, especially its belief that it has a right to great-power status. It has also created an image of Islam and Muslims as hostile "other" and as a source of actual or potential threat to Russia's security and even territorial integrity.

For Muslims, the encounter with Russia has performed similar tasks: It has etched an image of Russia in their collective memories as a conqueror and imperial power bent on weakening Islam and Muslims. This is especially true of those peoples who, over several centuries, were incorporated into the Russian Empire or were victims of Russia's imperial expansion. Therefore, in many Muslims' collective memory, Russia is perceived as the hostile other. This perception has helped shape the Muslims' sense of their own collective identity and their aspirations. In particular, it has endowed the Muslims' consciousness with a strong determination to retain their culture, religion, and traditions, and with a yearning for autonomy and even independence.

Meanwhile, because of its all-embracing character, Islam has contributed to the Muslims' ability not only to retain their religious and cultural traditions, but also to develop a sense of their own ethnic and national uniqueness and the worth of their own civilization. Indeed, it has been the conflation of religion and ethnonational identity among Russia's Muslims that has rescued them from total assimilation within the broader Russian culture. Similarly, it has enabled them periodically to seek to assert their identity and to strive for cultural and political autonomy whenever conditions have permitted it.

It is because of this conflation of religion and nationalism that Soviet-era authors were so concerned about the survival and, later, the revival of Islam in the Soviet Union. Writing in 1985, T.S. Saidbaev noted that among the USSR's Muslim population, a section "still considers religion and nationalism as similar and looks at religion as part of the national life. It is judged compulsory to follow the prescriptions of Islam. To reject them is disapproved as showing a lack of respect to the memory of one's ancestors, to the nation, and the national culture."[8]

Developments since the 1980s, both within Soviet/Russian Muslim communities and in relations between the Soviet Union and, later, Russia and some Muslim countries have tended to perpetuate these historically formed images and patterns of relating to one another between Russians and Muslims. The survival of Islam, despite decades of tsarist and Soviet efforts to eliminate it, followed by the revival of both Islam and ethnocentric nationalism among Russia's Muslims in the 1980s, coupled with the drive of some Muslims for autonomy and independence, revived Russia's historic fears of the potential threat posed by Islam and Muslims to its territorial and national integrity. Externally, the decade-long Soviet-Afghan War fought under the banner of Islam refreshed on both sides memories of past Russian-Muslim conflicts.

Recent Events

Developments in the last years of the Soviet Union and in the post-Soviet era, notably the continued desire of Russia's Muslims for greater cultural and political autonomy, have done little to alleviate Russia's historic fears of an actual or potential Muslim threat to its territorial and national integrity. In this context, Chechnya's drive for independence, which led to a bloody conflict, has played a critical role. In fact, the impact of the Chechen War has gone beyond merely reviving and strengthening Russia's and Muslims' old fears. Rather, it has affected many aspects of Russia's internal evolution, from the character of its national identity, its governmental system, and its attitudes toward religious and cultural issues to the direction of its external relations. The support extended by some Muslim states to the Chechen autonomists has meanwhile kept alive the perception of an external Muslim threat to Russian security and other interests. Moreover, such assistance, coupled with expanded ties between Russia's Muslims and the broader Islamic world, have led many Russians, especially those with nationalist leanings, to be concerned about what Alexei Malashenko has called "the integrationist potential of Islam, which is capable of not only rallying the Muslim states bordering on Russia, but also of mobilizing Muslims inside the Russian Federation itself."[9] These connections have also affected Russia's foreign policy perspectives and the character of its relations, not only with Muslim countries, but also with the West, China, and India.

Russian-Muslim Coexistence and Cooperation

Notwithstanding the foregoing, the history of Russian-Muslim encounter is not merely one of conflict, conquest, and resistance. Rather, relations between Russians and Muslims, both within Russia and between Russia and other Muslim countries, have also been marked by periods of coexistence, tolerance, accommodation, and even cooperation. For example, the period of Catherine the Great's reign provides an early and good example of such mutual accommodation and cooperation. Indeed, many Russians have an interpretation of their culture and history that sees Russia as a place where different peoples and cultures have lived in harmony for centuries. They also believe that many non-Russian, notably Muslim, peoples joined Russia voluntarily.[10] This may be too idealistic a view of the past, but the existence of past examples of Russian-Muslim coexistence justifies cautious optimism that this may be an achievable goal. However, in view of past and more recent experiences, success in this regard will require serious and sustained efforts on the part of the Russian government and peoples, as well as its Muslim population. Indeed, a major challenge for Russia will continue to be maintaining its territorial integrity while building a democratic society within which all peoples, religions, and cultures enjoy equal rights. A parallel challenge will be to develop a civic sense of Russian nationalism that allows for a degree of cultural plurality and a measure of autonomy for ethnic and religious minorities while ensuring that they remain loyal citizens of the Russian Federation.

To analyze the current status of Islam and Muslims in Russia, to assess the impact of the Islamic factor in the evolution of Russia's internal situation and its external relations while placing them in their proper historical context, and to identify the most likely direction in which the Russian society and polity will evolve and the position of Muslims within this evolving Russian society are the main objectives of this volume.

Conceptual Framework and Methodology

The basic conceptual framework for this study is the transformation of a multiethnic, multiconfessional, posttotalitarian, and postcolonial society. The methodology used will be historical and empirical. This case study of Islam in Russia will seek to develop concepts and ideas that could be applicable to other situations. It will thus try to answer a series of questions:

What are the dynamics of identity formation among ethnic and religious minorities within a society that is emerging from a totalitarian past, but in which elements of these minorities still see their relationship to the state as that of semicolonialism, and where the majority considers them as potential threats to the country's territorial integrity and cultural homogeneity?

Can such a state deal effectively with the historic, national, cultural, and political aspirations of these minorities?

Can it successfully develop a sense of national identity that encompasses and yet transcends a variety of competing traditions and aspirations?

Can it balance the objective of promoting national (or at least state) cohesion with the requirements of religious and cultural experiences that are at variance with the dominant ethos of the state?

In the process, can such a state transform itself into a pluralistic and democratic society?

How are all of these processes affected by the external environment—in this case, Russia's relations with the Muslim and Western worlds—as well as by the policies of external actors?

Finally, how do the foreign and security policies of the transforming state affect its ability to achieve its internal goals?

Thus this work is about Russia, about Islam, and about their relationship with one another over many centuries and continuing into the future. It is also about two separate concepts of identity, values, and cultures, one of which—Russian—has been dominant during the last 500 years and the other—Islamic—has been striving for self-assertion and self-determination for nearly the same period. By looking both at history and at the experience of the years since the end of the Soviet Union in 1991, this work tries to provide some answers to the question of whether diverse peoples and cultures can flourish in the context of a multiethnic and multicultural state without the quest for self-determination inevitably leading to conflict and ending either in separation or subjugation.

Organizational Structure

Based on the foregoing analysis of the dynamics of interaction between the Russian Federation's Muslims and the rest of the country's population, along with the greater linkages between these populations and the rest of the Islamic world, plus the broader international context, this study will be divided into three main parts. Part I of the book consists of two chapters. The first chapter provides a historical account of Russia's encounter with Islam and the current ramifications of this encounter. This will help establish patterns of continuity and change in the ongoing interaction between Russia and Islam. This is followed by a demographic, geographic, institutional, socioeconomic, ideological, and political profile of Russian Islam. The chapters in part II deal with the impact of Islam, especially its new and more politicized and extremist versions, on Russia's internal developments, including the development of its post-Soviet national identity and its political system. The third part of the book examines the role of Islam in the evolution of the Russian Federation's view of the outside world and its foreign policy perspectives. It will also evaluate Islam's role in shaping the character of Russia's relations with key international actors and different regions, most notably the Muslim countries, especially those that once formed part of the Soviet Union and their immediate and more distant neighbors.

I

Islam in Russia, Past and Present

An Overview

1

Islam in Russia

The Historical Background

It is difficult to establish exactly when Islam first appeared in Russia because the lands that Islam penetrated early in its expansion were not part of Russia at the time, but were later incorporated into the expanding Russian Empire. Islam reached the Caucasus region in the middle of the seventh century as part of the Arab conquest of the Iranian Sassanid Empire, many centuries before Russian expansion into this region,[1] and the archeological evidence points to the existence of links between the people of Bashkortostan, located in contemporary Russia's Ural Mountains region, and the Islamic world dating back to the eighth century.[2] By the tenth century, the Bulghar Kingdom on the banks of the Volga River had accepted Islam and incorporated Bashkortostan into its domain, almost half a millennium before Russia's conquest of the region under Tsar Ivan IV (Ivan the Terrible). Before the arrival of the Russians, the Bulghar Kingdom developed into an important center of Islamic civilization, with extensive ties to the rest of the Islamic world, especially Central Asia and Khorasan.[3] This fact prompted the nineteenth-century Russian philosopher and historian S.M. Soloviev to state, "When the Bulghar was already listening to the Qu'ran on the shores of the Volga and the Kama, the Russian Slav had not yet started to build Christian churches on the Oka and had not yet conquered these places in the name of the European civilization."[4]

Despite the proximity of these Muslim lands to Kievan Russia and their later incorporation into the Russian Empire, as long as they were beyond Russian rule, Islam remained only a neighbor of Russia and not a component of its religious fabric. Nevertheless, interaction between Russian and Muslim peoples, both peaceful and conflictual, dates back to at least the tenth century A.D. During this period, Russians conducted raids as far south as the Transcaucasus and in 942–44 destroyed a number of prosperous Muslim cities in South Caucasus.[5] If some legends are to be believed, Russia's embrace of Christianity instead of Islam owed as much to chance as to somber reflection. According to one such legend, Prince Vladimir of Kiev decided in the year 988 to choose a religion for his people—a common practice among ruling elites in those days—and met with representatives of the great religions. Although the prince was tempted by Islam, the religion's prohibition of alcohol persuaded him to reject it because, as Vladimir purportedly said, "The joy of Russia is drinking; we cannot be without it."[6] Although perhaps apocryphal, this legend underlines the growing importance of Islam as an external, if not yet internal, factor for the emerging Kievan Russian state.

During this period before Islam became an important internal social and political factor, Russians began forming a common identity, heightened by the adoption of Orthodox Christianity, that separated them from the Muslim peoples to the east and south. In the Russian perception, "in the early tenth century, the borderline between 'civilization' and 'barbarism' followed more or less exactly the frontier which today separates the Slavic 'European' people of the [former] USSR from areas populated largely by Muslims."[7] However, in the tenth century, it was not clear who were the barbarians and who were the civilized peoples. The Islamic world, from the tenth century to the middle of the thirteenth century, was experiencing its golden age, which would end with the Mongol conquests of 1206–1405. However, in due course, the various Turko-Mongol dynasties that ruled over vast areas stretching from Central Asia to the Urals would become significant centers of Islamic and Turko-Iranian civilization and would expand the frontiers of Islam to the Indian subcontinent. If the Russians viewed the Muslims as barbarians, the Muslims had a similar view of the "Rus" as "wild and primitive natives . . . and dangerous neighbors." Thus in the tenth century, from the Muslim perspective, " 'Barbary' was represented by the 'European' ancestors of the Russians."[8]

Mongol Conquest and Islam

Despite these mutually reinforcing negative views that the Russians and neighboring Muslim peoples had of one another, until the Mongol invasion, Islam and Muslims were only distant neighbors and not part of Russia's religious and political landscape. This occurred only after the Mongol conquest of Kievan Russia in the thirteenth century, and especially after the conversion to Islam by Özbek Khan of the Golden Horde in the early fourteenth century. The latter development was a pivotal point in the formation of the Russian view of Islam, with lasting influence and far-reaching consequences. Islam became identified with the Mongol conquest and the period of the "Tatar yoke," which is considered the greatest calamity that befell the Russians. Islam's introduction to Russia as a result of the Mongol conquest and Tatar rule has had significant implications for the development of Russia's perceptions of Islam and the character of its relations with the Muslim peoples and countries. A significant majority of Russians believe that their cultural and political development was thwarted by Tatar-Mongol domination because it created a gap between Russia and the rest of Europe. They attribute the worst aspects of Russia's political culture to Tatar-Mongol rule and maintain that the requirements of surviving and eventually overcoming Mongol rule forced Muscovy to adopt their ways, namely, tyranny, despotism, serfdom, and lack of liberty.[9]

Thus Islam and Muslims were seen by Russians as aggressors, conquerors, and oppressors from whose domination Russia must free itself and prevent future challenges by Muslims to Russian interests and independence. The latter concern contributed to Russian expansion into Muslim lands beginning in the sixteenth century with the conquest of the Khanate of Kazan in 1552 by Ivan the Terrible.[10] Even before that, the Russians had tried to rid themselves of Tatar rule. In 1380, Dimitrii, the prince of Moscow, defeated the Tatar-Mongols in the Battle of Kulikovo.[11] This victory, which is still celebrated today, became a source of tension between Kazan and Moscow in June 2001, with the Tatars demanding that the celebration be abolished.[12] This controversy illustrates how historic events and their legacy for the collective memories of Russians and Muslims affect contemporary developments. The centuries following the Russian capture of Kazan witnessed an inexorable—albeit, at times, difficult—process of Russian expansion into Muslim-inhabited regions of the Caucasus and Central Asia. By the time of the Bolshevik Revolution, the tsar's Muslim subjects numbered nearly 20 million.[13]

Throughout this centuries-long period of expansion, the memory of the Mongol conquest and the negative impact of Mongol rule heightened the Russian view of Islam and Muslims as "hostile others" against whom the Russians, to some extent, would define themselves and their national and cultural mission. Other rival cultures and external foes—notably the non-Orthodox Christian West—played a role at least as important as that of Muslim peoples in the Russian perception of external threats.[14] Nevertheless, two central aspects of the Russian view of Islam that developed during Mongol rule and the subsequent Russian expansion became fundamental components of Russian national identity and maintain significant relevance in Russia's present cultural and political contexts. First, Russia came to see itself as the eastern flank of the defense of Christendom against Islam and Asian nations, as Spain was in the west. Russians deeply believe that Europe would have succumbed to the Mongols and could not have either retained its Christianity or developed culturally and scientifically if Russia had not absorbed the shock of Mongol invasion. Therefore, they believe that the West owes a debt of gratitude to Russia. Moreover, Russia still sees itself as a bulwark against the Islamic South, which continues to threaten Europe. Second, Russia developed a sense of duty to perform a civilizing role, both in parts of Europe and in Asia, especially among its Muslim subjects. This experience, frequently viewed by Russians as suffering for the sake of others, has strengthened the messianic tendencies of Russian culture.[15]

As Russia pursued this mission and steadily expanded its reach, it became integrated, albeit incompletely, into the European political and, to a lesser degree, cultural system, especially following the reforms of Peter the Great and the Westernizing policies of Empress Catherine II (Catherine the Great). The Muslim world simultaneously entered a long period of decline. These parallel processes enhanced the Russians' sense of civilizational superiority and their belief in their civilizing role vis-à-vis the conquered peoples. Yet despite their decline and subsequent subjugation, Muslims of the Russian Empire retained memories of a rich cultural heritage, and a large segment of Russia's Muslim population rejected the notion of the inherent superiority of Russian civilization. This continued belief in the value of their civilization has been an important factor both in the preservation of Islamic traditions and ethnic identities of Russia's Muslims and in periodic efforts by successive generations at cultural revival, including those under way since the beginning of perestroika in 1987.

Over the nearly five centuries of this often troubled relationship between the Russian state and the subject Muslim peoples, Russia's treatment of its Muslim population evolved in accordance with the duration and difficulty of Russia's conquest of the different Muslim peoples, the basic characteristics and ideology of the Russian state, and the domestic and foreign policy priorities of the Russian government. Also important were the personality traits of key Russian figures in charge of governing Muslim regions. During the evolution of Russian policy through both the tsarist and Soviet periods, essentially four patterns of behavior dominated: (1) pervasive repression and, in some cases, elimination of national cultures and ethnic groups; (2) periodic tolerance; (3) assimilation; and (4) limited religiocultural autonomy and a measure of cooperation. In the post-Soviet era, there was a brief period of growing tolerance and moves toward accepting greater cultural and political autonomy for Russia's Muslims. However, since 1999, the dominant trends have been toward greater government control over Muslims' religious and cultural life, the reversal of trends toward cultural and political autonomy, and growing anti-Muslim sentiments—Islamophobia. In accordance with the historical pattern, Russia's troubles with some of its Muslim population, notably in Chechnya, and perceived threats to its security from Muslim autonomist aspirations have contributed to this trend.

Islam and the Russian Empire: Patterns of Russian Imperial Rule

From Ivan the Terrible to the Beginning of Catherine II's Reign: Repression and Assimilation

The period from the conquest of Kazan in 1552 to the coming to power of Catherine the Great in 1762 was marked by a policy of systematic repression of Muslims and the destruction of Muslim civilization within Russia's borders. According to the Russian historian M. Khudiakov, "The tragic day of 2 October [the day that Ivan conquered Kazan] caused the loss of a huge number of lives and immeasurable suffering and grief to the Kazan people, but it also destroyed the material prosperity which had been accumulated by many generations. Art treasures were torn from homes where they had been carefully preserved and mercilessly destroyed, damaged, and lost."[16] This destruction of outward manifestations of Islamic civilization was accompanied by efforts to cause its spiritual annihilation. Thus, as reported by historian N.N. Fissov, "With the arrival of the nobility and the monasteries, systematic religious persecution began. This persecution was initiated by Ivan IV, who was very much influenced by the Orthodox clergy. He destroyed the Tatar mosques and outlawed their reconstruction. The Muscovite clerics carried out their missionary work stubbornly, increasing the number of converts."[17]

This policy of destruction and assimilation reflected the character of the Muscovite state and its underlying ideology. By the time Russia began its expansion into Muslim lands during the reign of Ivan the Terrible, a certain idea of the basis of Russia's statehood and nationhood—to the extent that such concepts in their modern understanding existed at that time—had emerged. The most significant and deep-rooted aspect of this notion of Russia's statehood was the heritage of Byzantium, which had been founded on the principle of a fusion between religion and state. In the Russian context, this concept was expanded into a fusion of religion, ethnicity, and nationality. Consequently, being Russian meant being an Orthodox Christian and an ethnic Slav. As long as there were no Muslims or, for that matter, followers of other Christian traditions within the Russian realm, there was no conflict between the concepts of religion and nationality, religious community and national community, or, on the more aggregate level, religion and state. As Alexandre Bennigsen and Marie Broxup observed about this period of Russian history, "During this happy era, Muscovy was a nation-state or, rather, a religion-state."[18]

This situation changed with Russia's conquest and incorporation of Muslim lands, a process that broke the ethnoreligious unity of Russia. Given the large number of Muslims incorporated into the Russian Empire, the so-called Spanish solution—complete expulsion of Muslims—was not a viable option. The next best alternative, from the viewpoint of preserving Russia's Orthodox Christian character, was the assimilation of Muslims, which would safeguard the religious and hence national homogeneity of the empire. In this manner, the religious underpinnings of Russian statehood and nationhood were important factors in shaping the character of the Russian treatment of Muslims. Although total expulsion was not possible in Russia's case, over the centuries, certain Russian policies, such as Russia's system of land grants and the promotion of Russian and other non-Muslim migration into Muslim lands, led to a large exodus of Muslims from their ancestral homes either to less hospitable parts of the country or to other states, especially the Ottoman Empire. Thus in many areas—the Volga-Ural region, the Crimea, and parts of the North Caucasus—Muslims became minorities in their ancestral lands, a situation that persists today and creates special problems. Some ethnic groups such as the Cherkess (or Circassians) have nearly vanished.[19]

In the late sixteenth century, the policies of exclusion and discrimination pursued by Tsar Feodor toward the Muslim Tatars, combined with an extensive effort at Christian proselytization, led to a failed uprising by the Tatar feudal aristocracy and prompted a large-scale exodus of Tatars to Bashkortostan, the Kazakh steppes, and south toward Central Asia. This trend continued at different paces throughout the tsarist and Soviet periods. Consequently, today there are more Tatars living outside of the Republic of Tatarstan than within it.[20] Even under the relatively lenient rule of Empress Catherine II, following the conquest of the Crimean Peninsula, large numbers of Crimean Tatars fled the region. It is estimated that between 1783 and 1913, a million Tatars left Crimea for the Ottoman Empire.[21]

Russia's territorial expansion and Orthodox missionary activities first began under Ivan the Terrible, who had a relatively tolerant approach toward religious matters and accepted Muslims as his loyal subjects, especially if they belonged to the nobility. Nevertheless, his tolerance toward Muslim individuals was not sufficient to prevent the destruction of material and spiritual manifestations of Islamic civilization. His successors did not share even this moderate leniency toward Muslims. Consequently, during the seventeenth century and the first half of the eighteenth century, anti-Muslim activities intensified. In the period between the rule of the first Romanov tsar, Mikhail I, and Catherine the Great, Islam was treated as "an alien body." For example, in the span of seven years (1738–45), 418 out of 536 mosques of the Kazan district (*gubernia*) were destroyed. Other anti-Muslim measures included the confiscation of Muslim charitable property (*waqf*), the opening of special schools for the children of the newly converted Tatars, the intensification of missionary activities, and the expulsion of Muslims from villages where new groups of converts had gathered.[22] An aggressive policy of conversion was carried out in 1740–50, after the founding of the Kazan Office of New Converts. According to the edict creating the office, its purpose was to baptize all Muslims, forcefully if necessary.[23] Meanwhile, proselytization by Muslims was punishable by death according to an edict issued in 1649 by Tsar Alexei.[24] During this time, "Tombstones were removed from Tatar cemeteries and used as the foundations of monasteries, libraries were burnt, and other cultural monuments were destroyed. With the aid of such methods, the Tsarist autocracy aimed to make the Tatars forget their own history, culture, customs and traditions."[25]

These policies reflect the fact that despite changes in the composition of its population, Russia's rulers had not come to see it as a multinational empire that required different methods of governance to secure the loyalty of its new subjects. Rather, they continued to view the empire as a "Russian and Orthodox" nation-state.[26] The Muslims' presence challenged this concept of Russia, and the only way to meet this challenge successfully was to convert Muslims to Christianity. In stark contrast, and in accordance with the modernization strategy adopted by Peter the Great, the Russian government began encouraging foreign specialists to come to Russia and, as an enticement, was even prepared to accept them as equal to the Russian nobility. Consequently, foreigners came to play an important role in administering the Russian state; although this contingent of experts and bureaucrats consisted mostly of Catholics and Protestants, few spoke any Russian, and they certainly did not consider themselves to be Russian. Yet their position was far better than any of the tsar's Muslim subjects, and their presence was not viewed as diluting the Orthodox nature of the Russian state and society.

Catherine the Great: Relative Religious Tolerance and Limited Autonomy for Muslims

The rule of Catherine the Great is generally associated with a tolerant attitude toward Russia's Muslim population. Her more liberal and tolerant religious policy had much to do with her conception of the state, which she viewed as an empire more along the lines of other existing or emerging European empires rather than that of an ethnically and religiously homogeneous nation-state.[27] This vision, which was more reflective of Russia's realities, allowed it some room to accommodate other peoples and religions, treating them with some measure of fairness as citizens of the empire. It also permitted Russia's ruling elites to begin using their Muslim subjects to advance key state interests, a practice that has continued in different forms ever since.

Catherine's new approach toward Muslims was reflected especially in her policies toward the Crimean and other Tatars. Following the conquest of the Crimean Peninsula in 1771 and its final incorporation into the Russian Empire in 1783, Catherine followed a relatively liberal policy and treated the Muslim Tatars comparatively well. Under her reign, Muslims were treated as equals with the rest of the population and were free to exercise their religion, the Muslim religious leadership retained its control over *waqf* property and revenues that derived from it, Christian proselytizing was prohibited, and the Tatar landowning nobility was allowed to retain its privileges and was incorporated into the hierarchy of Russian society without having to convert to Orthodoxy. Forceful conversion was distasteful to Catherine, and in 1773 she instructed the Holy Synod to issue "a toleration of faiths" edict, which prohibited the destruction of mosques.[28] Catherine viewed Islam "as an impediment to social and political development, but not as a repugnant religion."[29] She hoped that a policy of "forceful modernization in the Crimea would show the Tatars the benefits and advantages to be gained from adopting the Russian model for their society."

Under advice from Baron O.A. Igelstrom, the viceroy of Ufa District, Catherine also adopted a policy of co-opting Muslim clergy, especially in the Crimea, and even bringing them into the bureaucracy as a means of controlling the population.[30] This policy led to the creation of Muslim institutions under direct government control. The creation by Catherine in 1789 of the first Muslim institution in Ufa, the Ufa Spiritual Muhammedan Assembly (Ufimskoe Dukhovnoe Magometanskogo Zakona Sobranie), headed by a high-ranking Sunni Muslim cleric called a mufti, was the first step in this direction. In 1796, it was renamed the Orenburg Muhammedan Spiritual Assembly (Orenburgskoe Magometanskoe Dukhovnoe Sobranie), indicating the expansion of the institution's area of jurisdiction, which at the time included the Ufa viceroyship (*namestnichestvo*) and the Orenburg governorship.[31] The mufti and the assembly were responsible for administering the religious life of the empress's Muslim subjects. The institutionalization of spiritual boards later expanded to other regions as Russia conquered more Muslim-inhabited territories, and even today it is a principal organizational form of the administration of Muslims' religious needs.

The creation of the board was the legal and institutional embodiment of Catherine's more enlightened vision, granting Muslims officially recognized cultural and religious status in the empire. However, in creating the Spiritual Assembly, Catherine also created an official Muslim clerical establishment that would be responsible to the government and would not act in an independent manner. Indeed, Baron Igelstrom in his petition to the empress proposed the creation of a state institution to "test" and "select" among the Muslim clerics those who would be "trustworthy" and thus would serve the state's interests.[32] In implementing this proposal, Catherine was following a more general trend in Russia, initiated by Peter the Great, of undermining the independence of religious establishments, including the Russian Orthodox Church.[33] In time, the Muslim spiritual administration evolved into a system of four spiritual assemblies each headed by a mufti: the Tatar mufti of Orenburg, the Crimean mufti of Bakhchisarai, and the Sunni and Shi'a muftis of Transcaucasus, all of whom were directly appointed by the imperial government.[34] This tradition of having subservient clergy survives in various forms today.

Catherine allowed the peaceful propagation of Islam in parts of the empire and its vicinity where Islamization was either superficial or nonexistent. Thus Catherine permitted the Tatars to build mosques and Qu'ranic schools in Bashkortostan and in the Kazakh steppes. This enlightened policy had many benefits for Russia, including the advancement of economic prosperity and cultural development of the Volga-Ural region. Cities such as Kazan, Ufa, and Orenburg became important centers of Islamic learning, and some of their medressahs acquired a high reputation in the Muslim world. Tatar merchants and other members of the Tatar elite helped create footholds for Russia in Central Asia, parts of Siberia, and China, which were not accessible to non-Muslims. Although many other aspects of Russian policy were detrimental to Muslims, Catherine made the first attempt to create a sense of unity and cooperation among the empire's increasingly diverse peoples by recognizing differences and trying to accommodate them, rather than by pursuing total religious and cultural assimilation. Catherine's policies also demonstrated that Russian-Muslim coexistence is possible and can be mutually beneficial.

Russian Advance into the Muslim World: Conquest of the Caucasus and Central Asia

The Tatars and Bashkirs were the first Muslims to be incorporated into the Russian Empire. Subsequently, Russia's southward expansion in the Caucasus and in Central Asia brought other Muslims under its rule and raised new issues about dealing with Islam and Muslim peoples.

The Caucasus

Russia's interest in the Caucasus, dating from the sixteenth century, was a direct result of the conquest of the Khanates of Kazan and Astrakhan. These conquests brought Russia to the shores of the Caspian Sea, thus making the Caucasus of geopolitical interest. Russia also became involved in regional politics of the Caucasus (North and South) and rivalries for influence in the region among neighboring powers, notably the Ottoman Empire, Iran, and the Khanate of Crimea. Internal problems for most of the seventeenth century, combined with troubled relations with European powers during the first part of the eighteenth century, prevented Russia from actively and systematically pursuing an expansionist policy toward the south. Nonetheless, Russia took advantage of opportunities for expanding its influence southward whenever they arose. Thus during the reign of Empress Anna (1730–40), the weakening of the Safavid Empire as a result of the Afghan rebellions and its subsequent end in 1736 prompted Russia to try, in collaboration with the Ottomans, to annex segments of Iranian territories, which at that time included parts of the Caucasus region. These efforts were frustrated by the rise of Nadir Shah Afshar, who expelled the Russians and the Ottomans from Iran.[35] During the rule of Catherine (1762–96), Russia resumed its southern expansion with the incorporation of Crimea in 1783.[36] After the elimination of the Crimean Khanate, Russia was free to advance into the North Caucasus.

The ethnically and linguistically diverse peoples and communities of the mountains of the North Caucasus had never formed a state and lacked the political and military structures of traditional states. Despite these shortcomings, they strongly resisted the advancing Russian army. The North Caucasian version of Islam facilitated the popular resistance with its wide network of Sufi brotherhoods of mostly, but not exclusively, the Naqshbandi school and proved an important unifying factor and a formidable foe for Russia.[37] The threat of Russian conquest also provided an impetus for unification among generally feuding North Caucasian peoples. Consequently, during a period lasting from 1785 to 1791, Sheikh Mansur Ushurma, a Chechen who had been initiated into the Naqshbandi Sufi rite, succeeded in uniting most of the North Caucasus in resistance to Russian advances and, on occasion, inflicted serious damage on the Russian army.[38] Ultimately, however, Sheikh Mansur succumbed to Russian military might, was captured by the Russians, and died in prison in 1793.[39]

The defeat of Sheikh Mansur caused the near disintegration of the network of Naqshbandi brotherhoods in the North Caucasus and for nearly thirty years ended resistance in the region.[40] Following his defeat, Russia made inroads in the lowlands and foothills of the North Caucasus, but the mountainous areas remained largely inaccessible. Sheikh Mansur's resistance left three important legacies for Russian-Muslim relations in the region: (1) it sowed the seeds of Sufi traditions, which evolved into Muridism; (2) it demonstrated that Islam could be a factor of unity and an impetus to resistance; and (3) in subsequent decades, it contributed to the expansion of Islam into the last remaining pagan enclaves of the North Caucasus.

The longest and strongest resistance to Russian advance was led by Imam Shamil, a Dagestani Avar who fought the Russian army from 1825 to 1859.[41] Shamil, too, was finally defeated by the Russian Empire, but his resistance left lasting marks on the North Caucasus and on the nature of Russia's relations with this region and its peoples. First, Shamil's activities led to the further spread and strengthening of orthodox Islam in the region, notably among the Chechens. Second, Shamil's resistance, known after the prophet Muhammad's campaigns as the Ghazawat, firmly established the tradition of defiance to Russian rule, a tradition that contributes to anti-Russian activities in the region today.[42] Russian rule in the North Caucasus, punctuated by periods of warfare and resistance, has contributed to mutually negative views between Russians and the North Caucasians, especially among the Chechens and the Dagestanis. Russians came to view Chechens and other followers of Sheikh Mansur and Imam Shamil as bandits, scoundrels, and ignorant people. By contrast, for the North Caucasians, especially Chechens, Russia's image as aggressor and oppressor is firmly established.[43]

Russia's advance into the South Caucasus was accomplished with greater ease. The ease with which Russia gained control of Georgia, the lands that now constitute the Republic of Azerbaijan, and those parts of Armenia that were not under Ottoman control had much to do with the state of weakness and decline that had befallen Iran following the assassination of Nadir Shah Afshar during his campaign in Dagestan in 1747. Christian Georgia, which had been chafing under the pressures of Iran and the Ottomans, had since the time of Catherine sought Russia's help. In 1795, Catherine's decision to help the Georgian king, Erekle II, brought Iran and Russia to the brink of war as the founder of the Qajar dynasty, Agha Muhammad Khan, organized an expedition to Georgia to reestablish Iranian suzerainty. The assassination of Agha Muhammad Khan in 1797 and the death of Catherine in 1796 averted a Russian-Iranian war. However, the decision of Tsar Paul I to respond positively to the request of the Georgian king Grigory XII to accept direct authority over his country, a decision later confirmed by Tsar Alexander I, rekindled Russian-Iranian rivalry. In a period extending from 1804 to 1828, with a pause between 1813 and 1824, due to Napoleonic wars in Europe, Russia fought two series of wars with Iran. They ended with Iran's defeat and the signing of the Treaties of Gulistan (1813) and Turkmenchai (1828), which led to Iran's loss of its Transcaucasian possessions.[44]

Central Asia

The Russian conquest of Central Asia was accomplished over a long period of time, extending from the 1820s to 1900.[45] Russian rule first displaced that of the khans in the Kazakh steppes. The Kazakh ruling class was a relatively willing collaborator, and the Russian policy of granting them a privileged status—without, however, admitting them into the Russian nobility—made the conquest of this region less difficult than Russian subjugation of the North Caucasus. Moreover, the Kazakh nobility, being more proud of its Kazakh origins than its religion, was only superficially committed to Islam, a fact that eliminated the possibility of using Islam as an instrument for organizing resistance as it was used in the Caucasus. Many members of the Kazakh elite were modernizers and were therefore willing to acquire the Russian language and culture, which they saw as a conduit to modern European civilization. They also disapproved of efforts made by the Tatars and people from Bukhara to spread and strengthen Islam among the nomads and viewed the Russian presence as a barrier to such activities.

Nevertheless, the complete subjugation of the Kazakh hordes of the steppe region was not accomplished quickly or easily. It took more than thirty years and occurred only after the Russians suppressed several widespread revolts. By 1854, the Kazakh hordes had been coerced into accepting Russian hegemony, allowing Russia to continue its southward expansion into the more urban parts of Central

Asia, where some of the most important centers of early Islamic civilization were located. After capturing Julek and Yani-Kurgan (1861), Tokmak and Pishpek (1862), and Chimkent and Tashkent (1865), Russia conquered Zerafshan and Samarkand and forced the emir of Bukhara to accept the status of a Russian protectorate. Khiva suffered a similar fate in 1873. With the defeat of resistance in the Turkmen region in 1884–85, Russia's conquest of Central Asia was complete.[46]

Russia's Treatment of Muslim Subjects during Imperial Expansion: Exclusion and Halfhearted Assimilation

As Russia expanded its frontiers to the south, it increasingly acquired the characteristics of a classic colonial empire. Catherine's successors generally did not pursue her enlightened policies, and by the 1860s, Russian authorities had reverted to a more imperialist and, to varying degrees, assimilationist policy toward Muslims, although these policies were applied with varying degrees of intensity at different times and in different parts of the empire. In the case of the Tatars, this new approach, which was based on the dual strategy of Christianizing Tatars while granting them linguistic and cultural freedom, was in some respects more dangerous for Islam's survival.[47] The ultimate goal of this policy was to create a new Christian Tatar intelligentsia that would perform the basic functions of proselytizing within the rest of the population. Nikolai Il'minsky established the educational foundations of this policy during the reign of Alexander II (1855–81). It was quite successful if judged on the basis of the number of converts to Christianity. Between 1868 and 1900, estimates of the number of Tatars who converted to Russian Orthodoxy surpassed 100,000. However, many of these Christian Tatars, or the "baptized ones" (*Kriashen*), retained many of their traditions and tried to rejoin the Muslim community.[48] From the assimilationist perspective, the long-term effect of this policy was largely negative, primarily because it created strong resentment toward Russia and the Russians among many in the Tatar community who remained faithful to Islam and its religious and cultural traditions.

In Central Asia and the Caucasus, Russia pursued an essentially colonialist strategy. Its principal goals were to establish Russia's political control without dismantling the structures of local political administration and to exploit conquered areas economically. The latter objective took three forms: providing land for Russian peasantry, acquiring sources of raw materials for Russian industry, and obtaining markets for Russian goods.[49] These policies were pursued systematically; the first wave of Russian and Ukrainian settlers reached the steppes in 1891, "not, as in the 18th or early 19th centuries, as a disorderly rush of peasants spurred by the prospect of rich land and freedom from serfdom, but as organized migration planned by the administration." By 1914, more than a million Slav peasants from central Russia and the Ukraine had settled in the richest areas of the steppes.[50]

During this period, Caucasian and Central Asian Muslims were not treated as "citizens" of the empire. However, in most cases, compared with the treatment of the Tatars—with the exception of the period of Catherine's rule—they were allowed relatively more religious and cultural freedom. With few exceptions, there was no aggressive Christian proselytization, and efforts at cultural Russification were generally halfhearted, although the intensity of this policy differed from region to region and from period to period.[51] Certainly there was no systematic effort at Russification similar to the one conducted among the Tatars of the Volga-Ural region. Instead, the cultural dimension of Russia's colonial strategy focused, with a few exceptions, on undermining Islam without attacking it directly. Critical factors in determining the method of pursuing this objective and, in particular, the degree of religious and cultural freedoms allowed to Muslims were the character and preferences of Russian authorities in charge of administering different Muslim regions. For example, General Konstantine von Kaufman, who was appointed governor general of Turkestan in 1866, opposed a policy of aggressive Orthodox Christian proselytization. He is reported to have said, "We [Russia] must introduce Christian civilization in Turkestan, but we must not try to propound the Orthodox faith to the native population."[52] Thus he did not attempt to prevent the performance of Muslim rituals, but focused his efforts on weakening the structure of Muslim religious authority.

Other Russian authorities attempted to weaken Islam by encouraging the development of a common identity based on pre-Islamic elements of collective consciousness, including memories of Mongol grandeur.[53] As part of this strategy, beginning in 1841, Russian authorities established Russian-Kazakh schools and admitted the children of the Kazakh nobility to Russian military schools and universities. However, rather than promoting nonreligious ethnic identity, these policies frequently fostered a sense of cultural inferiority on the part of many Kazakhs, a phenomenon similar to the emergence of widespread feelings of inferiority among modernizing nationalist elites of other Muslim countries at the time. For example, a nineteenth-century Kazakh writer and philosopher thought that "the Kazakhs without the Russians were no more than Asiatics."[54] However, the extent of these efforts was limited and did not reach enough people to have a major impact on the traditions and collective mentality of most Kazakhs. Moreover, the experiment did not last long enough to make possible a fair judgment about its viability. It became the victim of "economic and demographic realities" as population pressures from Slav immigrants combined with a deteriorating economy. These growing population and economic pressures culminated in severe conflicts between the Russian/European settlers and Kazakh nomads, the worst of which occurred in 1916.[55]

In the settled parts of Central Asia south of Kazakhstan, which today are located mostly in Uzbekistan, Russia was not as eager to encourage modern education and Russification. The natives, too, were suspicious of such schemes and saw them mostly a as means of undermining their existing large-scale infrastructure of Islamic education. Nevertheless, as part of the policy of spreading Russian culture, the imperial administration set up schools that would enroll both Russian and native students. Russian authorities even offered financial incentives to those parents who would enroll their children in mixed schools.[56] These efforts had little success in attracting Muslim students or fostering non-Islamic identity among the Central

Asians. Furthermore, at the turn of the twentieth century, a strand of Islamic reformism, the Jadid movement, became strong in Central Asia. The goal of the
Jadidists was to revitalize Muslim civilization by stripping it of outdated ideas and
policies—many of which were not rooted in the Qu'ran or early traditions of Islam—and by introducing modern scientific methods of analysis.[57] This movement
endangered Russian objectives in the region because it threatened the relative success of Russian-native schools and provided a means of revitalizing Islamic culture,
a development that could make Islam more resistant to Russification and much less
docile politically. In response to Jadidism and other attempts to strengthen Islam,
Russian authorities supported the most conservative and obscurantist elements
within the Muslim religious and educational institutions with the goal of keeping
the region both isolated from the rest of the world and "in a state of medieval
backwardness and deep economic and social stagnation."[58]

One of the basic components of Russia's colonial policy was that "any meaningful cultural change should be in the direction of Russification."[59] This policy of
isolation was only partially successful, especially since—unlike in the Soviet period—merchants and travelers from the region went to other Muslim and European
countries, and intellectual influences from Turkey and Iran and indirectly from
European sources reached the region.

Russia did not continuously and vigorously pursue Christian proselytization in
the Caucasus and Central Asia; however, the tsarist regime did attempt to weaken
the structures of Muslim religious authority in both regions. Among the Muslims
of the South Caucasus (mostly in present-day Azerbaijan), the Russians applied a
laissez-faire policy toward the general population, although a fair degree of Russification occurred at the elite level. The North Caucasus remained unstable for
most of the period of tsarist rule, with periodic revolts and uprisings. Thus Russia's
principal concern in this region was security related rather than cultural and religious. Nevertheless, there was a linkage between the region's religious life and
Russia's security concerns because religious groups and their leaders organized
most of the uprisings that occurred in the North Caucasus. Despite the defeat of
Imam Shamil's movement, the spirit of religious revival had survived, especially
in Dagestan, and continued to serve as an instrument of resistance to Russian rule.
The mountainous regions of Dagestan housed religious schools and theologians
whose fame spread throughout the Muslim world. In response, at times, the tsarist
government banned some religious practices and suppressed certain religious
groups, especially Sufi orders. In 1864, following a period of unrest, the Russian
government banned several practices of the Qadiriya Sufi order, notably *zikr* (the
religious ritual of loud chanting accompanied by the movement of devotees in
circles).

During this period of colonial conquest and alternating policies of toleration and
suppression of Islam, occasional gross abuses of Muslim subjects occurred, including massacres. A notable example is General Mikhail Skobelev's attempt to
exterminate Turkmen tribes during the Russian conquest of Central Asia in the late
nineteenth century.[60] The policy of mass killings was not employed in any extensive

and systematic fashion; nevertheless, large groups of indigenous Muslims were removed from their ancestral homelands through deportation and forced migration, a policy that led to the near annihilation of the Western Cherkess (Circassian) tribes, Abkhazian Muslims, and, to a lesser degree, the Crimean Tatars. The elimination of cultural and religious identity was also accomplished by cutting off populations from external influences and thus forcing their disappearance through backwardness and assimilation into surrounding ethnicities, including Russian. To varying degrees, this policy was applied to the Volga Tatars (sixteenth century), the Bashkirs (seventeenth century), the Crimean Tatars (eighteenth and early nineteenth centuries), the peoples of the northwestern Caucasus (late nineteenth century), and the nomads of the Kazakh steppes (late nineteenth and early twentieth centuries).[61] These policies abetted the more aggressive cases of assimilation discussed earlier through conversion to Orthodox Christianity, and were sometimes combined with linguistic and cultural Russification, as was applied at times to the Volga Tatars and the Kazakhs.

In light of these policies, it is not surprising that the Muslim response to Russian domination was characterized by armed resistance and periodic revolts, combined with less aggressive attempts to hold on to religious and cultural traditions. Yet Muslims were not averse to cooperation with their Russian rulers, provided the latter allowed them a degree of religious and cultural freedom and treated them as partners—albeit with a junior role. Despite the intermittently harsh treatment of Russia's Muslims, at times the tsarist regime practiced relative tolerance, including allowing limited autonomy for various Muslim peoples. The imperial government followed a policy of noninterference in Azerbaijan during much of the nineteenth century, and in Central Asia, notwithstanding the excesses of General Skobelev, Russia more often applied a strategy of co-opting the elites without interfering in the lives of the masses.[62] For brief periods, Russia pursued a policy of economic and political partnership with Muslims, such as Catherine's approach toward the Volga Tatars in the late eighteenth century and Tsar Alexander II's policy toward the Kazakhs of the southern steppes in the second half of the nineteenth century.[63]

These periods of Russian-Muslim accommodation and cooperation demonstrate that Islam and Russia, despite the troubled relationship during the reign of the tsars, need not be irreconcilable enemies and that Islam can be accommodated within the context of a multiethnic and multiconfessional Russia. Muslims' willingness to coexist with the Russians and within a Russian state provided they are given a sufficient degree of cultural, religious, and administrative determination is reflected in their active involvement in social and political reform efforts of the early 1900s and during the Provisional Government of Alexander Kerensky in 1917. Because of its contemporary significance, Muslim political activism of that period should be briefly discussed.

Muslim Political Activism in Russia, 1905–1914

By the turn of the twentieth century, political stirrings had begun to appear within Russia's Muslim population. Among the most important factors responsible for this development were Russia's defeat in the Russo-Japanese War of 1904–5, events in other Muslim countries—especially Iran's Constitutional Revolution of 1905–6—and, most important, a series of peasant uprisings, worker strikes, and protests within the military in 1904–7, collectively referred to as the Russian Revolution of 1905.[64] The events of 1905–7 initially prompted Tsar Nicholas II to embark on a modest program of political liberalization. This overall opening of political space allowed Russia's Muslims to engage in political activity aimed at achieving greater autonomy and equality. Early Muslim efforts at political mobilization were not well organized; rather, the awakening of Muslim political consciousness initially led to the emergence of an ill-defined and amorphous all-Russia movement of Muslim activists.[65] This movement brought to the fore a broad spectrum of demands with the overarching objective of achieving equality of Muslim nationalities with the Russian population. Although its direct participation in revolutionary activities was hardly noticeable, in the spring of 1905 the Muslim movement succeeded in formulating a unified political platform that included demands for religious self-determination, the fair distribution of land, and the prohibition of arbitrary expropriation and unauthorized sale of Muslim-owned lands.[66]

In August 1905, the development of a common platform was followed by the first major attempt to create a united organization of Muslim political activists with the convening of the first Congress of Muslims of Russia in the city of Nizhny Novgorod. The approximately 120 delegates who attended this event praised Tsar Nicholas II's manifesto of August 1905, which established a legislative body, the Russian Duma.[67] In addition, the delegates called for the inclusion of Muslims in the reform process and demanded equality for Muslims with Russians in regard to "political, religious, and property rights." The congress also passed a resolution emphasizing the need for Muslims to unite in order to pursue these objectives and reached a tentative decision on the creation of an all-Russia organization of Muslims.[68] The list of final resolutions passed by the first congress included the following goals:

1. Unification of Muslim citizens of Russia to support political, economic, and social reforms.
2. Legal equality of Muslim and Russian populations.
3. Establishment of a constitutional monarchy based on proportional representation of nationalities.
4. Freedom of press, convention, religion, and the like.[69]
5. Inviolability of personal property. Peasants with little or no landholdings should be given land from the holdings of the state and the crown.[70]

The second Muslim congress, which convened on 13–23 January 1906 in St. Petersburg, attracted about 100 delegates from Muslim regions across Russia.[71] The delegates to this congress officially announced the creation of a political party, Ittifaq-al-Muslimin (Union of Muslims), and ratified its charter.[72] This new party was liberal and proreform in outlook, without being radical or anti-Russian. According to Serge Zenkovsky, "In its social and economic program, Ittifaq was close to the Russian Constitutional Democrats (Kadets)."[73] This is explained by the fact that both parties' members consisted mainly of the bourgeoisie, intelligentsia, and landowning nobility. This membership gave the new Muslim party, like the Kadets, a liberal democratic character and placed it in the mainstream of the reform movement; however, as a loose association of influential members of the Muslim elite, Ittifaq suffered from a major weakness in that it was not representative of most of Russia's Muslim community.

In addition to creating a new political party, the second Muslim congress took the fateful decision of entering into political cooperation with the Kadets on the eve of elections to the first Duma.[74] Muslim activists hoped that their alliance with one of the prominent liberal political parties of Russia would enable them to win seats in the Duma and, therefore, to influence policies affecting the Muslim community. The Ittifaq leadership recognized that the party had a unique opportunity to join the Russian political mainstream and decided to seize it. To further this goal, party leader Reshid Ibragimov, in his letter to the Russian minister of internal affairs requesting the imperial government's permission to convene a third congress of Muslims, renounced any anti-Russian and separatist aspirations and pledged allegiance to the tsar.[75] This reversal reflected the tactical flexibility of Muslim activists in their desire to overcome the barriers hindering their participation in Russian politics. Almost a century later, this pattern of haphazard cooperation would be repeated by Muslim political forces in the context of the struggle to win seats in the State Duma of the Russian Federation.

The third All-Russia Muslim Congress was held on 16–21 August 1906 in Nizhny Novgorod with the official authorization of the Russian imperial government. This assembly, which attracted about 800 delegates, adopted a program that borrowed heavily from the political platform of the Kadets while incorporating some ideological elements of the Social Revolutionaries, National Socialists, and other parties. The Muslim congress elected an executive council (or presidium) of the congress and a Central Committee of Ittifaq.[76] After a heated debate, the congress also developed Ittifaq's political program. According to this document, Ittifaq's main objectives were the achievement of equality for all Muslim peoples of Russia; the delegation of administrative authority to the local level through the empowerment of the *zemstvo* institutions (local assemblies); and implementation of progressive educational reforms aimed at defending, preserving, and promoting the religious and cultural autonomy of Russia's Muslims.[77]

The third All-Russia Muslim Congress was more organized than the previous two congresses, as evidenced by the activities of working groups, or commissions, formed by the delegates to formulate common positions on the most pressing issues. The most significant commissions were those dealing with education and religious affairs. The commission on education, headed by A. Apanaev, promulgated a resolution that—apart from reaffirming the positions outlined in the political program of the Ittifaq—called for the introduction of Ottoman Turkish as the only language of instruction in all Muslim schools of Russia. This decision reflected a general gravitation of Russia's Muslim political forces toward pan-Turkist ideas. According to Serge Zenkovsky, this measure, if realized, "would have brought Russian Turks closer together culturally and oriented them politically toward Turkey."[78] The proposals of the commission on religious affairs, chaired by the prominent Muslim cleric Galimjan Barudi, called for a radical reorganization of the Muslim clerical establishment, including direct election of chief muftis by local communities and the creation of a central Islamic administration to oversee Muslim religious affairs. These measures were designed to curtail government interference in Muslim religious organizations and practice.[79]

While Russia's Muslim political leadership developed a common Muslim agenda through the All-Russia Muslim Congresses, Ittifaq struggled to establish itself in Russia's newly created parliament. This task was complicated by clashes between the Duma and Tsar Nicholas II, who responded by dissolving the first and second Dumas. The first Duma functioned from May to July 1906, and the second Duma from March to June 1907. Despite a degree of electoral success—Muslims won twenty-five seats as members of the Kadet caucus in the first Duma and thirty-nine seats in the second Duma—the short-lived legislatures offered little opportunity to pursue social and political reform. A notable exception was a speech by parliamentarian Shahaidar Syrtlanov at a session of the first Duma during which he pointed out the injustices suffered by Russia's Muslims and insisted on complete legal equality for them.

During the second Duma, despite the increase in the number of Muslim deputies, internal divisions and factionalism led to a decline of Ittifaq's political influence. Under the leadership of the Bashkir parliamentarian K. Hasanov, six Muslim deputies in the Duma split off from the Ittifaq-dominated Muslim faction and formed an explicitly leftist Muslim labor group called Musulman Hezret Taifasy (the Holy Muslim Assembly).[80] Activities of most of the remaining Muslim parliamentarians were coordinated, with varying degrees of success, by Ali Mardan bey Topchibashev. Despite these divisions, Ittifaq pushed forward with a reform program, proposing legislation aimed at promoting cultural and religious autonomy for Muslims through educational reform, reorganization of the Muslim spiritual administration, and fair land distribution, including the prohibition of the sale of Muslim-owned lands and allocation of agricultural plots to Muslim peasants with little or no land.

The dissolution of the second Duma in June 1907 coincided with the effective disintegration of Ittifaq, which by that time was beset by internal divisions stemming from differences based on ethnicity and ideology, and a weakening of the all-Russia Muslim movement. The fourth congress of Russia's Muslims was not held until June 1914 in St. Petersburg and attracted only thirty delegates. The congress unsuccessfully attempted to revive Ittifaq as a viable political party.

Although Ittifaq and the All-Russia Muslim Congresses faded in significance as Tsar Nicholas II reasserted his imperial authority and revolutionary sentiment faded, their legacy as vehicles for unified Muslim political action remained alive. The moderate bourgeois liberals who formed the majority of Muslim political activists abstained from discussing issues of political autonomy and limited themselves to demands for liberal reforms and equal rights regardless of ethnicity or religion. Their agenda could be summarized as (1) defense of cultural, educational, and religious rights of Muslim peoples of Russia; (2) mobilization of popular support among Muslims for political, economic, and social reforms to guarantee equality for Muslims in Russia; and (3) promotion of a democratic regime in which non-Russian nationalities would be represented by elected officials. Despite the relatively narrow, largely middle-class political base of the Muslim leadership, in advocating these moderate demands, Ittifaq and the Muslim congresses succeeded in organizing a potentially significant force for political change. After the collapse of the tsarist regime, this legacy helped bring to life a new all-Russia Muslim movement, this time much more willing to explore the limits of political autonomy within a postimperial Russian state.

Islam and the Bolsheviks: From Allies to Enemies

The collapse of the tsarist regime and the Bolsheviks' seizure of power ultimately proved even more destructive to the Muslim population than the policies of imperial Russia in nearly every respect, especially in religious and cultural matters. Yet the fall of the imperial system initially offered Russia's Muslims opportunities to obtain a greater measure of cultural, religious, and political autonomy. Some Muslims even aspired to total independence and, for a very brief period, even obtained it. An important aspect of this short-lived period of Muslim hopefulness was the revival of Muslim political activity during the struggle between the Bolsheviks and the Provisional Government in 1917.

Muslim Political Activism during the Revolutions of 1917

Arguably, one of the most significant developments in the modern history of Muslim political activism in Russia was the series of assemblies that were held in 1917 under the auspices of a revived All-Russia Congress of Muslims. In the aftermath of the February Revolution of 1917,[81] which brought about the collapse of the tsarist regime and the brief rule of the Provisional Government under Alexander Kerensky, Russia's Muslim political leadership revived the Muslim congress in an effort to influence the course of Russia's postimperial development.[82] The first posttsarist All-Russia Congress of Muslims, held in Moscow on 1–11 May 1917, attracted 800 delegates and 100 observers from various Muslim organizations and parties. Together they represented a wide political spectrum extending from "centralists" (proponents of the idea of a unified Muslim entity) to "autonomists" (adherents of the idea of separate Muslim entities),[83] from traditionalists to modernists, and from pan-Turkists to pan-Islamists. The modernists within the Muslim intelligentsia believed that excessive emphasis on Islam could undermine the Muslims' prospects for progress. Moreover, a major debate developed between those who could be characterized as ethnocentric nationalists and the pan-Islamists. Muhammad Amin Rasulzade from Azerbaijan expressed the view of the former in the following terms:

> They say that Islam in itself comprises a nation. They say that . . . Islam is unifying Muslims into forming a nation. If you ask a Turk what nationality he is, he will invariably say he is a "Muslim." This is an erroneous perception. . . . No doubt, Islam, like other religions of the world, has created a certain bond among its adherents. Yet this is not a national bond; it is an international bond. Just as an international bond was created among Christians to form what is called a "Christian Civilization," Muslim nations of the world have also created a common Islamic culture. This, nevertheless, does not mean that the Muslim peoples of the world have been incorporated into a single nation. Just as there is no such thing as a "Christian Nation," so there is no "Muslim Nation."[84]

Notwithstanding these differences, the congress reached agreement on certain important decisions: It voted against separatism and supported a unified Russian state, albeit with a federal system of government that would guarantee a degree of political, cultural, and national autonomy for non-Russian peoples; approved the creation of the All-Russia Central National Council of Muslims (Milli Shura) and entrusted it with the task of leading and coordinating the actions of Muslims throughout the country; and elected an executive committee, headquartered in St. Petersburg, to direct this new body.[85] Finally, the delegates agreed that the Russian army should be built on the basis of ethnicity, thus requiring the formation of separate Muslim regiments that would serve in areas where they resided.

The second All-Russia Muslim Congress of 1917 took place in Kazan from 21 July to 2 August 1917. In terms of attendance, this congress was less impressive: only 188 delegates participated. However, simultaneously with this second congress, Kazan hosted two other events: the tenth All-Russia Congress of Muslim Clerics (18–26 July 1917) and first All-Russia Muslim Military Congress (17–26 July 1917).[86] On 22 July, the three gatherings converged to hold joint discussions, unanimously adopted the "Declaration of National-Cultural Autonomy of Muslims of Inner Russia and Siberia," and designated 22 July as a national holiday for all Muslims of Russia.[87] Additionally, the delegates to the All-Russia Muslim Congress recommended that the Muslim peoples of Inner Russia and Siberia should resolve issues related to their territorial autonomy, religion, education, and language. To address these issues, the congress established a Milliat Mejlisi (National Assembly) to serve as the highest legislative body for Russia's Muslims and outlined a strategy to divide the territories inhabited primarily by Muslims into national administrative units (*gubernia*), each of which would be governed by a district-level assembly.[88] The Muslim congress also voted to create a Kollegia (Council), consisting of twelve members and headquartered in Ufa, Bashkortostan, to oversee the creation of a Muslim national-cultural autonomy (envisioned as an autonomous entity administered by Muslims) and to coordinate preparations for the first national assembly.

Posttsarist Muslim political activism culminated in the convening of the Milliat Mejlisi from 20 November 1917 to 11 January 1918 in Ufa. Attended mostly by the Muslim Turko-Tatar peoples of Inner Russia and Siberia, in terms of its social composition the assembly was quite representative—participants consisted of merchants, clergy, nobility, and Tatar officers of the Russian military. The Milliat Mejlisi negatively assessed the Bolshevik seizure of power from the Provisional Government in early November 1917[89] and declined an offer by the Russian People's Commissariat on Nationality Affairs (Narodny Komissariat po Voprosam Natsionalnostei, or Narkomnats in Russian abbreviation), a body set up by Vladimir Lenin to coordinate Communist policies toward Russia's national minorities and to encourage them to cooperate with the Bolsheviks. Furthermore, the Milliat Mejlisi adopted a resolution to create a Volga-Ural Republic (Idel-Ural)[90] plus a Constitution of "National Autonomy of Turko-Tatar Muslims of Inner Russia and Siberia" (Konstitutsia "Natsionalnaya Avtonomia Musulman Turko-Tatar Vnutrennei Rossii i Sibiri").[91] The assembly also created a Milli Idara (National Administration) comprised of separate agencies (*nazarats*) to administer the financial, educational, and religious affairs of the Muslim national-cultural autonomy, elected a delegation to attend the Versailles Peace Conference of 1919, and set the date for its future session in May 1918.

The proposal to create the Volga-Ural Republic should not be interpreted as an early attempt at secession on the part of the Muslims of Inner Russia and Siberia, although many Muslim political activists saw secession and political independence as their ultimate objective. Most Muslim leaders realized the impracticality of such a goal and strove only to achieve a significant measure of religious and cultural autonomy. In fact, the second All-Russia Muslim Military Congress, held in Kazan from 8 January to 18 February 1918, passed a resolution reaffirming the earlier decision of the Muslim national assembly to create such a republic that clearly stated that the new autonomous national-cultural territorial entity would be part of the new Russian state.[92]

The October Revolution and the Search for Muslim Allies

The year 1917 marked the peak of Muslim political activism in Russia. The fractured nature of central authority in Russia resulting from the collapse of the tsarist regime and the subsequent struggle for power between the Provisional Government and the Bolsheviks afforded Russia's Muslims an opportunity to organize politically and advocate a reformist agenda incorporating elements of national self-determination, especially religious and cultural. As Lenin attempted to consolidate power after the overthrow of the Provisional Government, he was aware that the attitudes of the non-Russian peoples of the former empire could be critical in determining the fate of the power struggle between the Bolsheviks and their opponents. In dealing with Russia's nearly 20 million Muslims, the new government's most significant challenge, in addition to the general issue of religion, was their ethnic and linguistic diversity, and the fact that these diverse peoples had been incorporated into Russia through conquest and imperial expansion. Therefore, Islam was not merely a "religious" matter, but also a "national" issue. The latter dimension became acute as Muslims began to voice national and political aspirations during the struggle for power in posttsarist Russia.

Recognizing this fact, Lenin avoided alienating Muslims and tried to gain their support. Under his direction, the People's Commissariat for Nationality Affairs issued the "Declaration on the Rights of Peoples of Russia," which proclaimed the equality and sovereignty of the peoples of Russia and recognized the right of non-Russian peoples to self-determination, including the right of secession.[93] Moreover, Lenin and his commissar for nationality affairs, Ioseb Djugashvili (Joseph Stalin), made a special appeal to Russia's Muslims, promising them religious and other freedoms. This "Appeal to All Laboring Muslims of Russia and the East" proclaimed:

> Muslims of Russia, Tatars of the Volga and Crimea, Kyrgyz, and parts of Siberia and Turkestan, Turks and Tatars of Trans-Caucasia, Chechen and Mountain Peoples of Caucasus, and all you whose mosques and prayer houses have been destroyed, whose beliefs and customs have been trampled upon by Tsars and oppressors of Russia: your beliefs and usages, your national and cultural institutions are forever free and inviolate.[94]

The results of these efforts to galvanize Muslim support for the Bolsheviks were mixed. In some cases, they had the desired impact. For example, during the Russian Civil War (1918–22), villages and, according to some reports, whole clans in the mountainous parts of the North Caucasus fought on the side of the Communists. They were joined by the so-called Shari'a squadrons, which served in the ranks of the Red Army, as well as the militia of Zaki Validi Togan in Bashkortostan and the Chechen Red Army under the leadership of Aslanbek Sheripov.[95] Some 70 percent of the Fifth Red Army, or the Turkestan Army, under the command of General Mikhail Frunze, consisted of Muslim soldiers.[96] They supported the Bolsheviks because they believed that the Bolsheviks gave Muslims greater religious liberty than the anti-Bolshevik (White) forces. Some segments of the reform-minded Muslims (Jadidists) in the Volga-Ural region and in Central Asia also felt that Muslim revival would be achieved more easily under the Bolsheviks. Most important, the Bolsheviks had strong allies in the Muslim National Communists, led by Mirsaid Sultan-Galiev, a Tatar nationalist and Marxist who became active in the antitsarist opposition in 1905 and joined the Communists in 1917.

However, skepticism regarding promises made by the Bolsheviks was strong in parts of Central Asia and the South Caucasus. In some cases, such promises had the paradoxical effect of reviving and intensifying old aspirations for political independence. Muslim nationalists of the South Caucasus declared the formation of an independent republic in 1918 and called it Azerbaijan.[97] Several autonomist movements emerged in Central Asia, such as the Kazakh nationalist party Alash Orda, which proclaimed the autonomy of the Kazakh people in December 1917. Farther south in Central Asia, an organization bearing the same name as the Tatar-dominated Ittifaq party in Russia proper, Ittifaq-al-Muslimin (the Union of Muslims), in November 1917 declared national autonomy for the Muslims of Turkestan.[98] This organization was formed by the merger of the two dominant Muslim parties of the region, Shura-i-Islamiya (the Islamic Council), which was comprised mostly of the Jadidist clergy, and the Ulema Jama'ati, which was dominated mostly by the conservative clergy. To the west, the Crimean Tatars elected a Constituent Assembly that adopted a constitution for the region, assumed legislative authority over the internal affairs of the Crimean Tatars, and appointed a military commander to oversee all Tatar military units in the Crimea and ministers for foreign affairs and war.[99]

Partly in response to these autonomist movements, in practice Bolshevik forces treated Muslims more harshly than formally advocated by Lenin. This divergence between declared and actual policy became publicly apparent in Central Asia, where the Bolsheviks aggressively dismantled Muslim organizations.[100] The Tashkent Soviet, formed by the local Russian supporters of the Bolsheviks, initially refused to include Muslims in its organization. Later, in defiance of Lenin's directives, it conducted antireligious campaigns, including profaning mosques, shooting clergy, confiscating the property of religious endowments, and closing religious courts and schools.[101] This behavior further alienated the region's Muslim population and contributed to the outbreak of the Basmachi revolt, which began in 1918 and continued, albeit at a reduced level, until 1928. The seeds of the revolt, however, had been sown earlier, in 1916.[102] As the Bolsheviks extended their rule eastward, they dissolved the governing bodies of the Idel-Ural Republic and arrested much of the Tatar nationalist leadership.[103] In accordance with a resolution of the People's Commissariat on Nationality Affairs and a corresponding decision by the Bolsheviks' Tatar-Bashkir Commissariat of 21 April 1918, the Milli Idara was dissolved. Subsequently, with the consolidation of Bolshevik control in Siberia, the Milliat Mejlisi ceased to exist.[104]

By 1921, although revolts continued in Central Asia, major challenges to Bolshevik power had subsided.[105] This situation permitted Lenin to focus on developing a comprehensive and long-term strategy to address the Islamic challenge with the ultimate goal of eliminating the Muslim religious infrastructure and its influence over the masses. However, as the nascent Communist regime continued to establish its authority in newly pacified regions, the Bolsheviks tried to maintain the fiction of a regime willing to cooperate with Muslim peoples and to permit them a degree of national, cultural, and religious autonomy. Accordingly, Lenin delayed the implementation of his antireligion program. Even certain positive actions were undertaken, such as returning *waqf* property and reopening mosques and religious schools, especially in Central Asia, to regain the trust of Muslims and the clerical establishments. The influence of the Muslim National Communists contributed to this decision.

The Bolsheviks in Power: Religion and the Role of Ideology

The anti-Islam strategy, which began to be implemented in 1924, had three principal components: (1) eradication of the Muslim judicial and educational infrastructure; (2) the elimination of the clerical establishment's financial independence by dismantling the *waqf*; and (3) anti-Islam propaganda. All religions were anathema to Communist ideology, but Islam was especially targeted for attack because it was viewed as reactionary and backward. This vision of Islam was not new. It had been common in prerevolutionary Russia and had been used in early anti-Islam campaigns. The characterization of the Qu'ran by the Russian poet Alexander Pushkin as nothing more than "a collection of new lies and old stories" captures the Russian view of Islam, which persisted after the revolution.[106] It is no wonder that the contents of Bolshevik propaganda against Islam and tactics employed to combat it were similar to those of the tsarist era.[107]

This aspect of the Soviet regime was the most damaging to Russian Muslims and their religious, cultural, and institutional heritage. Whenever state interests required it, Russia's new leaders were prepared to temporarily relent on their antireligious campaign. Nevertheless, the impact of antireligious agitation and coercion brought Russia's traditional Islamic institutions to the brink of collapse.

The ideology of the new regime was at the root of its approach toward Islam. Bolshevik ideology, as expounded by Lenin and his successors, was based on the philosophy of dialectical materialism developed by Karl Marx. An important component of this ideology was a strong antagonism toward religion, which was viewed as the "metaphysical manifestation of capitalist society."[108]

Marxism viewed religion as a historical phenomenon whose specific characteristics were determined by various stages of the development of human societies. According to Marxist theory, early religions arose because of human inability to comprehend natural forces and to control their environment. Thus humans attributed natural phenomena to supernatural sources on which they bestowed divine characteristics. According to Friedrich Engels, "All religion is nothing but the fantastic reflection in men's minds of those external forces which control their daily life, a reflection in which terrestrial forces assume the form of supernatural forces."[109] With the advancement of human societies accompanied by humans' growing ability to control their environment, belief in the divinity of natural forces was transformed into a more abstract and largely monotheistic concept of divinity. To the question of why man's increased knowledge of natural forces and his growing ability to control the impact of these forces on his daily life did not result in religion's elimination, Marxism offers this answer: With the development of human societies, the mode of production also changed, thus bringing about new patterns of socioeconomic relations based on domination and exploitation. This led to feelings of oppression and alienation on the part of the exploited. To cope with their unfavorable conditions, the alienated and the oppressed sought comfort in religion. As graphically put by Marx, religion thus became "the sigh of the oppressed creature, the heart of a heartless world just as it is the spirit of the spiritless conditions, the opium of the people."[110] Lenin shared this view of religion as an essential element in the capitalist order based on domination and exploitation. In his essay "Socialism and Religion," he wrote:

The economic oppression of the workers inevitably calls forth and engenders every kind of political oppression and social humiliation. . . . Religion is one of the forms of spiritual oppression which everywhere weighs down upon the masses of the people, overburdened by their perpetual work for others, by want and isolation. Impotence of the exploited classes in their struggle against the exploiters just as inevitably gives rise to belief in better life after death as impotence of the savage in his battle with nature gives rise to belief in gods, devils, miracles, and the like.[111]

Thus religion becomes "opium for the people, . . . a sort of spiritual booze in which the slaves of capital drown their human image, their demand for a life more or less worthy of man."[112]

However, before acceding to power and while they were still in search of allies against the tsar, the Bolsheviks under Lenin's leadership did not declare all-out war on religion. Rather, they stressed the need for making religion a "private affair" and establishing the principle of separation of church and state. Lenin even went as far as suggesting that the socialists should help those Russian Orthodox clergy who during the tsar's rule had joined in the demand for freedom and protested against the government.

This attitude, in addition to reflecting the practical bent of Lenin and his tactical flexibility when struggling to gain power, also derived from his view that religion, like nationalism, under certain circumstances and during certain periods of a people's history, can perform a progressive role, thus paving the way for the ultimate victory of socialism. Lenin's approach toward the Muslim subjects of the tsar and their aspirations for cultural and political self-determination reflects this perspective as well as crude power calculations. In his struggle against the anti-Bolshevik forces, Lenin appealed to the Muslims' desire for self-determination and partly succeeded in gaining the collaboration of some of them. The Bolsheviks' success in this regard had much to do with the fact that the level of the political consciousness and activism of Russia's Muslims had increased by the time of the October Revolution.

The Bolsheviks in Power: Islam and the Nationalities Problem

Historically, Islam and its role have been closely linked to the desire of Muslim populations to gain greater cultural and political autonomy, if not outright separation and independence from the Russian/Soviet Empire. As such, therefore, the question of how to deal with Islam has always been related to the issue of how to manage the non-Russian populations of the empire and their aspirations for cultural and political self-determination, both under the tsars and during the Communist period.

At the time of the Bolshevik victory, Islam formed the core of the individual and collective self-identity of the overwhelming majority of Muslims, who belonged to different ethnic and linguistic groups, although ethnicity, language, and regional and tribal affiliations were also important components of the Muslims' individual and collective identity. It was in recognition of this fact that despite the existence of administrative divisions based on geography and legal distinctions in terms of citizenship, under the tsarist regime, Muslims were treated as one people and other differences remained vague and secondary. Similarly, during the first years of the postrevolution period, 1918–23, the term "Muslim" was used to designate all those ethnic groups who professed Islam. As outward manifestations of this view, the administration of Muslim territories was carried out by Muslim Commissariats (Muskoms), and a Muslim Red Army and a Muslim Communist Party existed for a short period of time. More important, the Central Muslim Commissariat represented what Bennigsen and Broxup have aptly characterized as the institution that was the embryo of a "Muslim government."[113]

Similar perceptions of Muslims as forming, if not a single nation, at least a single religiocultural community, existed among Muslims themselves. Indeed, as noted earlier, the desire to create a large pan-Islamic state, even if not geographically contiguous, existed within considerable segments of Russia's Muslims.

Nevertheless, the idea of consolidating Muslim areas into a few large units in the context of a federal political system for Russia remained strong. In 1918, one popular vision, especially among pan-Turkist Muslims, was the creation of three major political-territorial entities, namely, (1) a Tatar-Bashkir state encompassing an area from Simbirsk and Kazan in the west to Chelyabinsk and Troitsk in the east with a population of six million. Its written language was to be the Volga Tatar dialect; (2) a Unified Turkestan, including Kazakhstan, with Chagatay Turkic (close to modern Uzbek) as the official language; and (3) a Muslim Caucasus—North and South—with Azeri Turkic as the official written language.[114] The Bolsheviks endorsed the plan of Muslim Communist leaders for the establishment of a Bashkir-Tatar republic, and in January 1919, an Autonomous Mountain Republic that incorporated Cherkess, Kabardin, Karachays, Balkars, Ossetians, Abazins, Chechen, and Ingush was created.[115] The Dagestanis were to set up their own republic in November of the same year. However, once the Bolsheviks defeated the counterrevolutionary forces, they came to see the formation of large political and cultural clusters of Muslims as potentially detrimental to their objectives and opted for a strategy of territorial, linguistic, and cultural fragmentation of the Muslim peoples. This strategy was perfected during Stalin's rule. Thus as early as the autumn of 1918, the Bolsheviks abandoned the idea of a Tatar-Bashkir republic; instead, they created two separate entities. The policy of fragmentation was pushed to the extreme in the North Caucasus.[116]

Over the following decades, the Communist regime also encouraged cultural fragmentation by developing various and closely related dialects into literary languages, a process aimed at enhancing a sense of separateness between closely related peoples, at times causing rivalry and animosity. Present feelings of mistrust between Tatars and Bashkirs owe much to this policy. However, given the existence of ethnic and linguistic differences and even animosities within Russia's Muslim populations, some of the schemes for creating larger clusters of Muslim linguistic and political units were unrealistic. For instance, it is difficult to see how the Tajiks, whose number at the time was larger and who are the heirs of Central Asia's Iranian civilization, would have voluntarily abandoned Persian and used Chagatay Turkic instead. These differences, coupled with ideological divergences noted earlier, made it easier for the Bolsheviks to fragment the Muslims politically and culturally. During the Stalinist period, two other dimensions were added to the nationality policies: (1) the inclusion of substantial ethnic minorities in various republics and autonomous regions and (2) large-scale transfers of populations from their native regions to other parts of the Soviet Union.

Examples of these new policies include the inclusion of the Tajik cities of Samarkand and Bukhara in Uzbekistan, while leaving large Uzbek minorities in Tajikistan and Kyrgyzstan; dividing the Ossetian people between Georgia and North Ossetia; and the transfer of Meskhetian Turks and large numbers of Chechens to Central Asia. Over time, the results of these policies proved counterproductive and detrimental to the interests of the USSR and later the Russian Federation. In particular, these policies failed to eliminate Islam's influence. On the contrary, in many cases, especially that of the deported nationalities, such as the Chechens, these policies strengthened religious feelings, as religion became a means of protecting one's native identity in unfamiliar environments. They also facilitated attraction to the stricter and less progressive versions of Islam.[117]

Islam and the Soviet Experience: From Near Annihilation to Remarkable Revival

Like other aspects of strategies dealing with the non-Russian peoples of the Soviet Union, the basic institutional framework for regulating Muslim religious affairs was developed during Stalin's rule. However, the ideological foundations of this framework were already laid by Lenin, and some institutional groundwork was done during his leadership.

Initially, while emphasizing the superiority of their materialistic ideology, the Bolsheviks tried to maintain a semblance of freedom of conscience. Thus the 1918 Constitution of the Russian Soviet Federated Socialist Republic (RSFSR) allowed both religious and antireligious propaganda.[118] Progressively, however, in practice such freedoms were abolished. Thus while religious propaganda was prohibited, the ideological and institutional basis of antireligious activities was strengthened. On the ideological front, Lenin's article "On the Significance of Militant Materialism" legitimized antireligious propaganda.[119] In 1920, an Agitation and Propaganda Department was established within the Communist Party's Central Committee. The Communists for Justice and Education, as well as the Communist Youth League (Komsomol), became active in organizing antireligious lectures and debates and helping in the publication of antireligious materials. In 1925, the League of the "Militant Godless" was created with the duty of coordinating all antireligious activity. This organization established branch offices in various Muslim-inhabited regions with names such as Allah-Sizler, Khoda Sizlar, and Din-sizlar.[120] In their essentials, these frameworks and policies survived until the time of Gorbachev's reforms. However, the vigor with which anti-Islam policies were implemented fluctuated during different periods under the influence of internal and external needs and the personalities of key leaders.

Muslims during the Stalinist Period, 1928–1953

Stalin's approach to Islam must be viewed in the overall context of building socialism in all its aspects, one of the most important of which was creating a Soviet Man (*Sovetskii Chelovek* or *Homo Sovieticus*). Success in this case was viewed as central to the overall success of the socialist experiment. To create such a human specimen, all peoples of the Soviet Union had to free themselves from the vestiges of the past, of which religion was an important element. Muslims were no exception. They were invited to abandon their Islamic culture in order to become sovietized and part of the new race.

The Communists felt that the fight against Islam must be harder because the comprehensive and all-embracing nature of Islam's juridical and moral code created stronger institutional and psychological barriers between Muslims and non-Muslims. Furthermore, Islam was accused of several flaws: (1) It was the most conservative and reactionary, and the least "social," of all religions because it emphasized the elders' authority, discriminated against women, and generated fanaticism, intolerance, and xenophobia among its followers; (2) Islam served as an instrument of the spiritual oppression of the workers, inculcated a spirit of resignation, and distracted them from revolutionary activities; (3) Islam was alien to the Muslim peoples of the Soviet Union since it had been brought into these regions—Central Asia and the Caucasus—by foreign invaders, such as Arabs, Iranians, and Ottoman Turks; (4) Islamic customs were barbaric and unhealthy, Islamic morals were anathema to socialist morals, and Islamic arts and literature were incapable of evolution and progress; and (5) despite their anti-Russian sentiments, Muslims and their leaders submitted to tsarist rule, which showed their reactionary tendencies. But first and foremost, Islam belonged to the past—not even to the capitalist stage of evolution, but to the feudal era. As such, it had no place in a society of "advanced socialism."[121]

These points were stressed during Lenin's time as well by the organizations noted earlier and in their publications. But during that early period, this type of propaganda had little effect on the population. This prompted Anatoli Lunacharsky, the commissar for education and enlightenment, to say, "Religion is like a nail; the more you hit it, the deeper it goes in."[122]

Stalin ruled over the Soviet Union for thirty-one years, and there were fluctuations in his attitude toward both the treatment of religion in general and dealing with Islam and Muslim populations in particular. Two distinct periods are especially significant.

Campaign of Eradication

Stalin launched his frontal attack on Islam in 1928. This attack included the massive closure of mosques. Before the revolution, there were about 26,000 functioning mosques in the Russian Empire, with 45,000 clerics (mullahs) serving the believers. By the end of Stalin's campaign in 1942, only 1,312 working mosques remained open.

This campaign of mosque closing was accompanied by large-scale persecution of the muslim clergy, who were accused of being "parasites of society" and "counterrevolutionaries." After 1935, they were also accused of being spies for Germany and Japan. As a result of this policy, the number of clergy throughout the Soviet Union was reduced to 8,000. A number of important legislative measures were also adopted that further undermined the position of religion, including Islam. In 1929, an amendment to the constitution abolished the right of religious establishments to proselytize while allowing antireligious indoctrination. The 1929 Law on Religious Associations provided strict functional guidelines for organized religion and authorized the state to supervise and control religious activities. The law placed severe limitations and barriers in the way of these associations.[123] In Islam's case, in addition to attacks on the clergy, Stalin targeted the Muslim National Communists, whose ideological mentor was Mirsaid Sultan-Galiev, because he considered these "national deviationists" to be threats to Soviet power in Muslim areas.[124]

Limited Rapprochement

The outbreak of the Second World War and, in particular, the abrogation of the Nazi-Soviet pact (the Molotov-Ribbentrop Non-Aggression Pact of 23 August 1939), which made the Soviet Union the target of German aggression, required reassessment of the USSR's domestic priorities. The defense and survival of the Soviet Union became the main objectives, goals that required the galvanization of all peoples, leading Stalin to soften his attitude toward both religion and nationalism. In the case of the USSR's Russian population, this policy was successful. In the case of Muslims, the new leniency did not have the same results. Some Muslims fought effectively for the Soviet Union, but others felt little loyalty toward it. It is estimated that of the 1,600,000 Muslim draftees, more than half defected to the Germans. At the end of the war, they paid a heavy price for their lack of total loyalty to the Soviet state. In 1943, Stalin accused all those Muslims whose territory had been occupied by the German armies and some others of treason and deported them to Siberia or other parts of the empire. It is estimated that the number of deportees reached 600,000.[125]

Despite the calamities that later befell them, initially the necessities of war allowed the Muslims to obtain some concessions from the government. In 1942, as a result of the initiatives of Abdurrahman Rasulaev, a Muslim leader from Ufa, the Soviet authorities agreed to normalize relations between Islam and the Soviet government. Consequently, Islam was granted an official Islamic Administration, roughly modeled after the Muhammedan Spiritual Assembly established during Catherine's rule in Ufa. It consisted of four Muslim spiritual boards: (1) Central Asia and Kazakhstan, based in Tashkent; (2) European Russia and Siberia, based in Ufa; (3) North Caucasus and Dagestan, based in Makhachkala; and (4) Transcaucasia, based in Baku. After the war, the foreign policy interests of the Soviet Union prompted Stalin to continue this relatively lenient policy toward Islam while at the same time pursuing atheistic propaganda. Stalin allowed a limited resumption of religious instruction and permitted the reopening of the Mir Arab theological school in Bukhara. However, after the school reopened in 1952, only 100 students were allowed to enroll for a five-year training program. Moreover, the level of religious training was not equal to that of other major Islamic institutions. Thus the school neither quantitatively nor qualitatively could respond to the need for Muslim jurists or *alims*. Islamic literature, mostly copies of the Qu'ran and Islamic calendars, were allowed to be published in small numbers, and a number of previously banned Muslim practices, including pilgrimage to Mecca (*hajj*), became permissible. The postwar period also saw the beginning of a practice that would become more common in the following decades as the Soviet Union's interests and ambitions in the Islamic and Arab worlds expanded, namely, the sending of official Muslim clergy on propaganda tours to Islamic countries and the appointment of Soviet citizens of Muslim origin to diplomatic posts in Arab and Muslim states.[126]

Muslims in the Post-Stalin Era: Khrushchev's "Thaw" and De-Stalinization

Stalin died on 5 March 1953. Following a brief period of collective leadership by Georgi Malenkov as premier and Nikita Khrushchev as first secretary of the Communist Party, the latter consolidated his power, demoted Malenkov, and by 1956 became the sole leader of the Soviet Union. The period of Khrushchev's leadership is best known for his policy of de-Stalinization of Soviet society, including the relative easing of social and political restrictions, and a return to what he himself characterized as "Leninist legalism" as opposed to the arbitrary style of Stalin's rule.

On the question of religion and how to deal with it, however, Khrushchev's instincts and inclinations were not liberal. Rather, he believed in a reformed and reinvigorated antireligious program. Khrushchev's antireligious tendencies were partly rooted in his belief that the Western powers had manipulated the persistence of religion in the Soviet Union in order to undermine the ideological claims of socialism. But Khrushchev's antireligious stands must also be viewed in the context of the resumption of the task of building a Soviet society and creating a Soviet Man, which had been put on hold during the Second World War.

In Islam's case, the religious dimension, as before, was linked to the question of nationalities and, in particular, the special role of the Russian people as the "elder brother" within the family of Soviet nationalities and in the process of building the new socialist society. Indeed, this trend had already begun by the late 1930s. It was believed that once the building of the Soviet system, which also implied the sovietization of all nationalities, was completed, the nationality problem would disappear through the "merging" (*sliyanie*) of various peoples. But before this goal could be achieved, people had to be brought closer together through the process of intense cultural Russification, greater interpenetration of populations, and mixed marriages (*sblizhenie*). Islam's survival as an alternative social, cultural, and moral order and as the core of most Muslims' identity would have seriously hampered the achievement of these goals. However, Khrushchev did not launch his antireligious campaign fully until 1960, except for a brief period in 1954. The worst period of the antireligious campaign was between 1960 and 1964.

In Islam's case, the Soviet Union's foreign policy objectives in the Middle East played an important role in determining the approach to anti-Islamic campaigns, as, indeed, it had done in Stalin's case. Because the Soviet Union wanted to expand its presence in the Middle East—especially in Egypt following the coming to power of Gamal Abdel Nasser, who espoused a militant and anti-Western Arab nationalism—Moscow could not be seen as persecuting the Muslims. In the intervening period, however, studies were conducted on the problems facing antireligious campaigns, including the holding of two interrepublican conferences in Tashkent and Baku to discuss the future state of atheistic propaganda regarding Islam.

By 1963, which was the height of the antireligious campaign, the full impact of Khrushchev's policies was felt on Islam's position in the USSR. The number of operating mosques was reduced to about 400 for the entire Soviet Union, and the number of clergy to between 2,000 and 3,000. A harsh campaign was conducted to discredit the remaining clergy by accusing them of all manner of wrongdoings, and many Islamic rituals were banned.[127] In brief, during the Khrushchev era, the existing antireligious laws were applied strictly.

Brezhnev's Period of "Stagnation," 1964–1982

Under Leonid Brezhnev, the antireligious campaign acquired a less hostile tone, although there was no tangible improvement in the conditions of religious institutions and the clergy. In October 1964, the Communist Party passed a resolution that acknowledged past mistakes and condemned the mistreatment of the clergy. Nevertheless, the mosques remained closed, and few, if any, of the official clergy were reinstated, although a few were released from prison. The basic difference between Khrushchev- and Brezhnev-era policies was that under Brezhnev, emphasis was placed on spreading atheistic philosophy rather than frontally attacking religion. This attitude is best reflected in the amendment to Article 52 of the Law on Religious Associations, which replaced the phrase "freedom of antireligious propaganda" with "freedom of atheistic propaganda." In short, gradually under Brezhnev, a more relaxed attitude toward religion was adopted in practice.

During Brezhnev's rule, too, the Soviet Union's foreign policy interests led the government to change its attitude toward Islam and made the practice of Islam, even if clandestinely, easier. By the mid-1960s, the USSR had made considerable inroads in the Middle East and was bent on the expansion of its influence in the Persian Gulf and the eastern Mediterranean. The prospects for achieving these ambitions were improved by the revolutionary and anti-Western wave that was sweeping through parts of the Middle East. This new environment meant that the traditional Russian/Soviet policy of denigrating Islam as a backward and barbarian religion would hurt its political ambitions in the Islamic world. Therefore, in a swift shift of policy, Islam was redefined as a progressive creed with revolutionary and anticolonial dimensions, and one whose many social principles were not incompatible with socialism. The Soviet government also began to encourage limited and tightly controlled contacts between its official clergy and the Islamic world, under the aegis of the Spiritual Board of Muslims of Central Asia and Kazakhstan, which was assigned the principal responsibility for coordinating these and other propaganda activities.

The Islamic Revolution in Iran in February 1979, which ended the long-standing presence of the United States, the Soviet Union's principal adversary, was characterized as a progressive and anti-imperialist phenomenon. Some Soviet commentators pointed out that the Iranian Revolution demonstrated the correctness of Lenin's view that at a certain stage of people's development, religion can play a progressive role. Leonid Medvedko, a political analyst, wrote that as recognized in classic works of Marxism-Leninism, "like nationalism, religion historically has two aspects: although it has been mostly at the service of the ruling classes, religion has on occasion been used by the oppressed to protest against national or social oppression."[128] Medvedko also referred to one of Lenin's works, *A Draft Programme of Our Party*, and stated that "political protests in religious guise are common to all nations at a certain stage of their development," which, according to Lenin, is one of upheaval, in which the "old order has been turned upside down," but one cannot see what kind of new order is taking shape.[129]

A number of conferences on Islam were held in 1979 and 1980 with the purpose of highlighting the Soviet Union's positive and accommodating treatment of Islam.[130] In the coming years, however, the souring of Soviet-Iranian relations and the Afghan War changed this benign view of Islam. But even during the early days of the Islamic Revolution, certain events in Central Asia demonstrated that Islam could be an instrument of opposition against the Soviet Union as well as Western powers. Among these events were anti-Soviet demonstrations in Tajikistan and Kazakhstan and reports of efforts to reopen mosques in Kyrgyzstan. In view of this factor, while on the one hand trying to co-opt Islam and Muslim countries, the Soviet authorities heightened security in the Muslim-inhabited regions, especially Central Asia because of its proximity to Iran and Afghanistan, and resumed periodic attacks on Islam as a reactionary force.[131]

Soviet Islam on the Eve of the Gorbachev Era: Factors behind Islam's Vitality

By the time Mikhail Gorbachev assumed leadership of the Soviet Union in 1985, more than six decades of intensive anti-Islam campaigns—despite periods of relative relaxation—had institutionally and intellectually devastated Islam. By the end of the Brezhnev era, the number of working mosques had been reduced even further (Table 1.1). In 1966, according to the official *Spravochnik propagandista i agitatora*

Table 1.1

Registered and Nonregistered Mosques in the Russian Federation, 1975–1986

Year	1975	1979	1980	1983	1984	1985	1986
Registered	175	159	166	182	185	187	189
Nonregistered	385	455	434	397	325	318	311

Source: Adapted from Igor Ermakov and Dmitri Mikulski, "Islam in Russia," in *Islam in Russia and Central Asia*, International Lotus Foundation for the Cultures of the Orient, Lotus Book Series no. 1–1993 (Moscow: Lotus Foundation/Detskaya Literatura, 1994), p. 18.

(Reference book of a propaganda worker and agitator), there were 400 working mosques in the Soviet Union. In 1979, according to the chairman of the Council for Religious Affairs of the USSR, there were only 300 registered mosques, plus 700 unregistered. However, the reliability of these figures is doubtful because Soviet religious authorities often cited higher numbers when dealing with the Muslim world, while figures cited for domestic consumption projected a steady decline in the number of working mosques. Therefore, in estimating the number of mosques, the semilegal and illegal institutions of "parallel" Islam must also be taken into account.[132]

Despite institutional weakness, in every other respect Islam remained very much alive and was experiencing a revival. Islam's vitality is attested by the expressions of alarm at its continued influence among the population and the widespread practice of some of its more social rituals, even by professed nonbelievers. On 30 August 1986, Kakhar Makhamov, first secretary of Tajikistan's Communist Party, had warned that "numerous facts show that the antisocial activity of Muslim clerics is growing and that the education of children in Islamic dogma is increasing. . . . We are especially worried by the fact that a certain portion of our youth is attracted to religion."[133] On 8 February 1987, *Kazakhstanskaya Pravda* reported that "the religious situation remains disturbing and the harmfulness of Islam is often underestimated. Backward customs and habits incompatible with the socialist way of life are being revived in some places."[134] More disturbing was the fact that those in charge of implementing atheistic propaganda were not immune to religious influence. Indeed, cases of members of the Communist Party who both observed Muslim social rituals and performed religious practices were not rare. In 1981, the case of a teacher of history and member of the Turkmen Communist Party was noted. After teaching the principles of scientific materialism to his pupils during the day, he would transform himself into a Sufi leader at night.[135] The issue of the so-called self-appointed mullahs and *ishans* (Sufi leaders) was raised at the 1981 Congress of Turkmenistan's Communist Party.[136] In Kazakhstan, in February 1981, the first secretary of the Communist Party, Dinmuhammad Kunaev, who was also a member of the Soviet Politburo, lamented that the observance of religious rituals was not declining in the republic, and even Communist Party leaders participated in them. Ironically, Kunaev himself, according to various reports, had been guilty of the same sin by holding a lavish feast to mark the circumcision of his son.[137]

Considering the long and extensive struggle against Islam by both the tsarist empire and the Soviet state, the following question arises: What factors contributed to Islam's survival and vitality? The main reasons are the following:

1. Islam's role as part of the Muslims' culture and the religious-national symbiosis in Muslim societies. In the Muslim parts of the Soviet Union—unlike some other Muslim countries such as Iran and Egypt that have had rich pre-Islamic cultures and traditions of statehood and nationhood—Islam and Islamic civilization have been the peoples' richest cultural heritage, although some Turkic nationalists have emphasized the richness and even superiority of Turko-Mongol traditions.

2. While Islamic traditions in many regions have been mixed with pre-Islamic and pagan elements, Islam has been the main organizing system of social and political relations and the provider of moral and ethical values in the Muslim-inhabited regions of the Russian/Soviet empires.

3. Soviet nation building was fundamentally different from the process of postcolonial nation building in many other Muslim countries. The most consequential difference was that under the Soviet system, ethnic cultures of various titular nationalities were emphasized to show the full development of various nationalities. Meanwhile, the further expression of national self-identity was stunted by simultaneous emphasis on the so-called socialist internationalism, which condemned any expressions of nationalism as "chauvinistic" and "antisocial behavior," especially in the political sense. The adoption of such a dualistic and contradictory policy was inevitable because the ultimate goal of the Soviet Union was to create a socialist society in which ethnic and national identities would be submerged under the socialist Soviet identity, culture, and ethics. The result of this contradictory policy was that Soviet republics could not develop national identities that could replace old concepts of identity and patterns of loyalty. Consequently, both religious and ethnolinguistic dimensions of identity remained strong.

4. There was a large-scale identification of Islam with nationalism and the expression of national peculiarities through religion. Soviet experts certainly saw this connection. According to S. Muslimov, an antireligious Dagestani expert writing in 1983, "It is well known that religious revivals are tightly tied to nationalistic trends. The nationalistic survivals often take on a religious appearance (*obolochka*), where religious revivals are propagandized under the flag of the defense of national traditions."[138] In an article, O. Redzhepova, a member of the Academy of Sciences of Turkmenistan, acknowledges domestic sources of religious revival: "There are also domestic contradictions and miscalculations (*proshchety*)

that result in deviations (*otstupleniya*) from internationalism which is the norm of the socialist way of life."[139] Because of this symbiosis, Soviet commentators acknowledged that it is difficult to fight Islam without being offensive to national traditions of the USSR's non-Russian peoples.[140]

5. The periodic relaxation of antireligious campaigns allowed the survival of Islam.

6. The often halfhearted manner in which local leaders and officials implemented the antireligious agenda, plus their lingering attraction to Islam, limited the effectiveness of antireligion policies.

7. The Soviet system offered limited benefits for most Muslims. Despite its egalitarian and internationalist dimensions, within the Soviet system, the Russians and other Slavic ethnic groups occupied the privileged positions. In most cases, after more than two centuries of Russian/Soviet rule, a disproportionate percentage of Soviet Muslims remained in rural areas and hence were highly influenced by religion.

8. The Sufi traditions of a significant portion of Soviet Muslims and the network of brotherhoods, which are more difficult to control. These traditions and networks have historically been strongest in the North Caucasus and parts of Central Asia. It appears that by the mid-1970s, the Sufi brotherhoods in the North Caucasus had become more openly active in social and political affairs. According to I. Makatov, an analyst writing in 1978, "Over the last few years religious groups have become more active and begun to meddle in public affairs which have nothing to do with the religious feelings of the believers."[141] The Sufis were also accused of representing Islam as the only depository of moral and national virtues and emphasizing the exclusiveness of Islam and thus trying to induce "a negative attitude toward the Soviet way of life and the friendship among nationalities of different creeds."[142]

9. Intellectual and political developments in the Muslim world in the 1970s, most notably the emergence of an ideologized and politicized Islam as an alternative both to Western and Soviet models of socioeconomic and political development, and the rise of Islamist movements contributed to Islam's survival. The Islamic Revolution in Iran had a significant impact on the reawakening of the political consciousness of Soviet Muslims by demonstrating Islam's potential for successful political mobilization against the existing power structure.

10. The Soviet invasion of Afghanistan in November 1979 and the ensuing ten-year war set in motion dynamics that deeply affected not only the evolution of Soviet Islam but also the fate of the Soviet Union.

The following three consequences of the Russian-Afghan conflict were particularly significant in revitalizing Soviet Islam, including its political dimensions: First, the war in Afghanistan galvanized both the Muslim and Western worlds against the Soviet Union and led to an extensive propaganda campaign against the USSR through a variety of radio programs based in Muslim and Western countries.[143] Even the Islamic Republic of Iran, despite anti-Western leanings, in its broadcasts to the Soviet Union's Muslim-inhabited areas took a consistently anti-Communist line, and its leaders condemned Soviet policies toward Islam in Central Asia and the Caucasus. These broadcasts certainly had an impact on the perceptions and attitudes of Soviet Muslims. The extent of this influence can be judged by the breadth and intensity of the Soviet government's and commentators' responses.[144] For example, in 1980, the head of the Azerbaijan KGB, Major General Zia Yusif Zade, denounced the "harmful influence of imperialist propaganda . . . on certain representatives of our [Azerbaijani] intelligentsia and young people."[145] Although Iran's policy in this respect changed by the mid-1980s, it continued to oppose Soviet occupation of Afghanistan.[146]

Second, the Afghan mujahedin and their Pakistani and Saudi supporters also established direct contacts with Central Asian Muslims.[147] Hundreds of illegal students from Central Asia and elsewhere in the Soviet Union went to study in the religious schools and train in the military camps that the government of President Muhammad Zia ul-Haq of Pakistan, with the financial assistance of Saudi Arabia, had built along the Afghan-Pakistani border. In these military camps and religious schools, young Muslims from the USSR and other volunteers studied, trained, and fought together. They also learned about other Islamic movements, their ideologies, and their tactics.[148] This is how P. I. Dzhabbarov characterized the threat posed by what he called the "Western anti-Communist reactionary Islamic clericalism" supposedly taught in these camps:

> Together with the Western anti-communist reactionary Islamic clericalism, closely linked with the ruling bourgeois-landlord clique which is against revolutionary, anti-feudal and anti-capitalist movements, is also attempting mass attacks, using widely reactionary religious organizations such as *Jamiat-e-Islami* in Pakistan, the Society for Struggle against Communism in Turkey, the Muslim Brotherhood, the Islamic World League and others.[149]

Third, the strength of Afghanistan's Islamic resistance and the forced withdrawal of Russian troops from Afghanistan shattered the perception of the Soviet Union's invincibility and enhanced the view of Islam as an effective instrument of resistance and liberation.

Perestroika, Glasnost, and Gorbachev's Policy toward Islam

There is consensus among specialists on the Soviet Union that among the USSR's leaders, Gorbachev was the least familiar with—or interested in—issues related to the non-Russian nationalities and the related question of religion. Consequently, Gorbachev's inclination was to continue the antireligious campaign. Thus in late February 1986, he stated that the Communist Party would use all forms of ideological influence for the wider propagation of a scientific understanding of the world and for overcoming religious prejudices without permitting any violations of believers' feelings.[150] The chief of the Central Committee cadres on ideological affairs, Yegor Ligachev, actively supported this policy.

Gorbachev's views on Islam reflected the traditional Communist perspectives. Moreover, he blamed Islamic culture for the widespread corruption in Central Asia and saw it as an impediment to his reform-oriented agenda.[151] In addition, until early 1990, Gorbachev had to contend with the influence of hard-liners within the Communist Party, largely identified with Yegor Ligachev, who favored the continuation of the antireligion campaign. However, Gorbachev's anti-Islam feelings and policies should not be attributed solely to Ligachev's negative influence. Rather, Gorbachev's own conviction that Islam's prevalence was a barrier to his reforms was mostly responsible for his attitude. Thus throughout 1986–87, there were calls for the strengthening of atheistic education, especially as applied to Islam, and attacks against the growing influence of Islam, even among educated segments of society. The result was an intensified anti-Islamic campaign, including arrests of unofficial clergy, especially in Central Asia. During the mid-1980s, Islam also came to be viewed as a potential political threat to the Soviet Union's integrity.

It was only in 1988, one year after the official launching of perestroika and glasnost, that Soviet policy toward religion, including Islam, began to change. This change was prompted by two factors: (1) The more democratic personalities and factions seem to have persuaded Gorbachev that economic reform was unlikely to succeed without an overall democratization of the system that would include the religious and spiritual sphere; and (2) beginning in 1986, a number of intellectuals and members of the clergy—mostly Orthodox Christian—had started to either "implicitly defend religion or passively criticize the Soviet Union's religious policies."[152] In particular, some intellectuals, notably Yevgenii Yevtushenko, had tried to establish a linkage between culture and morality and the place of religion as a component of culture.[153]

Two other factors contributed to Gorbachev's change of heart regarding the handling of religious matters, which is reminiscent of other episodes of the Soviet treatment of religion: (1) Gorbachev used the granting of religious freedom as an instrument to garner support for his reform program; and (2) he was sensitive to foreign policy considerations and obligations. Gorbachev was aware that granting some religious freedoms would improve the USSR's and his own image in the West. Moreover, as part of its policy of eliminating Cold War–era vestiges, the Soviet Union had signed the Helsinki Final Act, the concluding document of the Conference on Security and Cooperation in Europe (CSCE), which later became the Organization for Security and Cooperation in Europe (OSCE). Article 16 of the Final Act included provisions on religious freedom that forced Gorbachev's hand. The result was a law on the free practice of religion, approved on 1 October 1990. However, Muslims were the last to benefit from the law's passage, nearly a year after Christians and Jews had been enjoying the fruit of this new liberal policy. In fact, the Muslims did not feel the impact of the law.

Gorbachev's Reforms: Impact on Islamic Revival

The purpose of Gorbachev's strategy of economic reform and political liberalization was not to put an end to communism or to endanger the survival of the Soviet Union, although he did envisage a different type of federal structure for the country. Thus he was surprised and dismayed that the freedoms offered by glasnost were used largely for the expression of ethnic and religious grievances, thus setting in motion dynamics that ultimately led to the Soviet Union's disintegration. Yet in the period 1988–91, Islam and the Soviet Union's Muslim republics and regions were not in the forefront of separatist movements. Ironically, the fatal blow to the Soviet Union's survival was dealt by Boris Yeltsin and the Russian Federation and not by any of the Muslim republics. Perhaps Nursultan Nazarbaev, the President of Kazakhstan, has best expressed the peculiarity of the situation by asking a rhetorical question: since Russia and the Russians controlled the Soviet Union, from whom did they want to become independent?

Nevertheless, because of the following factors, the process of reform contributed to Islam's revival: (1) removal of restrictions on the expression of religious feelings and engaging in religious activities; (2) removal of barriers to increased contacts between Soviet Muslims and the rest of the Islamic world; and (3) the increased flow of funds and Islamic missionaries, in particular from Turkey, Saudi Arabia, Pakistan, and other Arab states and, in the case of some republics such as Azerbaijan, also from Iran. A graphic illustration of this increased level of linkage and interaction between Soviet Muslims and the rest of the Islamic world was King Fahd of Saudi Arabia's sending one million copies of the Holy Qu'ran to Central Asia.

As in 1917, however, traditional Islam was not the only element of the Soviet Muslims' ethnic and cultural consciousness that came to the fore. Rather, as had been the case seventy years earlier, ideas of ethnocentric nationalism, transnationalism, and, most important, pan-Turkism and pan-Islamism were also revived. In some cases, Islamic sentiments and ethnic feelings tended to reinforce one another, whereas in others, nationalist and Islamist tendencies competed and even conflicted. This was the case in Azerbaijan, where the Azerbaijan Popular Front (APF), one of the political groups that emerged during perestroika, espoused a secular, anti-religion ideology along Kemalist lines.

In Tatarstan, as reported by the Tatar scholar Rafik Mukhametshin, the first cautious demands for respectful treatment of Islam in the republican press were raised in March 1988. Later, in May 1988, during the All-Union Conference, the role of Islam in the history of Tatar social thought was discussed. But a deeper awareness of the meaning of Islamic values only began in 1989 during the celebration of 1,000 years of Russian Islam.[154]

Yet it appears that during these early years, there was not a massive popular return to Islam.[155] In fact, during the first years of Tatarstan's struggle for sovereignty, most prominent was political activity motivated by secular, nationalist objectives. Political and social organizations had more of a nationalist tinge, even those that characterized themselves as Islamic. Indeed, the growth of a nationalist movement helped the development of religious institutions in Tatarstan, including the Spiritual Board of Muslims. According to its deputy, Mufti Valliulla Yakub, these institutions grew out of social and nationalist organizations.[156]

Similar developments took place in other parts of the Russian Federation. In 1989, an Islamic religious school was opened in Ufa, Bashkortostan. Within the Russian Federation, the most extensive revival of Islam took place in Dagestan because the region has historically been an Islamic stronghold. Nevertheless, it was not until late 1990 and early 1991 that Islamic groups began to form in Dagestan and Islam-oriented publications appeared.

Islamic political activism was also revived. In this regard, an important development was the founding conference of the Islamic Rebirth Party (IRP) in Astrakhan in June 1990. The main base of this party was among the Avars, and its first leader was a Dagestani medical doctor, Akhmadkadi Akhtaev. Another early movement was the Islamic Democratic Party (IDP). The IDP was less Islamically oriented and wanted to create a synthesis between Islam and democracy. The party was highly critical of communism, and in the power struggles that were under way in Moscow, the IDP and its leader, Abdurashid Saidov, supported Boris Yeltsin because of his more liberal posture toward the Soviet Union's ethnic republics.[157] Another Islamic political grouping that emerged in the North Caucasus was the Party of the Islamic Way (Path) in Chechnya, which was established in 1990 and was led by Bislan Gantamirov. Smaller groupings based on ethnic or local affiliations also sprang up, but their impact was limited.

Meanwhile, a number of broader cultural and other institutions and groupings with headquarters in Moscow were created, including the Islamic Cultural Center of Russia, under the directorship of Abdul Vahid Niazov; the Moscow Institute of Islamic Civilization; the Religious-Cultural Center "Medina," based in Nizhny Novgorod; and the Voluntary Muslim Center (Oruzba) in the Volgograd region.[158] Many of these groupings either disappeared in the post-Soviet period or were transformed into totally different institutions, while other entities were established. The process of the evolution of Russia's Islamic institutions at both the federal and local levels is still continuing within the context of the broader developments in the Russian Federation and under the influence of internal and external stimuli.

Conclusion

The history of Russia's encounter with Islam spans nearly a millennium. For several centuries, Islam and Muslims remained more or less distant neighbors rather than part of Russia's religious, cultural, and political landscape. Russia's more intimate acquaintance with Islam was a result of foreign (Mongol) invasion that led to Russia's subjugation by peoples who later adopted Islam. Thus from the very beginning, in Russian minds Islam became identified with hostile alien forces against whom Russians must unite and from whose domination they must free themselves. Therefore, Tatar/Muslim rule arguably contributed to Russia's religious, ethnic, cultural, and eventually political consolidation. The next stage in Islam's spread in Russia was the result of Russian expansion into Muslim lands, beginning with the conquest of Kazan and continuing for four centuries. Thus the Muslims' collective memory of encounter with Russia is also that of an alien conqueror from whose domination they have striven to free themselves, or failing that, to try to maintain their religious and cultural traditions.

In sum, the underlying context of Russian-Muslim encounter has been that of conquest and reconquest. Russia's treatment of Islam and Muslims in the last 500 years has been mostly characterized by suppression and efforts at total elimination, especially under the Communists. However, this general policy was interspersed with periods of relative tolerance, mostly because of external threats or the use of Islam and Muslims as instruments of Russian foreign policy. These periods of relative relaxation enabled Islam to survive in Russia, albeit in a culturally and religiously debilitated form.

The relationship between Russia and Islam as cultural and political entities and between the Russian and Muslim peoples has essentially been colonial. This was true even in the Soviet period, despite the universalist aspirations of the socialist system. The consequence of this essentially colonial relationship was that whenever political circumstances permitted, Russia's Muslims agitated for self-determination, though to varying degrees of intensity. This was the case during 1905–7 as well as between 1917 and 1921 and in 1986–91.

Following the Soviet Union's demise, a large part of Russia's Muslim territories gained independence, but the issue of the place and role of Islam in post-Soviet Russia and the questions and dilemmas raised by the continued Muslim quest for self-determination are still evolving and, so far, have evaded easy answers and solutions. What is clear is that the Islamic component of Russia is still playing a considerable role in its internal evolution and in its relations with the outside world.

2

Islam in Post-Soviet Russia

A Demographic, Geographic, Institutional, Socioeconomic, Ideological, and Political Profile

Since the collapse of the Soviet Union, Islam's presence in Russia has vastly expanded. This expansion is reflected in the development of Islam's physical and intellectual infrastructure and in Muslims' rising awareness of their religious and cultural traditions and heritage. Meanwhile, because of a general decentralization in the Russian Federation and increased contacts with the Islamic world, Russian Islam has become organizationally, intellectually, and politically more diverse and complex.

Despite its revitalization, Islam has not eliminated the importance of ethnic, linguistic, and other factors as determinants of the collective self-identity of Russia's Muslims. Islam, nevertheless, has become a significant element in the process of identity formation of Russian Muslims and in the sociopolitical evolution of Russia's Muslim-inhabited regions. Most important, Islam has contributed to a greater Muslim cultural and political self-assertion, sometimes even leading to the emergence of autonomist and separatist movements, as best exemplified by Chechnya's quest for independence. In the process, Islam has become a more important variable in the overall development of Russia. This period of expansion and diversification of Islam, however, has reached a plateau and could experience a decline in the coming years. The following factors justify such a prognosis: (1) efforts of the federal government under President Vladimir Putin since 2000 to stop and reverse centrifugal tendencies—political, economic, and cultural—within the Russian Federation; (2) greater efforts to bring Muslim organizations under state control; (3) growing anti-Muslim sentiments among ethnic Russians, partly because of the Chechen War and its fallout, including acts of terrorism; (4) disenchantment of many Russian Muslims with the meager impact of religious revival on their living conditions and on the achievement of their cultural and political aspirations; and (5) the consequences of the 11 September 2001 terrorist attacks in the United States, which created greater sympathy in the West for Russia in dealing with the more restive elements within its Muslim population. This sentiment was further strengthened following the hostage-taking operation on 23 October 2002 in Moscow's Dubrovka Theater by a group of Chechen rebels. Despite these trends, because Islam is Russia's second-largest religion after Orthodox Christianity, both the number of its followers and its ethnocultural influence will ensure its continued importance as a factor in Russia's overall political and cultural development.[1]

How Many Muslims in Russia?

There is no agreement on the number of Muslims in the Russian Federation among different Russian institutions dealing with these issues, Russian scholars, and even Russia's Muslims themselves. There are no official statistics on the number of Muslims, and whatever official information exists is derived from census data on the number of predominantly Muslim ethnic groups in Russia.[2] Consequently, estimates of the number of Muslims produced by various surveys and unofficial and semiofficial studies diverge widely, ranging from 3 million to 30 million. The lower estimate of 3 million is based on a poll conducted by the All-Russia Center for Public Opinion in 1993 and covers only those Muslims who are fully observant.[3] Obtaining a more inclusive estimate more accurately reflective of Muslims' self-identity is hindered by the following factors: (1) the lack of nationwide census data on the religious affiliation of Russian citizens because neither the last census of the RSFSR in 1989 nor the first census of the Russian Federation in 2002 contained questions regarding religious affiliation; (2) the lack of consensus on the criteria by which the religious affiliation should be determined, namely, whether the level of religious observance or cultural affinity and self-identification are the best criteria; and (3) politically motivated estimates and manipulation of data regarding the number of Muslims by Russian and Muslim analysts. For example, the figure of 30 million is quoted both by those who want to stress the Muslim community's political influence and those who want to heighten popular fears about the growing Muslim presence in Russia and the risks that it poses to domestic demographic and political equilibrium.[4]

According to a series of surveys conducted by the Public Opinion Foundation in July 2000, 4.2 percent of Russian citizens, including 2.9 percent of Moscow residents, considered themselves Muslims. Similar surveys carried out in April 2001 yielded different results, with 5 percent of Russian citizens (7.75 million people), including 2 percent of Moscow residents, identifying themselves as Muslims. Mikhail Tulskiy suggests that a realistic estimate of the number of Muslims in Russia is between 7 and 9 million, of whom around 200,000 reside in Moscow.[5] Aleksei Maximov puts the number at approximately 8 million. He excludes from his estimate those Muslims residing in Russia who are not citizens of the Russian Federation. Maximov contends that of the 8 million Muslim citizens, at least half do not attend mosque on a regular basis.[6] A survey conducted in November 1999 by the Institute of Sociopolitical Studies of the Russian Academy of Sciences put the number of Muslims at 6 percent of the Russian population (8.7 million people). The same year, a group of scientists under the direction of academician Anatolii Vishnevsky estimated that based on information on natural increases and migration provided by the State Committee of the Russian Federation on Statistics (Goskom-stat), Muslims constitute 9 percent of the population (13.17 million people).[7]

More realistic assessments of some official and semiofficial Russian sources point to a population of 15 to 20 million, with the latter closer to the mark. R. Silantiyev maintains that between 8 and 10 percent (12 to 15 million people) of Russia's population profess Islam.[8] According to an article in the May 2001 issue of *Russian Federation Today* published by the Civil Service Academy of the Russian Federation, 13.5 million Muslims reside in Russia.[9] This number, however, does not include Muslims residing in Moscow, St. Petersburg, and other parts of western Russia. Personal interviews and conversations with Muslim religious figures, ordinary citizens, Russian officials, and experts indicate that a conservative estimate of the number of Muslims in Moscow and other parts of western Russia is around 2.5 to 3 million, of which 1.5 million to 2 million live in Moscow. Thus the total number of Muslims would be between 16 million and 16.5 million. The high number of Muslims in Moscow prompted the chairman of the Russian Council of Muftis (RCM), Mufti Ravil Gainutdin, who also chairs the Spiritual Board of Muslims of the European Part of Russia (Dukhovnoe Upravlenie Musul'man Evropeiskoi Chasti Rossii, DUMER), to say that "Moscow can be regarded as the main Muslim spiritual center on an all-Russia scale."[10] The estimate of the Muslim population of the Russian Federation by F.M. Mukhametshin and A.A. Dubkov also falls in the range of 15 to 20 million; they claim that more than 15 million citizens of the Russian Federation either profess Islam or adhere to some Muslim traditions.[11] In similar estimates, the embassy of the Russian Federation in Washington, DC, puts the number of Muslims at 19 million, and the representative of the RCM cites the 20 million figure, adding that this number is used to determine the Russian quota for the *hajj*. The ambassador of Saudi Arabia to the Russian Federation, Muhammad Hasan Abu aliWali, in an interview with *Nezavisimaya Gazeta*, confirmed that Russia's quota for the *hajj* is based on the 20 million figure.[12] At a press briefing on 27 January 2003, A.V. Yakovenko, the official spokesman of the Russian Ministry of Foreign Affairs, stated that there are more than 20 million Muslims in Russia.[13]

Once different estimates are taken into account, it appears that a figure of 18 to 20 million is the most realistic number. Thus Muslims constitute between 12 and 13.8 percent of the Russian Federation's population of 145 million. However, controversies regarding the number of Russian Muslims are likely to continue for the foreseeable future. Even Russia's 2002 census—the first one since the USSR's collapse—is unlikely to resolve the controversy, because although citizens were asked to identify their ethnicity, they were not queried about their religion.

Future Demographic Outlook

According to one estimate, by the year 2030, the number of Muslims in Russia will reach 30 million, although some offer even higher estimates.[14] In absolute terms, this is not a tremendous increase. However, viewed in the context of the declining birthrate among primarily Orthodox ethnic Russians, it may appear more significant. Some projections of demographic trends among the ethnic Russians are quite alarming.[15] Russian authorities, including President Putin, have expressed concern over the falling birthrate among Russians.[16] Irrespective of the seriousness of Russia's demographic crisis, a significant gap exists between the birthrates of ethnic Russians and Russia's predominantly Muslim ethnic groups: 1.7 births per 100 women for ethnic Russians, which is below the replacement rate,[17] and 4.5 births per 100 women for predominantly Muslim ethnic groups. In Moscow, for instance, according to the calculations of the Institute of General Genetics, in 1999 there were 1.24 births per 100 female Russian Muscovites, whereas Azeri Muscovites had 5.71.[18]

Declining birth rates are a by-product of the deterioration of Russia's socioeconomic conditions, including the degradation of its public health-care system, which affects all religious and ethnic groups, including Muslims. The discrepancy in demographic trends between ethnic Russians and Muslims stems from differences in lifestyles, notably the low level of alcoholism among Muslims and their proclivity for larger families. A continuation of this discrepancy could make Russia ethnically and religiously more diverse and increase the percentage of Muslims among the total population, thereby altering its social and political dynamics. However, even with an increase in the total number of Muslims and a declining birthrate among ethnic Russians, their relative percentages may not change much if Russia compensates for its population decrease by encouraging large-scale migration of non-Muslims, including ethnic Russians, living outside its borders. Nevertheless, should Russia become ethnically more diverse, its political and social dynamics would be affected, perhaps offering Muslims greater political weight. This is, however, by no means certain, and the reverse of such a scenario could materialize. Already, a body of opinion in Russia believes that the increase in the number of ethnic Muslims threatens Russian culture and potentially its territorial integrity and, therefore, should be counterbalanced through a policy of Russification and assimilation of non-Russians, especially Muslims. Such views have begun to influence aspects of the federal government's policies.

Geographic Distribution of Russia's Muslims

Muslim communities exist in all of the Russian Federation's eighty-nine territorial divisions (or federation subjects), including some of the most remote areas, such as Kamchatka Peninsula, which has about 30,000 Muslim inhabitants.[19] However, Russia's Muslim population is concentrated in two regions: the North Caucasus (or southern Russia) and the Volga-Ural region. According to R. Silantiyev, in the North Caucasus, Islam is the dominant religion in Dagestan, Ingushetia, Chechnya, Kabardino-Balkaria, and Karachaevo-Cherkessia.[20] Maksim Yusin of *Izvestia* states that Muslims constitute a majority in seven out of the eighty-nine subjects of the Russian Federation: Tatarstan, Bashkortostan, Chechnya, Dagestan, Ingushetia, Kabardino-Balkaria, and Karachaevo-Cherkessia.[21] According to the Russian Academy of Civil Service, the number of Muslims in the North Caucasus is approximately 1.285 million, which is a conservative estimate because it excludes smaller, largely Muslim ethnic groups in Dagestan as well as Muslims among the ethnic Ossets, a predominantly Orthodox Christian people. The largest concentrations of Muslims in the Volga-Ural region reside in the republics of Tatarstan and Bashkortostan, which have a combined estimated Muslim population of 4 million. Approximately 3.2 million Muslims live in central Russia. Additionally, between 2 million and 3 million Muslims live in and around Moscow and St. Petersburg. Major areas of Muslim concentration in Siberia and the Far East are Omsk, Tyumen, Tobolsk, Novosibirsk, Vladivostok, Khabarovsk, and Urengoi. Table 2.1 on pages 48–49 provides a selected list of Muslim populations in different regions of Russia.

Evolution of the Institutional Structures of Islam: Fragmentation and Reconsolidation

During the Soviet period, the religious life of Muslim-inhabited regions that are now part of the Russian Federation was managed by two central spiritual boards: (1) the Muslim Spiritual Board of the European Part of the USSR and Siberia, with headquarters in Ufa, Bashkortostan, and (2) the Muslim Spiritual Board of the North Caucasus based in Makhachkala, Dagestan. A third spiritual board, the Spiritual Board of Muslims of Central Asia and Kazakhstan, was also important because the only two Soviet institutions of higher Islamic education—the Mir Arab Medressah in Bukhara and the modern Islamic Institute of Al-Bukhari in Tashkent—were located in Uzbekistan.[22] These spiritual boards were under the supervision of the Council of the Affairs of Religious Cults, which was created by Stalin in 1944 and, with some modifications, continued overseeing religious affairs until the Soviet Union's disintegration.

This situation has changed drastically in the post-Soviet period. If the Soviet era was characterized by overcentralization, the post-Soviet period's distinguishing feature has been the administrative and institutional fragmentation of Muslim institutions. According to F.A. Asadullin, head of the Department of Science and Government Liaisons of the Russian Council of Muftis, in 1999, more than forty independent spiritual administrations were operating in the Russian Federation. Other sources put the number even higher: Alexander Ignatenko states that by September 1999, there were fifty-one spiritual boards of Muslims in Russia.[23] According to Mukhametshin and Dubkov, by 2000, their number had reached sixty.[24] Moreover, the pattern of allegiance of these spiritual boards vis-à-vis the centralized religious organizations (such as the RCM or the Central Spiritual Board of Muslims of Russia and European Countries of the Commonwealth of Independent States) has been quite fluid in the sense that they have tended to shift alliances and to form loose coalitions. This situation makes the exact identification of their structural affiliation very difficult. There are frequent cases of two or more—often rival—Muslim administrative structures coexisting within a single federation subject.[25]

Together with the fragmentation of the Islamic administrative structures, post-

Soviet Russia has experienced a proliferation of subregional Muslim organizations and local congregations with varying degrees of autonomy vis-à-vis the Muslim spiritual boards. By July 1999, 3,072 Muslim religious organizations had registered with the Russian Ministry of Justice.[26] According to the Commission on Affairs of Religious Associations (Komissia po voprosam religioznikh ob'edinenii), the total number of local Muslim organizations in the Russian Federation had reached 4,140 by the end of 2000.[27] Table 2.2 on pages 50–51 presents a detailed breakdown of the survey of sixty-five regions of the Russian Federation conducted by the commission and a picture of both the number and the pattern of distribution of Muslim organizations in the Russian Federation.[28]

Factors behind the Diversity of Russia's Islamic Organizations

The decentralization of Russia's Muslim religious establishment is partly the logical outcome of its broader democratization. It also reflects the ethnic, cultural, and geographic diversity of Russia's Muslims.[29] Under these conditions, regional and local organizations are often best able to represent and respond to religious needs of Muslim communities. However, this decentralization also reflects two other trends that could have negative consequences both for Russia's Muslims and for the state of interethnic and interconfessional relations in the Russian Federation: (1) increased religious and religio-ideological divergences within Russia's Muslim population and (2) growing rivalry among Muslim religious leaders for spiritual and political influence. The latter reflects personal ambitions, different ideological tendencies, and ethnic and cultural differences. To illustrate, the competition between Mufti Talgat Tadzhuddin, chairman of the Central Spiritual Board of Muslims of Russia and European Countries of the Commonwealth of Independent States (Tsentral'noe Dukhovnoe Upravlenie Musul'man Rossii i Evropeiskikh Stran Sodruzhestva Nezavisimikh Gosudarstv, CSBM) located in Ufa, and Sheikh Ravil Gainutdin, chairman of the RCM, based in Moscow, partly reflects the ethnic and political rivalry between the Tatars and the Bashkirs. According to R.A. Silantiyev, "The most negative consequences for the integrity of the Russian Islam stem from the tensions between the Tatars and Bashkirs."[30]

The proliferation of religious organizations prompted the government to regulate their activities and encourage the consolidation of smaller entities. Thus in September 1997, the federal government enacted the Law on Freedom of Conscience and Religious Associations. This law designates two categories of religious associations: officially recognized religious organizations (*organizatsiya*) that are registered with the authorities and informal religious groups (*gruppa*) that are not required to register, but have fewer legal rights.[31] Among the rights reserved for officially registered organizations are (1) owning buildings of worship, (2) publishing and disseminating religious literature, (3) establishing charitable organizations, (4) founding and operating religious educational institutions, and (5) inviting foreign nationals to Russia for professional religious activities.[32]

The 1997 law further stipulates that a religious organization must demonstrate

Table 2.1

Distribution of Muslims in Selected Subjects of the Russian Federation

Unit of Administrative Division: Republic, Krai, Oblast, Okrug	Estimates of Muslim Population	Source
Moscow City and Mocow Oblast	1.5–2 million	http://www.muslim.ru
Sverdlovsk Oblast	300,000	*What the Papers Say* (WPS) Russian media monitoring and newspaper digest service, http://www.wps.ru:8101tc_index.html
St. Petersburg and Leningrad Oblast	500,000	DUMER
Samara Oblast	200,000	http://mechet.perm.ru
Perm Oblast	100,000/300,000	http://mechet.perm.ru/obrashenie%20engl.html
Omsk	90,000	The fundraising letter by the head of the Spiritual Board of Muslims of Siberia and Far East, Mufti Zulckarnay Shackirzianov (undated, but after 6 August 1999), http://newsasp.omskreg.ru/culture/OmskIslam/info.html
Norilsk City	60,000	http://mechet.perm.ru
Republic of Karelia	20,000	http://www.murm.ru/~islam/activ.html
Republic of Marii-El	60,000	RFE/RL *Tatar-Bashkir Weekly Review*
Republic of Tatarstan	1,794,500	http://www.kcn.ru/tat_en/tatarstan
Republic of Bashkortostan	2,050,000	http://www.rferl.org/nca/features/1997/08/F.RU.970826152920.html
Republic of Dagestan	1,854,000	The official Web site of the State Council, Popular Assembly, and the Government of Dagestan, http://rd.dgu.ru/dagetn.html
Republic of Ingushetia	254,156	The unofficial Web portal of the Republic of Ingushetia, http://www.ingushetiya.ru:8080/article/34.html
Republic of Karachaevo-Cherkessia	202,560	http://www.geocities.com/wtoghuj/adiga.html
Republic of North Ossetia-Alania	408,100	A.A. Tsutsiev, *Certain Aspects of Language Situation and Language Policy in North Ossetia*, http://www.alanianet.ru/neokavkaz/n1/1-7.htm

(*continued*)

Republic of Kabardino-Balkaria	456,000	http://www.geocities.com/wtoghuj/adiga.html
Republic of Adygea	99,088	http://www.geocities.com/wtoghuj/adiga.html
Republic of Chechnya*	899,000	http://izvestia.ru/community/article7771
Kamchatka Oblast	30,000	http://www.assalam.dgu.ru/html14/a14-6.html
Total	11,077,404–11,577,404	

*The number of Chechens cannot be determined with reliable precision due to the ongoing war, which has generated massive civilian casualties and large flows of Chechen refugees into neighboring Ingushetia, Dagestan, Azerbaijan, Georgia, and Russia proper. This figure is based on the last Soviet census of 1989. Maksim Yusin, "Skol'ko u nas Musulman?" (How many Muslims do we have?), *Izvestia*, 16 October 2001 <http://izvestia.ru/community/article7771>. The preliminary results of the first Russian census of 2002 showed that the number of Chechens has actually increased to 1,088,000. However, this census result has been widely contested, and some observers noted that both the local administration and federal authorities were interested in deliberately inflating the number of Chechens— the former in the hope of receiving more federal funds for the so-called dead souls, the latter with the political purpose of demonstrating the normalization of life in Chechnya. See Olga Vandisheva, "Chechentsi ne stali tret'im narodom Rossii" (The Chechens have not become the third-largest nation of Russia), *Komsomolskaya Pravda*, 28 November 2002, the official Web site of the Russian census 2002 <http://www.perepis2002.ru/pe_publ/article_2002_11_28_N7.html> (at the time, this site was accessible, but this site is no longer valid). On the controversy of the census results in Chechnya see Timur Aliev, "Strannosti chechenskoi perepisi" (Peculiarities of the Chechen census), *Severny Kavkaz*, 28 October 2002, *Pravda.ru* <http://districts.pravda.ru/printed.html?news_id=2030>. For potential drawbacks in the methodology of the Russian census of 2002, see Valery V. Stepanov, "The 2002 Russian Census: Approaches to Measuring Identity" (paper presented at the convention of the Association for the Study of Nationalities, Columbia University, New York, NY, April 13, 2002) <http://www.iea.ras.ru/topic/census/discuss/stepanov_paper2002.doc>.

---

that it has been operating on Russian territory for fifteen years before registering and acquiring these rights.[33] A November 1999 Russian Constitutional Court ruling exempted religious organizations registered before the law's enactment from this fifteen-year waiting period; however, such organizations were required to reregister with the authorities within two years—later extended by amendment to three years (to December 2000)[34]—to maintain their legal status.[35] In July 2002, an amendment to the 1997 law, enacted as part of an initiative by President Putin to counter political extremism, established potentially harsher restrictions. The amendments grant authorities the power to ban any religious organization that engages in extremist activities, including such vaguely defined acts as undermining the security of the Russian Federation and interfering with the lawful activity of the authorities at any level.[36] Such language, loosely interpreted, could limit any religious activity deemed undesirable by the government.

Table 2.2

Distribution of Muslim Organizations in the Russian Federation, 2000

Unit of Administrative Division (Federal District/Republic, Krai, Oblast, Okrug)	Number of Muslim Organizations as of the End of the Year 2000*
Southern Federal District	
The Republic of Dagestan	1,099
The Republic of Kabardino-Balkaria	130
The Republic of Karachaevo-Cherkessia	92
The Republic of Chechnya	150
The Republic of Ingushetia	6
The Republic of Adygea	15
The Republic of North Ossetia–Alania	7
Krasnodar Krai	11
Stavropol Krai	39
Rostov Oblast	9
Volgograd Oblast	16
Astrakhan Oblast	38
Subtotal for Southern Federal District	**1,612**
Central Federal District	
Vladimir Oblast	4
Ivanovo Oblast	1
Orel Oblast	1
Kostroma Oblast	1
Tver Oblast	1
Ryazan Oblast	1
Kursk Oblast	1
Moscow Oblast	20
Yaroslavl Oblast	2
Subtotal for Central Federal District	**32**
Volga Federal District	
The Republic of Bashkortostan	560
The Republic of Kalmykia	6
The Republic of Marii-El	24
The Republic of Mordovia	11
The Republic of Tatarstan	985
The Republic of Udmurtia	25
The Republic of Chuvashia	38
Nizhny Novgorod Oblast	29
Penza Oblast	71
Samara Oblast	76
Saratov Oblast	20
Ulyanovsk Oblast	79
Perm Oblast	76
Orenburg Oblast	91
Subtotal for Volga Federal District	**2,091**

(*continued*)

Northwest Federal District

The Republic of Komi	1
Vologda Oblast	1
Kaliningrad Oblast	1
Murmansk Oblast	1
Pskov Oblast	1
Leningrad Oblast	1
Subtotal for Northwest Federal District	**6**

Ural Federal District

Kurgan Oblast	27
Sverdlovsk Oblast	51
Tyumen Oblast	93
Chelyabinsk Oblast	75
Khanty-Mansi Autonomous Okrug	21
Yamalo-Nenets Autonomous Okrug	10
Subtotal for Ural Federal District	**277**

Siberian Federal District

The Republic of Altai	2
The Republic of Buryatia	3
The Republic of Khakassia	2
Altai Krai	1
Krasnoyarsk Krai	9
Irkutsk Oblast	5
Kemerovo Oblast	11
Novosibirsk Oblast	22
Omsk Oblast	36
Tomsk Oblast	9
Subtotal for Siberian Federal District	**100**

Far East Federal District

The Republic of Sakha (Yakutia)	3
Primorsky Krai	3
Khabarovsk Krai	1
Kamchatka Oblast	1
Amur Oblast	1
Subtotal for Far East Federal District	**9**

Total for Russian Federation ** 4,127**

Source: F.M. Mukhametshin and A.A. Dubkov, "Musulmanskie Organizatsii v Rossiiskoi Federatsii" (Muslim organizations in the Russian Federation), Institut Gosudarstvenno-Konfessionalnikh Otnoshenii i Prava (Institute of relations between the state and religious denominations and law), 3 July 2001 <http://www.state-religion.ru/cgi/run.cgi?action=show&obj=1304>.

*These are the aggregate figures that include Muslim organizations that were registered with the Ministry of Justice of the Russian Federation, those that were undergoing the process of registration at the time of the survey, and those that were functioning without registration.

**This total excludes Muslim organizations located in the federal cities of Moscow and St Petersburg, which have 24 and two such organizations, respectively. However, even if we add these numbers we get the new total of 4,153, which still exceeds the total mentioned by the authors of the article (4,140) by thirteen. Mukhametshin and Dubkov fail to explain this discrepancy.

Principal Muslim Spiritual Boards

In the post-Soviet era, two principal Muslim organizations have been vying for the allegiance and control of Russia's Muslim community: the CSBM and the RCM. According to Dinara Mukhametshina, these two organizations are competing to establish their spheres of influence in more than 85 percent of Muslim congregations (*makhalliya*), constituting about 4,500 communities.[37]

The Central Spiritual Board of Muslims of Russia and European Countries of the Commonwealth of Independent States (CSBM)

According to Alexander Ignatenko, from a purely legal point of view, the CSBM is the successor to the Soviet-era Spiritual Board of Muslims of the European Part of the USSR and Siberia (Dukhovnoe Upravlenie Musul'man Evropeiskoi chasti SSSR i Sibiri).[38] In 1988, there were 142 officially registered Muslim communities under the jurisdiction of this organization. However, with the democratization of society and liberalization of religious life in Russia in the 1990s, the number of Muslim congregations increased almost tenfold.[39]

In response to the changes taking place in the Soviet political landscape, the Muslims of the European part of the USSR and Siberia convened in Ufa at the Fifth All-Russia Muslim Congress on 6–8 June 1990. Approximately 700 delegates from Russia and other Soviet republics, plus foreign guests from thirty-six countries and representatives of international Islamic organizations, attended this meeting. The Fifth Congress adopted a new charter for the Spiritual Board of Muslims (SBM) of the European Part of the USSR and Siberia, reelected Talgat Tadzhuddin as its chairman, and bestowed upon him the title of Sheikh-ul-Islam.[40]

Soon afterward, rifts emerged within the organization and set in motion the process of its disintegration. The first step in this direction was taken in August 1992 when the spiritual administrations of Muslims of Bashkortostan and Tatarstan decided to secede from the Spiritual Board of Muslims of the European part of the USSR and Siberia. Other major regional religious centers followed. Faced with the prospect of the imminent breakup of the Spiritual Board of Muslims of the European Part of the USSR and Siberia, the Sixth Extraordinary Congress of Muslims of the Russian Federation and the European Part of the CIS and Baltic states was organized in November 1992. The congress adopted a resolution expressing the desire of the participants to maintain the historical unity of the organization, but it fell short of implementing specific measures that could have prevented further disintegration.[41] The delegates to the congress adopted the present name, the Central Spiritual Board of Muslims of Russia and European Countries of the CIS (CSBM), thereby acknowledging the dissolution of the Soviet Union.[42] They hoped that most of the major autonomous Regional Spiritual Boards of Muslims (RSBMs) would continue to recognize the jurisdiction of the CSBM and abide by its decrees. The congress also created the new religious position of the supreme mufti and bestowed it upon Sheikh-ul-Islam Talgat Tadzhuddin.[43] On 8 April 1994, the CSBM registered its charter with the Ministry of Justice of the Russian Federation.[44]

The Seventh Extraordinary Congress of Muslims, organized on 1 November 1994 in Ufa, marked the most controversial event in the short history of the newly formed CSBM. In a display of dissatisfaction with Tadzhuddin, delegates to the congress revoked a provision of the spiritual board's charter stipulating that the supreme mufti be appointed for life, stripped Tadzhuddin of his position as supreme mufti and chairman of the CSBM, and voted to take away his religious title of mufti. In his place, the congress appointed Z. Khairullin to the positions of supreme mufti and chairman of the CSBM. However, Tadzhuddin and his allies convened another Extraordinary Session of the Congress of Muslims on 7 December 1994. Delegates to this session of the congress voted to revoke the previous resolutions of the Seventh Extraordinary Congress and called for organizing another Extraordinary Congress of Muslims. Meanwhile, Khairullin voluntarily resigned from the position of supreme mufti. On 17 January 1995, the Seventh Extraordinary Congress of Muslims of Russia and European Countries of the CIS reconvened with the participation of representatives from 2,034 out of a total number of 2,494 officially registered Muslim congregations of the Russian Federation.[45] This Congress reversed all resolutions passed by the previous November's congress and reinstated Talgat Tadzhuddin as supreme mufti.

As of late June 2003, it was not clear what the official title of the CSBM was. While the official website of the CSBM[46] featured the old title, there were indications that the name of the organization changed into either "Islamic Central Spiritual Board of Muslims of Holy Rus" (Islamskoe tsentralnoe dukhovnoe upravlenie musulman Sviatoi Rusi)[47] or "Central Spiritual Board of Muslims Obedient to God of Holy Rus" (Tsentralnoe dukhovnoe upravlenie musulman pokornykh Bogu Sviatoi Rusi).[48] The decision to rename the organization apparently took place on 31 March 2003.[49] According to Mufti Tadzhuddin, incorporation of the words "Holy Rus" into the official title of the organization demonstrates the commitment of Russian Muslims to peaceful coexistence among Russia's religions, namely Islam and Christianity.[50]

Organization and Structure of the CSBM

The organizational structure of the CSBM is characterized by a rigid and centralized hierarchy with heavy emphasis on vertical distribution of authority from the supreme mufti to Regional Spiritual Boards in the middle tier and on to local Muslim communities (see Figure 2.1). The supreme mufti is elected for life and has extensive powers; he appoints all regional muftis and approves the appointment of imams.[51]

The CSBM claims to represent the interests of Muslims from across Russia and some European countries of the CIS. According to one source, as of September 1999, 2,061 religious organizations both in Russia and in some CIS countries were

54

Figure 2.1 Organizational Chart of the Central Spiritual Board of Muslims of Russia and European Countries of the Commonwealth of Independent States (Located in Ufa and Headed by Supreme Mufti Talgat Tadzhuddin)

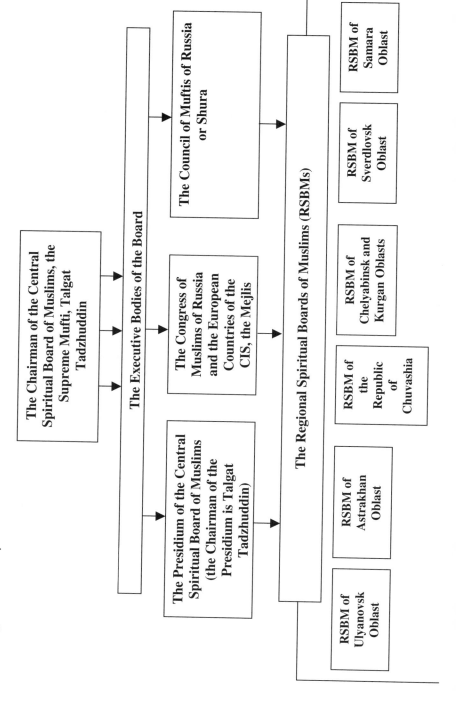

55

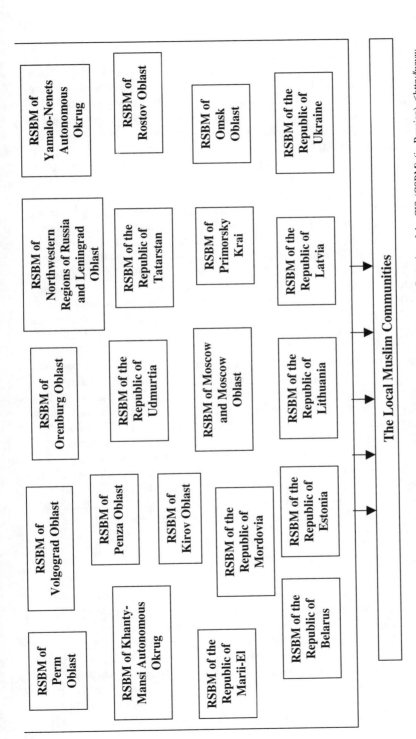

The Local Muslim Communities

Sources: The official server of the Central Spiritual Board of Muslims of Russia and the European Countries of the CIS (CSBM) (in Russian) <http://www .muslim-board.narod.ru/>; The official Web site of the Regional Spiritual Board of Muslims of Permskaya Oblast or Muftiyat of Permsk Oblast [in Russian] <http://www.raid.ru/customers/mufti/>; and Dinara Mukhametshina, "Ummah of Russia before Elections" [in Russian], *Nezavisimaya Gazeta* no. 4(51) (23 February 2000) <http://religion.ng.ru/islam/2000-02-23/3_umma.html>.

Note: The arrows in this figure represent the direction and source of authority, but the sizes of boxes are not intended to show the quantitative dimensions of respective congregations.

under its jurisdiction.[52] However, there is considerable disagreement regarding the number of Muslim religious organizations that are subordinate to the CSBM. Mikhail Tulskiy states that as of June 2000, out of the total of 3,048 Muslim congregations in Russia, 1,859 (more than half) accepted the CSBM's jurisdiction,[53] while the RSBM of Perm Oblast, which is subordinated to the CSBM, claims that by January 1996 there were 1,539 mosques and 2,034 Muslim communities under CSBM's jurisdiction.[54] F.M. Mukhametshin and A.A. Dubkov maintain that as of July 2001, only 868 local Muslim organizations were controlled by those regional spiritual boards that had accepted the leadership of the CSBM.[55] Meanwhile, according to Dinara Mukhametshina, by February 2000, Talgat Tadzhuddin controlled about 2,100 Muslim communities in Russia and other CIS countries. However, she speculated that this number could decrease to 1,600 because Muslim communities of Tatarstan would transfer their loyalty to the Spiritual Board of Muslims of Tatarstan, which had been established in 1998.[56] Silantiyev agrees with this assessment and claims that the number of Muslim communities controlled by Tadzhuddin's Central Spiritual Board is 1,600.[57] Despite different estimates on the exact number of congregations and Muslim organizations under its jurisdiction, in 2001, the CSBM was the largest centralized Muslim organization in the Russian Federation.

The most important religious centers subordinate to the CSBM are those of St Petersburg, Rostov, Ulyanovsk, Kazan, Yekaterinburg, Zelenodolsk, Astrakhan, Chelyabinsk, Penza, Perm, Salavat, Izhevsk, Samara, Volgograd, Nizhnevartovsk, Orenburg, Vilnius, Tallinn, Minsk, Kiev, Riga, and Cheboksary.[58] The geographic area of religious (canonical) jurisdiction of the CSBM encompasses all of the Russian Federation (with the exception of the North Caucasus republics) and the European countries of the CIS.[59] The CSBM, through its network of regional spiritual boards (RSBMs), maintains a dominant position among Muslim communities of nearly all regions listed in Figure 2.1. According to Silantiyev, excluding the Muslim communities of Tatarstan and the oblasts of Moscow, Rostov, and Penza, Tadzhuddin's regional spiritual boards unite between 70 and 100 percent of Russia's Muslim communities.[60] In Moscow, Rostov, and Penza oblasts too, Tadzhuddin maintains a relatively strong position, controlling between 30 and 50 percent of Muslim communities.[61]

The Russian Council of Muftis (RCM)

The principal impetus for the creation of the Russian Council of Muftis came from Mufti Ravil Gainutdin, one of the most prominent figures in Russia's Muslim establishment and head of the Spiritual Board of Muslims of the European Part of Russia (DUMER or the Moscow Muftiyat).[62] According to Aleksei Maximov, on 1 July 1996, the First Mejlis (Assembly) of Heads of Spiritual Boards of Muslims of Russia established the Russian Council of Muftis (RCM) and elected Mufti Ravil Gainutdin as its first chairman. Initially, only the muftis from the Spiritual Board of Muslims of the Central European Region of Russia, which was chaired by Gainutdin, formed the bulk of the council's members.[63] Subsequently the membership of this organization grew to encompass spiritual boards of other regions, as illustrated in Figure 2.2.

Organization and Structure of the RCM

Unlike the CSBM, the RCM is characterized by a less hierarchical and more lateral internal organization. The structure of the council is closer to that of a consultative body than to that of a centralized administration. As in the case of the CSBM, it is very difficult to establish the exact number of Muslim congregations that fall under the RCM's jurisdiction. There are many conflicting estimates. Some of these are intended to deliberately inflate the number of subordinate communities of believers in order to enhance the RCM's importance; others understate the number in order to diminish its religious power and authority. The council contends that it administers the spiritual affairs of all Muslim congregations of the Russian Federation. Farid Asadullin states that "practically since 1996, the Russian Council of Muftis has been the unifying center of the Muslim establishment of the Russian Federation."[64] According to Dinara Mukhametshina, the total number of communities controlled by the RCM's members exceeds 3,000, three-quarters of which are located in Dagestan and Tatarstan.[65]

The RCM brings together individual regional spiritual boards of Muslims, such as the Spiritual Board of Muslims of Tatarstan, as well as alliances or coalitions of regional spiritual boards, such as the Coordinating Center of Spiritual Boards of Muslims of North Caucasus. However, as illustrated by the dotted arrows in Figure 2.2, the degree of authority the RCM exercises over the two regional organizations just mentioned is ambiguous. This ambiguity justifies categorizing the Spiritual Board of Muslims of Tatarstan and the Coordinating Center of Spiritual Boards of Muslims of North Caucasus as "associate" or "collective" members of the council. It is noteworthy that the Coordinating Center of Spiritual Boards of Muslims of North Caucasus is also a member of the Supreme Religious Council of Peoples of Caucasus, which is controlled by the chairman of the Spiritual Board of Muslims of Caucasus (Transcaucasus), Sheikh-ul-Islam Allahshukur Pashazade.[66] The fact that Pashazade represents the majority Shi'a Azerbaijanis, whereas most of the North Caucasian peoples are Sunni (with the exception of pockets of Shi'a population in Dagestan and other republics of North Caucasus), implies that the doctrinal differences are of secondary importance in forming alliances of convenience.

At the international conference "Islam: Religion of the World" held in Nalchik, the capital of Kabardino-Balkaria, on 3–5 November 1999, the then chairman of the Coordinating Center of Muslims of North Caucasus and the mufti of Ingushetia, Muhammed-khaji Albogachiev, stated that the Coordinating Center is a "collective member" of the RCM.[67] The evidence that the Coordinating Center and Tatar Spiritual Board are "associate members" is strengthened by the pattern of their voting. Both Dinara Mukhametshina and Mikhail Tulskiy note that the muftis of North Caucasus, united under the aegis of the Coordinating Center of Spiritual Boards of

58

Figure 2.2 **Organizational Chart of the Russian Council of Muftis and Associated Spiritual Boards of Muslims (Headquarters in Moscow, Chaired by Mufti Ravil Gainutdin)**

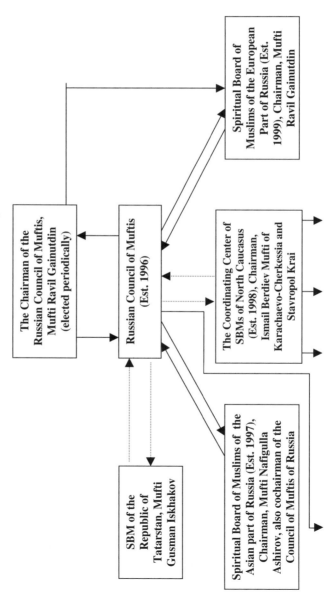

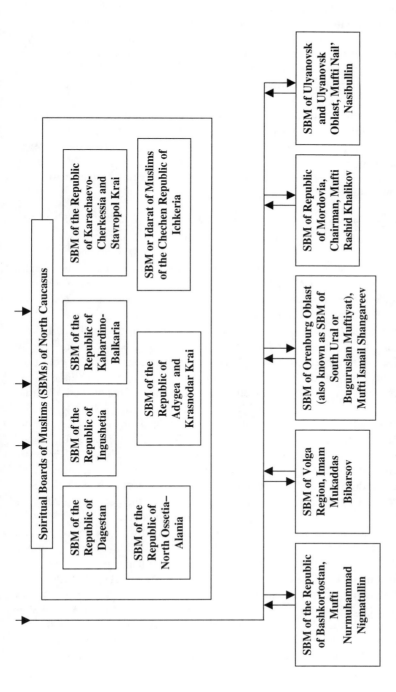

Sources: Mikhail Tulskiy, "Are Wahhabites Defeating the Moderate Muslims in Russia?"[in Russian], *Nezavisimaya Gazeta*, no. 108(2418) (19 June 2000) <http://www.ng.ru/printed/ideas/2001-06-19/8_vakhabit.html>; Aleksei Maximov, "The Leaders of Muslim Schism: Ravil Ganutdin" [in Russian], *Nezavisimaya Gazeta*, no. 12(75) (28 June 2001) <http://faces.ng.ru/printed/dossier/2001-06-28/7_split.html>; Dinara Mukhametshina, "Ummah of Russia before Elections" [in Russian], *Nezavisimaya Gazeta*, no. 4(51) (23 February 2000) <http://religion.ng.ru/islam/2000-02-23/3_umma.html>.

Note: The direction of arrows reflects the distribution of authority; the dotted lines represent associate affiliation between the entities, whereas the solid lines represent direct membership in the organization.

Muslims of North Caucasus, have repeatedly refused to sign declarations directed against Talgat Tadzhuddin, Mufti Ravil Gainutdin's principal rival.[68]

The most important component of the council is DUMER, which is the only spiritual board under the direct control of the chairman of the council. The office of the council's chairman is an elected position, and the heads of various spiritual boards that are members of the council become cochairman of the council on a rotating basis. In short, the chairman of the council is basically "the first among equals."

Another interesting feature of the council is that Muslim congregations frequently realign themselves among the council's member organizations, thus causing bitter disputes among them. In one of the most contentious disputes, in 1999, congregations from Penza Oblast that had previously been under the supervision of the Spiritual Board of Muslims (SBM) of Povolzhie shifted to the jurisdiction of the Moscow Muftiyat.[69]

The Spiritual Board of Muslims of the European Part of Russia (DUMER)

The DUMER is the successor to the Spiritual Board of Muslims of the Central European Region of Russia (DUMTSER). DUMER acquired its current name in December 1998 after reregistering with the Ministry of Justice.[70] DUMTSER was established at the founding Mejlis, which was organized on the initiative of Ravil Gainutdin, on 29 January 1994. The delegates to the assembly elected Ravil Gainutdin the chairman of the newly formed organization and bestowed the title of mufti upon him. The representatives of Muslim congregations from the oblasts of Moscow, Nizhny Novgorod, Yaroslavl, Vladimir, and Tver and the Krais of Stavropol and Krasnodar attended this meeting. At the time, Yaroslavl and Vladimir oblasts each had only one registered Muslim community. On 23 February 1994, DUMTSER was officially registered with the Russian Ministry of Justice. Yet despite all of the organizational changes and assertions of autonomy, for several months DUMTSER was reluctant to formally secede from the CSBM. However, on 23 September 1994, the presidium of DUMTSER adopted the "unanimous decision on the withdrawal from the structure of the CSBM." Meanwhile, DUMTSER established connections with the Supreme Coordinating Council of Spiritual Boards of Muslims of Russia, although it did not join it as a member.[71]

On 9 December 1998, at the regular assembly of Muslims of the European Part of Russia, the heads and representatives of Muslim organizations from twenty-two subjects of the Russian Federation decided to change the name from the Spiritual Board of Muslims of the Central European Region of Russia (DUMTSER) to its present official name, the Spiritual Board of Muslims of the European Part of Russia (DUMER). According to the official Web site of the RCM, DUMER unites under its jurisdiction the Muslim congregations and organizations in the following oblasts: Moscow, St. Petersburg, Nizhny Novgorod, Tver, Vologda, Kostroma, Kursk, Vladimir, Ivanovo, Tula, Tambov, Orel, Smolensk, Sochi, Penza, Kaliningrad, and Yaroslavl.[72] In total, DUMER extends its jurisdiction over 150 Muslim congregations and organizations.[73]

However, Dinara Mukhametshina maintains that this assessment overestimates the actual influence of DUMER. According to her, structurally DUMER mainly consists of the Spiritual Board of Muslims of Nizhny Novgorod Oblast headed by Mufti Umar Idrisov, which accounts for one-third of the congregations controlled by DUMER. The rest are several dozen communities scattered on a vast territory stretching from Sochi to Yaroslavl. Nonetheless, as is evident from its official name, DUMER contends to represent the interests of all Muslim congregations to the west of the Ural Mountains, but in reality its influence may be limited and concentrated in the Central and Central-Black Earth (Chernozemny) economic regions.[74]

As the chairman of DUMER, Mufti Gainutdin presides over the supreme executive body of the administration, the Presidium of DUMER, which consists of fourteen "reputable religious and social figures."[75] DUMER is comprised of the following administrative divisions: the Secretariat of the Mufti of DUMER, Science and Government Liaisons, Coordination of Religious Organizations, Islamic Education and Other Educational Programs, Administrative Affairs, Charities, Editorial Office, Press Service, Ritual Services, Advisory Board, Organization of Pilgrimages, and Distribution of *Halal* Foods.[76]

The Spiritual Board of Muslims of the Asian Part of Russia

The Spiritual Board of Muslims of the Asian Part of Russia was created by the initiative of Nafigulla Ashirov in August 1997 and registered with the Ministry of Justice on 14 December 1998.[77] It has about 100 Muslim organizations and congregations under its jurisdiction. Like DUMER, the Spiritual Board of Muslims of the Asian Part of Russia claims to represent the interests of all Muslims east of the Ural Mountains. Other sources, however, believe that after the withdrawal of the Tyumen Muftiyat, under the leadership of Galimziyan Bikmullin, from its jurisdiction in the fall of 1999, the number of Muslim congregations adhering to the board was reduced to twenty or thirty. Moreover, most of these communities are quite small and do not have mosques built specifically to serve as places of worship (purpose-built mosques).[78]

The Spiritual Board of Muslims of Tatarstan

In February 1998, the president of Tatarstan, Mintimer Shaimiev, organized the Unifying Congress of Islamic Clergy in Kazan to overcome divisions within the republic's Muslim community. The congress created the Spiritual Board of Muslims (SBM) of Tatarstan and elected Gusman Iskhakov as mufti of Tatarstan and chairman of the new spiritual board. The SBM of Tatarstan became one of the largest Muslim structures in the Russian Federation, uniting more than 900 communities, almost all Muslim congregations in Tatarstan. Dinara Mukhametshina suggests that the association of the SBM of Tatarstan with the RCM is prompted by the animosity of Tatarstan's SBM toward Talgat Tadzhuddin, who still hopes to return the lost Tatar communities to his jurisdiction.[79] Another contributing factor may be that a considerable portion of Russia's Muslim population is, like Ravil Gainutdin, of Tatar origin. Hence the affiliation of Tatarstan's SBM with the RCM is likely of a strategic and long-term nature.

Nonaligned Spiritual Administrations of Muslims in Russia

According to Dinara Mukhametshina, about 15 percent of Russia's Muslim communities are not affiliated with either of the two major Muslim religious establishments. These organizations function independently and include individual communities as well as larger, centralized organizations. Some of the independent Muslim communities consist of the puritanical believers influenced by Wahhabi teachings, which spread as a result of the intensified activities of foreign Islamic missionaries and the influx of foreign religious literature. Among such organizations, Dinara Mukhametshina cites the muftiyat of Tyumen Oblast and alternative spiritual boards of Muslims of Tatarstan, Dagestan, Karachaevo-Cherkessia, and Ulyanovsk Oblast.[80] The nonaligned Muslim spiritual administrations are concentrated in the European part of Russia, the Volga region, and Siberia. Mukhametshin and Dubkov include in this category the following organizations: the religious center Islam in the Republic of Kalmykia (headed by Sh. Magomedov), Sayanskiy Kaziyat in the Republic of Khakassia, Kurganskiy Kaziyat,[81] and Baikalskiy Kaziyat in Irkutsk Oblast.[82] An alternative spiritual board called the Association of Mosques of Russia and the newly formed association of Muslim organizations called Kazan Muftiyat also fall into the category of Muslim organizations that have an ambiguous attitude toward the two main religious establishments.[83] The continued rivalry between the RCM and the CSBM has contributed to the growth of autonomous Muslim organizations, thus further undermining Muslim unity and making Muslims more vulnerable to foreign influences and extremist ideologies.

The Coordinating Center of Spiritual Boards of Muslims of North Caucasus (CCSBMNC)

Although the Coordinating Center of Spiritual Boards of Muslims of North Caucasus (CCSBMNC) is considered a "collective" or "associate" member of the RCM, in reality, it is a completely autonomous entity. The Coordinating Center is an umbrella organization uniting more than 2,000 Muslim congregations in the North Caucasus. Figure 2.2 lists all the spiritual boards that are under the formal jurisdiction of the Coordinating Center. The Coordinating Center was established at the congress of the representatives of Muslim organizations of the region held in Nazran, the capital of Ingushetia, on 17 August 1998.[84] On 31 January 2001, North Caucasian Muslim leaders gathered in Moscow to celebrate its official registration with the Ministry of Justice.[85] In April 2003, Mufti of Ingushetia Muhammad Albogachiev, who had been serving as the chairman of the Coordinating Center since its inception, was replaced by Mufti of Karachaevo-Cherkessia and Stavropol krai, Ismail Berdiev.[86] The chairmanship of the Center is performed on a rotating basis in accordance with the provisions embedded in the charter of the organization.[87] The official inauguration of the new chairman took place in Moscow on 12 May 2003.[88] One of the objectives of the founders of the Coordinating Center is "to unite the Muslims of North Caucasus" and "to thwart the activities of organizations and persons directed at disseminating extremist ideas, religious exclusion, and intolerance."[89]

The question of which spiritual board plays a leading role within the structure of the Coordinating Center is a matter of continuous debate. According to R. Sil-antiyev, the Spiritual Board of Muslims of Ingushetia is the main structure and plays the leading role in integrating the Muslim community of the North Cauca-sus.[90] This explanation does not seem valid for the following reasons: First, the Mufti of Ingushetia no longer holds the Center's chairmanship; second, Dagestan has the heaviest concentration of institutions of higher Islamic learning and therefore potentially could exercise more influence over Muslim communities of the North Caucasus. This view is supported by Mukhametshin and Dubkov, who maintain that the Spiritual Board of Muslims of Dagestan is the oldest, most rep-utable, and largest religious board in terms of registered communities of believers and is, therefore, the undisputed leader of the region's Muslims.[91] Moreover, ac-cording to Mikhail Vagabov, director of the Center of Islamic Studies of North Caucasus and director of the Department of Religious Studies at Dagestan State University, in terms of religious observance, Dagestan occupies the first place among Russia's Muslim regions. This factor further strengthens the argument in favor of Dagestan's leadership role.[92]

An important feature of the Coordinating Center is that the majority of the congregations under its jurisdiction follow the Shafei school of Islamic jurispru-dence, whereas the Hanafi school is the most prevalent in the rest of Russia. This doctrinal difference is a contributing factor to the effective autonomy exercised by the Coordinating Center. As Dinara Mukhametshina has suggested, doctrinal dif-ferences between Muslim peoples of the North Caucasus and the rest of Russia are serious enough to make any attempts at their forceful unification under a single leadership unsuccessful.[93]

The Supreme Coordinating Council of Spiritual Boards of Muslims of Russia

On 30 September 1992, a group of influential Muslim leaders—Mufti Gabdulla Galiullin of Tatarstan, Mufti Nurmuhammed Nigmatullin of Bashkortostan, Imam Mukaddas Bibarsov of Saratov Oblast, Mufti Nafigulla Ashirov of Siberia, and the director of the Islamic Cultural Center, Abdul-Vahid Niazov—established the Su-preme Coordinating Council of Spiritual Boards of Muslims of Russia.[94] For four years, this organization, which registered formally with the Russian Ministry of

Justice in 1994, united Muslim organizations opposed to the CSBM of Talgat Tadzhuddin.[95] However, the influence of the Supreme Coordinating Council waned during this period, and by 1996, most of its prominent collective members had left. Nafigulla Ashirov took over the deteriorating organization, but was unable to revive it. Presently, the Supreme Coordinating Council is a nonfunctioning organization nominally headed by two directors, Nafigulla Ashirov and Abdul-Vahid Niazov.[96]

This analysis of the institutional structures of Russia's Muslim communities has pointed to a considerable degree of fragmentation following the collapse of the Soviet system, as well as to the efforts aimed at the consolidation of Muslim institutions within a few broad umbrella organizations. However, as Muslim communities and the dynamics of their interaction with the broader Russian society continue to evolve, it is quite likely that existing institutional structures will also undergo changes. Many of these changes may be initiated by the federal government.

Development of the Physical and Intellectual Infrastructure of Islam

Tsarist and Soviet rule destroyed the physical and intellectual infrastructure of Islam in the Muslim regions of the empire. However, in some regions, notably the Republic of Tatarstan, some historical mosques escaped destruction. The most significant damage was inflicted on Islam's intellectual foundations, notably its educational institutions and qualified clergy. Revitalizing these aspects of Russian Islam is an arduous task that will take more time and effort than the rebuilding of mosques.

This deterioration of indigenous Muslim intellectual capital has also proven politically harmful both to Muslims of Russia and to the Russian society as a whole by making them susceptible to exogenous religious and religious-political influences. These exogenous influences have added new layers of fragmentation to societies already divided along ethnic, sectarian, and other lines and have contributed to the rise of militant movements.

Rebuilding Muslim Institutions: Mosques

At the beginning of the process of liberalization under Gorbachev, only 94 mosques operated in the territory of what would become the Russian Federation.[97] However, many illegal and semi-legal places of worship continued to operate. Since then, however, there has been a proliferation of mosques. Table 2.3 gives an indication of the number of mosques in selected regions of the Russian Federation. According to Sergei Ivanenko and Alexander Shegortsov, from 1991 to 2000, the number of officially registered mosques in Russia grew from 870 to 7,000.[98] However, only a limited number of these mosques are purpose-built or cathedral mosques with domes and minarets. The rest are small prayer halls with rather rudimentary outward signs, such as tin roofs where the symbol of a crescent is displayed.

Table 2.3

Mosques in Selected Parts of the Russian Federation

Republic/Oblast/Krai/Okrug/City	Number of Mosques as of 2001
Northwest Region	
St. Petersburg	1
Central Region	
Moscow	4
Volga-Vyatka Region	
Nizhny Novgorod Oblast	35
Volga Region	
Republic of Tatarstan	700
Samara Oblast	41
Ulyanovsk Oblast	50
North Caucasus (Southern) Region	
Republic of Dagestan	1,200
Republic of Ingushetia	400
Republic of Chechnya	400
Republic of Kabardino-Balkaria	96
Republic of Karachaevo-Cherkessia	91
Ural Region	
Republic of Bashkortostan	490
Orenburg Oblast	75
Perm Oblast	39
Sverdlovsk Oblast	38
Chelyabinsk Oblast	36
West Siberian Region	
Tyumen Oblast	35
East Siberian Region	
Irkutsk	1
Far East Region	
Norilsk	1
Total	3,733

Sources: Islam and Muslims in Russia (Moscow: Russian Council of Muftis, Moscow Islamic University [College], 1999), p. 173; Aleksei Malashenko, *Islamic Rebirth in Modern Russia* (Moscow, Carnegie Center, 1998), p. 75; and the official Web site of the Perm-based Fund "Mosque" [in Russian] <http://mechet.perm.ru>.

In December 2000, the Russian Commission on the Affairs of Religious Organizations conducted a survey of sixty-five subjects of the Russian Federation with
substantial Muslim populations. The survey found 4,658 Muslim devotional buildings of different types, including mosques.[99] Of this total, 2,884 structures were
built in the 1990s, and 68 devotional buildings were under construction.[100] In accordance with the 1995 Law on the Transfer of Federal Property of a Devotional
Nature to Religious Organizations (O poryadke peredachi religioznym
ob'edineniam otnosyashegosia k federalnoi sobstvennosti imushchestva religioznogo znachenia), the process of returning religious property to the communities
of believers is continuing in Russia.[101] By the end of 2000, 522 devotional buildings
had been transferred to Muslim religious organizations, while the transfer of 42
was pending.[102] Meanwhile, the proliferation of unregistered, semiofficial, and illegal groups of Muslim believers complicates the task of conducting a thorough
quantitative assessment of the Muslim religious infrastructure in Russia, especially
because the unregistered Muslim groups often rent the property for religious purposes on a temporary basis. Nevertheless, the commission concluded that there has
been a surge in the construction of places of Muslim worship, which in some
regions outnumber the Muslim communities that would use them. The share of
federal funds in the construction of these facilities has been insignificant. Rather,
local authorities, foreign Islamic organizations, and private sponsors have been
major sources of funding.

According to the aforementioned study, the North Caucasus accounts for a large
portion of Muslim devotional buildings, with the number reaching 2,255, of which
1,585 are located in Dagestan. However, according to Maksim Shevchenko, there
is a surplus of mosques in Dagestan, and many, especially in remote villages that
people are leaving to search for jobs, remain unattended or poorly attended.[103] The
distribution of Muslim religious property in other republics of the North Caucasus
is as follows: 300 in Chechnya, 130 in Kabardino-Balkaria, 108 in Karachaevo-
Cherkessia, 85 in Ingushetia, 28 in Adygea, and 19 in North Ossetia.[104] In the
North Caucasus, 1,322 places of worship were built during the 1990s, and 39 were
under construction at the time of the commission's survey.[105] The government transferred 468 religious buildings to Muslim organizations, and the transfer of 32 more
is still pending. There are 2,403 Muslim religious buildings on the territory of the
European part of Russia, the Volga region, and Siberia. From 1990 to 2000, 1,562
buildings were built for Islamic religious practices, and 29 were under construction
at the time of the survey.[106] The government also transferred 31 buildings to Muslim
religious organizations, and the procedures for the return of 10 more were being
discussed as of July 2001.[107]

The Republic of Tatarstan, historically a major center of Islamic civilization,
has a number of historic mosques, especially in the capital city of Kazan. Table
2.4 lists the most important of these mosques, many of which were built in the
nineteenth and early twentieth centuries, although some go as far back as the eighteenth century. Nearly all of the earlier mosques were destroyed during the conquest
of Kazan by Ivan the Terrible. The only mosque remaining from that period is the

Table 2.4

Mosques of Kazan

Name	Dates of Construction
Marjani Mosque	1766–1770
Apanaev Mosque	1768–1771
Galeev Mosque	1798–1801
Mosque Iske Tash	1801–1802
Mosque No. 11	1801–1805
Mosque No.10	1808
Blue Mosque	1815–1819
Burnaev Mosque	1826–1898
Nurulla Mosque	1845–1849
Sultan Mosque	1867
Azimov Mosque	1890
Transkaban Mosque	1924–1926
Mosque Nur Islam	1988
Bulgar Mosque	1991–1993
Mosque Ramazan	1994
Mosque Islam	1996
Medina Mosque	1996–1997
Mosque Khuzaifa Ibn al-Yamani	1996–1997
Mosque Tinichlik	1998–1999
Mosque Kazan Nuri	1999
Kul Sharif Mosque*	

Source: Based on information gathered during Hunter's visits to Kazan in 2000–2001.

*The Kul Sharif Mosque is the only remaining mosque of the Kazan Kremlin that dates back to the period prior to the conquest of Kazan. The reconstruction of this mosque has been in progress since 1996.

one in the Kazan Kremlin (Kul Sharif), which has been undergoing a process of reconstruction. The plan is to complete the rebuilding of Kul Sharif in time for the celebration of Kazan's millennium in 2005.

In the 1990s, the industrial city of Naberezhnie Chelny emerged as a principal center of Islamic revival and, according to some, radicalism in Tatarstan. Several new mosques have been established in Naberezhnie Chelny, the largest of which is Al-Tauba Mosque. However, even this mosque is of modest proportions and is not very ornate or richly appointed.[108] The restoration of old mosques and the building of new mosques is an ongoing process in Tatarstan. One of the latest renovation efforts is taking place at the "Kshkar" mosque in the republic's Arskiy region. The mosque was built in 1777 by a Tatar merchant Bajazit al Kshkari. In 1865 his son added a minaret, which was torn down in 1930.[109] Historically, Ufa was another major center of Islamic religion and learning. The first cathedral mosque in Ufa was built in the 1830s by a local merchant, M. Tagirov; between 1960 and 1994, it was the only functioning mosque in Ufa. The second mosque was built in the 1880s but was closed in 1931 and was eventually destroyed. The third mosque, built in 1903 had a similar fate: it was closed in 1940 and now houses a sports complex. The fourth mosque was built in 1908 with funds provided by A. Khakimov and is known as Khakimovskaya Mosque. This mosque was closed for a period of time and was returned to the believers in 1991. The fifth mosque was built in 1909 but was severely damaged in a fire in 1960. The sixth mosque was built in 1918. It was closed in 1934 and eventually turned into a residence. Two new cathedral mosques were built during the 1990s: Gufran, which was designed by the architect I. Sabilov and built in 1994, and the mosque Lya Lya Tyulpan, the construction of which was finished in 1998.[110] A similar process of restoring old mosques is also occurring in Bashkortostan through private initiative. A recent example is the restoration of a historic mosque in the Abalyamovo village in the republic's Aurgazin district. The late village teacher Mausilya Ibragimova was the main initiator of this effort, and her entrepreneur son Marat Saitov provided most of the funding for the restoration of the mosque. The restored mosque is now called "Mausilya" in honor of Mausilya Ibragimova.[111] As of the end of 2002, the most recently constructed cathedral mosque was located in Nizhny Novgorod.

Public and Official Reaction to Construction of Mosques

During the Russian Federation's first decade, federal and republican authorities generally had a liberal approach toward the building of mosques. However, there was often opposition from the Orthodox Church and the non-Muslim population. In Murmansk, serious opposition arose in 1999 to the construction of a mosque on the grounds that its minaret, which was supposed to be twenty-four meters high, would dominate the skyline and become the city's symbol, and a petition was signed to halt its construction.[112] Efforts of Muslims in Kamchatka to build a mosque in the region's capital, Petropavlovsk, also encountered popular resistance. When the mosque's cornerstone was first laid, the local newspaper Novaya Kamchatskaya Pravda stated, "It is not a mosque . . . it is a stone of conflict which is laid by irresponsible bureaucrats led by the mayor."[113] The size of the mosque and its location in a majority Slavic neighborhood were principal causes of opposition, but religious rivalry and political suspicions on the part of the church were more important reasons.[114]

The case of the mosque in the city of Taganrog in the Rostov region is also instructive. When the Muslim community first tried to build a mosque in late 2000, members of the Communist Party, the Orthodox clergy, and Cossack paramilitary formations opposed it on the grounds that the opening of a mosque "will increase the threat of Wahhabi fundamentalism spreading to the region."[115] Following a protest to the presidential representative to the Southern Federal District, Viktor Kazantsev, Minister of Internal Affairs Vladimir Rushailo visited the region and advised the archbishop of Rostov and Novocherkassk and Mufti Jafar Bikmaev to reach an agreement on the issue.[116] After the visit, the community was permitted to build the mosque. But in March 2001, the Rostov Oblast court ruled that Muslims in the city of Taganrog must demolish their partially built mosque because the city's SBM had acted illegally by starting construction before having obtained the required permits. In response, Mufti Bikmaev claimed that he had in his possession a decree with fifteen signatures, including that of the mayor, and refused to demolish the mosque. Deputy Mayor Nikolai Savechenko insisted, "Court bailiffs will force the Spiritual Administration to carry out the court order."[117]

This situation is not surprising given the sentiments of the region's Russian population. During a visit to Novocherkassk in June 2000, the deputy mayor claimed that there were 2,000 to 3,000 Muslims in the area, mostly immigrants from the North and South Caucasus and other Muslim republics of the CIS. They wanted to build a mosque, but were deterred by strong popular opposition.[118] However, according to the independent Islamic information channel islam.ru, by December 2002 a mosque was near completion in Rostov-on-Don.[119] Meanwhile, as of May 2003, the efforts of Muslims in Sochi to build a mosque remained unsuccessful.[120] The region's proximity to the North Caucasus and the Chechen War is an important factor in popular anxieties regarding a more obvious Muslim presence. Nevertheless, often the threat of Islamic extremism is used to deny Muslims the right to organize their religious life.

Since late 1999, the attitude of federal and local authorities has become more cautious and less liberal. The following examples illustrate some of the obstacles to building mosques, especially in regions that are not traditional centers of Muslim concentration. The Muslim community in Karelia, which numbers 20,000 and is made up of Tatars, Karelians, and Russian converts,[121] has been refused permission to build a mosque in the republic's capital, Petrozavodsk, on the grounds that the individual behind the effort, Visam Ali Bardvil, is an Arab. Variously identified as Palestinian or Libyan, although he is a Russian citizen, he was accused of wanting to spread extremist ideas. In his own defense, Bardvil stated that "terrorists don't build mosques or recognize the state" and added that the application to purchase the land and build the mosque had been made "entirely according to the law."[122] Nevertheless, enhanced anti-Muslim sentiments led Karelia's minister of internal affairs, Igor Yunash, to write to the republic's president complaining about the mosque. Consequently, the community decided not to build the mosque in a central part of the city.[123]

Of even more importance is the case of the mosque in the city of Vologda, located 500 kilometers northeast of Moscow.[124] In 1997, a tender competition was announced for the construction of the mosque in which architects from Moscow, Vologda, Yaroslavl, and Vladivostok took part. However, when the mosque was completed, the regional prosecutor's office and the state directorate for the preservation of historic monuments began court action to have it removed. In December 2000, Mufti Ravil Gainutdin wrote to President Putin and complained about the lawsuits, comparing the campaign against the mosque to "an echo of the militant atheistic campaign of the 1960's."[125] He further added, "Unfortunately, we are encountering flagrant examples of Islamophobia on various levels in several regions, including Kamchatka, Taganrog, and Volgograd."[126] In response, the region's deputy governor assured Gainutdin that the moves against the mosque had nothing to do with Islamophobia.[127]

As of August 2002, it appeared that after nearly four years of controversy, the dispute of the Vologda city mosque was finally resolved. According to the leader of the Muslim community of Vologda, Nail' Mustafin, "Under the public pressure and with the support of President of the Russian Federation Vladimir Putin, the head of municipal government of Vologda Aleksei Yakunichev signed a resolution allowing the mosque to stand."[128] The breakthrough in the standoff over the Vologda city mosque was achieved after a meeting between President Putin and Mufti Ravil Gainutdin in January 2002. This episode once again highlights the crucial importance of personal involvement of high-ranking Russian politicians in resolving interdenominational conflicts in various regions.[129]

Parallel to the pattern of local opposition to the construction of mosques, the building of new mosques continued throughout 2002 and 2003. To illustrate, the first roadside mosque in Russia opened at the crossroads of federal highways Moscow-Ufa and Mamadysh-Kazan on 26 September 2002.[130] Another unprecedented event was the opening of a mosque at the Domodedovo airport in Moscow on 25 December 2002.[131]

Centers of Islamic Education (Medressahs)

The establishment of viable educational institutions that could revive the indigenous Islam of Russia and provide qualified and enlightened leaders for Muslim communities has proven more difficult than the rebuilding of the physical infrastructure. Yet this is an essential task, including from a political perspective, because it could help prevent the infiltration of extremist elements among poorly educated Muslims. The main obstacles to establishing adequate institutions of Islamic education are the following: a lack of adequate funds, inadequate human resources (especially a deficit of qualified instructors), and political factors. Despite much talk about large sums of money flowing to Russia from Middle Eastern sources, the actual funds received have not been substantial. Ravil Gainutdin, chairman of the RCM, in the summer of 1993 noted that Muslims in Russia received only $400,000 from Saudi Arabia, although they were promised $1.5 million.[132] Regarding political considerations, clearly there has been a great deal of skepticism on the part of federal, republican, and local authorities about the advisability of creating viable and independent institutions of Islamic learning. These misgivings have grown stronger since the late 1990s because of the infiltration of some Islamic schools by what governmental authorities have characterized as extremists or "Wahhabists."

The case of the Yulduz school in Naberezhnie Chelny intensified these fears and misgivings. The school was temporarily closed on 23 September 1999 after being accused of subjecting students to subversive ideas and training volunteers to fight in Chechnya and commit terrorist acts. At least one ex-student of the school, Dennis

Saitakov, was accused of having been involved in the 1999 apartment bombings in Moscow.[133] He attended the school for only one year and was expelled for nonattendance. Later he joined the radical Chechen rebel leader Shamil Basaev's forces in Chechnya, where he was killed.[134] Despite closure, the school continued its activities under a new name, Nur. In 2000, it was operating as an all-girl religious educational institution.[135]

In order to ward off accusations of extremism, many Islamic schools emphasize that their curriculum includes secular and scientific subjects. In September 2000, officials of the Muhammadiyya Higher Muslim Medressah in Kazan stressed the secular component of its curriculum. Moreover, the school seemed inadequately equipped to be a viable Islamic school, a medressah, on the level of serious institutes of Islamic learning, such as Al-Azhar, even if on a smaller scale. In 1999, the school had 120 students.[136]

A similar situation exists at the Russian Islamic University of Kazan, where instruction lasts eight years.[137] Instruction is evenly divided between secular and religious subjects, such as science, languages, and computer skills. The principal languages taught are English, Russian, Tatar, and Arabic. During the first few years, 75 percent of the subjects taught are secular. Later, students are taught Islamic philosophy and law (Shari'a) according to the Hanafi school. One of the university's officials said, "We do not allow the teaching of any nontraditional [non-Hanafi] schools." According to school officials, the goal of the school is to "create a modern personality who understands both secular and religious matters" and to show the students "how to live in a proper manner." To achieve this goal, each student is assigned to a tutor. At the time of Hunter's visit (September 2000), there were 107 students, ranging in age from seventeen to thirty-five. After graduation, the students can teach or work in religious institutes or other state organizations.

Despite the obstacles to rebuilding the educational infrastructure of traditional Russian Islam, institutions of various size and quality have emerged in different regions of Russia. According to the SBM of the Republic of Tatarstan, its Islamic educational infrastructure includes the following institutions of higher learning: (1) in Kazan, the Russian Islamic University, the Higher Muslim Medressah "Muhammadiyya," and the Higher Muslim Medressah of the 1000th Anniversary of Islam (with 955 students); (2) in Naberezhnie Chelny, the Intermediate Muslim Medressah "Yulduz," the Intermediate Muslim Medressah "Aq Mechet" (White Mosque), and the Naberezhnie Chelny Islamic Institute (which attracts many instructors from Istanbul and Ankara)[138] (3) the Intermediate Muslim Medressah "Risalliya" in the town of Nizhnekamsk; (4) and the Intermediate Muslim Medressah of Rizaeddin Fahreddin in the town of Almeteyevsk. Intermediate Muslim medressahs also operate in the cities of Buinsk and Nurlat. Each of these institutions hosts more than 1,000 students (shakirds) and has affiliated beginner-level schools where students are instructed in the basics of Islamic faith and its rituals.

In Bashkortostan, 419 Muslim organizations provide some form of Islamic education. There are five medressahs and two institutes, which are operated mostly by major mosques, including one by the Sobornaya Mosque, which was opened in

1990, and another by the Lya Lya Tyulpan Mosque. Other major centers of learning are Rizah Fakhretdin Islamic Institute and Maryum Sultanova Islamic Institute, which offers a four-year course.[139]

In the Nizhny Novgorod region, there are two major medressahs: Mahinur and Medina, which is a branch of Mahinur. Mahinur has been operating since 1994. It has eight affiliated institutions, three Sunday schools and five summer schools. This medressah also organizes cultural events and summer camps. Medina prepares male Muslims with secondary education for further religious studies at Mahinur. The term of study is two years during which students, in addition to religious studies, receive education in secular subjects.[140]

In the North Caucasus, the largest number of institutions of Islamic learning is in Dagestan (Table 2.5). Only nine of these institutions are officially licensed. An additional forty-five functioning institutions (filiali) are affiliated with the universities and institutes described in Table 2.5. As of December 2001, there were seventeen Islamic colleges, all of which were associated with the republic's SBM. There were 132 intermediate-level medressahs (srednie medrese) and 245 beginner-level schools (nachal'nie primechetskie shkoli).[141] Most of the latter schools function under the aegis of the mosques, and their main objective is to provide elementary religious education to believers (such as how to perform prayers and read the Qu'ran). Because of the irregular character of instruction at the beginner-level schools and their sporadic formation and dissolution, it is impossible to establish their precise number. The official newspaper of Dagestan's SBM, Assalam, provides different figures on the number of the republic's Islamic schools. According to it, in January 2001 in Dagestan there were seventy-two medressahs and more than one thousand mektebs (religious elementary schools attached to mosques).[142]

Among the institutions of higher Islamic learning in Dagestan, the Northern Caucasus Islamic University of Muhammad Arif, located in Makhachkala, represents a good example of the vibrancy of Dagestan's religious life. At this university, the religious instruction in Muslim dogma and law is based on the Hanafi and Shafei schools. In addition, the students are offered courses in Russian and English languages and in foreign literature. In September 2002, a women's department was opened at the university, where, in addition to the religious subjects, women can learn nursing, medicine and designing clothes.[143]

In Ingushetia, most mosques offer elementary Islamic education. The highest center of Islamic learning is the King Fahd Islamic Institute, which is located in the settlement of Ordzhonikidzevskaya and funded by Saudi Arabia.

Moscow has several important Islamic educational institutions, including the Moscow Islamic College, which trains imams. In July 1998, the first group of its imam-khatibs graduated and subsequently went to serve Muslim communities in Yaroslavl, Tver, Kostroma, Nizhny Novgorod, Vologda, and Moscow. The Moscow Islamic University registered with authorities in November 1998 and began accepting students in 1999. The Rasul Al-Akram Islamic College in the Solnechnogorsk District of the Moscow Oblast offers a four-year course of study and has thirty male students. The Ismailiya school, which operates from the Moscow As-

Table 2.5

Institutions of Higher Islamic Learning in the Republic of Dagestan (as of December 2001)

Islamic College	Location
Islamic University of Imam Ashari	Khasavyurt
Islamic University of Imam Shafii	Makhachkala
Islamic Institute of Imam Navavi	Village Novaya Serebryakovka, Kizliyar District
Islamic Institute of Imam Shamil	Kizilyurt
Islamic University of Saipula Kadiya	Buinaksk
Islamic Institute of Saiyed-Muhammad Abubakarov	Khasavyurt
Islamic University of Muhammad Arif	Makhachkala
Islamic Institute of Saipula Kadiya	Collective Farm (Sovkhoz) "Komsomolets," Kizilyurt District
Islamic Institute of Hasan Afandi	Village Gergebil
Islamic Institute "Nurul Irshad" of Said Apandi	Village Chirkei, Buinaksk District
Islamic Institute of Imam Shamil	Village Dylym
Islamic Institute of Yusuf-khaji	Khasavyurt
Islamic Institute of Mahmud Afandi	Village Noviy Batlukh
Islamic Institute of Muhammad Kharakhalilov	Settlement Shamkhal
Islamic Institute of Shamil	Khasavyurt
Islamic Institute of Said Afir	Khasavyurt
Islamic Institute of Khasanilasul	Village Noviy Chirkei, Kizilyurt District

Source: "Religioznoe Obrazovanie v Dagestane (Statistika)" (The religious education in Dagestan [statistics]), *Novoe Delo* No. 49, 12 July 2001 <http://www.ndelo.ru/4901/religija.html>.

sembly mosque, was established in 1998 and offers free elementary religious education.[144] These institutions are linked to DUMER. DUMER also provides gifted students with resources to study at religious schools in Egypt, Morocco, Syria, Saudi Arabia, Qatar, Turkey, and the Islamic Call University in Libya.[145]

In the Astrakhan oblast, the only institution of higher Islamic education is the Islamic Institute of Haji Tarhan in Astrakhan, which in late June 2003 celebrated the graduation of the first class of imams—a historical event because it was the first class of Muslim clerics to graduate in the Astrakhan oblast in the past one hundred years.[146]

In order to protect students from becoming unduly influenced by foreign teachers, non-traditional schools of Islam, or extremist ideas, the religious leaders of Dagestan in 2001 decided that no student should go abroad before getting some basic education in his own country.[147] This decision reflects an increasingly cautious attitude toward Islamic training abroad that is, on the part of Russia's Muslim establishment in general, in contrast to the practice of the early 1990s, when large numbers of students were sent abroad. The official reason as explained to Hunter at the Muhammadiya school in Kazan is that they were not satisfied with the results and quality of education that the students received, but the real reason is that religious and political authorities became concerned that the students were being exposed to nontraditional and potentially disruptive ideas and were being politicized and even radicalized. To avoid such dangers, the council of Dagestani *alims* (religious leaders) in 2002 decided to send a representative of the Dagestani SBM to Egypt, Syria, and Turkey to investigate the conditions of 600 Dagestani students who were studying there at religious institutions.[148] Another reason for not sending students abroad is that many of them abandon religious studies and work in various sectors of the economy.[149] Perhaps an even more important reason is that foreign-educated imams tend to be more independent minded and less amenable to control by the official Muslim and Russian establishments.

In general, under Putin, the government has attempted to exert more control over Islamic education in the country, notably by standardizing Islamic instruction throughout Russia. Sergei Kirienko, the presidential representative to Volga Federal District (Privolzhskii), expressed the government's position on this matter in early 2002 when he stated:

> We [the Russian government] clearly realize that unified teaching methodology for all the medressahs in Russia should be developed. Then we will understand the place and role of the country where the law is being violated and its safety is under threat. If our assistance is needed, we are ready to render it.[150]

This policy is part of a much broader process of Russification of Islam undertaken by Sergei Kirienko within the context of a long-term project entitled "Russian Islam."[151] The intellectual force behind this project is Sergei Gradirovsky. Since 2002, he has been a chief adviser to Kirienko. Another major contributor is Pyotr Schedrovitskiy, the director of the School for Cultural Politics (Shkola Kul'turnoy Politiki) in Moscow, and the former director of the Center for Strategic Studies in Nizhny Novgorod.

One of the objectives of this project is to conduct all Islamic education in Russian, to translate the Qur'an and Tafsir (interpretation of the Qur'an) into Russian, and in general to impose the use of Russian for all Islamic publications. It also requires that all sermons in the mosques be in Russian. Such changes would supposedly lead to the formation of a uniquely "Russian Islam" impervious to foreign, especially extremist, influences. It will also help develop a civic Russian identity transcending ethnic and religious boundaries. Interestingly, the project has generated fierce opposition both on the part of Orthodox Russians[152] and Muslims.[153] The former see Orthodoxy and Russianness as inextricably linked and thus object to the very term "Russian Islam" with its ethnic Russian connotations. Meanwhile, Muslims see the project as an insidious plan to undermine Muslim religion, institutions, culture, and identity. They warn that if fully implemented the project could lead to interreligious tensions.

Islamic Print and News Media

Since 1991, there has been an increase in the number of publications and various radio and television broadcasts dealing with Islamic issues. As of 2002, there were about forty newspapers and magazines of a Muslim character in Russia. However, like many other aspects of Muslim life in Russia, Muslim-oriented media are in a state of flux, with publications appearing and disappearing frequently.

In Moscow, the following are the most important publications: (1) *Islam Minbare*, a monthly newspaper published by DUMER that reflects the views of the RCM; (2) *Tribuna Islama* (The tribune of Islam), published by DUMER since 1994, with a circulation of 10,000 copies;[154] (3) *Islamskiy Mir* (The Islamic world); (4) *Zam-Zam*, published by the charity fund of the same name; and (5) *Al Fiqr*, a monthly bulletin published by the Islamic Congress of Russia.

In Tatarstan, Bashkortostan, North Caucasus, and other regions, the following are the principal Muslim publications: (1) *Din Va Magyyshat*, a Tatar-language publication of the SBM of Tatarstan; (2) *Iman* (The faith), both in Tatar and Russian; (3) *Muslima* (A Muslim woman), a magazine for Muslim women with a circulation of 5,000 copies;[155] (4) *Islam Nury* (The light of Islam), published in Tatar in Naberezhnie Chelny; (5) *Risalyat* (The message), a monthly publication by the SBM of the Republic of Bashkortostan in Bashkir and Russian; (6) *Musul'manskiy Vestnik* (The Muslim herald), published in Saratov, Volga District; (7) *Iman* (The faith), a newspaper published by the Religious Society of Muslims of Vologda; (8) *Solntse Islama* (The sun of Islam), published by the SBM of Penza Oblast; (9) *Kibla*, a newspaper published by the Religious Society of Muslims of Novocherkassk in southern Russia, close to Rostov-on-Don; and (10) *Azan* (Call to prayer), a newspaper published in Samara.

In the North Caucasus, Dagestan has the largest number of publications, including the following: (1) *Mezhdunarodnaya Musul'manskaya Gazeta* (International Muslim newspaper), an independent publication not affiliated with any religious board or other social and/or political organizations; (2) *Put' Islama* (The way of Islam), a monthly newspaper published by the Islamic Democratic Party; (3) *Nur-ul-Islam* (The light of Islam), published by the Russian Muslim social movement Nur; (4) *Assalam* (Peace), published twice a month by the SBM of Dagestan; and (5) *Islamskiy Vestnik* (The Islamic herald), a weekly newspaper circulated throughout the North Caucasus.[156] The newspaper *Minaret* is published by the Islamic cultural center in North Ossetia–Alania.[157]

The newspaper *Ummah* started circulation in August 2002 in Kazan. It is in Russian and is published by a charity fund and civic group, Ikhlas. Its goal, according to Rishat Khamidullin, who is in charge of this project, is to "disseminate objective information about Islam, primarily to Muslim youth."[158]

Union of Muslim Journalists (UMJ)

The creation of the Union of Muslim Journalists (UMJ) represents a watershed in the development of Muslim media in the Russian Federation. The founding convention of the UMJ took place in the conference hall of the Russian Council of Muftis (RCM) in Moscow on May 21, 2003.[159] The convention was organized by the RCM and the Eurasian Party/Union of Patriots of Russia. The participants at the convention included 35 journalists and editors representing various Muslim publications and media outlets.[160] Among the notable attendees were the chairman of RCM, Mufti Ravil Gainutdin; chairman of the Eurasian Party/Union of Patriots of Russia, Abdul-Vahid Niazov (leader of the Refakh movement); Rustam Arifdzhanov, the president of the media holding "Sovershenno Sekretno" and the chief editor of the newspaper *Versia*; the chairman of the Union of Journalists of Russia (UJR), Vsevolod Bogdanov; and the translator of the Qur'an and the member of the Russian Academy of Sciences, Iman Valeria Porokhova.[161] In his opening remarks Mufti Gainutdin noted,

> We should bring the truth about our religion and about the social activities of Muslims of Russia to the secular society, state and the peoples of other creeds. We should expose the false information spread about our religion and accusations made against Islam. . . . But in order to solve these problems we need a unified professional structure, in which a comprehensive all-Muslim (*obshchemusulmanskii*) approach to the existing problems will be developed.

The formation of the UMJ under the aegis of the RCM may signal a significant political realignment within a substantial part of the Muslim community in anticipation of the parliamentary and presidential elections in the Russian Federation, scheduled for December 2003 and March 2004 respectively. Moreover, this could also mean an increase in the influence of RCM because, as one of the founders of the UMJ, the RCM will no doubt significantly influence the shape and content of the activities and products of Muslim media in the Russian Federation. If successful, the UMJ may turn into an indispensable instrument for the mobilization of Muslim voters.

Radical Islamic Print

Since 1991, a number of periodicals with a radical and/or nontraditional orientation have also appeared. In early 1998, the Wahhabi organization Jama'at of the Chechen Republic of Ichkeria and the Scientific-Analytical Center "Al Qaf" founded the newspaper *Al Qaf* (Caucasus). Isa Gandaloev, a Wahhabi publicist and former public relations chief of the Department of Implementation of Punishments of the Supreme Shari'a Court of Chechnya, served as its editor in chief. The newspaper was printed in Grozny in the interim period between the first and second Chechen wars and achieved a circulation of 2,000 copies.

The materials published in this newspaper reflected the worldview of the Wahhabi elements within the Chechen leadership. Some articles had an openly anti-Semitic and anti-Russian character, but they were also harshly critical of President Aslan Maskhadov's administration and the activities of the traditional clergy, who supported him. In July 1998, the Chechen authorities temporarily halted the publication of the newspaper because of its antigovernment tone, but in September it resumed publication.[162] After the start of the second Chechen War, *Al Qaf* ceased to appear.

The popular educational magazine *Caliphate* was also founded by the Scientific-Analytical Center "Al Qaf" and the Wahhabi Jama'at. The Wahhabi publicist Ahmad Sardali served as its chief editor. The magazine was printed in Russian in Grozny. *Caliphate* was established in August–September 1998 as the official publication of the Main Headquarters for the Liberation of Dagestan (the military command of the Dagestani Wahhabis). The materials published in it were mainly of sociopolitical and religious character. They reflected the views of the Wahhabi leadership and included interviews with the representatives of Dagestan's Wahhabi community. The tone of the articles was similar to those of *Al Qaf*. The magazine had a supplement called *Musul'manka* (Muslim woman) directed at the female audience.[163]

Radio and Television Programs

Starting in 1992, DUMER, initially with the support of the government, created a number of radio and television programs on Islam, including "Minaret," "Now," and "Ruhi Miras" (Spirital heritage), which is a radio and television program in the Tatar language. Since the fall of 1998, the program "A Thousand and One Nights: An Encyclopedia of Islam" has appeared on the television channel Rossiya (Russia) every Friday. The program features relatively well known Muslim clergy, Islamic studies experts, and scholars of the Qu'ran. There are also two government-owned radio stations, Voice of Islam and Islamic Wavelength, that essentially serve to popularize the activities of DUMER. The following are radio and/or television programs in other Muslims regions of the Russian Federation: (1) "Din Va Tormysh" (Life and religion), a program on the local television in Kazan sponsored by the SBM of Tatarstan; (2) "Ihlas," a weekly television program in Ufa, Bashkortostan; (3) "Allahu Akbar," an informational and educational programming channel for Muslims as part of Saratov Tele-Radio Center; and (4) "For Unity and Stability" and "Peace to Your House," two radio and television programs in Dagestan that explain federal laws about the freedom of conscience and feature Muslim clerics.

However, conversations with the representatives of Russia's Muslim community, including key religious figures, indicate that they feel that they are not capable of countering what they see as anti-Islamic bias in the Russian media, especially television. Programs on the war in Chechnya, in particular, have spread fear of Islam among the non-Muslim population. The documentary "The Caucasian

Crescent" is one example of inflammatory reporting. It focuses on the rise of Wah-habism in the North Caucasian republics of Kabardino-Balkaria and Karachaevo-Cherkessia and claims that one of the main centers of Wahhabism is Tyrnyauz, a town west of the Kabardino-Balkarian capital of Nalchik.[164] The film sparked mass protests in both republics, and regional leaders appealed to President Putin, com-plaining that their peoples "had been slandered."[165] Muslim leaders complain that the Russian media and even officials do not make a distinction between law-abiding Muslims and rebels, extremists, or simple criminals who happen to be Muslims. Marat Murtazin, the rector of Moscow Islamic University, asks, "Is it sound to argue that all of a sudden those 20 million Muslims living in the Russian Federation have become potential bandits and terrorists? Should the whole nations, just like during the Stalin era, be punished for the crimes committed by individual citi-zens?"[166] In short, Russia's Muslim community does not have a sufficient media network to counterbalance the negative images of Islam that are often propagated by the Russian media.

Charitable Organizations: Types and Activities

DUMER and several other organizations provide a variety of social services and financial and other assistance to needy Muslims. To coordinate some of these char-itable activities, DUMER in 1995 created the Council of Guardians, which provides material aid to orphanages and hospitals. The council also provides financial as-sistance to the Higher Islamic Spiritual College, the Ismailiya Medressah, and scholars of Islamic studies. Additionally, the council provides funds for the building of mosques, including ones in Moscow (such as the one located on Moscow's Poklonnaya Hill), the nearby town of Solnechnogorsk, and in the oblasts of Nizhny Novgorod and Yaroslavl.

Alongside DUMER's charitable activities, the Ibragim bin Abdulaziz al Ibragim Fund, the Russian branch of an organization based in Saudi Arabia, provides food to patrons of Moscow's Assembly Mosque and scholarship funds for students at the Islamic College. It has helped organize competitions for Qu'ranic reading and has assisted in publishing efforts. The Bedir Fund, which was formed by Turkish and Russian citizens, is active in cultural, sporting, and youth-oriented events. The fund encourages cultural exchanges between Russian and Turkish citizens. It also maintains a youth club and has published a book on the life of the prophet Mu-hammad. Other charitable organizations include the Zam-Zam Fund, the Ikhlas Fund, the Al-Amal Fund, and the Hilal Fund, which has restored mosques in Omsk, Novosibirsk, Moscow, and Nizhny Novgorod.[167] Additionally, a wide range of youth and women's organizations operate in Russia. However, in the aftermath of 11 September, many of these organizations, especially those with ties to Arab countries, notably Saudi Arabia, have come under greater scrutiny, and their future is uncertain.

Muslim Political Movements

Twice, in 1905–7 and 1917, Russia's Muslims formed political organizations to unite the empire's Muslims in order to give them a larger role in determining their own destiny and shape Russia's postimperial government. Both times the Muslims' aspirations for autonomy, independence, or the creation of a truly federal system were frustrated, first by the reassertion of tsarist authoritarianism and then by Communist totalitarianism. After the USSR's collapse, once more Muslim political organizations emerged in Russia. However, as in the past, because of the diversity of Russia's Muslim population and factors related to Russia's broader political culture, none of the Muslim political movements has emerged as a viable force capable of speaking for Russian Muslims and acting as the advocate of their interests. Indeed, following the move under President Putin toward greater political centralization and cultural homogenization in Russia, along with other changes related to the process of the formation and functioning of political parties, even the most successful Muslim political party, Refakh, has transformed itself into a so-called Eurasian Party, which is part of the electoral coalition of Union of Patriots of Russia, and has abandoned its predominantly Islamic characteristics.[168]

Different Shades of Russian Islam

Historically, the dominant branch of Islamic Shari'a in Russia's Muslim regions has been the Hanafi school based on the teachings of Imam Abu Hanifa. The only exception is Dagestan, where the Shafei tradition is predominant. The dominance of the Hanafi school is partly due to the fact that Islamic teaching penetrated most Muslim-inhabited parts of the present-day Russian Federation from Central Asia, especially Bukhara. Imam Abu Hanifa was born in Central Asia and developed his views there. Dagestan, by contrast, was more influenced by intellectual and religious trends emanating from the Arab world. One attraction of the Hanafi school for the Central Asians, and later other Turkic peoples, was its greater tolerance toward pre-Islamic traditions and their incorporation into the fold of Islam. Some have attributed this aspect of the Hanafi school to the fact that Imam Hanifa was of Iranian origin. The Hanafi school generally has a more accommodating attitude toward political power and does not condone open rebellion against the state.[169] In recent decades, however, this characteristic has been criticized by the younger generations of Muslims. Some scholars have argued that this is one reason why they are attracted to more politically activist interpretations of Islam, including an activist interpretation of Wahhabism.[170]

In the North Caucasus, especially Dagestan, mystical traditions of Islam (Sufism) in its various forms and schools have been influential.[171] In the last twenty years, however, for a variety of reasons, other variants of Islam have penetrated Muslim regions of the Russian Federation. This process accelerated after the Soviet Union's collapse. The more open atmosphere of Boris Yeltsin's Russia, which allowed greater interaction between Russian Muslims and the rest of the Islamic world, combined with the increasing rivalry for influence in the post-Soviet Muslim space among some Muslim countries and transnational movements, contributed to this development. Presently, five major trends can be observed within Russian Islam: traditional Hanafism, Sufi traditions, Salafiyya (or Wahhabism), Jihadism, and Euro-Islam. In addition, in May 2001, the RCM in an important document titled "The Fundamental Principles of the Social Program of Russia's Muslims" (MSP) elaborated its positions on a number of critical social, cultural, and political issues.

Traditional Hanafism

Hanafism is the position of the official clergy, including those affiliated with the RCM and CSBM. In general, followers of Hanafism have a cooperative attitude toward governmental authorities at both local and federal levels. They wish to gain recognition for Islam as an important component of Russia's cultural heritage, and they defend Muslim interests. But they also emphasize the importance of coexistence and cooperation among the followers of different faiths, especially between Muslims and Orthodox Christians. Thus the RCM has been active in encouraging interfaith dialogue.[172] The Ufa center and Mufti Talgat Tadzhuddin are even more cooperative with the government. Both centers support the maintenance of Russia's territorial and political integrity, the secular character of its government, and the principle of the separation of church and state. For example, in a September 2000 interview with Hunter, Sheikh Ravil Gainutdin expressed his opposition to suggestions under discussion at the time in political circles in Russia that Orthodox Christianity and Islam be declared the two official religions of Russia. He said that this would be against the principle of equality of religions and could be damaging to interfaith harmony and coexistence, especially in regions where one religion is heavily represented. Many of these positions have been codified in the MSP. However, within this mainstream Islam, some religious figures favor a more assertive position for Islam and more extensive ties with the rest of the Muslim world. They are more openly critical of the anti-Islam statements and sentiments of segments of the Russian society, including those of some politicians and members of the Christian Orthodox establishment. This attitude often makes them vulnerable to charges of secretly harboring Wahhabist tendencies. For example, Mikhail Tulskiy accuses Ravil Gainutdin of having Wahhabi sympathies, while he praises Talgat Tadzhuddin for having "amply demonstrated his loyalty to Russia and Orthodoxy."[173]

Similarly, the chairman of the Spiritual Board of Muslims of the Asian Part of Russia, Nafigulla Ashirov, who studied at the Islamic University of Amir Abdul-Qadir in Algeria in 1990, has been considered to be on the radical spectrum of Russian Islam and has been suspected of having ties with Muslim religious extremists by the Russian authorities.[174] By mid-2001, he seemed to have joined the mainstream. For instance, along with Tadzhuddin, he was present at the opening ceremony of a new mosque and the subsequent roundtable discussion held in Nizhny Novgorod in June 2001. Gainutdin was absent from both of these events.

Since the plenipotentiary representative of the president in Volga Federal District, Sergei Kirienko, was one of the main initiators of this meeting, Ashirov's presence may have indicated that the Kremlin was changing its attitude toward him and viewed him as an important player in the government's efforts to form a unified Muslim establishment for Russia. However, given the volatility of Russian politics and the complex nature of relations between the Russian government and the Muslim establishment, the Kremlin's attitude may change again. Indeed, by early 2003, Ashirov's statements on a number of issues seemed to indicate that he had returned to his more independent position.

Sufi Traditions

In the North Caucasus, mainstream Islam is still dominated by various Sufi brotherhoods, notably Naqshbandya, Qadiriya, and Shaziliya, although increasingly, less mystical practices of Islam have been gaining ground (Figure 2.3). Thus a growing number of religious leaders in the North Caucasus, including Dagestan, have demanded the introduction of the Shari'a as the law of the land, as occurred in Chechnya during the period between the two Chechen wars. However, so far in Dagestan, the mainstream clergy have maintained that any such action must be compatible with Russian laws. One such figure was Said Muhammad Abubakarov, the mufti of Dagestan, who was assassinated by the more radical elements in early 1999. The dominant view in Russia still is that Sufism is essentially quietist and hence can be an antidote to extremist trends, but this perception is not entirely correct. The history of North Caucasus and Central Asia shows that Sufism can be turned into an activist creed. The most serious resistance to the Russian advance into the Caucasus was organized by a Sufi leader, Imam Shamil. During the Soviet Union's antireligious campaigns, Sufi brotherhoods were important centers of maintaining religious traditions.[175] Under certain circumstances, the emergence of a more activist version of Sufism cannot be ruled out. Nor is Sufism inherently apolitical. Indeed, some Sufi leaders are actively involved in Dagestani politics.[176]

Nontraditional or Radical Islam: Salafiyya or Wahhabism?

Since the time of perestroika, other forms of Islam that are not traditional to the Muslim-inhabited regions of the Russian Federation have become popular among Russia's Muslims. The most influential of these schools, especially in the North Caucasus, has been inspired by the teachings of Muhammad Ibn Abdul Wahhab, or Wahhabism. Meanwhile, because some of those who are attracted to the Wahhabi school have been involved in violent acts, and because Russian authorities have indiscriminately applied the term "Wahhabi" to all Muslims who engage in violence or simply advocate strict observance of Islamic rules, many scholars have come to shun the use of the term "Wahhabism," and the Wahhabis prefer to use other terms of self-identification. Many of these nontraditional Muslims call themselves Salafiyya or Salafis. The question to be asked, therefore, is the following: Is there a difference between the Salafis and the Wahhabis, or are they the same?

Figure 2.3 **Main Sufi Brotherhoods and Religious-Political Organizations of Dagestan and Chechnya**

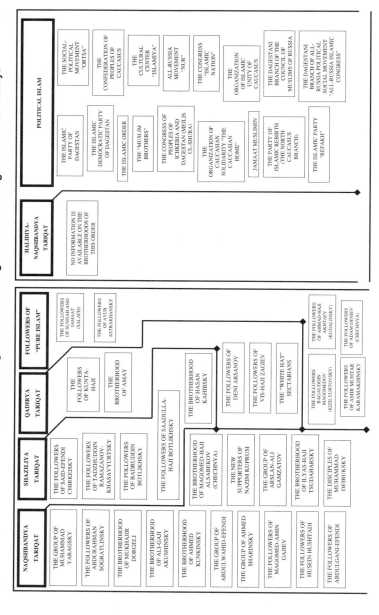

Source: Zagir Arukhov, deputy minister of Nationality Policy, Information, and External Affairs of the Republic of Dagestan and deputy director of the Center of Islamic Studies of North Caucasus, from Hunter's personal collection.

In its strict sense, Salafiyya means those who follow only the teachings of the Qu'ran, the Prophet, and his companions—*Sahaba*, the *Taibun*, and the *Taba Tai'bun*—"the righteous ones" and the two or three generations after them. However, there has never been a school of Islamic law (Shar'ia) called Salafiyya, partly because all four main Sunni schools, including the Hanafi school, give the highest priority to traditions of early Islam. Periodically in the course of Islam's history, religious leaders have invoked the "Salaf" (ancestors) as part of a strategy of reforming Islam, ridding it of foreign influences, and justifying their own prescription for reform and renewal. Yet Muslim religious scholars have not agreed on who exactly are the "Salaf." To illustrate, the nineteenth-century reformist movement formed by Sheikh Muhammad Abduh and Jemaleddin al-Afghani was called Al-Salafiyya after the Salaf. Yet Muhammad Abduh included later generations of theologians in his definition of the Salaf and, rather than advocating a reductionist definition of Islam, called for a synthesis of Islam and modernity.

Contemporary Salafis, by contrast, generally include only the first few generations of Islamic leaders in their definition of Salaf. This view is close to Muhammad Ibn Abdul Wahhab's interpretation, and his teachings are influential in today's Salafi movements. Pakistani movements inspired by the Deobandi school, which was influenced by Abdul Wahhab's teachings, have played an important role in the dissemination of Salafi/Wahhabi tendencies in the Russian Federation and elsewhere. The adherents of Salafi ideas are more numerous in Dagestan and other parts of the North Caucasus, but they are not limited to this region. According to one official of DUMER, "They [Salafis] can be found anywhere, even among the clergy."[177] Some Salafis have an activist interpretation of Islam and impute characteristics to early Islam that are not supported by historic evidence. Some go as far as seeing Islam more as a political ideology and tool. For example, Geidar Jemal, the chairman of the Islamic Committee of Russia, espouses such a view. He believes in "the ideology of real, true Islam, the Islam of the 'Sahhaba' of the Prophet, which is not a clerical direction (*klerikal'noe napravlenie*), but Islam that is militant, purely political."[178]

Jihadism

As in the rest of the Islamic world, those Russian Muslims who adhere to strict and reductionist interpretations of Islam and are committed to establishing the rule of Shari'a differ in their methodologies of achieving their goal. They fall into two broad categories: (1) those who want to bring about Islamization through peaceful means and (2) those who believe that if necessary, these goals should be achieved by violent means or through the waging of holy war (jihad), as they interpret this concept. This tendency is called Jihadist.[179] The Jihadist phenomenon is a varied one reflecting the peculiarities of individual Muslim countries. Some sources credit the Egyptian Muhammad Abd al-Salam Faraj as being the theoretician of the Jihadist movement.[180] According to Faraj, jihad was the sixth pillar of faith in Islam, but was later abandoned. He believed that the concept of jihad was distorted and came to be seen as struggle against an individual's lower instincts, whereas initially it meant to take up arms and to compel everyone to submit to Islam. This view is not supported by major Islamic sources, but because the purpose of the theory is political mobilization of Muslims, not religious enlightenment, it is less concerned with doctrinal authenticity.

Jihadist ideas gained credence and a significant number of adherents as a result of the Soviet-Afghan War. The war was characterized as "jihad" by both Muslims and the West, and the Afghan resistance movement came to be known as the Mujahideen (holy warriors). Volunteers from Arab countries, Central Asia, and the Caucasus went to fight in Afghanistan. Some continued to fight in the Afghan civil war, which raged following the collapse of the Soviet-supported Afghan government in 1992. After the breakup of the Soviet Union and the outbreak of ethnic and other conflicts in the Caucasus, some Afghan War veterans became engaged in the region's conflicts, notably the Chechen War. It appears that following the rise of the Taliban government in Afghanistan in 1996, a close relationship developed between Chechen extremists and the Taliban and such Jihadist movements as that of Osama bin Laden.[181]

Shahidism

An offshoot of the Jihadist movement that has recently appeared in Russia and the North Caucasus is that of the Shahidists, whose members celebrate martyrdom as a way of achieving their goal. The hostage-taking operation in Moscow's Dubrovka Theater in October 2002 and the suicide bombing of the headquarters of the pro-Moscow Chechen administration in Grozny in December 2002 were examples of translating Shahidist ideology into violent acts.[182]

Other recent acts of terror illustrative of growing Shahidist influence include the suicide bombing of the government compound in the village of Znamenskoe in the Nadterechny district of northern Chechnya on 12 May 2003,[183] the suicide bombing at a Muslim religious celebration in the village of Ilaskhan-Yurt (Belorechye) in the Gudermes district on 14 May 2003,[184] the suicide attack on the bus with the Russian military personnel, which occurred on the outskirts of the city of Mozdok in North Ossetia on 5 June 2003,[185] and the suicide attack at the Krylya rock festival, which was held at the Tushino airfield near Moscow on 5 July 2003.[186] The suicide bombings of both the pro-Moscow Chechen administration building in Grozny and the government compound in the village of Znamenskoe were particularly devastating. In both cases, the Shahidists used trucks laden with explosives in order to inflict maximum damage. As a result, the first attack left 80 dead and 150 wounded, and the second attack killed 54 people and injured about 200.[187]

The increasing participation of women in these suicide bombings represents a novel and disturbing trend with parallels with similar occurrences in the zone of the Arab-Israeli conflict. The suicide attacks on the bus in North Ossetia and at the rock concert at Tushino airfield, which were carried out by women, also indicate that the potential area of suicide attacks is not circumscribed by Chechnya proper, and indeed can be expanded into the North Caucasus region and even further into the Russian Federation.[188] The mastermind behind the Dubrovka theater hostage-taking tragedy[189] and the recent wave of suicide attacks appears to be Shamil Basaev, the radical Chechen field commander.[190] According to the Moscow-appointed Chechen Prosecutor General Vladimir Kravchenko, Shamil Basaev had trained thirty female suicide bombers for carrying out attacks against Russian federal troops stationed in Chechnya and Chechnya's pro-Moscow Administration.[191]

The Appeal of Extremist Islam

Several factors account for the appeal of nontraditional and extremist versions of Islam among segments of Russia's Muslims. These factors can be divided into three categories: (1) institutional; (2) social and economic; and (3) ethnocultural and political.

Institutional Weakness

Tsarist and Soviet policies seriously weakened traditional educational and institutional foundations of Russian Islam, resulting in a shortage of Muslim religious institutions and properly educated clergy. Consequently, the Muslim religious revival during perestroika triggered a crisis within Russia's Muslim community caused by what Marat Murtazin, the rector of Moscow Islamic University, has characterized as "a lack of educated Imams, preachers, lecturers, scientists-theologians, and experts of Shari'a and other Islamic sciences."[192] The result was the sending of students abroad for religious education and an influx of foreign missionaries and lecturers to Russia. According to Murtazin, foreign missionaries chose the very young students—between the ages of twelve and eighteen—and sent them abroad for further studies. The students were influenced by various types of extremist ideas without necessarily becoming good scholars. Clearly some of the foreign-educated imams may have acquired extremist tendencies, but it is difficult to apply this rule generally.

Another cause of Islam's institutional weakness has been the identification of the official Muslim establishment with the government and its image as dependent and subservient. This perception still persists to a great extent and taints the image—albeit to different degrees—of some religious figures. The post-Soviet evolution of the official Muslim establishment, including rivalries among its key leaders, has not inspired popular confidence in official Islam. More seriously, the behavior of some Islamic leaders has given rise to doubts about their Islamic credentials.

Social and Economic Factors

In some Muslim-inhabited regions, notably North Caucasus, the deterioration of social and economic conditions has contributed to the appeal of extremism. According to Anatoly Savateev, "The flawed policies conducted both by the federal center and the republican leadership, the Russian pseudo-reforms hit the North Caucasus particularly hard. The overall fall in industrial output; the breakdown of agriculture; massive unemployment (especially among the youth, who account for 80 percent of the unemployed); [and] the drastic deterioration of living conditions of people (around 80 percent of local residents are at least four times poorer than the average citizen of Russia)" were partly responsible for the growth of extremist ideas, notably those inspired by the Wahhabi doctrine.[193] Economic disparities in the North Caucasus—within individual republics, notably Dagestan, and between a few clans and the rest of the people—are another contributing factor. According to Savateev, the 200 families in Dagestan that constitute the republic's ruling elite "hold 85 percent of the republic's wealth."[194]

Other parts of the North Caucasus also face problems of economic underdevelopment and unemployment. For some republics, such as Ingushetia, the fallout of the Chechen War has created additional difficulties in the form of refugees; by the end of 2002, there were 160,000 Chechen refugees in Ingushetia.[195] The harsh conditions in the refugee camps and anger over human rights abuses by the Russian military in Chechnya may make these refugees more receptive to extremist ideologies.

These economic problems, combined with other consequences of the USSR's collapse and various types of strife that it created, also undermined the social fabric of Muslim communities, thus creating a psychological and moral crisis. Old guidelines for societal relations disappeared, but new ones were long in taking root; in the case of the North Caucasus, because of the Chechen War and other smaller conflicts in the North and South Caucasus, a chaotic situation developed, with criminal groups gaining undue political and economic influence, largely through corrupt practices. This resulted in a situation whereby amid widespread poverty, a small minority holds wealth that by the standards of the North Caucasus is enormous.

Under these circumstances, many of the deprived—notably unemployed youth and poor peasants—became attracted to the extremist discourse with its "condemnation of luxury, self-indulgence and materialistic excesses."[196] Meanwhile, "the ideas of equality, ethics of brotherhood, and unity of all Muslims, as well as social harmony," became more attractive.[197]

Alexei Malashenko also recognizes these factors as contributing to some Muslims', including nonextremists', turn to Islam as the only way out of the crisis. According to Malashenko, "In Dagestan, and in the North Caucasus in general, a considerable segment, perhaps even the bulk of the population, is disillusioned with the ethnic elites. They are also disillusioned because of the center's inability to help the Muslim regions emerge from their crisis."[198]

Cultural and Political Factors

For some Muslims, the attraction of the extremists lies in their claims to protect Islamic culture from the negative influences emanating from the Moscow-based media and the West. The danger of cultural dilution in these Muslims' views has increased with the communication revolution. Many areas, such as the Kadar District in Dagestan, which even in Communist times had persevered in its traditional lifestyle, are particularly sensitive to the greater intrusion of external cultural influences. The cultural factor seems to be important in attracting even those Muslims who are relatively well off economically. Muslims who have aspirations of political self-determination find some strands of extremist thought, especially those that emphasize the establishment of Islamic rule as the only way to independence, quite appealing. Mufti Ravil Gainutdin seems to view sociopolitical and cultural factors as mainly responsible for this phenomenon, as the following comment illustrates:

> The reason for the emergence of extremists who are in one way or another related to Islam, in my opinion, should be looked for not in Islam, but in the living conditions of Muslims. If we approach this problem from this position, then the threat is real, and, moreover, it is constantly growing. And it is understandable—it is precisely among the Muslim youth that unemployment is highest in the country and the living conditions are the lowest. This youth experiences big difficulties in adapting to the contemporary conditions. This process is much more difficult for Muslims than for the followers of other religions. The Muslims are experiencing the crisis of traditional values and the lifestyle.[199]

Muslim Extremist Groups in the Russian Federation

Any analysis of the emergence, evolution, and present status of Muslim extremist groups in Russia involves an initial problem of defining what is meant by extremism and who is an extremist. In nearly all Russian sources, all of those who adhere to the so-called Wahhabi school are either actively or passively (potentially) extremist. Some Salafis because of their affinity with the Wahhabis also fall in this category.

However, here extremism is defined as an ideology that justifies resorting to violence in order to create systems of governance and/or independent states based on the establishment of a puritanical (Wahhabi-Salafi) Islam. In other words, extremism is equated with Jihadism and Shahidism. As a first step toward achieving the goal of creating Islamic governments and/or states, these groups advocate the establishment of communities often referred to as *jama'at* within which strict Islamic rules will be enforced. Such enclaves are also referred to as "Separate Islamic Territory" (*Otdel'naya Islamskaya Territoriya*), as was the case with the villages of Karamakhi and Chabanmakhi village in Dagestan. However, *jama'at* at times also refers to broader organizations at a national level that espouse the same strategy, such as Islamic Jama'at of Dagestan or Islamic Jama'at of the Chechen Republic of Ichkeria. Some of these groups of religious extremists have their own paramilitary forces. The principal center of Islamic extremism in the sense defined here has been the North Caucasus, specifically Chechnya and Dagestan.

Chechnya

In Chechnya, the emergence of extremist groups has been directly linked to the power struggles that emerged within the Chechen leadership following the assassination of the first president of Chechnya, Dzhokhar Dudaev. An additional factor was the influence of outsiders, notably the veterans of the Afghan War.

In a speech delivered in July 1998, Chechen president Aslan Maskhadov referred to the political ambitions of some Chechen personalities with Wahhabi sympathies and expressed regret that he had initially tried to accommodate them. Maskhadov noted, "After the war, without understanding the situation and their ideology we [the Chechen government] began to distribute the responsibilities amongst us. Suddenly everyone wanted to become a president or a minister. We wanted to have the Wahhabis on our side, and that is why we played (*zaigrivali*) with them, complied with their whims. And today we are reaping the fruits of our behavior."[200] Maskhadov also blames foreign elements for creating dissent in Chechnya and spreading extremism. In a clear reference to the Arab commander Khattab, Maskhadov accused him of not having any feelings for Chechens or Chechnya, as the following passage from the same speech illustrates: "I told him, 'You came here from Jordan and you have no pity for Chechens, but we are supposed to take care of each other—and that's why you should abandon the battlefield.' He did not comply, and did not leave. I told him again that he had violated the laws of the state, and demanded the cessation of hostilities and retreat. And again he did not listen to me. Then the confrontation escalated as new forces joined the warring sides. Now there are killed and wounded."[201]

The period between the end of the first Chechen War (August 1996) and the beginning of the second (September 1999) was particularly fertile in terms of the formation of military groups. The main difficulty in describing and classifying various militant Islamic groups is that they are ill defined and constantly change their names, organizational structures, and the nature of relations among themselves. Of the Islamic military formations, the most important in Chechnya has been the Islamic Regiment/Battalion of Special Forces (Islamskii Polk Spetsial'nogo Naznachenia) under the joint command of Khattab and Shamil Basaev. The Islamic Regiment was created between 1998 and 1999 as part of the process of Islamization of the Chechen political and governmental infrastructure and formed part of the official military establishment of the nascent Chechen Republic of Ichkeria. The Chechen military also included the National Guards (Natsional'naya Gvardia), which was an essentially nonreligious formation loyal to President Maskhadov, and the Shari'a Guards (Shariatskaya Gvardia), which had an explicitly Islamic character. However, with growing dissent within the Chechen leadership and fighting among various military groups, Maskhadov decided to disband the Shari'a Guards. After the disappearance of the Shari'a Guards and the total breach between Maskhadov and Basaev over the issue of the Chechen incursion into Dagestan in August–September 1999, the Islamic Battalion came to represent the main military faction of Muslim extremists in Chechnya. This group also became an important force during the confrontation between the local Wahhabi militants and the police in the village of Karamakhi, Dagestan, in May 1998, when the former seized and disarmed the village police station. According to some sources, Shamil Basaev warned that he would deploy his Islamic Battalion to Dagestan if the republican authorities decided to use military force against the Wahhabi *jama'at* of Karamakhi.[202] Finally, it is worth mentioning the group that was responsible for the hostage-taking disaster in Moscow's Dubrovka Theater, the Reconnaissance and Sabotage Battalion "Riyadh as-Salihin" (The gardens of the righteous).[203] A survey of publicly available resources provides little information on this group except that it specializes in suicide attacks and is controlled by Shamil Basaev.[204] It cannot be ruled out that the December 2002 suicide bombing of the pro-Moscow Chechen administration building in Grozny was also committed by members of this group.

Dagestan

Timur Muzaev, the author of *Dagestan: Vlast, Narody, Konflikti* (Dagestan: Authority, peoples, conflicts) identifies the most extremist Islamic movement in Dagestan, which he characterizes as Wahhabi, as Jama'at of Dagestan. According to Muzaev, this movement has been engaged in armed struggle against the republican authorities and the Russian troops stationed in Dagestan since 1997. In September 1998, in response to repression by the republican authorities, the movement's headquarters was moved to Chechnya. D.V. Makarov notes that the Jama'at of Dagestan (Islamic Jama'at of Dagestan, or IJD) "factually was not a centralized organization but rather represented a conglomerate of separate [local] jama'ats, which were united by common ideas and values, but were not necessarily in agreement with one another on all issues."[205] Makarov observes that the relocation of the headquarters of the IJD to Chechnya coincided with the division of the Wahhabis of Dagestan into two cores: (1) the "outer core," consisting of those with more radical aspirations who moved to Chechnya and were committed to ousting the Dagestani republican government by force, and (2) the "inner" core, which comprised the moderate Wahhabis who advocated the establishment of an Islamic state in Dagestan, but favored a conciliatory approach toward republican authorities and preferred the gradual transformation of Dagestan's sociopolitical order.[206] Since the resumption of warfare in Chechnya, the fate of this organization is not clear.

At the local level, the most significant *jama'ats* were in the Dagestani villages of Karamakhi, Chabanmakhi, and Kadar. In August 1998, they established separate Islamic territories or so-called Shari'a zones.[207] This action led to clashes with other communities that did not approve of the Wahhabis' particular interpretation of Islam because the latter viewed many of the region's traditional practices as un-Islamic. Initially, violent confrontation was averted by the signing of an accord between Magomedali Magomedov, chairman of Dagestan's State Council, and representatives of the three villages. Later, Russian minister of internal affairs Sergei Stepashin met with the leaders of the villages to further reduce tensions.[208] However, in September 1999, when the second Chechen War started, these villages also were attacked by the Russian military.

The Islamic Army of Caucasus (Islamskaya Armia Kavkaza)

The first reference to the Islamic Army of Caucasus surfaced on 23 March 1999 when the leaders of Salafi *jama'ats* of Dagestan and Chechnya announced jihad against Russia and appealed to the youth of Caucasus to join their ranks and come to designated areas. Muhammad Tagaev, an active supporter of jihad, stated in the spring of 1999, "We shall liberate Dagestan by all means. . . . And then without any suspension of activities, together with the liberation of Dagestan, we will liberate Caucasus. . . . The summer of 1999 should become the beginning of the decisive battles against the Empire."[209]

The Unified Command of Dagestani Mujahideen (Ob'edinennoe Komandovanie Dagestanskikh Modjakhedov)

The principal military arm of the Jama'at of Dagestan is the Unified Command of Dagestani Mujahideen. This organization was created at a meeting of the leaders of the Jama'at of Dagestan on 25 January 1998 in Gudermes, Chechnya. They adopted the "Manifesto of the Jama'at of Dagestan to Muslims of the World," which declared the "situation between the Jama'at and pro-Russian leadership of Dagestan [as] one that can be characterized as military with all ensuing consequences." The manifesto called for "full-scale activation of the Islamic call and for waging Jihad against unbelief and everyone who represents it."[210] The newly formed organization was supposed to coordinate and direct all the military-political activities of the Islamic forces. During the armed clashes in Dagestan in the summer of 1998 in the villages of Karamakhi and Chabanmakhi and in their aftermath, this organization was referred to as the Unified Command of Dagestani Mujahideen. After the clashes, the Unified Command issued the strongly worded "Urgent Appeal to All Power Structures of the Republic of Dagestan," which explicitly warned military and law-enforcement agencies in Dagestan that all those who dared "to interfere with the establishment of the will and authority of Allah" would be destroyed. The document further warned that any attempts at "extracting and appropriating weapons or property which belong to Jama'at, and also efforts at detention or apprehension of the Mujahideen, will be mercilessly and severely punished."[211]

Army of the Liberation of Dagestan (Armia Osvobozhdenia Dagestana)

The Army of the Liberation of Dagestan was first mentioned in the media in September 1999 when a journalist working for the Agence France-Presse (AFP) in Grozny received a phone call from someone by the name of Khasbulat. The caller identified himself as a member of the Army of the Liberation of Dagestan and claimed that it was responsible for the explosion at Manezhnaya Square in Moscow on 5 September 1999. He added that similar acts would occur throughout the Russian Federation until the Russian soldiers left Dagestan. According to Khasbulat, the Army of the Liberation of Dagestan was a subdivision of the Islamic

Army of Caucasus led by Sheikh Muhammad Bagauddin. The leader of the Wahhabi community, Sheikh Bagauddin, a native of the village of Karamakhi, had created this army in response to the assault of federal troops on his birthplace. However, Sergei Bogdanov of the Federalnaya Sluzhba Bezopasnosti (FSB, the Russian Federal Security Service) press service in Moscow and Moscow Oblast stated that the words of a previously unknown individual representing a semimythical organization should not be considered as reliable. Furthermore, as Bogdanov suggested, the Dagestani religious extremists, who were surrounded by the Russian troops, used the explosion to substantiate their promises of unleashing "wide-scale terrorist actions across Russia." Bogdanov, however, insisted that this organization had nothing to do with the bombing.[212]

The Dagestani Rebel Army of Imam (Dagestanskaya
Povstancheskaya Armia Imama)

The Dagestani Rebel Army of Imam is the military wing of the anti-Russian Caucasian Confederation of Zelimkhan Yanderbaev. The leader of this group was Muhammad Tagaev, an ethnic Avar. It had engaged in armed clashes with Russian troops since the beginning of 1999 independently of the military operations conducted by the forces of the Islamic Jama'at of Dagestan.[213]

Other Extremist Groups

The emergence of guerrilla training camps in Chechnya between 1996 and 1999 led to the proliferation of small groups of extremists across the North Caucasus. After the death of Chechnya's first president, Dzhokhar Dudaev, in April 1996, the sociopolitical movement the Way of Dzhokhar was formed in Chechnya. The military wing of this organization was the Army of Dzhokhar, a small detachment of battle-hardened veterans of the Chechen War led by a prominent field commander, Salman Raduev. However, after the capture of Raduev by federal forces on 16 March 2000, this group disbanded.[214] In September 1999, Russian and Ingush security forces apprehended members of an Islamist group called the Ingush Regiment and confiscated a schedule of military training sessions and a manual on laying mines.[215] Further west, Valerii Kokov, the president of Kabardino-Balkaria, attributed a series of bombings against government buildings in the capital, Nalchik, to Wahhabis.[216] In Adygea, Russian authorities charged the organization Islamic Appeal with attempting to spread Wahhabism among college students in Adygea.[217] The discovery of an Islamist group in the summer of 2001 that federal authorities alleged was plotting to topple the republican governments in Kabardino-Balkaria and Karachaevo-Cherkessia further raised fears of religiously inspired violence.[218]

Euro-Islam: The Modernist Face of Russian Islam

There is also a modernist trend within Russian Islam, especially in Tatarstan. Its most prominent representative is Rafael Khakimov, a Tatar intellectual and academician and a former adviser to the republic's president, Mintimer Shaimiev. He bases his theory of Euro-Islam on the philosophy of the Jadid movement of the late nineteenth and early twentieth centuries, which extended from Tatarstan to Central Asia. This movement was part of the greater reformist phenomenon that spread throughout the Islamic world under the influence of figures such as Jemaleddin al-Afghani. Several Tatar religious and intellectual figures became part of this movement. Notable among them were Shihabeddin Marjani, Rizaeddin Fahreddin, and Ismail Bey Gaspirali (Gasprinsky).[219] The basic goal of the Jadidists was to revitalize Islamic peoples and free them from foreign domination. To achieve this goal, they believed that Islam must be stripped of superstition and other static forms of behavior, and that Muslims should master science and technology.[220]

Some contemporary Tatar intellectuals have offered new interpretations of Jadidism and have tried to give it a more specifically Tatar character. Thus, according to Khakimov, "The Jadids offered a 'Western' interpretation of Muslim culture. Or it could be called the 'Oriental' interpretation of European culture, for the Tatar theologians found in Islam the concepts that were consonant with European trends."[221] He also maintains that Tatarstan's special geographic position (on the periphery of the Muslim world) and its political conditions (close interaction with Russia) led to the creation of an "Islamic subcivilization" among Tatars best exemplified by Jadidism.[222] In Khakimov's view, a new, vibrant, and modern Islam can be developed on the foundations of Jadidism, especially in Tatarstan. This modern Islam can be emulated by other Muslims. According to him, Jadidism's advantages lie in that "it encourages individualism, has a creative premise, and welcomes all sorts of social activities as pleasing to God; it is a stimulus for a transition to a market economy. Reform Islam does not stand in the way of present day European norms and values. On the contrary, it permits traditional Tatar and Islamic values to be organically united with the ideas of liberalism and democracy."[223] He then adds, "The pragmatism of Tatar Islam brings it closer to the European mentality."[224]

In his latest writings, including an essay titled "Gde nasha Mekka?" (Where is our Mecca?), Khakimov has altered some of his earlier views and now argues that Russia's Muslims should reorient themselves toward taking advantage of the opportunities offered by the globalization and information revolution in the third millennium. Hakimov discounts the significance of the Arab language and even claims that "Arabic language brings about a backward mentality, whereas Western European languages allow us to strive for greater achievements [this means in scientific, economic, and other fields]."[225] Khakimov maintains that the modern world has new requirements for people and society, a significant aspect of which is the importance of the individual. For Khakimov, "Righteousness is about becoming civilized and educated."[226] He discounts the significance of a global Muslim community or *ummah* and instead offers a new interpretation of this concept as a conglomerate of international rules and organizations that embody them. Khakimov believes that "the times of Caliphates are long gone," and that Russian Muslims should conform to the way of life in Russia, where the majority of the population is Orthodox Christian and Shari'a is not practiced.[227] He attributes the success of the Protestant missionaries' proselytizing activities in Russia, as compared to Muslim clerics or Orthodox priests, to their more contemporary interpretation of biblical texts. Khakimov concludes by stating that "Islam will inevitably become Europeanized," by which he implies that it will adapt to the requirements of the modern world and will rid itself of the vestiges of the past, which impede progress.[228] This change in Khakimov's views can be explained in light of the internal evolution of Russia in a culturally more Russocentric and politically more centralized direction. It also reflects the influence of regional and international changes triggered by the events of 11 September.

The ideas presented by Khakimov are intriguing. However, his views are infused more by a strong sense of Tatar cultural nationalism and superiority, as well as an unrealistic reading of the vast panorama of Islam in Tatarstan. The fact is that not all Tatar Muslims, including some intellectuals and political figures, do not adhere to the Jadidist way of thinking. Khakimov is a "cultural Muslim" who believes that for many Tatars, "Islam is more an element of culture than of cult [religion]."[229] This may be so, but for many others, Islam is both culture and faith. Some Muslims view Jadidist ideas and Euro-Islam as subversive of Islam's essence. Nevertheless, his new interpretation of the Jadidist school and the development of a theory of a European Islam can, under proper conditions, be a bridge between the Russian Federation's Russian and Muslim peoples and cultures. It can also help Russian Muslims to combine the requirements of modernity and a globalizing world with the desire to retain their culture and traditions. However, his later overemphasis of the European dimension of this new interpretation can alienate more devout Muslims and hence prove counterproductive.

Developing an Official Muslim Position: RCM's Muslim Social Program

The adoption of "The Fundamental Principles of the Social Program of Russia's Muslims" (MSP) by the Russian Council of Muftis (RCM) on 25 May 2001 was a watershed in the ongoing process of developing and explaining the views of a substantial portion of Russian Muslims on key social and political issues, including state, citizenship, and Muslim relations with the followers of other faiths. It is an important document because it elucidates Muslim views on vital issues related to modernity and lays the groundwork for defining the collective identity of Russia's Muslims. By delineating the rights and responsibilities of Russia's Muslims, it also acts as an effective instrument to counteract prevalent stereotypes of Muslims and misconceptions regarding Islam in popular Russian culture. Finally, by formulating a social and political platform for Russian Muslims, it serves as a starting point for constructive dialogue between the Muslim community and the Russian government at federal and local levels.[230] Perhaps more important, the MSP explains in an accessible form and language Islam's basic tenets and the main aspects of the Muslim understanding of contemporary issues to average Russian citizens. According to its authors, "The necessity of developing such a document derives from the fact that objective information on Islam was and still is inaccessible to the majority of Russian citizens."[231] The authors view the MSP as a reference document intended "for the people, who do not have sufficient information on Islam's true teachings."[232] However, the MSP is not representative of the attitudes and opinions of the entire Russian *ummah*. Rather, it represents the views of that part of Russia's Muslim population that recognizes the RCM's authority. The following four sections of the MSP are particularly worth noting.

Section 1, "Foundations of Religious Teaching of Islam"

Section 1 reiterates the basic tenets of Islam. It explains the main divisions within Islam (Sunnism and Shiism) and states that the majority of Russian Muslims are Sunni.[233] It points out that of the four schools of Sunni jurisprudence (*mazhabs*), Hanafi and Shafei are the most prevalent in Russia, while the Maliki and Hanbali schools are less popular. However, it emphasizes that despite their doctrinal and methodological differences, all four schools of Sunni jurisprudence are considered equally legitimate.[234] Although Sufism does not represent a separate branch equivalent to Sunnism or Shiism, it "does express the mystical-ascetic tendency of both of these mainstream branches" and is described as "an extremely multifaceted phenomenon, in which many spiritual and moral teachings are intertwined."[235]

Section 6, "The Attitude of Muslims toward the Representatives of Other Religions"

On behalf of the Russian *ummah*, the MSP resolutely denounces terror and extremism perpetrated in the name of Islam. The document states that "Russian Muslims object to the attempts of certain journalists and political figures to equate the actions of extremists with the teachings of Islam. This approach misrepresents Islam and divides people along religious lines."[236] Another passage notes that President Putin's assertion that criminals have neither nationality or religion "adequately corresponds with the Sunnah of Prophet Muhammad, who stated, 'He who commits a theft ceases to be a Muslim. He who commits a murder ceases to be a Muslim.' "[237] The MSP also refers to the "Declaration on Inadmissibility of the Use of Islamic Symbols for Nonreligious Purposes," which was adopted by the Russian Council of Muftis on 30 June 2000 and which denounces all forms of extremism and terrorism, including Wahhabism.[238]

Section 7, "The Muslims and the State"

Section 7 outlines the Muslim attitude toward such issues as the role of the social accord, secular authority, war and peace, and the notion of jihad. Social accord is defined as a "norm of social existence dictated from above" and is compared to the "covenant of humanity with Almighty Allah."[239] The concept of accord in social teachings of Islam (*Ahd* or *Moahedah*) corresponds to the notion of *dar as sulkh* or "the abode of agreement [peace]," which embodies the formula for concluding agreements with non-Muslim social groups and states with the purpose of maximum protection of rights and freedoms of Muslims.[240] Moreover, agreements and treaties concluded by the prophet Muhammad with polytheists, Jews, and Christians and with non-Muslim rulers of Ethiopia, Persia, and Byzantium are invoked as examples of the importance assigned to the principle and practice of the accord in Islam.[241] Hence "the state and its laws are viewed as a form of social contract, in which the most viable compromise is achieved and an equilibrium among interests of various social groups and religious organizations is established."[242] Furthermore, this section asserts that "the attitude of Muslims toward the state is based on the rational principles that defend freedoms, support justice, and instill law-abiding behavior."[243] According to this section, Muslims view the state and state laws "as the result of an agreement among all social groups on general norms of coexistence within a defined territory and within one legal and economic system."[244] Therefore, the state and state laws "are means of guaranteeing natural and basic rights and freedoms of all citizens."[245]

When state laws are designed to protect basic human rights and freedoms of all citizens, "it is not only a civil but also a religious duty for Muslims to follow the laws of their country, as they represent the highest accord among citizens."[246] The MSP unequivocally condemns the failure to comply with state laws by stating, "The failure to fulfill civil duties and calls for civil disobedience and rebellion on behalf of the believers and religious communities are inadmissible in Islam."[247] However, should disagreements with the laws arise, the document urges Muslims to resolve them "exclusively in the framework of the existing legislation" and to "avoid taking any actions that might violate social harmony and lead to bloodshed and unrest."[248]

The MSP extensively discusses the concept of jihad and its different categories, such as "jihad of a heart," which implies individual struggle with sinful inclinations, "jihad of a tongue," which calls for public statements endorsing good and prohibiting evil, and other examples.[249] However, the primary focus is on the "jihad of a sword," which is defined as a defensive warfare to protect religious freedom and to repel external aggression. The MSP makes it clear that "the interpretation of 'jihad' by certain extremist and pseudo-Islamist groups and segments of the Russian mass media as a 'war with religious purposes' is false and contradictory to the Qu'ran and the Sunnah of the Prophet. This is so because offensive warfare is inadmissible in Islam."[250] It further emphasizes that in Islam only the state has the right to declare and conduct warfare. This must be warranted by the threat of external aggression and the necessity of defending the freedom of religion. By recognizing the Constitution of the Russian Federation as a "supreme accord" regulating the life of the country, the Russian *ummah* recognizes the right of the highest institutions of state authority "to resolve the questions of war and peace" in accordance with the constitution and "for the benefit of all Russian citizens."[251]

Section 8, "The Muslims in the Russian State"

The MSP considers the contemporary legal system of the Russian Federation the most favorable for Muslims in the history of Russia because "for the first time it guarantees freedom of religion and the juridical equality of Islam with other religions."[252] The application of the Islamic concept of the "abode of agreement" (*dar-ul-Moahedah*) implies the fulfillment of mutual responsibilities of the state and the Muslim establishment toward one another. The state is obligated to guarantee religious freedom and equality of all religions under state laws; prohibit discrimination against citizens based on their religion; prevent religious conflicts; and invite representatives of religious organizations to participate in discussions related to legislative and other governmental initiatives that would affect the interests of the believers.[253] Muslim organizations, meanwhile, are required to recognize the legitimacy of the laws of the Russian Federation; exhibit loyalty to the legally elected state authorities; strengthen patriotic feelings among Muslims toward their motherland (i.e., Russia); promote spirituality, high moral standards, religious tolerance, and brotherly relations among various nationalities; resolve conflicts and disputes only by legal means and within the existing legal framework; and avoid interfering in governmental activities on both federal and local levels.[254]

One of the principal elements of this arrangement, in accordance with the Russian Law on Freedom of Conscience and Religious Associations, is that the state should honor internal regulations and charters of religious organizations as long as they do not contradict federal laws.[255] The MSP demands that the state symbols of the Russian Federation (such as the national anthem and government rewards) "adequately reflect the multinational and multireligious character of the country" in order to make Muslims feel that they are Russian citizens with equal rights. Otherwise, the document warns, "the national unity and patriotic feelings of citizens will be undermined by the state itself."[256]

The concluding part of this section focuses on the international connections between the Russian *ummah* and Muslim states and governmental and nongovernmental Islamic organizations. It stresses that ties with the Muslim world contribute to the "revival of Islamic religious education in Russia and the construction of mosques, creation of funds, widespread charitable activities, and spiritual and cultural growth of Russian Muslims."[257] The document categorically states that "the Russian Muslims do not cooperate with radical Islamic organizations with terrorist and extremist orientation."[258] In its final part, the MSP stresses the idea of forming a comprehensive social partnership between the Russian Council of Muftis and the federal government as a means of "defending national interests of Russia in relation to Islam both inside the country and from a geopolitical perspective."[259] The realization of this ambitious objective would ensure the Russian Council of Muftis a dominant role in guaranteeing "effective interaction between the secular state and the believers."[260]

Economic Profile of Russian Muslims

Compared to the rest of the population of the Russian Federation, Muslims are in an economically less advantageous position. This is the case not only in the traditionally poor, agricultural, and underdeveloped regions with high concentrations of Muslims, such as the North Caucasus, where the only major industry was prewar Chechnya's petroleum sector, but also partly in such Muslim republics as Bashkortostan and Tatarstan, which have more mineral resources and industries and in which overall wages approach the national average.

Several reasons of earlier and more recent origin account for this situation. Among the earlier causes are the particular characteristics of the Soviet economic system. In the Muslim regions, an important aspect of the Soviet Union's econome policy was that most managerial and technical positions were occupied by ethnic Russians and other Slavs, while a disproportionate percentage of Muslims were employed in agriculture or lower-end industrial jobs. This meant that their average income was lower than that of the rest of the population. The USSR's economic development policies were also geared toward meeting the overall needs of the country as determined in long-term plans developed by the central planning organization. Little attention was paid to the development of viable regional economies. Furthermore, in drawing the borders of various republics, no account was taken of existing regional economic linkages, nor was there any effort to make political divisions economically viable. This aspect of the Soviet-era policy, which is having a negative impact on the economic conditions and social stability of the North Caucasus today, is noted in an article by Sergei Polyakov and Valentin Bushkov of the Moscow-based Institute of Ethnology and Archeology titled "Socioeconomic Situation in the North Caucasus."[261]

In the Southern Federal District, which incorporates all republics of the North Caucasus plus the krais of Krasnodar and Stavropol and the oblasts of Astrakhan, Volgograd, and Rostov, Russians and other Slavic ethnic groups cultivate cash crops such as grains. This type of agriculture requires a high degree of capital investment. In the more solidly Muslim areas, agriculture consists of vegetables cultivated on small plots of lands, thus creating what Polyakov and Bushkov characterize as a "kitchen economy."[262] Fewer people are employed in public enterprises, agricultural or otherwise, and those who are not have no reliable source of income. Whatever manufacturing capacity exists is mostly concentrated in the largely Russian-inhabited parts of the region. This situation inevitably leads to large disparities in income along regional and ethnic lines. Thus by the end of 1998, the average monthly income of a Russian citizen was estimated at 900 rubles, whereas in the North Caucasus it varied from 300 rubles in Ingushetia to the maximum of 600 rubles in Krasnodar and Rostov Oblasts.[263] According to I.G. Kosikov and L.S. Kosikova, the authors of the 1999 socioeconomic guide to the North Caucasus, all territorial-administrative units that comprise what the authors termed the North Caucasus Economic Region (NCER), with the exception of relatively well off and predominantly Russian-populated Rostov Oblast, are characterized by poverty. The poverty rate in the North Caucasus is one and a half to two times higher than the average for Russia (Table 2.6), and the income level is barely half that of Russia.[264] The percentage of people living in poverty is particularly high in Ingushetia, followed by Dagestan and Karachaevo-Cherkessia. The authors contend that "the difficult economic situation, consequences of the Chechen War, and local conflicts have caused the North Caucasus region to become a zone of real social disaster."[265]

The comparative examination of the monthly salary averages of the Muslim-populated parts of the Russian Federation with the Russian national average reveals a wide disparity. Among the regions, too, there are obvious inequalities, with the more solidly Muslim territorial-administrative entities having a much lower salary average, as Table 2.7 (p. 100) illustrates.

Dagestan, the most solidly Muslim republic, has the lowest monthly salary average, whereas regions and republics with a high percentage of ethnic Russian inhabitants, such as Krasnodar Krai and Astrakhan and Volgograd Oblasts, have a higher average. Adygea, in which ethnic Russians comprise 68 percent of the population, also has a higher average income. Moreover, the regional salary average for the Southern Federal District (2,382.4 rubles) is significantly lower than those of the industrially developed and urbanized Northwestern Federal District (4,060.3 rubles), which includes St. Petersburg, or the Central Federal District (3,646.1 rubles), which includes Moscow.[266] Only the republics of Bashkortostan and Tatarstan have salary averages (3,134.2 rubles and 3,080.5 rubles, respectively) that are close to the national average (3,578 rubles) and are actually higher than the average for the Volga Federal District (2,768.3 rubles). This situation is explained by the fact that Tatarstan and Bashkortostan are located in the traditionally economically developed Volga-Ural region of Russia, where for decades Soviet economic planners pursued large-scale industrial development and which also are well endowed with mineral resources, including hydrocarbons.

In terms of employment, the Muslims are more represented in the unskilled labor category, including a variety of low-paying agricultural occupations. Russia's post-Soviet political and economic transformation has negatively affected the economic position of some of Russia's Muslim-inhabited regions. The most severely affected is the North Caucasus, largely because of the fallouts of the Chechen War. The rapid deterioration of the regional economy is manifested in dramatic job cuts in virtually all sectors of the economy. A regional meeting of Russian government officials devoted to the problems of unemployment that was held in Pyatigorsk on 16–17 November 1999 highlighted the fall in the level of employment between 1995 and 1999. For example, the number of those employed in the manufacturing sector decreased by 286,000, in construction by 168,000, and in agriculture by 210,000. These estimates are significantly higher than the comparable national figures.[267]

Table 2.8 (p. 101) presents the official estimates of the number of individuals who have undergone unemployment registration with the regional branches of the State Employment Service (Gosudarstvennaya Sluzhba Zanyatosti) of the Russian Federation, which is part of the Ministry of Labor and Social Development. How-

Table 2.6

Poverty Level in the North Caucasus (Defined as the Percentage of the Population with Income below the Minimum Income Level)

Year	1994	1995	1996	1997	1998
Republic of Adygea	46.3	46.4	56.7	42.0	45.7
Republic of Dagestan	—	71.2	64.7	53.8	57.5
Republic of Ingushetia	—	—	—	—	76.0
Republic of Kabardino-Balkaria	36.7	42.5	40.7	40.5	44.5
Republic of Karachaevo-Cherkessia	28.3	45.7	55.3	40.3	52.0
Republic of North Ossetia-Alania	33.1	42.8	38.5	34.2	33.8
Republic of Chechnya	—	—	—	—	—
Krasnodar Krai	23.7	32.4	25.1	25.0	32.0
Stavropol Krai	36.5	39.6	30.3	34.8	40.0
Rostov Oblast	31.0	33.4	21.2	19.8	33.0
Russian Federation	**22.4**	**24.7**	**22.1**	**20.8**	**21.0**

Source: Adapted from I.G. Kosikov and L.G. Kosikova, *Severny Kavkaz: Sotsial'no-Ekonomicheskii Spravochnik* (The Northern Caucasus: A socioeconomic guide) (Moscow: Mikron-Print, 1999), p. 36.

Note: The minimum income level (*prozhitochny minimum*) is calculated periodically on an annual, semiannual, and quarterly basis. It is supposed to represent the monetary value of the basket of goods and services that are necessary for the physical survival of an individual. The methodology of the calculation of the minimum income level is regulated by the Federal Law no. 134 of 24 October 1997, "On Minimum Income Level in Russian Federation."

ever, due to a variety of factors, including a pervasive lack of knowledge among the North Caucasians regarding the state employment services and unemployment registration procedures, these figures underestimate the level of unemployment. Despite the confusing methodology used to assess the number of unemployed who are officially registered, data in Table 2.8 show that Dagestan has the highest rate of unemployment in the Southern Federal District (i.e., the North Caucasus).

The understatement of unemployment figures becomes evident upon examination of statements by Russian government officials, regional political leaders, and experts. For instance, by the end of 1999, according to the weekly information bulletin issued by the Ministry of Labor and Social Development of the Russian Federation, in Ingushetia alone, more than 50 percent of the labor force (*trudo-sposobnoe naselenie*) was unemployed. Figures for Dagestan and North Ossetia were 30 percent and 26 percent, respectively.[268] The representative of Saratov Oblast in the Russian Federation Council, Ramazan Abdulatipov, stated at a conference titled "North Caucasus: Islam in Politics or Politics in Islam?" held in August 1999 that as much as 80 percent of Dagestan's population was unemployed.[269]

Russian officials have been aware of the gravity of the unemployment problem in the North Caucasus especially because of its prevalence among young people, who are potentially more susceptible to social unrest and, in the case of Muslims,

Table 2.7

Monthly Salary Averages for Selected Muslim-Populated Regions of the Russian Federation (as of November 2001)

		As a percentage of	
	Rubles	**November 2000**	**October 2001**
Russian Federation	3,578.2	143.3	101.8
Southern Federal District	2,382.4	142.4	100.9
Republic of Adygea	2,065.6	143.0	104.4
Republic of Dagestan	1,313.3	140.5	106.7
Republic of Ingushetia	2,431.3	150.5	97.3
Republic of Kabardino-Balkaria	1,718.3	134.5	101.7
Republic of Kalmykia	1,975.1	138.8	110
Republic of Karachaevo-Cherkessia	1,728.8	129.5	102.1
Republic of North Ossetia-Alania	1,938.0	137.5	104.5
Republic of Chechnya	N/A	N/A	N/A
Krasnodar Krai	2,806.3	145.4	100.3
Stavropol Krai	2,249.5	136.6	101.7
Astrakhan Oblast	2,723.5	125	94.6
Volgograd Oblast	2,636.9	141.1	101.1
Rostov Oblast	2,340.3	148.6	101
Volga Federal District	2,768.3	138.3	99.9
Republic of Bashkortostan	3,134.2	140.5	99.7
Republic of Tatarstan	3,080.5	134.8	98.3
Orenburg Oblast	2,559.4	124.2	99.5
Samara Oblast	3,385.1	139.8	100
Saratov Oblast	2,089.5	137.4	101.3

Source: Adapted from *Sotsial'no-Ekonomicheskoe Polozhenie Rossii 2001 god* (Socioeconomic situation in Russia in 2001) Moscow: State Committee of Russian Federation on Statistics [Goskomstat], (2001), pp. 396–97.

Islamic extremism. I.G. Kosikov and L.G. Kosikova state that almost 70 percent of people under the age of thirty are unemployed in the North Caucasus.[270] Moreover, they warn that if appropriate measures are not taken, unemployment "might become the source of heightened social tensions accompanied by crime increase, a worsening of interethnic relations, and strengthening of the influence of extremist groups."[271] In 1999, the Russian minister of labor and social development, Sergei Kalashnikov, stated, "The employment problem in the North Caucasus is more acute than elsewhere in the country. . . . Indeed, the unemployment rate is the highest here. In Dagestan, for instance, it has reached 30 percent."[272] Furthermore, according to Kalashnikov, "The problems of peace in the North Caucasus and the efficiency of socioeconomic policy in this region, as well as geopolitics, are in many respects tied to the unemployment problem."[273] This echoes the opinion of

Table 2.8

Unemployment Statistics for Muslim-Populated Parts of the Russian Federation (as of November 2001, in Thousands)

		Number of Citizens Unemployed	
	Number of Citizens Not Engaged in Productive Activities	Total	Unemployed Who Received Unemployment Payments
Russian Federation	1,291.5	1,065.3	945.5
Southern Federal District	158	141.9	121.1
Republic of Adygea	3.1	2.8	2.4
Republic of Dagestan	56.5	55.5	43
Republic of Ingushetia	10.5	7.9	7.4
Republic of Kabardino-Balkaria	8.6	8.1	6
Republic of Kalmykia	3.8	3.5	3.2
Republic of Karachaevo-Cherkessia	2.4	2.3	2.1
Republic of North Ossetia-Alania	6	3.2	2.7
Republic of Chechnya	N/A	N/A	N/A
Krasnodar Krai	16	14.6	13.3
Stavropol Krai	11.8	10.3	9.5
Astrakhan Oblast	9.3	8.4	7.9
Volgograd Oblast	12	10.6	9.6
Rostov Oblast	18	14.7	9.6
Volga Federal District	250	214	194.2
Republic of Bashkortostan	25.1	21.9	19.7
Republic of Marii-El	11.4	10.4	9.8
Republic of Mordovia	9.7	8.8	8.1
Republic of Tatarstan	21.3	17.5	16.1
Republic of Udmurtia	23.7	19.3	17.4
Republic of Chuvashia	14.1	13.3	12.2
Orenburg Oblast	6.6	5.5	4.9
Perm Oblast	18.3	14.6	13.4
Samara Oblast	24.9	21.9	19.6
Saratov Oblast	17.3	16.3	15
Ulyanovsk Oblast	13	11.8	10.7

Source: Sotsial'no-Ekonomicheskoe Polozhenie Rossii 2001 god (Socioeconomic situation in Russia in 2001) (Moscow: State Committee of Russian Federation on Statistics [Goskomstat], 2001), pp. 400–401.

Note: The information in this table is based on the data gathered by the Ministry of Labor and Social Development of the Russian Federation and indicates the number of those unemployed registered with the State Employment Service.

the deputy prime minister of the Russian Federation, Valentina Matvienko, who considers unemployment in the Caucasus a political problem.[274]

Anecdotal evidence indicates that most Muslim communities in other parts of Russia have employment and income levels below the national average, although reliable and readily available data on their size and socioeconomic conditions are lacking. Possible exceptions are Tatar communities in Moscow and other parts of Russia because a substantial number of Tatars are engaged in business activities. According to an article in the *Tatar Gazette*, the Tatars living in the Republic of Mordovia "are the most successful in business. There are among them some large and plenty of small businessmen."[275] However, because of the semicolonial status of Muslims in the Soviet Union and the ensuing low educational and economic conditions of Muslims, combined with the particular characteristics of Russia's post-Soviet transition to a capitalist economic system, there are very few Muslim businesspeople of any weight. Certainly there is no Muslim who could even approach the status of Russia's minor oligarchs, even though Muslims constitute anywhere between 10 and 14 percent of Russia's population.

The Muslim Establishment and the Russian Society and Government

The revival of Islam in post-Soviet Russia and the desire of Russia's Muslims to assert their cultural and political presence and become more involved in Russia's social, cultural, and political life have created new dynamics in their interactions with the Russian society and government, including the Orthodox Christian establishment. The Russian Muslims' efforts to gain more recognition and to become an integral and important part of the Russian society and polity have been hampered by a variety of factors. These include Muslims' inferior social and economic position and the continued political strife in parts of Russia's Muslim-inhabited regions, notably Chechnya, which has had extremely negative consequences for Islam and Muslims' image and position in Russia. Another important factor has been intra-Muslim divisions, including ones at the highest levels of the Muslim religious leadership.

An important consequence of the fragmentation and decentralization of official Muslim organizations, combined with the growing political, religious, and ideological diversity within Russia's Muslim population, has been the emergence of sharp differences and, at times, acute rivalries within the Muslim religious leadership at local and national levels. These rivalries have resulted from a variety of religious and secular differences. They also reflect the legacy of the tsarist and Soviet eras, during which the consolidation of an independent leadership was prevented. These rivalries have been damaging to the Muslim community and to the character of interaction between Moscow and the Muslim leadership and hence the Muslim community in general. In particular, they have provided the central government with the opportunity to exercise greater control over much of the Islamic establishment and perhaps to work toward its complete restructuring. This is illustrated by the comment made at the roundtable "The Islamic Factor in Russian Politics," held in Nizhny Novgorod on 24 June 2001, by Sergei Kirienko, the presidential representative to the Volga Federal District. Kirienko noted, "Changing realities of life necessitate changes in relations between the state and the traditional religious denominations. I am deeply convinced that we are now at the new stage of the formation of these interactions because the existing system of relations does not satisfy either side."[276]

The problem with this strategy is that it is likely to cause the further erosion of Muslims' confidence in official organizations, already undermined by intra-Muslim disunity and personality clashes within the Muslim religious leadership. These divisions have led to the emergence of "parallel" or "alternative" Muslim organizations. The most serious and potentially most damaging intra-Muslim rivalry is that between the spiritual administrations under the RCM, headed by Mufti Ravil Gainutdin, and the CSBM of Mufti Talgat Tadzhuddin. This intense competition for the leadership of Russia's Muslims is characterized by mutual accusations of adherence to Wahhabi orientation, which the Russian media have made synonymous with "religious fundamentalism" and "extremism," and competition for Moscow's attention.[277]

Gainutdin versus Tadzhuddin: Sources of Rivalry and Dispute

A variety of factors, ranging from ethnic differences—Gainutdin is Tatar, whereas Tadzhuddin is Bashkir—to doctrinal and political disagreements have contributed to the rivalry between the two principal leaders of Russian Muslims. This competition came into the open in September 1994 when Tadzhuddin attempted to remove Gainutdin as leader of the Moscow Cathedral Mosque as he was leading the prayer.[278] In response, on 23 September 1994, Gainutdin withdrew from the structure of the CSBM. Subsequently, during the Seventh Extraordinary Congress of Muslims of Russia and European Countries of the CIS, convened at the initiative of Tadzhuddin in Ufa on 17 January 1995, the delegates representing 2,500 Muslim communities revoked the religious title of Mufti Ravil Gainutdin and prohibited him from performing his duties as a Muslim religious leader under the pretext that he was "supporting divisive actions of Arab organizations" and "violating traditional canons of Russian Islam."[279]

Since then, accusations of Wahhabism against Gainutdin and deviation against Tadzhuddin have become a hallmark of their rivalry. Tadzhuddin, on a number of occasions, has accused Gainutdin and his organization of being secret sympathizers of Wahhabism (i.e., religious extremism). On one occasion, he called the All-Russian Islamic University established in Kazan with the support of the RCM the "source of Wahhabi cadres for entire Russia."[280] The Gainutdin-led RCM responded with the following statement:

> In the television program "Itogi" of 14 November 1999, one of the leaders of Muslims, Talgat Tadzhuddin, . . . accused practically all Muslims of Russia, and

nearly all spiritual administrations of the country, of being the "enemies of the people" and "Wahhabites." . . . We pray to the Almighty Allah that He would forgive the unfortunate man, but we resolutely oppose those forces that unleashed with his hands the Islamophobic campaign in the mass media.[281]

A particularly dramatic manifestation of this rivalry occurred at the fourth meeting of the Inter-Religious Council of Russia on 22 March 2000. Tadzhuddin, who was invited for the first time to the official proceedings of the Inter-Religious Council, openly opposed the participation of Gainutdin's Council of Muftis in the United Nations–organized International Summit of World Religious and Spiritual Leaders scheduled for August 2000 in New York.[282] Tadzhuddin's objections sparked an emotional exchange between the two men. Gainutdin left the meeting and addressed the council members in a memorandum explaining the reasons for his sudden departure.

The principal sources of dispute between the two leaders are doctrinal differences and diverging interpretations of Islam. Tadzhuddin's religious beliefs are rather eclectic and, according to more orthodox Muslims, even heretical. His unorthodox views and behavior have dismayed many Muslims and are a source of conflict between the two men. In the early 1990s, Tadzhuddin made statements and staged events that many Muslims viewed as heretical. Tadzhuddin has repeatedly stated that the pre-Islamic pagan belief of ancient Turkic peoples in the deity Tengre (the universal spirit) was the first true form of monotheism. In his comments, Tadzhuddin even claimed that by worshipping Tengre, the ancient ancestors of Tatars actually worshipped Allah long before the appearance of the prophet Ibrahim (Abraham).[283] He also tried to create a fourth holy site for Muslims in Russia, in the small Volga town of Bulgar in the Republic of Tatarstan. On a number of occasions, he participated in Muslim services wearing the mantle of an Orthodox Christian priest. In an interview with *Nezavisimaya Gazeta* during a religious conference in Ufa, Gainutdin claimed that Tadzhuddin appeared at the Ufa Cathedral Mosque dressed as an Orthodox Christian cleric and proposed the idea of unifying all religions. He then proceeded to place Orthodox Christian icons in the mosque until the members of the local congregation disrupted his actions.[284] On another occasion, he tried to place a star of David in a mosque in Tatarstan. Tadzhuddin's unorthodox beliefs and eccentric behavior contributed significantly to his alienation from the rest of the Muslim establishment. In an interview with *Nezavisimaya Gazeta*, Gainutdin alluded to this fact when he noted, "The irresponsible and immoral behavior of Talgat caused the schism between him and the rest of the Russian Muslim clergy."[285]

The two also have sharply different approaches to the question of Wahhabism in Russia. While Tadzhuddin has consistently opposed the spread of Wahhabism in Russia, Gainutdin's reactions have oscillated between mild objection to the Kremlin's anti-Wahhabi policies and rhetoric and reluctant approval. On 10 June 2001, when President Putin visited the newly built mosque Lya Lya Tyulpan in Ufa, Tadzhuddin expressed his views on the incursion of foreign Islamic missionaries into Russia. Supporting the Kremlin's official position on this subject, Tadzhuddin stated, "We do not want to have Wahhabis in our country and also those who come from foreign lands and want to educate us. . . . From ancient times Orthodox Christianity and Islam went hand in hand and for almost 300 years they were the foundation of our statehood."[286] During this visit, Tadzhuddin and President Putin held a private forty-five-minute meeting. The specifics of their discussions were not revealed, but they were characterized as "productive."[287] Tadzhuddin believes that the most serious challenges faced by Russia's Muslim establishment are the adverse impact of foreign-inspired doctrines and the necessity of revitalizing traditional Russian Islam. In an interview with *Nezavisimaya Gazeta,* he said, "The main problems of Russia's Muslims are to rebuild traditional Islam and to fight against religious extremism, terrorism, and one of its manifestations—Wahhabism."[288] Thus Tadzhuddin sees any increase in Wahhabi influence in Russia's Muslim community as not only undermining his personal influence, but also unraveling the religious unity of Russia's Muslim *ummah.* However, his statement could also mean that Tadzhuddin considers any independent thinking among Muslims as politically and culturally subversive and thus accuses all independent Muslims of Wahhabi deviation. On other important issues related to Islam and Muslims, Tadzhuddin has been supportive of the government's position. Regarding Chechnya, he has said that "the Chechen people should not be the hostage of the so-called Islamist gang formations, Wahhabites, or similar pseudoreligious figures, regardless of what they use to hide their criminal intentions. The actions of the authorities fully correspond to international and religious laws."[289]

By contrast, on these issues Gainutdin has on many occasions adopted a more independent posture. For example, his position has been rather cautious regarding the war in Chechnya and Wahhabism. Over time, however, he has to some degree adjusted his opinions to changing conditions. This becomes clear when his statements during the first and second Chechen wars are compared. Concerning the first Chechen War, in an interview with *Literaturnaya Gazeta,* Gainutdin stated, "The minority, Chechens, are confronting the majority and the Russian army as a whole: We should have known their national character, their patriotic attitudes, responding to the call of the Holy Qu'ran."[290] In his remarks regarding the second Chechen campaign, Gainutdin, adopting a less sympathetic stand toward the Chechen cause, stated, "Perhaps from a theological point of view Ahmad Kadyrov could have interpreted the invasion of Russian troops [in the first Chechen War] as an attempt to thwart the freedom of Chechen people. Then he had the right to do so. But now the situation is entirely different. The Chechen armed formations invaded the territory of Dagestan and drew fire upon themselves."[291]

On the problem of foreign Islamic proselytizing in Russia and, in particular, on the allegedly widespread Wahhabi indoctrination, Gainutdin's views have ranged from tacit approval to explicit condemnation. In the interview with the newspaper *Nezavisimaya Gazeta,* Gainutdin characterized Wahhabism in the following way: "If we interpret Wahhabism as the media and politicians interpret it daily, then, of course, I would view it negatively. The sad truth is that Wahhabism is understood only as the ideology of extremism and terrorism. However, Wahhabism is the official ideology of the Kingdom of Saudi Arabia, where there is no terrorism or extremism that would be rooted in Wahhabism."[292] This view is not unconventional and corresponds to that expressed by many Western commentators—at least until the 11 September 2001 terrorist attacks in the United States—who criticized the characterization of Chechen and other Muslim activists by the Russian authorities and media as Wahhabist. Geraldine Fagan and Lawrence Uzzell of the Keston Institute note, "The very term 'Wahhabism' has become a tool for discrediting anyone of Muslim background who is out of favor with the government for any reasons, regardless of his actual doctrinal views or actual connections with terrorist activities. It is likely that non-mainstream followers of Islam in Russia will continue to be special targets for restrictions on their religious freedom."[293]

Gainutdin has also had a less alarmist view of the dangers of the spread of Wahhabism in Russia. In November 2000, he stated, "I think all talks about some sort of targeted religious expansion against Russia by Muslim states are entirely unfounded."[294] He further cautioned against the adoption of any laws that would limit religious activities of Muslim organizations, thus admonishing, "The adoption of any legislation that would prohibit Wahhabism would be undoubtedly discriminatory to the rights and constitutional freedoms of Muslims of Russia."[295] Gainutdin maintains that the most effective means of offsetting religious extremism is to facilitate moderate religious education in order to stress the importance of religious tolerance and interfaith dialogue. It seems that most of Gainutdin's concerns stem from his fear that the application of laws forbidding Wahhabism would be biased and therefore would be directed against any Muslim organization that maintains connections with other Muslim countries or is somewhat independent from the government. Gainutdin is also skeptical of the criteria the authorities would use to judge whether a given religious organization is Wahhabi or not. Yet he welcomed the decision of the head of the provisional administration of Chechnya, Ahmad Kadyrov, to prohibit Wahhabism on the territory of the republic and stated, "By prohibiting Wahhabism in Chechnya, Ahmad Kadyrov made the right decision."[296] During a press conference on 6 March 2001, he attempted to deflect criticism of his ambivalent stand on Wahhabism by noting that "the Muslims of Russia have always adhered to moderate interpretations of Islam."[297] This evidence indicates that Gainutdin is a more orthodox and independent-minded personality who is also very sensitive to the shifts in the agenda of Russian political elites. Thus by adjusting his positions, he tries to maintain a strong presence and influence in any future discussions and decisions affecting Russia's Muslim communities.

Implications of the Tadzhuddin/Gainutdin Rivalry for the Muslim Community

The rivalry between the leaders of the CSBM and the RCM and hence their organizations has broad and mostly negative ramifications for Muslim life and organizations at various levels. The dispute transcends the administrative boundaries and results in struggles among Muslim congregations that are under the religious jurisdiction of competing centralized spiritual administrations. This pernicious process engulfs entire cities, towns, settlements, and villages. For instance, the Spiritual Board of Muslims of Omsk Oblast (Omskiy Muftiyat) under the leadership of Mufti Zulkarnai Shakirziyanov is aligned with the CSBM and is bitterly opposed to the Spiritual Board of Muslims of the Asian Part of Russia, headed by Nafigulla Ashirov and associated with the RCM. Similar disagreements and conflicts exist elsewhere, notably in the oblasts of Penza and Tyumensk, the autonomous okrugs of Yamalo-Nenets and Khanty-Mansi, Krasnoyarsk Krai, and the Altai Republic.[298] Disputes over religious affiliations of the mosques of Bulgar and Perm illustrate this negative trend.

An intense struggle for control over the mosque of the town of Bulgar in Tatarstan has been raging since 1997 between the Spiritual Board of Muslims of the Republic of Tatarstan, headed by Mufti Gusman Iskhakov, and the self-proclaimed mufti of Tatarstan, Farid Salman; Salman represents the interests of Mufti Talgat Tadzhuddin in Tatarstan. At the Unifying Congress of Muslims of the Republic of Tatarstan held in February 1998, he was one of the six candidates for the position of chairman of the autonomous Spiritual Board of Muslims (SBM) of the Republic of Tatarstan. After losing his bid to become the mufti of Tatarstan, Salman worked in the newly formed SBM of Tatarstan as the chairman of the Commission on Compliance of Literature with the Shari'a. However, after accusing the SBM of misappropriating funds and adhering to Wahhabism, he left and declared himself the mufti of Tatarstan under the religious supervision of Tadzhuddin. With a small group of supporters, Salman occupied the mosque in the city of Bulgar. Repeated attempts to gain access to the mosque by a commission appointed by Tatarstan's SBM to investigate the dispute failed.[299] Finally, in February 2002, the Tatar SBM, with the support of local authorities, regained control of the mosque.[300]

A similar controversy surrounds the religious affiliation of the Perm city mosque. At the core of the controversy is the conflict between members of the congregation and the Regional Spiritual Board of Muslims of Perm Oblast, represented by its chairman, Mufti Magomedgali Khuzin.[301] Debate over control of the mosque revolves around the following issues:

1. Ethnic diversity and tensions within the congregation, which consists mainly of newly arrived Azerbaijanis, Uzbeks, and Dagestanis, and the longer-established local community, consisting primarily of Tatars and Bashkirs.[302] In fact, the mosque is located close to the city market, which is dominated by immigrants from the Caucasus and Central Asia. The influx of these immigrants has changed the ethnic composition of the congregation of the Perm city mosque, while there has been no corresponding change in the community's leadership. The result has been a rift between the new members and the mosque's official clerical administration, leading to its expulsion.

2. The newly arrived members represent parts of Russia and the former Soviet Union where Islamic religious practices are of a more orthodox nature. These new members consider the spiritual and religious leadership of the mosque's clerical

administration as inadequate. This has been partly due to the affiliation of the Regional Spiritual Board of Perm Oblast (Perm Muftiyat) with the CSBM of Mufti Talgat Tadzhuddin. Therefore, the more active members of the congregation, represented by Khamit-khaji Guliyauddinov, decided to join Mufti Ravil Gainutdin's DUMER, which they considered to be more in line with orthodox Islamic practices.[303] This initiative drew the strong criticism of Khuzin, who realized that he might lose the mosque's leadership to a rival spiritual administration. In order to discredit the members of the congregation, who were advocating accession to DUMER, Khuzin launched a campaign in the local media in which he accused the congregation of having Wahhabi sympathies. Thus in the summer of 1998, Khuzin made an unsubstantiated public statement in which he warned the authorities that Perm might become a center for the dissemination of Wahhabism.[304] Moreover, in an interview on 16 August 2001, he stated, "We [the CSBM of Talgat Tadzhuddin] cannot recognize the DUMER and its leader Ravil Gainutdin as a legitimate religious and juridical structure."[305]

3.   The intentionally ambiguous position of municipal authorities, who are ultimately responsible for resolving such disputes, hinders resolution of the conflict. Procedural and legal issues are partly responsible for their ambiguous position, but other reasons are also at work. For example, in order to join DUMER, the congregation of the mosque must reregister with local authorities, yet the congregation of Perm city mosque has had difficulties in accomplishing this simple task for almost two years.[306] The local administration's behavior thus could be attributed either to its desire to remain impartial in intra-Muslim disputes or to an interest in keeping the Muslim community divided and, therefore, weak. The dispute culminated in the seizure of the mosque by thirty supporters of Khuzin on 8 March 2001 and the declaration that in accordance with the decision of Supreme Mufti Talgat Tadzhuddin dated 27 February 2001, the Perm city mosque would be returned to the religious jurisdiction of the Perm Muftiyat of Khuzin.[307] Under pressure from outraged members of the mosque's congregation, local authorities convinced Khuzin to order his supporters to open the doors of the mosque.

Competing for Moscow's Affection

Another manifestation of this rivalry has been a keen competition between the two leaders of Russia's official Muslim establishment for the attention and favor of federal authorities. Thus they periodically issue public statements endorsing government policies. To illustrate, on 16 March 2000, Supreme Mufti Talgat Tadzhuddin supported the counterterrorist campaign in Chechnya and said that "the war in Chechnya is not against Islam, but for the restoration of law and order."[308] In his speech commemorating the end of the holy month of Ramadan at the Moscow Cathedral Mosque in January 2001, Mufti Ravil Gainutdin echoed this sentiment; commenting on President Putin's speech on the same occasion, he said, "By speaking in defense of our religion from groundless accusations, he [Putin] stressed that Russia does not fight with Islam, nor does she wage war against peoples practicing

Islam."[309] In short, it seems that both Muslim leaders strive to demonstrate their loyalty to the regime.

For most of the 1990s, under President Boris Yeltsin's generally liberal policy in religious and political spheres, Tadzhuddin's eccentric behavior tended to undermine his influence and led to his relative isolation. However, this situation might also have been due to the fact that Tadzhuddin had supported the failed coup against Mikhail Gorbachev of August 1991, which alienated the first wave of Russian reformers and democrats who assumed power. Consequently, according to some Bashkir experts, for most of the 1990s, Tadzhuddin's Ufa-based CSBM was not "represented in the Muslim clergy's dialogue with Zyuganov, Primakov, and other political figures of Russia, or with representatives of Muslim countries."[310]

Meanwhile, Gainutdin devoted much time and effort to cultivating contacts within both executive and legislative branches of the Russian government. According to Farid Asadullin, "Ravil Gainutdin established regular consultations and meetings with the members of the cabinet of ministers of the Russian Federation as well as with influential political figures of all-Russia scale, such as President Vladimir Putin, Ramazan Abdulatipov, Gennady Zyuganov, Valerii Kokov, Yuri Luzhkov, Mintimer Shaimiev, Boris Gromov, and others."[311] As a result, the spiritual structures controlled by Gainutdin enjoyed the support of officials from the presidential administration and the Moscow mayor's office. The distribution of federal funds to Muslim religious organizations is a good indicator of the quality of the relationship between the government and various spiritual administrations. In 1995, the Supreme Coordinating Council of Spiritual Boards of Muslims of Russia received 1.2 million rubles in government subsidies, Gainutdin's Spiritual Board of Muslims of the Central European Region of Russia (the official predecessor of the Spiritual Board of Muslims of the European Part of Russia) received 3.5 million rubles, and the CSBM of Tadzhuddin received 2.2 million rubles.[312] Until the late 1990s, according to Aleksei Maximov, the presidential administration under Putin supported Gainutdin and his organization because they galvanized Muslim constituencies in favor of Vladimir Putin in the presidential elections of March 2000.

Gainutdin, for his part, has stressed his loyalty to President Putin whenever he has had a chance to do so. In "The Fundamental Principles of the Social Program of Russian Muslims," discussed earlier, he compared Putin's statements to the *hadiths* or the sayings of the prophet Muhammad.[313]

Since 2000–2001, however, the Russian government has attempted to bridge the gap between rival groups of Muslim clerics. The first step in this direction was taken by the participants in the aforementioned roundtable discussion "The Islamic Factor in Russian Politics" on the occasion of the inauguration of the Tauba (the repentance) Mosque in Nizhny Novgorod.[314] The participants did not come to a comprehensive agreement on all issues of concern. Nevertheless, they signed a joint resolution that outlined their common aspirations. In particular, the declaration expressed the signatories' willingness to work together on unifying standards in all Muslim educational institutions of the Volga Federal District, irrespective of their official religious affiliations (meaning subordination to different spiritual boards).

The participants also unanimously pledged "to oppose the spiritual and moral decay of society, not to allow interethnic and interconfessional animosity, to counter religious deviation and sectarianism that are potentially dangerous for the society, and to implement multilateral programs aimed at lowering the level of crime, alcoholism, and drug addiction."[315] The fact that Talgat Tadzhuddin and Nafigulla Ashirov, who represented the interests of the RCM and its leader Ravil Gainutdin, sat at the same table was in itself remarkable. In a sign of reconciliation, Ashirov noted:

> Canonical [doctrinal] disagreements with Mufti Talgat should not affect our collaboration on resolving the issues that are vital for both of us. On the contrary, we need to intensify cooperation in such areas as harmonization of religious educational standards, achievement of interethnic harmony in Russia, and stabilization of relations with government structures.[316]

The Nizhny Novgorod meeting potentially could be a promising development and, under favorable conditions, could promote the normalization and stabilization of Muslim spiritual life in Russia. Yet despite Ashirov's participation in the conference, Moscow still plays the two leaders against one another, depending on the circumstances. For example, in 2000, Moscow began shifting its favors from Gainutdin to Tadzhuddin. Several reasons accounted for this weakening of the relationship between Gainutdin and the Russian government. First, the relative deterioration in relations between the federal government and the Republic of Tatarstan, where Gainutdin has many supporters, gave rise to disagreements between Gainutdin and the Kremlin, especially concerning the cultural and religious rights of Tatar Muslims. These disagreements are partly related to Moscow's recentralization strategy and partly due to the Tatar leadership's decision to change the alphabet in the republic from Cyrillic to Latin, thereby raising Russian fears of Turkification in Tatarstan.[317] Second, as ties between the Russian Council of Muftis and the government have deepened and broadened, Gainutdin has displayed more assertiveness and independence. On a number of controversial subjects, including the war in Chechnya and the Wahhabi presence in Russia, Gainutdin's opinions, although not always consistent, have frequently demonstrated ambivalence toward, and occasionally divergence from, the official position. This show of independence has led to a certain degree of disillusionment among government officials who previously favored Moscow's mufti. Third, to some degree, the Orthodox Church has promoted Tadzhuddin. The suggestion to invite Tadzhuddin to participate at the meeting of the Inter-Religious Council of Russia came from the representatives of the Russian Orthodox Church, which has the leading role in the council. This position on the part of the church is not surprising in view of Tadzhuddin's more relaxed and less orthodox beliefs, which appear less challenging to the church.

According to Andrei Kovalev and Sergei Mikhailov, the Kremlin's recent support of Tadzhuddin reflects the view in certain circles of the Russian government that it is more expedient to have strong relations with Tadzhuddin and his center in Ufa rather than with Gainutdin and his headquarters in Moscow.[318] Another indication of support for Tadzhuddin was his participation at the founding conference of the All-Russian Political and Social Movement "Eurasia," organized on 21 April 2001. In fact, Tadzhuddin was voted into the newly formed movement's governing body, the Central Council.[319] This move signified Tadzhuddin's alliance with the leader of the "Eurasia" movement, Alexander Dugin, who is on friendly terms with many influential people in the Russian government, such as the former chairman of the State Duma of the Russian Federation, Gennady Seleznev. Vitalii Khliupin maintains that this change in the government's attitude is also related to the Kremlin's decision to employ various Islamic authorities to popularize pro-Moscow policies, especially in those parts of Russia that are increasingly dissatisfied with Putin's centralization drive.[320] Under these circumstances, Gainutdin's more independent streak and his relations with foreign Muslim organizations make him a less attractive partner for the Russian government, which is bent on exerting more control over the Muslim religious establishment. However, subsequent events, notably changes triggered by post–11 September developments, have caused the Kremlin to reassess its position toward the two leaders yet again.

Post–11 September Developments in Russia's Muslim Clerical Establishment: Impact on Intraclerical Rivalry

The terrorist attacks in the United States on 11 September 2001 had a significant, albeit not decisive, impact on the balance of influence within Russia's Muslim community, specifically regarding rivalry between the CSBM and the RCM. It appears that for several reasons, the Russian government has again shifted to a position of developing closer relations with Mufti Ravil Gainutdin's RCM at the expense of Mufti Talgat Tadzhuddin's CSBM.

First, both rival groups of clerics in early 2001 aligned themselves with the emerging political structures. Tadzhuddin's CSBM is supporting the All-Russian Political and Social Movement "Eurasia" headed by Alexander Dugin, while RCM leaders Gainutdin and Nafigulla Ashirov have established good relations with the Eurasian Party of Russia. This party was created by the prominent Islamic activist and member of the Russian State Duma Abdul Vahid Niazov following the dissolution of the Islamic movement Refakh. The events of 11 September radically reoriented the course of Russia's political leadership toward building a new strategic partnership with the United States in the context of the global war on terrorism. This reorientation had profound consequences for Russia's domestic political scene and affected the alignments between rival Muslim clerical groups and political entities. According to Aleksei Krymin and Georgi Engelgardt of the Laboratory of Crisis Monitoring, "The movement 'Eurasia' failed to adjust to the new reality because it could not perceive the necessity of revising the rigid anti-American paradigm, which permeated its political platform and rhetoric. By contrast, A.V. Niazov's Eurasian Party of Russia (EPR) effectively capitalized on the changes in the political situation."[321] Therefore, Gainutdin's choice proved to be more effective and brought him political dividends, whereas Tadzhuddin's alliance with Dugin proved a miscalculation.

Second, as Krymin and Engelgardt point out, the appointment of Vladimir Zorin to the position of Russia's minister-coordinator for nationality and confessional affairs on 6 December 2001 further weakened the position of the CSBM, partly because prior to his promotion, Zorin worked as a deputy to the presidential representative for the Volga Federal District, Sergei Kirienko. In this capacity, Zorin advised Kirienko on regional interethnic and interreligious issues, a task that brought him into close contact with Muftis Ravil Gainutdin, Gusman Iskhakov, and Mukaddas Bibarsov. Furthermore, Zorin has expressed skepticism about Tadzhuddin's allegations that his opponents have Wahhabi sympathies. Regarding this issue, Zorin stated that "the harsh criticism . . . creates tension not only among the Muslims, but in the entire society. . . . an average citizen is puzzled."[322]

An important indication of the shift in the government's favor toward the RCM was a meeting between Gainutdin and President Putin on 25 January 2002.[323] At this meeting, Gainutdin presented a report on the conditions of the Muslim community. Putin then asked Gainutdin to provide him directly with regular reports on issues of importance to Russia's Muslims. This act demonstrated the positive rapport between Putin and Gainutdin and signified that the executive branch trusted the RCM, not the CSBM, as the principal source of information on developments in the Muslim community.

According to Maksim Shevchenko, federal authorities are working toward the creation of a High Islamic Council. The council's membership will include Muftis Ravil Gainutdin (RCM), Talgat Tadzhuddin (CSBM), Mukaddas Bibarsov (SBM of Volga Federal District), and Umar Idrisov (SBM of Nizhny Novgorod).[324] The primary purpose of this institution will be to work with and advise the Russian government on policies affecting the Muslim community. The exclusion of Mufti Nafigulla Ashirov from the tentative list of the council's members indicates that in the post–11 September atmosphere, Ashirov's past statements in support of the Taliban movement have made him unwelcome to the Russian authorities. Shevchenko notes that the success or failure of this initiative would be largely determined by the evolution of Russia's political situation and by the state of rivalries within the Muslim clerical establishment. Regarding the latter point, post–11 September events indicate that existing divisions within the Muslim establishment will not be easily resolved. They also indicate that Moscow may prefer the current situation, which is allowing it to manipulate Muslim leaders in order to advance the federal government's agenda. An event illustrative of this policy was the failed conference on "Islam against Terrorism."

The "Islam against Terrorism" Conference: Muslim Disunity and Moscow's Shifting Position

The idea of organizing the conference "Islam against Terrorism" was agreed upon at the meeting of Muslim religious leaders with President Putin on 24 September

2001.[325] The main objective of the conference was the issuance of a collective religious decree (*fatwa*) by Russia's main Muslim religious figures strongly denouncing all attempts to justify extremism and terrorism by reference to the Qu'ran or the Sunnah. The organization of the conference took a long time, and it was finally scheduled for 29 May 2002. However, on the eve of the conference, in an interview with *Gazeta*, Mufti Talgat Tadzhuddin attacked the RCM for its alleged support of nontraditional Muslim movements in Russia, including Wahhabi-oriented groups, and accused it of creating "parallel Islamic structures."[326] Tadzhuddin's remarks followed the established pattern of accusations against the rival RCM, but their timing caused suspicions that Tadzhuddin wanted to sabotage the conference. The following day, the RCM issued a press release announcing that given the negative media campaign unleashed against the RCM on the eve of the conference, it had decided not to participate in the conference. Instead, it issued its own *fatwa* stressing the inadmissibility of justifying terrorism and extremism according to the Qu'ran and the Sunnah.[327] The RCM's refusal also led to the abstention of the head of Tatarstan's SBM, Mufti Gusman Iskhakov.[328] There are conflicting accounts regarding the participation of the Coordinating Center of Spiritual Boards of Muslims of North Caucasus (CCSBMNC) in the conference.[329] It appears that only the head of the SBM of Chechnya, Mufti Ahmad Shamaev, and the plenipotentiary representative of the CCSBMNC in Moscow, Harun Batsarov, took part in the conference.[330] The absence of a significant number of influential muftis rendered the conference largely meaningless and turned it into a "one-man show" for Tadzhuddin. Flanked by twenty other muftis, he denounced the activities of Wahhabi-oriented groups in Russia and demanded that the government take firm actions against radical Islamic groups.[331] The conference issued a collective *fatwa* "On Inadmissibility of Justification of Extremism and Terrorism by Norms of Holy Qu'ran and the Sunnah of the Prophet," but its effect was diminished because of the absence of a substantial number of important muftis.

The conference's failure reaffirmed the divided nature of Russia's Muslim community and leadership and indicated that the idea of unifying major Muslim religious organizations into a single entity such as a High Islamic Council would not be easily realized.[332] According to Maksim Shevchenko, this failure was partly due to the fact that influential elements within Russia's political leadership that are competing for power have different preferences regarding this issue.[333] The conference's failure also reflects the ongoing rivalry between the two main Muslim clerical groups, the RCM and the CSBM, for the allegiance of the CCSBMNC, which, in the opinion of some observers, might become a decisive factor in determining the eventual balance of power within Russia's Muslim religious establishment.[334] Most important, it suggests the Kremlin's involvement in instigating intraclerical feuds and the possible reemergence of Tadzhuddin as Moscow's favorite. These developments support earlier observations regarding the cyclical nature of Moscow's favoritism vis-à-vis key figures of the Muslim clerical establishment, which is partly the result of differences of opinions in the Russian leadership.[335] In light of the foregoing, it is most likely that relations between the government and the Muslim clerical establishment will continue to evolve, and the periodic shifts in the government's favor from one organization to the other will be an integral part of this process. In fact, events prior to and after the Iraq War proved this diagnosis correct.

The Iraq War: Source of Further Intra-Muslim Dispute

The war launched against Iraq by the United States and Britain together with their allies on 19 March 2003 caused perhaps the deepest ever split within the Muslim clerical establishment, renewed hostile verbal exchanges between Muftis Gainutdin and Tadzhuddin, and may have irremediably damaged the reputation and position of Mufti Tadzhuddin.

Opposition to the War and Tadzhuddin's Declaration of Jihad Against America

Russia's religious establishment—Christian and Muslim alike—was against the war with Iraq as was the Russian government and the majority of the Russian people. Thus, the Russian religious establishment lent its support to the efforts of the Russian government and those of many other countries, which tried to resolve the Iraqi crisis without resort to war. As part of these efforts, a delegation headed by Mufti Talgat Tadzhuddin and including representatives of the Orthodox Church visited Baghdad on 17 March.[336]

President Putin, in particular, received praise from Russia's Muslim leaders for his efforts to prevent the war and, once it began, to end it rapidly. Thus an official statement signed by Mufti Ravil Gainutdin and issued by the Russian Council of Muftis on 20 March 2003 expressed support for "the well considered policy of Vladimir Putin, the President of Russia, who has called the military action against Iraq a 'big political mistake' and declared that Russia 'insists on the earliest cessation of the military actions' and a solution of the problem on the basis of the UNSC resolutions."[337]

Criticism of the war was widespread within Russia's Muslim communities and a majority of them felt that it would be harmful to Muslim interests worldwide. Some Muslim political leaders, notably Geidar Jemal, went even so far as criticizing Russia's position on the Iraq war as being too weak.[338] Part of the clerical leadership called for the boycott of American goods by Muslims. However, others such as Gusman Iskhakov, head of the Tatarstan's SBM, considered such acts as ineffective.[339]

Tadzhuddin Declares Jihad

The first reference to the possibility of declaring a jihad against America appeared in *Izvestia* on 25 March 2003. According to an article published in *Izvestia*, Mahmud Velitov the Mufti of Moscow and Moscow Oblast told the newspaper that he intended to call on the Russian Muslims to participate in jihad against the United States and was going to coordinate his efforts with the heads of the Muslim establishments of CIS countries at the extraordinary meeting of the Muftis of the CIS countries on 26 March.[340]

These calls, however, did not go very far and did not attract much attention. What caused a significant stir as well as surprise was the declaration of jihad by Talgat Tadzhuddin, the head of Central Spiritual Board of Muslims of Russia, on 3 April 2003. He mainly justified his call to jihad on the grounds that the war in Iraq would ultimately pose a security threat to Russia because the United States and Britain were pursuing long-term strategic goals in the region. He stated, "They [the United States and Britain] want to enter Iran, Azerbaijan and Armenia from Iraq, come to their ally Shevardnadze, and approach Russia's borders."[341] Considering the fact that Tadzhuddin has consistently supported the official position of various Russian governments and is the preferred Muslim leader of Russia's Orthodox establishment, his call to jihad is out of character and surprising. Consequently, it raises the suspicion that Tadzhuddin might have been put up to doing so by some elements within Russia's political and religious establishments who would like to portray Islam as a dangerous phenomenon and Muslims as backward. The fact that the Russian Ministry of Justice initially showed a relaxed attitude to Tadzhuddin's declaration of jihad, stating, "If it is a matter of moral and material support for people of the same belief, there is nothing reprehensible about it," gives some credence to this theory.[342] Furthermore, the Moscow Patriarchate characterized Tadzhuddin's call as an emotional outburst and added that it was unlikely that he truly meant to incite any illegal or extremist actions.

Moscow Times in an article on 15 May seemed to endorse the view that Tadzhuddin was manipulated to serve Putin's political needs. According to the *Moscow Times*, the jihad story coincided with a shift in Russia's policy toward a more cooperative approach toward the United States and it enabled Putin "to make sure that the United States understands the difficulties he faces as the head of a country with a huge Muslim population, and that it appreciates the firmness of his response."[343] Others have speculated that by declaring jihad Tadzhuddin hoped to rectify his image as a person closely connected to the Russian government and, according to some rumors, to the intelligence services and thus gain greater credibility and popularity among Muslims.[344] Whatever Tadzhuddin's reasons, shortly after his declaration, and despite the initial mild reaction of the authorities, the prosecutor of Bashkortostan sent an official warning to Tadzhuddin and his organization according to the Law "On Countering Extremist Activity." Meanwhile, the spokesman for the office of the Russian Prosecutor General Leonid Troshin said that the warning by the Bashkortostan Prosecutor was issued after a probe carried out under Prosecutor General Vladimir Ustinov's instructions. On 4 April the Prosecutor General's office declared that Tadzhuddin's organization may be liquidated. As of the winter of 2003, Tadzhuddin's organization had not been dismantled.[345]

These warnings were followed by a barrage of criticism directed at Tadzhuddin by Muslim religious and political leaders who thought that his action was harmful to Muslim's interests in Russia.

Gainutdin Asserts His Position

The imprudent behavior of Tadzhuddin provided a golden opportunity for Ravil Gainutdin to consolidate his image as the most dignified, reasonable and hence dependable Muslim leader and a better interlocutor for the Kremlin. As a first step, the Russian Council of Muftis in a statement declared that it regretted that there were elements within the Muslim community who do not seek peace in Iraq but rather want a Third World War. It then went on to express support for Putin's policy in dealing with the Iraq War.[346] Then on 14 April, at a meeting in which muftis from various regions of Russia, including the Asian part of Russia, the North Caucasus, Tatarstan, Bashkortostan, and Karelia among others participated, Tadzhuddin's call to jihad was severely criticized. The participants justified their criticism on the grounds that it damaged the authority of Muslim organizations and harmed Russia's foreign policy objectives. They also stated that Tadzhuddin could not remain as the spiritual leader of Russian Muslims and effectively dismissed him from his position in absentia. However, the RCM has no legal authority to remove Tadzhuddin from his position. Indeed, as Mikhail Tulskiy pointed out, this was the fifth time Tadzhuddin had been dismissed from his position.[347]

Since then mutual recrimination between Tadzhuddin and Gainutdin has continued with negative consequences for Russia's Muslim community, especially in terms of their public image. Meanwhile, Gainutdin has emerged as the more favored Muslim leader of at least the Russian Presidential apparatus.[348] However, it is not clear how long this situation will last. Most likely the Kremlin will revert to its policy of playing Muslim leaders against each other. If it is proven that Tadzhuddin has outlived his usefulness, another leader may be groomed to replace him in order to act as a counterweight to Gainutdin.

Islam and Orthodoxy: Dynamics of Competition and Cooperation

The process of Islam's revival in Russia, especially the Muslims' quest for greater cultural self-determination and their effort to gain official recognition of Islam's status as the country's second religion, have introduced new dynamics into Muslims' relations with the Russian Orthodox Church. In many areas, including Islam's greater physical visibility, the nature of relations between Islam and Orthodoxy has been complex, involving elements of competition and cooperation. Several reasons account for this situation; the most significant is the fact that in post-Soviet Russia, the Orthodox Church has acquired an important social and political position and a good deal of influence in decision-making circles. According to its 1993 constitution, the Russian Federation is a secular state and does not have an official religion. Nevertheless, the 1997 Law "On Freedom of Conscience and Religious Associations" in its preamble recognizes "the special contribution of Orthodoxy to the history of Russia and to the establishment and development of Russia's spirituality and culture."[349]

Post-Soviet leaders from Boris Yeltsin to Vladimir Putin have emphasized the special place of the Orthodox Church within Russia by attending church services and including the leader of the Orthodox Church in official ceremonies.[350] Orthodoxy has become an important intellectual force affecting the debate about Russia's national identity and its fundamental underpinnings. The church has also experienced a substantial physical expansion with the renovation and reopening of old churches and the establishment of new ones.

To a large extent, this situation is natural and the consequence of two factors: (1) the adherence of at least 50 percent of Russia's population to the Orthodox creed and (2) the historic symbiosis between Russian nationhood and statehood and the Orthodox faith. Indeed, the Russian Orthodox Church is portrayed as a force unifying all ethnic Russians, who, regardless of their individual religious beliefs, are assumed to form their national identity from their association with the Orthodox creed. Thus, as Inna Naletova points out, "The Russian Church regards itself as an ethnic church."[351] This organic linkage between the concept of Russian national identity and Orthodoxy is further evidenced in the public comments of one of the most active representatives of the Russian Orthodox Church, the chairman of the Department for External Relations of the Moscow Patriarchate, Metropolitan Kirill of Smolensk and Kaliningrad. In an interview with the Russian newspaper *Vremya Novostei,* he stated that "one simply must know Russia's history. The church always has been present in the center of the life of the nation. This is the church's historic place."[352] The following statement by Father Aleksander, the priest of the Holy Trinity Church in Moscow, further illustrates the growing national role of the church, especially in the political sphere. After a visit of then Acting President Putin to the church on 7 January 2000, Father Aleksander said, "We welcome it when politicians come to pray, whatever the reason." He added, "It shows that we have reached a new threshold of acceptance, when it is no surprise that a President goes to Church."[353] In its official statements, the church denies the existence of any kind of "special relationship" between the federal authorities and the clergy, but other pronouncements give a different picture of the church's view of the nature of its relations with the government. The following statement by Metropolitan Kirill is particularly instructive because he draws parallels with Islam's position in Russia:

> It is true that the Russian government officials at the highest levels openly declare their affiliation to the Orthodox Christianity by attending religious services, but we forget that the leaders of a secular state are not supposed to be atheists and have inalienable rights to adhere to their religious beliefs. By contrast, the heads of the Islamic regions of Russia do not conceal their affiliation to Islam—they openly participate in prayers and join the *Hajj.* Moreover, there are cases of

introduction of the Shari'a premises into regional legislations of certain subjects of the Russian Federation, in particular those related to the legalization of polygamy and prohibition of the use of alcoholic beverages in the month of Ramadan.[354]

Officially the Russian Orthodox Church upholds the principle of the separation of church and state. This official position is reflected in the decision of the Holy Synod (the highest authority within the Russian Orthodox Church) that prohibits priests from assuming political office or supporting political parties.[355] Nonetheless, the church often finds creative ways to circumvent this ban and manages to show its affinity toward authorities indirectly. This practice often leads to the participation of high church officials in important events whereby their very presence indicates the church's tacit endorsement of government policies. This ambiguous modus operandi of the Russian Orthodox Church—on the one hand, remaining neutral in regard to domestic political power struggles while, on the other hand, selectively engaging in public debates on a variety of issues—was embodied in the development and implementation of the concept of "active neutrality." In its essence, this concept implies that the church does recognize the separation of civil and religious authority, but at the same time it has the responsibility to objectively assess, and if necessary criticize, those actions of the government and other political forces which have an impact on people's lives.[356] Thus social and political activism of the church is represented by its involvement in events affecting not only Orthodox Christians, but also a global community of nations.[357] Despite these advances, clearly this situation underscores the fact that the character of the relations between the Orthodox Church and the state in Russia is still evolving.

Despite its many successes, the Orthodox Church has also faced serious challenges in the context of a more open post-Soviet Russian society, the most serious of which has been the proselytizing activities of other Christian denominations and foreign cults. Many non-Orthodox Russians, including nonbelievers and atheists, have been attracted to these new creeds, while the Orthodox Church has been losing some of its adherents.[358]

The Muslim religious establishment has also been concerned about the activities of nontraditional (to Russia) religions and pseudoreligious sects. According to some reports, Mufti Ravil Gainutdin shares the view of the Orthodox Church that activities of foreign missionaries should be tightly regulated.[359] Thus resisting the intrusion of nontraditional faiths into Russia is one area where the Orthodox Church and the Muslim establishment can cooperate. However, Islam's rising profile and the aspirations of some Muslim religious leaders for Islam to be treated on a more or less equal level with Orthodoxy, have been seen as a challenge by a portion of the Orthodox leadership, who consider this phenomenon as diluting Russia's Orthodox Christian essence. During the controversy over the construction of an Islamic Cultural Center in Moscow in 1994, Father Georgy, the priest of the Church of the Archangel Michael, expressed this feeling when he noted: "Moscow has always been and will continue to be a holy city for the Orthodox Christians. It has always been known as the oldest capital, as a golden-domed city built of white stag [a symbol reflecting light and beauty seen in Russian churches]. But they want to make us into nobodies with no heritage. We pray to God that everything turns out alright. But all the same, Moscow is the Third Rome, not the Second Mecca"[360] In terms of its relations with the Muslim establishment, this attitude of the church results in its preference for malleable Muslim leaders, notably Mufti Talgat Tadzhuddin.[361]

Other factors affecting the dynamics of competition and cooperation between the Orthodox Church and the Islamic community and leadership in Russia include the following:

1.   Diverging views and attitudes within the Orthodox Church regarding Islam. According to one scholar, in respect to their attitude toward Islam, the Orthodox clergy fall into three broad categories; (a) those who ignore Islam's role in Russian history and culture; (b) those who believe in an inherent antagonism between Islam and Orthodoxy; and (c) those who see Islam as a tactical ally in the fight against Western influences.[362] Depending on their inclinations, each of these groups approach the Muslim community differently, hence the diverse nature of comments about Islam coming from leaders of the Orthodox Church.

2.   Internal divisions within the Orthodox Church. Like its counterparts within the Muslim establishment, the Russian Orthodox Church is also experiencing internal rivalries and divisions. The proliferation of splinter groups, which are usually led by young priests dissatisfied with the highly centralized and hierarchically rigid structure of the church, has become a matter of grave concern for the senior church leadership, partly because of its consequences for the disputes over property.[363] The progressive segment of young priests feels alienated because of the church leadership's consistent intolerance of innovative interpretations of Orthodox dogma.[364] Irrespective of their causes, these internal divisions have prevented the emergence of a consensus within the church that would have enabled it to speak with one voice to Muslims in Russia and thus perhaps have hampered the cause of interfaith harmony.

3.   Moscow versus the periphery. There is also often a divergence of attitude vis-à-vis Islam between the central leadership of the church in Moscow and local priests. While not relishing the rising profile of Islam, the central leadership nevertheless emphasizes the theme of interreligious dialogue and cooperation to combat social ills. The church has even tried to create institutions to formalize interreligious contacts. The most important of these institutions is the Inter-Religious Council of Russia (IRCR).[365] The IRCR was created in December 1998 at the initiative of the Orthodox Church. The representatives of Russia's four traditional religions—Christianity, Judaism, Islam and Buddhism—are represented in the Council. The IRCR's principal goal is to maintain an ongoing dialogue among Russia's traditional religions and to "jointly discuss the problems facing the contemporary Russian society in an attempt to develop a common position on them in order to testify in front of the people and government."[366] However, at the local

level, the Orthodox Church and its representatives often oppose the construction of mosques, if not in principle, then in certain localities.

4. Political dimensions. The relationship between Islam and the Orthodox Church cannot be separated from political issues and developments, including the character of each religion's relation to the state. At least three factors account for the existence of a political dimension to the relationship between Orthodoxy and Islam in the Russian Federation. The first factor, as Alexei Malashenko has pointed out, is that both Islam and Orthodoxy, especially Islam, have political dimensions, and Orthodoxy, like Islam, "actively interferes in secular, including political, issues."[367] But the Orthodox Church, or at least some powerful elements within it, "aspire to a monopoly on Russia's national and state ideology."[368] Consequently, the church and many Russian politicians are against any Muslim political activism, and especially any religiously based Muslim political parties and movements.[369] Meanwhile, the relationship between the Orthodox Church and the state has been growing closer.[370] The church supports most of the government's policies, notably its campaign in Chechnya.[371] In particular, the relationship between the military and the church has been growing steadily closer. As symbols of this growing closeness, in January 2000 the patriarch of Russia's Orthodox Church presented religious medals or icons to Armed Forces Chief of Staff Anatolii Kvashnin and his deputy and also conducted prayers for the 93,000 servicemen fighting in Chechnya.

The Chechen War has played an important role in this respect. It has offered opportunities to some military commanders to cast the war in religious terms. Although Russian leaders, to varying degrees, have tried to avoid such characterizations, at times the temptation to do so has proven too strong.

For example, during the first Chechen War, both some foreign observers and representatives of Russian republics observed that at times President Yeltsin and his administration edged too close to characterizing the Chechen War as a religious war. According to Donna E. Arzt, in a televised speech in December 1994, Yeltsin "attempted to portray the Chechen rebellion, with its ethno-religious trappings, as camouflage for organized drug and weapon traffickers."[372] Although such inferences may have been made from Yeltsin's speech, the clearly anti-Islam rhetoric increased during the second Chechen War, especially by some military personnel. The following statement by Colonel Alexander Kovalyov, an instructor at the Northern Caucasus Red Banner Military Institute in Vladikavkaz, North Ossetia, is a good example: "We are fighting Islamic fascism, that's what we are doing. In the Great Patriotic War, we fought German fascism. . . . now we are fighting Islamic fascism."[373]

There are also clergy in the army catering to the spiritual needs of the soldiers. Some sources claim that the clergy is used for Orthodox proselytization of the soldiers.[374] Some Muslim minorities whose members serve in the Russian army have wondered whether this proselytization extends to them, especially since according to these sources, many religious ceremonies are compulsory. Thus an article in the *Tatar Gazette* asks, "What happens to Tatar soldiers during such ceremonies? Are they forced to take part, or do they have to perform manual jobs instead?

Whatever the case may be, one thing is certain: there are no military mullahs in the Russian Army."[375] Some sources indicate that there are efforts at Christian proselytization in the North Caucasus. The following statement by Father Innokenty Vasetsky, based in Vladikavkaz, if correct, gives some credence to these reports: "In our hospital, how many Tatars and Muslims have we baptized? After fighting in Chechnya, they understand the difference between Christianity and Islam."[376]

The feelings expressed earlier do not fully or accurately represent the sentiments and attitudes of the whole body of the Orthodox establishment. On the contrary, important figures within the Orthodox establishment want to maintain dialogue and peaceful and in some areas—for example, opposing the intrusion of other religious sects—cooperative relations with Muslims and their official representatives.

What the Orthodox Church does not countenance, however, is any pretension to equal status at the official level between Orthodoxy and Islam. Islam can be acceptable only as a junior and docile partner that does not aspire to any political role beyond what the Moscow leadership is willing to assign to it. Alexei Malashenko has explained this point very aptly by pointing out that Russian politicians and, one might add, the Orthodox leadership want " 'a domesticated,' artificial Islam, one that will not interfere with their lives."[377]

Significant numbers of Russian Muslims and part of the Muslim establishment resent being treated as second-rate citizens. The late Nadirshakh Khachilaev, a onetime member of the Duma from Dagestan who was later accused of extremism and terrorism by Russian authorities, during the first Congress of the Union of Muslims of Russia (UMR), explained the rationale behind the movement's creation in 1995 in these terms: "Our Union [of Muslims] was an answer to the discrimination against part of the [Muslim] community, especially the people referred to as 'members of the Caucasian nationality.' They sense that Muslims are somehow second rate and that they should be playing a subordinate role in this country."[378] Ravil Gainutdin, the chairman of the RCM, has also complained about this secondary status assigned to Islam. To remedy this, the MSP demands that Russia's state symbols reflect its multireligious character.

Be that as it may, the trend in Russia, including the Orthodox Church, since the mid-1990s and increasingly so since the late 1990s has been toward limiting Islam's role in the country's social and political life and the promotion of those Muslim leaders who are willing to play a secondary role. This situation is unlikely to change in the foreseeable future for essentially three reasons: first, an increase in anti-Islam feelings in Russia to a large extent due to the Chechen War, developments in Afghanistan and Central Asia in the late 1990s, and more recently the terrorist attacks of 11 September in the United States and the hostage-taking operation in Moscow in October 2002; second, the emphasis that the Russian media put on everything negative regarding Islam; third, the greater determination of the Russian government under Putin to bring religious establishments, except the very tame, under its control—a process that would be more favorable to the Orthodox Church than to the Muslim establishment.

The Limited Impact of Islam on Russia's Cultural, Social, Economic, and Political Scenes

While developments within Russia's Muslim regions and among its Muslim citizens, most notably their quest for greater self-determination, have deeply affected the evolution of Russia's governmental institutions and have strengthened the trend toward a Russocentric culture, Islam's influence in shaping other aspects of sociopolitical and economic processes has been limited. This has been especially true in the area of political and cultural discourse despite the emergence of nascent political entities, some of which aspire to enrich the cultural and political discourse in Russia with Islamic values.[379]

The combination of four main factors explains the relative insignificance of Islam as compared to the power and influence wielded by Orthodox Christianity in Russia. First, Russia still is an essentially monocultural country, where the ethnic Russians constitute the overwhelming majority. Despite the frequent public statements of high-ranking Russian politicians and public officials, including President Putin himself, the idea of Russia as a multicultural and multiethnic country remains alien to the majority of its people, as evidenced by the emergence of certain extreme right movements in Russia, some with openly racist tendencies. Second, the lack of an adequate Muslim educational infrastructure and the acute shortage of qualified clergy and Muslim intellectuals inhibit the representation of the views, values, and interests of the Muslim community in an adequately accessible and attractive manner and hinder becoming engaged in public debates. Leonid Sukiyainen, a prominent Russian scholar of Islamic law at the Institute of State and Law of the Russian Academy of Sciences, supports this view. According to him, the nascent Muslim educational infrastructure is insufficient for producing educated religious cadres who would be able to engage in sophisticated public debates on controversial issues.[380] The problem of the shortage of educated Muslim clerics is compounded by the fact that the existing Muslim establishment mainly consists of the Soviet-era Muslim religious functionaries, who are mostly poorly educated. Moreover, as Sukiyainen suggests, this old leadership hinders the intellectual evolution of Russian Muslims.[381] In fact, the old generation of clerics feels threatened by the young Muslims, who have received religious education abroad, because they see them as ultimately undermining their authority. Third, whenever Muslims have taken an active political stand, their proposals and initiatives have been largely ignored by the Russian political mainstream. This was the case with the recommendation of the Muslim political party Refakh that Russia should join the Organization of the Islamic Conference as an observer.[382] More recently, because of the new dynamics unleashed by the Iraq War, Russia appeared to show greater interest in joining the OIC. Unfortunately, other manifestations of the Muslims' political ambitions were often channeled through separatist movements and sometimes even terrorist acts. These aspects of Muslim politics have negatively impacted the public perception of Muslims in Russia. This worsening of Muslims' image has severely limited their options in terms of assuming an active role in the sociopolitical, cultural, and economic spheres. This negative perception of Muslims has been magnified by the Russian media. Fourth, the interethnic tensions within the Muslim community itself have prevented the Muslims from reaching an internal consensus, and, consequently, Muslims have been incapable of projecting a coherent and appealing image of Islam to society at large, which could have made a contribution to post-Soviet Russia's political, social, and spiritual ethos.

Conclusion

Even after the separation of the Muslim republics of the former Soviet Union, Muslims constitute a substantial minority in the Russian Federation, although estimates as to their exact number vary widely. If current demographic trends continue, the Muslim element may become even more important, although apocalyptic views of Russia soon becoming a Muslim state are totally unwarranted.

Islam in the post-Soviet period has experienced a quantitative and qualitative expansion and has become more visible. Muslims today enjoy more religious freedom than they ever did before. However, Islam is not yet a fully accepted part of Russia's cultural fabric. Some of Islam's newfound visibility has been caused by negative developments, notably the two wars in Chechnya, the spread of certain extremist ideologies, and an influx of refugees and other immigrants from the Caucasus and Muslim republics of Central Asia, and thus has been damaging to Muslims. Consequently, Islam has acquired a strongly negative image that has deep roots in earlier history, and anti-Muslim sentiments have become more widespread. Even peaceful and moderate expressions of Islam have elicited resentment and fear. Differences of opinion and acrimonious exchanges between Russia's principal Muslim leaders, which often reflect ethnic animosities and Islam's inability to overcome such divisions, have been extremely detrimental to the development of Russian Islam in a coherent fashion. This situation has led to a repeat of the old pattern of creeping governmental control over Muslim organizations and Islam's limited role in the context of the ongoing debate about Russia's post-Soviet identity and values.

Russia's Muslims also remain among the least advantaged social and economic segments of the population. Similarly, their political and cultural influence remains negligible. This situation is mostly the result of the inadequacies of the Muslim communities themselves, but it is also reflective of centuries of policies of socioeconomic and cultural discrimination. With the growing tendency in Russia toward political centralization and cultural homogenization, Islam will remain on the margins of Russian social and political life. However, the trend toward a physical and cultural revival of Islam will not be easily reversed. Moreover, the Muslim quest for self-determination, albeit to varying degrees, is likely to continue, even if in a more subdued fashion. Thus Islam will continue to influence Russia's political and cultural development, even if its role will be that of a force against which Russia defines itself and perceives a need to protect itself.

II

Identity Politics in the Russian Federation

The Islamic Factor

3

The Evolution of Russia's Post-Soviet National Identity

The Impact of the Islamic Factor

In 1996, President Boris Yeltsin stated that what Russia needed most was a national idea (*natsionalnaya ideia*) suited to the conditions and needs of the post-Soviet environment. Following his reelection in June 1996, Yeltsin set up a commission of philosophers, historians, linguists, and other experts to devise such an idea within a year. The commission failed in this task; instead, it issued a report titled "Russia in Search of an Idea" that explained the need for such a unifying idea.[1] By establishing this commission, Yeltsin acknowledged the existence of a widespread and deep sense of uncertainty within Russia about where the country was headed, what guiding principles the nation should adopt for its internal organization and foreign relations, and what Russia's place and role should be in the post-Soviet world.

Many Russian scholars and philosophers have also been preoccupied with this condition, which nearly all characterize as "a crisis of identity and national self-consciousness."[2] In November 1999, Vladimir Putin, campaigning for the presidency, acknowledged the lack of a unifying concept for the Russian nation. During a meeting with several university presidents, he stressed the need to develop a national idea based on "patriotism in the most positive sense of the word."[3]

Considering the dramatic changes triggered by the collapse of the Soviet system in every aspect of the Russian people's lives, in Russia's geopolitical situation, and in its international status, this sense of collective disorientation is natural. Some Russian scholars even believe that in magnitude Russia's post-Soviet crisis is more serious and on a larger scale than the convulsions caused by the revolutions of 1917, the abolition of serfdom, and even the Time of Troubles (1598–1613); this crisis can only be compared to the collapse of the Kievan state in the thirteenth century and the development in the coming centuries of the Russian state and civilization.[4] This statement may be an exaggeration; nonetheless, the Soviet Union's collapse has been a traumatic experience for the Russians. It has shattered most premises of their collective identity, has caused great confusion regarding the basic rules governing social and political relations and institutions, and has rendered Russia's international role and purpose ambiguous. In short, both a crisis of national identity and a search for a new identity have been natural outcomes of the Soviet Union's collapse.

The Soviet Union: A Colonial Empire?

The traumatic impact of the Soviet Union's collapse for the Russian people derives from the very nature of the Soviet system. The Soviet Union—territorial successor to the tsarist Russian Empire—culturally and politically resembled a colonial empire. With the exception of the first fifteen years after the revolution, ethnic Russians, later joined by other Slavs, held most high leadership posts in the central government and Communist Party organs. For most of Soviet history, there were no high-ranking officials from Muslim republics present in the Politburo of the Communist Party. The first Muslim elevated to such a position was the Kazakh Dinmuhammad Kunaev in 1971, followed by Heidar Aliev of Azerbaijan in 1982. It was only in 1990 that other Muslims were elevated to Politburo membership.[5] Some scholars have speculated that had the USSR not disintegrated in 1991, this trend might have strengthened as the Muslim population of the USSR increased.[6]

Ethnic Russians were also assigned a civilizing role of the "elder brother" toward the non-European populations of the Soviet Union. Thus although Soviet authorities throughout the 1920s created new literary languages for some national minorities and encouraged the development of well-established cultures and languages, this policy of *korenizatsia* (indigenization) primarily maintained the fiction of the Soviet system as a voluntary federation. Indeed, Soviet nationalities policies ultimately advanced the process of Russification and undermined indigenous cultures. Most official business was conducted in Russian, and few high-ranking officials or members of the intelligentsia in non-Russian republics were fluent in their native languages.[7] The change in script of the Muslim republics' languages adversely impacted their civilizations and eroded their ability to communicate with cultural kin.[8] Despite these shortcomings, the creation within the USSR of union republics, autonomous republics, and national territories—all bearing the names of their titular nationalities—paradoxically strengthened the sense of a separate ethnic identity of non-Russian peoples. This sentiment was reinforced by the industrialization and modernization of the non-Russian areas. According to Teresa Rakowska-Harmstone, two decisions of the early Bolshevik government, the establishment of a federal or pseudofederal state and an accelerated tempo of industrialization, determined the pattern of the evolution of the nationalities problem in the Soviet Union.[9]

The Soviet approach to the history of relations between Russia and the non-Russian peoples was more complex and fluctuated as the system evolved. John Dunlop has noted that the Soviet regime "pursued erratic and at times contradictory policies vis-à-vis the minority nationalities."[10] These minorities were initially treated sympathetically; some ideologues of the Russian state justified the minorities' struggles against the Russian tsarist conquest and attributed revolutionary dimensions to this resistance. The first edition of the *Great Soviet Encyclopedia*, published in 1939, states the following about Imam Shamil's campaign in Dagestan and Chechnya:

> The movement was aroused by the colonial policy of Russia, which robbed the native population of their forests, tore away the best parts of their land for Cossack colonization, and in every respect supported and sustained the despotism of the local feudalists.[11]

Even in this early period, however, the Russian conquest of the Caucasus and Central Asia was viewed as a "lesser evil" for the indigenous people than being conquered by the British. Later, Russian conquest was characterized as being a "greater good." Figures such as Shamil and others who resisted Russian domination were treated as "insidious reactionaries."[12] By 1947, the authorized view of Russian expansion into the Caucasus was that Russian annexation of the Caucasus "played a positive and progressive role for the people of the Caucasus." Moreover, the people welcomed union with Russia.[13] Nevertheless, the Soviet Union was in some fundamental ways different from classical colonial empires, including the tsarist Russian Empire.

Socialist Utopia and the Soviet Man

Previous colonial powers had all had civilizing and culturally messianic impulses, but none of them had tried to create a utopian society transcending ethnic, religious, and class distinctions as the Soviets aspired to do. Nor had previous empires tried to create a new individual, the Soviet Man (*Homo Sovieticus*), an individual with a new identity disconnected from any preexisting identities, first by *sblizhenie* (bringing various peoples closer together) and then *sliyanie* (merging them within a socialist family). This utopian scheme was never achieved, and ethnic and religious identities remained tenacious. There was resistance to the idea of merging diverse peoples, both among Muslims and ethnic Russians. Muslims feared this merging because they were numerically inferior and risked losing their national identities; the Russians feared for the survival of their distinct cultural and biological identities. In the late 1960s, the notion of "merging" was abandoned in favor of the concept of *polnoe yedintsvo* (full unity), or "the clustering of Soviet peoples around commonly held ideals without any implication of biological unity."[14] Even this more limited goal was not achieved. Nor did periods of intense anti-religion, particularly anti-Islam, campaigns, atheistic propaganda, and internationalist education eliminate religion and religiocultural traditions. These distinct and diverse traditions, along with identities based upon them, survived and came to the fore in the late 1980s with the opening offered by Mikhail Gorbachev's reforms.

Other contradictory aspects of the Soviet system, notably its nationalities policies, contributed to the failure of this utopian program. One aspect particularly stands out: the encouragement of migration of Russians and other Slavs to less developed areas of Central Asia and other regions with substantial non-Russian populations. These better-educated and technically more qualified immigrants helped the process of regional industrialization. However, this type of development caused economic stratification along ethnic lines: the indigenous population remained mostly rural with low incomes and maintained its traditional way of life. These disparities in economic conditions and lifestyles of indigenous peoples and immigrants elicited resentment from the former. Thus rather than creating greater interethnic amity, the policy caused, at best, mutual mistrust and, at worst, animosity.

External events, notably the Second World War (or "Great Patriotic War") and the German invasion of Russia, accelerated the process of the growing apart of Soviet ethnic groups by encouraging the nationalization or, more precisely, the Russification of socialism that was already under way. This phenomenon was natural, given that "the powerful urge to particularism" has nearly always diverted universalistic and utopian schemes from their intended path.[15] Utopian schemes harbored by revolutionaries who accede to power generally come face to face with two irresistible forces: the need for order and the pull of historic continuity.[16]

Yet the Soviet Union did develop a territorial and politicocultural space that was different from both the classic colonial empire and the traditional nation-state. A Soviet identity, albeit amorphous and ambiguous, evolved, often coexisting with and sometimes superseding the more ethnocentric, religious, and local identities. This was especially true of the Russians because of their dominant position in the Soviet Union. The following statement by Mikhail Gorbachev illustrates how, in the minds of many Russians, Russia and the Soviet Union were nearly one and the same: "What is Russia? It is the Union. What is the Union? It is mostly Russia."[17] The Russians were therefore more prone to see the entire Soviet Union as their rightful patrimony where they should be able to move freely, in contrast to the majority of Muslims, who remained tied to their native lands.

Because Russian was the USSR's lingua franca and Russians held all levers of power, Russian attitudes and subsequent behavior appeared legitimate and realistic. In short, because of the predominance of the Russian element in the Soviet Union, Russians viewed conquered parts of the Soviet Union as their homeland and found it easier to consider themselves as Soviets. Thus Boris Yeltsin, in a 1990 interview, said:

> I recognized myself to be a citizen of the country [i.e., the USSR] and not of Russia. Well, I also considered myself to be a patriot of Sverdlovsk, in as much as I had worked there. But the concept of Russia was so relative to me that, while serving as first secretary of the Sverdlovsk party Obkom [the regional organization of the Communist Party of the Soviet Union (CPSU)], I had not turned to the Russian departments on most questions. I would first turn to the Central Committee of the CPSU, and then to the union government.[18]

In the case of those Russians who had lived for generations in the outlying, notably Muslim, regions of the empire, this was an understandable attitude. Less understandable today is why so few Russians ever took the trouble to learn the local languages or become acquainted with their civilizations. According to a well-educated Tatar woman, "The Russians never learn our names and prefer to call us by Russian names that sound closest to our native ones."[19] Because of this pervasive lack of knowledge on the part of the average Russian about Soviet national minorities and the nonrecognition of the fact that they had lived in those lands centuries before the Russians arrived, many Russians in the outlying regions viewed the collapse of the Soviet Union as the loss of their homeland. This explains why so many Russians have had great difficulty accepting the former Soviet republics as independent states and adjusting to the new circumstances, including the need to learn native languages.[20] Irrespective of the merit of such attitudes, the important question is how they influence the debate about post-Soviet Russian identity and its principal components.

Is Russia Going the Way of the Soviet Union?

The rise of nationalism and separatism among ethnic minorities, which contributed to the disintegration of the Soviet Union, also spread among minority nationalities of the RSFSR and its successor, the Russian Federation, generating fears that the Soviet Union's collapse would be a prelude to the disintegration of the Russian Federation. The event that most crystallized these fears was the 1994 outbreak of war in Chechnya, which raised Russian fears that events in Chechnya might trigger a domino effect, potentially culminating in the Russian Federation's complete or partial disintegration. This apprehension is reflected in a January 1995 statement by Grigory Karasin, a spokesman with the Russian Foreign Ministry, who justified military intervention in Chechnya by arguing that "the alternative, not to counteract the separatist and the criminal regime [in Chechnya], could lead to a repetition of the Yugoslav scenario in Russia."[21] Oleg Lobov, secretary of the Russian Security Council, expressed similar fears when, in a warning aimed at Western criticism of Russian actions in Chechnya, he stated that Chechnya's secession would "open the door to Russian disintegration" and "most likely [lead to] a Yugoslav variant."[22]

The introduction of Islam as an instrument of Chechen nationalism exacerbated the perceived danger to Russian territorial integrity by deepening ethnic differences and, in the view of many, incompatibilities that separated the ethnic Russian majority from Muslims. The 1994–96 Chechen War was a complex phenomenon, with many causes that are still debated. To the extent that the war was a manifestation of the Chechen desire for self-determination, it was similar to other wars of national independence: it was rooted in two centuries of Chechen resistance to, and rebellion against, Russian domination rather than being a religiously motivated conflict. However, the Chechen separatist leadership employed Islam to foster a sense of Chechen national identity, transcending family and clan loyalties, and to rally opposition to continued Russian rule. The use of Islam by the Chechens as an instrument of separatism, combined with the rise of nationalist movements among other Muslim minorities, including the Tatars, intensified the perceived threat posed by Muslim peoples to the Russian Federation's territorial and national integrity.

To these fears was added the threat of cultural dilution and, in the case of some Russian communities, oppression or absorption by more numerous nationalities. The Soviet Union's collapse left an estimated 25 million ethnic Russians outside the Russian Federation. During the 1990s, approximately 8 million of these "new Russian minorities" migrated to the Russian Federation; however, a large Russian population (approximately 18 million, or 12 percent of the former Soviet Union's Russian population) remains outside the Russian homeland. Thus the end of the Soviet Union geographically fragmented the original Russian ethnic group, thereby enhancing the overall sense of loss of national identity and a strong sense of ambivalence regarding the essence of a collective identity.[23]

Ideological and Cultural Vacuum

The collapse of the Soviet system also created an ideological and cultural vacuum. By the time of Mikhail Gorbachev's reforms, most Russians had lost faith in the Soviet Union's ideology and utopian aspirations. They were also choking under its manifold restrictions on basic freedoms. Nevertheless, the Soviet system and its socialist ideology had after seventy years provided a degree of economic and social stability and predictability in the lives of Soviet citizens, some important cultural guideposts and social values, and thus a degree of psychological comfort. In short, the Soviet experience had given rise to a particular way of life, many aspects of which were valued by the people. According to Richard Sakwa, by the time of the system's collapse, while communism had receded as an attractive goal, it had become more attractive as a way of life.[24] Soviet citizens did not embrace the system's values, but neither did they oppose it. Rather, they created their own countervalues, which "did not so much oppose the system as ignore it."[25]

This latter dimension of the system was particularly important for the Russian population because despite the transcendental pretensions of Marxism, in cultural terms, Soviet socialism was based on Russian culture and history.[26] Some Russian intellectuals and philosophers claim that communism is anathema to traditional Russian culture. Some even claim that the 1917 Russian Revolution was a grand conspiracy against Russia by anti-Russian (Russophobic) minorities. Russian politicians such as Boris Yeltsin have portrayed the entire Soviet system as an anti-Russian enterprise, especially under Stalin. He noted that during the Soviet era, the Russian Supreme Soviet performed only ornamental tasks because Stalin "was afraid of Russia. . . . God forbid [Stalin thought] that Russia should rise up and become a counterweight to the center and its power."[27] This statement and the sentiments behind it are ironic and even demagogic. Indeed, after 1934, Stalin, a Georgian, persistently emphasized the importance of the Russian element in the building of the Soviet system and encouraged the rise of Russian nationalism. It was under Stalin that historic Russian military and literary heroes, including Ivan the Terrible, Peter the Great, Alexander Nevsky, and General Mikhail Kutuzov, were rehabilitated and even glorified. Terms such as *rodina* (homeland) that had disappeared from the vocabulary reentered public speech. Other components of Russian national culture, notably the Orthodox Church, also received better treatment, and even Fyodor Dostoevsky's novels enjoyed a revival.[28] After the defeat of Germany, Stalin "singled out the Russian people during victory celebrations, praising them as the backbone of Soviet power": John Dunlop states that some Russian historians believe that the triumph of Stalin's theory of Russia-centered socialism over Trotsky's militant internationalism was the beginning of the rise of Russian nationalism in the Soviet period.[29] Thus, irrespective of whether it was the system of Soviet values or the people's hidden countervalues that collapsed, the Soviet Union's dissolution left an important void.

Search for an Alternative Model

Initially, it appeared that the post-Soviet ideological and cultural void could be filled with the wholesale importation of the West's liberal democratic political model, its market economy, and its culture. However, the first years of transition from totalitarianism to a democratic system in Russia were highly disruptive and caused many dislocations and disappointments. The end of communism did not result in rapid and substantial improvement of Russia's economy and its people's living standards. Rather, economic reforms caused much pain and impoverished a large portion of the population. Reforms were accompanied by rapid erosion of Russia's industrial base and the emergence of a small rich elite who acquired their wealth through financial speculation or by taking over state-owned industries, a process characterized by some analysts in Russia and the West as "*nomenklatura* privatization," or elite-based capitalism.[30] Particularly disorienting for the Russians, who had been used to a system that took care of their basic needs, was the new philosophy underlying post-Soviet economic policies, namely, that everyone must fend for oneself. Yevgenii Yasin, a key government adviser, told the public that because the country was going through difficult times, "people must understand that they should not rely on others."[31] Alfred Kokh, who as deputy prime minister and director of the Committee on State Property Management in the mid-1990s played a key role in administering Russia's massive privatization of state assets, stated, "This is a time of Social Darwinism, during which a process of natural selection must take place."[32]

Other aspects of the early economic reforms, such as disregard for environmental and health safety standards, contributed to a feeling among the population that "a fundamental violation of the implicit contract between government and society had taken place."[33] The erosion of Russia's industrial base was also very disturbing because Russia's industrialization was a source of national pride. Thus it was frequently lamented that Russia was turning into a Third World–type country, with raw materials, especially energy, as its main exports and source of income. The pain caused by the steady degradation of the Russian economy soon led to the emergence of conspiratorial theories: the West had orchestrated the Soviet Union's fall to turn Russia into a supplier of raw materials for the West, to eliminate a rival in the global export markets, and to turn Russia into a consumer of Western goods. According to General Alexander Lebed, "The West is attempting to turn Russia into a cheap supplier of raw materials, a reservoir of free labor, and a huge hazardous waste dump for the industrial world."[34] Moscow mayor Yurii Luzhkov expressed similar sentiments. After the 1998 collapse of financial markets in Russia, he asked, "Why should we be commanded by Western economists and countries, which want to face no competition on the Russian market after suppressing Russian producers and making Russia just a supplier of natural resources?"[35]

The decline of the Russian economy and the ensuing hardships dealt a serious blow to the Russians' faith in the efficacy and superiority of the Western economic model. They found the philosophy of social Darwinism favored by Russia's new capitalists especially disorienting because Russian popular culture had always put a high value on communal solidarity and the state's responsibility to satisfy people's needs.

Political developments were also discouraging. Because Russia lacked some of the basic components needed for building democracy, the Soviet Union's collapse did not lead to a truly democratic system. Rather, politics in post-Soviet Russia evolved in the direction of what has been described as "presidential authoritarianism" and led to a system based on dictatorial executive power.[36] This development is not surprising. Even before the Soviet Union's collapse and Boris Yeltsin's rise to power, the desirability of a "democratic" dictatorship for Russia was debated within reformist groups and press. The main argument in defense of such a system was that given Russia's conditions, democratic methods would, in effect, lead to a stalemate because "the people would not accept the pain necessary for the birth of a new economic and political system."[37]

President Yeltsin's tendency to rule by decree was a natural outcome of this way of thinking. However, with the growing tendency of various regions and their powerful leaders to act independently and to ignore the official channels, the dictatorial presidency was more fiction than fact. Nevertheless, Yeltsin's style of governing perpetuated the long-established, traditional Russian belief in leaders who could perform miracles rather than those who could generate confidence in well-founded institutions.

Thus while the deeply rooted Russian tradition of belief in a strong leader persisted, the faith in government and its institutions suffered. The growth of criminal and semicriminal organizations, often linked to local and national power structures, contributed to this process. According to Tim McDaniel, a survey taken in June 1992 in the cities of Moscow, St. Petersburg, and Vladimir showed that "only six percent of Russian citizens considered that power in fact belonged to the visible official organs of government. Almost thirty percent believed that the mafia was the most powerful political force in the country, while fifteen percent were convinced that the old party elite was still dominant."[38]

Politics in post-Soviet Russia also remained highly personal; power was sought as a means to gain access to economic advantages. Parties were formed and dissolved according to electoral calendars. Because the new system was superficially democratic, the general population perceived its failures as failures of the Western political model. Culturally, the elite's excessive greed and lust for conspicuous consumption were viewed as products of the West's culture of materialism and threats to Russia's spiritual values and, according to some prominent figures, even to the health and survival of its people. General Lebed encapsulated the feelings of those who thought along these lines when, commenting on the crass materialism, he stated, "Our children have already picked up their first words: *raket* [racket], *krysha* [cover, or protection provided by an organized crime syndicate], *babki* [cash], *baksy* [bucks]. . . . We should pass on to them a cleaner heritage." Lebed reportedly said that the Russians were being "turned into drunkards, spiritually and morally poisoned by the violence and sex rubbish that has filled the screens of television sets and theaters."[39]

The combined effect of these developments was the serious erosion of popular belief in the superiority of the Western model and its applicability to Russia, and hence the intensification of debate about the principal framework for a new order in Russia. A fundamental part of this debate related to what the nature of a post-Soviet Russian identity should be: ethnic, religious, ethnoreligious, or even civic. The outcome of this debate will largely define Russia's entire political structure and underlying cultural tendencies. Since Muslims constitute the largest group of non-Russians, and given Islam's role as a coherent belief system and way of life, the way Islam and Muslims are dealt with in the process of constructing Russia's post-Soviet identity will have a considerable impact on its basic characteristics. Similarly, the evolution of Russia's Muslim communities—the process of post-Soviet identity formation, their behavior toward the ethnic Russians and the federal government, and especially the character and extent of their quest for self-determination—will influence this debate. Already, developments in parts of Russia's Muslim regions, most notably the Chechen War, have had a significant impact.

Nostalgia for Lost Power and Search for a New Role

Western powers attempted to treat Russia as an equal partner, at least symbolically, as illustrated by its inclusion in the Group of Seven—now Eight—industrial countries. Yet the inescapable fact is that the Soviet Union's disintegration, coupled with Russia's multidimensional crisis, ended its great-power status on a par with the United States or the European Union.

In the post-Soviet world, in many respects and in many regions, Russia found itself almost irrelevant, and in the view of some Westernizers it became, in Sergei Kortunov's words, a "superfluous country."[40] The United States emerged as the dominant power on the international scene, and frequent references to America as the sole superpower were naturally jarring to the Russians. Most frustrating and humiliating was the fact that the West was replacing Russian influence not only in the ex–Warsaw Pact countries of Central Europe, but also in the former republics of the Soviet Union. More disturbing was the fact that historical rivals such as

Turkey were becoming major actors in the post-Soviet republics, and other Muslim countries were also becoming more involved in the post-Soviet space and were even making inroads in Muslim-inhabited republics and regions of the Russian Federation itself. In sum, not only was Russia no longer a key player in deciding world events, it was also witnessing the penetration of its traditional spheres of influence by other actors, including some of its historic rivals.

Consequently, nostalgia for the past was inevitable because whatever complaints the Russians might have had about the Soviet system, they were proud of the Soviet Union's superpower status.[41] This phenomenon led Russian constitutional scholar and legislator Oleg Rumyantsev to say that Russia was suffering from "the psychological detritus of a super-power."[42] Former U.S. ambassador to Moscow Thomas Pickering said that "many Russians certainly regret the loss of empire, and many would favor a resumption of Russian hegemony if the price is right."[43] These feelings were natural because for three centuries, the Russians had believed in their destiny as a great power. Even Andrei Kozyrev, the liberal Russian foreign minister, wrote that "Russia is predestined to be a great power. It remained as such for centuries in spite of repeated internal upheavals."[44] The combination of a deep-rooted belief in Russia's great-power destiny and the actuality of its loss of power led to a soul-searching about Russia's future goals and aspirations and how it should define its new concept of greatness. Should Russia continue to see its greatness in the vastness of its empire, in the strength of its military power, as Yuri Luzhkov indicated,[45] or in its ability to achieve better living conditions for its citizens, as Kozyrev seemed to advocate?

Here it should be noted that Russia's traditional sense of greatness did not derive solely from its military prowess or the size of its empire. Rather, it stemmed from its belief in having a superior civilization before and during the Soviet era, especially in moral terms, and its sense of special mission, whether to be the guardian of true Christianity or the creator of a utopian world order. Therefore, the Soviet Union's collapse and the penetration of Western culture into Russia undermined the other two pillars of Russian greatness. The erosion of Russia's cultural influence in regions considered part of its historic sphere of influence increased the Russians' feeling of national humiliation. This loss was particularly bitter in the case of those peoples, notably in the Muslim republics of the former Soviet Union, whom the Russians considered culturally inferior.[46] Yet Russia, like any other country, cannot clearly define its internal goals, its priorities in the outside world, or a sense of mission transcending mere material interests without first defining its national identity, its basic components, and the values that underpin it.

Nationalism and National Identity: Diverging Concepts

Before discussing the basic components of Russian identity, its evolution, and its various definitions by different schools of Russian political thought, often within the framework of the so-called Russian idea, it is important to address the following question: What is "national identity," and in what ways does it differ from other forms of identity, such as ethnic, religious, and class?

To define national identity, it is necessary first to explore the following questions: (1) What factors constitute a nation? Are nation and ethnos the same? Is the "political nation," as expressed through the medium of state structures, the same as "ethnic nation"? (2) Can a cohesive national identity be forged among different ethnic groups through the actions of centralized power structures? What is required to make such efforts successful and lasting? (3) Under what circumstances do such forcibly forged identities begin to fracture and perhaps disintegrate into their constituent components, including efforts by different ethnic groups to establish political identities by creating separate states?

The relationship between "nation" in the political sense—namely, the state, which is not always coterminous with the ethnos—and "nation" in the sense of a largely homogeneous ethnic and cultural entity is a controversial issue within the modern international system. Many so-called nation-states are, in fact, multiethnic entities, some of which may have active or latent ambitions of forming separate states wherein political and ethnic boundaries coincide. Moreover, often an ethnic group is divided between two or more countries, hence the newly developed notion of "nations without states." However, ethnicity—descent from common ancestors—does not always determine a group's or collectivity's sense of identity, meaning its concept of "self" and the values that give meaning, form, and purpose to it. In certain cases or at particular moments of history, religion can be a more binding force and defining component of collective identity than ethnicity. Examples include the Catholics and Protestants in Northern Ireland; Serbs and Croats; Serbs and Bosnians; and the Lebanese Maronites and Muslims.[47] Often, communities slide from one type of identity to another, and overlap is frequent. Anthony Smith has noted that "for the greater part of human history religious and ethnic identities have been very close, if not identical."[48] The experience of having lived under different sociocultural structures can create significant differences within an ethnic group that prove insurmountable. This "growing apart" makes unification of territorially scattered ethnic groups unachievable, even if other barriers could be eliminated.

Also significant is the point at which a dormant feeling of distinctiveness based on ethnicity or religion becomes a conscious sense of nationhood, seeking political expression within a particular territory by creating a state, thus transforming latent grievances into a quest for national self-determination.[49] This leads to consideration of the relationship between nationalism and national identity. Are these two concepts the same? Or do they represent different notions of the "collective self"? That the two are intimately connected cannot be denied. According to one author, "Nationalism is the expression of the community's sense of identity and purpose as articulated by a myth-symbol complex."[50] Because nationalism can also serve as a political ideology with detailed prescriptions for the society's organization and its behavior toward other collectivities, nationalism and national identity are not always synonymous. Nevertheless, nationalism, as the expression of a community's sense of identity, and national identity represent a single phenomenon.

Nature of Nations, Nationalism, and National Identity

The concept of national identity—its origins, its meanings, and the attitudes imputed to it—is closely bound up with the debate on the origins of nations, their core constituents, and the nature of nationalism. Scholarly opinion on the origins of nations and their core components, and hence the origins of nationalism and national identity, is divided. The main divide is between the "primordialists" and the "modernists." The primordialist interpretation of nation is based on the idea that "national and ethnic communities are the natural units of history and integral elements of human experience."[51] Therefore, "there is nothing particularly modern about nationalism, nor is it likely to disappear with any marked alteration of 'modern conditions.' "[52] The primordialists see examples of nationalism in the ancient world: (1) nationalism based either on a sense of superiority over others, incorporating concepts such as "chosen people" or "civilized versus barbarian peoples," and (2) nationalism based on a need to resist foreign encroachment or on a desire to liberate conquered lands. In the primordialists' concept of nation, ethnicity plays a central role and is often accompanied by linguistic and religious similarity and attachment to a particular territory. These ties are strengthened by shared myths of common descent and struggles against hostile others, as well as by more mundane traditions of everyday life. These myths can have a real basis in history, can be borrowed from other cultures, or can be totally invented. The function of this complex set of myths, symbols, and traditions is to maintain or create a common identity and sense of purpose.

In the modernists' view, nations are neither natural or necessary components of society and history; they are a purely modern phenomenon and the result of the rise of capitalism and extensive bureaucratic organizations, which are both the consequence of and a contributor to the rise of centralized states and secular utilitarianism. There are different strands within the modernist perspective. Ernest Gellner emphasizes economic factors, especially the requirements of growth-oriented industrial societies, including a mobile, educated, and skilled workforce, which can only be provided within a modern state. The state, in turn, needs an ideology—nationalism—to legitimate itself.[53] Others acknowledge the supremacy of economic factors, but accord an instrumental function to ethnicity; ethnic and national units provide a useful environment for generating mass support in the struggle of various elites for wealth, power, and prestige. In the global struggle for scarce resources in a world of rapid communication, ethnic symbols and boundaries generate greater commitment and help to reconcile diverging interests under a single banner. Thus ethnicity and its symbols ultimately serve the economic and power interests of elites rather than the cultural goals that are proclaimed to be its objectives.[54]

Another strand of modernist theory, expounded in Benedict Anderson's "imagined communities," is cultural-psychological, although it also has strong economic motivations. In Anderson's view, the emergence of nations and nationalism is closely related to two modern phenomena: the erosion of religion in modern societies, which provided at least partial answers to the problem of mortality, and the development of so-called print capitalism. According to Anderson, the decline of religion creates the need to find alternative modes of association and affiliation that can help individuals grapple with problems of mortality. The spread of print capitalism or, even more intensely, the communications revolution makes it possible to create such associations and affiliations in the form of imagined communities. These form the basis of nations, which are both sovereign and limited, through which a sense of immortality can be evoked, and with which otherwise anonymous individuals can identify. Such imagined communities thus come to serve both psychological and economic needs.[55]

The structuralists see a direct link between nations and modern capitalism. "Nations" are created by developing particular types of economic and political institutions according to the model that developed in Europe—the nation-state— and hence the structuralists emphasize the notion of "nation building." In the structuralists' scheme, concepts of ethnicity and ethnic cultures play little role in the process of nation building. Rather, they see the persistence of such feelings, which they often characterize as tribalism, as an impediment to nation building. All modernists agree that nationality means citizenship and is devoid of ethnic connotations and that nationalism is a civic concept meaning loyalty to the state.

Alternatives to Primordialism and Modernism

There are two other schools of thought on the origin of nations that try to bridge the gulf between the modernists and the primordialists. The first school is neoprimordialism, whose principal proponent is Walker Connor.[56] According to this school, ethnicity is at the core of nations, and nationalism is loyalty to a particular ethnic group. They play down the impact of economic factors in the emergence of nations and nationalism. They believe that the age of the multinational state may be over and that there may be a new upsurge in ethnonationalism. The rise of ethnocentric nationalisms in many of the so-called nation-states, which were created according to the structuralist model of nation building and their drive to establish ethnically based states, gives some credence to this theory. Neoprimordialists believe that the homogenizing, centralizing, and intrusive modern states have contributed to the rise of ethnocentric nationalisms by increasing local resentment.

The second school, mostly identified with Anthony Smith, combines elements of the modernist and primordialist schools. Smith admits that "nations and nationalism are modern phenomena in the sense that the basic features of the modern world require nations and nationalism." However, unlike other modernists, he does not see nations and nationalism as merely products of economic change.[57] He believes that "nations require ethnic cores if they are to survive. If they lack one, they must reinvent one."[58] He points to the persistence of ethnic ties and cultural sentiments in many parts of the world as evidence that "modern political nationalism cannot be understood without reference to the earlier ethnicities and memories and, in some cases, to pre-modern ethnic identities and communities."[59] Smith does not believe that "every modern nation must be founded on some antecedent ethnic ties," but he asserts that "many such nations have been and are based on these ties, including the first nations in the West."[60] According to Smith, paramount among these ties are certain common myths related to a nation's origins in time (when the community was born), origins in space (where the community was born), ancestry and migration (from where the community came to its present dwelling place), liberation (how a people was freed from foreign domination), and "golden age" (how a people became great). This last myth is often accompanied by one of decline and rebirth, how a people decayed and how it can be restored to past glory.

Types of Nationalism

Different interpretations of the origins of nations also result in different interpretations and types of nationalism. There are essentially two views regarding nationalism and hence two types of nationalism. One is the so-called Western view, which, in more recent times, has been characterized as "civic" nationalism. In this interpretation, citizenship, not ethnic origin, determines a person's nationality. According to this definition of nationalism, what binds people into a society is a set of common legal and ethical principles, especially its egalitarian nature, at least theoretically. It is assumed that civic (Western) nationalism is benign, nonexpansionist, and nonaggressive. These attributes of civic nationalism are disputed. Michael Ignatief notes that French revolutionary nationalism was intensely civic, with its definition of national identity based on the ideals of liberty, equality, and fraternity, yet these values "underwrote the messianic imperialism of Napoleon and the French revolutionary armies."[61] Ignatief goes further, arguing that some forms of civic nationalism, because of a belief in the superiority of their values, have expansionist tendencies.[62]

The other type of nationalism is the Eastern perspective. This view emphasizes the ethnic element as the core of national identity. A third form is characterized as the "Southern view," wherein religion forms the basis of nationality and national identity.[63]

In reality, the nature of nationalisms and hence of national identities is not clear-cut and evades neat categorization. Civic nationalisms have ethnic cores, while ethnocentric nationalisms have civic elements. As Ignatief points out, the line between "civic" and "ethnic" is often muddy because even the most "civic" nationalist societies depend on certain "ethnic" elements to sustain nationalist sentiment, while most "ethnic" societies ostensibly safeguard a host of "civic" principles. Ignatief notes that the British view themselves as an expression of a "civic nationalist paradigm," but when asked why they love their country, they often use "ethnic" justifications, such as the "English way of life."[64] Moreover, in many multicultural and multiethnic societies, "the majority community is willing to grant its citizens equal rights but feels possessive about the country and insists that, for democratic, historical, and other reasons, the definition of national identity should reflect its centrality and enshrine its deepest cultural aspirations."[65]

Even in communities and nations where religion is both the defining and the binding element, other factors, notably ethnicity, play important roles. National identities, in short, are composite phenomena within which ethnic, religious, and civic loyalties coexist, overlap, and, at times, clash.

However, if within a state a large gap develops between, on one hand, the aspirations of particular communities with common ethnic roots, historic memories, and specific myth-symbol complexes and, on the other hand, the broader society held together by civic ties, the risk of breakup becomes serious. As Anthony Smith has pointed out, the "civic kind of nationalism is a nationalism of order and control and suits existing states and their dominant ethnies, but it has little to offer many submerged ethnic minorities."[66] It is because of this factor that the intelligentsia of such communities turns to ethnic nationalism, which is often directed toward symbolic goals, such as education in a vernacular language and preservation of certain sites.

Lastly, nationalism and national identities are not static, but evolve under the influence of changing internal and external developments. Identities often develop and crystallize, sometimes in response to some form of external or internal threat. Peoples and communities become aware of their specific identities when they sense the danger of their loss.

The Evolution of Russian Identity:
Ethnic and Religious Basis

Where does Russian nationalism and hence national identity fit in the context of this conceptual framework? In what direction has it evolved historically? What direction is it likely to take in the future? To answer these questions, a brief review of the history of the development of Russian nationalism is necessary.

By the time of the Bolshevik Revolution, Russia was a multiethnic and multireligious empire, following five centuries of imperial expansion. Prior to this expansion, the Muscovite state, founded in the fourteenth century by the Great Russians, was ethnically and religiously homogeneous, with Orthodox Christianity as the most binding element of Russian society beyond village-based communal links. Despite challenges to the authority and independence of the church by powerful monarchs, such as Peter the Great and his successors, until the Bolshevik Revolution, Orthodox Christianity was a determining element of a sense of "Russianness" and Russian identity. Thus the early idea of Russian identity corresponded to the Southern concept of nationalism, with religion as its core.

In the Russian myth-symbol complex, however, the birth of the nation and the state embodying it is traced to the Kievan Rus and the state created in the ninth century, which lasted until the thirteenth century.[67] The origins of the Kievan Rus state and how it was formed are not clear. Especially, the role of the Scandinavian Vikings in its formation—and even in coining the term Rus—is highly controversial.[68] There was also a 200 year hiatus between the fall of the Kievan state and the consolidation of the Kingdom of Muscovy. There are considerable cultural, social, and political continuities between the Kievan Rus state and the Kingdom of Muscovy, although the role of these traditions in the formation of the Muscovite state's cultural and political identity and their relative weight compared to other influences, including the legacy of Mongol rule, are debated by historians.

Nevertheless, in Russia's myth-symbol complex, the legacy of the Kievan Rus is very important for several reasons. First, the perception of Muscovy as the continuation of the Kievan Rus provides Russia with historic depth. Second, the experience of the Kievan Rus provides Russia with a myth of grandeur and a sense of being beleaguered, and later defeated, by inferior peoples, notably the Mongols, and a yearning to recover lost glory. Third, religious and cultural values of the Kievan state and its social and political traditions have influenced Russia's later political and social institutions, basic values, and national identity.

Orthodox Christianity

The most important legacy of the Kievan state to Russia was Orthodox Christianity, as practiced in Byzantium. The choice of Orthodox Christianity by Prince Vladimir was largely the result of practical considerations, but it had deep cultural and value-related consequences, including effects on Russia's perception of the outside world, Christian and non-Christian.[69] The embrace of Orthodox Christianity imbued Russia with a sense of moral superiority vis-à-vis other Christians because of Orthodoxy's supposed antimaterialist and "otherworldly" dimensions and its emphasis on communal solidarity rather than on the cult of individualism, which developed in other parts of the Christian world in the following centuries, especially after the rise of Protestantism. It also made Russia feel that it was the embodiment of true Christianity after Byzantium fell to the Ottoman Muslims in 1453, hence giving rise to the view of Russia as the Third Rome.

This perception imbued Russia with a sense of uniqueness as a sui generis civilization, different both from the Catholic and Protestant West and from the Islamic East ("East" is used here in a cultural rather than geographical sense), a sense of mission and spirit of messianism. In practical terms, this led to a belief that (1) in every aspect of life, Russia must find its own special way and that foreign models flounder on Russian cultural soil; (2) Russia has a duty to protect Christianity from encroachment by others, meaning principally Muslims, but potentially other non-Orthodox Christians; and (3) Russian lands are coterminous with the true realm of Christianity. Thus Orthodox Christianity and its history became inextricably linked to Russia's cultural heritage and its national identity; to be Russian meant to be Orthodox Christian. However, the reverse was not the case, and conversion to Christianity did not make a Russian. Efforts at Christian proselytizing among the Tatars in the nineteenth century failed because "the belief that only a Russian could be a full-fledged Orthodox was strong among the ecclesiastical thinking of the Russian church. The prospect of a Christian Orthodox priest performing the Holy Mass in the Tatar language was therefore a bitter pill to swallow."[70]

Need for a Strong Center

In political and social institutions, too, Byzantium was the inspiration for the Kievan state. Yet in the structure of the state, "Byzantine ideas could never quite overcome more traditional concepts and institutions and therefore had their greatest impact . . . in the Muscovite period of the tsars."[71] Unlike Byzantium, the Kievan state was not tightly structured and resembled a feudal system, in which princes with rival claims to supremacy often warred against each other. This constant internecine strife weakened the Kievan state, making it vulnerable to attacks by Asian nomads, culminating in its fall to the Mongols.

The lesson for the new Russian state that developed around Muscovy was that to prosper and expand, Russia needed a strong government. This statist streak has proved tenacious, becoming part of Russian national ethos and identity despite periods of state breakdown.

The Role of the "Other" in the Formation of Russian Identity

The process of collective, including national, identity formation entails the need for communities not only to determine who they are and what they value, but also to decide who they are not and what they do not value. Some scholars believe that the latter may be more important. According to Samuel Huntington, "We know who we are only when we know who we are not and often only when we know whom we are against."[72] Thus the process of identity formation includes the setting up of boundaries between "us" and "them," between external and internal enemies and friends, by "a process of exclusion and inclusion." Hence the importance of the "other" or "others" in identity formation.[73]

Other scholars have challenged the theoretical value of this concept, but the history of nations and proto-nations of the ancient world demonstrates that the process of boundary setting and defining oneself in terms of opposition to an "other" has been a constant part of collective identity formation. Anthony Smith notes that throughout history, the names of many nations have been coupled together because of the function of "other" that they have performed for each other.[74]

The relationship between self, notably the collective self, and other, meaning different, need not always be hostile. However, this relationship often is hostile, sometimes extremely so.[75] In such cases, the "other" migrates from being something merely different from the self and is transmuted into the "enemy." The way in which the other is viewed takes different forms. "There are some others who are . . . perceived in less human terms, below human beings in hierarchical terms, or, in extreme cases, as non-human beings, dangerous animals that can and must be killed."[76]

The identity and character of the "other" may change, and the intensity of animosity toward it often fluctuates. In modern societies, there is seldom universal
agreement about the identity of the other or others. The picture of the "other" often
emerges as a result of a clash of competing ambitions and values, religions, or
ideologies. Invasion and occupation by foreigners are two of the most important
factors in the development of the image of "other." If a nation manages to survive
such traumatic events with the core of its culture and identity intact, it often seeks
revenge and reconquest and, if successful, conquest beyond its original borders.
This chain of action-reaction results in a tradition of viewing certain peoples or
religions as the hostile other—the enemy. These perceptions are transmitted to
future generations through a process of socialization.

Islam as the Hostile Other

The Mongol Invasion and Its Consequences for Russian Identity

An important element in the development of Russian identity has been Russia's
vulnerability to foreign invasion. The Kievan state was challenged by many adversaries from within and without and, by the time of the Mongol invasion, had been
reduced to a collection of warring princedoms. Nevertheless, it was the Mongol
conquest that led to the Kievan state's disappearance, ushering in 200 years of
Mongol domination that caused a significant rupture in Russia's historic evolution.
Besides its direct effects, the Mongol invasion opened Russia to the intrusion of
other peoples and states. It enabled Poland and Lithuania to absorb parts of Russia,
thus marking "a point of no return in the branching of the Russian people into
Belorussians in the east, Ukrainians in the southwest, and the Great Russians in
the northeast." It also "facilitated the occupation of the lands along the Baltic Sea
by German knights and later by Swedes."[77] The Mongol invasion devastated major
urban centers of Russia, although this devastation was on a much smaller scale
than that inflicted on the Central Asians and Iran.[78]

Yet in the consciousness of the Russians, the Mongols—later mixed with other
Turkic peoples—stand as one of two "hostile others," and perhaps the primary one.
A wide range of Russia's later problems and deficiencies, including those related
to its social attitudes and political culture, are attributed to the Mongol influence
and the period of the so-called Tatar yoke. Three of the most important examples
are Russian beliefs that (1) the Mongol invasion and later Mongol-Tatar dominion
sapped Russia's energies and greatly contributed to its backwardness; (2) Mongol-
Tatar domination severed Russia from the West for centuries, thus preventing the
country from benefiting from the scientific and economic changes that transformed
Europe from the time of the Renaissance onward; and (3) Russia inherited the
dictatorial and authoritarian tendencies of the Mongols, and, therefore, democracy
did not flourish in Russia.[79]

Most Russian and other Western historians dismiss any positive contribution of the Mongols to Russia's cultural development because they believe that the Mongols did not have much to contribute. According to Nicholas V. Riasanovsky, "they [the Mongols] had to borrow virtually everything from alphabets to advisers from the conquered peoples to enable their states to exist. As one of these advisers remarked, an empire could be won on horseback, but not ruled from the saddle."[80]

In the late 1920s, however, one branch of the Eurasian school of thought developed what might be called a revisionist view of the Mongols, giving them a more positive interpretation. The Eurasianists emphasized the political role of the Mongols in the development of the Muscovite state and considered the "Muscovite Tsar and the Muscovite state as successors to the Mongol Khan and the Golden Horde."[81] They maintained that the Mongols exerted a great deal of influence in "transforming weak and divided appanage Russia into a powerful, disciplined and monolithic autocracy."[82] In the Eurasianist theory, "Institutions, legal norms, and the psychology of Muscovite Russia have all been described as a legacy of Jenghiz Khan."[83] Tatar intellectuals in recent times have also emphasized the positive impact of the Mongols, not only in helping to create the Muscovite state, but also in helping the Russians resist pressures from the Germans and the Lithuanians.[84] According to Rafael Khakimov, "A union with the Mongols protected Rus' from invasion from the West . . . [and] it laid the foundation of a new statehood. The unification of the Russian lands around Moscow began and took place thanks to the Golden Horde."[85]

The question of where the balance of negative and positive falls regarding the impact of the Mongols on Russia's evolution is hard to settle.[86] What is clear is that in the Russians' myth-symbol complex, the Mongol invasion and the ensuing Mongol-Tatar domination constitute major calamities. Moreover, ending Mongol-Tatar rule is interpreted as the beginning of Russia's national renaissance. Mongol rule also contributed to the unification of Russia's warring princes, the consolidation of the Orthodox Church, and the deepening of Christian belief among the Russians.

When they first invaded Russia, the Mongols were pagans, but Özbek Khan (1312–1343) converted to Islam, linking in the Russians' minds the images of Islam and the Mongols. Thus Islam acquired the image of hostile "other," although on religious matters the Mongols were tolerant and the Orthodox Church was allowed to operate freely. They also avoided efforts to proselytize or Islamize the Russians. The Mongol invasion "made unity and cohesiveness a high priority value in Russian society and the Russian state."[87] Moreover, "Out of that experience and the necessity of building a strong state to overthrow the Mongol yoke came an emphasis on the strength to be found in a common religion, Orthodoxy, and in a common allegiance to the grand prince (later the tsar)."[88] These characteristics have formed important parts of Russian identity and nationalism throughout its history, including the Soviet period, although during Soviet rule, communism replaced Orthodoxy as the country's religion in the official creed. Thus the conquest of Kazan by Ivan the Terrible was also viewed as the triumph of Christianity over Islam, symbolized by the cross placed above the crescent atop Russian churches.

Muslim resistance to Russian expansion, especially in the North Caucasus, where it was carried out under the banner of Islam, along with conflicts with Muslim states—the Ottomans and Persian dynasties—solidified Russia's view of Muslims as hostile "others." Russian-Ottoman rivalry in particular may have been driven largely by geopolitical factors and worldly interests, but it also had a religiocultural dimension: the Ottomans considered themselves to be caliphs and thus defenders of Islam, while Russia saw itself as the Third Rome. These religiocultural factors contributed to the aspirations of Catherine the Great and her successors to free Constantinople from Muslim rule. These aspirations were shared by such intellectuals as Dostoevsky.

In sum, Russia has never viewed Islam as an intellectual and spiritual rival to Orthodoxy or to the Russian culture, as it has the West and Western Christianity. Nevertheless, Islam and Muslims, although they may have been perceived as inferior, have been seen as a threat to Russian interests and a hindrance to Russia's territorial and cultural expansion.

Fears of a Unified Muslim Bloc

Historically, divisions within the Muslim world and the preponderance of state interests over consideration of Islamic solidarity have always prevented the formation of a united Muslim front against Russian expansion. Nevertheless, throughout its modern history, Russia has been concerned about any potential cooperation among Turko-Muslim peoples. These fears were rekindled by the time of perestroika and the ensuing increase in contacts between the Soviet Union's Turkic speaking populations and Turkey. The Soviet Union's collapse opened further opportunities for intra-Turkic collaboration. Turkey embarked on an aggressive program of cultural expansion in the newly independent republics of Central Asia and the Caucasus and within the Russian Federation. It built mosques and religious and secular schools in the former Soviet republics and the Russian Federation, sponsored thousands of students from various post-Soviet Muslim republics and the Turkic populations of the Russian Federation to study in Turkish universities, and promoted the replacement of Russian by modern Turkish as the lingua franca for Muslims of Central Asia and Russia.[89]

Russian officials generally do not openly express concerns about the rising Turkish cultural influence or the fear that such influence may be a prelude to political unification of the Russian Federation's Turkic-speaking peoples, but Russian politicians and analysts do, especially those of a nationalist orientation. Vladimir Zhirinovsky, leader of the nationalist Liberal Democratic Party of Russia (LDPR), has reportedly said, "Pan-Turkism threatens Russia, for in Russia there are a large number of Turkish-speaking people."[90] This will offer Turkey the opportunity to extend its influence. Consequently, "The great and talented Turkish people will be worthy of living in the very center of the world . . . while this weak, powerless Russian nation must perish. Will the history of mankind thus be arranged? No, this is impermissible."[91]

The president of North Ossetia, Alexander Dzasokhov, also expressed concern about the rise of "pan-Turkic moods" in the North Caucasus.[92] Russian ex-officials are more open about Turkey's activities, particularly its military and clandestine services in the promotion of pan-Turkism.[93]

Certain developments within the Russian Federation itself, such as the establishment of the Assembly of Turkic Peoples in 1991 and talk about the creation of a Volga-Ural (Idel-Ural) Turkic Confederation (comprising Tatarstan, Bashkortostan, Chuvashia, Mordovia, Marii-El, and Udmurtia), even if limited to small and not very influential circles, help solidify these fears and are manipulated by ultra-nationalists.[94] The following statement in a *Komsomolskaya Pravda* article titled "The Idea of Ottoman Empire Lives on, and Is Already Winning?" is attributed to Vyacheslav Timofeev, chairman of the Turkic Assembly (1993–97) and onetime member of the Chuvash Republic's parliament:

> We need to proceed toward independence through unity. We have to strive toward the unity of language, opinions, and actions, unity of statehood, army, and flag. So how are we going to unite? Very simple. We shall begin to communicate in Turkish. As we have learned Russian, so we shall learn Turkish. We do not have an alternative. Either continue to live under the yoke or pave the way to independence.[95]

The article suggests that some of those non-Muslim Turkic peoples who go to Turkey or study in Turkish schools set up in the Russian Federation often convert to Islam and adopt Islamic names.[96] Here it should be noted that many Russians, notably nationalist elements, see the variant of Islam sponsored by the secular Turkish government as more dangerous than extremist or stricter versions because it pretends to be progressive. Thus Alexei Malashenko points out that Zhirinovsky views Islamic fundamentalism more favorably than the Turkish variant.[97]

The first step toward achieving these objectives is to change the alphabet from Cyrillic to Latin, a step that Tatarstan has already taken.[98] In light of these developments, in 2000, the State Duma of the Russian Federation asked committees on security, science and education, and nationality to assess the potential threat that such a change would pose to Russia's security. Their joint report concluded that such changes "will have negative political consequences by causing the isolation of the population of Tatarstan from other peoples of the Russian Federation, including those who are Turkic. Moreover, the implementation of such reforms will further distance the subjects of the Federation from the federal center."[99] The report notes that because "written Turkish employs the Latin alphabet, the perspective of its implementation as an official language in the Republic of Tatarstan will give renewed incentive to cultural expansion of Turkey in this subject of the Russian Federation, which, in turn, will contribute to the realization of the long-term geopolitical aspirations of Ankara."[100] It also accuses the Turkish-sponsored mosques and schools in Dagestan, notably in Makhachkala, of "popularizing the ideology of Pan-Turkism . . . [and] encouraging among the listeners a desire toward national self-assertion and separatism."[101]

Pan-Turkism and Islam historically have had an ambiguous relationship. One strain of pan-Turkism views Islam as having been harmful to the Turks, whereas others see Islam and Islamic civilization as creating common bonds among Turkic peoples and enhancing their unity. Although within the Russian Federation there are divisions between the pan-Turkists and Islamists, in Russia's "image of the other" the two are closely linked.

Non-Turkic Muslims and Russia

The Turkic peoples are not the only Muslims with whom the Russians have had troubled relations. There were conflicts with various Iranian dynasties in the course of Russia's southern thrust until Iran's decadence and weakness eliminated it from the regional power equation. In the 1940s, the Soviet Union tried to divide Iran by establishing socialist puppet regimes in Iranian Azerbaijan and Kurdistan. Russia's embroilment in Afghanistan during the 1980s, which ended in its withdrawal after failing to subdue the Islamic resistance, is another example of its adversarial encounter with Islam.

Since the USSR's disintegration, the Russians have been concerned about potential linkages between the non-Turkic Muslims within Russia and the other states on the territory of the former Soviet Union (FSU) and their kin in the neighboring regions. Thus Zhirinovsky is worried not only about the potential emergence of a pan-Turkish bloc, but also about Iran's desire to create a so-called Greater Iran.[102] Even former Russian prime minister Yevgenii Primakov once accused Iran of wanting to create a "Farsistan" land of Persian speakers.[103]

In short, the confrontation with Turkic and other Muslim peoples solidified the Russians' self-identity as Russians and Orthodox Christians and confirmed their sense of cultural superiority.[104] Consequently, even during the Soviet period, when there was an effort to blunt ethnic and religious identities, Muslims were never considered to be full and equal citizens. This treatment, in turn, contributed to the consolidation of Muslims' separate sense of identity.

The Chechen War and Its Consequences: Enhancing Islam's Image as the Hostile Other

Russia's encounter with the Chechens, beginning in the eighteenth century, has been very bitter. Nowhere else in their conquest of Muslim lands did the Russians face such an unyielding enemy. To overcome the Chechens' resistance, the Russians, notably the famous general Aleksei Yermolov, employed especially harsh measures that were criticized even by a number of Russian intellectuals and literary figures as well as foreign observers.[105] The Chechen experience under the Soviet system, which included mass deportation directed by Stalin in 1944, was equally traumatic.

In view of this experience, it was perhaps natural that Gorbachev's reforms should lead to the emergence of nationalist and proindependence groups in Chechnya. However, a Russian-Chechen war was not inevitable. Rather, the war occurred because of power struggles at the center and the contradictions that Gorbachev's reforms had created within the USSR's political system. This situation led Moscow to pursue contradictory policies toward the Chechen nationalist movement, including a halfhearted use of force in November 1991.[106]

The conduct of Russia's policy toward Chechnya after the republic became effectively independent in 1991 until the outbreak of full-scale war in 1994 also left much to be desired. It is difficult to explain how the Russian military allowed so much of its hardware to fall into Chechen hands.[107] Other contributing factors were the growing disunity within the Chechen leadership, Chechen president Dzhokhar Dudaev's inability to resolve it, and his growing tendency to authoritarian rule, which exacerbated these divisions and rivalries.[108] Other difficulties rooted in the character of the Chechen and Russian constitutions and ongoing presidential-parliamentary power struggles in Chechnya and in the Russian Federation further diminished chances of reaching an agreement between the two actors during this period.[109] Personality clashes between Yeltsin and Dudaev were also significant factors.

More important, it appears that by 1993 Russia had abandoned the idea of reaching an agreement with Dudaev and was helping his opponents. According to John Dunlop, "The cornerstone of the Yeltsin-Shakhrai [Sergei Shakhrai was one of Yeltsin's principal advisers on Chechnya] strategy for managing the Chechen crisis was to avoid all personal contact with Dudaev. This, of course, was not acceptable to Dudaev."[110] It was thus that both sides drifted into a devastating war. There is a wide range of conspiratorial theories about the origins of the Chechen War, including those involving rivalries among criminal gangs. These factors may have played a role, but they cannot be used in an analysis of the causes of the war. Theories of miscalculation or bureaucratic rivalries offer more appropriate explanations. The war ended up not being the blitzkrieg that the military had apparently promised President Yeltsin, but a long-drawn-out-war that claimed the lives of nearly 4,000 Russian military personnel, plus nearly 18,000 wounded and 1,906 missing. Some observers have attributed the "ineffectiveness and the snail's pace of the initial assault on Chechnya" to the reluctance of "Russian officers to involve themselves in a matter properly assigned to the Ministry of Internal Affairs and the 'Internal Troops.' "[111] Others have cited personal failings of the defense minister, Pavel Grachev.[112] Finally, Russia was forced to sign a cease-fire agreement with the Chechens because of mounting opposition to the war among the Russian population and the approaching presidential election of December 1996.[113]

After months of negotiations beginning in March 1996, a cease-fire was finally signed in the Dagestani town of Khasavyurt on 31 August 1996 by General Alexander Lebed, secretary of the Russian Security Council, and Aslan Maskhadov, then the Chechen military chief of staff and later Chechnya's president.[114] The Khasavyurt agreement was a vague document that in some respects was in direct contradiction of the Russian constitution; this characteristic made its implementation without constitutional revision impossible. This may explain why neither President Yeltsin nor Prime Minister Viktor Chernomyrdin endorsed the agreement formally.[115] More cynical observers attributed this attitude to the fact that the Russian leadership had no intention of implementing the agreement. However, on 12 May 1997, President Yeltsin and Chechen president Aslan Maskhadov signed a formal peace agreement, the Treaty on Peace and the Principles of Relations between the Russian Federation and the Chechen Republic of Ichkeria. This accord committed both sides to "refrain in their international relations from the threat or use of force" and to "build [their] relations in accordance with the generally accepted principles and norms of international law."[116]

The period between September 1996 and September 1999, when Russia first resumed bombing Chechnya because of the incursions of the rebel forces led by Shamil Basaev and Khattab into Dagestan, was not used effectively either by the Chechen leadership or by the Russians to stabilize the situation. Rather, the evolution of events in Chechnya took a negative turn. The most destructive development was the proliferation of various armed groups, including those that used extremist Islam as their organizing principle, ultimately plunging the country into disorder.[117]

The Islamic Factor in the Chechen Conflict

The question of the main impetus—Islam or nationalism—behind the Chechens' drive for independence can never be settled conclusively because Islam has been integrated into Chechen national identity and nationalist mythology. More important, it is not even clear if the Chechens' goal in the beginning was total independence, which would have effectively ruled out any possibility of compromise with Russia, or if the interplay of a complex set of factors—ranging from power struggles in the Kremlin and tribal politics in Chechnya to international and regional geopolitical rivalries over the domination of oil and gas transportation routes from the Caspian Sea (both functioning and proposed)—made a Russian-Chechen armed conflict inevitable. Nevertheless, Islam did have a role in strengthening the Chechens' drive for independence. Some Chechen leaders were more Islam oriented and, indeed, wanted to create an Islamic state in Chechnya.

Dzhokhar Dudaev, who became identified with Chechen independence, was not a particularly observant Muslim. He was a product of the Soviet system and, as a fighter pilot during the Soviet-Afghan War, had participated in bombing raids on Muslims. Russian authorities used this fact to undermine his Islamic credentials. Sergei Stepashin, the former head of Russia's Federal Security Service (FSB), noted, "Dudaev did not create any Islamic state. In general, if one can put it, he is an anti-Islamist. He carpet-bombed his fellow Muslims in Afghanistan."[118] Most likely, Dudaev was not a religious person. Nevertheless, it is conceivable that once he became engaged in the Chechen independence movement, he discovered his

Muslim roots and, more significantly, the usefulness of religious zeal in achieving his political goals.[119] What is clear is that Muslim groups in Chechnya, such as the Islamic Path, supported Dudaev's bid for independence.[120]

Yet in his early statements, Dudaev made little reference to Islam and, during his first year in power, ruled out the establishment of an Islamic state.[121] On the contrary, he made specific statements opposing the creation of an Islamic state. In an interview with *Literaturnaya Gazeta* in August 1992, he said, "Where any religion prevails over a secular constitutional organization of the state, either the Spanish Inquisition or Islamic fundamentalism will emerge."[122] To ensure that this would not happen, the 1992 constitution of the self-declared sovereign Chechen republic stated that "religious organizations are separate from the state, administer their affairs autonomously, and operate independently from state organs."[123] However, growing Chechen-Russian tensions, Moscow's clandestine activities in the republic, and the growth of Islamic sentiments—partly because of the factors already mentioned and partly because of the influence of external forces, notably various foreign Islamist groups and missionaries—led Dudaev to resort to Islam as a mobilizing and legitimizing instrument. Thus in August 1994, the National Congress of the Chechen Peoples adopted a resolution giving Dudaev the power to declare an Islamic uprising in the tradition of *Gazavat* of Imam Shamil and other Muslim leaders in Chechnya.[124] In November 1994, Dudaev declared Chechnya an Islamic state and formed an Islamic Battalion to counter the activities of opposition forces supported by Moscow. He further suggested the application of Shari'a in the republic in order to counter Russian aggression at a special congress of religious and clan leaders.[125]

Once the Russian military campaign began in full, the Chechen public's identification with Islam intensified, and the Chechen fighters took to wearing green headbands with the words "Allahu Akbar" (God is great)—the battle cry of all Islamists—written on them, participated in public prayers on a regular basis, and abstained from alcohol.[126] Zelimkhan Yanderbiev, who became Chechnya's acting president after Dudaev's assassination in April 1996, went even further in using Islam for political ends. He declared that he would "take the lead in a war, in a 'jihad' of the Chechen people in the name of Allah and in the name of the freedom of the Chechen people."[127]

The end of the first round of the Russian-Chechen War did not reduce Islam's function as an instrument in the hands of both the government and opposition forces in their struggle to gain popular legitimacy. Shortly after the signing of the Khasavyurt agreement, Yanderbaev abolished secular courts, created a supreme Shari'a court, and implemented a criminal code for Chechnya based on the Shari'a.[128] Among the crimes listed in this new criminal code was apostasy, defined as openly advocating the rejection of Islam, the punishment for which was death.[129]

The Islamization trend continued after Aslan Maskhadov's election as Chechen president in January 1997. During a trip to Turkey, Maskhadov announced his intention to create an Islamic state in Chechnya and to change the republic's name to the "Islamic Republic of Ichkeria."[130] Moreover, he signed a decree that extended Shari'a to all aspects of the state and formed a commission of religious leaders to draft a constitution based on the Qu'ran and the Shari'a.[131]

In short, if Islam was not the main impetus behind the Chechen independence movement, in the course of the Russian-Chechen conflict it became the main unifying factor and later the cornerstone of postconflict Chechen nation building. Paradoxically, Islam also became a major cause of the failure of such efforts as different interpretations of Islam divided the Chechens.

The growing trend toward Islamization in Chechnya widened the political and cultural gap between Grozny and the federal center, thus reducing the chances of reaching a mutually acceptable compromise about the country's final status, which the Khasavyurt and Yeltsin/Maskhadov agreements had left unclear, even if other barriers to such a final compromise could be removed. For example, beginning in September 1997, Chechen authorities televised a series of public executions, which led to protests from Moscow. Chechnya's deputy prosecutor general dismissed Russian concerns and noted, "It does not matter how much Russia shows its indignation. We are living in an independent state, we have our own Shari'a courts, and we shall punish criminals according to Shari'a law."[132]

Radicalization of Chechen Islam: External Influence and the Contagion Effect

Resort to Islam as a source of unity and an instrument of nation building proved disastrous in Chechnya. The process of Islamization created new sources of division in an already highly fragmented society and became an ideological tool to propel ambitious individuals to power. Since Maskhadov had already gone a long way toward molding Chechnya's social and political system according to an Islamic blueprint, his competitors had to adopt an even more radical version of Islam in order to make his program appear inadequate. This dynamic played an important role in the spread of a more puritanical interpretation of Islam inspired by the Wahhabi school. Thus Shamil Basaev and his collaborator, Khattab, adopted the Wahhabi vision as a vehicle to advance their ambitions.

Islamization also intensified the level of external involvement, mostly nongovernmental groups and organizations, but often with the knowledge and acquiescence of the governments of certain countries. Foreign involvement in Chechnya began before the first Russian-Chechen War and had many reasons in addition to the Islamic factor. Particularly important was the regional and international rivalry in the post-Soviet space, notably over the issue of pipelines carrying Caspian oil to world markets.[133]

Details of external involvement in the Chechen War will be discussed in part III of this volume in the sections dealing with the impact of the Islamic factor on Russia's external relations. Here, suffice it to say that foreign involvement in Chechnya was substantial, leading to intensified Russian fears of the threat from the Muslim South and strengthening the Russian view of Muslims as hostile "others."

The Contagion Effect

The Chechen conflict helped spread radical Islamist ideas to other parts of the Russian Federation, especially areas in its immediate vicinity, most notably Dagestan.[134] In the North Caucasus, Islam has historically had the deepest roots in Dagestan, and by late 1989 an Islamic revival was already under way in the republic. Nevertheless, the Chechen conflict gave a decidedly radical tone to Dagestan's Islamist movement. As Arab and other missionaries and fighters poured into Chechnya, they also crossed into Dagestan. Their preaching and activities caused deep rifts between them and the followers of the region's long-established Sufi traditions, at times leading to violent clashes.

The Russian-Chechen cease-fire of 1996 did not stem the tide of Islam's radicalization in Dagestan; rather, it contributed to it because many Islamists who had left Dagestan to fight against the Russians in Chechnya returned home. Dagestan's internal dynamics—deteriorating economic conditions, widespread unemployment, and crime—helped the recruitment efforts of the Islamists.[135] In the summer of 1998, Islamist influence culminated in the creation of a miniature Islamic state, also known as an "autonomous Shari'a territory," on the territory of the three villages of Karamakhi, Chabanmakhi, and Kadar.[136]

The activities of various Chechen leaders inspired by Islamist views, irredentist aspirations, and geopolitical ambitions also contributed to this expansion of Islamic extremism. Parts of eastern Dagestan, including the village of Khasavyurt, where the 1996 cease-fire agreement was signed, once formed part of Chechnya and are now predominantly settled by the Akkin Chechens. Thus uniting Chechnya and Dagestan under the banner of Islam would have satisfied the Chechens' territorial ambitions. Furthermore, the Chechens wanted to gain access to the Caspian Sea, which would have been possible only by incorporating Dagestan and its port capital of Makhachkala. The nationalist and Islamist aspirations of Chechens toward Dagestan met in the vision of creating an Islamic state by uniting the lands that supposedly had once been ruled by Imam Shamil. To prepare for the realization of this ultimate goal, in August 1997, Movladi Udogov, Chechnya's first deputy prime minister (and later its foreign minister), organized a meeting of more than thirty groups representing Muslim nationalities from across the North Caucasus to found the Nation of Islam. In April 1998, at Udogov's insistence, representatives of the two republics, Chechnya and Dagestan, met in Grozny to found the Congress of the Peoples of Chechnya and Dagestan. Shamil Basaev, at that time acting Chechen prime minister (although he later broke ranks with Maskhadov), was elected as leader of the congress. Upon his election, Basaev declared the congress's ultimate goal to be the unification of Chechnya and Dagestan.[137]

There were also efforts at coordination among various armed Islamist groups in

Chechnya and Dagestan. In December 1997, Salman Raduev, leader of a detachment of Chechen war veterans known as the Army of Dzhokhar (named after Dzhokhar Dudaev) and organizer of a 1996 Chechen raid on Kizilyurt, Dagestan, signed an agreement with the Unified Command of Dagestani Mujahideen, an armed wing of the Jama'at of Dagestan. The agreement, which formalized an anti-Russian military union, stated, "Our common enemy, the Russian Empire, does its utmost to preserve its presence and influence in the Caucasus and prevent Shari'a from striking deep roots in our region so that an integral Islamic state should not be formed."[138]

Yet the Islamists could not unite Chechnya and Dagestan. On the contrary, their activities intensified internal divisions and personal rivalries in both republics. In July 1998, there were clashes between members of the Chechen National Guard loyal to Maskhadov and 2,000 militants, including members of Chechnya's Islamic Regiment and the Shari'a Guard, in the city of Gudermes.[139] Following these events, the breach between Wahhabi-inspired Islamists and the Maskhadov government became inevitable; Maskhadov banned Wahhabism in Chechnya, disbanded the Islamic Regiment and Shari'a Guards, and expelled Arab missionaries, accusing them of wanting to impose an alien ideology on the country.[140]

These ideological and other rivalries accelerated the process of the breakdown of law and order in Chechnya and exerted a destabilizing influence on Dagestan. One aspect of this phenomenon was increasing attacks on Russian and Dagestani military installations. Another manifestation was conflict between militant Islamists and traditional Muslims. In May 1997, a violent confrontation took place between 400 Islamist combatants and local inhabitants—followers of traditional Sufism—in the village of Chabanmakhi. The conflict was stopped by the intervention of Dagestan's Ministry of Internal Affairs.[141] In December 1997, a group calling itself the Central Front for the Liberation of the Caucasus and Dagestan claimed responsibility for an attack on a Russian army base in the Buinaksk region of Dagestan.[142]

In the summer of 1999, large-scale warfare erupted in the North Caucasus as several thousand Muslim militants crossed into Dagestan from Chechnya with the stated objective of liberating Dagestan from Russian rule and establishing an Islamic state.[143] Chechen president Maskhadov condemned the raid; however, Basaev and Khattab assumed leadership of the invading forces. According to villagers and reporters in the region, in addition to Chechens and Dagestanis, the insurgents included Arabs, Central Asians, and other foreigners.[144] Within days of the incursion, an organization called the Shura (Islamic Council) of Dagestan announced the formation of an Islamic state and appealed to "mujahedin and defenders of the religion of God, who have raised the banner of Islam and the honor and dignity of the Muslim *Ummah* (Community) with a call to support the Muslims of Dagestan."[145] This attempt by Islamist militants to push Russia out of the region and establish Shari'a rule led to the reintroduction of large-scale Russian forces into the North Caucasus and provided one of the principal reasons for the renewal of the Russian-Chechen conflict.[146]

In addition to reigniting warfare, the expansion of Islamic extremism hardened

Russian views of Islam as a hostile other. Although Russian officials were often careful to distinguish between the extremists and the rest of Russia's Muslim population, the actions of Islamists enhanced both elite and popular fears of an Islamic threat to Russian security and territorial integrity. In February 1998, Sergei Stepashin said, "We believe the greatest threat comes from Islamic fundamentalism, namely Wahhabism. It is a special form of extremism similar to terrorism. We should not wait for this fire to spread to Moscow and St. Petersburg."[147] The 1999 incursion by Muslim militants into Dagestan confirmed these fears within the Russian government and population.

Terrorist Attacks in Russian Cities

Shortly after these incursions, Russia experienced a series of terrorist bombings in Moscow and other Russian cities that intensified its fears of an Islamic threat and contributed to an unprecedented surge of anti-Muslim feelings. The first bombing, which occurred on 31 August 1999, targeted Moscow's Okhotny Ryad shopping center, killing one person and injuring dozens. Because the blast happened following the incursions into Dagestan, Russian minister of internal affairs Vladimir Rushailo said that he was not ruling out the possibility of a linkage between Dagestani extremists and the bombings. Meanwhile, a little-known extremist group called the Islamic Army for the Liberation of Dagestan claimed responsibility for the act and warned, "Terrorist acts will continue on the territory of Russia until all Russian troops withdraw from Dagestan."[148] Yet some Russian officials expressed skepticism about this claim; Yevgenii Ryabtsev, the Internal Affairs Ministry spokesman in Dagestan observed, "I think [the militants] are just trying to give themselves more weight. [The claim] doesn't ring true."[149] There were other suspects as well. A flyer found at the scene of the explosion indicated that a so-called Revolutionary Writers Union opposed to materialism and consumerism may have been responsible for the attack.[150]

More devastating both in human and psychological terms was a series of attacks on apartment blocks that rocked Moscow and other cities in September 1999, resulting in the death of more than 300 people. In the Dagestani city of Buinaksk, a bomb destroyed a military housing complex near the site of ongoing fighting between Islamist insurgents and federal forces.[151] Further north, an apartment building in the city of Volgodonsk in Rostov Oblast and two apartment buildings in Moscow were destroyed.[152] Although both the Maskhadov government and Basaev denied knowledge of or involvement in the crimes, Russian authorities claimed that Chechen or Chechen-trained Islamic extremists were responsible. A few months after the attacks, Vladimir Putin, at that time Russia's acting president, announced that security forces had identified a camp in Chechnya's Uras-Martan region where the terrorists were trained.[153]

Six Dagestanis were later convicted of the bombing in Buinaksk,[154] and Russian authorities announced that the bombings in Moscow and Volgodoansk were carried out on the orders of Chechen rebel commanders Khattab and Sheikh Abu-Umar.[155]

However, despite Russian claims, the question of responsibility for the attacks remains a controversial subject, with some people accusing Russian security services of having orchestrated them in order to justify a military assault on Chechnya. In 2001, former FSB officer Alexander Litvineko and historian Yurii Felshtinskii claimed in their book *The FSB Blows Up Russia* that the Russian Federal Security Service orchestrated the bombing.[156] Russian oligarch Boris Berezovsky aired similar accusations in his 2002 documentary film *Assault on Russia*.[157]

The greatest loss of life occurred during a terrorist attack in October 2002, when a group of Chechen extremists calling themselves the "Guardians of the Righteous" took over the Dubrovka Theater in Moscow and held about 800 people, including several foreigners, hostage for fifty-eight hours. The crisis ended after three days when the Russian Special Forces, in an attempt to incapacitate the militants, released a nerve gas into the theater, resulting in the death of all the hostage takers and at least 120 hostages.[158] The leader of the hostage takers was Movsar Baraev, nephew of Chechen rebel leader Arbi Baraev, who was killed in 2001. Their principal demand was that Russia withdraw its troops from Chechnya. Russian authorities claimed that the hostage takers were operating with the knowledge and approval of Aslan Maskhadov, in concert with accomplices in Arab and other Muslim countries.[159] According to some reports, a Russian law-enforcement source claimed that they had been "contacting accomplices in the United Arab Emirates and Turkey."[160] A distinguishing feature of the hostage takers was their avowed willingness to die. In a video shown on the Qatar-based television Al-Jazeera, one of the militants said, "I swear by God, we are more keen on dying than you are on living. . . . Each one of us is willing to sacrifice himself for the sake of God and independence of Chechnya."[161] This attitude reflects the influence of Shahidism (martyrdom seeking), an offshoot of Jihadism, among segments of the younger generation of Chechens. Another distinguishing characteristic was the presence of women among the rebel ranks. Shahidist tendencies appeared again two months later when suicide bombers destroyed the main administrative building of the pro-Moscow Kadyrov government in Grozny, killing dozens and wounding more than 100.[162] Suicide bombings continued in the northern Caucasus and Moscow during the course of 2003. In early July, two female suicide bombers blew themselves up at an outdoor rock concert in Moscow killing fourteen people.

Consequences of the Chechen Conflict for Russian Identity

The Chechen conflict and its consequences, notably terrorist attacks within the Russian heartland either perpetrated by Islamist extremists or attributed to them, deepened the religious and ethnic chasm in Russia and in general helped develop a more monoethnic, monoreligious, and monocultural collective consciousness among ethnic Russians. It also enhanced the enemy image of Islam and the Muslim world as an active or latent threat to Russia's security and identity.

On the religious level, the growing use by the Chechens of Islam and Islamic symbols led the Russians to employ Christian symbols. Thus Russian soldiers departing for the Chechen war front were blessed by high-ranking clergy during special ceremonies. It was also reported that some Russian tanks had religious pictures on them, and to the Muslim cry of "Allah-u-Akbar!" Russian soldiers responded with the cry of "Christ has risen!" Following an agreement between the Orthodox Church and the Defense Ministry, priests were sent to war fronts in Chechnya. According to Father Safrony, chaplain to the Russian paratroopers fighting on the Chechen-Dagestani border, the main goal was "to raise the fighting spirit of the army and explain to the soldiers that they are performing an important duty."[163] Although not clearly stated, part of this duty was to defend Christianity against Islam. The Chechen War has brought the military and the Orthodox Church closer together, resulting in the establishment of more than 100 churches and chapels on Russian military bases.[164] Other sources claim that military academies have employed priests to instruct recruits in Orthodox beliefs.[165] But since the Russian army also includes Muslims, some of whom have fought in the Chechen War, this development has elicited negative reactions from Muslim leaders. Mufti Ravil Gainutdin has said that "we [Muslims] are seriously concerned that certain leaders of the Defense Ministry are creating a split along ethnic and religious lines by placing Orthodoxy over other religions. . . . Is the army made up only of Orthodox?"[166] Anti-Muslim feelings, particularly toward Chechens, have also intensified, as has animosity toward other non-Slavs, especially those from the Caucasus region, who mostly have darker complexions and are referred to as *chyornie* (blacks). This animosity was translated into official harassment—verbal and more substantive—in the form of large-scale expulsions and mistreatment by the police.[167]

Attacks by groups of right-wing (neo-Nazi) youth known as skinheads have become more frequent, especially against North Caucasians. According to Valerii Solovei, while in the early 1990s skinheads "had only a few dozen members, from the mid-1990s onwards their numbers started expanding swiftly, and the movement itself became more politicized—a side effect of the first war in Chechnya."[168]

Examples of such attacks include one carried out on 23 April 2001 against people of Caucasian origin working in a Moscow market.[169] Racist attacks have also occurred in military installations, and recruits of North Caucasian background have been "mercilessly bullied by the older hands."[170] The victims of such acts "blame the war in Chechnya and the growing wave of Russian nationalism which has swept through the army in its wake. The war has sparked widespread hatred for all Caucasian nationalities and a bitter distrust of the Islamic faith."[171] Terrorist attacks deriving from the Chechen conflict have further intensified these feelings. More disturbing is the fact that the use of racist actions and language is not limited to the extreme right. Rather, it appears that the expressions of xenophobic and racist sentiment have gained a degree of acceptance that was not the case before.

Alexei Levinson, a sociologist with the Russian Centre for Public Opinion and Market Research (VTSIOM), has observed, "Taboos have been broken. Violent opinions have received a kind of official sanction. Therefore, racist verdicts that were expressed before mainly as a private view can now be voiced without the feeling of violating morality."[172] He also maintains that "anti-Caucasian sentiment has largely replaced anti-Semitism."[173] There has also been a rise in anti-Arab and African sentiments, leading to attacks not only against foreign students and ordinary citizens, but also against diplomats and their family members. The latter fact is becoming a matter of embarrassment for the Russian authorities.[174]

The more extreme rightists are equally hostile to Christian Caucasians, notably the Armenians. But for the majority of the people, religious and ethnic prejudices are mutually reinforcing. Notwithstanding the crucial role that the war in Chechnya and its fallouts have played in exacerbating anti-Caucasian and anti-Islam sentiments, the roots of such prejudices are very deep. These feelings have become stronger as a result of social and economic problems and greater stratification of the society.[175] This is especially evident in recruitment of the nationalist youth because of its loyalty and commitment to Russian traditions and explicit hatred toward other religions, especially Islam.[176]

Alexei Malashenko has noted that during the Soviet era, ethnophobia toward the people of Central Asia and the Caucasus was widespread. This phobia was not evident at a person-to-person level, but became visible when these people were evaluated as a group—in other words, in their function as the "other." Malashenko adds that any sympathy toward the Tatar was mixed with a distrust and dislike of his religion—Islam—and his manner and culture.[177] Furthermore, ethnic Russians felt that the Caucasian and Central Asian people were a burden on the Soviet state, and that they were not even grateful for all the benefits that the Russians in pre- and post-Soviet periods had bestowed upon them.

The rise of nationalist movements during perestroika and the eventual collapse of the Soviet Union intensified these feelings. The migration of large numbers of Caucasians to Russia's major cities and their involvement both in small-scale trade and in criminal activities further made them a good target for the venting of the pent-up frustrations of many Russians. These frustrations, according to Levinson, are rooted in "defeats in Afghanistan and Chechnya [the first Chechen War], the loss of world power status and failure of economic reforms. Blame for these losses is hard to assign. But Caucasians, particularly Chechens, are a practical target."[178]

Malashenko, too, attributes ethnic phobias to material factors such as sentiments that Caucasians are taking the jobs of Russians, but he maintains that religious phobia has deeper identity-related roots: it derives from an instinct of self-preservation, a desire to protect one's national and cultural identity. Religious phobia is directed mainly against Muslims, some of whom happen to be from the Caucasus. According to Malashenko, religious phobias are largely promoted by the Russian Orthodox Church, which is afraid of losing adherents.[179]

In sum, the collapse of the Soviet Union and its fallout, especially the Chechen War, have enhanced the image of Islam as the hostile other. The dissolution of the Soviet Union, according to Malashenko, brought about an "inferiority complex" that led many Russians to compensate for it by clinging more forcefully to the belief in the unique status and mission of Russia.[180] The threat from the revival of Islamic and non-Russian ethnic consciousness, best crystallized in the Chechen

War, also strengthened other components of Russian identity, notably belief in a strong and centralized state and in charismatic leadership.

The dynamics of interaction between ethnic Russians and the Muslim citizens of Russia and prospects for the nature of these relations cannot be understood only in light of the Russian experience. For example, harsh statements by high Russian officials regarding Chechens and negative and sometimes alarmist reports about Islam and Muslims in the Russian media reverberated negatively within Russia's Muslim community, including its leadership. Mufti Ravil Gainutdin noted that not all of the nearly one million Chechens are bandits and terrorists. In short, the Chechen conflict also rekindled the Muslims' grievances at their treatment by the Russians, thus strengthening their sense of ethnic and cultural separateness and their view of the Russians as hostile "others." This view corresponds to the larger myth-symbol complex of the Muslim peoples, which has played an important role in the Russian-Muslim interaction and will continue to do so in the future.

Islamo-Turkic Myth-Symbol Complex: Russia as the Hostile Other

As can be gleaned from earlier discussions, there is a counter myth-symbol complex that is largely accepted by Turko-Muslim peoples of the Russian Federation, although some of them emphasize its Islamic and some its Turkic aspect, while still others see a symbiotic relationship between the two. Whether these competing Russian and Turko-Islamic myth-symbol complexes will be reconciled or remain antagonistic will to a very large extent determine the nature of Russia's post-Soviet identity. The most important components of the Turko-Islamic myth-symbol complex are (1) the large Muslim presence in Russia, (2) the longevity of the Turkic presence in Russia and neighboring areas, (3) a more favorable interpretation of the Mongol-Tatar civilization and its impact on Russia, (4) a long history of conquest and resistance, and (5) a view of Russians as exploiters of Muslim lands.

Regarding the first component, Muslims were present in parts of Russia, notably in the Volga-Ural region and in the Caucasus, long before the Russians. Muslims point out that the Bulghar Kingdom was already an Islamic power before the Kievan Russian state adopted Christianity, or any Slavs in substantial numbers settled in this region. Similarly, regarding the second component, pan-Turkists emphasize that Turkic peoples have been present not only in most parts of Russia but also in the Caucasus and parts of the Middle East for several millennia. They dispute the theory that Turkic peoples in substantial numbers did not arrive in the Caucasus, southern Europe, especially the Black Sea region, and the Middle East before the ninth or tenth century. Rather, they claim that many peoples identified as being Indo-Europeans of the Iranian branch were Turkic. Thus M. Zakiev claims that the Scythians and Sarmatians were all Turkic. He even considers the Sumerians as Turkic. According to him, "Objective data show that in those days (BC) there were more non-Persian speaking tribes rather than Iranian speaking ones." He even claims that the Etruscan language is likely a branch of Turkic languages.[181] He attributes the anti-Turkism of the Russians and other Europeans to the conquest of

Jerusalem by the Turkic-Muslim Seldjuks in the eleventh century.[182] Many Turkic intellectuals in the Russian Federation, notably in Tatarstan, either firmly believe in these views or at least are receptive to them.

Third, the Turkic peoples have a much more favorable view of their civilization and believe that Mongol-Tatar rule had more a positive rather than a negative effect on the post-Kiev state building in Russia around Muscovy. According to Rafael Khakimov, "The Mongols were distinguished by religious tolerance and did not break the cultural traditions of either the Bulgars or the Russians."[183] He also credits the Mongols with having helped Russia resist pressures from the West.[184] Khakimov also asserts the existence of a Turkic civilization of which the Turkic peoples of the Russian Federation are an inalienable part. Moreover, as a Tatar historian, Khakimov understandably emphasizes the contributions of the Tatars to "the development of pan-Turkic culture and to an actual ideology of Turkism itself."[185] Additionally, he expresses the feelings of nearly all Russian Muslims when he asserts that "a Muslim civilization exists."[186] What all this amounts to is that Russia's Turkic and Muslim population does not accept the Russocentric interpretation of the country's history, which views it as an uninterrupted political and cultural chain from Kievan Rus to the present day, with only a few dark episodes of foreign domination, such as the period of the Mongol-Tatar yoke.

Fourth, Muslims reject the view—prevalent among Russians—that Muslim peoples joined Russia voluntarily because they recognized the civilizing benefits of being part of Russia. This idealized Russian view is far from the historical reality. Muslims, in fact, saw Russia as a colonial power bent on dominating them. Furthermore, their view of this encounter is one of domination and resistance, expulsion and exile, and efforts to revive their culture and identity against the assimilating and homogenizing influence of Russia both under the tsars and the Soviet Union. As the Russians celebrate the victory of Ivan over the Tatars, the latter mourn this event as the beginning of the destruction of their civilization. These memories, so dramatically opposed to Russian perceptions, are alive today, as illustrated by large demonstrations in Kazan on 14 October 2001 "to mourn those who defended the city against Ivan the Terrible in 1552."[187]

Fifth, Muslims reject another prominent Russian belief concerning the benefits Muslims gained through their incorporation into the Russian Empire and the Soviet Union. According to this view, the Muslim population benefited from Russia's civilizing impact, including some level of industrialization, but is now ungrateful, either gaining independence, as did the Muslim republics of Central Asia and the South Caucasus, or wishing for independence, as the Chechens do. The Muslims' view, however, is that Russia exploited their lands, disrupted their way of life, and ruined their environment and health. Where the balance of credit or blame lies is hard to establish. Certainly both sides can conjure up painful memories of their interaction. However, the weight of evidence—the drying up of the Aral Sea, the distorting impact of the cotton monoculture in Central Asia, and the health hazard of nuclear facilities in Muslim lands—underlines the harmful impact of Russian/Soviet colonization. Many of these negative consequences did not result from consciously anti-Muslim policies. Russian and non-Muslim peoples also suffered from the misguided policies of the Soviet era.

The strengthening of these diametrically opposed myth-symbol complexes will be damaging to both the Russians and the Muslims. Yet post-Soviet developments—notably the rise of Muslim demands for greater self-determination, Russia's resistance to these demands, and ensuing conflicts—have intensified antagonistic views of the past.

Russia's Other "Hostile Other": The West

Historically, Russia has defined itself as much in opposition to the West as to the Turko-Muslim world. The Western challenge has been the greatest in terms of Russia's efforts to define its national identity and decide where it belongs in civilizational terms for two reasons: (1) the intellectual and civilizational challenge of the West and (2) the West's challenge to Russia's security.

Civilizational Challenge from the West

Religious and cultural differences between Russia and the Muslim world have always been too deep for Russia ever to consider itself as part of that world. The conquest of Kazan was a watershed event in this context as well as in terms of Russia's relations with Muslim peoples. Arguably, from then on, the nature of Russia's relations with Muslim peoples and declining Muslim empires became that of the conqueror and conquered, dominant and dominated. Thus Russians had no sense of inferiority toward the Islamic civilization. Russia may have viewed the Muslim challenge within its borders as a nuisance, but Muslim culture did not challenge Russia's self-identity or cultural self-confidence.

The problems with the West were of a deeper and more complex nature. On the one hand, despite deep doctrinal differences between Russian Orthodoxy and Western Catholicism and Protestantism, Christianity created strong bonds between Russia and the West. In fact, via Christianity, Russia in a sense was always part of the West. Yet Western culture, both in the pre- and post-Enlightenment periods, in many respects was different from Russian culture. The Russians believed that Western Christianity, especially Protestantism, had been too much influenced by rationalist thinking, which had weakened the element of "faith" and ultimately had contributed to the Enlightenment and the growth of secularism, individualism, and materialism. Orthodoxy had retained its sense of community, faith, and lack of materialism. Consequently, many Russians believed that they were culturally superior to the West.

Yet even by the time of Peter the Great, when Russia scored its greatest victories against its Western rivals—such as that over Sweden in 1709, the watershed event that marked the beginning of Russia's career as a great European power—it had become clear that in scientific and industrial progress, Russia was lagging behind Western Europe. As Russia became an important player on the European scene, major European powers and their leaders still viewed it as an Asiatic and barbaric entity. The British "had not overcome their initial impression dating back to the days of Queen Elizabeth that Russia was a great and cold land of 'barbarous manners, ignorance, and arbitrary violence.' "[188]

Napoleon Bonaparte, who tried to conquer Russia and failed, viewed it as an Asiatic empire. Yet in Asia, Russia was viewed as a European power, and the Russians were considered Europeans.[189] Thus the West's challenge to Russia was very serious. In order to compete with the West and win, Russia had to adopt Western ways, including its rationalist philosophy and its utilitarian and materialistic—and hence, according to some Russians, corrupt—culture. But to do so would mean to lose what was best in Russia and in its culture, and, therefore, a sense of Russian cultural authenticity. It was this dilemma that ruptured the unity of Russian identity and generated the debate about the path that Russia should pursue, a debate that is still ongoing. Thus the West became the civilizational paradigm according to which Russia would define itself, either by opposing it or by imitating it.

Security Challenge from the West

The West also posed a security challenge to Russia. From the time of the Kievan Rus, Russian security had been threatened from the West. After the Mongol conquest, Russia faced the risk of total disintegration and the absorption of large portions of its territory by countries to its west; ironically, this danger was averted with the Mongols' assistance.

Napoleon's invasion of Russia, occurring soon after Russia's substantial Westernization under Peter the Great and Empress Catherine, confirmed its suspicions that the Western threat to Russia went beyond the civilizational realm. The intensified Russian-British rivalry beginning almost immediately after the end of the Napoleonic Wars created the phenomenon that one historian has described as "Russo phobia." This sentiment culminated in the formation of an unprecedented alliance of Christian Britain with the Muslim Ottoman Empire against Christian Russia in the Crimean War, thus consolidating Russia's view of the West as a threat to its great-power aspirations.[190]

Germany's invasion of Russia during the Second World War, followed by nearly five decades of intense competition with the West in the context of the Cold War, has left a strong imprint on the Russians' collective psychology, which views the West as an active or potential threat, or at least a serious competitor. Yet it is the West's civilizational challenge and the dichotomies that episodic efforts to emulate the West created in the Russian society and collective psyche that have had the most complex effect on the evolution of Russia's national identity.

Westernization versus Russian Authenticity

As the experiences of other countries in the nineteenth and twentieth centuries have demonstrated, the process of modernization along the model of post-Enlightenment

Europe creates significant social, economic, and cultural divisions in the fabric of traditional society. These disruptions have two particularly important features that invariably lead to counterreactions, ideological and otherwise. First, the processes of modernization affect the balance of economic and political power within the society and often result in the emergence of new categories of citizens who impinge on the privileges of the old elites by gaining wealth and consolidating power. Second, modernization creates—at least in its early stages—a cultural duality that produces a gulf between the elites and the masses. Furthermore, an imitative and imported process of modernization is often incomplete, particularly in its political dimension, thereby distorting the entire process and ultimately turning it against its originator(s).

This is especially true of modernizing processes undertaken by single individuals, who in the political parlance of the second half of the twentieth century have been called "modernizing dictators." Peter the Great, the father of Russia's modernization designed after the European model, was the first in a long line of modernizing dictators. Social, economic, political, and cultural dislocations caused by the process of modernization led to a counterreaction, notably an effort to recapture the lost sense of unity and cohesiveness and cultural authenticity. In short, modernization, especially when it is imported, creates an identity crisis.

Peter's Reforms and Their Motivation

The reign of Peter the Great (1682–1725) and his multifaceted reforms marked an important watershed in Russia's political and cultural history. During Peter's reign, conscious and systematic efforts were made to turn Russia into a European country culturally and politically. The outward manifestation of this policy was the construction of the city of St. Petersburg (modeled after the major Western European cities) and eventually making it the capital of the empire. Peter also introduced educational and cultural reforms, amounting to a "cultural revolution," accompanied by an unprecedented overhaul of administrative, military, and political structures and institutions.

It appears that Peter's inspirations for these reforms were the Renaissance, the Reformation, the age of discovery, and the scientific revolution.[191] In carrying out his reforms, Peter heavily relied on foreigners, some of whom achieved influential positions in the Russian government. Peter's reforms created superficial resemblances between parts of Russia and Western Europe, but the European civilization did not have a profound impact on the Russian population and society.

Political ideas that Peter imported from Europe were of an authoritarian nature and were based on the theory of the divine right of the king to rule without any religious intermediary; this view was popular in early-eighteenth-century Europe, where the Protestant schism and the consolidation of the post-Westphalian state system (1648) had eroded the power of Rome. Thus the main political idea that Peter borrowed from Europe was that of "enlightened despotism."[192] In the application of this concept, Peter eliminated traditional limitations and hindrances to absolute power prescribed in the European concept and severely limited the influence of such traditional Russian institutions as the church, the *zemskii sobor* (local councils), or the Boyarskaya Duma (Council of Nobles) that existed in Muscovy.[193] Even the title of emperor, which Peter adopted, had more secular connotations than that of tsar and implied more distance between the ruler and the ruled.[194]

Peter's principal purpose in modernizing Russia was to make it "a feared and powerful state" so that past experiences of foreign domination would not be repeated.[195] Because "the Russia of Peter's time appeared vulnerable in the presence of the technologically advanced west," it was necessary that it should narrow this gap.[196] But Peter had no intention of allowing political ideas of liberalism and egalitarianism that were gradually spreading in Europe to enter Russia.

Catherine's "Enlightened" Reign

The next ardent Westernizer was Catherine the Great. Catherine continued the outward Europeanization of Russia, but she also sought to find a new basis for the legitimacy of the Russian Empire and its emperor in classical Europe. This was quite natural since Catherine's reign coincided with the neoclassical period in Europe, with its fascination with Rome and Athens. Thus by using classical imagery, Catherine tried to link Russia to contemporary Europe. The eighteenth century expansion of Russia in nearly all directions "had little to do with the Byzantine and Mongol legacies" that in the past had been invoked to "legitimize territorial claims and even validate the mantle of leadership."[197] Therefore, "The soaring leap across space and time to establish cultural ties with classical empires—which have made similar grandiose claims—became an ideological imperative."[198]

Catherine did much both to consolidate Russia's image as a European power and to popularize European culture, including principles of the Enlightenment and styles of education.[199] However, Catherine was no more able than Peter to envisage the political consequences of these policies. Like Peter, she was unwilling to embrace the emerging European ideas of liberalism. Rather, in her version of enlightened absolutism, "which combined faith in reason and reform with the recognition of the absolute authority of the monarch," she declared Russia to be both European and an absolutist state.[200]

At the time, this was not exceptional because many Western European countries were still absolute monarchies. But European countries, either in an evolutionary manner or through revolutions, were moving toward political liberalization. In Russia, such movements were to be stifled in the coming decades, despite periodic and halfhearted efforts at political reform. The failure of liberalizing efforts during the first half of the nineteenth century led Russian Westernizers to look to other European political and ideological movements, notably romanticism, Hegelianism, and socialism. Modernization and Europeanization in Russia, to the extent that they happened, tended to strengthen the state at the expense of the citizenry. Russia's modernizing dictators faced the dilemma of how to benefit from scientific and technological fruits of modernity without suffering from its side effects such as the transformation of traditional society, and, more important, how to forgo the social and political requirements of this process. Apparently they repeatedly failed to realize that "modernity comes in a single package."[201]

Reaction to Modernization: Reasserting Russian Authenticity

According to Nicholas Berdyaev, "Peter's reforms were absolutely inevitable."[202] As he explained:

> Russia could no longer exist as a closed country in a backward condition both military and naval and economic without education and technical civilization. In such circumstances the Russian people not only could not fulfill its great mission, but its very independence was exposed to danger. . . . Russia was obligated to break out of its isolation and join in the swirling life of the world. Only in such a way could the Russians make their contribution to the life of the world.[203]

Berdyaev, however, is very critical of the way the Westernizing reforms were implemented, especially the way the Westernizers "denied any original distinctive character to the Russian people and Russian history. They clung to naïvely simple views of the progress of enlightenment and civilization and saw no mission of any sort for Russia except the necessity of catching up with the West."[204] Berdyaev further maintains that Peter's reforms, as they were implemented, "did terrible violence to the soul of the people and to their beliefs."[205] His methods also ruptured Russia's historical and cultural evolution because "he wanted to destroy the old Muscovite Russia, to tear up by the roots those feelings which lay at the very foundation of its life."[206] In their brutality, Berdyaev compares Peter's methods to those of the Bolsheviks.[207]

The modernizing policies also created a wide cultural gap between a narrow and superficially Europeanized elite and the masses. According to Berdyaev, "Peter secularized the Orthodox kingdom and guided Russia into the way of enlightenment."[208] However, "This process took place in the upper levels of Russian society among the nobility and the civil servants. . . . But the people went on living by the old religious beliefs and regarded the gentry as an alien race."[209]

The inordinate use of foreigners in the setting up and managing of the new institutions and other privileges that they enjoyed under Peter and even more under Catherine intensified the feelings of estrangement between the elite and the masses. The arrogant behavior of the foreigners added to the people's resentment. Thus, as Wayne Allensworth has pointed out, many people came to see themselves "only as common fodder for Peter's wars and human material for his many collectivist projects."[210]

Some extreme Westernizers saw no value in the Russian culture, including the bedrock of its traditional civilization, Orthodox Christianity. Pyotr Yakovlevich Chaadaev thought that Russia had contributed nothing to the world civilization. In his letters on the philosophy of history, Chaadaev claimed, "Alone in the world we [Russians] have given nothing to the world, taught the world nothing; we have not added a single idea to the fund of human ideas; we have contributed nothing to the progress of the human spirit, and we have disfigured everything we have taken out of that progress."[211] Chaadaev, who converted to Roman Catholicism, saw Orthodoxy as a main cause of Russia's cultural barrenness. He wrote, "What were we doing while the edifice of modern civilization was arising out of the struggle between the energetic barbarism of the Northern peoples and the high idea of Christianity? Obedient to our fatal destiny we turned to miserable Byzantium, the object of profound contempt among these peoples, for a moral code on which to base our education."[212]

Such harsh opinions expressed by some extreme Westernizers, combined with the way modernization was carried out and its slow pace and limited scope, inevitably led to a reaction. This took various ideological forms. It also gave rise to a still ongoing debate: where does Russia belong? In the West? Or is it a sui generis civilization, a third way between the East and the West?

Birth of Slavophilism and the Early Slavophile Thinkers

Slavophilism as a cohesive philosophy, based on Russia's indigenous traditions that could serve as an alternative to the perspectives of the Westernizers, emerged in the late 1830s.[213] Its origins, however, are rooted in earlier criticism of Peter's policies, which surfaced during the reign of Catherine the Great.

The first opponents of these policies emerged from the ranks of the nobility, such as Prince Mikhail Shcherbatov. He felt that the emerging bureaucratic state system and the growth of careerist individualism, which engendered autocracy and servility, eliminated all the old checks and balances provided by the privileges of the nobility and the church. In his criticism, Shcherbatov juxtaposed the society of ancient Russia, which was based on mutual obligations and responsibility and was tempered by Christian mercy and restraint, to that of the autocratic and bureaucratic state that Peter had started to create.[214]

Nikolai Karamzin was another defender of Russian authenticity in the face of creeping Westernization. He praised the "virtuous and simple life" of old Russia, when "Russians were Russian."[215] Old Russians spoke Russian, whereas the post-Petrine Russian nobility and the new upper classes spoke French. Under the influence of the French Revolution and Napoleon's assault on Russia, Karamzin revised some of his earlier more liberal views and came to view autocracy as the only system capable of safeguarding society. Nevertheless, he believed that the tsar's power should be limited by the revival of such ancient Russian institutions as the *veche* (citizens' assembly), the observance of customs in relations between state and society, and the granting of a more independent role for the church.[216]

Karamzin's ideas had a significant impact on the development of the Slavophiles' views. Mikhail Pogodin was another early critic of Petrine and post-Petrine Russia, although as a person of nonnoble birth he owed his education and position to Peter's reform. Pogodin influenced the Slavophile thinking indirectly by emphasizing Russian distinctiveness and its special destiny. In some essential ways, his views sharply differed from those of the Slavophiles, especially Slavophilism's more liberal strain; Pogodin did not have any particular affection for ancient Russian communalism or the spirit of Orthodox Christian fellowship. In his view, what was specifically Russian was the uncompromising nature of absolutism.

Pogodin's ideas were used by a variety of political schools of thought attempting to create a separate path of development for Russia and a Russian way of political, social, and economic evolution. Despite their differences, Pogodin influenced Slavophiles by, in the words of Yuri Samarin, showing them that "it was possible to look at Russian history and Russian life in general from a completely new angle. Western formulas are not applicable to us; the way of life is an expression of specific principles unknown to other nations; our evolution is subject to its own laws that have not yet been defined by scholarship."[217]

Slavophilism was a complex phenomenon, and its emergence is rooted in cultural, social, economic, and political factors. But above all, like all authenticist movements, it was a response to the pressures of modernization and the rupture of what is often erroneously viewed as a fully integrated and organic collective personality and community. The juxtaposition of "ancient Russia" as the ideal prototype of an organic society to "post-Petrine Russia" as a model of a disconnected society, and of Russia to Europe, is a direct consequence of this encounter of old and new, indigenous and foreign. Slavophilism, like other authenticist ideologies, was a utopian philosophy, but not in the sense of wanting to create a new society, but rather to resurrect a preexisting ideal society that had vanished because of external influences.

The following aspects of the Slavophile philosophy are particularly important and worth noting since, in different and subtle ways, they affect the current direction of Russia's social evolution: (1) religiosity and spirituality as opposed to rationalism and materialism of Europe; (2) emphasis on national self-consciousness (*narodnost*), which refers both to the spirit of Russia and the belief in its spirit and is both the cult and the essence of Russian national identity; (3) belief in Russia as a "historical nation" and hence belief in Russia's historic mission;[218] and (4) preoccupation with the question of national identity. Regarding the latter, the Slavophiles sought to "discover 'correct social principles' that would serve as antidotes to the errors committed by the Europeanization of Russia and would put Russia back on a genuine historical path."[219] In terms of their social philosophy, the Slavophiles were populist and communalist. Berdyaev has pointed out that Slavophiles opposed the ideas of Roman law on property and were defenders of the commune, which they saw as the only original Russian structure of economic life.

Pan-Slavism

Despite some affinity with Slavophilism, pan-Slavism is a different ideology and has different objectives. Most Slavophiles were primarily interested in the fate of the Russians and in the inner regeneration of the Russian society in the spirit of Christian and ancient Russian traditions, not in uniting Slavs under Russian influence and/or protection.[220] However, the Crimean War ignited a significant interest in the fate of Slavs under Turkish (Islamic) rule. Thus Ivan Aksakov, a prominent Russian intellectual and publicist, proclaimed that "the 'holy aims' of the Crimean War was to conquer Constantinople and unite the Slavs under the Russian Tsar."[221] Consequently, the rise of pan-Slavism had important consequences for Russia's relations with the Islamic world in the past and, to some degree, continues to exert influence today.

Pan-Slavism also had anti-Western tendencies, with Austria being a particular object of animosity. It emphasized Russian nationalism and the need to make Russia "a nation with a powerful instinct for statehood with expansionist and hegemonic tendencies."[222]

Here it should be noted that the modernizing and authenticist dichotomy has also bedeviled the Islamic world, including Muslim-inhabited parts of Russia, for more than a century. As with Russia, this dichotomy is partly due to the fact that within Islamic thinking, too, there exists a strand of retrospective utopianism. This strand has been popular with many Islamists and aims to re-create the ideal society that supposedly existed in Medina under the spiritual and temporal rule of the prophet Muhammad.[223] The existence of this utopian trait in both civilizations is another potential source of conflict in the respective Russian and Islamic myth-symbol complexes and a challenge to the formation of a post-Soviet Russian identity acceptable to all of Russia's ethnic and religious groups.

Westernizers and Authenticists: A Continued Chain of Interaction

The experience of nearly all nations shows that efforts to transform a society according to borrowed models will neither be entirely successful nor have the intended consequences. Historical experience also demonstrates that efforts to completely reverse the changes that have taken place and return to an idealized and utopian past are doomed to failure.

Imported ideas often transmute in the context of a country's history, traditions, and cultural proclivities, thus giving rise to new versions of original ideas or generating a new synthesis. This process occurred in Russia and gave rise to a totally Russian interpretation of various European philosophies regarding state, nation, and society, from Hegelianism to Marxism. According to Nicholas Berdyaev, communism was the extreme form of Russian Westernism. Paradoxically, he also states, "Russian Communism is the Communism of the East."[224] Clearly, communism was the Russian version of modernism, which was supposed to be superior to that of the West.

The Westernizing policies of some Russian tsars had brought Russia closer to Europe and had deeply engaged it in European politics to the point that disengagement from Europe was not a viable alternative. Thus the question had changed from whether Russia should be in Europe to what its role and mission in Europe should be. In his famous speech on the occasion of the unveiling of the Pushkin monument (8 June 1880), Dostoevsky defined Russia's role as defender of Europe and reconciling Europe's contradictions, reflecting a peculiarly Russian penchant for messianism and all-encompassing notions. He said that the desire to serve all humanity was the impulse behind Peter's reforms and the policies of the Russian state. He asked:

> For what else has Russia been doing in her policies during these two centuries, but serving Europe much more than herself? . . . I believe we, well, not we but the Russians of the future to the last man, will comprehend that to become a genuine Russian means to seek finally to reconcile all European controversies, to show the solution of European anguish in our all human and all unifying Russian soil, to embrace in it with brotherly love all our brothers and finally, perhaps, to utter the ultimate word great, universal harmony, of the fraternal accord of all nations abiding by the law of Christ's gospel.[225]

Russia tried to do just this, but not according to the gospel of Christ, but that of Marx or, rather, the Russian interpretation of Marx in the context of its revolution of 1917. Western ideas of liberalism and social reform did not take root in Russian soil because they appeared unrealistic. Bolshevism looked more suitable for Russia partly because it was "more faithful to certain primordial Russian traditions, to the Russian search for universal social justice, understood in a maximizing sense, and to the Russian method of government and control by coercion."[226]

Eurasianism as Another Expression of Russian Authenticity

The totalitarian uniformity that the Communist system imposed on Russia meant an impoverishment of intellectual life, especially in the sphere of political ideas. It was only in the 1960s that an underground intelligentsia emerged and began offering either new interpretations of old ideas or completely original ideas in literary works or in underground publications (*samizdat*). Nevertheless, during the first decade of the new regime, another theory of Russian identity was developed within the Russian émigré community, namely, Eurasianism. New and different interpretations of this idea have acquired considerable currency within post-Soviet Russian political circles. The intellectual fathers of the movement were Prince N.S. Trubetskoy, P.N. Savitskii, P.P. Suvchinski, and G.V. Florovski, who in 1921 published a collection of essays titled *Iskhod k Vostoku* (The way out [or exodus] to the East).

The Eurasianist school has certain similarities with the Slavophiles, particularly in its religiospiritual aspects, but first and foremost, its founders were proponents of the view—so pervasive even among Westernizers, albeit sometimes subconsciously—of Russia's unique character and mission. The Eurasianists even more than the Slavophiles were of the opinion that Russia could not derive much benefit from European culture. In this respect, they were close to the extreme nationalists and pan-Slavists, notably Nikolai Danilevsky. A principal component of the Eurasianist theory is the characterization of the European and Asian subjects of the tsarist empire as neither Asian nor European, but rather forming "an organic United

Eurasian people."[227] Some Eurasianist theoreticians have based this interpretation on the historic intermingling of Slavic and Turko-Mongol peoples. This tendency was stronger in that branch of Eurasianism that is called ethnocultural Eurasianism and whose most ardent representative is Professor G.V. Vernadsky. He stressed "the decisive influence of the steppe and the forest societies on the enormous plain, the ethnic and cultural complexities of Russia, and the major and organic contribution of eastern peoples, especially the Mongol, to Russian history."[228] Other figures who espoused similar views regarding a synthesis between Slavic and Turko-Mongol peoples were the philosopher Vladimir Soloviev and the poet Alexander Blok, who wrote the famous poem "The Scythians."[229]

However, others believe that Slavs in themselves and without the interference of Turko-Mongols are Eurasian people. Another component is the view that the Russian Empire was a tolerant place where diverse peoples were free to fulfill themselves, albeit under the tutelage of the Russian people. The third element is the perception of Russia's cultural evolution as neither a fully Western nor Eastern society and state. Some Eurasianists, mostly the new ones, believe that Russia's deep religiosity brought it closer in many ways to the mystical East than to the materialist West.

The early Eurasianists had an ambiguous view of the revolution of 1917, combining positive and negative interpretations. They considered it a negative development because it was a "destructive rebellion against God."[230] Moreover, they viewed the Bolsheviks as "extreme Westernizing intellectuals perpetuating the split between the intelligentsia and the people."[231] On the positive side, they hoped that "the 'wise people' would sweep them [the Bolsheviks] away and unite under the Orthodoxy and the rule of a 'Eurasian Party.' "[232]

It appears, however, that the messianic and expansionist streak of Russian thought influenced the development of the Eurasianist school; they believed that the changes unleashed by the First World War meant that "the East was about to rise" and that Russia "could lead the emerging colonial peoples."[233] The Eurasianists believed that Russia was uniquely qualified to do so because it itself had become a "colonial [colonized] country" and thus "could lead other colonial countries, especially her 'Asiatic sisters' in a decisive struggle against the Romano-Germanic colonizers."[234]

The problem, however, as Nicholas Riasanovsky points out, is that "while Eurasianism wanted to make Russia into a future leader of the colonial world, its past activities in such countries as China or Persia ranged it with the colonizers. . . . Much more important, the Russian empire itself, and after it the Soviet Union, contained very many non-Russian nationalities."[235] In light of these realities, Riasanovsky concludes that in the final analysis Eurasianism was "a determined defense of Russia, one and indivisible in an age when empires crumbled," because "if the Russian empire were a symphonic unity of peoples—more than that, if there were no Russian empire at all but only one organic Eurasia—the issue of separatism lost its meaning."[236]

Another strand of Eurasianism worth noting is the "geopolitical" version, which sees Eurasia as a self-contained geopolitical entity.[237] This version of Eurasianism was strongly influenced by German geopolitical theories, but it also reflected the patriotism of its creator, Savitskii. Geopolitical Eurasianism was more acceptable to other intellectual trends than its ethnocultural version because even anti-Westernizers and Slavophiles essentially identified with Europe. As Riasanovsky has pointed out, even archconservatives "formulated their conflict with the West as a fraternal one, perhaps all the more bitter for that reason."[238] Moreover, "Self-identification in terms of Orthodoxy, the Byzantine heritage, the Russian people or Slavdom almost inevitably implied a close relationship to other Christians, other heirs of the classical world and other European peoples or groups of peoples," and not with the Asiatic people.[239] Nevertheless, fascination with Asia and Asiatic peoples had grown in Russia by the turn of the twentieth century within literary and artistic movements and contributed to the rise of Eurasianist schools.[240]

Lastly, it seems that the experience of exile for a group of Russian intellectuals who had not had a chance to play a role in their country before the revolution and could expect none under the revolution and their sense of alienation from the foreign societies in which they were living contributed to the emergence of Eurasianism. Riasanovsky maintains that in a sense, "Eurasianism constituted a desperate bid to reestablish vanished Russia, to transmute fragmented and rootless existence in a foreign society into an organic and creative life at home."[241] This theme can be observed in the post-Soviet neo-Eurasianists in the sense that they too want to re-create the vanished world of the Soviet Union, albeit in a new context.

The Nature of Russian Nationalism and National Identity

Before moving to a discussion of the spectrum of political thought in post-Soviet Russia, and in particular the emerging dominant view among the Russian ruling circles, especially President Vladimir Putin's vision, it is necessary to answer the following questions: Where does the Russian definition of nationalism and national identity fit within the typology described earlier, and what have been its implications for non-Russian populations, notably Muslims?

Put briefly, pre-Soviet Russian nationalism was a combination of the Southern (religious) and Eastern (ethnocentric) types. The crucial role that Orthodox Christianity played in forging a common bond among Russian peoples, its role in endowing Russia's imperial expansion with a higher purpose, and the symbiotic relationship developed between the religious concept of Orthodoxy and the ethnic concept of Russianness justify this characterization. This character of Russian nationalism and identity had significant implications for the fate of those Muslims who were absorbed by Russia.

Because of the religious and ethnic symbiosis underpinning Russian nationalism and identity, non-Russians who converted to Orthodoxy were not accepted as full citizens, as exemplified by the case of the Christian Tatars. This conflation of Orthodoxy and Russianness and the central role assigned to Orthodoxy as part of Russian identity meant that Muslims could never be really accepted as full citizens.

This factor was also behind the Russian government's sporadic and often half-hearted efforts at proselytization and the opposition of some Orthodox priests to such proselytizing efforts. Moreover, although by the 1860s Muslims constituted a considerable minority within the empire, they remained confined to the margins of Russian society. Even the culturally and linguistically Russified Muslims remained outside the boundaries of Russianness. The distinction between *Russkii* (ethnic Russian) and *Rossiiskii* (pertaining to the territorial and legal space of Russia) was a linguistic manifestation of this tacit division. However, the Russian Muslims' sense of identity and nationalism was also a combination of Southern and Eastern concepts of identity in the sense that religion and ethnicity were important components of their identity. Consequently, they too were not keen to submerge their religionational identity within a broader civic Russian identity.

Furthermore, despite Russia's eastern expansion, both in the cultural (the Muslim world) and the geographical (Far East) sense, and notwithstanding bitter disputes between Westernizers and supporters of variants of what is best defined as Russian authenticity, Russia, from an identity point of view, was always closer to the West than it could ever be to the Islamic world. This was not merely because of common bonds of Christianity; it also derived from the existence of a separate and, at least theoretically, cohesive Islamic civilization with its own worldview and aspirations that often competed with those of Russia.

However, it was not just those Russians who saw themselves as "Asiatics" or subscribed to Eurasianism, with its symbiosis of Slavic and Turko-Mongol peoples, who refused to see Russia as a fully European country. Western Europeans also saw Russia as apart from European civilization. This refusal to accept Russia as European contributed to anti-Western feelings and movements in Russia. According to Vilho Harle, "Western hostility to Russian reforms played an important role in frustrating Russians. . . . The more Peter attempted to modernize Russia according to the Western model, the more hostile the West Europeans became."[242] It is impossible to judge whether Russian development would have taken a different direction if it had been treated differently by the West. Given Russia's particular geographical, historical, and cultural characteristics, Russia was bound to evolve in its own special way. In particular, Russia's sense of its moral superiority and its penchant for idealistic and utopian schemes should not be underestimated. Indeed, Russia always has believed itself to represent what is best in the West, be it in a religious sense (Orthodox Christianity) or a secular form (the Russian version of socialism). But the chasm might have been less deep if the Western response had been different.

Furthermore, despite the fact that the dynamics of imperial rivalries had at times pushed Western European countries to side with the Muslim Ottomans against Russia, Western Europeans were not averse to making deals with the Russians against Muslims either. The 1907 Russian-British agreement known as the Anglo-Russian Entente to divide Iran and to declare Afghanistan a neutral or "buffer" state illustrates this propensity. Thus the dichotomy was not so much between

Russia and the West, but rather different interpretations of what the West was and should be, and the rivalry over the leadership of the West.

The Soviet Experience and the Failure of Civic Nationalism

The goal of the Soviet Union was to do away with ethnic, religious, and other loyalties and to create a new Soviet identity and a system of loyalty based on citizenship and commitment to the goals of socialist internationalism. Compared to the tsarist regime, in terms of citizenship, the Soviet system, at least superficially, was egalitarian. However, the following aspects of the Soviet system undermined the development of civic nationalism: (1) the establishment of ethnically based republics; (2) the central role assigned to ethnic Russians, which led to the near equation of the Soviet Union with Russia; and (3) recurrent antireligious—especially anti-Islam—campaigns. The practice of mass deportations of Chechens and other ethnic groups from their homelands to other parts of the Soviet Union, a slackening of internationalist education, and Brezhnev's policy of allowing local party bosses greater freedom in running their republics (provided they kept the peace and met their assigned agricultural and industrial production quotas) also hampered the consolidation of civic identity and nationalism while strengthening ethnocentric and religious identities. Especially important was a revival of Russian nationalism in various official and nonofficial underground forms. Stalin even eased pressures on the church, which created high expectations on the part of some church leaders that after the war, he "would disband or completely reform the Communist Party and proclaim the country a pan-Slavic Orthodox empire."[243]

Although Stalin officially used Russian nationalism during the 1930s and 1940s, he retrenched on this front in the last years of his life. The trend continued after his death, and once more, most of the Soviet Union's achievements were attributed to socialism rather than the virtues of Russian nationalism. Andrei Zhdanov, an associate of Stalin, attributed the victory in the Great Patriotic War to socialism rather than to Russian nationalism and love of the homeland.[244] The process of the rehabilitation of writers and philosophers such as Dostoevsky and Berdyaev was reversed. Yet, as John Dunlop notes, "The genie of Russian nationalism, or a mixture of religion and nationalism, could not, once released, be so easily returned to the bottle. In a sense, Stalin's concessions began, slowly and gradually, to take on a life and momentum of their own."[245]

Khrushchev's attacks on Stalin and his revelations of the crimes committed in Stalin's era deeply affected the Soviet youth, eroded their faith in communism, and sent them searching for new ideological alternatives, including nationalism. This is ironic because Khrushchev was antipathetic toward Russian nationalism and was militantly antireligious. Nevertheless, his policies revived various types of Russian nationalism and even reopened old debates between Westernizers and Slavophiles in various underground (*samizdat*) publications.

The evolution of Russian nationalism in the following years followed an erratic course, particularly in terms of the attitude of Soviet authorities to its covert and overt manifestations. The attitude of the Russian nationalists of the post-Stalin period to non-Russian populations was not uniform. Some of them felt that non-Russian minorities—Uzbeks, Tatars, Georgians—should be allowed to "concern themselves with their antiquity, their history. . . . Let them pride themselves on their individual cultures."[246] Some, such as Alexander Solzhenitsyn, even advocated partial dismemberment of the Soviet Union.[247] Others, by contrast, insisted on the maintenance of a "single and indivisible Russia" and argued that the Russian Empire was historically justified.[248]

Within the non-Russian population, the contradictory and paradoxical cultural policy of the Soviet Union, coupled with the strength of local ethnic and religious identities, prevented the development of a civic Soviet identity and nationalism. However, the main reasons for the failure of civic identity formation during the Soviet era were the continuing centrality of the ethnic Russians and their national myth-symbol complex throughout the Soviet Union's political and cultural space and the lack of any effort to synthesize the myth-symbol complexes of other major ethnic groups beyond the superimposition of a socialist mythology of a utopian society in the making. In short, to the extent that a civic form of nationalism and national identity was attempted in the Soviet Union, it was based, as Ignatief has pointed out, on a core ethnic and cultural—namely Russian—element.

Post-Soviet Spectrum of Russian Political Thought: Diverging Approaches to Nationalism, National Identity, and Islam

The Soviet system did not succeed in developing a widespread culture of civic nationalism, although it was more successful than the tsarist empire in the Russification of non-Russian ethnicities and in their alienation from their indigenous cultures. However, this was mostly true of the non-Russian elites and part of the urban populations. Even in the case of the elites, this process was not complete, as was reflected in the persistence of certain religiocultural practices among party bosses in the Muslim republics.

Most important, many ethnic Russians came to see communism and the Soviet system as a violation of their identity, their values, and even their souls. Alexander Solzhenitsyn wrote that Marxism "swept on us from the West at the end of the last century and has tormented and ravaged our soul."[249] Indeed, it is ironic that the Russian nationalists of the Soviet era believed that the Russian people had been particularly victimized by the Soviet system. Despite this, at the beginning of Gorbachev's assumption of power, the general official view was that there were "no serious problems" on the national front. In 1986, the official Communist Party of the Soviet Union (CPSU) Program declared that the national question had been "successfully resolved."[250] The implication of this assessment is that the question of national identity and its character was also answered. There was a Soviet identity and Soviet nationalism, or "patriotism," that was transethnic and transreligious—in other words, civic—in nature.

This vision of collective identity in the Soviet Union did not correspond to external realities. Nevertheless, it became a guiding principle of Gorbachev's strategy of reform. What was needed was an economic reform and a degree of liberalization to regenerate the Soviet Union. Since the problem of national identity was solved, no need was felt to develop a new concept of identity and nationalism suited to a more open—economically, politically, and culturally—Soviet Union. Yet notwithstanding the fact that the problem of nationalities had not been resolved in the Soviet Union, there was no massive nationalist resurgence among non-Russian peoples, notably Muslims, for independence, nor were demands for the dismantling of the Soviet Union prevalent. For example, as late as March 1991, 76 percent of the electorate voted to preserve the USSR as a renewed federation during a popular referendum.[251]

The strongest and earliest nationalist movements advocating separation emerged in the Baltic republics and, to a lesser degree, in the Caucasus. During this period, within the RSFSR, the strongest nationalist and autonomist movements emerged in Tatarstan and later (1990) in Chechnya. The main concern of the Tatar nationalists was the elevation of Tatarstan to the level of a full union republic, although the extreme nationalists had the goal of ultimate independence.[252] In Chechnya, too, early stirrings were for greater autonomy within the Russian Federation rather than outright independence. Considering the nature of the Turko-Muslim myth-symbol complex in the RSFSR, such movements were to be expected. However, the separatist component of these movements was small. Of equal interest is the fact that while, from 1988 onwards, Islamic sentiments were more openly expressed and politically motivated Muslim groups emerged, the most ardent nationalists, autonomists, and independence-seeking groups, both in the RFSFR and in the rest of the Soviet Union, were secular and were often influenced by pan-Turkist ideas, as were the Azerbaijani popular front Berlik, the Uzbek movement Erk, and the All-Tatar Public Center in Tatarstan.

One of the most significant and puzzling aspects of the Soviet Union's collapse is that it was not caused by the challenge from the periphery, especially the Muslim parts. Rather, the rise of Russian nationalism and the declaration of sovereignty by the RSFSR in 1990, combined with Boris Yeltsin's active encouragement of other republics to do the same and his decision in December 1991 to declare the Soviet Union defunct—caused its disintegration. It is difficult to judge whether Yeltsin had thought out the consequences of his actions—not just for the Soviet Union, but also for its main successor state, the Russian Federation—or whether his actions were motivated by a desire to gain power irrespective of the consequences. There is no evidence to show that Yeltsin's actions were the result of a clear vision regarding what should be the basic characteristics of post-Soviet Russian identity, its essential components, and its implications for Russia's domestic and foreign policies. This lack of vision, combined with other mistakes committed in the implementation of his economic reforms and the poor results of his foreign policy, created the crisis of identity that forced Yeltsin in 1996 to declare that Russia needed a national idea—in other words, a national identity.

Diverging Views on Russian National Identity

By and large, there has been a broad consensus that Russia needs a new national identity. The problem has been that there are various ideas about what such an identity should encompass and what its core elements should be. Nevertheless, despite differences in emphasis, nearly all schools of thought see the "Russian experience," or the historical experience of the ethnic Russians and their culture, as the foundation of an emerging Russian identity. Others can accept it; certainly there can be legal and other protections for minority cultures. But there can be no duality of cultures. For instance, a Muslim culture cannot achieve equal status with the Russian culture, even in Muslim-inhabited regions, especially in the political and legal spheres.

The fact that the ethnic Russians presently constitute more than 80 percent of the total population has led many politicians and public figures to express the opinion that Russia is, in fact, a monoethnic country, much more so than France, Spain, or Belgium, not to mention the United Kingdom.[253] Thus the dominant political thought in post-Soviet Russia is more or less ethnocentric rather than embracing civic nationalism. Differences relate to other characteristics of nationalists. In this regard, they can be divided into the following broad categories: (1) religious (Christian) nationalists; (2) Communist nationalists; (3) geopolitical nationalists; (4) fringe nationalists (ultranationalists or neo-Nazis); and (5) reform nationalists.

Christian Nationalists

Broadly speaking, Christian nationalists believe that religion, namely, Orthodox Christianity, has a vital role in reviving the Russian nation and remains the central element of Russian identity. However, Christian nationalists differ in their geopolitical definitions of Russia and in their methodology for achieving their stated goals. Some are inclined toward democratic methods and tolerance of other groups, whereas others tend to have antiminority sentiments. Two major trends within this movement and two personalities who represent them and whose views have influenced the shaping of the nascent, albeit still ambiguous, concept of Russian national identity deserve attention.

Alexander Solzhenitsyn

To include Solzhenitsyn in the category of Christian nationalists may not be strictly justified because he has developed a vision of Russia that, while drawing on many historical sources, is uniquely his own. The single most important characteristic of Solzhenitsyn's system of thought is a belief in Russia's uniqueness and the necessity for Russia to find its own path of national development and regeneration.[254] Nevertheless, because of the central place that religion and spirituality (i.e., Orthodox Christianity) have in Solzhenitsyn's philosophy, he should be included among Christian nationalists.

Two major themes dominate Solzhenitsyn's thinking: (1) Russia's and the modern world's crises derive from man's rebellion against God and his assumption of the role of God, and (2) Russia must find its own way to fulfillment. In developing the former theme, Solzhenitsyn claims that man's attempt to play the role of God, in effect, his repudiation of God, has had two destructive consequences, both of which were fully manifested in communism and the Soviet system. First, the destruction of the natural and social environment results from an excessive belief in man's ability to mold the world according to his own designs and in the possibility of achieving utopian perfection. Second, rejection of God eliminates the spiritual dimensions of human life and thus absolves human beings of responsibility by identifying the material environment as the root of all problems.[255] The latter theme in Solzhenitsyn's belief system is based on the necessity of preserving the unique features of Russia's historic national identity. He believes that, as Oswald Spengler pointed out, "the very concept of the state is differently understood in different cultures and there is no definitive best form of government which needs to be borrowed from one culture for use in another. . . . For a given people with its specific geography, history, traditions, and psychological makeup, the task is to set in place a structure that will lead to a flourishing of this people rather than its decline and degeneration."[256] Therefore, he prescribes a path of development for Russia that, in his words, can "save Russia's traditional character and national culture, helping it resume its historic development," which was "sidetracked by [Russian] imperialism, pan-Slavism, and most of all communism."[257] He believes that this natural path of development has been threatened since the end of communism by an explosion of a capitalist version of materialism.

In Solzhenitsyn's view, the proper path for Russia includes a greater role for religion—Orthodox Christianity—and the creation of a more ethnically and culturally homogeneous Russian society. Accordingly, he is a great advocate of the uniting of Russia's Slavic peoples. He is also very conscious of the existence of Russians outside the borders of the Russian Federation and believes that the Russian government must protect them. Thus Solzhenitsyn's view of national identity is, at its core, ethnocentric rather than civic. However, he does make room for "cultural Russians" by saying that when he refers to nationality, he does not mean bloodline, but rather a spirit, a consciousness. Consequently, whoever belongs to the Russian culture is Russian.[258]

Nevertheless, there are groups that fall outside the cultural and spiritual realm of Russia as envisioned by Solzhenitsyn. Alexei Malashenko has pointed out that the point of view that unequivocally places Islam beyond the pale of Russian civilization and classifies it as merely "a confessional and cultural community" was expressed most explicitly, and perhaps for the first time, by Solzhenitsyn.[259] In his book *How We Can Reconstruct Russia,* Solzhenitsyn advocated detaching the non-Slavic (primarily Muslim) republics from Russia.[260] However, following the second

Chechen War, he seems to have changed his mind. On 29 April 2001, Interfax News Agency in Moscow reported Solzhenitsyn as having said that he "favors the application of the supreme [death] penalty to Chechens who seek independence from Russia."[261] Solzhenitsyn's attitude of mistrusting Islam and forced coexistence with it is natural, given the central role he assigns to Orthodox Christianity in the spiritual and political rebuilding of Russia and his monoethnic and monocultural conception of Russia. Yet Solzhenitsyn's nationalism is not imperialist: it is introspective and focused on Russia's inner regeneration. However, some peoples and countries, notably the Ukrainians and the Kazakhs, may find that his ideas of Slavic unity entail a degree of imperialist impulse and hence are disquieting.

Christian Democrats: Viktor Aksiuchits

According to Wayne Allensworth, the difference between Solzhenitsyn and other Christian nationalists is that his embrace of Orthodox Christianity "has not led him down the path to imperialism."[262] This, he argues, contrasts with other Christian nationalists, in whose thinking Russia's national, imperial, and religious missions are often fused. This is, however, natural because nationalist movements often use religion to mobilize the rebirth of the nation. In Russia's case, this is particularly apt since there is such a symbiotic relationship between Christian Orthodoxy and the Russian sense of nationhood. According to Viktor Aksiuchits, a preeminent Russian nationalist and leader of the Christian Democrats, the first act of Russian national consciousness was a religious act—the adoption of Orthodoxy.[263] Consequently, as early as the last years of Gorbachev's rule, a variety of organizations espousing different versions of Christian nationalism emerged, including the liberal brand of nationalism frequently espoused by Christian Democrats and a more xenophobic strand with fascist, antiminority, and especially anti-Semitic dimensions. This latter strand, sometimes referred to as the "Black Hundred" movement, is no longer a significant force on the Russian political scene, although in some circles the ideas promoted by its proponents resonate in contemporary politics.[264]

Russian Christian Democratic Movement

Among the various movements calling themselves Christian Democrats, the largest and most influential was Aksiuchits's Russian Christian Democratic Movement (RCDM), which later registered as a political party. However, the party was weakened as a result of differences between two of its leaders.[265] In 2002, it was denied registration as a political party under new rules stipulated by the 2001 Law on Political Parties, that banned parties based on religious affiliation.[266] It is not easy to present the various contradictory strands of thought in Aksiuchits's philosophy as a coherent whole. Nevertheless, some of its fundamental features, with implications for the nature of Russian identity and the place of nonethnic Russians in such a scheme, can be noted. First, in Aksiuchits's view, it is the *Russkii narod* (ethnic Russian people) that are "the subjects or agents" of Russian national consciousness. Second, Orthodox Christianity is the core of this consciousness and its coordinating agent. According to him, it was after baptism into Christianity that the Russian people became unified. Third, the Russian people are the *gosudarstvo obrazuiushchy narod* (state- and civilization-creating people). They created the civilization and organized the state, into which other groups may enter and into which other cultures, languages, and religions feed. Fourth, Russian civilization and national consciousness have a metaphysical and universal dimension that enabled them to solidify a vast multinational and multireligious state under the umbrella of Orthodox civilization without committing the genocidal acts of other empire builders. According to him, during Russia's expansion, not a single culture was destroyed, nor, unlike other empires, where the imperial center exploited the colonies for its own material benefit, did Russia enrich itself at the expense of conquered lands.[267]

This interpretation, of course, does not correspond to reality. The Russian conquest of the Circassian (or Cherkess) people caused their geographic dispersal (especially to the Ottoman Empire) and disappearance as a cohesive ethnic group with a common identity.[268] In Central Asia, Russia pursued economic objectives similar to those of other colonial powers, turning the Ferghana Valley into a supplier of cotton for expanding Russian textile industries.[269] When, in an interview with Aksiuchits, I raised these issues, he admitted that there had been excesses, but he insisted that Russian colonialism had been of a more benign type than that of others.

These core beliefs had implications for the behavior of Aksiuchits and his fellow Christian nationalists prior to the fall of the Soviet Union and in subsequent years. Given his interpretation of the nature of the Russian Empire, he supported the declaration of sovereignty by the RSFSR's Supreme Soviet in 1990 because he saw it not as a prelude to the possible disintegration of the Soviet Union, but as "an assertion of Russian identity and national rights against . . . a denationalized and completely depraved Soviet regime."[270] For the same reason, it was difficult for Aksiuchits and his followers to believe that the non-Russian republics would want to separate from Russia. Thus Aksiuchits is reported to have said, "I am absolutely convinced that the nations on the borders of our country are trying to escape from the communist regime, not from Russia."[271] It is also for this reason that Aksiuchits supports the reunification of the former Soviet republics, albeit through peaceful means. Initially, the RCDM had included in its program a range of democratic concepts in the context of its overarching paradigm of "enlightened patriotism," including rejection of "national hatred," "discrimination," and "national egotism."[272] However, the emergence of the secessionist movements in the North Caucasus and the spread of Western culture in Russia, combined with international events, especially the crisis in Yugoslavia and the international isolation of Serbia, led Aksiuchits to take a sharp turn toward *gosudarstvennost* (statist) positions.[273] Thus the restoration of Russian statehood and, with it, Russia's status as a great power became his main preoccupation, leaving democratization, even in its Christian variety, as a secondary issue.

Other Types of Christian Nationalism

In the context of the typology described earlier, Christian nationalism in its various forms is not of the civic variety. In this scheme, other religions and cultures, notably Islam, may be tolerated, but certainly not treated as equals, even though the principle of equality among Russia's traditional creeds is recognized in most nationalist manifestos. The exclusionary nature of Christian nationalism was demonstrated in February 2003 when the Russian region of Penza adopted a regional flag bearing an image of Jesus adopted from a Russian Orthodox icon. The adoption of this new flag led to protests by the local Muslim community.[274] Additionally, Christian nationalism considers the Russian ethnic element the most important core of the state.

Other Russian intellectuals who construct their political and social philosophy on the basis of various aspects of Orthodox Christianity include Vladimir Malyavin and Natalia Narochnitskaya. Malyavin represents the Slavophile understanding of the Russian identity. He maintains that Slavophile teaching is deeply rooted in the mysticism of Russian Orthodox Christianity.[275] According to Malyavin, this particular version of Slavophilism "represents a serious alternative to the contemporary technocratic civilization. It offers a way out of the boredom of one dimensional existence embedded in technologicial systems."[276] The main problem of the Slavophiles, according to Malyavin, has been their inability to formulate and explain their ideas.

Communist Nationalists

One of the latest versions of combining Russian nationalism with communism has been that of Gennady Zyuganov, leader of the Communist Party of the Russian Federation (CPRF). Zyuganov's vision of Russian nationalism and identity is composite and draws on many sources, including religion.[277] Other elements of Zyuganov's nationalist vision include the ethnic Russians' sense of beleagueredness, encompassing age-old theories of internal and external conspiracies against Russia by "those who hate Russia," a sense of continuity in the historical evolution of Russia, and the importance of reviving Russian statehood and Russia's status as a great power. On economic issues, however, Zyuganov has softened traditional Communist doctrines and accepted a mixed economic system. He considers this important for Russia's internal development and its world outlook. Two aspects of his view of Russian history and its implications for Russia's future are worth noting: (1) the idea that during the Soviet period, the Communist Party was divided by an internal conflict between two factions, patriotic ethnic Russians and internationalists who eschewed national identity, and (2) the belief in a centuries-old conspiracy by the West and certain national minorities to weaken and, if possible, dismember and enslave Russia.[278]

According to the first idea, during the Soviet period, there were, in effect, two

Communist parties that competed with one another in a fierce, albeit quiet, struggle for power. Zyuganov calls one of these parties the party of "our country," meaning Russia. To this party belonged "Zhukov and Gagarin [and] the largest part of the functionaries and administrators."[279] Competing with this party was the party of "that country," meaning the denationalized Soviet Union, whose members saw "that country" and "those people" as "merely the arena for the realization of their own ambitions and reckless experiments. It was the party of Trotsky and Kaganovich, Beria, . . . Gorbachev and Yeltsin. Its legal successor today is Democratic Russia (*Demrossiya*)."[280] Those who belonged to the party of *nasha strana* (our country) were populist and patriotic Russians. The members of the party of *eta strana* (that country) consisted of internationalists, cosmopolitans, and mercenary elements coming largely from national minority communities. According to Zyuganov, the first group "saw the particular talents and spiritual qualities of the Russian people rather than dogmatic adherence to Marxism as the essential element in the construction of *derzhava* (a Great Power) and its socialist system, which for all its shortcomings achieved much that is worth preserving."[281]

The second aspect of Zyuganov's blend of communism and nationalism identifies the West, especially the United States, as the main villain because Western leaders want to weaken Russia, destroy its great-power status, and turn it into an appendage of a "supra-national world regime."[282] Zyuganov views the Yeltsin-era reformers as the heirs to the earlier cosmopolitans and internationalists (the party of that country), who did not have Russia's interests at heart. To prevent the realization of these anti-Russian plots, Russian statehood must be restored by re-creating the Soviet integrated state; this would be a multinational, but unitary, state and would be ruled by Russians and their Russified allies. To some degree, this goal contrasts with statements Zyuganov made during his presidential campaigns, during which he posed as a defender of ethnic minorities and religions. However, these goals need not be as antagonistic as they appear since a degree of cultural diversity is achievable within a unitary state.

Zyuganov approaches the question of Islam in Russia and its impact on the development of Russia's post-Soviet identity and statehood essentially from the angle of Russia's external relations and its role in the outside world, especially in terms of warding off the West's geopolitical and cultural threat. From a cultural perspective, Zyuganov has a positive view of Islam due to what he believes are its antimaterialist and anti-individualistic characteristics. His belief that the Russians "are a nation of idealists, a nation of dreamers and heroes who in practical life are often driven by immaterial spiritual impulses," gives him a natural affinity with Islam.[283] Zyuganov, who has made "spirituality" one of the three pillars of his vision for a revitalized Russia, has stated that this goal should be achieved, among other means, through "the constructive interaction with traditional religious confessions."[284] The official program of the CPRF mentions Judaism along with Orthodox Christianity, Islam, and Buddhism as Russia's traditional religions. In other statements, notably an interview with the newspaper *Orthodox Moscow*, Zyuganov has said that it is in the Russian national interest to support three religions, Russian Orthodoxy, Islam, and Buddhism, which "are traditional for Russia and which put spiritual and moral values above consumerism."[285]

During his campaign for the presidency in 1996, Zyuganov sent a message to Russia's Muslims that was reminiscent of the famous 1917 Lenin-Stalin letter to Muslims. In his message, titled "To Russia's Muslims," he acknowledged and condemned past wrongs committed against them and promised that they would not be repeated.[286] He also stressed the common danger that the spread of Western values and Americanism is posing to Russia's traditional values, Islamic and Christian. Further, he referred to the historic "interaction between Christian and Muslim peoples and the inter-penetrations of their cultures" through which "a unique Eurasian civilization has emerged."[287]

Despite such proclamations, the Communists' "Election Appeal" issued in 2000 was much more Russo-centric, illustrating the overall trend in the country. While stating that no people will be discriminated against, Zyuganov says that "ethnic Russians will occupy a place and position in the Russian state that accords with their status as a great people, the custodians of our distinctive character and unifier of the fraternal peoples."[288] The latter phrase is reminiscent of the "elder brother" notion of the Soviet era. Zyuganov advocates an alliance between state and church, meaning all traditional Russian denominations, but he emphasizes "Russian Orthodoxy's special role in the people's life."[289] He attempts to demonstrate that the West has targeted both Orthodoxy and Islam and suggests that Western powers have sent terrorists to Chechnya as part of a general campaign against these two religions.[290] Unlike some Russian nationalists, Zyuganov does not see—or, at least, he has not said anything to indicate otherwise—radical Islam as a useful ally for Russia in challenging the forces of globalization and what he sees as the hegemony of the United States. However, he cautions that Russia should not antagonize Muslims or attempt to act as a buffer between the West and the Muslim world.

Geopolitical Nationalists: Zhirinovsky, Dugin, and the Neo-Eurasianists

The views of Vladimir Zhirinovsky, Alexander Dugin, and the neo-Eurasianists differ considerably. For example, Dugin's views have a religious and even mystical dimension, which makes them radically different from those of Zhirinovsky. However, they agree on one fundamental point, namely, the importance of geopolitical factors in shaping states' characteristics and the impact of geography and climate in forming peoples' characteristics; hence all three qualify as geopolitical nationalists. According to Zhirinovsky, "There are specific geopolitical factors that have played a part in the development of the Russian soul. Russia is situated in bad climate zones with bad neighbors. For 700 years, there have always been wars, . . . the Tatars for 300 years, with Turkey alone, thirty wars, with others dozens, hundreds of wars."[291] To end this geopolitical disadvantage, Russia must not only secure and pacify its southern front, but should expand further, incorporating countries such as Iran, Afghanistan, and Turkey, eventually reaching the warm waters of the Indian Ocean. According to him, "The warm [Indian] ocean breeze will soothe everyone living in this new geopolitical area within the new borders of Russia. . . . We [Russians] will be able to relax more, we will become calmer."[292] Zhirinovsky believes that in this manner, Russia will also render a service to the world by eliminating the "Islamic threat."[293]

Zhirinovsky has an essentially negative view of Islam, and not merely its extremist variants; he believes that Islam is a principal source of religious wars.[294] He has a colonial attitude toward Muslim nations, both those within the CIS and others. Muslim countries are supposed to provide raw materials, markets, cheap labor, and places of leisure for Russians. Zhirinovsky is more fearful of progressive Islam. Yet, according to Malashenko, "he is ready to recognize fundamentalism and Islam itself as natural for the other, un-Orthodox world with which one [Russia] can have dealings and which one [Russia] can, in the final account, subordinate to one's [Russia's] own ends."[295]

Alexander Dugin: The Eurasist Movement and Islam

Dugin, too, emphasizes geographical characteristics of nations as fundamental to their cultures and even their sense of purpose and mission. In the early 1990s, Dugin developed his particular concept of Eurasianism, stressing the importance of "Russia's geographical location at the center of the European heartland in determining Russian culture and politics."[296] He also pointed to "the urgency of Russia's imperial mission in the face of mondialism (globalization)."[297] Dugin's views border on geopolitical determinism. He maintains that geographic conditions create particular civilizations with totally different values, aspirations, and dynamics. In Dugin's view, the two most characteristic and, at the same time, antagonistic prototypes of geographically determined civilizations are those of "continent" (or "land-based") and "island." In their ultimate forms, they represent two types of empires: the *tellurokratiya* (continental) and *talassokratiya* (island). The best examples of the latter are the British Empire and what Dugin considers its successor, the United States. The island civilization's ideology, which Dugin calls "Atlanticism," is based on instability, rootlessness, and materialism.[298] In contrast, the continental empire is an integrative, spiritual, and nonexploitative civilization, and its ideology is "Eurasianism."

Dugin believes that since ancient times, these two civilizations have been in competition.[299] Dugin has written that the Atlanticists search for global domination in the form of mondialism, trying to subject the traditional cultures of Eurasia.[300] In his early writings, Dugin stated that Russia's main duty was "to unite the anti-Atlanticist, anti-mondialist forces of Eurasia in a new imperial alliance."[301] Dugin thought that in advancing this goal, Islam could potentially be an ally of Russia because it shares with Russian Orthodoxy a deeply "Eastern" and "continental" spirituality and rejects materialism. For a long time, Dugin was on the periphery of Russian national politics, but in 2000, he became part of the political mainstream by supporting President Putin and appearing in various conferences with Russian officials.

Dugin's Eurasist Movement. A major development in Dugin's evolving political role was the founding on 21 April 2001 of the All-Russia Political and Social Movement "Eurasia" and its registration with the Russian Ministry of Justice. In its manifesto, the movement laments the fact that the early Eurasianists (Eurasists) were not appreciated. But in the late 1980s, a new version of Eurasianism emerged and laid the basis of modern Russian geopolitics. The manifesto states that Russia's new realities, including its new government (Putin), created a favorable atmosphere for the translation of Eurasist principle into concrete policies. According to the manifesto, "The present authorities, their specificity, their social image, considerably differ from the [immediate] post-Soviet period and from the times of uncritical passion for reckless liberalism. A new state worldview, a new domestic pattern of political correctness have surfaced. This is testified by that persevering search for a national idea in which the authorities are today engaged."[302] The manifesto further states that the movement is open to all ethnic and confessional groups of Russia, provided that the prospective applicant "loves Russia, . . . cannot think of himself without it, . . . [and] wants, passionately wants, that all of us at last would rise in a mighty power . . . above the country, the continent, the world, our solar Russian ideals—Ideals of Freedom, Equity, Fidelity to the Origins."[303]

The movement describes itself as the "radical center, . . . neither leftist nor rightist . . . neither slavishly compliant to the authorities, nor oppositionist at any cost, barking with a reason or without."[304] It expresses support for President Putin as long as he acts "for the sake of [State] power, for the sake of the people." The manifesto describes five priorities for the movement: (1) constructive dialogue among the creeds traditional to Russia; (2) placing the public principle above the individual and subordinating economic policies to solving strategic social problems; (3) revival of the traditions of the Russian people and the recovery of ethnic Russian demographic growth;[305] (4) Eurasist federalism, meaning a combination of strategic unity and ethnocultural (in certain cases, economic) autonomies that permits different ways of life at a local level alongside strict centralism in the basic moments, linked to state interests; and (5) reconstruction on the basis of the CIS of a solid Eurasian Union (analogous to the USSR) on a new ideological, economic, and administrative basis.

In terms of Russia's relations with the outside world, Dugin promotes four basic objectives. First, he emphasizes the need for what he calls the "strategic integration of the internal spaces of the CIS to . . . a wider area . . . [encompassing] the countries of the Moscow-Tehran-Delhi-Beijing axis." Such a Eurasist policy will "open for Russia an exit to warm seas, not through war and suffering, but through peace and open friendly cooperation."[306] Second, Dugin believes that Russia should promote close relations with Europe because, in contrast to the time of the early Eurasist movement, in the contemporary international system, Europe no longer represents "the source of 'world evil.' " Instead, it is the United States that has assumed this role.[307] According to him, "Eurasist Russia should play the role of deliverers of Europe, but this time from American political, economic, and cultural occupation."[308] Third, Dugin promotes active cooperation with the countries of the Pacific region, especially Japan. "The economic giants of this area should see in the Eurasist polices of Russia the orienting point for a self-supporting political system and also for a strategic potential of resources and new markets."[309] Finally, Dugin stresses the need for active and universal opposition to globalization because "Eurasianism defends the blossoming complexity of peoples, religions, and nations. All anti-globalist tendencies are intrinsically Eurasist."[310]

Dugin's Views of Islam. Dugin has long considered Islam a potential ally of Russia. In recent years, he has further developed his views on Islam, the religion's different forms, and the implications of each for Russia and its relations with the Islamic world, both within Russia and outside the country. Dugin elaborated his views on this subject in an article titled "Islam against Islam" published on 15 February 2000, and in a speech he delivered at a conference titled "Islamic Threat or Threat to Islam," held in Moscow on 28 June 2001. The Moscow conference was held under the auspices of the Eurasia Movement and the Central Spiritual Board of Muslims of Russia, led by Mufti Talgat Tadzhuddin with the support of President Putin and under the tutelage of the chairman of the Russian State Duma, Gennady Seleznev. Central to Dugin's argument is the notion that the concept of "Islamic threat" is a Western invention designed to foster rivalries between international actors that might otherwise form alliances to resist Western influence. He further argues that by encouraging tensions between Russia and the Islamic world, the West is striving to weaken both and to enhance its own position globally.[311]

Dugin applies his geopolitical theories to the world of Islam and states that "the Islamic world has its own geopolitical dualism. It is not so clearly outlined and expressed as in the case of Christianity. Nevertheless, using the same typological criterion, we see that there is a specific Eurasist Islam (deep, contemplative, mystical, not paying excessive attention to the ordinary aspects of life)."[312] According to Dugin, Shi'a Islam and mystical Sufi sects of Sunni Islam belong to this Eurasist Islam, which, like its counterpart in Christianity, Orthodox Eurasian Christianity, is "open, contemplative, multi-polar, anti-totalitarian, and traditional."[313] This Islam has its opposite in the "Atlanticist" Islam, which, like the Atlantist version of Christianity, "ignores the divine side of man, rejects contemplation and multi-polarity, and imposes on all its unidimensional, flat, purely ritualistic practice."[314] To this category, according to Dugin, belong Wahhabism, the Jama'at Tabligh (the Tablighis) and the Ikhvanists (Muslim Brotherhood).[315]

Dugin identifies two additional forms of Islam: so-called socialist Islam and "Enlightened Islam." According to Dugin, the former type is primarily associated with the Ba'ath Party and at one time was strong in Iraq, Syria, Libya, and (South) Yemen. This Islam is potentially Eurasist.[316] Enlightened Islam, best represented by Turkey and Tunisia, is "oriented toward copying Western models of politics and economics, . . . imposes the secular model of Atlanticist nature, . . . [and] is completely pro-Western and strategically dependent." According to Dugin, the West supports Atlanticist Islam and fights against Eurasianist Islam. In Russia, the West uses both types of Atlanticist Islam—the Enlightened Islamism of Turkey and the Wahhabism of Saudi Arabia.[317] In Chechnya, according to Dugin, these two forms of Islam united to defeat the Eurasianist Islam of Chechnya inspired by Sufi traditions—which is alien to Wahhabi morality—and Chechen Islamic socialists.[318]

Implications of Dugin's Ideas.   Beneath its metaphysical and pseudospiritual veneer, Dugin's theory of Eurasianism is essentially a Russocentric nationalist ideology with strong statist and, if not imperial (in the classic sense of the term), then great-power tendencies. This is how the neo-Eurasianist theory is seen by many non-Russian intellectuals, especially those with nationalist and/or pan-Turkic (in the cultural sense) tendencies. Rafael Khakimov of Tatarstan states that "Eurasianism in the present day treatment is an ideological cloak for the old, tried and true policy of territorial claims. This is an attempt to restore the [Russian] state within the borders of the [former] USSR or of the Russian Empire."[319] He further argues that Eurasianism is also a vehicle to thwart "the already-started process of the rebirth of the non-Russian peoples."[320]

Dugin's analysis of various categories of Islam is both faulty and reminiscent of the Soviet-era literature, albeit put into a new ideological framework.[321] His basic distinctions are between "quietist" and "assertive" Islam on the domestic front and, on the international front, between those who are friendly to Russia and those who are allied with the West. The fact that Talgat Tadzhuddin, the head of the Central Spiritual Board of Muslim of Russia and the European Countries of the CIS, is a founding member of the Eurasist movement illustrates what kind of Islam Dugin thinks is best for Russia, namely, a quietist and culturally subservient Islam that at times can be useful as a tool of foreign policy. Following the September 2001 terrorist attacks in the United States and the Russian-American rapprochement, Dugin's political fortunes have suffered. However, some of his views still resonate with segments of the Russian population and intelligentsia.

Alexei Kara-Murza and the Concept of Russia's Dual Identity

A different variety of Eurasianism is offered by Alexei Kara-Murza's theory of Russia's dual identity. According to Kara-Murza, Russia has a dual identity (*dual'naya identichnost*) consisting of two halves: (1) a European civilizational identity (*tsivilizatsionnaya identichnost*) because Russia's ethnocultural core belongs to the Eastern branch of the European Christian civilization and (2) a Eurasian geopolitical identity (*geopoliticheskaya identichnost*). The latter, however, is acquired and derives from the historical accident of Russia's location on the European platform. The stability of this identity is based on the cultural-political union of Slavic, Finno-Ugrian, and Turkic peoples, who have developed the ability to coexist without losing their identities.[322] However, Kara-Murza, like Aksiuchits, ignores the fact that at least as far as Turkic Muslims are concerned, this coexistence was based on Russian domination and has resulted in the dilution of their identity. Yet in criticizing both Westernizers and Eurasianists for forcing a choice on Russia between these two poles of its identity, he reveals himself to be a cultural imperialist when he says that "Russia's finest hours occurred when its civilizational (European) identification and its geopolitical tasks harmonized in the course of the realization of European cultural 'mission' in its own Russian East."[323]

According to Kara-Murza, dogmatic adherence to either of Russia's identities would be potentially dangerous. The embrace of Eurasianism as a phenomenon different from, and perhaps in opposition to, the West risks Russia's cultural degradation consequent to its separation from its European roots, while "the Vulgar Westernizing drive towards presenting Russia as merely 'part of the West' and dismissing everything in Russia that does not belong to the West leads toward absolute civilizational identification of Russia with the West at the expense of its geopolitical interests—and, therefore, logically toward the surrender of geopolitical positions."[324]

Put crudely, Kara-Murza believes in the cultural Westernization of Russia while retaining its dominant position in its traditional sphere of influence. In other words, Eurasianism is an ideological justification for the spread of Russian influence rather than one of true synthesis of Russian and non-Russian (Turko-Muslim) cultures. Therefore, Kara-Murza too is a geopolitical nationalist, albeit with Westernizing traits.

Fringe Nationalism: Russian National Unity and the Ultrarightists

Russian National Unity (RNU) and its leader, Alexander Barkashov, expound a type of extreme ethnocentric nationalism that is akin to racism, and a political and ideological belief system that has close parallels with Nazism. One of the underlying ideas behind the philosophy of RNU and Barkashov is the belief in the existence of a distinct Russian racial "genotype" whose purification from all alien elements, as well as less than perfect Russian elements—such as alcoholics, drug addicts, and the like—is a first and necessary step toward the restoration of a feared and powerful Russian empire.[325] Barkashov's movement further believes in Russia's historic mission to create a just world order and to be the guarantor of justice. However, in RNU's conception, justice does not mean equality or even attempts to create equal opportunities.

Another distinguishing characteristic of RNU's ideology is its ambiguous attitude toward Orthodox Christianity. The organization sees Christian qualities of charity, mercy, and humility as obstacles to achieving a genetic regeneration of the Russian people and to instilling the combative spirit that is needed to gain greatness. Rather, RNU promotes the cult of paganism, with its emphasis on heroic actions.[326] However, realizing the importance of the religious impulse and the hold of at least cultural Orthodoxy on many Russians, RNU followers are willing to use it and its rituals to instill in the people a powerful sense of will and belonging. This is why Wayne Allensworth has characterized Barkashov's view of Russian Christianity as "Orthodox Paganism." Some RNU followers also see Christianity as an antipeople, antination phenomenon. The organization also believes in violent actions to achieve its goals. RNU members have fought in various trouble spots of Russia and in the Yugoslav civil war on the side of the Croats.[327] Another central belief of RNU is that Russia is threatened by internal and external enemies.

Russian National Unity does not exhaust the list of racist nationalist groups in Russia. Rather, the list of groups with similar ideas is fairly long. The most overtly racist groups include the National Front of Ilya Lazarenko (Nazis and skinheads), the League of the Defense of Russia's National Assets (LZDDR) of Alexander Savastyomov (Slavic-Aryan racists), and Russian Aim of Semyon Tokmokov (a group of skinheads).[328]

In February 2002, another nationalist party, the National Power Party of Russia (Natsionalno-derzhavnaya Partiya Rossii, or NDPR), attracted 193 delegates from sixty-five regions for its founding congress in Korolev (Moscow Oblast). Most of the attendees were senior military personnel and representatives of seven Cossack armies, the Russian diaspora (including guests from Belarus, Ukraine, and the Trans-Dnester region of Moldova), and right-wing elements of the antiglobalization movement. According to some sources, the party opened regional branches in fifty-three regions and gained 1,300 members in its first year.[329] Due to the NDPR's strong anti-Semitic tendencies, the party's registration with the Russian Ministry of Justice in September 2002 caused a serious controversy and forced the ministry to order an investigation into the party's real goals.[330]

An interesting aspect of the party's philosophy, as expressed by one of its co-chairmen, Boris Mironov, is its belief that only those people who are indigenous to Russia and do not have ethnic or other connections to "other state formations" should have the right to vote or run for office.[331] This effectively disenfranchises naturalized citizens and Soviet-era citizens of Caucasian and Central Asian descent. The rationale behind this position is that such people can be subject to conflicting loyalties or even put another country's interests above those of Russia. The NDPR considers as Russians all peoples who are indigenous to Russia because, according to Mironov, Russia "has always been part of a multi-ethnic family."[332] Therefore, logically, people belonging to ethnic minorities native to modern Russia's territory, including Muslims, should have equal rights in terms of political participation. However, given their cultural, religious, and ethnic links with Muslims in other countries, Russia's Muslims are potentially suspect. Consequently, they may not be fit to play a significant role in Russia's political life or occupy high positions on the federal level.

Regarding the implications of these groups for Russia's Muslims, Alexei Malashenko has pointed out that "extreme radical nationalists are not afraid of Islam. . . . Thus, in the programme of the movement for Russian National Unity headed by Alexander Barkashov, Islam is not mentioned at all among the enemies of the Russian people. . . . Nor are there anti-Islamic motifs in the programmatic tenets of the Front for National Revolutionary Action."[333] This may be so; however, the racist dimension of their philosophy is clearly detrimental to Russia's Muslim population. If the renaissance of the Russian nation depends on genetic purification, then Muslims will be victimized. For example, the National Republican Party of Russia advocates the creation of a "national regime" in Russia that "would wage war on what the party terms the 'Black Hydra', the most immediate threat being the 'blacks,' the Turkic and Caucasian hordes of the former Soviet empire's southern underbelly."[334] Since the overwhelming majority of these people are Muslims, the ultranationalists are clearly anti-Islamic. Cases of attacks have increased steadily in recent years and have been taking more organized form, leading some observers to speculate that some government agencies or elements within them may be sympathetic to the ultranationalists' goals. It is widely believed, for example, that the police are sympathetic to ultranationalists. Some even believe that the FSB and other government officials are aiding them.[335]

One of the most alarming aspects of these ultranationalist groups is the fact that they are attractive to a large portion of Russia's youth. According to some opinion polls, of the 4 to 6 percent of Russian youth interested in politics, more than half (2 to 3 percent of the total youth population) tend to be attracted to ultranationalist neo-Nazi and fascist ideas.[336] This is not surprising, given the social and economic turmoil Russia has experienced and given that the destruction of Russia's old values has left Russian youth adrift and socially alienated.[337] Moreover, "Two wars in Chechnya have given strong momentum to nationalist and racist moods."[338]

Reformist Liberal Nationalism

Reformist or liberal nationalism, although the degree of liberalism in regard to various issues from economics to interethnic and religious relations to concepts of citizenship may differ, combines the requirements of modernization—political and economic—with enhancing Russia's statehood, restoring its great-power status, and maintaining its cultural distinctiveness. Reform nationalism, rather than being a single unified political movement expressed through the institutional framework of one or more political parties, is a philosophy that aims at harmonizing Russia's historical and cultural realities with the need for social, political, and economic modernization. Reform nationalism is also a reaction to the disruptions caused by the reforms of Gorbachev, the revolutionary reformism, best exemplified by economic "shock therapy," of the early Yeltsin era, and a recognition of the new realities created by these reforms. After 1993, even President Boris Yeltsin pursued a variant of reform nationalism as he moved away from domestic economic reforms, initiated a war in Chechnya to preserve Russia's territorial integrity, and pursued a foreign policy more independent of the West.

Nationalism in Reform Nationalism

The nationalist dimension of reform nationalism derives from its emphasis on the centrality of Russia and Russian interests and its overriding goal of making Russia strong, independent, and prosperous. This aspect is best encapsulated in the concept of Russian *derzhavnost* (greatness) as espoused by the late General Alexander Lebed, a presidential candidate in 1996, former secretary of the Russian Security

Council, and governor of Krasnoyarsk at the time of his death in a helicopter crash in April 2002. In Lebed's conception, all the other questions are of secondary importance because they do not relate to the fundamental goal, but to instruments of achieving this goal. *Derzhavnost* is as much a goal as a state of mind and a vision of what Russia should be. This view consists of the following components:

A Sense of Belonging and Rootedness That Breeds Patriotism. According to Lebed, to achieve this sense, "A man must stand on his own land, he must have something of his own . . . something to defend, something to fight for, and, if necessary, die for."[339]

Self-Reliance and Self-Respect. Russia should rely on its own resources and abilities to develop and prosper, economically and culturally, and should "not look to foreigners to save her."[340] This does not imply economic autarchy, but it does entail the protection of Russia's productive capacity and the limiting of imported products, be they goods or culture.[341]

Pragmatism over Ideology. Russia should no longer be an arena for wild experimentation with various ideologies. Rather, the political leadership should pursue pragmatic and flexible reforms that could help achieve the stated goals and that are compatible with Russian traditions. For example, Lebed did not see democracy as an end in itself, nor did he believe in a total transplantation of Western-style democracy to Russia. Rather, he believed that the democracy that would come to Russia "will be a distinctly 'Russian' democracy, and it must evolve over time."[342] Some of Lebed's statements indicate that under certain conditions, a degree of authoritarianism may be necessary.[343]

Importance of Historical Continuity and the Central Role of the Armed Forces. Having a sense of historical continuity and acknowledging the past without becoming its prisoner is a main theme embedded in Lebed's vision. He said, "We [Russians] cannot cancel out our history. The past is with us, it is inside us. Without the past, there is no future." But he also said that the Russians cannot live always looking back. He believed that the military, through its rituals, symbols, and organization, can help "maintain the sense of continuity between past, present, and future that is a necessary element of patriotism, of the sense that one owns a piece of the national patrimony."[344] This view is based on the belief that Russian statehood was built by the army, and that the Russian army developed into a people's army that defended the country and turned it into a great military power.

On the specific question of who is a Russian and the role of ethnic Russians in the rebuilding of Russia, Lebed's view can be characterized as moderately ethnocentric, but not exclusivist, and allowing for nonethnic Russians to be members of the Russian nation and state. The following statement perhaps best sums up his philosophy in this regard: "I am a Russian [*Rossiiskii*] general, but first of all, I am a Russian [*Russkii*] man."[345] In terms of religious issues, Lebed again embraced a middle-of-the-road position: he adhered to the view of Russia as an essentially Orthodox country, but also recognized the rights of adherents of what are often referred to as the other traditional religions of Russia, namely, Islam, Judaism, and Buddhism.

Other reform nationalists share many of the beliefs just described, such as the supremacy of Russian national interest over ideology and the necessity of reform, including a degree of Westernization in the sense of utilizing Western economic and political concepts, but they believe that these ideas should be implemented within the boundaries set by the "Russian mentality" and "Russian historical roots."[346] The notion of collective self-respect is also important for other reform nationalists, as Vladimir Lukin, who, along with Grigorii Yavlinsky and Yurii Bold-eryev, formed the Yabloko electoral bloc. According to Lukin, for Russia, at stake are her national interests, her identity, and her self-respect. While he does not see automatic and inevitable conflict between Russian and Western interests, he insists that Russia can never become a mere colony of the West.[347] The reform nationalists favor a moderately strong central government with a dose of local autonomy. They support democratization and economic reform, but not as ends in themselves and not without concern for the consequences for Russia's vital interests, notably its territorial integrity. Although there are variations among the reform nationalists on the role of religion—some are more secular—in general, they are tolerant of minority religions, provided that the aspirations of religious minorities do not threaten Russia's national interests, especially its territorial integrity.

Vladimir Putin and His Vision of Russian Nationalism and National Identity

While campaigning for the presidency, Vladimir Putin admitted that there was a lack of a unifying concept for the Russian nation and pointed to the need to develop a national idea. Since becoming president, however, Putin has not tried to offer a coherent view on this question, nor has he appointed any special commissions to develop such a concept, as Yeltsin did. On the contrary, at times, Putin has made statements to the effect that there was no need to develop an overarching ideological or philosophical concept explaining the nature of Russian identity or setting guidelines for Russia's internal and external behavior. In an interview with the editor of *India Today* prior to his visit to India in October 2000, Putin, when asked about the issue of developing a Russian national idea, stated that "the country [Russia] was not in a position to develop anything new and should not attempt to do so."[348] During the interview, Putin "made a point of repeating that Russia was not going to invent anything new and that the country and people were not going to be radically different from any other people in the world."[349] In another interview, Putin stated that "the introduction of the national idea is, in my view, an empty and completely senseless venture. It cannot be invented just like that. People's moral and ethical values develop over centuries—people are changing and so is their understanding of life. And I am convinced that the outlines of the new general national ideology are already being defined now."[350] Thus the outlines of Putin's vision of Russian national identity and the nature of Russian nationalism must be pieced together from his statements on various aspects of Russian statehood and nationhood, and, even more important, from his actions and the type of individuals he appoints to his government.

Chechnya: Stepping-Stone for Putin or Reassertion of Russian Territorial Inviolability?

In understanding Putin's view of Russian nationalism and its basic components, it is important to remember the role that the second Chechen campaign played in propelling Putin to the presidency. Unlike the 1994–96 Chechen War, which was greeted with widespread condemnation from the Russian public and media, the war beginning in 1999 received broad popular support across the country. Several reasons account for this change in popular attitudes. First, developments in Chechnya in the 1996–99 interwar period reduced expectations that the dispute between Moscow and Grozny on the status of Chechnya could be resolved through political means short of granting the republic full independence. Second, the turn of events in Chechnya and the heightened risk of instability spreading beyond Chechnya into Dagestan and perhaps other parts of the North Caucasus increased fears regarding the territorial integrity of the Russian Federation. Third, terrorist acts committed by Chechen militants or attributed to them by the Russian government increased popular anxieties about terrorist threats and intensified anti-Chechen sentiments. Fourth, the Russian military achieved some initial success in 1999 (as opposed to its disastrous performance in the previous war), especially in routing out Islamist militants in Dagestan. Fifth, a heightened sense of injured pride and popular anger over criminal activities in Chechnya, especially kidnapping for ransom, combined with a desire for revenge for Russia's military defeat in the 1994–96 war, increased Russian support for the use of force to subdue Chechen separatism. Sixth, Moscow's ability to exercise greater control over reporting in Chechnya, along with a dramatic decline in sympathy for the Chechens among Russian journalists during the interwar period, virtually eliminated negative reports in the Russian media about military operations in Chechnya.

Putin's handling of the Chechen War and how he used the sentiments just noted greatly contributed both to sustaining public support and to increasing his own popularity. Putin's actions and statements regarding Chechnya helped to clarify one important aspect of his vision of Russia's future, Russian nationalism, and hence Russia's national identity. First and foremost was Putin's emphasis on the inviolability of Russia's territorial integrity, his goal being to maintain a Russia "whole and indivisible." Thus Putin's nationalism—even though he avoids using the term, preferring to talk about "patriotism"—has a definite territorial dimension.

In an interview with *Izvestia* on 19 July 2000, Putin, when asked about the Chechen problem, categorically stated that "one thing is clear: Chechnya will not become independent outside Russia."[351] It is important to note that such a view had already been expressed by President Yeltsin's administration. In an interview with the *Financial Times* in October 1999, the presidential press spokesman, Dmitri Yakushkin, stated, "Our position is that Chechnya is Russian territory and nothing has changed."[352] He went on to explain that the ultimate goal was to prevent the contagion effect of Chechnya and "to send a message to all the North Caucasian republics. . . . Re-imposition of order in Chechnya would help quell unrest in [Russia's] other [North] Caucasian republics, such as Karachaevo-Cherkessia, Dagestan, Ingushetia, and Ossetia."[353]

The territorial dimension of Putin's version of Russian nationalism is not limited to the maintenance of the present borders of the Russian Federation; rather, it includes the aspiration of integrating parts or all of the former Soviet Union into a more cohesive political entity than the CIS, with priority given to the largely Slavic states of Ukraine and Belarus, which are ethnically close to Russia. However, this goal did not originate with Putin. Rather, such views have been popular with large segments of the Russian population and political groups. On 8 December 1999, Boris Yeltsin and Belarusan president Alexander Lukashenko signed a treaty signaling their intention to create a new Soyuznoe Gosudarstvo (Union State) uniting Russia and Belarus.[354] In fact, Putin is rather ambivalent about the usefulness of such schemes. Certainly the record of his presidency indicates that he is unlikely to sacrifice Russia's other important goals, most notably its economic revitalization and maintaining relations with Europe and the United States, to realize this aspiration. Rather, for Putin, this is a secondary and more distant goal that could provide a framework for the reassertion of Russia's great-power status in the future should other conditions make such a move possible. To the extent that Putin moves in this direction, it could be argued that his vision of Russian nationalism contains both Slavophile and Eurasianist influences, although neither plays a decisive role in his ideology.

Centrality of the State: Putin as Statist

In a speech titled "Russia at the Turn of the Millennium," delivered at a ceremony celebrating the dawning of the third millennium of Christianity, Putin stated, "Russia needs a strong state power and must have it," but he added, "I am not calling for totalitarianism. History proves all dictatorships, all authoritarian forms of government, are transient. Only democratic systems are intransient."[355] On another occasion, Putin stated that the process of democratic change and movement toward a market economy was irreversible. Putin has also talked about the importance of a strong civil society and a free press.[356] Judged solely on the basis of these and similar statements, Putin's statism, as Astrid Tuminez has pointed out, would appear to be of a moderate character.[357] However, Putin's other statements—and, even more important, his actions—since becoming Russia's president indicate a more robust statism, at least in the political sphere. While emphasizing that the process of democratization is irreversible, Putin seems to think that its completion will take some time and that Russian democracy will have its own special features. At one point, Putin rejected the notion that Russia "can ever become a second edition of the United States or Britain with their centuries-old traditions of political liberalism."[358]

Putin's efforts to assert the authority of the federal center over Russia's provinces, although originating in the policies of Yeltsin's second term as president, demonstrate that his interpretation of federalism is of a restrictive nature. Putin's approach to freedom of the press also indicates that his liberalism is of a mild nature. Indeed, actions taken in 2001 against the independent television station NTV and the closures of the daily newspaper *Segodnya* and the weekly *Itogi* led one prominent American specialist on Russia to write that "more than any event in the Putin era, the recent closing of NTV, Russia's only independent television network, demonstrates unequivocally that Putin seeks to destroy Russia's already fragile and weak democratic institutions."[359] This statement may be an exaggeration of Putin's intentions, but the record of his presidency indicates that the reassertion of state power, economic revitalization, and the maintenance of the country's territorial integrity—not the consolidation of democratic institutions—are his priorities.

Russia Firsters and Historical Continuity

While Putin has not been specific about his version of Russian nationalism and identity and has at times made contradictory statements on this subject, the bulk of his statements and actions, symbolic and otherwise, demonstrate an ethnocentric tendency with elements of traditional Russian nationalism. In his millennium speech, Putin stated that in addition to universal values embedded in a democratic system, "the traditional values of Russia" can best unify society.[360] In his interview with *India Today,* Putin defined these traditional Russian values, which he asserted should form the basis of a Russian national idea. In response to a question about Russia's national idea, Putin stated, "The basic values are none other than patriotism, love of one's own home, one's people, religious and cultural values, everything that forms the foundation of our life. . . . Everything that makes us a nation, that is the source of our uniqueness, everything that we can be proud of—all this is the foundation of the idea you mentioned."[361] In his millennium speech, Putin elaborated on his interpretation of patriotism. He began by saying that "this term is sometimes used ironically and even derogatively. But for the majority of Russians, it has its own original and positive meaning. It is a feeling of pride in one's country, its history and accomplishments. . . . Patriotism is a source of the courage, staunchness and strength of our people. If we lose patriotism, and national pride and dignity, which are connected with it, we will lose ourselves as a nation capable of great achievements."[362] Indeed, the theme of dignity, individual and collective, appears often in Putin's speeches.

There is nothing alarming in these statements, including the indirect allusion to the deeply rooted notion of "Russian uniqueness," if one considers Russia a monoethnic society (a condition rarely achieved in history) or, more realistically, a monocultural society. However, in addition to a Russian national myth-symbol complex, there is a Turko-Islamic one that views those episodes of Russian history that Russians consider glorious stages in the development of Russian statehood and greatness as stages in the loss of their own identity and independence. Consequently, allusions to Russian patriotism and uniqueness tend to isolate and marginalize non-Russians. Additionally, in practice, only purely Russian motifs have been used in developing new symbols of Russian statehood and identity, as illustrated by the readoption of the old Soviet anthem with new lyrics as the anthem of the Russian Federation. According to a report, "Putin's voice cracked" when he told a television audience that this "was necessary to heal the wounds of the past and fuse the Soviet era with Russia's thousand-year history."[363] Putin added that to reject the Soviet era would mean that "the lives of our mothers and fathers were useless, meaningless, and lived in vain."[364] He added that "neither in my heart nor in my head" could he accept the total rejection of the country's past, a past that included "the victory of the Russian people in the Great Patriotic War against fascism."[365]

Similarly, a law signed by Putin adopted the post-Communist Russian tricolor flag and the Romanov double-headed eagle as official state symbols and designated the "red banner of victory" as the official standard of the Russian armed forces. According to one commentator, "By mixing both pre- and post-Soviet symbols, Putin was clearly attempting to fuse positive memories of both periods (Russia as the Orthodox third Rome, home of Pushkin, Tolstoy, and Dostoevsky; Russia as a 'new democracy,' the triumph of the Great Patriotic War) as the building blocks of a post-Soviet Russian national identity and resolve."[366] Such positive symbolism resonates with ethnic Russians and Orthodox Christians, and some non-Russians may share some nostalgia for the Soviet period, the only era where a conscious— albeit failed—attempt was made to create a civic and transethnic identity and patriotism. But this symbolism is disturbing to Muslims.

Putin has also emphasized the religious aspect of Russian traditions. Just before the March 2000 presidential election, Putin participated in a Christmas service even though he had not demonstrated previously that he "faithfully adhered to intricate Orthodox rituals."[367] After Putin was elected president, he attended "a festive service delivered by Patriarch of Moscow and All Russia, Alexiy II."[368] During the ceremony, the patriarch said, "It is now most important for Russia to revive the spiritual strength of the nation and its loyalty to genuine moral values." The patriarch also stressed that "the Russian Orthodox Church will invariably assist the temporal power in the deeds aimed at the revival of the fatherland." He also presented Putin with an icon of St. Prince Alexander of Neva (Nevsky), the patron saint of Russia.[369] In response, Putin thanked him for the church's help "to preserve many traditional and spiritual values."[370] Even more important, Putin asserted, "Russia is a European country with Christian traditions."[371]

Russian Greatness

Putin also emphasizes the theme of Russian greatness and sees "belief in the greatness of Russia" as a major component of Russian patriotism. According to Putin, "Russia was and will remain a great power. It is preconditioned by the inseparable characteristics of its geopolitical, economic, and cultural existence. They determined the mentality of Russians and the policy of the government throughout the history of Russia, and they cannot but do so at present."[372] Emphasis on the geopolitical factor as predetermining Russia's fate as a great power has hints of Eurasianist thinking, although without its ideological anti-Westernism. Moreover, Putin emphasizes the point that the Russian mentality should be expanded by the introduction of new ideas, particularly those concerning the underpinnings of a nation's greatness. According to Putin, "In the present world, the might of a country as a great power is manifested more in its ability to be a leader in creating and using advanced technologies, ensuring a high level of its people's well-being, reliably protecting its security, and upholding its national interests in the international arena, than its military strength."[373] This, however, does not mean that Putin does not see military strength as an important ingredient of Russia's power; it simply shows that he knows that without technological and economic prowess, military strength is not sustainable. Indeed, Putin is reported to have said, "Russia has two allies: the army and the navy."[374]

Modernization and Pragmatism

Putin's nationalism, however, while incorporating certain basic components of traditional Russian nationalism, is not based on a desire to resurrect a utopian vision of old Russia. Rather, his vision is forward looking and directed at creating a new framework for Russia's material modernization, consolidating Russian statehood, and regaining Russia's international status. In practical terms, to the extent possible, Putin wants to co-opt Russia's various social classes and political-ideological tendencies. In advancing his goals, Putin shows the same kind of pragmatism on the international scene, shifting positions—notably in terms of relations with the West—whenever this is beneficial to Russian interests.

Some analysts have attributed the rather eclectic nature of Putin's nationalism and his vision of the principal values that should underpin Russia's future development to the necessities of acquiring and maintaining power. Thus Lilia Shevtsova, a prominent scholar of the Russian presidency, has written that "Putin still must not make his image concrete. Consequently, he is obliged to keep groups with varying aspirations and ideologies as his base of support—from advocates of a strong state to liberals."[375] However, this approach may be the result of a recognition of Russia's contemporary realities and needs, which require a combining of Westernizing trends with certain deeply rooted Russian traditions. This requirement is reflected in the fact that more than 70 percent of the Russian population "continues to believe in the uniqueness of their country and its 'special path.' "[376] The test for the future ultimately lies in the balance between modernizing and Westernizing trends, on one hand, and Russia's political traditions, including statist and autocratic tendencies, on the other.

Putin and Islam

Putin was propelled to power by his tough stand in regard to Chechnya and his determination to stamp out Islamic militancy in the North Caucasus and the terrorism associated with it. Putin has also been harsh in words toward these extremists.[377] However, he has been careful to distinguish between Muslims and extremists. Putin's official views on Islam have not been much different from those expressed by other Russian political leaders, for example, that Islam is one of Russia's traditional religions and, as such, has a place in society, and that Muslims and Christians have lived in harmony for centuries in Russia. Interestingly, during a call-in interview on television, in response to a question from a Muslim viewer in Kazan, Putin attributed Christian-Muslim harmony to the fact that in Russia, "the majority of Christians are Orthodox Christians, which is eastern Christianity, and we have a great deal in common with Islam."[378] In the same interview, Putin also stated that Islam, as a traditional Russian religion, "merits the support of the state."[379] In practice, however, Putin's approach has been a combination of suppression of extremists, control of Muslim institutions, the curbing of activities of the more independent-minded Muslim clerics, and the co-option of the Muslim population.

Moreover, Putin has viewed extremist Islam and its global network, extending from the Caucasus to Southeast Asia, as an existential threat to Russia. Putin has not been averse to tactical cooperation with some Muslim states, but he sees no spiritual affinity between Islam and Orthodox Christianity, notwithstanding some of his statements addressed to Muslim audiences citied earlier. Culturally, Putin is more of a Westernizer, but as a pragmatic leader, he realizes the importance of showing appreciation for Russia's deeply held values and traditions.

Religion, Ethnicity, and Identity Formation among Russian Muslims: Diverging Trends

Russian Muslims have not escaped the identity crisis that has gripped post-Soviet Russia. A major aspect of this crisis relates to the relationship between, on one hand, the Russian state and society and, on the other hand, Muslim minorities involved in issues of national self-determination, albeit to varying degrees of intensity. In some cases, the alienation from the Russian state and society has been so intense that it has led to attempts to gain total independence, most dramatically illustrated in Chechnya. Another aspect of this identity crisis deals with internal dynamics of Muslim societies and tensions within these societies between the ethnic and religious poles of their collective identities. In most of these cases, Muslims do not want separation from the Russian state. In fact, most share a "civic" sense of Russianness with other citizens of Russia. This situation derives from the fact that despite its central role in shaping the Muslims' identity and way of life, Islam has neither blunted ethnic differences and loyalties nor eliminated pre-Islamic traditions in the Muslim world. Russia's Muslims have not been immune to this general rule. Thus in the post-Soviet era, a dichotomy has emerged among Russia's Muslims—albeit to different degrees—between Islam and an ethnocentric and largely pre-Islamic concept of identity.

This dichotomy is most clearly observable in the case of Tatarstan and, to a lesser extent, in Bashkortostan, where a Turkic ethnic and cultural identity competes with a predominantly Islam-based collective identity. As with the rest of the Muslim world, there is also a third trend that tries to reconcile Islam and a more ethnocentric sense of identity by ethnicizing religion. These three trends are observable most clearly in Tatarstan because of the Tatars' particular historical experience as successors of the Chengizid Empire and major participants in Islam's and Turkism's intellectual evolution.

Turkic Neopaganism: An Alternative to Islam?

The tendency among Muslims, especially non-Arab peoples, to idealize their pre-Islamic culture and to resurrect it as an alternative to Islam as a system of values and guidelines for the social and political organization of society became quite common during the late nineteenth and twentieth centuries. The main impetus behind this trend was the Muslim world's decline, which contributed to its eventual domination and colonization by Western European powers and by Russia. These developments caused a deep soul-searching among Muslims regarding the causes of their decline. Some Muslims attributed their decline to Islam, whereas others saw a falling away from Islam's pure teachings as the main reason. A third group thought that it was not Islam per se that was the cause, but rather the narrow-minded clergy who interpreted its principles in ways that made them appear incompatible with science and progress. Many Islamic reformist movements of the nineteenth and early twentieth centuries, including Jadidism in Central Asia, Tatarstan, and the South Caucasus, are reflections of this third tendency. Because the period of decline of the Islamic world coincided with a rise of nationalism in Europe, many Muslims saw ethnocentric nationalism, including a cultural element, as an appropriate alternative to Islam.

A certain trend within the Turkic nationalist and transnationalist thinking (pan-Turkism) tended to mythologize the history of various Turko-Mongol peoples and glorify their past achievements. Some Tatar intellectuals of the nineteenth and twentieth centuries, notably Yusuf Akchutin and Ismail Bey Gaspirali, were among the pioneers of this trend and the founders of the pan-Turkist ideology and movement.[380]

One of the principal arguments of ethnocentric nationalists against Islam is that it is of foreign—Arab—origin and, therefore, is alien to the ancestral beliefs and traditions of non-Arab Muslims, which they consider to be superior to Islam. Within the context of present-day Tatarstan, this anti-Islam cultural ethnocentrism is reflected in the movement of Tengrism or Tengrianity. The movement gets its name from Tengre, the pre-Islamic god of the Turkic peoples. The proponents of this school of thought believe that the Turko-Tatar people must build an ideological and philosophical foundation for their future development on the basis of their own traditions. These traditions include religious principles as well as philosophical concepts and worldview, including issues of relations of humankind to its environment and the cosmos, or what they call the "sky." In addition to providing a framework for social and political action, they believe that Tengrism could serve as a unifying factor for Turkic peoples. Their main criticism of Islam is that it has no relevance to what they see as "the traveled path" of the Turkic-Tatar people nor to their contributions to world civilization. An article published in the movement's newspaper *Beznen Yul* (Our way) expresses this feeling by stating, "In the holy books there is no description of the traveled path, of the history of our Turkic-Tatar people. There, the Semitic (Jewish and Arab peoples) present their traveled path, their history as the history of mankind. We, the Tatar people, must find our way with higher forces."[381]

The Tengrists are also wary of the universalist, transethnic, and transnational essence of Islam. The Tengrists who are Tatar nationalists and pan-Turkists fear that those Tatars who are committed to Islam will put the interests of the broader Islamic world ahead of the national interests of Tatars. Again according to *Beznen Yul*, "One cannot expect anything good from modern leaders, Imams and their reforms. Who can say that they will not go against their people under any banner, for example, under the direction of international Islam?"[382]

There is also a class dimension to the Tengrists' perspective in that they equate Islam with the dominance of rich classes. They believe that the principle of submission to the will of God inherent in Islam, as indeed in Christianity, works in favor of the privileged classes. They also believe that the lack of an ethnically rooted religion has prevented Tatarstan from achieving independence and has led to the impossible "Tatar model."[383] No such elaborate theories have been developed in other Muslim-inhabited regions of the Russian Federation. However, in some regions, such as Bashkortostan, there has been growing interest in the Bashkirs' pre-Islamic history and traditions. Various congresses dealing with these issues were held during the early 1990s. A number of books and articles glorifying Bashkir history have also been written. A principal proponent of this trend is Salavat Gallyamov, among whose publications is "The Ural-Batyr Epic Is 4000 Years Old." According to Aislu Yunusova, the goal of these writings and other artistic works, despite their often "unscientific nature," is "to make Bashkir history appear older than it really is" and "to extend Bashkir history and exaggerate the importance of its pre-Islamic culture."[384] They also conclude that Islam has not and will not dominate "Bashkir mass consciousness."[385]

This phenomenon is less evident in the North Caucasus because of the diversity of ethnic groups and the fact that most North Caucasian people do not belong to the Turkic family of peoples and hence cannot fall back on their real or imagined collective history. Moreover, unlike the Tatars, for example, none of the North Caucasian peoples has an established and more or less continuous history of statehood built at least partially around the notion of ethnicity. The efforts of Imam

Shamil to create a state based on Islamic principles that could unite various peoples of the region failed following his defeat by the Russian Empire. However, the failure of his effort was also due to internal divisions among the North Caucasian tribes, showing that commitment to Islam is incapable of overcoming other divisions.

Given these circumstances, in some parts of the North Caucasus, especially in Dagestan, despite the persistence of ethnic divisions and identities, Islam has emerged as the most important component of collective identity within some of the largest ethnic groups. Nevertheless, there is also a fear that the new process of Islamization, which is influenced by external, especially Arab, forces, could erode the region's cultural uniqueness and dilute its peoples' rich customs and traditions.

Islam as the Principal Core of Identity and Instrument of Independence

On the other extreme of the ideological spectrum is the view that maintains that Islam was and once again should become the core of the identity of Muslims, the basic framework of their social and political organization, and the main instrument of their independence and liberation from the rule of nonbelievers (that is, the Russians). The proponents of this perspective further maintain that the type of Islam that should perform all these functions should be pure Islam based on the Qu'ran and the Sunnah and cleared of what Fauzia Bairamova, the Tatar Islamic nationalist leader, characterizes as "Paganism, Sufism, Jadidism, Polytheism."[386] Speaking in the Tatar context, she says that Tatars were a Muslim people who became enslaved by the infidels (Russians) 500 years ago. Thus deprived of an environment within which they could live according to legal, moral, and ethical canons of Islam, the Tatars fell prey to all sorts of anti-Islamic influences.

In Bairamova's view, the most damaging aspect of this situation has been the intellectual and spiritual fragmentation of the Tatars and the loss of national pride and the will to fight for their independence and their faith (jihad). She sees two major obstacles to the refocusing and restructuring of a Tatar national identity around Islam: (1) external forces, which she identifies as aligned to the Judeo-Christian world and civilization, which "has developed a strategic plan directed at the destruction of Tatars from within and pushing them into unbelief,"[387] and (2) various non-Islamic groups of intelligentsia ranging from the proponents of Turkism to the advocates of Euro-Islam. She explains these attitudes of the Tatar intelligentsia in light of their secular and Russified character. She argues that this intelligentsia views religion as a philosophical concept and as an instrument for advancing state's objectives and policies. Bairamova considers the largest part of the clergy, who for such a long time worked under state control, also responsible for this situation.[388] What Bairamova seems to forget, as do most other Muslims who reason along similar lines, is that what should be described as historical Islam as lived by various peoples—as opposed to Islam as a divinely revealed religion—

has never been a static phenomenon. Rather, it has been an ever-evolving organism in the context of a continuing encounter with, and opposition or adaptation to, other forces and stimuli, including forces that were present before its arrival and those that subsequently penetrated Muslim societies.

This trend of viewing Islam as the core of the identity of Muslims is strongest in Tatarstan and is institutionalized in the framework of the Ittifaq political party. It also exists in other republics, notably Bashkortostan, but is not as well articulated as in Tatarstan. In the North Caucasus, the most significant manifestation of this trend is the merger of Islam and Chechen nationalism and the emergence of groups in Dagestan that tried to establish Islamic rule in the Dagestani villages of Karamakhi, Chabanmakhi, and Kadar.

Nationalizing Islam

In terms of Islam's place as a component of national identity and a force in the sociopolitical restructuring of the Muslim-inhabited regions of the Russian Federation, the extreme trends discussed previously do not have large popular appeal. Rather, the most common trend, although less organized and conceptually less well developed, is what can be called nationalized or ethnicized Islam. This is not surprising. Indeed, it reflects an old phenomenon in the Muslim world. To illustrate, one hears about Iranian, Turkish, East Asian, and African Islam, each with its own peculiarities reflecting the influence of pre-Islamic cultures and sense of identity, doctrinal variations, and adherence to various schools of Shari'a. These factors also allow for the expression of ethnic pride and sense of uniqueness without separating a particular group from the rest of the Islamic family. The broadest tendency is to view Islam as an important, but not the sole, component of a people's collective identity. Thus even Tatar modernists and proponents of reformist Islam see it as an integral part of Tatar national identity and as a unifying factor.

Those Turkists who are not hostile to Islam also consider it an important part of the Turkic peoples' identity and civilization. The program of the assembly of Turkic people, promulgated in Tatarstan in 1991, notes the special role of Islam for Turkic peoples. The same could be said about the Bashkirs. Consequently, Islam will remain an important component of the collective identity of Russia's Muslim peoples, but often in a nationalized or, in more ethnically fragmented societies, like those of the North Caucasus, ethnicized form. This does not mean that Islamocentric notions of identity will disappear. Rather, it means that it is unlikely that they would be able to garner enough support among Russia's Muslims to overcome other differences. The only exception would be a situation of deep economic crisis and excessive political and cultural pressure from the center. In short, the revitalization of Islam in the post-Soviet era has enhanced its role in the process of identity formation of Russia's Muslims and reopened old debates about the relative roles of Islam, ethnicity, and other factors in determining the collective identities of various Muslim peoples.

Conclusion

The Soviet Union's disintegration and the discrediting of the philosophy underpinning it reopened the debate about Russian identity and its principal components. Meanwhile, it reawakened traditional identities of Russia's Muslim populations and led to an upsurge in demands for greater self-determination, notably more freedom to openly practice Islam and obtain for it a legitimate place within Russia's social, cultural, and political landscape.

As has been the case in the last 300 years, since Peter the Great's Westernizing reforms fractured the cultural homogeneity of the ethnic and Orthodox Russians, debate about Russia's post-Soviet identity has been centered on three thematic questions: (1) What is the role of Russian culture? (2) Where does Russia belong culturally? (3) Should Russia emulate the West or find a unique Russian path? The first question largely concerns the role of the Russian language and Orthodox Christianity as the main underpinnings of a post-Soviet Russian identity. The main issue is whether Russia should be an essentially Russocentric and Orthodox society and culture into which other ethnic groups can be accepted, provided they undergo a large degree of Russification. This does not necessarily mean total assimilation, but it does mean the acceptance of the supremacy of the Russian culture. In other words, should Russian identity and hence its nationalism take on a primordial cast with elements of civic nationalism, or should Russia move toward a more multi-ethnic and multicultural identity and hence a civic sense of nationalism?

The second question revolves around the centuries-old issue of whether Russia is a part of the West or a unique Eurasian entity, culturally and geopolitically, that has harmonized within its underlying Russian-Orthodox civilization many cultures, religions, and ethnic groups. This view of Russia has suffered setbacks largely, but not exclusively, because of the Muslim quest for self-determination, which regrettably at times, as in Chechnya, has taken a violent form. This development has undermined the cultural claims of Eurasianism as a harmonious synthesis, as Sergei Stankevich has put it, of Russian and other cultures. Many Russians still see themselves as a unique culture and entity that straddles Europe and Asia, has a special role to play, and has a rightful claim to great-power status.

For non-Russians, notably many Muslims, Eurasianism is merely a cover for Russia's imperial ambitions. Certainly those Eurasianists who saw the West as Russia's main cultural and political rival and advocated alliance with non-Western cultures to counteract the West's cultural and political encroachments have been largely discredited. Russia's problems with parts of its Muslim population and territories, plus a growing fear of a security and cultural threat from the Muslim periphery, have led many Russians to view the West as much more of a cultural kin and natural ally than as an adversary, certainly in facing the real or imagined threat of Islam. The events of 11 September 2001 and the Russian response, while partly determined by practical calculations, nevertheless were indicative of these broader cultural and identity-related issues. Many Russians still feel uncomfortable with aspects of Western culture and are not willing to submerge their cultural authenticity under an all-embracing and advancing Western culture. They also do not relish the West's economic and military superiority and Russia's subordinate international role. But they certainly feel more affinity with the West than with either the Islamic world or the Chinese cultural milieu.

The question of whether Russia should emulate the West or seek a unique path of social evolution remains a central issue in Russian self-perception, as it has in previous centuries. In the post-Soviet era, Russia has been grappling with the same dilemma that it has faced since the time of Peter, namely, does modernization mean abandoning all that is specific to Russia, or can Russia modernize without losing its authenticity or its soul? In confronting this dilemma, Russia is similar to other countries that have wanted to benefit from the material advantages of modernism without abandoning their authentic cultures. This dilemma derives from the fact that modernity is a Western phenomenon and a consequence of a deep intellectual transformation of Western traditions over 300 years. Others have borrowed from the West and grafted modern concepts into traditional societies, thus fracturing the social and cultural cohesiveness of the society and engendering debates. This is what happened in post-Petrine Russia. For a period, the Soviet system appeared as the Russian alternative to Western modernism. Its failure has forced Russia once more to search for a new model and a new synthesis. Return to an idealized past—ancient or Soviet Russian—as some philosophers dream, is not an option. Even since 1992 the society has undergone some fundamental changes. But the question of what form Russian modernism should or will take—liberal or more corporatist—remains unclear.

In sum, since 1992, after long and still ongoing debates, the basic contours of a new Russian identity have been gradually emerging. In this process, interaction with the West and the challenge from the Muslim South, both within the borders of the Russian Federation and on its periphery, have played important roles in shaping this new identity, as they had done throughout Russia's history. This identity is largely ethnocentric and monocultural, as illustrated by the Russian Ministry of Education's decision in November 2002 to develop a course on Orthodox culture for the Russian public school system.[389] Recent writings by prominent Russian experts on nationalities, such as Valerii Tishkov, the director of the Institute of Ethnology and Anthropology of the Russian Academy of Sciences, argue that multiculturalism on the model of Australia or Canada is not possible in Russia because it would lead to further fragmentation of its population into smaller groups. Tishkov further argues that excessive emphasis on cultural specificities can lead—and has led—to conflict.[390] The controversy created by the project "Russian Islam" further indicates that neither the Russians nor Muslims have yet reached a consensus on what multiculturalism means in the Russian context.[391] In short, Russian nationalism, even in its moderate form, is not yet of a civic type. Russia's new identity is closer to the West than to other cultures within Russia or in its close neighborhood to the south and to the east.

The reassertion of the cultural supremacy of the Russian element, given the Russians' numerical superiority, is to some degree natural, as is a greater feeling of closeness with the West because of the common bonds of Christian civilization, despite the historic breach between Eastern and Western Christianity, and other common cultural roots. The challenge for Russia, a multiethnic and multireligious entity, is how to ensure that the reassertion of Russianness and the affirmation of the Russian culture and identity will not be at the expense of other major ethnic and cultural groups, notably the Muslims. Failure to reconcile the competing claims of its diverse people for self-determination within a broad and all-encompassing civic Russian identity, encompassing loyalty to the Russian state after a period of reawakening and reassertion of ethnic, cultural, and religious peculiarities and efforts to achieve greater self-determination, could presage continuous interethnic strife and the strengthening of nondemocratic forces. Such a development could set back Russia's development and modernization—economic, social, and political—and possibly endanger Russia's stability.

Developing a broad-based democratic and civic Russian identity will not be easy, especially since Russian Muslims too have different notions of collective identity that compete for allegiance. However, the effort must be made if Russia is to achieve political stability and interethnic accord, avoid further narrowing the parameters of ethnic, cultural, and political self-determination, and prevent the loss of the democratic gains of more than a decade.

4

The Evolution of Russian Federalism

The Islamic Factor

Vladimir Putin's first major initiative as Russian president was a sweeping reorganization of the country's federal system. Within a week of his inauguration in May 2000, Putin initiated this reorganization with a presidential decree that declared his objectives of "ensuring the exercise of the Russian Federation President's constitutional powers [and] increasing the effectiveness of the activity of federal organs of state power."[1] In light of the weakened state of Russia's federal government at the time, coupled with the fact that Russia was fighting a war in Chechnya to preserve its territorial integrity, this initiative was not surprising. A reevaluation and restructuring of the pattern of relations between the federal center and various regions had become necessary because, a decade after the dissolution of the Soviet Union, the Russian Federation had failed to construct a coherent system to manage these relations. The federal government remained incapable of consistently exercising authority over Russia's eighty-nine provinces (or federation subjects) while regional leaders claimed varying degrees of political and economic autonomy and—in the case of Chechnya—independence.[2]

During the 1990s, centrifugal tendencies in Russia were not limited to Muslim and other non-Russian provinces; in many cases, predominantly ethnic Russian regions led the way in appropriating powers from the weakened federal government.[3] Nevertheless, the most significant challenges to post-Soviet Russia's central authority and, potentially, its territorial integrity arose in Muslim areas, especially in the republics of Tatarstan and Chechnya, where a combination of ethnic nationalism, cultural and religious revival, and claims of regional autonomy strained the limits of Russian federalism. In Tatarstan, calls for greater autonomy—and for outright independence by extreme nationalist groups—impelled federal authorities to assent to the Russian Federation's first bilateral power-sharing treaty between the federal government and a federation subject. This arrangement provided a model for the asymmetrical and largely improvised federalism that developed during Boris Yeltsin's rule. More dangerously, the rise of ethnic nationalism in Chechnya, coupled with the inability of Moscow and Grozny to reach a mutually acceptable formula that would satisfy Chechen demands for autonomy and Russia's desire to retain its territorial integrity, led to the 1994–96 Russian-Chechen War. This conflict, which lasted twenty-one months and cost the lives of tens of thousands, ultimately resulted in a de facto independent republic in Russia's North Caucasus region.

It is difficult to measure the extent to which these challenges strengthened centralizing tendencies in Russia. However, Chechnya's de facto independence, combined with its potentially contagious impact on the North Caucasus region and the rise of militant Islam in the republic after Russia's military intervention in December 1994, intensified fears of Russia's possible fragmentation and provided strong popular support for Putin's recentralization drive. Developments between the end of the 1994–96 Russian-Chechen conflict and the resumption of warfare three years later—especially the establishment of a network of local and foreign Muslim militants in Chechnya, incursions by Chechen-based militants into neighboring Dagestan, and a series of terrorist bombings in Russia widely blamed on Chechen militants—produced an upsurge in popular support for military action to restore order. Beginning with his use of military force and uncompromising rhetoric toward Chechnya, Putin established a reputation as a decisive leader capable of restoring order and even reviving Russia's status as a world power. After Yeltsin resigned as president in December 1999, Putin utilized this image to propel himself to the presidency and to mobilize support for his project to reform Russian federalism and restore central authority.

Islam played an important role in the Russian-Chechen conflict, both as a cultural factor differentiating predominantly Muslim ethnic groups from the numerically superior Russians and as a political instrument used to mobilize support for national self-determination and to oppose Russian rule. It was also a factor in other challenges to the federal government's authority, especially in Dagestan and elsewhere in the North Caucasus and, to a lesser degree, in Tatarstan. To the extent that it intensified frictions between the federal center and these Muslim regions, Islam contributed to the reawakening of the Russians' traditional support for a strong, centralized government and to growing popular sentiment in favor of reasserting the dominance of Russian cultural traditions in the post-Soviet Russian state.

These sentiments proved central to the broad popular backing Putin received for his recentralization initiative. They also raised fundamental questions about the place of non-Russian minorities and cultures in post-Soviet Russia. Foremost among such questions was whether the Russian Federation would develop into a federation that protects and encourages national and cultural traditions of non-Russian peoples who are indigenous to—or have inhabited for centuries—its territory or into a unitary nation-state dominated by a single ethnic group and its cultural ethos. Critical aspects of this question and possibly the most important barometers of how it will be answered are Russia's treatment of its Muslim minorities and the degree of regional self-rule and religious and cultural autonomy granted to Russia's Muslim communities.

Soviet Federalism: Ethnic Autonomy versus Centralized Rule

Putin's efforts to reassert central authority over a decentralized multiethnic state do not constitute the first such attempt in Russian history. Following their seizure of power in 1917, the Bolsheviks initiated a sweeping campaign to reunite the territory of the defunct Russian Empire under a highly centralized governing structure. In addition to confronting the advance of German and Turkish forces during the final months of the First World War and resistance from anti-Bolshevik (White) forces during the 1918–21 Russian Civil War, the Bolsheviks had to contend with the fragmentation of Russia's immense territory along ethnic lines.[4] The collapse of central power and the fall of the tsar elicited demands for national self-determination from non-Russian nationalities, including the tsar's Muslim subjects, albeit to varying degrees. By early 1918, several former imperial possessions had declared independence, while others proclaimed the formation of self-ruled autonomous territories.

The Bolsheviks initially embraced demands for national self-determination to gain the support of non-Russian peoples. Thus after seizing power in early November 1917, the Bolsheviks issued both the Declaration on the Rights of the Peoples of Russia, which guaranteed national self-determination for non-Russian ethnic groups, and the Appeal to Laboring Muslims of the East, which proclaimed Islamic beliefs, practices, and cultural and national institutions to be sacrosanct.[5] However, after consolidating their authority in Moscow and the former imperial capital of St. Petersburg, the Bolsheviks forcibly extended their control over the former empire's territory. By the conclusion of the Russian Civil War in 1921, they had conquered most of the former empire.

Federalism and the Soviet Constitution

To mask this reassertion of centralized rule and to differentiate the emerging Soviet system from the Russian-dominated imperial regime, the Bolsheviks created a federal structure for the Soviet Union. In theory, this structure was based on territorial autonomy for non-Russian nationalities, hence allowing them a significant degree of self-determination. The legal basis of this system was provided by the 1922 Union Treaty, which created an ostensibly voluntary union of sovereign, ethnically defined republics.[6] Within these constituent (or union) republics, the Bolsheviks created a hierarchy of lesser national homelands consisting of (1) autonomous republics, which were granted the highest level of autonomy after the union republics; (2) autonomous *oblasts* (autonomous regions); and (3) autonomous *okrugs* (autonomous districts). These lower-level autonomous territories were designed for ethnic minorities who inhabited territories that did not have external (Soviet) borders, were numerically small, or were deemed by the Bolsheviks to lack fully developed national consciousness. The Russian republic, the largest of the union republics, contained more than half of these lower-level national territories and, accordingly, was granted the status of a federated republic, the Russian Soviet Federated Socialist Republic (RSFSR).

Even before the formal creation of the Soviet Union in 1922, the Bolsheviks began developing a constitutional system governing relations between the federal center and the regions under its control. In July 1918, the nascent Communist regime promulgated a constitution that declared, "The Russian Soviet Republic is established on the principle of a free union of free nations, as a federation of Soviet national republics."[7] After the signing of the Union Treaty, the Bolsheviks adopted a new constitution in January 1924 extending this federal structure over the newly created Soviet state. This constitution declared the Soviet Union to be a voluntary association of sovereign republics with the right to secede from the union and the right to adopt their own constitutions.[8] The Stalin constitution of 1936 and the Brezhnev constitution of 1977 reaffirmed these national rights. Amendments adopted in 1944 granted union republics the additional authority to engage in direct relations with foreign states, including exchanging diplomatic representatives.[9]

The Communist Party and the Unitary Soviet State

Despite the formal rights granted to ethnic minorities, several key features of the Soviet political system—notably the monopoly of power exercised by the Communist Party of the Soviet Union (CPSU)—allowed the Soviet leadership to concentrate political power within the central government in Moscow. After deposing Alexander Kerensky's Provisional Government, the Bolsheviks systematically eliminated alternative poles of power. They disbanded the popularly elected Constituent Assembly in early 1918 and created the Extraordinary Commission for Combating Counterrevolution and Sabotage (Cheka) to suppress dissent. During the 1918–1921 Russian Civil War, the Bolsheviks eradicated most major pockets of political and nationalist opposition and erected a comprehensive system of repression and coercion to maintain CPSU domination. The 1977 Soviet constitution reaffirmed the Communist Party's monopoly of power, stipulating that "the leading and guiding force of Soviet society and the nucleus of its political system, of all state organizations and public organizations, is the Communist Party of the Soviet Union."[10]

Following the Bolsheviks' consolidation of power over the former empire's territory, they constructed a highly centralized party structure based on the principles of democratic centralism. Accordingly, strict party discipline forbade open dissent from majority opinion, and the decisions of higher party organs were absolutely binding on the lower levels.[11] Consequently, the party's Political Bureau (Politburo) and its most powerful member, the CPSU general secretary, disseminated policy decisions down through the party hierarchy. Separate Communist Party organizations were established in union and autonomous republics; however, they served primarily as a means of transmitting central directives from Moscow to the republics. The Communist Party program of 1919 reflected this centralized nature by stating, "There must exist a single centralized Communist Party. . . . All decisions of the Russian Communist Party [later transformed into the CPSU] and its directing organs are unconditionally binding on all branches of the party, regardless of their national composition."[12]

The Communist Party's monopoly of power, combined with the centralized control exercised by the party leadership in Moscow, reduced Soviet federalism to a legal facade concealing the regime's true nature as a unitary state. Periodically, the Soviet leadership experimented with decentralization: Nikita Khrushchev replaced central ministries with *sovnarkhozy* (regional economic councils), and Leonid Brezhnev loosened central control over the internal affairs of the union republics. However, Khrushchev's reforms maintained the Communist Party's monopoly on decision making, including economic planning.[13] Similarly, although Brezhnev allowed elites in non-Russian republics to consolidate regional power, which in many cases led to rule based on ethnic patronage and corruption, he kept republican leaders dependent on Moscow for financial and material resources. Republican leaders thus retained their power only as long as they remained loyal to the central party leadership in Moscow.[14]

Multiculturalism versus Soviet Uniformity

The same dual character that defined the Soviet political system—structured formally as a multinational federation, but operating as a unitary state—characterized the Soviet approach toward national and cultural identity, which simultaneously promoted local nationalism and socialist internationalism. In the early years of the Soviet state, the Bolsheviks openly promoted the development of non-Russian identities and cultures. Although they forcibly extended their rule over most of the former empire, after consolidating control, the Bolsheviks initiated a strategy of *korenizatsia* (indigenization). Designed to alleviate historic fears of Russian imperialism and to promote sociocultural development in non-Russian regions seen as backward by the Bolsheviks, this strategy entailed encouraging the use of native languages and certain cultural practices in the national territories while promoting non-Russians into leadership positions within the Communist Party in their home regions. Many non-Russian languages were assigned alphabets using the Latin script, which was seen as a modernizing instrument that would encourage non-Russian peoples to break with their traditional cultures.[15]

This strategy corresponded to the Bolsheviks' internationalist ideology; it promoted Communist solidarity among different nations and granted—on the surface—equality to all ethnic groups. In many ways, *korenizatsia* devalued indigenous cultures and continued the imperial-era process of separating non-Russian ethnic groups from their traditions and national identities. The creation of Latin-based alphabets weakened many indigenous literary traditions and corrupted some languages. The promotion of non-Russians in the party, while giving a voice to ethnic minorities in the CSPU, also served as a socializing instrument that increased loyalty to the party and the Soviet state. Moreover, cultural traits, especially religious beliefs and practices, deemed backward were suppressed.

In the 1930s, *korenizatsia* was abandoned for a more direct process of under-mining indigenous cultures through varying degrees of Russification. The Latin script was condemned as a tool of Western imperialism and was replaced with variants of the Cyrillic script.[16] Russian-language instruction was made obligatory in all schools in the national territories.[17] Meanwhile, Stalin initiated widespread purges within the Communist Party during which thousands of non-Russian cadres were expelled from the party and, in many cases, imprisoned or executed on charges of "nationalist deviation." This mass cleansing of the party, which culmi-nated in the Great Terror of 1937–38, reduced the participation of ethnic minorities in the CPSU markedly. By 1946, less than half of party members living in national territories belonged to the indigenous nationalities.[18]

Throughout both the *korenizatsia* period and Russification under Stalin, Soviet authorities pursued an antireligious campaign, varying in intensity over time, to eliminate obstacles to mass acceptance of official Communist ideology and to sup-press alternative sources of social authority. This campaign had an especially dam-aging impact on Islamic institutions and the Muslim population. By the time Mikhail Gorbachev came to power in 1985, although Islam's religious and cultural influence had survived and was experiencing a revival, its institutional and intel-lectual foundations had seriously eroded.[19]

Mikhail Gorbachev and the Rise of Ethnic Nationalism

Once the Bolsheviks had suppressed political opposition, ethnic- and religious-based challenges to the Soviet regime remained subdued for almost sixty years. Until the mid-1980s, few serious signs of internal or structural instability appeared within the Soviet Union's centralized, pseudofederal system. Cases of ethnic-based activism occasionally arose: nationalists in Ukraine and the Baltic republics fought for independence against Soviet forces during the Second World War, clashes broke out between Armenians and Azeris over the status of the Armenian enclave of Nagorno-Karabakh in 1968, and thousands of Georgians protested in Tbilisi over attempts to remove Georgian as the official language of the republic in 1978.[20] Nevertheless, expressions of nationalist sentiments from ethnic minorities remained irritants that could be suppressed or co-opted by the leadership. The dual nature of Soviet federalism provided a viable model for authoritarian rule over a multi-national state for several decades. Reforms initiated by Mikhail Gorbachev in the mid-1980s, however, altered this pattern of relations between the federal center and the national territories and precipitated the fragmentation of the Soviet Union along ethnic lines.

Gorbachev's Reforms

By the time Mikhail Gorbachev assumed leadership of the CPSU in March 1985, the Soviet economy had been declining steadily for nearly two decades. According to some estimates, real economic growth had come to a complete halt as early as

1978.[21] The Soviet economy's poor performance threatened not only the people's standard of living, but also the USSR's international competitive position, especially in the technological and military fields. As Gorbachev explained:

> Analyzing the situation, we first discovered slowing economic growth. In the last fifteen years, the national income growth rate had declined by more than half and by the beginning of the 1980s had fallen to a level close to economic stagnation. A country that was once quickly closing in on the world's advanced nations began to lose one position after another. Moreover, the gap in the efficiency of production, quality of products, scientific and technological development, the production of advanced technology and the use of advanced techniques began to widen, and not to our advantage.[22]

Gorbachev initiated his economic strategy of perestroika to reverse this trend. Shortly afterwards, he launched a campaign of openness, or glasnost, and limited democratization to mobilize public support for his reforms and to weaken his opponents by exposing mismanagement and corruption within the Soviet bureaucracy. These political reforms loosened censorship of the media, allowed relative freedom of speech and political association, and introduced competitive elections to government office. In early 1990, at the urging of Gorbachev, the Soviet constitution was amended to abrogate the Communist Party's official monopoly of political power.[23] This act led to a proliferation of political parties and movements, including some based on ethnic or religious identity.

Ethnic Fragmentation of the Soviet Union

To the dismay of Gorbachev and his supporters, political liberalization, instead of facilitating a reform of the Communist system, elicited opposition to the Soviet regime itself, notably from nationalist and proindependence elements within the Soviet Union's ethnic minorities. By the late 1980s, movements advocating various degrees of national self-rule had arisen in several of the union republics. With the introduction of popular elections, these elements gained control of some union republic governments. In the space of two years—from Estonia's declaration of sovereignty in November 1988 to Kyrgyzstan's similar declaration in December 1990—all of the Soviet Union's fifteen union republics issued formal declarations of sovereignty. In most cases, the term "sovereignty" remained ill defined; at a minimum, it meant that union republic laws took precedence over the laws and constitution of the Soviet central government. Before the end of 1990, the three Baltic republics had proclaimed their complete independence.

Nationalist and proindependence forces were strengthened by intraleadership power struggles within the Soviet central government and the Communist Party. During the period 1987–90, Yegor Ligachev, second secretary of the CPSU, led a core group of conservatives who staunchly resisted Gorbachev's reforms. He was aided by the Soyuz (Union) faction in the Soviet parliament, which advocated halting—by force, if necessary—any devolution of authority to the union republics.

This division within the Soviet leadership weakened its ability to respond to the centrifugal forces and contributed to the central authorities' erratic response to them. There is even some evidence that both sides manipulated ethnic problems to demonstrate the dangers of their opponents' positions: the conservatives encouraged interethnic conflict to show the dangers of glasnost, while the reformists did the same to demonstrate the risks of repression.[24] The conservative coalition ultimately lost the battle; however, intraleadership power struggles did not end. Rather, Gorbachev's victory over Ligachev was followed by an intense battle for political supremacy with RSFSR leader Boris Yeltsin. Again, Yeltsin used nationalism among non-Russians to gain political advantage, with devastating consequences for the USSR.

After his election as president of the RSFSR in May 1990, Yeltsin openly encouraged nationalist sentiments among the union republics in an attempt to weaken Gorbachev and the Soviet central government. In May 1990, he announced his intention to conclude separate treaties with the secessionist Baltic republics and proclaimed that the Russian republic would not support efforts by Gorbachev to suppress separatism in the union republics. In June 1990, at Yeltsin's urging, the RSFSR parliament adopted a declaration of sovereignty. This act served as a catalyst for the so-called parade of sovereignties as other union republics made similar declarations. Afterward, Yeltsin continued his efforts to weaken Gorbachev's government. In December 1990, he signed a treaty with Ukraine in which both parties agreed to recognize one another as sovereign states, and in January 1991, he traveled to Estonia at the height of a Soviet crackdown in the Baltics to formulate a common strategy for resisting pressure from the central authorities.[25]

Gorbachev's response to proindependence forces fluctuated between coercive measures—including an economic blockade of Lithuania and the use of military force in Georgia, Azerbaijan, and the Baltic republics—and tentative compromise. The latter approach is exemplified by the April 1990 Law on the Procedure for the Secession of a Republic from the Union, which specified the steps necessary for the union republics to secede from the USSR.[26] Meanwhile, Gorbachev sought to curb secessionist tendencies and weaken Yeltsin's position as leader of the RSFSR by demonstrating the potential consequences of ethnic-based separatism for the union republics. The law on secession contained a provision allowing autonomous republics within the larger union republics to decline participation in referenda on secession, giving them the option of remaining in the USSR should the union republics opt for independence.

Despite efforts to preserve central authority, by the end of 1990 Gorbachev recognized the need to fundamentally restructure the relationship between the federal center and the USSR's various republics and autonomous territories. In November 1990, he proposed a new Union Treaty to replace de facto centralized rule with a functioning federation. Initially, this approach was moderately successful: nine union republics, including all six Muslim republics, agreed to sign the new treaty and remain in a unified state. The August 1991 coup d'état by hard-liners to prevent the devolution of central power, however, thwarted this final attempt to preserve the Soviet Union, even in a diminished form. The open division within the Soviet leadership and the strong show of popular opposition led by Boris Yeltsin illustrated the central organs' inability to retain power. Over the next three months, most union republics declared independence from the rapidly disintegrating Soviet Union.

On 8 December 1991, the leaders of Russia, Ukraine, and Belarus signed the Agreement on the Establishment of the Commonwealth of Independent States. This agreement, which was later coauthorized by all remaining former union republics except the three Baltic states, declared that "the Union of Soviet Socialist Republics, as a subject of international law and a geopolitical reality, hereby terminates its existence." The treaty further established the Commonwealth of Independent States (CIS) as a voluntary association of independent states to replace the ethnically defined union republics of the USSR.[27]

Boris Yeltsin and Decentralization of the Russian State

It is debatable whether the disintegration of the Soviet Union was inevitable once national reawakenings became widespread or was triggered by the intraleadership power struggle that encouraged these nationalist challenges and eroded the central authorities' ability to restrain them. In either case, by the beginning of 1991, nationalist and proindependence sentiment among non-Russian ethnic groups had altered fundamentally the relations between Moscow and the national minorities. Moreover, these centrifugal forces were not unique to the Soviet central government and its relations with the union republics. In the final years of the Soviet Union, the RSFSR was also threatened by demands for national self-determination and regional self-rule. Spurred on by Yeltsin's efforts to weaken Gorbachev and consolidate his own base of support, this trend survived the Soviet Union's collapse at the end of 1991 and continued to threaten the viability of the newly constituted Russian Federation.

Ethnic Nationalism in the RSFSR

The RSFSR was a multiethnic entity containing thirty-one national homelands for non-Russian nationalities and approximately 100 ethnic groups, some of which numbered only in the hundreds, while a few consisted of more than one million people. The rekindling of ethnic nationalism across the USSR affected many of these nationalities. As ethnic nationalism arose in many areas of the Soviet Union, various ethnic groups of the RSFSR began asserting claims of national and cultural self-determination. By the end of 1990, encouraged by the Russian Republic's own declaration of sovereignty, fourteen autonomous republics and three autonomous oblasts within the RSFSR had declared themselves sovereign republics.

Trying to secure his base of political power and win the contest with Gorbachev, Yeltsin made concessions to non-Russian ethnic groups of the Russian Republic, such as incorporating into the RSFSR's June 1990 declaration of sovereignty a provision guaranteeing the right of "every people to self-determination in their chosen national state and national cultural form."[28] In September 1990, during a speech in Kazan, Yeltsin called on regional leaders to "take as much sovereignty as you can swallow."[29] In 1991, his administration altered the RSFSR's administrative structure and elevated all autonomous republics and four autonomous oblasts to the status of constituent republics of the larger Russian Republic.[30] These concessions may have increased Yeltsin's support in many of the RSFSR's regions in his battle with Gorbachev; however, this strategy sowed the seeds of later troubles as some national minorities, and even some predominantly ethnic Russian regions, claimed a greater degree of autonomy than he had envisioned.

Centrifugal Forces in the Independent Russian Federation

The centrifugal tendencies that had arisen in the RSFSR carried over to the post-Soviet period and the independent Russian Federation, which retained a dual system of federalism characterized by fifty-seven nonethnically defined (predominantly Russian) regions and thirty-two national homelands for ethnic minorities (see Table 4.1). According to the Russian Ministry of Justice, nineteen of Russia's ethnic republics adopted constitutions that violated provisions of the federal constitution. The constitution of Ingushetia declared federal legislation lawful in the republic only if it did not violate the republic's sovereignty, while the constitution of Sakha stipulated that federal legislation must be approved by the republic's parliament before becoming valid on the republic's territory.[31] Several republics claimed territory beyond their recognized borders, including some demands on territory outside the Russian Federation, such as Tyva's claim over territory in neighboring Mongolia and pressure from Osset nationalists to unite North Ossetia with South Ossetia in neighboring Georgia.

Centrifugal tendencies were not confined to the national homelands. Many ethnic Russians saw special autonomous status for national minorities as an unjust anachronism and agitated for greater regional autonomy. Several ethnic Russian regions asserted the right to self-rule, including some that declared sovereignty or claimed the status of republic.[32] In some cases, strong regional leaders, such as Moscow mayor Yuri Luzhkov and Primorsky Krai governor Yevgenii Nazdratenko, openly defied federal laws and court rulings. Several regional groupings tried to challenge federal authority by creating larger territorial units. Eduard Rossel of Sverdlovsk Oblast led an attempt to create a sovereign Urals Republic, some regions around Moscow attempted to form a larger Central Russian Republic, and regional leaders in Siberia founded Siberian Accord, a regional association designed to secure economic and political autonomy for a number of regions in Siberia.[33]

A principal impetus behind regionalism was economic necessity. To recover from the collapse of the integrated Soviet economic system, provinces adopted extraordinary measures, including the withholding of regionally collected tax revenues from the Ministry of Finance. The problem of regional autarky became par-

Table 4.1

Subjects of the Russian Federation

Regions (Territorially Defined)		National Homelands (Ethnically Defined)	

Oblasts (49)

Amur	Omsk	
Arkhangelsk	Orenburg	
Astrakhan	Oryol	
Belgorad	Penza	
Bryansk	Perm	
Chelyabinsk	Pskov	
Chita	Rostov	
Irkutsk	Ryazan	
Ivanovo	Sakhalin	
Kaliningrad	Samara	
Kaluga	Saratov	
Kamchatka	Smolensk	
Kemerovo	Sverdlovsk	
Kirov	Tambov	
Kostroma	Tomsk	
Kurgan	Tula	
Kursk	Tver	
Leningrad Oblast	Tyumen	
Lipetsk	Ulyanovsk	
Magadan	Vladimir	
Moscow Oblast	Volgograd	
Murmansk	Vologda	
Nizhny Novgorod	Voronezh	
Novgorod	Yaroslavl	
Novosibirsk		

Republics (21)

Adygea
Altai
Bashkortostan
Buryatia
Chechnya
Chuvashia
Dagestan
Ingushetia
Kalmykia
Kabardino-Balkaria
Karachaevo-Cherkessia
Karelia
Khakassia
Komi
Marii-El
Mordovia
North Ossetia
Sakha
Tatarstan
Tyva
Udmurtia

Autonomous Oblast (1)

Jewish Autonomous Oblast

Krais (6)

Altai	Krasnoyarsk
Khabarovsk	Primorye
Krasnodar	Stavropol

Federal Cities (2)

Moscow
St. Petersburg

Autonomous Okrugs (10)

Aga-Buryatia	Koryakia
Chukotka	Nenetsia
Evenkia	Taimyria
Khant-Mansi	Ust-Orda Buryatia
Komi-Permyakia	Yamalo-Nenetsia

Source: Constitution of the Russian Federation, Article 65 <http://www.russianembassy.org>.

ticularly acute during Russia's 1998 financial crisis, when several regional governments halted all financial and tax revenue transfers out of their regions or republics. The governor of Kaliningrad even declared a state of emergency in his oblast, a power reserved for the Russian president in the federal constitution.[34] By the end of Yeltsin's rule, from one-quarter to one-third of all provincial legislation violated federal legislation or the Russian constitution.[35]

The Muslim Challenge to Moscow's Rule

During this period of economic and political disarray, some of Russia's Muslim nationalities were among the most active in seeking a greater measure of self-determination. In most cases, Muslim republics demanded greater cultural and administrative autonomy rather than outright independence. The Republic of Ingushetia, for example, legalized some traditional and religious activities that violated federal law, such as polygamy for men and the abduction of women by their prospective bridegrooms.[36] The Republic of Adygea adopted a constitution stipulating, in violation of the federal constitution, that the republic's president must speak the Adygei language and that 50 percent of the posts in the republic's governing bodies must be reserved for ethnic Adygei, although the titular nationality constituted only 22 percent of the republic's population.[37] All eight Muslim republics of the Russian Federation declared various levels of sovereignty, emulating the actions of the union republics of the USSR.

In Bashkortostan, intra-Muslim ethnic rivalries between Tatars and Bashkirs served as a catalyst for the rise of nationalism. Beginning in 1989, several Tatar nationalist groups emerged in the republic, including the Tatar Social Center, the Tatar Democratic Party "Idel-Ural," and the Bashkortostan branch of the Tatar youth movement Azatliq (Freedom). Largely in response to Tatar activism, the Bashkir People's Center "Ural" (BPC) held its founding congress in December 1989 and demanded that Bashkortostan be elevated to the status of a union republic in the USSR. In February 1991, the BPC's second congress attracted approximately 1,200 delegates from Bashkortostan and across Russia. Allied groups such as the Baskhir People's Assembly, the Bashkir People's Party, and the Bashkir Youth League advocated the creation of an independent Bashkortostan, while Bashkir extremists called for the expulsion of non-Bashkirs in order to ensure a Bashkir majority in the republic.[38]

Bashkortostan's government, led by republican president Murtaza Rakhimov, took advantage of this enhanced nationalist sentiment to increase the republic's administrative autonomy. Under Rakhimov's leadership, Bashkortostan ratified a constitution proclaiming the republic's sovereignty and requiring the president to speak Bashkir.[39] The constitution further affirmed Bashkortostan's right to "freely leave the Russian Federation."[40] The Bashkir minister of education advanced a nationalist agenda in 1993 by requiring compulsory study of the Bashkir language and literature by all students in first through ninth grades regardless of their linguistic background.[41] In August 1994, Bashkortostan gained recognition of its sovereignty in an agreement negotiated with the Russian federal government.

In some cases, Muslim nationalist movements advocated more drastic measures to secure their national rights. In the dual-ethnic republics of Kabardino-Balkaria and Karachaevo-Cherkessia, nationalist movements sought to divide the republics into separate national homelands. Several nationalist movements arose to represent different ethnic groups in the multiethnic republic of Dagestan; most notably, a Lezgin nationalist movement advocated the creation of an independent Lezginstan on traditional Lezgin territory in Dagestan and neighboring Azerbaijan. Movements also arose to support the creation of larger multiethnic homelands, including Adyge Khase, which sought to unify the Circassian peoples of the North Caucasus, and the Confederation of Peoples of the Caucasus, which supported the formation of an independent multinational Caucasian Republic. At times, rising nationalist sentiment among Muslim ethnic groups led to interethnic conflict, including violent clashes between Chechens and Laks in Dagestan and between Ingush and Ossets in North Ossetia.[42] These conflicts illustrated the limits of Islam in blunting ethnic differences in the post-Soviet era, reminiscent of the failure of earlier Muslim attempts to achieve greater self-determination and unity.

However, during the final years of the USSR (and the RSFSR) and throughout the decade of Boris Yeltsin's presidency, national awakening in Russia was dominated by the rise of nationalism in the Muslim republics of Chechnya and Tatarstan. An enhancement of Islamic awareness—a principal component of collective identity among Tatars and Chechens, especially those seeking to assert their distinctiveness from the surrounding Russian culture—accompanied this rise in nationalist sentiment. The pursuit of Muslim national autonomy, intermingled with growing religious consciousness, and the response of federal authorities played determining roles in the evolution of Russian federalism throughout Yeltsin's rule and defined some of the most important issues in center-periphery relations faced by his successor.

Tatarstan's Nationalist Challenge

In Tatarstan, nationalism emerged as a strong political force in January 1989 as delegates from Tatar communities across the USSR met in Kazan to found the All-Tatar Public Center (ATPC). The delegates demanded a reduction in ethnic Russian immigration into the republic and the designation of Tatar as Tatarstan's official language. The ATPC also expressed the goal of raising the status of Tatarstan from an autonomous republic to a full union republic of the USSR, thereafter moving gradually toward complete independence. By October 1989, the ATPC estimated its membership across the Soviet Union at one million.[43] The following year, several other nationalist organizations joined the ATPC, including Azatliq and the Sovereignty Committee. Additionally, the political party Ittifaq (Unity) emerged as the most anti-Russian of Tatar nationalist organizations and espoused a particularly harsh anticolonialist (anti-Russian) position. The name Ittifaq evoked memories of the early-twentieth-century Ittifaq-al-Muslimin and the Tatars' earlier attempts to assert national self-determination. In October 1991, Ittifaq's leader, Fauzia Baira-mova, wrote:

> The great tragedy is that the [Tatar] nation has lost its pride. Would a nation that has any pride really allow such self-mockery in its history; would it really sell the Russians its language, religion, and customs; and would it really accept their much inferior traditions? Would a Tatar who had any pride really mix his ge-nealogy with that of his enemy? Would a Tatar who had any pride really look on calmly as his sacred lands were parceled out to others? Would a Tatar who had any pride really toil like a donkey for four centuries, pulling along the Rus-sian newcomers? . . . Tatar lands form half of Russian territory. . . . It is time to raise the question of joining to Tatarstan the lands that belonged to Tatars of old and where they live now.[44]

In February 1991, the more radical of these nationalist groups organized an all-Tatar *kurultai* (congress) in Kazan, bringing together Tatars from across the Soviet Union. The congress declared Tatarstan independent and elected a seventy-five-member Milli Mejlis (National Assembly).[45] During its first meeting the following month, the Milli Mejlis declared itself the supreme legislative body of all Tatars and proclaimed that it had the authority to abrogate acts of Tatarstan's government that contravened the interests of the Tatar people.[46] In October 1991, these forces organized a massive rally in Freedom Square in front of Tatarstan's parliament building to protest the anniversary of Ivan the Terrible's conquest of Kazan. Vio-lence resulted when a large group of protestors attempted to storm the republican legislature after the parliament refused to adopt a declaration of independence.[47]

Religion did not play a dominant role in the formation of these Tatar nationalist movements, which almost unanimously advocated the creation of a secular auton-omous or, in some cases, independent republic. As a fundamental component of Tatar identity, however, Islam served as a unifying cultural symbol even for secular nationalists. In its 1991 political program, the ATPC extolled the virtues of Jadid-ism, a reformist interpretation of Islam prevalent in Tatarstan, as a modernizing force and included the revival of Jadidism among Tatars as one of its principal objectives. The center also declared that the republic should have its own Muslim religious board headquartered in Kazan. The ATPC later reiterated its commitment to Islam as a part of Tatar national culture in the following official statement: "The history of Tatar culture and enlightenment, the entire way of life, is closely con-nected to Islam. Therefore, Islam cannot be separate from national policy or from the national movement, and is closely connected to and cooperates with them."[48] The Islamic Democratic Party of Tatarstan, a nationalist party founded in 1991 to seek a secular independent state, also appealed to Tatars' desire to reassert their Islamic heritage.

Other movements drew a much tighter association between Islam and Tatar nationalism. The Islamic Youth Center "Iman," in a statement to the Organization of the Islamic Conference, presented the following appeal:

> To preserve their Muslim religion, our ancestors refused riches, left their native places, and faced death. And we, their descendants, serve as evidence to you that they protected our common faith and passed it on to us. At the same time, we appeal to you to variously support the natural striving of our state toward independence and freedom, for in conditions of the strong spiritual and material expansion of Christianity, only that will allow for the future preservation of the Islamic faith of our people.[49]

Bairamova's Ittifaq party and the Milli Mejlis espoused an equally radical, although still secular, view of Islam as an instrument to distance Tatars from Russians. In 1991, they issued a joint program proclaiming, "The ancient culture, the entire life of the Tatar people are in an intimate way connected to Islam. And in the complex modern situation, religion must defend the nation, and the nation must defend religion."[50]

In the latter half of the 1990s, as nationalism receded, Ittifaq and the Milli Mejlis adopted more extremist pan-Islamist positions to renew their declining support. In December 1997, at Ittifaq's fourth party congress, party leaders issued a pronouncement stating, "We declare the national liberation struggle we are waging against the Russian empire to be henceforth known as jihad aimed at liberation from the infidels' slavery. We, Muslim nationalists, are launching a struggle for the creation of an Islamic state in Tatarstan."[51] Meanwhile, the Milli Mejlis also adopted a more Islam-oriented posture and in January 1996 approved a new unofficial Tatar constitution (never recognized by the government of Tatarstan) that included the goal of reviving Shari'a as envisioned by Jadidism in the republic. In June 1996, both organizations participated in the founding of the Muslims of Tatarstan, a sociopolitical organization, with former Tatar mufti Gabdulla Galiullin as its leader.[52]

The rise of Tatar nationalism, minus its religious overtones, in the final years of the Soviet Union was reflected in the policies adopted by Tatarstan's government. In August 1990, Tatarstan's parliament proclaimed the republic's sovereignty and renamed it the Tatar Soviet Socialist Republic–Republic of Tatarstan, implying equal status with the USSR's union republics. Mintimer Shaimiev, chairman of Tatarstan's parliament, signed the declaration and resigned from the Communist Party.[53] Just two days after the failed August 1991 coup d'état, Tatarstan's parliament, at Shaimiev's urging, adopted the Act of State Independence of the Republic of Tatarstan authorizing a future referendum on the nature of sovereignty for Tatarstan.[54]

In March 1992, four months after the USSR's dissolution, Tatarstan held the proposed referendum, which asked voters, "Do you agree that the republic of Tatarstan is a sovereign state, a subject of international law, building its relations with Russia and other republics and states on the basis of equitable treaties?"[55] Despite threats by the Yeltsin administration to bring criminal charges against officials conducting the referendum, Tatarstan's residents responded positively by a wide margin: with 81.6 percent of the electorate participating, 61.4 percent voted in favor of sovereignty.[56] In November 1992, Tatarstan's parliament ratified a new constitution reiterating Tatarstan's status as "a sovereign state, subject to international law."[57] This assertion of self-rule was accompanied by overtures to ethnic Russians and other non-Tatars in the republic, including a provision making Russian (along with Tatar) an official language of the republic and guaranteeing equal protection for all citizens regardless of their ethnicity.[58] However, the constitution, without directly proclaiming Tatarstan's independence, implied that the republic was outside the legal jurisdiction of the Russian federal government, pending the negotiation of a treaty delineating Tatarstan's status, if any, within the Russian Federation.

Chechnya's Declaration of Independence

Parallel to the rise of Tatar nationalism, a Chechen independence movement posed another challenge to the federal center. In November 1990, a self-proclaimed Chechen National Congress met in Grozny, the capital of the then dual-ethnic Republic of Chechnya-Ingushetia, and elected Soviet air force general Dzhokhar Dudaev as chairman of its executive committee and commander of a newly formed Chechen National Guard.[59] A few days later, the formal government of Chechnya-Ingushetia, headed by Doku Zavgaev, attempted to appease the rising nationalist sentiment by issuing a declaration of sovereignty for the republic, much as Shaimiev had done in Tatarstan. However, Dudaev and the Chechen National Congress (renamed the National Congress of Chechen People, NCCP, in June 1991) continued to rally the more radical elements among the Chechen nationalists. After the abortive 1991 coup d'état against Gorbachev, which Zavgaev failed to condemn, the NCCP proclaimed the dissolution of the ruling Chechen-Ingush Supreme Soviet and declared its own executive committee, led by Dudaev, the ruling authority of the republic. Early the next month, Dudaev and his national guard briefly seized control of the republic's Supreme Soviet building. Under pressure from Moscow and Dudaev's forces, the Communist-dominated ruling body subsequently voted to dissolve itself and surrender power to a Provisional Supreme Soviet, which would rule the republic until elections scheduled for the following November.[60]

Although several Chechen nationalists served on the new Provisional Supreme Soviet, Dudaev and the NCCP declared the provisional government dissolved in October 1991 and seized government assets across the republic, including the regional headquarters of the Committee for State Security (KGB). Despite warnings from Moscow that the results of any illegitimate elections would be declared invalid, Dudaev also organized presidential and parliamentary elections for a new Chechen republic. In late October 1991, Dudaev decisively won the presidential election, taking 85 percent of the vote, while supporters of Chechen independence won the majority of seats in the new parliament.[61] Within days of his election, Dudaev issued his first presidential decree, stating that by "the will of the citizens of the Chechen republic, expressed by direct and general elections, the state sovereignty of the Chechen Republic is declared."[62] The next day, the pro-Dudaev Chechen parliament ratified his declaration.

As in Tatarstan, Islam played a secondary role in the early years of Chechnya's bid for greater national self-determination. Although he associated his rule with Islamic institutions traditional to Chechnya, at first Dudaev did not use religion overtly as an instrument to rally support. He encouraged the revival of the traditional clan structure and religious communities characteristic of Chechnya's version of Sufi Islam and brought back to prominence the Council of Elders and other Islamic institutions and traditions of pre-Soviet Chechnya.[63] However, he remained a secular nationalist in the first years of his rule and supported a secular government for Chechnya. Not until Russian military intervention in 1994 did Dudaev link Chechen independence directly with Islam. Once hostilities began, he appealed to Islamist sentiment in Chechnya, the Caucasus, and even beyond Russia's borders to foment opposition to Russian intervention in Chechnya and to consolidate his power in the republic.

In response to Dudaev's rejection of federal authority in 1991, Yeltsin embarked on a short-lived policy that hinted at his willingness—confirmed three years later— to rely on military force to resist separatism in Russia. In November 1991, Yeltsin declared a state of emergency in Chechnya and dispatched several hundred troops to arrest Dudaev and disperse proindependence forces. Upon landing at the airport in Grozny, however, Russian forces were surrounded by the Chechen National Guard. After a two-day standoff, the Russian Republic's parliament voided Yeltsin's state of emergency decree, and the Russian president, faced with the risk of bloodshed on a large scale, backed down from further confrontation. Chechen and Russian forces subsequently reached an agreement on a Russian withdrawal from the city, ending Yeltsin's first experiment with military force to subdue ethnic nationalism and separatism.[64] In the following months, Chechen forces quickly took over military facilities and weapons on Chechen territory and built a formidable arsenal, including tanks, armored personnel carriers, and several thousand automatic weapons.[65]

Yeltsin's Attempts to Halt Decentralization

From the time he assumed the presidency of the RSFSR in June 1990, Yeltsin faced a rapid deterioration in the governing power of his administration, plus a secessionist crisis in Chechnya and potentially in Tatarstan. Through an evolving set of policies, Yeltsin tried to halt decentralization and, where possible, reassert federal authority. These policies, which did not amount to a cohesive strategy and contained many contradictions, took five forms: (1) direct appointment of regional officials; (2) negotiation of a comprehensive treaty defining relations between the federal center and the republics and regions; (3) ratification of a new constitution increasing the federal government's authority; (4) negotiation of bilateral power-sharing treaties with individual provinces; and (5) the use of military force.

Yeltsin's Agents in the Provinces

Even before the Soviet Union's dissolution, Yeltsin initiated his first efforts to re-store central authority with the promulgation of two presidential decrees. The first decree, issued in August 1990, assigned regional presidential representatives to the provinces in order to ensure that federal legislation and directives were imple-mented.[66] Three months later, Yeltsin issued a second decree, endorsed later by the Russian parliament, authorizing him to appoint and dismiss governors of Russian regions (but not ethnic republics) with the approval of regional legislatures. Yeltsin retained this power until 1995, when the Russian parliament passed legislation mandating that all regional and republican chief executives be elected.[67]

Despite the theoretical power these decrees gave Yeltsin to intervene in the prov-inces, his regional representatives remained largely ineffective. This failure was due partly to the political power of the regional legislatures, which, as elected bodies, could claim a popular mandate when defying the actions of Moscow-appointed governors and representatives. Provincial authorities also exercised significant lev-erage over federal officials residing in their regions through the provision of goods and services, including affordable housing and transportation.[68] At times, appointed governors pursued their own objectives at the expense of federal directives; the most embarrassing case occurred in 1993 when Eduard Rossel, the Yeltsin-appointed governor of Sverdlovsk Oblast, attempted to create an autonomous Urals Republic. In Tatarstan, the Shaimiev government blocked the appointment of a presidential representative in his republic, while in Chechnya, Dudaev, although he allowed several federal officials to be based in the republic during negotiations with the Kremlin, did not allow them a significant voice in the republic's decision making.[69]

The 1992 Federation Treaty

Yeltsin initiated a more comprehensive effort to define the limits of regional au-tonomy after the Russian Federation attained independence. In early 1992, he opened negotiations with provincial governments on a Federation Treaty to provide a legal basis for relations between the federal center and the federation subjects. In March 1992, the Kremlin reached agreement with eighty-six provinces (exclud-ing Tatarstan and Chechnya-Ingushetia, formally still a united republic) on the provisions of the treaty. The Federation Treaty did not recognize the right of ethnic republics to secede and stated that republican laws and constitutions could not violate those of the federal government. However, like Gorbachev's 1991 Union Treaty, the new treaty defined the ethnic republics as sovereign and granted them significant powers, including the authority to conduct independent foreign and in-ternational trade policies, to assert ownership over land and natural resources of their territories, and to determine their own governmental structures. By contrast, the other federation subjects were not described as sovereign and were denied the authority to have their own constitutions or to determine the structures of their governing bodies.[70]

The treaty's concessions to the ethnic republics formalized a significant degree of decentralization and national autonomy, but also served Yeltsin's interests by gaining agreement from most republics not to seek secession and by curtailing ethnic nationalism at a time when he was consolidating his power. Yeltsin exercised substantial political authority as Russia's elected president; however, he encountered powerful resistance to his policies from Russia's parliament, which, having been elected in March 1989, contained a large core of Soviet-era Communists and others opposed to Yeltsin's reform strategy. Chairman of the Russian Supreme Soviet Ruslan Khasbulatov and Yeltsin's own vice president, Aleksandr Rutskoi, emerged as leaders of the opposition.[71] Yeltsin agreed to a formal treaty creating a federal structure that granted republics significant autonomy largely to avoid antagonizing nationalists among non-Russian ethnic groups in the same manner that he sought to gain the support of ethnic minorities during his struggle with Gorbachev.

The 1993 Russian Constitution

In 1993, Yeltsin succeeded in marginalizing the remaining Soviet-era opposition to his rule, after which he attempted to curb many of the national rights recognized in the Federation Treaty. In the autumn of 1993, after dissolving the parliament by an unconstitutional presidential decree, Yeltsin employed military force to break up violent demonstrations and to expel recalcitrant members of the legislature from the parliament building. He then called elections for a new lower house of parliament, the State Duma, held simultaneously with a referendum for a new constitution. The new constitution, approved by 58 percent of voters in December 1993, granted Yeltsin extraordinary presidential powers and curtailed much of the national autonomy given to the ethnic republics in the Federation Treaty. The new federal constitution did not describe the republics as sovereign and placed many of the rights recognized as belonging to the republics under joint jurisdiction with federal authorities.[72]

Despite Yeltsin's consolidation of power and his clearly demonstrated willingness to use force against the parliament toward this end, the enhancement of federal authority contained in the constitution did not translate immediately into effective power over the provinces. Conflict between the Yeltsin administration and the new parliament, which contained a large number of nationalists and Communists, combined with a prolonged economic crisis, hindered the Kremlin's capacity to exert effective influence over Russia's vast territory.[73] Moreover, in twelve republics, either the constitution was not approved by a majority of voters or turnout for the referendum was under the 50 percent minimum required to validate the results.[74]

The Muslim republics of Tatarstan and Chechnya continued to pose the boldest challenges to the federal center. Leaders of both republics refused to participate in negotiations on the Federation Treaty and did not sign the final document. During the same month in which the treaty was signed, Tatarstan held its own referendum on sovereignty and the Chechen parliament ratified a new constitution for the self-proclaimed Republic of Chechnya. In December 1993, although Shaimiev allowed Tatarstan's citizens to vote during the referendum on the Russian constitution, his administration actively discouraged voter participation and kept turnout in the republic to less than 15 percent of eligible voters.[75] In Chechnya, the Dudaev government did not permit voting on the referendum. To overcome the open challenge presented by these two republics, Yeltsin employed two sharply divergent strategies: bilateral negotiation in Tatarstan and military force in Chechnya.

Tatarstan: The Negotiation Option

Yeltsin's strategy of negotiating with regional leaders began to take shape early in his presidency. Throughout the early 1990s, despite the long-running dispute over Tatarstan's status in the Russian Federation, federal authorities and Shaimiev's government quietly engaged in diplomacy to resolve practical policy issues (primarily economic) in their relations. From March 1992 to the end of 1993, the two governments concluded a series of bilateral accords covering such diverse topics as ownership of oil fields and defense industries in the republic, environmental protection, the republic's education system, and customs regulations.[76] Following Yeltsin's consolidation of power in Moscow and the ratification of the 1993 constitution, both sides expanded on these agreements to reach a comprehensive accord on Tatarstan's relations with the federal government. The result was the first power-sharing treaty, signed in February 1994, between the federal government and a federation subject.[77]

To secure this agreement, the Shaimiev government agreed that Tatarstan would be a subject of the federation and permitted language in the treaty that referred to Tatarstan as a state "united with the Russian Federation"[78] rather than being simply "associated with Russia," as stated in Tatarstan's constitution.[79] Neither sovereignty nor the right of secession was mentioned in the document. The treaty did not identify the republic as a subject of international law, as did Tatarstan's constitution and declaration of sovereignty. In return, Tatarstan gained powers reserved in the Russian constitution for the federal government or for joint federal-republican jurisdiction, including the authority to engage in foreign and international economic relations, to determine the republic's budget and tax policies, and to establish forms of alternative civil service for citizens of Tatarstan eligible to substitute such activity for service in the Russian military.[80]

Shaimiev's willingness to make concessions on the nature of Tatarstan's sovereignty largely reflected geographic and demographic weaknesses. Despite its size, Tatarstan has no external borders and is completely surrounded by the territory of the Russian Federation. Additionally, at the time of the signing of the power-sharing treaty, Tatarstan's titular nationality accounted for less than half the republic's population, with Tatars comprising about 48 percent and Russians comprising about

43 percent.[81] This ethnic mix, which resulted from the Bolsheviks' strategy of delineating Tatarstan's borders in a way that guaranteed that the majority of Tatars resided outside the republic, presented the risk of internal interethnic strife in the event of outright secession from Russia. Most important, Shaimiev was more interested in supporting nationalist sentiment as a means of consolidating his own power in the republic and limiting federal interference in his rule than in establishing an independent Tatar state. Consequently, he was willing to sacrifice the veneer of sovereignty to enhance his own federally recognized powers.

The resulting power-sharing treaty between Tatarstan and the federal government established a model for resolving disputes in Russia's center-periphery relations, although Sergei Shakhrai, chairman of the commission designated by Yeltsin to negotiate agreements with the provinces, claimed that the treaty with Tatarstan was born of political necessity and was not intended as a model for center-periphery relations.[82] Regardless of the federal government's original intent, the treaty set a precedent for negotiations with other republics and regions. By the end of 1998, the Yeltsin administration had concluded forty-two power-sharing treaties with forty-six provinces (some of the treaties covered more than one province), including several republics and regions with substantial Muslim populations.[83]

The Yeltsin administration's use of power-sharing negotiations introduced a new element of stability in Russia's center-periphery relations. It bound republics and regions to the federation within a mutually agreed upon formula and addressed the most contentious points of conflict between federal authorities and the provinces. Most important, the agreement with Tatarstan eased a crisis in the Kremlin's relations with Kazan that had emerged prior to Russian independence in December 1991. However, the price of realizing these advantages was the institutionalization of both the de facto decentralized nature of Russian federalism and the asymmetry in Russia's center-periphery relations. Because most power-sharing treaties were negotiated on a bilateral basis, the contents of individual treaties differed substantially from one another and recognized different levels of autonomy for different federation subjects, sometimes in violation of federal law and the Russian constitution.

These treaties thus codified the uneven devolution of power that had occurred during the first years of Yeltsin's rule.[84] For example, the agreement with Bashkortostan described the republic as a "sovereign state within the Russian Federation," the only time a republic was called "sovereign" in any of the forty-two treaties, while the treaty with North Ossetia referred to the republic simply as a "full subject of the Russian Federation," and the agreement with Udmurtia called the republic merely "a republic" and stated that Udmurtia's relations with the federal center were regulated by the Russian constitution.[85] Similar disparities emerged among agreements with ethnic Russian regions. Sverdlovsk Oblast, for example, gained important attributes of autonomy, including the authority to establish its own civil service, to remove leaders of federal agencies on its territory (in consultation with federal authorities), and to suspend certain federal government acts on its territory.[86] By comparison, many other regions gained no extraconstitutional rights, and some never signed power-sharing treaties with the federal center. Consequently, Yeltsin's reliance on power-sharing negotiations left to his successor the task of addressing the decentralized and asymmetrical nature of Russian federalism.

Chechnya: The Military Option

Despite the Yeltsin administration's success in negotiating a resolution to its dispute with Tatarstan, the Kremlin abandoned this option in dealing with the Dudaev regime in Chechnya and opted for military intervention to restore federal authority. A number of factors, many of which may never be identified, contributed to this deviation from the negotiated power-sharing option. First, the bitter historic experience of the Chechens during Russia's conquest and rule over the region left a legacy of mistrust and, among many Chechens, antagonism. Chechen resistance to Russian conquest, led by Sheikh Mansur and Imam Shamil, an ethnic Avar from Dagestan, was among the strongest the empire faced, and its memory still constitutes an important component of Chechen national identity.[87] Periodic Chechen uprisings continued under the tsars and, later, Soviet rule into the 1930s. Stalin's deportation of Chechens to Central Asia in 1944, which caused the death of nearly a third of the Chechen population, intensified historic Chechen-Russian antagonism, especially for survivors of the deportation and those like Dzhokhar Dudaev who spent their formative years in exile.[88] This troubled history hindered assimilation of the Chechen people into the larger Russian (and Soviet) society and increased their willingness to resist Russian rule.

A second factor that hindered negotiations was the antagonistic relationship between the Dudaev regime and the Yeltsin administration. Unlike Shaimiev, who was elected to the Tatarstan presidency, Dudaev seized power in a military coup d'état and only later legitimized his rule through questionable elections. Yeltsin originally acquiesced in the overthrow of Doku Zavgaev, the purportedly antireform leader of the Chechen-Ingush Republic, but Dudaev's subsequent seizure of government assets in the republic and his decision to hold elections for a separate Chechen Republic alienated him from the Kremlin. Mutual antagonism increased in 1994 as Yeltsin's liberal period drew to a close following the strong performance by Communists and nationalists in the December 1993 parliamentary elections.[89] Thus Yeltsin began relying increasingly on a core group of hard-liners, the "party of war," who advocated a more aggressive posture toward Chechnya.[90]

Third, Chechnya's proximity to, and potential influence on, the other Muslim republics and ethnic groups of the North Caucasus also raised concerns about a "domino effect" that could lead to a rise in anti-Russian nationalism as well as pan-Muslim or pan-Caucasian separatist sentiments. These fears may have been exaggerated since many of the other Caucasian peoples feared the spread of unrest emanating from Chechnya. Nevertheless, Russian fears were intensified when Dudaev stated during a 1994 interview published in a Turkish newspaper, "My plan foresaw the creation of a union of Caucasus countries directed against Russian imperialism. . . . Our chief goal was the achievement of independence and liberation, acting together with the Caucasus republics which have been oppressed by Russia over the course of 300 years."[91]

Fourth, Chechnya was a major transportation corridor, linking Russia to the South Caucasus via railway, highway, and oil pipeline. Until its replacement by an alternative route in the spring of 2000, a critical segment of Russia's vast network of pipelines, which linked Russian and Caspian Sea oil to the Black Sea and international markets, passed through Chechnya.[92] From Russia's perspective, the importance of securing this route increased when proposals were made for the construction of an alternative Baku-Tbilisi-Ceyhan pipeline bypassing Russia and ending in the Turkish Mediterranean port of Ceyhan. Turkey actively lobbied for this alternative, fueling suspicions in Russia that Turkey and other international actors were helping the Dudaev regime and fomenting unrest in Chechnya, partly to make pipeline routes through Russia less viable.[93]

Despite these obstacles to a peaceful settlement, shortly after the failure of Yeltsin's first attempt to forcibly depose Dudaev in November 1991, Russia and Chechnya opened talks. In December 1992, negotiations produced a draft power-sharing agreement, the Treaty on the Separation of Power and Authority between the State Governing Bodies of the Russian Federation and the Governing Bodies of the Republic of Chechnya. During negotiations, however, the Yeltsin administration attempted to isolate Dudaev, partly to deny him enhanced legitimacy and public standing. Instead, federal negotiators dealt with other members of the separatist Chechen government, including Dudaev's political rivals Yusup Soslambekov, chairman of the Chechen parliament's committee on foreign affairs, and Yaraghi Mamodaev, Chechnya's acting prime minister and head of the Confederation of Peoples of the Caucasus. In response, Dudaev dismissed the December 1992 draft treaty as a private affair. In January 1993, Dudaev's guards turned away Russia's chief negotiators, Sergei Shakhrai and Ramazan Abdulatipov, when they arrived in Grozny to discuss the treaty with members of the Chechen parliament.[94]

Chechen-Russian tensions intensified through early 1994, even as Russian-Tatar negotiations culminated in a compromise agreement. In January 1994, Dudaev issued a decree declaring the formation of the Chechen Republic of Ichkeria, a name derived from the republic's mountainous Shatoi and Vedeno districts.[95] This act was designed to consolidate the support of Chechnya's mountain population, which historically has been highly resistant to rule from Moscow. The next month, during a speech to the Russian parliament, Yeltsin declared the Dudaev regime illegitimate and ruled out Chechen independence. Reflecting Russia's hardened stance on Chechnya, Deputy Prime Minister Sergei Shakhrai declared that a power-sharing treaty with Chechnya was possible only after the election of a new Chechen government.[96] With this declaration, the option of negotiation was effectively eliminated, and Russia and Chechnya drifted into a devastating war.

Consequences of the First Chechen War

The Russian-Chechen conflict had three major consequences: (1) it contributed to the rise of Islamic extremism in Chechnya and other parts of the North Caucasus; (2) it intensified anti-Muslim (especially anti-Caucasian) sentiments and fear of an Islamic threat to Russia; and (3) it increased support for the reassertion of central authority over restive regions and national minorities while strengthening popular support for a stronger central government. Although Islamist sentiment in Chechnya was relatively weak prior to Russian military intervention in 1994, the beginning of warfare enticed Dudaev to resort to Islamic symbolism to mobilize popular resistance and to gain external support for Chechen independence. Consequently, Islam—including extremist versions—became firmly entrenched in Chechnya's internal politics, and Islamic extremism, aided by deteriorating socioeconomic conditions, spread to other parts of the North Caucasus, especially Dagestan. By the mid-1990s, Islamist congregations had extended beyond Dagestan and Chechnya to Ingushetia, Karachaevo-Cherkessia, Kabardino-Balkaria, and Muslim areas of Stavropol Krai.[97]

In August 1999, this rise in Islamic extremism culminated in the incursion of several thousand Islamist militants from Chechnya into Dagestan with the objective of establishing an Islamic state in the region. Combined with the 1999 terrorist bombings in Moscow and other cities, the renewal of warfare in the North Caucasus provoked strong anti-Chechen as well as anti-Caucasian and anti-Muslim sentiments within the Russian population. In the immediate aftermath of the bombings, approximately 60 percent of the Russian public favored the expulsion of all Chechens to prevent further terrorist attacks.[98] Support for military action also increased dramatically. In July 1999, one month before the incursions into Dagestan, 82 percent of the Russian public expressed a willingness to accept the secession of Chechnya from Russia. Just three months later, 65 percent favored subduing Chechen separatists by any means necessary.[99]

Vladimir Putin's Reassertion of Central Authority

In this altered political environment, Vladimir Putin embarked on an ambitious initiative to reassert federal authority, using Chechnya as the testing ground of his polices. His first and most forceful effort to advance this objective began immediately after the Chechen incursion into Dagestan. As Russia's newly appointed prime minister, Putin mobilized the Russian military for a large-scale counteroffensive to restore order in the North Caucasus. After several weeks of fighting, during which the Russian military forced insurgents to withdraw from Dagestan, he ordered the military to reestablish government authority in the Islamist-dominated Dagestani villages of Chabanmakhi, Kadar, and Karamakhi. By the end of September 1999, Russian forces had eliminated large-scale organized resistance in Dagestan. Russian officials claimed that more than 2,000 militants died in the fighting,[100] while Russian casualties reached 281 dead and 930 wounded.[101] Approximately 22,000 Dagestanis were displaced.[102]

After repelling the insurgents and defeating Islamists in the rebellious villages in central Dagestan, Putin ordered the military back into Chechnya, this time, in contrast to the 1994–96 military operation, without significant popular opposition or ambivalence. After weeks of air strikes against retreating insurgents and their bases inside Chechnya, Russia widened its military offensive to include the reimposition of federal authority in the republic. Crossing the Chechen border in late September 1999, the Russian military mobilized approximately 80,000 troops. In February 2000, Russian forces captured the Chechen capital of Grozny after a prolonged and devastating assault that resulted in the deaths of approximately 1,500 Russian soldiers and an unknown number of Chechen rebels and civilians. By the spring of 2000, although guerrilla warfare and terrorist attacks continued, the Russian military had forced the separatist Chechen regime, now headed by Aslan Maskhadov, elected Chechen president in the spring of 1997, underground and had established control over the republic's major population centers.

This military campaign had an important antecedent in the months prior to Putin's rise to power. In the spring of 1999, Sergei Stepashin, then Russia's prime minister and a former director of the FSB (during the 1994–96 Russian-Chechen War), oversaw preparations for a large-scale military operation in Chechnya. After the abduction of General Gennady Shpigun, Russia's representative to Chechnya, federal authorities drafted plans to take control of the northern third of the republic (a largely flat territory north of the Terek River), seal off Chechnya's borders, and destroy terrorist and guerrilla training camps.[103] According to Stepashin, the military failed to launch this plan because it was preempted by the incursions into Dagestan, which brought about a much larger military response from Russia. The disclosure of this plan revealed that the Yeltsin administration—which included Putin, who served simultaneously as both FSB director and secretary of the Russian Security Council—had planned to restore federal control by force over parts of the increasingly anarchic Chechnya before the Islamists' incursion in August 1999.

Putin's Federal Reforms

Popular support for the war increased Putin's approval rating dramatically, thus enabling him to win the Russian presidency in March 2000. As Russia's president, Putin initiated a comprehensive strategy to restore what he called the "vertical chain of executive power,"[104] or *vertikal' vlasti* (vertical of power), as it was popularized in the Russian media. In May 2000, he announced the formation of seven large administrative federal districts, each encompassing a subset of Russia's eighty-nine federation subjects (see Table 4.2). Putin then appointed a presidential representative to each new federal district and tasked these new representatives with overseeing the performance of federal agencies in the provinces and monitoring the implementation of federal policy. In assigning these representatives, who re-

Table 4.2

Seven Federal Districts of the Russian Federation

Southern (North Caucasus) District	**Greater Volga District**
Headquarters: Rostov-on-Don Presidential Representative: Viktor Kazantsev (former commander of Russian armed forces in Chechnya) Muslim Republics: Adygea, Chechnya, Dagestan, Ingushetia, Kabardino-Balkaria, and Karachaevo-Cherkessia	Headquarters: Nizhny Novgorod Presidential Representative: Sergei Kirienko (former prime minister) Muslim Republics: Bashkortostan and Tatarstan

Central District	**Urals District**
Headquarters: Moscow Presidential Representative: Georgi Poltavchenko (formerly served in the FSB and federal tax police)	Headquarters: Yekaterinburg Presidential Representative: Petr Latyshev (former deputy minister of internal affairs)

Northwestern District	**Siberian District**
Headquarters: St. Petersburg Presidential Representative: Viktor Cherkesov (formerly served in the FSB) Deputy Prime Minister Valentina Matvienko replaced Cherkesov in March 2003.	Headquarters: Novosibirsk Presidential Representative: Leonid Drachevsky (former diplomat and minister for CIS affairs)

Far Eastern District

Headquarters: Khabarovsk
Presidential Representative: Konstantin Pulikovsky (Former deputy commander of Russia armed forces in the North Caucasus

Sources: U.S.-Russia Business Council, "Russia's Federal Districts and Presidential Representatives," 2 February 2002 <www.usrbc.org>; and "Putin Replaces Cherkesov in Northwest," *Russian Region Report*, 8, no. 5 (8 April 2002).

placed the regional envoys introduced by Yeltsin, Putin chose from veterans of Russia's military and security services, with all but two being former officers in the armed forces, Ministry of Internal Affairs, or Federal Security Service. The new representatives to the provinces were made ex officio members of the Russian Security Council[105] and were granted authority to attend cabinet-level meetings of the federal government.[106]

In the months following his creation of the new federal districts, Putin introduced a series of measures to reduce systematically the power of regional leaders. He began with a broad legislative agenda consisting of the following measures: (1) a law that banned regional chief executives from serving in the upper house of parliament, the Federation Council, where they served as ex officio members; (2) legislation that granted the president authority to disband regional legislatures that passed laws violating federal norms and to dismiss any regional chief executive who was charged with a federal crime;[107] (3) a new tax code that reduced the resources available to the regions and republics by requiring them to surrender a greater share of their tax revenue to the federal government (70 percent according to some regional leaders);[108] and (4) a measure granting the Russian president enhanced authority over regional law enforcement, including the power to appoint and dismiss police chiefs in the provinces.[109] Putin created a new body, the State Council of the Russian Federation, to which he appointed all regional chief executive as compensation for their dismissal from the Federation Council. However, this body played an ill-defined advisory role and was given no formal powers in the government.

Parallel to this legislation, Putin introduced administrative measures to assert his authority over the provinces. During the summer of 2000, he issued several decrees annulling regional laws and policies that contradicted federal guidelines. In the process, Putin unilaterally cancelled legislation and governmental edicts in the Muslim republics of Adygea, Bashkortostan, and Ingushetia.[110] In June 2001, he signed a decree creating a presidential commission responsible for redefining the distribution of powers between the federal center and the provinces, with a special focus on bringing the power-sharing treaties into compliance with the federal constitution. In October 2001, the commission's chairman, Dmitri Kozak, announced that all power-sharing treaties with provisions violating the Russian constitution would have to be amended or face cancellation.[111] This sentiment was echoed by President Putin, who stated in his April 2002 State of the Nation address that the power-sharing treaties had led to "inequality in relations between the constituent parts of the federation . . . and between citizens who live in different territories of Russia."[112]

There were dissenting views about the risk of overcentralization and the creation of a so-called hierarchical state for Russia's future stability. The strongest opposition came from the ethnic republics, notably Tatarstan. The Tatar intellectual Rafael Khakimov maintained that democracy and federalism were synonymous in Russia and that one was impossible without the other. He further argued that attempts to abolish Russia's ethnic-based federalism would lead to interethnic conflict.[113] Some Russians expressed similar views. Emil Pain, former adviser to Yeltsin on nationalities issues, stated that Putin's policies would increase Russian xenophobia and nationalism, which would stimulate a backlash from national minorities. He particularly decried the war in Chechnya, which he claimed enhanced Islamic and ethnic solidarity among non-Russian nationalities.[114] Former Russian deputy prime minister Sergei Shakhrai also claimed that Russian federalism under Putin was in decline and would die without being fully developed.[115]

Putin's federal reforms, however, received broad popular support and acquiescence from most regional governments. In May 2000, 63 percent of the Russian public supported Putin's polices (compared to 20 percent who opposed them), and 51 percent supported the president gaining "complete control over parliament and the governors."[116] Russian analyst Boris Lagutenko of the Institute of Economics at the Russian Academy of Sciences summed up the prevailing attitude when he stated, "Russia's current administrative-territorial division is not only absurd, but also dangerous. It in no way corresponds to the democratic spirit of the Constitution . . . and results in inequity for citizens of a supposedly united country. . . . They only hasten the collapse of the state."[117]

In this political environment, several regional leaders acted quickly to align themselves with the president. Shortly after the creation of the Kozak commission, several federation subjects renounced their respective power-sharing agreements.[118] By June 2002, according to Kozak, thirty of the original forty-two power-sharing treaties had been abrogated.[119] Further conceding to this trend, the governors of Bryansk and Kursk oblasts suggested that elections for regional chief executives be abolished in favor of allowing the Russian president to appoint them.[120] The pro-Putin political party Unity introduced a bill in late 2000, later rejected by the State Duma, which would have put this concept into practice.[121] The governors of Vologda and Saratov oblasts endorsed the idea of merging various provinces to reduce the number of federation subjects.[122] Even Eduard Rossel, the rebellious governor of Sverdlovsk Oblast, faced with the threat of having his region's legislature dissolved, signed a decree that brought his region's laws into compliance with federal norms.[123] Similar intense pressure from the Kremlin forced Governor Yevgenii Nazdratenko of Primorsky Krai, a persistent foe of the federal government under Yeltsin, to resign in February 2001.[124]

Is Ethnic Federalism in Russia Obsolete?

Putin's initiative to reassert federal authority, coupled with the popular response to it, raised fundamental doubts about the continued viability of Russia's system of ethnic federalism. Within months of his inauguration as president, two court decisions placed the special status of the ethnic republics in doubt. In June 2000, the Russian Constitutional Court ruled that declarations of sovereignty issued by most republics were unconstitutional. According to the court, "The Constitution of the Russian Federation does not allow any kind of state sovereignty beyond the sovereignty of the Russian Federation."[125] The court further stated that the Russian constitution took precedence over the 1992 Federation Treaty and that clauses in the treaty "providing for sovereignty for the republics . . . are at odds with the Russian Federation Constitution and therefore are invalid and are not to be enforced."[126] The following month, the Constitutional Court ruled that provisions within the constitutions of six republics—Adygea, Bashkortostan, Ingushetia, Komi, North Ossetia, and Tatarstan (all but one, Komi, with large Muslim populations)—violated the Russian constitution. Among these provisions were assertions that republican law took precedence over federal law, that the republics were subjects of international law, and that the republics owned the land and natural resources on their territory.[127]

Following these court decisions, officials within the Putin administration began questioning the legitimacy of the national territories and their special status within the federation. In April 2001, Deputy Minister for Federation Affairs Valery Kirpichnikov stated that the Russian Federation's ten autonomous okrugs constituted an anachronistic "legacy of the Soviet Union," and some were "destined to merge with larger regions."[128] Four months later, his superior, Minister for Federation Affairs Aleksandr Blokhin, extended doubts about the future of the autonomous okrugs to include the ethnic republics. Explaining why he opposed restoring the German Autonomous Republic, which Stalin had abolished in 1941, Blokhin stated that if an ethnic group does not form a majority of the population within a compact territory, it should not be given territorial autonomy.[129] If adopted as policy, this formulation would eliminate fifteen (possibly sixteen) of Russia's twenty-one ethnic republics, including all Muslim republics except Chechnya, Ingushetia, and possibly Tatarstan.[130] Echoing this sentiment, Vladimir Zhirinovsky, Liberal Democratic Party of Russia (LDPR) leader and deputy speaker of the State Duma, stated during his party's annual conference that Russian federalism should be replaced with a unitary state system and that ethnically defined autonomous territories should be abolished altogether.[131]

Several of Russia's national territories quickly conceded to this atmosphere of growing antagonism toward the right of self-determination for national minorities. Many republics amended their constitutions to bring them into compliance with the Russian constitution and federal court rulings, thus removing claims of sovereignty and other assertions of autonomous status. Some took the extraordinary measure of officially rescinding declarations of sovereignty issued in the early 1990s.[132] Governments of a few autonomous okrugs even expressed support for merging their territories with larger Russian regions.[133] With the exception of an ultimately unsuccessful lawsuit filed jointly by the republican governments of Adygea, Chuvashia, and Sakha against Putin's reorganization of the Federation Council,[134] leaders of the national territories refrained from cooperative efforts to resist recentralization. Resistance to the fading of ethnic-based federalism remained largely isolated within a few republics, notably the Muslim republics of Chechnya, Tatarstan, and, to a lesser extent, Bashkortostan.

Muslim Nationalities in a Recentralized Russian State

In the first years of Putin's presidency, the disparagement directed at the national territories had a chilling effect on dissent to recentralization based on the right of national self-determination. In those few cases where significant resistance arose, the Putin administration took corrective—sometimes punitive—measures to ensure that neither resistance from regional ruling elites nor nationalist mobilization among non-Russian ethnic groups threatened federal reforms. Among Russia's eight Mus-

lim republics, this pattern of acquiescence and, when challenges did emerge, retaliation from the Kremlin or its allies in the parliament reversed many of the gains
in national autonomy acquired during Yeltsin's rule.

Response of the Muslim Republics' Ruling Elites

In the North Caucasus, most Muslim republican leaders acquiesced to recentralization with surprising speed. In May 2001, despite its participation in an ultimately
unsuccessful lawsuit against aspects of Putin's federal reforms, Adygea amended
its constitution to comply with federal standards. As part of these constitutional
changes, Adygea removed a provision stating that 50 percent of all positions in the
republic's ruling bodies must be reserved for ethnic Adygei.[135] Similarly,
Kabardino-Balkaria adopted a new constitution in July 2001 that excluded several
provisions within the republic's previous charter that violated federal law, including
clauses proclaiming the republic's sovereignty and stating that republican laws took
precedence over federal laws.[136] Perhaps most surprisingly, Ingush president Ruslan
Aushev, a vocal critic of Putin's policies in Chechnya, offered no resistance when
the courts ruled that many of the Ingushetia's laws, including a provision legalizing
polygamy, were unconstitutional. In December 2001, Aushev abruptly resigned as
republican president, according to some reports to avoid corruption charges from
federal authorities.[137]

In Chechnya, the remnants of Maskhadov's government remained defiant despite
the loss of Grozny and most of the republic's territory. However, the Russian military dismantled the separatist regime, reducing it to a guerrilla insurgency with no
governing capacity and questionable influence over the Chechen population. With
Maskhadov effectively deposed, Putin installed a pro-Moscow leadership. In June
2000, he appointed Chechen mufti Ahmad Kadyrov, a former ally of Maskhadov,
to head a provisional Chechen administration until the republic could be pacified.
Two months later, Putin permitted the election of Chechnya's first deputy to the
Russian State Duma, a contest won by Aslambek Aslakhanov, a former general in
the Russian Ministry of Internal Affairs and leader of the All-Russia Islamic Congress.[138] Both Kadyrov and Aslakhanov criticized human rights abuses by federal
forces in Chechnya, but they refrained from asserting a Chechen right of national
self-determination. Although Aslakhanov went so far as to accuse the military of
genocide,[139] he insisted, "[Russia] is my country. I never separated [in my mind]
Chechnya from the Soviet Union, nor from Russia."[140]

Dagestan presented a special case for Putin. An impoverished multiethnic republic with a history of interethnic rivalries and, more recently, sectarian tensions
between Islamists and supporters of traditional Islam, Dagestan struggled to maintain stability after the collapse of the Soviet Union. To help Dagestani authorities
preserve relative peace, the Kremlin underwrote the republic's budget throughout
the 1990s, providing the republic more subsidies per resident—accounting for 90
percent of the republic's budget—than any other province.[141] The federal government also permitted Dagestan to maintain an internal political system that flagrantly
violated the federal constitution. This system, designed to secure parity between

the republic's largest ethnic groups, guaranteed proportional ethnic representation in the republic's executive and legislative branches. In doing so, it helped maintain relative stability—albeit occasionally interrupted by short bursts of interethnic violence—in the republic's internal politics throughout the 1990s.[142] Dagestani scholar Enver Kisriev maintained that efforts to alter this model to fit federal norms would cause political instability and leave bureaucratic enforcement from the center as the only thing holding the republic together.[143]

In recognition of the role ethnic power sharing played in preserving stability in Dagestan, the Putin administration initially remained cautious about challenging the constitutionality of the republic's political system, which the Dagestani population approved by popular vote in three separate referenda.[144] In return, Dagestan remained one of the federal government's most loyal allies among the ethnic republics. The republican government organized local militias in August 1999 to fight alongside federal troops to repel the incursions from Chechnya and supported Putin's candidacy for president in 2000.[145] In June 2000, while maintaining proportional ethnic representation in the republic's governing bodies, Dagestan became one of the first republics to remove claims of autonomy vis-à-vis the federal government from its constitution. In the process, Dagestan surrendered several attributes of self-rule, including authority to suspend federal laws that violated the republic's sovereignty, to participate independently in international relations, and to unilaterally alter the republic's status within the Russian Federation.[146] Nevertheless, in July 2003, the Kremlin forced Dagestan to adopt a new constitution that complied with federal standards, thus eliminating official arrangements for proportional ethnic representation.

To the east, unlike most of their counterparts in the North Caucasus, the republican leaders of Bashkortostan and Tatarstan challenged aspects of Putin's efforts to curtail ethnic federalism. In the first years of Putin's presidency, both republics sought to preserve some of the most important attributes of autonomy and national self-identity, through compromise with federal authorities whenever possible. Illustrative of this approach, in December 2000, Tatarstan and Bashkortostan reached an agreement with the Putin administration to settle a three-year dispute on internal passports. Since 1997, both republics had insisted that new passports issued to replace Soviet passports indicate the nationality of the holder. Federal authorities, seeking to eliminate ethnic distinctions in passports, refused this demand. In the agreement reached in 2000, the two republics dropped their insistence on listing ethnicity in return for the authority to insert a title page in each passport giving the holder's biographical data in the titular national language.[147] In this manner, Tatarstan and Bashkortostan sought to assert their ethnocultural distinctiveness from the rest of the Russian Federation.

Bashkortostan and Tatarstan attempted similar compromise solutions to disputes with the federal government over their respective republican constitutions. Both republics bowed to pressure from the Putin administration and amended their constitutions to reduce the degree of autonomy claimed vis-à-vis the federal center. However, both new charters retained language that asserted the sovereign status of their republics and claimed governing powers reserved for the federal government in the Russian constitution. Bashkortostan ratified a new constitution in November 2000 stipulating that the republic had the right to (1) enter into international treaties; (2) assert ownership of natural resources on the republic's territory; and (3) establish an independent republican citizenship. The new Bashkir constitution also incorporated the text of the 1994 power-sharing treaty between Bashkortostan and the federal government, a document that proclaimed the republic to be a sovereign state. According to Russia's general prosecutor, eighty provisions violated federal norms.[148]

In April 2002, Tatarstan followed Bashkortostan's example and adopted a new constitution that surrendered some aspects of autonomy, but also asserted the republic's right to engage in international relations, dispose of natural resources on its territory, and maintain a separate republican citizenship. The new constitution also described Tatarstan as a "state united with the Russian Federation" and identified the republican president as the "guarantor of sovereignty" of the republic. Moreover, it incorporated the 1994 Moscow-Kazan power-sharing treaty into the Tatar legal system and declared the treaty, along with the Tatar and Russian constitutions, to be the defining determinant of Tatarstan's status within the larger federation.[149] These provisions implied that Tatarstan maintained a separate statehood and was bound to Russia on a voluntary basis. Russian federal authorities claimed that fifty provisions of the new constitution contradicted federal law.[150]

Muslim Nationalist Mobilization

Within Russia's Muslim population, popular reaction to Putin's policies largely mirrored the response of the Muslim ruling elite, with only a limited mobilization of nationalist opposition. Even in Bashkortostan, where Rakhimov's government resisted federal encroachment on the republic's autonomy, the ethnic Bashkir population did not experience significant nationalist mobilization, as it had in the early 1990s. This acquiescence can be attributed in part to ongoing assimilation into the dominant Russian culture—a process under way for centuries in some cases—and to a decline in both the novelty and the expectations for social change associated with the national awakenings of the late 1980s and early 1990s. The lesson of Chechnya was also an important factor; few were willing to risk military confrontation with Russia to assert a right of greater national self-determination. Interethnic rivalries also served to redirect nationalist ambitions away from the federal center and toward competing national minorities. This trend proved prevalent in regions where past Soviet policies had fostered interethnic tensions through the formation of multiethnic homelands and the deportation and resettlement of entire nationalities during the Second World War.

The Bolshevik policy of establishing multiethnic national territories, each serving as a homeland for two or more national minorities, affected interethnic relations as titular nationalities competed for political influence and ethnic preeminence. In multiethnic Dagestan, despite the republic's system of ethnic power sharing, interethnic friction persisted, occasionally leading to violent confrontation, such as the

May 1998 takeover of government buildings in the republican capital of Makhach-kala by militia members (primarily ethnic Laks) retaliating for the attempted arrest of their leaders. Similarly, in Karachaevo-Cherkessia, the April 1999 electoral victory of Vladimir Semenov, an ethnic Karachai running for republican president, sparked months of violent protests and a threat by Cherkess nationalists to declare a separate Cherkess republic. In relatively quiet Kabardino-Balkaria, nationalist tensions nearly resulted in a crisis in 1997 when Balkar nationalists declared their intention to form a separate Balkar republic and some Chechen rebel commanders offered to provide them military support.[151]

In the case of Stalin-era deportations, interethnic friction resulted when members of exiled nationalities attempted to return to their homelands. Excluding the wars in Chechnya, the two largest incidents of interethnic violence in post-Soviet Russia occurred in Dagestan and North Ossetia in 1992 when previously exiled national minorities attempted to regain control of their ancestral lands, which had been settled during their exile by other ethnic groups. In Dagestan's Novolaksk district, federal authorities declared martial law to end violent confrontations between Ak-kin Chechens, who were attempting to reclaim lands from which they had been deported in 1944, and ethnic Laks, who had been settled in the area subsequently by Soviet authorities. In North Ossetia, violence broke out as ethnic Ingush and Ossets clashed over control of the Prigorodny district, which had been under Ingush jurisdiction before Stalin deported the Ingush to Central Asia in 1944.[152] Such interethnic competition impeded the development and expression of nationalist grievances against Russian rule.

Despite the lack of popular national resistance to recentralization among most ethnic minorities, popular opposition to Putin's policies did arise in Russia's two most troublesome republics, Chechnya and Tatarstan. In Chechnya's case, this opposition took the form of a guerrilla insurgency. Estimates of the number of guerrillas opposing the Russian military in Chechnya range from several hundred to several thousand, including those motivated by Chechen nationalism, Islamist sentiment, or a combination of the two. In October 2002, Chechen insurgents conducted the stunning terrorist attack on the Dubrovka Theater in Moscow, and two months later, suicide bombers destroyed the Kadyrov government headquarters in Grozny.[153] At the end of 2002, Russian military sources reported that 4,700 Russian soldiers had been killed and 13,000 wounded in Chechnya since Russian forces reentered the republic in October 1999.[154]

Islamist-based resistance to Russian federal authority, although not pervasive in the region, arose elsewhere in the North Caucasus, partly in reaction to Russia's military campaign in Chechnya. In March 2000, an armed contingent captured and killed a group of forty-two police officers near the Dagestan-Chechnya border. One year later, a multiethnic group, including residents of Dagestan, Tatarstan, and Karachaevo-Cherkessia, was arrested for the crime and accused of undergoing training in Chechen camps.[155] To the west, a series of bombings in Karachaevo-Cherkessia left 26 people dead and 153 injured in March 2001.[156] In subsequent months, security forces arrested a group of militants from Karachaevo-Cherkessia and Kabardino-Balkaria for carrying out these terrorist acts. During the course of the investigation, police uncovered a network of Islamist militants who, authorities claimed, were planning an armed insurgency in the two republics.[157] Although these acts lacked popular support in the region, they demonstrated the tenacity of a small cadre of Muslim extremists resisting Russian rule in the North Caucasus.

In Tatarstan, although nationalist mobilization to protest Putin's policies did not reach the levels attained in the late 1980s and early 1990s, nationalists consolidated an active constituency in favor of preserving Tatarstan's autonomy. Within weeks of Putin's creation of the seven federal districts, the All-Tatar Public Center organized rallies across Tatarstan to protest the regional reorganization and burned copies of a map illustrating the new federal districts.[158] The ATPC and Azatliq organized rallies in Kazan's Freedom Square on Heter Koene (Memory Day) to commemorate the anniversary of the fall of Kazan to Ivan IV in 1552. In October 2001, the Heter Koene rally attracted more than 2,000 demonstrators and was marked by speeches denouncing Putin's policies and calling for the formation of an independent state.[159] This rally was followed by a meeting of the Milli Mejlis, which denounced the growing threat to Tatarstan's autonomy and criticized the Shaimiev government for "choosing sovereignty without any ethnic identity."[160] Early in 2002, fifteen different organizations met in Kazan to create a national alliance, the Popular Front for the Defense of Human and People's Rights and Tatarstan's Sovereignty, with the stated objective of defending the Tatar people's right of national self-determination.[161]

Religious and cultural self-awareness played a role in the Tatar nationalist resistance to the reassertion of Russian central authority. In a rare case of violent extremism in Tatarstan, militants blew up two major natural-gas pipelines in Tatarstan in December 1999. According to one of those convicted of the crime, "Dagestanis from Karamakhi asked us to help [our] Islamic brothers fighting in Chechnya. They said that if we blew up the gas pipeline, the Western public would take notice of the war."[162] Two of the perpetrators were students of the Yolduz Medressah in Naberezhnie Chelny.[163] In 2002, several thousand Muslim women, protesting a federal regulation banning head coverings in passport photographs, refused to be photographed without their traditional headscarves. They gained the support of several prominent Muslim and Tatar leaders, including Mufti Talgat Tadzhuddin, Tatar State Council chairman Farid Mukhametshin, and Tatar mufti Gusman Iskhakov.[164] In a formal statement issued in July 2002, the Spiritual Board of Muslims of Tatarstan claimed that the prohibition against wearing headscarves "humiliates Muslim women who are forbidden [from removing their head coverings] in the presence of any strangers."[165] After a lengthy, but inconclusive, court battle, the Russian Ministry of Internal Affairs relented in June 2003 and agreed to allow the use of head coverings (as long as the face remained uncovered) in passport photographs if required by an individual's religious beliefs.

Putin's Reaction to Muslim Dissent

The Putin administration responded to challenges to recentralization with both broad measures to secure federal supremacy and targeted actions to subdue individual republics. In Chechnya, the Kremlin pressed its anti-insurgency campaign throughout Putin's first three years as president despite growing popular support among the Russian public for negotiations with Chechen separatists. By the time of the 2002 terrorist attacks in Moscow and Grozny, which greatly reduced prospects for a near-term negotiated settlement, the conflict had entered its fourth year and had lasted more than a year longer than the 1994–96 Russian-Chechen War. During this time, the Russian military consistently denounced any repeat of the 1996 Khasavyurt cease-fire agreement, and Russian authorities derided all Chechen insurgents as bandits or Islamist terrorists. In February 2002, FSB spokesman Sergei Ignatchenko claimed that rebels fighting in Chechnya "are not nationalists or independence-seekers, they are disciplined international terrorists, united by a single aim: to seize power and bring in a new world order based on sharia law."[166]

Alongside Russia's military campaign, the Putin administration attempted to establish a new ruling elite in the republic loyal to Moscow and to build a pro-Moscow indigenous police force consisting primarily of ethnic Chechens to take over key aspects of maintaining security in the republic.[167] This strategy of *Chechenizatsiya* (Chechenization) of the conflict was illustrated in Putin's choice of Chechen mufti Ahmad Kadyrov to be Chechnya's chief administrator. Although Kadyrov resigned his post as mufti shortly after assuming this position, the Kremlin attempted to capitalize on his status as a Chechen religious leader during much of the 1994–96 Russian-Chechen War—he became mufti in April 1995—and a former supporter of Chechen independence to add a much-needed appearance of legitimacy to the Russian-installed Chechen government.

In a further attempt to enhance the legitimacy of Moscow's authority in Chechnya, Russian officials announced plans to hold a referendum in the republic in the spring of 2003 on proposed legislation that would provide a legal basis for electing a new Chechen government and on creating a new Chechen constitution. The new legislation, which would allow for the election of a Chechen president and parliament, constituted an effort by federal authorities to delegitimize Maskhadov, Chechnya's last elected president, and undermine support for separatist and Islamist forces. Similarly, the proposed constitution offered an alternative to the Islamist constitution adopted by the Maskhadov government in 1999, while offering the Chechen people some degree of participation in forming a republican government to eventually replace the Moscow-imposed Kadyrov administration.

Not surprisingly, the draft constitution rejected separatism, thus declaring, "The territory of the Chechen Republic shall be united and indivisible and shall be an inalienable part of the territory of the Russian Federation."[168] The proposed constitution further stated, "The Chechen Republic is a secular state. No religion can be established as a state or compulsory religion."[169] However, contradicting Constitutional Court rulings and Putin's own policies of eliminating vestiges of regional autonomy, the new Chechen constitution declared, "The sovereignty of the Chechen Republic is expressed in its possession of all powers (legislative, executive, and judicial) which the Russian Federation does not hold [and] powers jointly held by the republic and the federation, and is an inalienable quality of the republic."[170] Although "sovereignty" in this case was defined in a highly proscribed manner, referring only to those powers not claimed by the federal government, the surprising addition of this once harshly derided term illustrated the Putin administration's determination to proceed with Chechenizatsiya while undermining separatist and Islamist forces.

As the date of the constitutional referendum in Chechnya approached, this strategy of Chechenizatsiya failed to boost the popularity of the Kremlin-supported Chechen government. According to an opinion poll commissioned by the Kadyrov administration in early 2003, in elections for a new Chechen president, 36.6 percent of Chechens would prefer a candidate from the Chechen diaspora in Moscow, 19.5 percent would be willing to vote for an ethnic Russian or a candidate chosen by Moscow, and only 16.5 percent would vote for Kadyrov. Furthermore, mistrust of the federal center remained high: 62.5 percent of Chechens blamed the Russian leadership for the "tragic events in Chechnya," while only 14.6 percent blamed Wahhabis and 9.6 percent blamed separatists. Moscow did receive some good news from the survey: only 1 percent of Chechens would support a separatist candidate, and a plurality opposed peace talks with separatist leader Maskhadov (41.5 percent opposed talks, while 23.4 favored negotiations).[171] However, popular Chechen sentiment against both the Kadyrov administration and the Russian leadership cast doubt on the prospects for the establishment of a stable government in Chechnya acceptable both to Moscow and Chechens.

In this atmosphere of popular mistrust of both federal authorities and separatist forces, the Chechen people voted in the Moscow-sponsored referendum in March 2003. In a resounding rejection of calls by separatists to boycott the referendum, Chechens voted overwhelmingly in favor of both the new constitution and the draft legislation on electing a new republican government. According to the Chechen election commission, with a turnout of almost 90 percent of eligible voters, more than 95 percent voted in favor of the new constitution while a similar percentage voted to approve the two new election laws.[172] The overwhelming support for the referendum raised speculation that fraud and vote-tampering undermined its legitimacy—claims that derived enhanced credibility from the fact that tens of thousands of federal troops serving in Chechnya were allowed to vote.[173] However, the one-sided nature of the results indicated a strong desire on the part of the Chechen people for security and stability, as well as a popular rejection of further bloodshed on behalf of separatist or Islamist aims.

Hoping to take advantage of this rejection of separatism, the Putin administration attempted to further undermine support for Maskhadov and the separatist opposition with two new initiatives. Following the referendum, Putin announced plans to negotiate a power-sharing agreement with Chechnya that would "provide broad autonomy" for the republic and announced his support for a limited amnesty for guerrillas who agreed to cease hostilities against Russian forces.[174] In May 2003, Putin signed an order creating a working group, consisting of federal and Chechen representatives, to submit proposals for a power-sharing treaty by the following October.[175] In June 2003, the Russian parliament passed a law allowing Chechen insurgents not involved in grave crimes—such as murder, rape, and kidnapping, and killing or attempting to kill federal personnel—to receive amnesty if they surrendered their arms.[176] Through these measures, the Putin administration hoped to further isolate separatists by gaining broad popular support for a new Chechen regime and by providing a mechanism for the participation of Chechen elites in negotiating relations with the federal government.

Despite these compromises on Putin's recentralization strategy, the prospects for peace in Chechnya remained doubtful following the March 2003 referendum. In the summer of 2003, a series of suicide bombings in the republic—including an attempt to assassinate Kadyrov during a crowded religious celebration and a truck bombing of government offices that left at least 59 people dead—illustrated the inability of Russia to subdue or coopt the most dedicated and dangerous elements of the Chechen insurgency.[177] In an article in the June edition of the Chechen separatist newspaper *Dzhikhad Segodnya* (Jihad Today), Maskhadov declared, "We should not listen to their empty talk about amnesties, elections, and referenda. . . . Neither a referendum nor amnesty will stop this war. This war will end only when we cleanse this land of the last occupier. There is no other way to peace!"[178] One month later, on the day after Putin signed a decree authorizing Chechen presidential elections in October 2003, two women—one of whom was identified as a twenty-year old Chechen woman—conducted a suicide bombing attack at a large music festival outside of Moscow, killing at least thirteen people and wounding more than fifty.[179] Two days after the attack, Putin urged Russian security forces to hunt down Chechen militants, declaring, "The bandits operating in Chechnya are part of the international terrorist network. . . . It is useless to try to work with them. They should be plucked out of the basements and caves where they are hiding and destroyed."[180]

As the Kremlin pressed its military campaign in Chechnya, federal authorities took measures to ensure that Kadyrov remained in power, including systematically removing his most popular rivals from Chechnya's presidential election race. State Duma deputy Aslanbek Aslakhanov and businessman Umar Dzhabrailov abruptly withdrew from the race just weeks before the election while businessman Malik Saidullaev was disqualified as a candidate due to violations in his registration petition. Consequently, Kadyrov appeared headed for an electoral victory despite his lack of popular support and peace in Chechnya seemed as distant as ever.

In the Volga-Ural region, federal authorities relied on a series of legal measures to counter assertions of national autonomy from Bashkortostan and Tatarstan. In April 2001, the Russian Supreme Court ruled that the federal government had the authority to take legal action, without further authorization from the courts, against republics that refused to remove declarations of sovereignty from their constitutions. This ruling granted Supreme Court approval for the Putin administration to begin legal procedures to dismiss republican presidents and disband republican legislatures for noncompliance with federal law. Shortly after this court decision, Sergei Kirienko, Putin's presidential representative to the Greater Volga Federal District, publicly announced that the clauses on sovereignty in the constitutions of Bashkortostan and Tatarstan would have to be removed.[181] In June 2002, the Rus-

sian Supreme Court further ruled that thirty-seven articles of the Bashkir constitution violated federal law and were thenceforth invalid.[182] Six months later,
Bashkortostan succumbed to federal pressure and adopted a third republican constitution. Unlike the republic's previous charters, the new Bashkir constitution
avoids any mention of "sovereignty" for the republic and contains neither the text
of the 1994 power-sharing treaty between Bashkortostan and the federal government nor provisions for a separate Bashkir citizenship.[183]

In a more targeted action, the Putin administration, in accordance with the census
law approved by the State Duma in November 2001, divided the Tatar nationality
into seven separate ethnic groups during the 2002 Russia-wide census, Russia's
first post-Soviet census: Tatars in general, Kazan Tatars, Siberian Tatars, Crimean
Tatars, Astrakhan Tatars, Mishars, and Kryashen (Christian Tatars).[184] Depending
on how these census data are employed in the future, this division could reduce
dramatically the officially recognized number of Tatars nationwide and could alter
significantly the demographic balance in Tatarstan. According to the 1989 census,
Tatars comprised 48.5 percent of the republican population, while Russians comprised 43.3 percent. By some estimates, population growth after 1989 raised the
Tatar population to an outright majority in the republic. The ethnic differentiation
of Tatars could erase these demographic gains from official statistics and give ethnic
Russians a plurality in the republic. Such an outcome would reduce the perceived
legitimacy of the republic's claims of national autonomy and foster political divisions within the Tatar population.[185]

The Putin administration also enlisted the support of the Russian parliament to
suppress challenges from Bashkortostan and Tatarstan. In February 2002, the State
Duma easily defeated a bill that would have legalized separate citizenship for Russia's republics, ending an attempt to legalize clauses in the constitutions of Tatarstan
and Bashkortostan that allow for separate republican citizenship (along with Russian citizenship).[186] During the same month, the Russian State Duma's Committee
on Nationality Affairs recommended for approval a measure mandating that all
ethnic republics use the Cyrillic alphabet for their titular national languages. This
requirement derailed Tatarstan's plans, initiated in 1999, for a phased introduction
of the Latin script for the Tatar language. The Russian parliament passed the measure in November 2002, and Putin signed it into law the following month. According to Kaadyr-ool Bicheldei, the State Duma deputy from Tyva who proposed
the bill, this measure was initiated by the Putin administration specifically to re-
taliate against Tatarstan.[187]

Conclusion

The challenge posed by the rise of nationalist movements in Russia's predominantly
Muslim regions—especially in Chechnya, where separatists fought partly under the
banner of Islam—influenced the evolution of post-Soviet Russian federalism and
contributed to the current trend of recentralization. Largely in response to the
Chechen challenge, President Putin initiated his sweeping reassertion of central

authority, abruptly ending Russia's ad hoc experiment with asymmetrical and de-centralized federalism. After a decade of decentralized rule, based in large part on the ability of regions and republics to appropriate governing powers from a weak-ened federal government, the Russian tradition of centralized rule reclaimed a prin-cipal role in both popular and elite attitudes. Consequently, the future structure of the Russian Federation looks increasingly more unitary in nature, with regional governments surrendering—either willingly or under the threat of coercion—many of the gains in political autonomy they acquired in the aftermath of the Soviet Union's dissolution. Even those powers granted to regional governments in formal power-sharing treaties during Boris Yeltsin's rule are subject to reclamation by federal authorities. More ominously from the perspective of Russia's regions and republics, calls from government and parliamentary officials for regional consoli-dation raise the possibility that some federation subjects, including Muslim repub-lics, will be eliminated altogether.

Under these circumstances, the idea of creating a true ethnic federation to replace the now-defunct pseudofederal system of the Soviet Union is itself effectively de-funct. Vestiges of national autonomy for some national minorities are likely to remain, including ethnically designated homelands in the form of republics and autonomous okrugs, the right of republics to have their own constitutions, and the retention of the title "president" instead of "governor" for republican chief execu-tives. However, significant attributes of ethnically based political autonomy gained in the 1990s are incompatible with the reassertion of central authority under Putin. In fact, any initiative to consolidate regions is likely to begin with the autonomous okrugs, whose confusing dual status as federation subjects and constituent com-ponents of the oblasts or krais in which they are contained has given rise to spec-ulation that some or all of them are destined to be abolished.

This turn back toward centralized rule should not automatically entail a turning away from democracy or cultural pluralism. Unitary states can be both democratic and respectful of different national and cultural heritages. However, without a com-mitment to maintaining a political system and social environment in which national minorities can peacefully practice their traditions and express their national self-identities unmolested, centralizing tendencies can lead to suppression and forced assimilation. This danger is especially prevalent in societies where a dominant nationality feels threatened by minorities viewed as hostile "others." As demon-strated by Stalin's brutal deportation of several predominantly Muslim Caucasian nations en masse during the Second World War, racial intolerance and xenophobia exerted significant influence even in the Soviet regime that created the national homelands for non-Russian minorities. Moreover, the evolution of Russian identity and Russian nationalism, especially since the renewal of warfare in the North Cau-casus in 1999, has acquired an ethnocentric and monocultural character—a devel-opment detrimental to the assertion of cultural self-determination by minorities.

After a decade of uncertainty, as Russia defines the nature of relations between the federal center and the federation subjects, the treatment of Islam and Russia's predominantly Muslim ethnic groups will serve as an important barometer of whether the reassertion of central authority devolves into intolerance and suppression of national minority rights. The dominant role of some Muslim nationalities, most notably Chechens and Tatars, in pursuing self-determination and the rise of militant Islam among a small but dedicated cadre of Muslims have placed Islam and those associated with it—religiously, ethnically, and culturally—among the most likely targets of ethnic or religious intolerance, whether emanating from the state or disaffected segments of the population. Especially important in this respect are the incursions into Dagestan by Islamist militants, the ongoing conflict in Chechnya, and terrorist bombings in Moscow and other cities, which mobilized public support for Putin's reassertion of a strong centralized state and strengthened popular perceptions of Islam as a hostile "other."

Russia's ability to overcome this trend and provide an environment that is conducive to the free expression of Islamic religious and cultural practices and that protects the rights of Muslim national minorities while maintaining the country's security will be a crucial determinant of how the Russian political system evolves in the twenty-first century. The reversal of centralizing trends after the decade of dramatically weakened federal authority and sometimes dangerous decentralization experienced in the 1990s is unlikely. Nevertheless, Russia still faces a major challenge in the coming years: preserving the state's integrity—territorial and political—while granting an adequate measure of self-determination to its ethnic and religious minorities and protecting their fundamental human rights. Russia's treatment of its Muslim regions and peoples will be an important test of its ability to combine these two principles—a difficult but not impossible task and a measure of the strength of its democracy.

5

Democratization and Multiparty Politics in Post-Soviet Russia

Impact on Muslim Political Mobilization and Participation

The ability of Russia's Muslims to organize politically and play an active role in the nation's political life is heavily dependent on the influence of two separate but interconnected contexts: the Islamic context and the Russian context. Especially important in the Islamic context are (1) the role of Islam in the formation of Muslims' individual and collective identities relative to other attributes—ethnicity, language, and so on—and (2) the ability (or inability) of Muslims to coalesce for common political action. This second factor is linked to the compatibility of Islam with a democratic society in which political parties play an important role. In the Russian context, the structure of Russia's post-Soviet political system and the legacy of a political culture that distrusts pluralism and admires potentially authoritarian social traits such as social unity, a strong state, and a forceful, charismatic leader have produced an underdeveloped civil society and political party system. Additionally, legal barriers to religious and ethnic-based political parties have eroded the ability of Muslims to organize around a common identity to participate in Russian politics. To these factors must be added Russian distrust of Muslim political activism, heightened by the conflict in Chechnya, and, among many Russians, persistent perceptions of Muslim peoples and other ethnic minorities as culturally inferior and a potential threat to Russia's political stability and even its territorial integrity.

The Islamic Context

Islam, Ethnicity, and Muslim Identity

Islam is a universalist and egalitarian creed that transcends racial, ethnic, and linguistic boundaries and aims to unite believers within a single Muslim *ummah* (community). Islam does recognize and respect ethnic and other differences. The Qu'ran says that God has divided humanity into tribes and nations so they may learn about one another; otherwise, he would have created only one people. Nevertheless, Islam aspires to become the core of its adherents' identity and focus of loyalty.

Despite this universalist goal, the development of Muslim societies presents a different image, one of an Islamic community divided along ethnic, sectarian, and other lines. In the course of Islam's history, many schisms, secular and religious, developed and fractured the unity of the Muslim world, often leading to internecine conflicts. Moreover, the decline of the Islamic world at a time when the West was entering a period of scientific and industrial transformation, which translated into military supremacy, led to the subjugation of Muslim lands by European powers. Subjugation by outside powers caused soul-searching among Muslims about the causes of their civilization's decline, a process that resulted in large-scale social, economic, and, to a lesser extent, political reforms based on models borrowed from Europe. Later, many Muslim countries also experimented with the socialist model of development. These reforms created a further divide within the Islamic world between the modernizers and the traditionalists, who not only wanted to retain Islam's authentic traditions, but to return to a purist form of Islam and an imagined utopian Islamic society. Such divisions have made reaching a broad social and economic consensus within Muslim societies, especially the ethnically heterogeneous ones, difficult.

All of these divisive factors exist within Russia's Muslim population. Ethnic peculiarities and loyalties, combined with doctrinal differences, cause divisions and rivalries within Russia's Muslim religious establishment. In regions such as Dagestan, ethnic and tribal rivalries, plus doctrinal differences both within the Sufi brotherhoods and between them and other Muslims, prevent the formation of broad-based institutions with the goal of representing and defending Muslim interests. The conflicting interests of Muslim elites, who often use religious or ethnic identity to advance their personal agendas, further fracture Russia's Muslim community politically, economically, and socially.

Thus while Islam, at least in a cultural sense, is an important component of nearly all Muslims' self-identity, it is not the sole or, in most cases, even the most important component of their individual and collective identities. This diversity was a main reason for the ability of foreign powers, including Russia, to effectively divide and rule Muslim peoples during the age of imperialism. Furthermore, it prevented Russia's Muslims from taking effective advantage of the opportunities presented to them in 1917 to form a solid Muslim bloc and obtain extensive cultural and political rights. This pattern was repeated during perestroika and continues to severely limit the Muslims' ability to form a strong political bloc within post-Soviet Russia.

Islam and Democracy

The low level of Muslim political mobilization has also been attributed to the presumed incompatibility of Islam with democracy. The fact that there is debate within and without the Islamic world on whether Islam and democracy are compatible is beyond dispute.[1] Those who believe in the incompatibility of Islam and democracy often refer to the fusion of spiritual and temporal domains in Islam—in other words, the inseparability of religion and politics in Islam. Bernard Lewis has encapsulated this view by saying, "In the universal Islamic polity as conceived by Muslims, there is no Caesar but only God, who is the sole sovereign and the sole source of law."[2] This view, however, is simplistic. The history of the Muslim world shows a greater degree of actual separation of religion and politics—or rather the subordination of religion to politics—than is generally assumed. Moreover, certain principles of Islam such as *shura* (consultation), *bay'a* (pledging allegiance to the ruler), and *ijma* (consensus of society) create the basis of developing democratic or at least participatory systems of government.

Certainly there are political parties in most Muslim states. Although in many cases their independence is questionable, the main problem in this regard is not Islam, but any system of belief based on divine law. The question is, Can manmade law contravene God's commands? On this question, Islam is no different from other religions. The issue is not whether there can be political pluralism in Islamic societies, but whether state policy and legislation can contradict Islamic law. Here, too, much depends on how Islamic principles are interpreted. Thus it is not Islam as a religion that impedes the development of democracy among Muslim countries, but the political traditions of Muslim societies based on authoritarian rule—native or foreign imposed—and the level of their social and economic development, most notably their lack of a strong middle class. This principle applies to Russia's Muslim regions, where post-Soviet political leaders often have preferred authoritarian methods of rule.

The Russian Context

The broader political context of Russian culture and politics has also hindered Muslim political activism. Two aspects of this political context are especially important: (1) the structural features of Russia's political system that marginalize political parties and (2) the persistence of an essentially monocultural mind-set that fosters resistance to treating Muslims and other minorities as equals and promotes a distrust of Muslim political activism. The spectacular proliferation of advocacy groups, trade associations, and other independent organizations since Gorbachev's reforms has expanded civil society in Russia and given Russia the broad outlines of a nascent pluralist society. However, this trend is still fragile and has not yet produced a political system characterized by competition among broadly based and stable parties with clearly defined agendas and platforms. This failure is due, in part, to historic and cultural factors that have undermined popular confidence in pluralism and political parties. Additionally, the design of Russia's post-Soviet political system has marginalized the influence and appeal of political parties. Combined with an undertone of endemic distrust toward Muslim cultural and political activism, these features of Russian politics hinder the formation and effective political participation of Islamic parties. Legislation designed specifically to ban religious and ethnic-based parties from electoral politics has further undermined Islamic parties.

Uniformity and Intolerance in Russian Political Culture

According to the nineteenth century pan-Slavic intellectual Nikolai Danilevsky, Russian tradition calls for a monarchy to safeguard social harmony by ensuring that individual interests are subordinated to the common good. Accordingly, he derided the role of political parties, the principal means of pursuing self-defined political interests in a pluralist democracy, and declared that "the Russian people [are] completely alien to the idea of political parties."[3] Although this observation is by no means a universally held opinion in Russia, it reflects a strand in Russian political thought that endured through centuries of tsarist rule and, more recently, found expression in the Soviet political system (despite its reliance on the Communist Party). This outlook is based on the premise that society should pursue one transcendental truth or common vision that supersedes the everyday concerns of the citizenry. Extolling the virtues of a polity united in pursuit of such a truth, adherents of this view call for political uniformity and hold in disdain political pluralism and competitive party politics, which lead to the political fragmentation of the citizenry. Tim McDaniel has pointed out that proponents of this political philosophy believe that truth is "unitary and compulsory" and that "individuals and groups will have a legitimate place and voice in the country to the extent that they conform to this truth. . . . Opposition and diversity is falsehood and therefore deserves no hearing."[4]

Conservative Russian political philosophers, particularly those reacting against the encroachment of Western ideas, expressed exceptionally harsh criticism of liberal democratic values and extolled the institution of autocracy. Nikolai Karamzin, while accepting limits on the tsar's power based on traditional institutions such as the *veche* (citizens' assembly) and the church, rejected attempts to restrict autocratic rule based on parliaments or other instruments of liberal democracy. While serving as state historian for Alexander I, he argued against any moves toward a constitutional monarchy and admonished the tsar with the following assertion: "Russia, taught by long disasters, vested before the holy altar the power of autocracy in your ancestor, asking him that he rule her supremely, indivisibly. This covenant is the foundation of your authority, you have no other; you may do everything, but you may not limit your authority by law."[5] Toward the end of the nineteenth century, Konstantin Pobedonostsev expressed similar sentiments when he stated that parliamentary democracy divides power among those seeking personal benefit, while a unified state is an expression of social truth and represents the national will.[6] According to him, parliamentary democracy leads to "the tyranny of the masses and the abandonment of the general good to the mercy of the brutal struggle of particular interests."[7]

Others, notably Aleksei Khomyakov, Danilevsky's Slavophile contemporary, rejected democratic pluralism because it was spiritually inferior to Slavic traditions.

These traditions emphasized the search for truth and a single consciousness transcending the individual. By contrast, Western traditions emphasized the individual and his pursuit of narrow, personal interests.[8]

The commitment to political uniformity reached beyond Russia's conservative and Slavophile thinkers and influenced other ideologies. Even Pyotr Chaadaev, who advocated emulation of the West, insisted that the individual is significant only to the extent that he subordinates himself and his interests to the collective good. On Russia's political left, members of the agrarian-socialist Populist movement of the late nineteenth century, recognizing the link between political liberalism and capitalism in the West, rejected pluralism and parliamentary democracy. Petr Tkachev, one of the most radical Populists, asserted that uniformity of needs is a prerequisite for a just society and that individual needs exceeding the established norm—as determined by a society's level of economic development—must be suppressed because they can only be satisfied at other people's expense.[9] Thus the greater common good necessitates political uniformity and the suppression of dissenting views. This principle was echoed by Vladimir Lenin, who mocked political pluralism as an element of the unjust bourgeois social order and embraced both the suppression of dissent and tight centralization—both of the ruling party and society—to achieve the collective welfare.[10]

This rejection of pluralist democracy and its principal instrument, competitive political parties, persists to varying degrees in Russian political culture. In his neoisolationist conception of "Island Russia," contemporary Russian political theorist Vadim Tsymbursky alludes to the need for cultural autarky and the exclusion of outside influences until Russian civilization fully develops. Vladimir Malyavin's embrace of "vertical socialization" also implies a need to restrict pluralist tendencies and the political compromises necessary in a pluralist society. This idea is reflected in Malyavin's assertion that the "Russian man does not like calculations and compromises; he lives by extreme feelings."[11] In short, an enduring aspect of Russia's political culture engenders an aversion to democratic pluralism and multiparty politics, which require compromise and political tolerance.

Russian History of Authoritarian Rule

This aspect of Russian political thought helped produce, and in turn was reinforced by, Russia's centuries-long experience with authoritarian rule. From the declaration by Ivan III in 1493 that he was sovereign of all Russian lands to the Bolsheviks' creation of a totalitarian system, Russia's successive regimes have relied on authoritarian political systems to govern. Ivan the Terrible conducted a reign of terror through his *oprichniki* (political police) to suppress political dissent and consolidate his autocratic power, and even modernizing monarchs like Peter the Great and Empress Catherine strove for the establishment of an absolutist monarchy. Attempts at political liberalization did not begin until the nineteenth century under Alexander II (1855–81) and a reluctant Nicholas II (1895–1917), and even these reforms fell far short of measures necessary to promote the emergence of representative democracy and independent political parties. Only after the Russian Revolution of 1905 were political parties legalized and a national parliament established.[12]

Numerous political parties emerged during liberalization under Nicholas II, including revolutionary parties such as the Party of Socialist Revolutionaries (Narodniks) and the Social Democratic Labor Party (predecessor to the Communist Party), moderate proreform parties like the Octoberists and the Constitutional Democrats (Kadets), and Russian nationalist and proimperialist parties such as the Nationalist Party and the Union of Russian People. During this period, an upsurge of Muslim political activism illustrated that provided other conditions were propitious, religious factors would not be an insurmountable barrier to Muslim participation in the political process. However, Nicholas II resisted the consolidation of a liberal political order; he banned the most ardent revolutionary parties, gradually retreated from the reforms announced in his 1905 October Manifesto, and dissolved parliament on three separate occasions.[13]

After the downfall of Nicholas II, Alexander Kerensky's Provisional Government began a more aggressive process of political liberalization, including the legalization of several previously banned political parties and the introduction of freedom of speech and assembly.[14] However, the Bolshevik seizure of power abruptly ended this process. Immediately after deposing the Provisional Government, the Bolsheviks began to eliminate systematically alternative poles of political power, including the Constituent Assembly, a popularly elected body to which the Provisional Government had originally planned to yield power.[15] After the defeat of the anti-Bolshevik forces during the Russian Civil War, the Communist Party leadership established its dominance over the Soviet political system and silenced dissenting political voices.

The Bolshevik victory and the subsequent formation of the Soviet political system ended Russia's first, brief experiment with competitive political parties and extended Russia's history of authoritarian rule for another seventy years. During this period, informal groups such as the *samizdat* (self-publishing) movement and various human rights and dissident organizations conducted underground activities outside the control of the state.[16] In the Muslim regions, the institutions of underground or parallel Islam, including various Sufi brotherhoods, performed similar functions. However, despite their growing support in the final decade of the Soviet Union, these movements were excluded from formal participation in politics and were suppressed with varying degrees of severity by Soviet authorities. Consequently, the Soviet public had no historic or cultural experience with, much less a personal knowledge of, a pluralist system based on political parties. The one long-term experience of Soviet citizens with party politics provided a strongly negative example: the Communist Party's monopoly of power and its role in erecting the oppressive Soviet regime left much of the population with a hostile view of mass-based political parties.[17] This deep distrust of parties was expressed most famously by Boris Yeltsin, who proclaimed after he resigned from the Communist Party in 1990 that he would never join another political party, a promise he kept throughout his decade of rule.[18]

Gorbachev's Reforms: Emergence of Civil Society and Political Parties

Throughout the Soviet period, the various social, cultural, and professional institutions that normally constitute civil society were created and controlled by the Communist Party. Thus, rather than serving as independent organizations representing citizens' interests to the political leadership, Soviet-era labor unions, youth groups, and other civic organizations served the interests of the party and the state. Minority communities, especially in Muslim regions, suffered from additional restrictions on the practice of their national, cultural, and religious traditions, a condition that exacerbated the underdeveloped nature of their local civil societies. The opening offered by Gorbachev's reforms led to a proliferation of various civic organizations as environmental groups, trade and labor unions, human rights organizations, and religious societies expanded.[19] The central and regional governments promoted several proreform groups, such as the Interregional Association of Democratic Organizations and Movements, the Moscow Social Democratic Association, and the Perestroika Support Organization, to support Gorbachev's reforms. By the end of 1989, more than 60,000 informal organizations had formed.[20]

One of the most important aspects of the Soviet Union's emerging civil society was the birth and rapid expansion of independent political parties. The expansion of political parties began in May 1988 with the formation of Democratic Union, the first independent opposition party in Russia since the Bolshevik consolidation of power in the 1920s.[21] After the formal lifting of the CPSU's domination of Soviet politics in the spring of 1989, several democratic and reform-oriented parties emerged, including the Social Democrats, the Christian Democrats, and two rival Constitutional Democratic parties that attempted to revive the constituency of the early-twentieth-century Kadets.[22] Several nationalist organizations joined these reformist parties, including the National Patriotic Front, commonly called Pamyat (Memory), and the Liberal Democratic Party of Vladimir Zhirinovsky.[23] By the end of 1989, more than 100 parties were operating on Russian territory.[24]

During this period, the Communist Party became the midwife to the birth of several opposition parties as it became highly factionalized at the end of its monopoly of power. The largest new faction, representing 58 percent of the CSPU's membership, was the Communist Party of the RSFSR, the first Communist party organization established for the Russian Republic since the founding of the Soviet Union in 1922.[25] In the larger CPSU, three competing factions emerged: the proreform Democratic Platform, the democratic-socialist Marxist Platform, and the hard-line Movement for Communist Initiative.[26] These factions provided the foundation and much of the membership for a number of independent parties, from reformist to nationalist and reactionary movements.[27] Few of these parties, however, succeeded in capturing stable constituencies. By February 1991, despite the proliferation of parties in the USSR, only three—the Democratic Party, the Social Democrats, and the Russian Christian Democratic Movement—had succeeded in gaining the minimum 5,000 members required to register formally as political parties with the right to participate in elections.[28]

For a brief period, several proreform parties united to form Democratic Russia, a large alliance of disparate parties representing the full range of democratic alternatives to communism.[29] Democratic Russia gained hundreds of thousands of supporters and provided the principal vehicle of support for Boris Yeltsin during his successful campaign for RSFSR president in 1991.[30] However, this democratic alliance quickly disintegrated when the collapse of the Soviet state and the CPSU eliminated its raison d'être. Although fear of a return to Communist rule has been employed since the demise of the Soviet Union, most notably during Russia's 1996 presidential election campaign, the largely bipolar political order in which democratic parties mobilized popular support through anti-Communist alliances disappeared with the Soviet regime.

Evolution of Multiparty Politics under Yeltsin

After the collapse of the bipolar political order pitting Communists against democrats, a confusing array of political parties and movements emerged to represent diverse interests and segments of society, many of which had not yet—and some of which never would—coalesce into stable constituencies. Among these organizations were several Gorbachev-era political parties that attempted to capture or hold on to constituencies in the newly formed Russian Federation, including the Christian Democrats, the Social Democrats, and the Constitutional Democrats. Zhirinovsky's nationalist party renamed itself the Liberal Democratic Party of Russia (LDPR), while the Communist Party of the Russian Federation (CPRF) emerged from the remnants of the RSFSR's Communist Party organization. Many new parties joined these holdovers from perestroika. Some, such as the Agrarian Party, Women of Russia, and Russia's Party of Unity and Accord, were successful initially and won seats in the Russian Federation's first parliamentary elections in December 1993.

Most new parties, however, remained relatively insignificant and had little impact on Russian politics. Parties such as the Dignity and Charity Party, the Constructive Ecological Movement, the Beer Lovers' Party, and many more disappeared as quickly as they emerged. The majority of the new political parties and movements had negligible memberships, poorly defined programs, and inadequate public recognition. In 1993, only 22 percent of Russians identified with a party they believed represented their interests, compared with 87 percent in the United States and 92 percent in the United Kingdom. In the same year, only thirteen parties collected the 100,000 signatures necessary to appear on the ballot for the Russian Federation's first parliamentary elections.[31] Even among those parties appearing on the ballot, the degree of popular support they could claim remained tenuous: of the eight parties that won parliamentary seats in 1993, only three managed to repeat their success in Russia's second round of parliamentary elections just two years later.

By the late 1990s, Russian politics had largely recovered from the collapse of the perestroika-era bipolar order, and much of the electorate had coalesced around four electoral blocs: (1) Zyuganov's CPRF, representing the political left; (2) Zhirinovsky's LDPR, representing the nationalist right; (3) Grigorii Yavlinskii's Yabloko, representing those favoring economic reforms with greater social protections; and (4) the Union of Right Forces, representing the right-of-center proreform electorate.[32] An electoral system imposed by a presidential decree issued in 1993 and later voted into law by the parliament contributed to the consolidation of this fledgling multiparty order by creating a system of proportional representation in the Russian State Duma. According to this system, all political parties that succeeded in gathering 100,000 signatures (200,000 beginning in 1995) were placed on the ballot for elections to the State Duma. Parties receiving 5 percent or more of the party-list vote were granted parliamentary seats, divided proportionally, from the 225 seats reserved for parties. The other 225 seats were filled through simple majority vote for individual candidates in electoral districts (single-mandate districts), regardless of party affiliation.[33] In December 2002, Russia enacted a new election law stipulating that beginning with the 2007 parliamentary elections, political parties must receive 7 percent of the party-list vote to gain party-list seats in the State Duma. This electoral method helped raise the importance of political parties to the public and created an incentive for their consolidation.

Presidential Supremacy and Political Party Weakness

Despite the proportional representation system, institutional aspects of Russia's political system have continued to undermine the importance of political parties at the national level. Foremost among these institutional characteristics is Russia's strong presidential system, sometimes referred to as "presidential authoritarianism." Among his extraordinary formal powers, the president appoints members of his government regardless of their party affiliations or the party composition of parliament. He also has the authority to dissolve the State Duma and call new elections if the legislature rejects his nominee for prime minister three times or passes a vote of no confidence in the government twice in a three-month period.[34] Additionally, the president retains authority to make policy unilaterally by issuing wide-ranging ukazi (decrees).

These presidential powers were incorporated into the 1993 Russian constitution after a presidential-legislative struggle that solidified the supremacy of the presidency. Buoyed by a nationwide referendum in April 1993 that confirmed public support for his presidency, Yeltsin convened a constitutional convention to draft a new constitution establishing a strong presidential system.[35] A conservative bloc in the Russian parliament, which had been elected in 1991 before the fall of the Soviet Union, resisted this effort, causing a political deadlock that prevented Yeltsin from proceeding with his reform agenda. In September 1993, Yeltsin responded by dissolving parliament and employing military force to expel recalcitrant parliamentarians and to put down violent antigovernment demonstrations. This show of force, which included tanks shelling the parliament building, left an estimated 146 people dead.[36] The new constitution was ratified by referendum in December 1993.

The presidential powers incorporated in the new constitution, combined with the violent defeat of Yeltsin's opposition, raised the political importance and stature of the presidency well above those of other governmental institutions, especially the parliament, Russia's primary incubator of broad-based political parties. This arrangement served Yeltsin's short-term interests by undercutting the influence of political parties and curtailing the formation of a strong opposition party. On two occasions, the Yeltsin administration attempted to further hinder the organization of alternative poles of political power by introducing legislation to overturn the proportional representation system in parliamentary elections. In both cases, parliament voted against the administration's proposal.[37]

Personality-Based Politics

Another characteristic of Russia's political system that has undermined the consolidation of political parties is the prominent role of the new political elite in forming parties and controlling their agendas. Reflecting the personality-based nature of Russian politics, in October 1993, Russian prime minister Yegor Gaidar and other Yeltsin allies created Russia's Choice (later renamed Russia's Democratic Choice) to mobilize support for Yeltsin's reforms. Other members of the political elite followed Gaidar's example, although many attempted to advance their own agendas rather than implementing coherent programs of social, economic, and political reform. Viktor Chernomyrdin, following his appointment as prime minister to replace Gaidar in December 1992, formed a second, more centrist, pro-Yeltsin party, Our Home Is Russia. Later, former Russian vice president Aleksandr Rutskoi founded Derzhava (Great Power), former Finance Minister Boris Fyodorov formed Forward Russia! and former Security Council secretary Yury Skokov created the Congress of Russian Communities with the help of the late Alexander Lebed (who, before his death in a helicopter crash in April 2002, also served as Security Council secretary and later as governor of Krasnoyarsk). Such organizations often had no party structure or membership to speak of, preferring instead to remain hollow organizations through which their leaders could pursue their personal objectives. As one Russian commentator noted of Russia's political parties, "In many cases they are merely offices with (or even without) facsimile machines or [serve as fronts for] commercial enterprises."[38]

Personality-driven political parties attained a new height of influence with the rise of presidential electoral blocs. During the 1999 parliamentary election campaign, two such blocs emerged to rally popular support for presidential candidates Yevgenii Primakov and Vladimir Putin, respectively. In April 1999, Moscow mayor Yurii Luzhkov's Fatherland movement joined forces with All-Russia, an alliance of regional leaders, to support Primakov, Russia's former foreign minister and prime minister. Similarly, at the instigation of the Kremlin, the electoral bloc Unity formed around the leadership of Russia's minister for emergency situations, Sergei Shoigu, primarily to counter Fatherland–All-Russia and to garner public support for then Prime Minister Vladimir Putin's presidential campaign. Despite the fact that neither movement offered a strong party platform, Fatherland–All-Russia and Unity won a combined total of 36 percent of the party-list vote, with the pro-Putin bloc gaining 23 percent and the pro-Primakov alliance taking 13 percent. Only the CPRF won more votes, placing first in the party-list voting with 24 percent.[39] Yabloko, the Union of Right Forces, and the LDPR each gained less than 10 percent. No other party crossed the 5 percent threshold required to win party-list seats in the Duma.

Renewed war in Chechnya may have increased the standing of Putin and Unity, in the process temporarily distorting Russia's political system, but the ability of presidential electoral blocs to displace support for more established political parties indicates that Russia's multiparty system has yet to evolve into a party-based democracy. This is reflected in the fact that many candidates for political office have shunned association with political parties or movements. Throughout the 1990s, individual candidates with no party affiliation won a large percentage of the single-mandate seats in the State Duma. Out of 225 seats reserved for geographically defined districts, independent candidates won more than half (130 seats) in 1993, 34 percent (77 seats) in 1995, and 47 percent (106 seats) in 1999.

In several cases, individuals with financial means and political clout have been successful in elections without association with political parties. The electoral victory of Russian financial oligarch Boris Berezovsky in 1999 illustrates this trend. Running for the parliamentary seat representing Karachaevo-Cherkessia, a republic with which he had no previous connection, Berezovsky promoted his ties to the Kremlin and influence with Yeltsin rather than his affiliation with a political party. His electoral victory was mirrored by the success of other oligarchs and representatives of powerful firms. In December 2000, oil and financial magnate Roman Abramovich won the governorship of Chukotka Autonomous Okrug, although he was not associated with a party active in the okrug. Similarly, Aleksander Kholponin, an executive with Norilsk Nickel (Russia's largest metal-producing company), and Boris Zolatarev, an executive of Yukos (Russia's second-largest oil producer), won governorships without being affiliated with a political party. One analyst of Russian politics has referred to this phenomenon as "the rise of business states in Russia's regions."[40]

In this distorted political environment, public regard for and identification with political parties has remained low. According to a poll conducted by Russia's Public Opinion Foundation almost two years after the December 1999 parliamentary elections, more than 60 percent of Russians did not identify with a political party, and the majority of those that did could give only general reasons for their attachment.[41] Similarly, a multiyear survey conducted from 1996 to 2000 assessing popular support for democratic institutions found that only one-third of Russians believed that party competition strengthened Russia's political system, while another third believed that Russia should have one-party rule. The survey also indicated that between 50 and 55 percent of Russians during this period supported outlawing all political parties.[42]

Legal Barriers to Islamic Parties

The endemic lack of respect for political parties and the structural features of Russia's political system that marginalize their political influence have affected Muslim parties as strongly as, if not more than, other parties. Additionally, legislation passed with Putin's support banning parties based on religion or ethnicity raised new and possibly insurmountable barriers to the Muslim parties, whether organized around religious or ethnic identity. In January 2001, the Putin administration submitted to the State Duma a bill drafted by the Central Election Commission, ostensibly to rationalize Russia's multiparty system. Passed by the Russian parliament in July of that year, the Law on Political Parties provided a legal definition of "political parties" for the first time in the Russian Federation's brief history and stated that only such entities could nominate candidates for political office in federal or regional elections. The law stipulated that to be recognized as a political party, organizations must have at least 10,000 members nationwide and regional party organizations—each with at least 100 members—in at least half of Russia's eighty-nine republics and regions. The law further stated that parties already registered with the Ministry of Justice would have to reregister within two years or lose their rights as legally recognized parties, including the right to run in parliamentary elections at the federal or regional levels.[43] In addition to establishing these requirements for party registration, the law instituted a broad prohibition on parties based on religious or ethnic identity. The measure stated:

> It is prohibited to form political parties based on professional, racial, national, or religious affiliation. Political parties that indicate in their charters or political programs that their goals include defending the professional, racial, national, or religious interests of their members fall under this category. Parties that reflect such agendas in their official names are also subject to these restrictions.[44]

This prohibition expanded earlier restrictions placed on religious organizations by the Law on Freedom of Conscience and Religious Associations. In addition to restricting the activities of religious congregations and other organizations, this measure stipulated that religious organizations "shall not participate in elections to institutions of state power or local government [and] shall not take part in the activities of political parties or political movements, or provide them with material or other assistance."[45] Thus since 1997, Muslim parties have been prohibited from receiving assistance from Muslim congregations and other groups that engage in religious activities. By expanding this prohibition to include an outright ban on parties based on religious identity, the Putin-sponsored Law on Political Parties further distanced Islam and other religions from the political process. In a sign of its seriousness about enforcing this restriction, in 2002, the Ministry of Justice rejected the registration applications of the Christian Democratic Party and the Islamic Party of Russia, citing the unlawful use of religious identification in their titles.[46] Such a strict interpretation of the law will affect Muslims and other religious minorities more than the predominantly Christian ethnic Russians, who, because they comprise the majority of the Russian population and dominate Russian politics and culture, are less in need of outlets to express their unique collective identity.

Muslim parties potentially could evade this ban by avoiding reference to Islam or Muslims in their names and excluding provisions that refer to a predominant focus on Islam from their charters. Although such measures would dilute their Muslim character, a handful of Muslim parties employed similar techniques during the 1990s to broaden their bases of support. However, the Law on Political Parties raised an additional impediment to Muslim parties by requiring that parties have regional organizations with at least 100 members each in more than half of Russia's provinces, a severe constraint on parties that rely on national minorities for support. Even parties representing Russia's Tatars, the most numerous and widely dispersed of Russia's predominantly Muslim nationalities, may have difficulty mobilizing supporters in forty-five different republics and regions. Pan-Islamic parties face similar difficulties in attracting supporters in a large number of overwhelmingly non-Muslim regions and, even if they are successful in disguising their religious or ethnic focus, are too small to be truly competitive in the parliamentary elections. In the fall of 2001, Deputy Justice Minister Yevgeny Sidorenko suggested that the new law would reduce the list of political associations (consisting of 59 parties and 139 more loosely defined political movements and organizations in 2001) to no more than 10.[47]

In July 2002, the Russian parliament passed a second measure, the Law on Countering Extremist Activities, that could further restrict the activities of political parties and possibly lead to the disbanding of some. This measure defines several activities as extremist, including actions designed to forcibly alter Russia's constitutional system, violate Russia's sovereignty, form illegal armed groups, and incite ethnic, racial, or religious hatred. The law further grants federal authorities the right to suspend the activities of any organization engaged in such actions and, if supported by a court order confirming that it is participating in extremist acts, liquidate the organization and all companies and institutions providing it with financial or material assistance.[48]

Although the law is aimed principally at racist groups, especially neo-Nazi skinheads who had committed several highly publicized hate crimes in the months leading up to the law's passage, it raised concerns that federal authorities would use it to silence political opposition, including opposition parties. Tamara Pletneva, a State Duma deputy of the CPRF, claimed, "We're in favor of fighting fascism, racism, and ethnic chauvinism, but these are all included in existing laws. The goal here is to silence all opposition."[49] Yabloko leader Grigorii Yavlinskii, concurring with these concerns, stated that the measure was "very, very dangerous law."[50]

In light of the Putin administration's identification of Islamic extremists and "Chechen terrorists" as Russia's most pressing security threats, political parties and organizations associated with Muslim—and especially Chechen—causes have reason to be wary of the new law. Tatyana Kasatkina, director of the human rights group Memorial, expressed fears that her organization could be liquidated because

it is active in Chechnya and frequently criticizes the military's abuses in the republic.[51] Expressing similar concerns, Russia's Eurasian Party announced in February 2003 that it was expelling Salambek Maigov from the party after the latter
announced his intention to serve as Chechen president Maskhadov's representative
in Moscow. Eurasian Party leader Abdul Vahid Niazov said that he feared that the
Justice Ministry could rule that the party has "links with terrorist organizations" if
Maigov remained a member.[52]

Muslim Parties and Movements in Russian National Politics

For Muslims of all ideologies, the combination of presidential supremacy and elite-
based party formation, as opposed to popular political mobilization, tends to deter
identification with political parties and reliance on parties to represent their interests. Additionally, Russia's tradition of authoritarian rule and aspects of Russian
political culture that denigrate democratic pluralism exert influence on much of the
Muslim population, especially Muslim communities that have lived under Russian
rule for centuries or have experienced heavy Russification under the imperial and
Soviet regimes.

Muslim political activism is further handicapped both by internal dynamics
within the Muslim population and by active intervention by the Kremlin. In the
former case, geographic and socioeconomic variation among different Muslim communities in Russia hinder identification with a larger Russian *ummah* and foster
divergence in interests and political objectives. Tatarstan and Bashkortostan both
lie several hundred miles east of Moscow—Kazan is about 500 miles from the
Russian capital, while Ufa is about 580 miles away—and have experienced four
and a half centuries of exposure to Russian culture and political traditions. They
are also highly industrialized and economically successful by Russian standards,
with per capita incomes and standards of living above the national average.[53] In
contrast, the Muslim republics of the North Caucasus, lying more than 1,000 miles
southeast of Moscow, are less Russified—the region was conquered by Russian
forces approximately three centuries after the conquest of the Volga-Ural region—
and less developed economically. These divergences in historic experience,
economic and political development, and ethnocultural background impede the development of shared interests and common political identities.

Alongside these intrinsic factors impeding the development of a common political identity, both the Yeltsin and Putin administrations, along with their allies in
the Russian parliament, pursued policies designed to marginalize or co-opt the few
national parties that have attempted to unify the Muslim electorate. Although some
Muslim organizations entered national politics during the 1990s, their ability to
serve as viable national Muslim parties was hindered further by the Kremlin's use
of informal means to restrict their ability to run in national elections and to co-opt
their leadership. Even for Russian Muslims who surmount the historic, cultural,
and socioeconomic barriers to gaining a broad Muslim-based political self-
awareness, the legal and informal measures employed by the Kremlin have thwarted

efforts to form and sustain national-level parties effectively representing Muslim interests.

Perestroika and the Reemergence of Muslim Activism

The opening offered by Gorbachev's reforms led to a flourishing of Muslim activities, including many that took political form. Some of the most active Muslim political groups that emerged during perestroika were nationalist movements and parties representing ethnic minorities. In November 1988, one of the most influential of these movements emerged in Uzbekistan with the founding of Birlik (Unity). In subsequent months, nationalist parties emerged in the other four Central Asian republics, including Agzybirlik (Unity) in Turkmenistan, Rastokhis (Revival) in Tajikistan, and Askar (Mutual Aid) in Kyrgyzstan. In Kazakhstan, nationalists attempted to revive the spirit of the anti-Bolshevik Alash Orda party by founding a new movement named Alash.[54] These movements were matched in the Caucasus by the founding of the Circassian movement Adyge Khase, the Confederation of Peoples of the Caucasus, the Chechen National Congress, and several other nationalist parties and movements. The social cohesion of multiethnic Dagestan was particularly threatened by the rise of nationalist movements, including the Lezgin movement Sadval (Unity), the Kalmyk nationalist movement Tenglik (Equality), and the Avar Nationalist Movement.[55]

This rise in ethnic identity was accompanied by an increase in cultural and religious awareness. Sparked by renewed contact with Muslims outside the Soviet Union during the 1979–89 Soviet-Afghan War and accelerated by political liberation under Gorbachev, a Muslim revival spread throughout much of Central Asia, the Caucasus, and Muslim areas of the Volga region. This revival was marked by a rejection of Moscow-appointed religious leaders on the Muslim spiritual boards and a proliferation of unofficial Islamic organizations and illegal religious practices. Growing discontent with official Islam was illustrated early during Gorbachev's reforms when the arrest in August 1986 of Mullah Abdullah Saidov, the leader of an illegal Islamic movement in Tajikistan, provoked violent demonstrations, including an attack on a local police station and courtroom.[56] That same month, the first secretary of the Tajik Communist Party organization expressed the alarm of the regional Communist leadership:

> The level of religiosity of the population of our republic has noticeably increased. Numerous facts show that the anti-social activity of Muslim clerics is growing and that the education of children in Islamic dogma is increasing. Production and distribution of ideologically dangerous literature is growing. Also, more religious video films, which are brought from abroad, are being shown. . . . For every official mullah in the Navai district of Uzbekistan, there are 15 self-appointed ones.[57]

This statement was echoed in 1987 by the chairman of the Chechen-Ingush Supreme Soviet, who claimed that "60,000 people of working age in the North Caucasus belong to *murid* groups [Sufi: religious congregations formed around a charismatic leader], work and live outside the Soviet sphere," and that "religious tribunals often overrule Soviet [government] tribunals."[58]

The rise in national and Islamic identity among Muslims of the USSR coalesced in 1990 with the splintering of the official Muslim spiritual boards along ethnic lines. This process began in June 1990 when an assembly of Kazakh Muslim clerics founded the Muslim Spiritual Board of Kazakhstan and elected Ratbek Nisanbaev, the Kazakh representative to the official Muslim Spiritual Board for Central Asia, as the new board's director and Kazakh mufti. This act was followed by the effective dissolution of the Muslim Spiritual Board of Dagestan and the North Caucasus. An assembly of Muslim clerics from the North Caucasus declared the board defunct and proposed the formation of separate Muslim religious centers for each of the autonomous national territories of the region. Although neither Moscow nor the official Muslim spiritual boards recognized these acts, the state-sanctioned Islamic institutions were unable to prevent the ethnic-based fragmentation of their organizations as Muslim self-identity became incorporated into ethnic nationalist sentiment.[59]

Parallel with the rise in Muslims' religious and cultural consciousness, often fused with ethnic identity, several Islamic political parties surfaced during perestroika. The Turkestan Islamic Party emerged in Central Asia's Ferghana Valley in 1989 and opened the first mosque to operate openly outside the jurisdiction of the official Muslim spiritual boards. Alongside the new mosque, the party founded a medressah to provide religious training to all students, in contrast to officially sanctioned religious schools designed to train only students who wished to become clerics.[60] In Dagestan, Abdurashid Saidov and other pro-reform Muslims founded the Islamic Democratic Party in 1990. The party's principal objective was the ouster of Dagestan's Communist leadership and the construction of a democratic republic based on the principles of Islam. Al-Islamiyya, a more radical Dagestani organization, advocated the creation of an independent Islamic state in Dagestan.[61] The Jamaat-ul-Muslimin (Society of Muslims) also became active in Dagestan during this period and advocated increasing Islamic influence in the republic, including expanding the number of mosques and introducing separate educational facilities for girls and boys.[62]

The most successful of the Gorbachev-era Islamic parties was the Islamic Rebirth Party (IRP), which gained a significant following in Tajikistan, Uzbekistan, and to a lesser extent Dagestan. In June 1990, delegates from various parts of the USSR met in Astrakhan for the party's founding congress and elected Akhmadkadi Akhtaev as its leader. This pan-Muslim party advocated political reform by peaceful means, religious freedom for all Soviet citizens, and a rejuvenation of the Islamic faith after seventy years of persecution. By early 1991, the party claimed thirty thousand members spread out among three different regional organizations covering Central Asia, the Caucasus, and European Russia and Siberia.[63] Three months after the founding of the IRP, a group of Tatar political leaders formed the Tatar People's Democratic Party, commonly known as Vatan (Homeland), to support the creation of a Tatar state on the territories of the historic khanates of Astrakhan, Kazan, and Siberia. This party later changed its formal name to the National-Democratic Party and expanded its activities to advance Muslim interests throughout Russia.[64] In later years, Vatan organized demonstrations against Russian military operations in Chechnya, the treatment of Muslim minorities (such as Meskhetian Turks), and the Kremlin's policy of resisting international intervention to protect the ethnic Albanian population of Kosovo in 1999.

First Attempts at Muslim Political Mobilization in the Post-Soviet Era

The dissolution of the Soviet Union fractured the IRP along national lines and effectively ended attempts to create a pan-Islamic party to represent Muslims of the former union republics (now independent states). Party cofounder Akhtaev returned to his home republic of Dagestan and founded a successor party, the All-Russia Islamic Rebirth Party (ARIRP). Despite its national pretensions, the ARIRP focused principally on Dagestan, advocating the peaceful and gradual formation of an Islamic state on the territory of the republic (without, however, demonstrating any strong separatist tendencies).[65] Despite the initial success of its predecessor in mobilizing support, especially in Central Asia, the ARIRP quickly faded in political significance. The party failed to register for the Russian Federation's first round of parliamentary elections in 1993 and the following year failed to renew its registration with the Russian Ministry of Justice.[66] This failure to renew its legal status ended the ARIRP's ability to run in elections or to operate effectively as a political party.

In the turmoil that characterized the first years of post-Soviet Russian politics, Muslim political parties remained largely confined to regional politics, as illustrated by the ARIRP's inability to expand its activities beyond Dagestan. Not until the approach of the Russian Federation's second round of parliamentary elections in December 1995 did Muslim political leaders organize national parties and more loosely structured political movements to participate in electoral politics. In July 1995, the Islamic Committee of Russia emerged to represent more radical elements of Russia's Muslim electorate. Geidar Jemal, an Islamist activist since the 1980s and one of the more radical members of the Gorbachev-era IRP, emerged as the organization's leader. According to some sources, the Islamic Committee of Russia began as part of a loose Islamist alliance that formed in Khartoum, Sudan, and quickly established affiliates in Iran, Chechnya, France, the United Kingdom, and elsewhere.[67]

In preparation for the 1995 elections, the Islamic Committee joined forces with a moderately leftist electoral bloc, the Trade Unions and Industrialists of Russia–Union of Labor. Cooperation with this electoral alliance of Soviet-era enterprise managers and labor groups, which opposed Yeltsin's reforms, provided the Islamic Committee with a respectable vehicle for participating in the elections. However, as would become apparent during the next round of legislative elections in 1999, the Islamic Committee's alliance with this left-of-center opposition group belied the radical positions held and later openly espoused by Jemal and his organization.

The 1995 parliamentary elections served as an impetus for the formation of two additional Muslim movements, the Union of Muslims of Russia (UMR) and the All-Russia Muslim Social Movement, commonly known as Nur (Light). These movements presented a more moderate image than the Islamic Committee of Russia, emphasizing secular aspects of Muslim identity and advocating continued economic reforms with greater social protection. While seeking to capture a unified Muslim electorate, both organizations attempted to gain support from non-Muslim ethnic minorities to broaden their respective bases of support. The UMR's political program, in addition to calling for an increase in federal investment in Muslim-populated regions and an expansion of Russia's relations with Muslim countries, identified the protection of the rights and economic interests of all national minorities as one of its principal tasks.[68] Similarly, Nur, while advocating the strengthening of Muslim traditions and a peaceful settlement of the conflict in Chechnya, adopted a platform that called for defending the civil, political, economic, and cultural rights of all Russia's minority peoples.[69]

State Manipulation and Muslim Electoral Defeat

Despite their efforts to broaden their support by appealing to non-Muslims or by joining larger electoral alliances, a practice reminiscent of Muslim activism between 1904 and 1907, none of the three Muslim movements formed in 1995 performed well in the parliamentary elections. The UMR suffered the worst defeat of the three: in November 1995, Russia's Central Election Commission disqualified the UMR from the elections for irregularities in its registration documents.[70] The Russian Supreme Court rejected the UMR's subsequent legal appeals, leaving Nur the only Muslim organization to appear independently on the ballot. The UMR's disqualification fits a pattern of interference in the operation and political participation of Muslim movements and parties. In the larger context of Russian politics, this pattern of interference is one aspect of the arbitrariness with which Russia's electoral laws have been enforced or ignored at the national and regional levels. The denial of registration requests, disqualification from elections, and other means of interference by regional and national authorities to eliminate political rivals have occurred regularly in Russia's electoral politics. Muslim organizations and candidates have not escaped this trend.

One of the most blatant cases of electoral abuse occurred in 1999 when the local electoral commission of Stavropol Krai disqualified Aleksander Traspov, who was running for a seat in the Russian State Duma, ruling that his appearance on local television to answer questions about his candidacy constituted bribery of the electorate. The Russian Constitutional Court declared this ruling invalid, but only in January 2002, more than two years later.[71] The Russian Supreme Court's disqualification of Khamzat Gutseriev, a candidate for the presidency of Ingushetia and a competitor of the Kremlin's favored candidate, the day before the election in April 2002 is another example of abuse of electoral laws. Alexander Veshnyakov, chairman of the Russian Central Election Commission, commented on this problem during a June 2002 interview. After praising the passage of legislation in the summer of 2002 designed to eliminate such abuses, Veshnyakov stated, "In previous practice, there was no small number of curiosities: some [candidates] were eliminated from the electoral game for [not reporting extra income of] eighty rubles, while others were forgiven for 1000 rubles. With cars, there is a complete mess. One person was punished for [not reporting ownership of] an old Zhiguli. Another's Mercedes was overlooked."[72]

Following the elimination of the UMR, Nur and the Islamic Committee participated in the 1995 elections as planned, the former by appearing directly on the ballot independently and the latter as a member organization of the Trade Unions and Industrialists of Russia–Union of Labor bloc. Despite the lack of direct competition for the Muslim electorate, Nur received less than 1 percent (0.57 percent) of all votes cast.[73] Nur's electoral performance was slightly better, although still disappointing, in some predominantly Muslim regions. In Tatarstan and Bashkortostan, Nur gained 5 percent and 1.25 percent of the vote, respectively. The movement's showing of 12 percent in Chechnya was significantly better, but still constituted a small portion of the republic's Muslim voters.[74] (Voting in Chechnya during 1995 may have been distorted by ongoing warfare, the displacement of hundreds of thousands of Chechen residents, and the pervasive presence of the Russian military.) The Islamic Committee's electoral alliance performed slightly better nationally, capturing 1.6 percent of the national vote, but fell far short of the 5 percent threshold required to achieve party representation in the State Duma.[75] Consequently, of the 225 party-list seats in the Duma, none was allocated to Muslim movements or parties.

In addition to the cultural, institutional, and socioeconomic factors impeding political mobilization around any Muslim party, a credibility problem may have hindered the performance of Nur while also curtailing popular support for the Islamic Committee and the disqualified UMR. Ironically, despite the emphasis they placed on national minority rights, both Nur and the UMR suffered from an association with Vladimir Zhirinovsky's ultranationalist Liberal Democratic Party. Akhmed Khalitov, a member of the LDPR, was the UMR's first general secretary and one of the movement's principal organizers. The UMR's own membership criticized him for his association with the LDPR and rejected his candidacy for chairman of the movement.[76] Similarly, Khalid Yakhin, the elected leader of Nur, served on the staff of LDPR State Duma deputy Alexei Mitrofanov.[77] The Islamic Committee's leader suffered from a similar association with right-wing nationalism: in the late 1980s, Jemal joined the quasi-fascist Pamyat and served on its coordinating council, although he subsequently claimed that he did so at the instruction of Islamist allies in Tajikistan to explore possible contacts with Russian nationalists.[78]

The Failure of Muslim Unity and the Decline of Nur and the UMR

Following their failure in the 1995 elections, Muslim leaders made several attempts to establish more effective political parties and movements. The first major attempt occurred in April 1996 with the founding congress of the Muslims of Russia movement (not to be confused with the Union of Muslims of Russia, the UMR) in Saratov Oblast. The congress, which attracted delegates from thirty-nine Russian regions and republics, elected former UMR leader Mukaddas Bibarsov as its chairman.[79] The new organization gained the support of Mufti Ravil Gainutdin, chairman of the Russian Council of Muftis, whose backing ostensibly enhanced its legitimacy as a Russia-wide movement.[80] However, the movement failed to transcend Muslims' diverse regional, ethnic, and political identities and never significantly extended its influence beyond the Volga-Ural region. As Bibarsov admitted, "From a psychological standpoint, the problems facing Muslims in different parts of Russia differ. For Tatars and Bashkirs, for instance, the greatest danger is assimilation, while the main problem for Muslims of the northern Caucasus is the Chechen tragedy, as well as Moscow's imperial ways."[81]

In May 1996, Nur and the UMR agreed to form a united Muslim political organization in a second attempt to form a united Muslim bloc. Meeting in the Dagestani capital of Makhachkala, leaders of the two organizations signed an accord stating their intention to unite to form a new Russian Muslim Union. This new organization, which the cofounding movements planned to open to all Islamic movements and parties, sought to unite the Muslim electorate and rally Muslim support behind a single candidate in the approaching 1996 presidential election.[82] However, this attempt proved ineffective in attracting support from other organizations and quickly collapsed, leaving Nur and the UMR as separate and competing organizations.

Compounding the failure of Nur and the UMR to form a larger association, both movements suffered major setbacks in the months leading up to the 1999 parliamentary elections. Ironically, in the case of the UMR, a crippling loss of credibility followed one of the most significant achievements of Russia's Muslim movements and parties. In 1996, during by-elections held to fill a vacant seat for Dagestan in the State Duma, UMR chairman Nadirshakh Khachilaev won a seat in the Russian parliament and joined Viktor Chernomyrdin's pro-Yeltsin electoral bloc, Our Home Is Russia.[83] Thus less than a year after being disqualified from participating in the 1995 elections, the UMR succeeded in placing its leader in Russia's national parliament. However, two years later, this victory was erased by Khachilaev's involvement in a violent confrontation with police and a subsequent riot in Makhachkala. In May 1998, an attempt by Dagestani police to search the motorcade of Nadirshakh Khachilaev and his brother, Magomed Khachilaev, leader of Dagestan's Lak national movement, resulted in a clash that left several police officers dead. The confrontation escalated as armed supporters of the Khachilaev brothers seized several municipal office buildings, including the Dagestani parliament building, in Makhachkala's main square.[84]

Although peace was restored after Dagestani leaders reached an agreement with the Khachilaev brothers, both were later arrested by federal authorities, Magomed Khachilaev in September 1998 and Nadirshakh Khachilaev in October 1999 after hiding in Chechnya for more than a year. After the State Duma voted to lift Nadirshakh Khachilaev's parliamentary immunity, the Khachilaev brothers were convicted for their roles in the May 1998 violence. Both men were immediately released under the terms of a general amnesty enacted by the Russian parliament to commemorate the fiftieth anniversary of the Allied victory in the Second World War, leaving Nadirshakh Khachilaev, although no longer a member of parliament, free to pursue his political career.[85] However, neither he nor the UMR succeeded in regaining political credibility. Support for UMR eroded steadily, virtually disappearing in the Volga-Ural region and diminishing substantially even in Khachilaev's native Dagestan.[86] As Russia's third round of parliamentary elections approached in December 1999, the battered UMR failed to register to appear independently on the ballot.

Alongside the decline of the UMR, Nur suffered a preelection defeat at the hands of Russia's Central Election Commission. In October 1999, the commission disqualified Nur, citing the movement's failure to pay a mandatory campaign fee on time and a violation of federal disclosure law by one of its major contributors, the Uzbek commercial bank Mesed.[87] Nur's leader at the time, Maksud Sadikov, raised suspicions that the movement's disqualification was a politically motivated attempt to prevent the independent Muslim movement from participating in the elections. Noting that the Central Election Commission had stretched the rules for other parties and movements, he claimed, "The main reason [for Nur's disqualification] is that Muslims are not considered to be very convenient [to state authorities], even though the Muslim electorate accounts for more than 20 million votes."[88] Sadikov's protests proved futile, and Nur experienced the same humiliating preelection disqualification that the UMR had suffered four years previously.

Muslim Political Mobilization for the 1999 Parliamentary Elections

Like the 1995 parliamentary elections, the Russian Federation's third round of elections for the State Duma provided a catalyst for renewed efforts to unite the Muslim electorate. In December 1998, the All-Russia Islamic Congress (ARIC) and the Refakh (Welfare) movement registered with the Ministry of Justice in preparation for elections scheduled for the following December. The ARIC elected as its leader Aslambek Aslakhanov, an ethnic Chechen who served as chairman of the Union of Chechen Peoples and had formerly represented the Gudermes District of Chechnya in the Russian parliament. As a retired general from the Ministry of Internal Affairs and president of Russia's Association of Law Enforcement Agencies and Personnel, Aslakhanov combined an image as a strong leader of national stature with his ethnic roots to present a potentially compelling candidate for Muslim voters.[89]

Refakh's leader, an ethnic Russian named Abdul Vahid Niazov (formerly Vadim Medvedev), was also a highly visible political figure; he had served as both a founding member of the Union of Muslims of Russia and as leader of the Moscow-based Islamic Cultural Center.[90] Other prominent members of Refakh included Brontoy Bedurov, president of the Congress of Turkic Peoples of Russia; Ali Polosin, a former Russian Orthodox priest who had converted to Islam and had become editor of the newspaper *Musulmanskaya Gazeta* (Muslim gazette); and Ahmet Palankoyev, chairman of the Assembly of Muslim Youth. Like Nur and the UMR, Refakh developed a political program designed to expand its support among Muslims and other national minorities. The movement's political priorities included legal protection of the political and cultural-religious rights of national minorities, increased state funding for the restoration of mosques and other sites of religious and cultural significance to minorities, the strengthening of Russia's relations with the Muslim world, and censorship of indecent television programming offensive to Mulism values.[91] Refakh also acquired semiofficial endorsement when, like Mukaddas Bibarsov's Muslims of Russia movement three years earlier, it gained the support of Mufti Ravil Gainutdin, who agreed to serve as director of Refakh's Council of Spiritual Mentors.[92]

In July 1999, in yet another attempt to present voters with a unified Muslim electoral bloc, the ARIC and Refakh joined with Nur and the Muslims of Russia movement to form the political alliance Mejlis (Assembly). Leonard Rafikov, the new alliance's leader, claimed that Mejlis could capture up to 8 percent of the vote in the 1999 parliamentary elections.[93] However, just one month later, the events that triggered Vladimir Putin's rapid rise to power also splintered the nascent Muslim political alliance. The incursions by Islamist militants into Dagestan, followed by the terrorist bombings in Moscow and other Russian cities, led to both the second Russian-Chechen War and the sudden rise in popularity of the previously unknown Putin. With the growth in Putin's stature as the newly appointed prime minister and the rise of the pro-Putin Unity movement, an alternative and potentially more realistic path to electoral victory emerged. Refakh, hoping to capitalize on Putin's growing popularity, agreed to join the pro-Putin Unity bloc for the December 1999 elections. Other members of Mejlis allied with Chernomyrdin's electoral bloc, Our Home Is Russia, and, in contrast to Refakh, were critical of Russia's policies in Chechnya. Mejlis leader Leonard Rafikov claimed that the "Russian government has already destroyed Chechnya's economy. It is natural that the situation there is not stable, since people have neither jobs nor bread," while Nur leader Maksud Sadikov stated, "What is being done right now [in Chechnya] is a crime. There are plenty of peaceful options that can be used to resolve the situation."[94]

The Radical Fringe

Alongside these politically moderate Muslim movements, Geidar Jemal's Islamic Committee entered the electoral race. In contrast to its attempt to adopt a moderate appearance for the 1995 elections, the Islamic Committee openly embraced a far-right nationalist-patriotic platform, combining Islamic fundamentalism and Eurasianism, without the chauvinist pan-Slavic sentiments espoused by many Eurasianists. According to Jemal, the peoples of Central Eurasia, especially Muslims and Russians, are the world's best hope for resisting Western imperialism. In support of this position, the Islamic Committee joined forces with the Movement in Support of the Army, led by Viktor Ilyukhin and Albert Makashov, both of whom represented the radical nationalist wing of the Communist Party. In July 1999, during a conference in St. Petersburg titled "Orthodoxy and Islam: Spiritual Basis of Unity and Patriotism of the Peoples of Russia and Its Allies," Jemal announced, "The Movement in Support of the Army is a patriotic movement that opposes Yeltsin's pro-Western policy. We are uniting . . . based on the fact that Muslims and Orthodox Christians have common goals and tasks. Russia must be ready to wage the next world war on the side of the Islamic world."[95] In a subsequent interview, Jemal expanded on this position, stating that "one of the principal objectives of the Islamic Committee is to strategically position Russia closer to the international Muslim ummah, because they are natural allies in the struggle for the common Islamic and Russian ideals of justice, brotherhood, and equality."[96]

Jemal added to this hybrid Islamist-Eurasianist ideology a strong nostalgia for the Soviet Union. Ignoring the Soviet regime's repression of religion and the human rights violations it had inflicted on many Muslim nationalities, such as the mass deportations from the Caucasus during the Second World War and the forced Russification under Stalin, Jemal extolled the Soviet Union as a force that united the Eurasian peoples. He advocated the construction of a strong Russia that could replace the Soviet Union and join the Islamic world to resist the West. Jemal presented this position in a 1999 radio broadcast during which he asserted:

> Since the collapse of the world socialist system, the peoples of the world have been without shelter or support. The Soviet Union, which fought the West's imperialist desires, has collapsed. The overwhelming majority of Muslims always opposed the disintegration of the USSR. The overwhelming majority of Muslims know that this is a blow to ordinary people and a threat to the future of all our nations. Today, Muslims have the political will to help reunite the nations of the former USSR and the will to build a life together in Great Eurasia's boundless spaces. . . . Today, we Muslims and Russians must form a single front against our common enemy.[97]

Muslim Moderates Prevail

As an electoral strategy, Refakh's alliance with Unity proved the most effective. Capitalizing on Putin's growing popularity, Unity won 23 percent of the votes cast and came in a close second place in the party-list voting, with Zyuganov's Communist Party surpassing the pro-Putin bloc by just 1 percent of the vote.[98] As a member organization of Unity, Refakh was awarded five of the sixty-six party-list seats won by the electoral bloc, with Niazov taking one of the seats. Refakh thus became the first Muslim movement or party to win party-list seats in the State Duma. After the election, seven other Muslim parliamentary deputies joined Refakh, bringing the movement's parliamentary membership to twelve.[99] By contrast, the experience of other Muslim movements proved disastrous. Our Home Is Russia, which remained closely associated with the unpopular Yeltsin, won just 1.2 percent of the vote. The performance of the Movement in Support of the Army, Jemal's chosen electoral bloc, was even worse: it gained less than 1 percent (0.58 percent) of the vote.[100] As a result, neither electoral alliance won party-list seats.

Muslim Parties under the Putin Regime

The failure of its rival Muslim movements left Refakh as the only political movement or party explicitly representing the Muslim electorate in the State Duma. In less than a year, Aslambek Aslakhanov of the All-Russia Islamic Congress joined Niazov and his fellow Refakh members in parliament. Emulating Khachilaev's electoral success in Dagestan two years earlier, Aslakhanov defeated twelve other candidates in August 2000 to win a special election for a State Duma seat representing Chechnya.[101] However, despite their electoral success, the All-Russia Islamic Congress and Refakh remained in weak positions in the State Duma. Aslakhanov won his parliamentary seat through elections in a single-mandate district (as opposed to a party-list vote), and his movement lacked the popular endorsement gained by other parties and movements that had acquired party-list seats. In the case of Refakh, although the number of parliamentary seats gained by the movement may have corresponded to the movement's electoral significance, it constituted barely 2.5 percent of all seats in the State Duma. Additionally, although Refakh was the first Muslim organization to gain party-list seats in the Russian parliament, this accomplishment was possible only after Refakh allowed itself to be absorbed into a larger electoral alliance with no connection to Muslim-specific issues.

To overcome these weaknesses, Niazov and Aslakhanov attempted to unite their organizations. In October 2000, Refakh and the ARIC signed an agreement to form a single political party, which Niazov later announced would be called Blagodenstviye (Prosperity).[102] Soon afterwards, Nur and the UMR joined negotiations on the formation of this new Muslim party.[103] However, as with previous attempts to establish a unified Muslim political party, efforts to found Blagodenstviye soon faltered as competing ambitions and ideological differences prevented Muslim leaders from uniting their organizations. In June 2001, Niazov abandoned the idea of a larger Muslim bloc and joined forces with several political parties and movements, including Christian Unity and the Congress of Buddhist Peoples, to form the Eurasian Party of Russia (not to be confused with Alexander Dugin's Eurasia Movement).[104] Claiming that Muslims formed the vanguard of the new party, Niazov, the new organization's elected chairman, nevertheless described it as a vehicle to unify Russia's disparate peoples through their unique Eurasian traditions.[105] Four months later, Aslakhanov joined the Fatherland-All-Russia bloc, which subsequently merged with the pro-Putin Unity movement to form the United Russia party.[106]

As Refakh prepared for the formation of the Eurasian Party of Russia, the movement's political vulnerability was demonstrated by the tenuous nature of its partnership with Unity. Refakh supported Unity's agenda during the 1999 parliamentary election campaign and publicly supported Putin's candidacy for president the following year. In January, in an appeal urging Muslims and members of other minority religions to vote for Putin, Refakh's presidium issued the following statement:

> The priority task today is to ensure social stability in the country, to strengthen the statehood and integrity of Russia. It is common knowledge that the national minorities suffer most of all from wars, upheavals, instability, and political chaos. This is why they particularly need a strong political leader, capable of being a guarantor of the country's sovereignty and territorial integrity, a guarantor of the equality of its citizens, irrespective of nationality and faith.[107]

However, a year after Putin's election as president, Unity expelled Niazov from its ranks, allegedly for speaking on behalf of the pro-Putin bloc without authorization, especially concerning issues related to the Middle East and the larger Muslim world.[108] This abrupt dismissal of Refakh's leader despite the party's strong show of support for Putin during the election campaign reflects the low level of significance that Unity placed on its continued association with the Muslim movement after the election. Although the Muslim movement was useful as an electoral ally to attract some Muslim voters and give both Unity and Putin the appearance of inclusiveness, it proved to be expendable as a political partner when the time came to exercise power in the State Duma.

Shortly after Niazov's expulsion from the Unity coalition, the Russian parliament passed the 2001 "Law on Political Parties," which banned parties based on religion or ethnicity, and Niazov began building his Eurasian Party as a more broadly based alternative to Refakh. By adopting a broader Eurasianist theme, Niazov hoped to create a viable party that could meet the new law's stricter requirements and gain sufficient support to win seats in the December 2003 parliamentary elections. In the closing months of 2002, Niazov's party expanded its name to the Eurasian Party-Union of Patriots of Russia and registered formally with the Russian Ministry of Justice.[109] In January 2003, Niazov announced that the party, which he claimed had gained more than 100,000 members, would lead a left-of-center coalition that would promote Eurasianism as the basis for "the creation of a new union in place of the former USSR."[110] He subsequently entered his party into an electoral alliance with other political parties, including the newly formed Russian Party of Peace, co-chaired by former Ingush president Ruslan Aushev. During an interview concerning this new coalition, simply called the Union of Patriots of Russia, Niazov claimed, "Probably we shall be unable to compete with either the powers that be [a reference to the pro-Putin United Russia party] or the Communists, but we shall certainly become a third force."[111] To advance this goal, however, Niazov progressively abandoned Islamic themes and subsumed Refakh within a larger coalition with little Muslim-specific character.

Islamic Party of Russia

Despite the new ban on religion-based parties, a new Islamic party emerged during the same month that Niazov was expelled from Unity. In March 2001, the Islamic Party of Russia held its founding congress and announced plans to participate in future elections. Emulating the strategies of past Muslim movements, the Islamic Party adopted a broad political program to gain support from national and religious minorities. The program's principal objectives included the advancement of minority rights, opposition to racial and religious intolerance, and reformation of Russia as a multiethnic federal state. Similar to Niazov's Eurasian Party and the more radical Islamic Committee, the Islamic Party of Russia combined aspects of a Muslim-centered agenda with a Eurasianist ideology. The movement advocated a less Western-oriented foreign policy and, focusing on Russia's historic role as a nexus of civilizations, supported Russian culture as a means of expressing "Eastern traditions in the language of the West and the West's dreams of happiness through the traditional monotheist spirituality of the East."[112] The organization's political program promoted the use of Islamic traditions to advance these objectives.

During its third party congress in April 2002, the Islamic Party of Russia resolved to transform itself into an officially recognized political party capable of meeting the new requirements set forth in the Law on Political Parties. Party chairman Muhammad Rajabov announced that the new party had established regional branches in sixty-three regions and republics and had gained a total membership of 1.5 million (an almost certainly exaggerated claim). He predicted that the new party would be the only Muslim party to register with federal authorities and take part in the 2003 parliamentary elections. According to Rajabov, although the party would consider changing its name, the word "Islam" would remain in the title. Adopting the formulation of Islam expressed by Geidar Jemal, Rajabov claimed that Islam was not only a religion, but also a set of cultural characteristics accessible to, and accepted by, different religions and nationalities. As such, the ban on religion-based parties contained in the Law on Political Parties would not prevent the party from participating in Russia's 2003 parliamentary elections.[113]

Just six months after Rajabov made these claims, however, the Islamic Party of Russia succumbed to growing pressures to further submerge or even abandon its Islamic identity in order to remain active in Russian politics. In September 2002, approximately 200 members of the party met in Moscow for the founding congress of a new party, the True Patriots of Russia. Abandoning the reference to Islam in its title and forgoing Islamic aspects of its original political program, the revised party declared itself a strictly secular organization.[114]

Regional Islamic Parties in Russia's Muslim Republics

The political environment in Russia's republics and regions exhibits many of the same characteristics that hinder the development of democratic pluralism and party formation at the national level. Russia's authoritarian tradition and reliance on centralized rule impede identification with either national or regional parties. Additionally, as effective political power was decentralized throughout Russia during the 1990s, ruling elites in many republics and regions established regional political orders that—as in Russian politics at the federal level—marginalized the influence of parties. Regional political elites often merged with financial and business interests, with executives of large companies serving in the administrations of governors and republican presidents, a trend that intensified with the rise of the oligarch-governors.[115] Regional chief executives frequently filled their provinces' legislatures with their subordinates: between 1995 and 1996, 332 city and district administration heads, who report directly to the regional governor or republican president, won seats in forty-five regional parliaments.[116] In some cases, regional leaders engage directly in repressive measures such as closing independent media outlets and banning the activities of opposition parties to marginalize political opposition.

The prevalence of this environment in Russian regional politics ensured the political dominance of the regional chief executives in most regions and republics and, in many cases, gave rise to a form of "democratic authoritarianism" or "managed democracy" that surpassed presidential dominance at the federal level. In early 2002, State Duma deputy Vladimir Ryzhkov claimed, "Competitive, free elections would put [these systems] at risk and are thus viewed [by their beneficiaries] as undesirable. Today, authoritarian regimes of differing degrees have taken root in at least 60 of Russia's 89 regions."[117] The limited role of political parties under these circumstances is illustrated by their marginal influence in elections over the last decade. In the first round of regional legislative elections in 1993 and 1994, in which seventy-nine republics and regions elected new legislatures, just 13.8 percent of victorious candidates were affiliated with either a national or regional party. In the second round of regional legislative elections from 1995 through 1997, in which seventy-two republics and regions participated, only 16.8 percent of winning candidates were members of a party,[118] and in seventeen provinces, the newly elected regional parliaments had no members affiliated with a political party.[119]

Democratic Authoritarianism in the Muslim Republics

Democratic authoritarianism—with dominant chief executives able to employ dictatorial measures to restrict or eliminate alternative poles of power, including competitive political parties—can be found to varying degrees in Russia's Muslim republics. In several cases, republican heads have dominated politics in their respective republics since before the collapse of the USSR. With the exception of Chechnya, single individuals dominated the first decade of post-Soviet politics in Russia's Muslim republics.

In Bashkortostan, Murtaza Rakhimov served as the chairman of the republic's Supreme Soviet beginning in 1990. After winning the republic's first presidential election in December 1993, he pushed through the republican legislature a new constitution granting him extraordinary powers, including the authority to appoint and dismiss the heads of district and city administrations, leaving only villages and collective farms with the power to elect their local leaders. He consolidated his power in March 1995 when elections for Bashkortostan's new bicameral parliament resulted in a legislature dominated by his allies. In a clear violation of the principle of separation of executive and legislative powers, approximately three-quarters of the 154 members of the new parliament's upper house (the Chamber of Representatives) held governmental posts that placed them directly under President Rakhimov's authority. During Bashkortostan's second presidential election in 1998, republican officials disqualified four major contenders, including two members of the Russian State Duma and a former Bashkortostan prime minister. When the Russian Supreme Court ruled their disqualifications illegal, Bashkir authorities responded that the Russian courts had no jurisdiction in the republic.[120]

A similar quasi-authoritarianism exists in Dagestan. In 1994, Magomedali Magomedov, chairman of the Dagestani Supreme Soviet since 1990, was elected head of the republic's newly formed executive body, the State Council. After holding that position for eight years, he was reelected overwhelmingly by the republic's Constitutional Assembly, 228 votes to 4, to a third term in June 2002.[121] To maintain his position, Magomedov has manipulated the republican parliament and eliminated rival poles of influence. In 1994, the Magomedov administration helped engineer dismemberment of the Islamic Democratic Party of Dagestan. With the administration's support, Surakat Asiyatilov, chairman of the Dagestani legislature's Committee on Civil and Religious Affairs, was elected leader of the party, which subsequently adopted the name Islamic Party of Dagestan and dropped demands for democratizing the republic's political structure.[122] Two years later, Magomedov convinced the parliament to extend his term from two to four years and, in 1998, pushed through a constitutional amendment allowing him to run for a second term. In 2001, Dagestan's legislature again acquiesced to Magomedov's demands and granted him the right to run for a third term as State Council chairman, an action that permitted his essentially uncontested victory a year later.[123]

Elsewhere in the North Caucasus, the near monopoly of political power held by republican presidents has undermined the development of democratic systems. In Kabardino-Balkaria, Valerii Kokov has served as president since 1992; he was reelected with 99 percent of the vote in 1997[124] and with 87 percent in 2002.[125] In Karachaevo-Cherkessia, Vladimir Khubiev headed the republican government for twenty years, from 1979 to 1999, before being ousted in the republic's first presidential election.[126] Similarly, Aslan Dzharimov served as Adygea's president for ten years before losing his reelection bid in 2002 to millionaire gold magnate Khazret Sovmen. As president of Poyus, one of the world's largest gold firms, Sovmen became one of Adygea's largest benefactors and gained sufficient influence to overcome Dzharimov's powers of incumbency.[127] Ruslan Aushev of Ingushetia also dominated his republic's politics until he suffered a similar loss of influence, in this case at the hands of the federal government. After abruptly resigning in December 2001, Aushev supported one of his allies in the Ingush government to succeed him. However, the Russian Supreme Court disqualified Aushev's favored candidate, Ingushetia's internal affairs minister Khamzat Gutseriev, one day before the election. This act allowed pro-Moscow Murat Zyazikov, a general in the FSB and President Putin's deputy presidential representative to the Southern Federal District, to win the presidency.[128]

The Example of Tatarstan

One short-lived exception to this pattern occurred in Tatarstan in the late 1980s and early 1990s, when Tatar nationalist organizations gained temporary prominence. During this period, Mintimer Shaimiev loosely aligned with Tatar nationalists to consolidate his power and maximize Tatarstan's autonomy vis-à-vis Moscow. In February 1989, Shaimiev, at that time chairman of Tatarstan's Council of Ministers, initiated this cooperative relationship by sending an official delegation to the founding congress of the All-Tatar Public Center (ATPC). Shortly afterwards, Tatarstan's government granted the new organization access to the republican mass media and helped it expand its organizational structure outside the republic. In September 1989, Shaimiev, by this time first secretary of Tatarstan's Communist Party *obkom* (regional organization), appointed Rafael Khakimov, one of the ATPC's most important figures, deputy head of the obkom's ideology department.[129]

In subsequent years, Shaimiev enlisted the support of the ATPC, Fauzia Bairamova's Ittifaq party, the Tatar youth movement Azatlik, and other nationalist organizations to secure his dominant political position and enhance the republic's autonomy. In August 1990, during debate in the republican parliament on Tatarstan's status within Russia, approximately 50,000 proindependence demonstrators gathered in Liberty Square outside the parliament building. Prompted by this show of popular support for the nationalist cause, the legislature agreed to many of the elements of political autonomy demanded by Shaimiev. Most important, the republican parliament passed a resolution declaring Tatarstan's sovereignty, affirmed the republic's control over natural resources and industry on its territory, and agreed to adopt a new constitution. Perhaps most central to Shaimiev's plans, Tatarstan's parliament agreed to hold a referendum on creating the post of president for the republic.[130] In June 1990, Shaimiev, with the endorsement of the ATPC, was overwhelmingly elected Tatarstan's first president.

In addition to helping him establish his dominance in the republic, this strategy of cooperating with Tatar nationalists aided Shaimiev in his struggle with federal authorities. Following the failed 1991 coup d'état against Gorbachev, which Shaimiev tacitly supported by quelling prodemocracy demonstrations and suppressing criticism of the conspirators in the republic's media, officials in Moscow began calling for Shaimiev's removal from power. When Sergei Shakhrai arrived in Kazan to engineer Shaimiev's removal, he was greeted with extreme hostility by crowds of demonstrators decrying Russian imperialism. Tatar nationalists organized demonstrations on Liberty Square, while Ittifaq called for the creation of a national guard to defend the republic's sovereignty. This nationalist pressure helped subdue criticism of Shaimiev in the Tatar Supreme Soviet. During Shakhrai's visit, the republican parliament refused to discuss Shaimiev's removal and rejected claims that Tatarstan had supported the attempted takeover.[131]

Despite his reliance on Tatar nationalists during the early part of his rule, once he had consolidated his political authority and the republic's autonomy, Shaimiev began taking steps to marginalize Ittifaq, the ATPC, and other nationalist groups. In October 1991, after violent demonstrations in protest of the Tatarstan Supreme Soviet's refusal to unilaterally declare independence, Shaimiev condemned the violence and supported a referendum on Tatarstan's status that fell far short of the nationalists' demands.[132] Ittifaq and other nationalist organizations retaliated early the following year by convening a Tatar national congress, which subsequently founded the Milli Mejlis (National Assembly) to serve as an unofficial parliament of the Tatar people.[133] In response, Shaimiev persuaded Tatarstan's parliament to declare the Tatar congress and the activities of the Milli Mejlis illegal. Additionally, he organized an alternative World Tatar Congress consisting of delegates representing Tatar communities worldwide. Convening in June 1992, the congress endorsed Shaimiev's strategy of pursuing sovereignty through negotiation with Moscow and rejected nationalist desires to unilaterally declare independence.

In the following years, Tatarstan's authorities continued efforts to weaken nationalist parties and movements, many of which moved into open opposition to Tatarstan's government. The republican government banned Ittifaq's publication, *Altyn Urda* (Golden horde), and removed officials associated with the nationalists from government positions.[134] Denied their former political and material support from republican authorities and largely shunned by the republic's media, Tatar nationalists faded in political relevance. In 1995, Fauzia Bairamova, the most visible leader of the nationalists, lost her seat in the parliament, while membership in the ATPC declined dramatically, leaving the once formidable nationalist organization without significant popular support or political influence.

This loss of political relevance prompted Ittifaq to search for new methods of gaining support, including turning to Islamist rhetoric—such as advocating the formation of an Islamic state in Tatarstan—and joining forces with other opposition groups. In June 1998, Ittifaq participated in the founding congress of the Muslims of Tatarstan movement, an alliance of Tatar nationalists and former members of the Spiritual Board of Muslims of Tatarstan. The congress elected Gabdulla Galiullin, the former mufti of Tatarstan, as its chairman and adopted a political program committing the movement to support Tatar nationalist revival and to protect the rights and interests of Muslims in the republic. Coupling Tatar nationalism with Islamic identity, the movement adopted the "Canon of Tatars" originally promulgated by the Milli Mejlis. According to the canon, the three pillars of the Tatar nation are Islam, Tatar ethnic identity, and Turkism.[135] In November 1998, the Muslims of Tatarstan movement joined with the Communist Party of Tatarstan and other opposition groups to found the party Omet (Hope). Galiullin was again chosen to lead the opposition alliance.[136]

However, the nationalist opposition to Shaimiev, even after merging nationalist and Islamist agendas, failed to gain a significant voice in the republic once Shaimiev had consolidated power. After his re-election as president in 1996, Shaimiev gained approval in the republican parliament for an amendment to Tatarstan's constitution that removed a provision prohibiting presidents from serving more than two consecutive terms.[137] In 2001, Shaimiev faced no credible opposition in his bid for a third term as republican president and was reelected with 80 percent of the vote.[138] In parliamentary elections later that year, 78 of the 130 deputies elected to the Tatar State Council held governmental posts that made them directly subordinate to Shaimiev, including Tatarstan's prime minister, the director of Shaimiev's presidential administration, and more than fifty heads of district and city administrations throughout the republic.[139]

Putin's Electoral Reforms and the End of Regional Parties

The rise of democratic authoritarianism in Russia's Muslim republics has limited the influence of regional political parties in those areas where Islamic parties are most likely to build bases of support. As the experience of Tatarstan demonstrates, even nationalist parties and movements that once seemed ascendant in regional politics are subject to demobilization. In the first two years of his presidency, Putin gained parliamentary approval for two measures that further undermined regional parties in these and other republics and regions: (1) the 2001 Law on Political Parties and (2) the 2002 Law on the Main Guarantees of Election Rights and the Right to Take Part in a Referendum of Citizens of the Russian Federation (henceforth the Law on Elections). The first of these measures provides a legal definition for political parties and stipulates that only legally recognized parties can participate formally in elections. By imposing this restriction on regional as well as national elections, the law requires regional parties to meet the new stringent requirements, including gaining at least 10,000 members and establishing regional organizations in no fewer than forty-five regions and republics. In effect, the law requires regional parties to expand and become national parties if they wish to participate in elections even at the regional level.

This requirement, which became effective in the summer of 2003, revokes the legal status of most current regional parties, including Ittifaq in Tatarstan and the Islamic Party of Dagestan, leaving large national parties such as United Russia, Yabloko, the Communist Party, and Zhirinovsky's LDPR to run in regional legislative elections. Political organizations denied the legal status of political parties may continue functioning as activist or lobbying groups, as Vatan has done since it was denied reregistration in 2000. However, they are not eligible to participate in legislative elections. In the Muslim republics of Bashkortostan and Tatarstan, this law adversely affected twenty-two regional parties and movements previously registered with republican officials.[140] In some cases, national parties may absorb regional parties, which may be able to maintain some political cohesion as regional factions of the larger parties. However, such means of indirect representation are unlikely to halt the erosion of support for regional parties that no longer appear on the ballot or formally hold seats in the legislature. Moreover, regional factions would have to support the platform of the main party and thus would be incapable of fully representing local concerns.

In June 2002, President Putin signed the Law on Elections, which specified that regional legislatures must be elected using the same format of single-mandate and party-list seats employed in elections to the Russian State Duma. Accordingly, half of all deputies in each regional legislature will be elected in single-mandate districts and half must be chosen from party lists.[141] Because only parties that meet the requirements of the Law on Political Parties (i.e., are able to gain nationwide memberships) are eligible to participate in elections, national parties will dominate regional parliaments for the foreseeable future. This development raises the influence of national parties while reducing what little relevance regional parties might maintain following the loss of their right to run formally in elections. Islamic parties in Russia's Muslim republics will face an uphill battle to retain their already limited influence, let alone develop into more viable institutions.

Conclusion

As demonstrated by the performance of the All-Russia Islamic Rebirth Party, Nur, the UMR, and other Muslim parties and movements, Muslim political organizations have not gained influence in Russian politics commensurate with the size of Russia's Muslim constituency. To a large degree, this failure can be attributed to the Muslim population's internal divisions—economic, geographic, ethnic, and theological—which hinder the formation of a united Muslim electorate, even at the regional level. Additionally, Russia's post-Soviet political environment has limited the effectiveness of political parties, especially those representing ethnic or religious minorities. Although Russia has many of the attributes of a democratic system, most important, free and regular elections to determine political leadership, the political system erected under Yeltsin contains several features that hinder the formation of broadly based parties. The dominance of national and regional chief executives who retain extraordinary powers to suppress political opposition, heightens the lingering effects of Russia's authoritarian tradition. In this environment, political parties, with a few notable exceptions, have remained marginal to Russian politics.

Muslim parties, whether organized around religion or ethnicity, have been particularly ineffectual. State manipulation and interference at both the federal and regional levels have impeded their operation and participation in elections. In some cases, Muslim parties have experienced qualified and temporary success by aligning with stronger factions or individual political leaders. However, as demonstrated by the cooperation of Ittifaq and other Tatar nationalist groups with Mintimer Shaimiev and Refakh's collaboration with the pro-Putin Unity movement, such alliances have proved fragile and ultimately ineffective in building broad bases of support or enhancing political influence. In other cases, the political ambitions of Muslim party leaders—notably Nadirshakh Khachilaev's actions as leader of the Union of Muslims of Russia—have led to diminished credibility and loss of support.

With the advent under President Putin of new obstacles to the formation of political parties, the prospects of parties based on Islam or Muslim ethnic identity will deteriorate further. New requirements for parties to gain 10,000 members spread out over at least half of Russia's republics and regions, combined with prohibitions on ethnic- and religion-based parties, will lead inevitably to the elimination of most of the country's existing parties while substantially impeding the emergence of new ones. As political organizations competing in elections and serving as links between Muslim citizens and Russia's political leadership, Muslim parties will likely disappear, either through absorption by or metamorphosis into larger non-Muslim parties or by simply becoming moribund, as the All-Russia Islamic Rebirth Party in Dagestan did in the early 1990s. Niazov's efforts to recreate Refakh as the Eurasian Party and Aslakhanov's decision to join the Fatherland–All-Russia movement (now United Russia) attest to this trend. The 2002 Law on Countering Extremist Activities, depending on how broadly federal authorities apply it toward Islamic-based organizations, could further erode opportunities for Muslim political activism.

The disappearance of any opportunity for Muslims to participate directly in the political process on the basis of ethnic or religious identity will lead to the disenfranchisement of many. Combined with restrictions on the activities of religious groups contained in the 1997 Law on Freedom of Conscience and Religious Associations, the elimination of Muslim parties will significantly curtail Muslim political and social activism. This could enhance their sense of alienation—already encouraged by Russia's renewed emphasis on political centralization and moves toward monoculturalism—and encourage many to opt out of the political process or find alternative means of expressing their political and other concerns. Under these circumstances, Islamist alternatives, including extremist ones, may become more attractive to some Muslims, especially those looking for ways to resist Russian cultural and political influence. Central Election Commission chairman Alexander Veshnyakov alluded to the dangers of alienating political forces from mainstream politics in a May 2002 interview when he stated, "[Parliamentary] deputies represent the interests of various political forces. These interests should be realized in a representative body. If this does not take place, political forces will defend their interests in street events in far from always civilized forms."[142]

278 IDENTITY POLITICS IN THE RUSSIAN FEDERATION

Such activities, however, will remain the choice of a small, albeit sometimes vocal and dangerous, minority. For the majority of Russia's Muslim population, the already circumscribed political space available for ethnic- and religions-based self-identity and expression will shrink even further. This development, combined with other trends in Russia toward greater governmental centralization and a Russocentric culture, will further reduce the degree of cultural and political self-determination for Russia's Muslims.

III

Russia and Islam

The Islamic Factor in Russia's External Relations

6

The Evolution of Russia's Foreign Policy Perspectives in the Post-Soviet Era

One of the most critical questions raised by the collapse of the Soviet Union was the following: What would be the direction and the guiding principles of the Russian Federation's foreign policy? Charting the course of Russia's foreign policy has proved difficult and complicated, mainly because Russia had been an empire during its entire history as an active international player. Moreover, unlike other European empires, Russia has never been a nation-state, although Russia "as one of fifteen constituent republics of the [Soviet] Union had some accoutrements of a nation state." Yet unlike other Soviet republics, Russia did not have its own separate Communist party organization and thus "was actually intertwined with the USSR in a manner that no other republic was. It was pro-forma one of the co-equal republics of the Union and at the same time it was at the apex of the power in the USSR: the Union itself."[1]

Notwithstanding its federal structure and its transnational ideology, the Soviet Union was in many respects a multinational empire whose borders largely corresponded to those of tsarist Russia. In short, despite the ideological rupture with the past, geopolitically the USSR was the continuation of the tsarist empire and inherited many of its geopolitical imperatives, impulses, and policies.[2] The USSR's ideology was periodically adjusted to meet internal needs and external challenges, but it still provided a long-term vision of the world and guidelines for its realization. The Russian Federation may be the legal successor state of the Soviet Union, but clearly is not the Soviet Union's geopolitical successor, nor is it the geopolitical or cultural heir of the tsarist empire. Because of these historic realities, prior to the Soviet Union's collapse, Russia had not thought of its security, national interest, and place and prestige within the community of states outside of an imperial or supranational framework.

Therefore, since the USSR's demise, Russia's foreign policy has faced a series of crucial questions: Can Russia free itself from the imperial mode of thinking and behaving?[3] If so, how long will it take to shift from an imperial to a national mode of thinking? Finally, can Russia's imperial impulse take a more indirect shape, as did those of France and Britain?[4] The evolution of Russia's foreign policy ideals and practices since 1991 shows the difficulties and uncertainties involved in such a transition.

The difficulty of Russia's transition to a postimperial status and frame of mind is sharpened by the fact that while it is ethnically more homogeneous than many other European countries, it embraces a sizeable Muslim minority. This minority has a different national and cultural sense of identity and memory of the Russian-Muslim historical encounter. Moreover, some of its members want to assert their own identity and to acquire a large measure of autonomy and, in some cases, complete independence.

The presence of this indigenous Muslim minority endows the Russian Federation with some characteristics of empire. Inevitably, this influences Russia's worldview, security perspective, and foreign policy choices and generates diverse opinions on these issues. Thus at least some of Russia's Muslims want extensive relations with other Muslim countries and prefer Russia to be sympathetic to issues of concern to Muslims worldwide. The presence of the Muslim community also makes Russia vulnerable to developments in the Islamic world. In theory, this should make Russia conscious of the impact that its treatment of its Muslims has on the character of its relations with the Islamic world, but, as amply demonstrated by Russian conduct in the Chechen War, such concerns are overshadowed by more important interests, including the maintenance of the federation's territorial integrity.

The relative impact of the Islamic variable, both on Russia's security perspective and on its foreign and security policy, is affected by other factors, most notably economic and financial considerations, the nature of the international system, competing strategic concerns and interests, geographic location, historic experience, and national and elite value systems. The interplay of these factors determines the broad outlines and specific characteristics of Russia's, and indeed all nations', foreign policies, although at times one or two variables may exert greater influence. Any significant alteration in one or more of these variables affects the direction of foreign policy. Since 1991, these fundamental determinants of state behavior, combined with factors specific to Russia, have influenced the evolution of Russian foreign policy theories and practices.

The Impact of Geography

A country's geographic characteristics affect its worldview and hence its actions because these traits form important aspects of its culture and its collective self-perception and psychology. They also determine the character of a country's neighbors as well as the nature, type, source, and severity of threats to its security, and thus many of its policy options and limitations. A landlocked country's security concerns, foreign policy options, and aspirations are different from those of a country with an extensive coastline. A country on the crossroads of major migratory movements and without significant natural defenses such as high mountains or vast oceans develops its own particular psychological sense of threat.

In Russia's case, for at least 500 years, geography has played a crucial role in shaping its collective identity and psychology, worldview, perceptions of threats, and foreign policy. Paramount has been Russia's vastness, stemming largely from its territorial expansion in a continual effort to break out of its semilandlocked condition. Even post-Soviet Russia is a continent-size country. According to many Russian historians and political scientists, notably Sergei Medvedev, this fact has determined many salient characteristics of Russian culture. It has strengthened a feeling of entitlement to great-power status and made Russia part of different continents and neighbor to several civilizational zones.[5] This led Medvedev to suggest that "Russian space is a conglomeration of peripheries."[6]

Vastness has made Russia a Eurasian country. Barring the territorial disintegration of the Russian Federation, geography would prevent it from disengaging from Asia, even if culturally and politically it wanted to integrate into the West. The fact that many of Russia's southern neighbors belong to the Islamic civilization makes South and Central Asia, the South Caucasus, and the Middle East of significant strategic interest. This would have been true even if there were no Muslims within the Russian Federation or if Russia had had no imperial history in the Muslim world.

Russia's lack of direct access to warm waters has also deeply influenced its collective psychology, values, and security perceptions. Medvedev's statement that Russia possesses "the greatest number of seas on which no one sails"[7] helps to explain its acute concern with the Baltic and Black Sea regions and the nature of its relations with the countries that abut them. Here, as in Asia and the Muslim South, the option of nonengagement is unrealistic.

Historical Experience

Historical memories and experiences color nations' assessments of present reality, shape their vision of the future, and form their national ethos. Not all members of a nation share the same view of the past, especially if, as is the case with Russia, it is multiethnic and multireligious. There may be competing memories, as is clearly true in Russia. The "past" is also subject to reinterpretation, especially when a country experiences revolutionary change under the impulse of a new ideology. Russian history, written in both Soviet and post-Soviet periods, provides graphic examples of such reinterpretations. Nevertheless, experiences that have left an enduring imprint on a nation's collective memory and psychology always reassert themselves, and ideological precepts are modified in order to bring them into conformity with historical experiences. The Soviet period in Russia provides many examples of this process.[8]

Past experiences do not always determine future behavior. Nations can overcome destructive legacies under new and more favorable circumstances. Europe's experience after the Second World War, notably Franco-German reconciliation, proves that this is possible, provided systemic conditions are favorable. The transformation of the international political system, especially through the creation of the North Atlantic Treaty Organization (NATO) and the European Community, was instrumental in this process.

In Russia's case, too, systemic changes and its interaction with other countries can help it overcome its negative historic legacies. So far, however, Russia's past has influenced the formation of its post-Soviet identity and its vision of the outside world. Russia's historic adversaries, including some Muslim nations both inside and outside Russia, have also not been successful in overcoming the influence of their experience with Russia. Furthermore, in contrast to opportunities provided to Europe by the post–Second World War system, the contemporary international setting has not provided Russia with a propitious environment for shedding its negative historic legacy.

National Identity

A nation's definition of itself—its national identity—determines its goals, its aspirations, its discrimination between friend and foe, and hence its attitude toward other nations. Many elements, including geography and history, help shape a nation's self-identity, which is not static and is continuously being rebuilt. At various times, different elements—ethnicity, religion, ideological affinity, and notions of citizenship—acquire greater or lesser significance. Different segments of a nation may have diverging, competing, or even conflicting concepts of the nation's identity. At times of great change, established notions of identity are challenged, as has been the case in the post-Soviet era. A crisis of identity often is accompanied by competing and volatile worldviews. Shifts in Russia's foreign policy directions in the post-Soviet era have reflected the ongoing debate about its identity. This identity is still being developed in the context of competition between internal and external forces to shape it. The outlines of a broad consensus on the basic components of Russia's national identity are emerging, but the identity debate is not over. Thus Russia's external behavior is still subject to periodic shifts, although the magnitude of these shifts will be determined by systemic factors and the resources Russia can devote to international affairs.

Value System/Ideology

The Soviet Union's disintegration ended the era of ideologically determined international politics. However, conflicts deriving from divergent value systems, both within states and among them, did not end. They may even have become sharper and acquired larger dimensions. Some analysts, following the lead of Samuel Huntington, believe that civilizational clashes are replacing past ideological battles. In this theory, religious beliefs mainly determine the underlying characteristics of various civilizations and hence decisively influence states' internal structure and external behavior.[9] In fact, value and belief systems, including religions, today perform many of the roles that ideology performed in the past.[10]

This theory is certainly controversial.[11] Nevertheless, even in the postideological era, values, especially those of the ruling elite, do affect state behavior. It is necessary to assess their role relative to other determinants of state behavior. In Russia's case, the difficulty lies in the fact that since 1991, opinions have differed widely regarding the values that should guide the country's internal evolution and external behavior. The emerging consensus, at least within the Russian ethnic majority and in the context of the interaction between internal developments and external events, including the interface between Islam and Russia's Muslim and non-Muslim peoples, is still fragile. Therefore, it is not clear whether this consensus will be consolidated or, under the impact of internal and external events, altered.

Domestic Context: Political Systems and Public Attitude

F.S. Northedge wrote that foreign policy is a dialogue between the inside and the outside. In this view, domestic considerations significantly affect a state's external behavior.[12] An important aspect of this interplay is the way that foreign policy decisions affect public attitudes toward political leaders, especially when such decisions adversely impact the citizens' well being. Ultimately, even autocratic leaders cannot be oblivious to public attitudes. But the impact of popular attitudes on foreign policy differs widely within different political systems. The composition, character, and priorities of political elites and important interest groups—economic, ethnic, bureaucratic, and regional—are of even greater importance. The content and direction of foreign policy are often the result of either a compromise among these groups or the ascendancy of some over the others. Because different foreign policy orientations affect the interests of various interest groups, foreign policy–related intraelite disputes are often intense.

Russia's post-Soviet behavior is a good example of the impact of competition between established and emerging elites, notably new financial and industrial magnates, on the formulation and implementation of foreign policy. These intraelite disputes have been particularly intense in Russia because, according to Alexei Kara-Murza, "generally in Russia, a change in regime brings about a complete change in foreign policy priorities. And conversely, a reversal in foreign policy in Russia has usually precipitated a complete change of the political class."[13] Thus those who have won because of change want to retain their gains, and those who have lost want to regain their privileges or prevent their further erosion.

Although their relative impact has varied,[14] the most influential post-Soviet Russian interest groups have been the following: (1) ministries and government agencies that often have different foreign policy priorities; (2) the military-industrial complex; (3) export-oriented sectors, notably the energy sector; and (4) financial groups and certain key individuals with large financial and other interests, known as Russia's "oligarchs."[15] Other interest groups include some ethnic and religious lobbies and various nongovernmental organizations (NGOs), including human rights groups.

Diverging interests of these groups have affected Russia's approach toward different countries and issues. For example, the interests of military and nuclear industries, which benefit from sales to countries such as Iraq under Saddam Hussein and Iran, have partly shaped Russian policy toward these countries, although other, competing interests have limited their influence. The collective influence of Russia's pro-Israel lobby, certain key oligarchs, and, according to some sources, Tatarstan president Mintimer Shaimiev and some influential Azerbaijanis has prevented the full expansion of Russian-Iranian relations. At times, influential groups have pursued policies that diverge from that of the Russian Foreign Ministry, as LUKOIL did regarding Azerbaijan.[16]

The evolution of the Russian military's attitude toward the West and on other issues has impacted the state of Russian-Western relations. In the future, the extent of this impact will depend on the military's power within the Russian polity relative to other groups and other policy requirements.[17]

More important, the structure and basic characteristics of a country's political system deeply influence its foreign policy. In a presidential system with a weak legislature, the president's preferences determine the main elements of policy, whereas in systems in which the executive and legislative powers are more evenly distributed, the legislature exerts more—sometimes decisive—influence. In nontransparent political systems, narrowly based interest groups can exert disproportionate influence. However, with the exception of countries whose governments rely only on coercion, even the most powerful president or a combination of interest groups cannot conduct a foreign policy totally at odds with the most widely held public views. Nevertheless, strong leaders can shape public attitudes, especially in a country like Russia with a long tradition of belief in the abilities of charismatic leaders. In post-Soviet Russia, the impact of public preferences on foreign policy has been marginal.

Ends and Means: Resource Constraints and Their Consequences

The realization of a country's foreign policy aspirations requires political, economic, and military means. Countries with sizeable economic and military resources have a broader range of foreign policy options than those poorly endowed. Although the nature of today's international economic and financial system renders autarky impossible, countries with advanced technological bases, strong, diversified economies, and the ability to generate capital needed for economic development have greater ability to achieve their foreign policy goals. Through their actions, such countries largely determine the character of the international system, thereby influencing the policy choices of other actors and their ability to achieve them.

For sixty years, the Soviet Union pursued a policy of economic near autarky and developed vast and self-sufficient military power, which enabled it to pursue a foreign policy of global reach. The countervailing power of the United States and its allies, later coupled with the Chinese challenge, prevented the USSR from achieving its external goals, but the Soviet Union influenced virtually all major international issues and the foreign policies of other states, thus prompting Andrei Gromyko, the USSR's foreign minister (1957–85), to boast that no important international issue could be decided "without the Soviet Union or in opposition to it."[18] Indeed, "Moscow may not have had the power of veto over any and all international issues, but its conflict with the West was certainly felt in every corner of the world."[19] Furthermore, the USSR bought influence and clients, more or less on a par with the West, by providing economic and military assistance.

By the mid-1980s, the Soviet Union's deteriorating economic condition necessitated a process of reappraisal of Soviet foreign policy priorities, culminating in Mikhail Gorbachev's "New Thinking." In the post-Soviet era, Russia's deteriorating economic conditions, growing dependence on external official and private financial resources, and a shrinking military base have limited its policy choices and eroded its international influence. Resource constraints have made impossible such goals as reunifying the former Soviet space under Russian influence or pursuing a global diplomacy. These resource constraints are unlikely to be removed in the foreseeable future and, therefore, will continue to limit Russia's policy options.

The Impact of Systemic Factors

Foreign policy is also about managing a state's relations with the outside world to maximize gains and minimize losses. The perception of what constitutes gains and losses can change with alterations in a state's political structure, value system, collective identity, and priorities, but the basic function of foreign policy remains unaltered.

The external environment—the international system and regional subsystems—greatly determines states' policy choices and their ability to realize them because a state's policies are framed largely in response to the actions of other states and, increasingly, nonstate actors. The nature of the international system and the relative influence of its major actors are primarily determined by the way economic and military power is distributed. During the nineteenth century and the first half of the twentieth century, the international system was characterized by a multiplicity of power centers, nearly all based in Europe. With its entry into the First World War, the United States emerged as a major power center and a key international actor. European countries, and later the United States, controlled the destinies of the world, either directly through colonial rule or indirectly by establishing exclusive spheres of influence. By the end of the nineteenth century, the pattern of alliances and rivalries had become quite rigid and ultimately led to the outbreak of the First World War. The Russian Empire was one of these centers of power, and it was deeply engaged in imperial rivalries, including competition with Britain in Central Asia, the Middle East, and the Black Sea region.

Until the 1917 Bolshevik Revolution and, later, the rise of fascism and Nazism, international politics were determined by power rather than ideology. However, the United States did justify its entry into the First World War on the ideological grounds of "making the world safe for democracy." The First World War also marked the intrusion of what today is called "identity politics" into international relations through President Woodrow Wilson's introduction of the concept of national self-determination as the legitimate foundation of the state.

After the Second World War, dramatic changes in the international system—the expansion of the Soviet sphere of influence in Eastern Europe, the growth in Soviet power, the rise of anticolonial movements, the erosion of the major European actors' global role, and the accumulation of vast nuclear arsenals by the United States and the USSR—reduced the principal centers of power to two clusters of countries grouped around the USSR and the United States, thus giving rise to a bipolar system. International politics also became highly ideologized as the socialist USSR and its allies and the liberal capitalist West embarked on an existential battle to determine mankind's destiny. The East-West rivalry pervaded all major aspects of international life. By the 1960s, conflict between the rich North and the poor South began to impact international relations, although it remained subordinate to East-West competition.

Because of the socialist system's economic and political crisis, by 1987, the Soviet Union abandoned the ideological struggle with the West, thus transforming the climate of the international system. The Cold War's end greatly enhanced the West's and its allies' position and undermined that of their antagonists. This shift in power offered the West new possibilities for projecting its political and military power. The Persian Gulf War of 1991 reflected this systemic change.

The Soviet Union's subsequent disintegration and the rapid decline of Russia's economic and military power triggered another fundamental systemic change: they heralded the end of bipolarity and the beginning of the ascendancy of the West and, most important, the United States, thus creating what is often referred to as a "unipolar" system.[20] Dominance does not mean omnipotence, and sheer power is not always translatable into influence in the sense of "making others do what one wants them to do." Nevertheless, since the Soviet Union's collapse, the United States, either alone or with its allies, has exerted pervasive influence globally. Therefore, when other countries—at times, including some U.S. allies —have disagreed with U.S. policies, they have been unable to prevent their implementation.

However, few have been willing to jeopardize their relations with the United States over policy differences that involve third countries or broader systemic considerations. Thus, despite much talk about the risks of a "unipolar" world, including statements by some European leaders, notably French president Jacques Chirac, the desire to change this situation, even in the months after the Iraq War, has not been sufficiently strong to overcome other interests and prompt the creation of a counterweight to U.S. power. The end of the Cold War led to growing asymmetry in the interests of various countries, thereby introducing fluidity and complexity to regional and international alliances.

It is within this new international system and its constraints that Russia has tried to develop and implement its policies. New systemic factors have influenced the evolution of Russia's foreign policy doctrines and hence Russian polices. They have also limited the range of Russia's policy options.

Russia's Post-Soviet Foreign Policy Doctrines

The evolution of Russia's post-Soviet concepts of security and foreign policy began before the dissolution of the USSR with Mikhail Gorbachev's introduction of "New Thinking" (*Novoe myshlenie*). It stemmed from the same factors that produced perestroika and glasnost: the Soviet Union's economic crisis. Although the reason for its formulation was never stated by either Gorbachev or Soviet foreign minister Eduard Shevardnadze (1985–90), New Thinking followed a realization that the Soviet Union could not economically afford a policy of global reach and all-out competition with the West. The failure of some of the Soviet Union's more adventurous policies during the 1980s, such as its entanglement in Afghanistan, miscalculations about the direction of Iran's Islamic Revolution, and meager returns from past investments in the Third World, contributed to this process.[21] This record highlighted the shortcomings and, in some cases, disastrous consequences of an ideologically driven foreign policy.

Yet situational factors were not the only impetus behind New Thinking. Rather, as Alexander Dallin stated, "The success of New Thinking was greatly helped by a new generation of Soviet international affairs specialists and diplomats who during the preceding years had become acquainted with Western thinking and practice, and who had, continuously and sporadically, begun to integrate the lessons of this experience into their own worldview."[22] Other analysts assign a greater role to the Soviet leaders' learning process, especially during the Afghan War.[23] Although these factors were important, they took second place to domestic considerations, especially economic imperatives.

New Thinking evolved over time; therefore, it is difficult to present a coherent view of what it actually meant. Moreover, various Soviet analysts and policy makers interpreted it in different ways. Still, two tenets of the New Thinkers had the most far-reaching and lasting implications for Soviet and post-Soviet Russian foreign policy: the strengthening of the Soviet economy as the ultimate goal of foreign policy and the deideologization of Soviet foreign policy. Regarding the former, in addition to its domestic importance as the foundation of social well-being and political stability, a strong economy was important for international status. "Economic strength was proving more decisive than military strength in resolving many global issues. . . . [Thus], only by reversing its precipitous economic slide and establishing linkages to the international economy could the USSR qualify as a true 'superpower.' "[24] In the second case, deemphasizing ideology in foreign policy became necessary because Soviet foreign policy could no longer be guided by classic tenets of Marxism-Leninism, especially the notions that class struggle is the principal determinant of state behavior and that international relations constitute a zero-sum game.[25]

These were arguments for change, but they provided no clear guidance for the Soviet Union's post–Cold War foreign policy or for determining major threats to Soviet security in this new environment. Yevgenii Primakov, at the time the head of the Institute of World Economy and International Relations (IMEMO), maintained that Russia's foreign policy should be guided not by ideology, but by its traditional national interests. But there was no agreement on what these traditional interests were. However, the Soviet Union's policy priorities during the New Thinking period were to reduce tensions with the West, thus eliminating the need for large military expenditures, and to abandon costly entanglements in the Third World. The principal focus of New Thinking was to change the character of Soviet-Western relations. Policy changes toward various regions derived from this basic concern.

New Thinking and Islam

Statements regarding the main determinants of New Thinking and its principal goals made no reference to Islam, including the revolutionary type as practiced in Iran, which had not yet quite exhausted itself. Yet the Islamic factor played an important, albeit unacknowledged, role in changing Russia's thinking on foreign policy, both because the Soviet defeat in the Afghan War contributed to the reassessment of past policies and because resistance to the Soviet occupation in Afghanistan had been organized under Islam's banner and in close collaboration between a number of Muslim countries and the United States.

There was also concern that Islamist thinking could spread to the USSR's Muslim peoples and encourage proindependence sentiments among them. This perception of an Islamist threat enhanced the USSR's desire to improve relations with the West. Given the West's concern with some types of Islamic extremism, notably that practiced by Iran, the West became more responsive to Soviet overtures. Meanwhile, the USSR used the threat of Islamic extremism to limit Western criticism of its action in some of its Muslim republics, including sending troops into Baku in January 1990 following clashes between Azerbaijanis and Armenians under the pretext of preventing the spread of Islamic fundamentalism to the Caucasus.[26]

Kozyrev and Euro-Atlanticism

Although progressive for its time, New Thinking was the outcome of the Cold War and the competing-bloc system, plus the USSR's very nature as a multinational empire. Therefore, following the Soviet Union's collapse, debate began on a new foreign policy concept. Some questioned whether an overarching concept was needed. Russia's first foreign minister, Andrei Kozyrev, criticized what he described as "a habit of thinking in terms of blueprints," adding that the Russians seemed to "need Das Kapital or a CPSU program that gives a schematic answer to all questions. But there can be no blueprint. What exist are reactions to a specific situation, and those reactions display Russia's national interests. No country has an official description of its national interest."[27] These comments did not mean that Kozyrev had no opinions about the primary objectives of Russia's foreign policy or the principal paradigm defining post-Soviet international relations. He had strong views on both subjects, although, under pressure from other political groups and Russia's changing internal dynamics, he adjusted his opinions over time.

Debate about the broad concept of Russia's post-Soviet foreign policy is closely linked with the more important debate on its national identity. In the immediate aftermath of the Soviet collapse, the Westernizing pole of Russian tradition and its more recent variant dominated the debate. Consequently, the first foreign policy concept to become dominant in Russia was Euro-Atlanticism. This concept consisted of five principal components: (1) opposition to Islamic extremism in the South; (2) promotion of an external environment conducive to Russia's internal reforms; (3) restoration of Russia's status as a great power; (4) integration of Russia into the Western-dominated global order; and (5) preservation of Russia's role as a civilizing agent and preeminent power in Central Asia and the South Caucasus.

The South as a Source of Threat: Islamic Radicalism

According to the Euro-Atlanticists, confrontation between East and West was being replaced by confrontation between South and North.[28] This version of a North-South paradigm was different from that of the Cold War period; then, East and West competed for "hearts and minds" as well as for the South's (Third World) markets and resources. In its new version, the North-South paradigm meant that the rich North was increasingly threatened by the poor South through "migration, terrorism, Islamic fundamentalism, and even aggression from the developing countries in the south."[29]

Since Russia was adopting the same values as the West—democracy, market economy, and human rights—it would be subjected to similar threats.[30] The Euro-Atlanticists saw major threats to Russia's security emanating from ethnic and nationalist conflicts in the former Soviet Union (FSU) and the spread of Islamic radicalism within the Russian Federation and elsewhere in the FSU.[31] Since Islamic militancy was also posing a threat to the West, it could serve as an added argument for Russian-Western partnership. During the Russian-American honeymoon (1992–94), President Boris Yeltsin "proposed the creation of a joint political system for the northern industrial states [and] . . . called for the formation of a joint U.S.-Russian defense system (directed against potential aggressors in the south)."[32] In reality, this meant Muslim states, especially Iran, Afghanistan, and some other Middle Eastern countries. The Euro-Atlanticists perceived Russia as the front line of defense against the threat of Islamic radicalism, much as imperial Russia had been the eastern defensive front of Christianity against Muslim incursions.[33]

These ambitious schemes for a Russian-Western political and security alliance did not materialize. Euro-Atlanticism in its early, idealistic version lost its intellectual validity and operational influence. A number of events and corresponding Western policies extending from the Caucasus (Chechnya) to Bosnia, Kosovo, and Afghanistan created an impression and, among some Russians, a deep belief that somehow the West was playing the Islamic card, especially in relation to radical elements in Chechnya and Afghanistan (the Taliban), to undermine Russia's interests and even threaten its security.[34]

The Russians particularly resented the fact that the West did not see parallels between Russia's fight against what they saw as Islamic terrorism in the North Caucasus and the West's battle with the same phenomenon in other parts of the Muslim world. Prime Minister Vladimir Putin in an article in the *New York Times* titled "Why We Must Act" drew parallels with what Russia was doing in Chechnya and past U.S. antiterrorist acts:

> No government can stand idly by when terrorism strikes. It is the solemn duty of all governments to protect their citizens from danger. When two United States embassies in Africa were blown up, American warplanes were soon dispatched to bomb suspected terrorist facilities in Sudan and Afghanistan. . . . The same terrorists who were associated with the bombing of America's embassies have a foothold in the Caucasus. We know that Shamil Basaev, the so-called Chechen warlord, gets assistance on the ground from an itinerant guerilla leader with a dossier similar to that of Osama bin Laden.[35]

The idea that the common threat of Islamic radicalism could be used to develop converging U.S. and Russian approaches toward certain regions and countries reappeared in 2001, this time on the U.S. side. In an article, "What to Do with the New Russia," Henry Kissinger wrote:

> On the political plane, the challenge of Islamic fundamentalism is probably the dominant Russian concern. . . . America has its own concerns about the spread of fundamentalism toward Saudi Arabia, Pakistan, and into the Middle East. An effort should be made to achieve concurrent or at least compatible policies with Russia on the Middle East, including Central Asia, Afghanistan, Iran, and at least as far as Russia is concerned, the Balkans.[36]

However, the limitations of the threat of Islamic radicalism as the organizing principle of Russian-Western relations were apparent to both sides. Kissinger admitted this reality:

> There are limits beyond which neither country may be able to go. America cannot, in the name of opposition to Islamic fundamentalism, acquiesce in Russia's methods for suppressing upheavals in Chechnya. Nor can America be indifferent should Islamic fundamentalism become a pretext to force the newly-independent states of Central Asia back under Russian strategic domination.[37]

Domestic Primacy and External Environment

The Euro-Atlanticists believed that the first goal of Russia's foreign policy should be to create an external environment that would enable it to become a "democratic, market-oriented and civilized nation." A primary test of Russia's becoming a civilized state would be the living standards of its people.[38] During the two years following the collapse of the Soviet Union, the Euro-Atlanticists' view of the international environment as it affected Russia was essentially benign, and they saw threats to Russia as only coming from the South.

Russian International Integration

The Euro-Atlanticists believed in "the need to integrate Russia into the 'civilized world.' " Without this integration, achieving the second goal would not be possible. To become a member of what Kozyrev called a "special civilized club," Russia must subscribe to the universal values expressed in the United Nations Charter, the CSCE (later OSCE) Charter, and the Paris Charter of Human Rights. It should renounce the ideological vestiges of its past, tsarist and Soviet, and overcome any messianic temptations and "excessive Russian-ness."[39] In short, Russia must embrace Western culture in its totality.

A Normal but Great Power

Russia "needs to become a normal power, while remaining a great power." Thus it should continue to carry out the "historical responsibility" conferred on it by the fact of possessing nuclear weapons and a permanent seat on the United Nations Security Council.

Russia as Civilizer

"Russia should be a bridge and an agent of civilization." Even the Euro-Atlanticists could not escape from Russia's Eurasian geography, its historical legacy, and its sense of mission. Thus, despite their belief that Russia should abandon messianic ambitions, the Euro-Atlanticists saw Russia's role in Central Asia and the Caucasus as that of a "civilizer" and bridge, indeed, the "only" bridge between these regions and the West. According to Kozyrev, through its persistence and dynamism, Russia would transform these regions and thus enable them, over time, to become part of the civilized Euro-Atlanticist family.[40] Yevgeniy Gusarov openly spoke of an "enlightened Russian big brother."[41] The Euro-Atlanticists thought that Russia would perform this civilizing role in collaboration with the West. During their ascendancy, the West was willing to entrust Russia with a civilizing and stabilizing function in the Asian parts of the FSU. In sum, in Euro-Atlanticist thinking, two principal components of Russia's security strategy were (1) partnership and eventual alliance with the United States and Europe through confidence-building measures and disarmament, leading to a global security system "which stretches from Vladivostok to Vancouver," and (2) the creation and consolidation of the Commonwealth of Independent States (CIS) collective security structure under Russian leadership as part of this global system.[42]

This vision was reflected in the Charter of Russian-American Partnership and Friendship, signed in Washington on 17 July 1992.[43] However, Western support for a prominent Turkish role in this sphere and Western promotion of the so-called Turkish model of development in the Muslim republics of the FSU inevitably diluted Russia's role in this envisaged Russian-Western partnership. Moreover, the CIS countries increasingly began to pursue independent foreign policies and, in the process, established direct ties to various international and regional actors and refused to surrender to Russia their representation in the global system. Later, other developments made the realization of this vision problematic.

Eurasianism and the Quest for a Multipolar World

The Euro-Atlanticists had an unrealistic expectation of how effectively and quickly joining the West would help Russia solve its economic, political, and cultural problems, accumulated over several decades. Because of their unrealism, they were doomed to disappointment. In turn, disillusionment with the effectiveness of a West-centered foreign policy opened the way for other views to gain credence and acceptance with policy-making elites and the population.

Main Criticisms of the Euro-Atlanticist School

The failure of the Euro-Atlanticist school to realize its principal objectives led to widespread criticism of its proponents and their policy prescriptions. The most serious attacks on the Euro-Atlanticists are listed here.

Naïveté and Idealism. The Euro-Atlanticists' view of a Russian-Western partnership was "naïve." The end of the Cold War and ideological conflict had not eliminated other motives of state behavior, most important, national interest. Therefore, the West would act on the basis of its own interests and not those of Russia. Moreover, these interests might not always coincide. Additionally, the Euro-Atlanticist vision of the West was too idealized and approached romanticism, as demonstrated by ardent Euro-Atlanticists who acted on the unrealistic assumption of the convergence of Russian-Western interests. Some critics believed that Euro-Atlanticism had developed into a dogmatic ideology with global applications. According to Andranik Migranyan,

> In effect Kozyrev and the other Russian leaders replaced one ideological postulate, the Marxist-Leninist one, in accordance with which it was necessary to bring about the expansion of the Soviet model everywhere in the world and counteract the policy of the U.S. and the West in all respects, with another ideological postulate, one in accordance with which, following the elimination of the CPSU and the Marxist-Leninist ideology, a complete unity of goals and values exists between the U.S. and the West and Russia.[44]

Clearly, Migranyan did not agree with this postulate. These critics, in particular, doubted that the West wanted Russia to be strong. Ednan Agayev warned that the West was not interested in a strong Russia.[45]

Inequality. Euro-Atlanticist policy was too "concessionary" toward the West and hence "unequal" in nature since rewards for Russian concessions were small.

According to Migranyan, in exchange for all their concessions, Gorbachev and Shevardnadze received "symbolic sums of assistance, idle talk, noisy applause and friendly pats on the shoulder . . . [and] the Russian Ministry of Foreign Affairs inherited this foreign policy from the Union ministry."[46]

Lack of National Mission. Sergei Stankevich, onetime state counselor to Boris Yeltsin, was one of the first analysts to raise the issue of a lack of national mission. Writing in *National Interest* in 1992, he noted that frequent and categorical assertions had been made that Russia must renounce messianism and that pragmatism should be the leading principle of its foreign policy. However, "Pragmatism not balanced by healthy idealism would with us [the Russians], alas, most likely degenerate into extremes and cynicism. Russia's foreign policy must provide for goals and tasks elevated above opportunistic pragmatism."[47] In other words, Stankevich believed that Russia needs a "mission," although care must be taken that this sense of mission does not degenerate into "messianism."[48]

If one accepts Henry Kissinger's analysis that for most of its history, Russia "has been a cause looking for an opportunity," then Stankevich's view that Russia needs a mission does not sound unrealistic.[49] Russia's mission should be "to initiate and support a multilateral dialogue of cultures, civilizations, and states." This is "Russia the conciliator, Russia connecting, Russia combining; . . . a country imbibing West and East, North and South, unique and exclusively capable, perhaps, of the harmonious combination of many different principles of a symphonic harmony."[50]

Inadequate Attention to the South and East. Another criticism directed at Euro-Atlanticists was that they did not pay enough attention to the former Soviet republics, their Muslim neighbors, and the East, especially China. For the critics of Euro-Atlanticism, this neglect was dangerous both from a foreign policy perspective and in terms of Russia's domestic concerns. Sergei Goncharov pointed out "that in the event of a North-South conflict Russia and not the West-European community would become the target of attack since Russia, unlike Western Europe and the United States, has common borders with the South."[51]

These critics also noted that overidentification with Western policies would alienate China and the Islamic world. According to Stankevich, there was a domestic angle to this criticism as well, namely, the need for Russia to "search for accord, mutual understanding and cooperation with the Turkic and Muslim components which have performed a tremendous role in the history of Russia."[52]

Criticism of the Euro-Atlanticist school and, specifically, the way Andrei Kozyrev had interpreted and implemented it came from a variety of sources. These critics ranged from what Margot Light has characterized as "pragmatic nationalists"—equivalent to "reform nationalists"—to "fundamentalist nationalists," a category that covers a wide spectrum, including people with traditional pan-Slavist leanings.[53] These criticisms affected the evolution of Russian foreign policy in both theory and practice for most of Kozyrev's tenure as foreign minister. But the most coherent alternative to the Euro-Atlanticist theory was offered by the Eurasianist school.

Intellectual Underpinnings of the Eurasianist School

The ideas of the Eurasianist school have at times echoed traditional Eurasianist views of Russian history and identity. However, the new Eurasianists' philosophy is not the same as traditional Eurasianism, nor does it subscribe to the polarized vision of Alexander Dugin's Eurasianism, which is informed by the principle of irreconcilable differences between continental (Eurasian) and sea or island (Atlantic) powers and civilizations. The new Eurasianist school of foreign policy is essentially inspired by the realist theory of international relations and a desire to retain Russia's great-power status, even if it is diminished.

Foreign Policy and Russian Statehood.   The Eurasianists, too, see the creation of a favorable external environment that would enable Russia to pursue internal reforms as a primary purpose of Russian foreign policy. However, they differ in their conception of reform and requirements for its success.[54] They believe that a major precondition for the success of reform is the reassertion of Russian statehood. In their view, because the Soviet Union's collapse ruptured Russia's historic notion of statehood, foreign policy must play a role in shaping its post-Soviet sense of statehood. Sergei Stankevich, after noting that post-Soviet Russia does not yet have the attributes of statehood and a clearly formulated system of national interests, argued that "foreign policy practice frequently based on search, analogies and intuition is helping Russia become Russia. Dealings with the surrounding world are helping shape Russian statehood and helping Russia recognize its interests."[55] In short, according to the Eurasianists, there is a dynamic and mutually supportive interaction between a more assertive and realist Russian foreign policy and the strengthening of its statehood.

Interests over Ideals.   According to Eurasianists, even in the post-Soviet era, interstate relations are determined by the pursuit of interests rather than ideals, and they are influenced by perennial determinants of state behavior, notably geopolitics. In 1993, the speaker of the Russian Parliament, Ruslan Khasbulatov, expressed this view when he asserted:

> We [Russians] must always bear in mind that the struggle for economic and political influence is continuing in the world. There remains a complex hierarchy of relations conditioned by the real power of this or that country, even if the struggle may have taken a more civilized as well as a more complicated form than before.[56]

The Eurasianists emphasize the importance of geopolitical factors and argue that Russia's geopolitical realities demand a multidimensional policy that is not disproportionately focused on the West. Yevgenii Primakov was an early proponent of recognizing the importance of geopolitical factors in shaping Russia's foreign policy. He believed that Russia could not be a great power if its foreign policy was not geopolitically expansive and globally encompassing not only the United States and Europe, but also China, India, Japan, the Middle East, and the Third World.[57]

Russia's Cultural Superiority or Equality with the West? Ardent Euro-Atlanticists consider Western civilization superior to that of Russia. This view is explicit in Kozyrev's frequent calls for Russia to join the club of civilized nations. His early statements are reminiscent of the views of nineteenth-century ultra-Westernizers, some of whom saw little merit in Russian culture. The Eurasianists recognize that Russia could benefit from some aspects of Western civilization, but believe that Russian civilization, with its spiritual dimension, is superior to the West's materialistic culture.[58] This belief lies behind the Eurasianists' sense of Russia's mission.

The Eurasianists, however, are not inherently anti-West, nor do they underestimate the importance for Russia of good relations with the West. But they favor a more balanced foreign policy that also encompasses relations with China, other Pacific Rim countries, the former Soviet republics, and Muslim countries of the Middle East and South Asia. Initially, the more nationalist Eurasianists argued that the former Soviet republics should be declared Russia's exclusive sphere of influence. Andranik Migranyan wrote, "It seems to me that Russia should declare to the world that the entire geopolitical space of the former USSR is a sphere of its vital interests."[59] Likewise, Yevgenii Ambartsumov advocated that Russia should develop its own version of a Monroe Doctrine in the post-Soviet space.[60] Such exclusivist ideas have proved to be unrealizable and have thus lost most of their attraction and credibility. Russia is now mainly concerned with maintaining a sufficient presence and influence in the FSU. However, Eurasianist influence is felt in Russia's foreign policy, although the term Eurasianism is not used. Instead, reference is made to Russia's "multidimensional" or—in Russian foreign minister Igor Ivanov's words—"multivector" foreign policy.[61]

Eurasianists and Islam. Various Eurasianist schools have had different and at times contradictory perceptions of Islam. Moreover, their views have changed in response to developments in the Muslim world, especially the evolution of ideological trends within Islam and developments within Russia's own Muslim regions.

In many respects, the Eurasianist view of Islam has not been much different from that of the Euro-Atlanticists. The Eurasianists also fear the prospect of Russia facing a Turko-Muslim front. Consequently, they have been concerned about growing links between the former Soviet Muslim republics and neighboring countries. They are also concerned about the threat of extremist Islam and its expansion into the former Soviet republics and the Russian Federation.

What distinguishes the Eurasianists from the Euro-Atlanticists in dealing with Islam and the Muslim world are their tactics. The Eurasianists emphasize Russia's geopolitical imperative to focus on the Muslim world, especially the former Soviet republics and immediate neighbors. They are also conscious of the long history of Russian/Soviet ties with the Islamic world and believe that this investment, as put by Alexei Malashenko, should not be allowed to "melt" away.[62] The Eurasianists maintain that, for the foreseeable future, Russia, in Malashenko's words, "is doomed to play the role of a loved but bankrupt 'distant relative' of the West. The fate of 'second class Europeans' for Russians, apparently, is unavoidable." Therefore, the Eurasianists conclude that Russia must have a more nuanced and independent policy toward the Islamic world. According to Malashenko, "The Russian approach to Islam should not be comparable or equal to that of the Americans or Europeans."[63] Alexei Vassiliev asserts that "equating Russia's interests with those of the United States is fraught with many dangers. One of these is a threat to Russia's position in the Moslem world."[64] Therefore, they advise that Russia should not join the West in an anti-Islamic front. Malashenko notes that this is the wrong approach because many Muslim states are friends of America and Americans "are actually trying to find the common language with the Muslim peoples. This is especially noticeable when it comes to the activities of American diplomats in the Muslim regions of the Commonwealth of Independent States."[65] Eurasianists believe that in certain cases, Russia should use tensions in the West's relations with the Muslim world to further its own interests and in general view the Muslim world as a "potential, if not a necessary friend."[66]

The influence of this school began to be felt as early as late 1992, and even Kozyrev adopted many of its precepts, especially regarding Russia's special role in the CIS.[67] However, the Eurasianists' views of a potential Russian-Muslim grand alliance proved as naïve as the vision of a total convergence of Russian-Western interests. Two factors doomed such an alliance: the dynamics of Russia's Muslim population, most notably demonstrated by the Chechen War, and the West's superior presence in the Muslim world. In some cases, it appeared that there was more Western-Muslim cooperation against what, by 1994, looked like a reappearance of Russia's imperial impulse than Russian-Muslim coalition building against the West. This was true of U.S.-Turkish and U.S.-Pakistani collaboration in the Caucasus and Central Asia. Some Russians, in fact, believed that the West was playing the Muslim card to undermine Russia's position in the Caucasus and Central and South Asia.

Primakov and the Quest for a Multipolar World

A primary concern of those who did not embrace the Euro-Atlanticists' vision was that the West was attempting to "use the disintegration of the former Soviet Union in order to create a unipolar structure of the world." This structure was lacking in balance because it attempted "to reduce world order to the priority of the United States' objectives" and was therefore inherently destabilizing.[68] The conclusion was that counterweights should be developed to "counter-balance the destabilizing factors."[69]

Initially, it was thought that the CIS could be transformed into something akin to the European Union and NATO and thus could provide such a counterforce. Kozyrev tried to turn the CIS into a regional organization with a security dimension on the basis of Article 51 of the United Nations Charter, but the CIS's failure on nearly all fronts made this an inadequate solution to the post-Soviet disequilibrium in the international power equation.[70]

Realizing the limits of a CIS-based strategy, Russia adopted multipolarity—dubbed the "Primakov Doctrine" in the West because of his role in promoting it—as the principal framework for its foreign policy.[71] But it would be a mistake to see the concept of multipolarity solely as Primakov's brainchild. Rather, pro-Western analysts, politicians, and journalists also had accepted the idea that Russia should pursue a policy based on "a more balanced interaction on all directions." This is evident in the fourth and final draft of Russia's Strategy to the XXI Century, prepared by the Council on Foreign and Defense Policy.[72]

The essence of multipolarity is to create a counterweight to America's predominance and to limit its ability to act unilaterally on international issues and to set rules of conduct for all countries. Of course, multipolarity need not be anti-American in the sense of posing a security threat to the United States or being antagonistic to all U.S. interests. Rather, as Peter Rodman has pointed out, it reflects the natural tendency of international actors to try to balance the influence of an actual or potential dominant power. America's unease has ideological roots, namely, "the traditional Wilsonian bent" of its foreign policy. Since America believes that it is acting "in the name of universal moral principles," it becomes "genuinely puzzled" when others see its assertiveness as unilateralism. Yet the "fact is that the rest of the world is reacting to American power in thoroughly classical, un-Wilsonian balance of power fashion."[73]

Nor is the quest for greater balance in power relations limited to Russia, China, or some Middle East countries concerned about American predominance. Rather, America's European allies, too, are uncomfortable with the current configuration of power. Thus during French president Jacques Chirac's visit to China in May 1997, France and China signed a joint "Declaration on the Establishment of a Comprehensive Partnership," that stated: "Both parties have decided to engage in reinforced cooperation, to foster the march towards multipolarity, to support efforts to create wealth and well-being, on the basis of respecting plurality and independence . . . and to oppose any attempt at domination in international affairs."[74] Nevertheless, it has been Russia that has most tried to redress the imbalance in the international system.

Objectives and Instruments of the Strategy of Multipolarity

There are four key objectives in the Russian strategy of multipolarity. First, limit U.S. ability for unilateral action and reduce its international predominance. In particular, the multipolar strategy challenges the U.S. right to delegitimize and internationally isolate countries, either because it disapproves of their policies or has difficult relations with them. Thus in his speech to the fifty-second General Assembly of the United Nations in September 1997, Primakov stressed Russia's strong support for the campaign against terrorism and then stated, "Individual U.N. member states should not be stigmatized forever as international rogues irrespective of changes in their policies or simply because of suspected links to terrorists."[75]

Second, counter Western belief in the universal applicability of its economic, political, and cultural model. This Russian goal was reflected in the statement issued following Chinese president Jiang Zemin's visit to Moscow in April 1996: "People of every country have the right to independently choose, in light of their respective national conditions and free from outside interference, their social system and course and mode of development."[76] On various occasions, President Yeltsin echoed the themes developed by Primakov, even going so far as to endow the concept with a moral quality. In an interview with the Italian newspaper *Corriere della Sera*, Yeltsin said:

> We don't see multipolarity as a utilitarian means to achieve some kind of aim. . . . A multipolar world is the wisest and most democratic system for the world. Only in such a world will all countries regardless of the size of their military power have a voice and preserve their unique character. . . . Attempts by some countries to force a unipolar model, in other words, their exclusive leading role on the world are unrealistic and perhaps even dangerous.[77]

Third, increase Russia's international weight and its involvement and influence in managing international affairs. This strategy aimed to render Russia more relevant in managing and resolving regional conflicts beyond those in its immediate proximity, especially the Arab-Israeli conflict. In his speech to the fifty-second session of the United Nations General Assembly on 23 September 1997, Primakov stated, "In the present day world, no country should hold a monopoly on any conflict resolution effort. This fully applies to the longest-standing conflict in the Middle East, where the settlement process has been stalemated."[78]

The final objective of Russia's strategy of multipolarity is to provide a more congenial atmosphere and environment for Russia's international and trade activities.

In the view of Russian supporters of a multipolar world, the principal instrument for pursuing it is development of a close Sino-Russian strategic alliance, to be joined by India.[79] At some point, the EU could also play a role in building this multipolar world, and Russia certainly has encouraged Europe to move in this direction.[80]

Multipolarity and Islam

The potential role of the Islamic world in building this multipolar world is ambiguous. According to Western observers critical of this concept, Iran is an important, albeit "junior," partner in its creation.[81] Some Russian analysts, too, early on talked of a Russia-China-Iran triangle.[82] The concept of a multipolar world is attractive to Iran, especially the more conservative elements who oppose U.S.-Iranian reconciliation.[83] Yet Russia has been ambivalent about including Iran in its multipolar schemes. Thus, despite frequent visits to Moscow by the highest-ranking Iranian officials, including two presidents, and despite Iran's eagerness for a return visit by President Yeltsin or even prime ministers Viktor Chernomyrdin or Yevgenii

Primakov, there have been no high level Russian visits to Iran, whereas Presidents Yeltsin and Putin both visited China and India.[84] A principal reason for this ambivalence is U.S.-Iranian animosity and Russia's fears that granting Iran a prominent role in its projected multipolar structure could antagonize the United States unduly and damage Russia's other interests. Moreover, while Moscow has been conscious of Iran's prudent behavior in the Caucasus and Central Asia and its collaboration with Moscow in settling such difficult issues as the Tajik Civil War, some Russian leaders are still suspicious of Iran because of its Islamic ideology. Some powerful interest groups are also anti-Iran.

Because of long-standing and close ties with Iraq during the Soviet era, under different circumstances, Iraq would have been a more acceptable partner in this multipolar structure, but Iraq's being under international sanctions made such a partnership unlikely. Following Iraq's occupation by U.S. and British forces and the establishment of America's controlling influence in determining Iraq's future, this option became totally unrealizable. More generally, providing a significant role to any Muslim country in a multipolar system would be problematic because of shared concern by Russia, China, and India over what they view as extremist Islam but that, in reality, includes any form of Islamic assertiveness or quest for self-determination among Muslim minorities. Post-Soviet Russia's close ties to Israel also argue against an Islamic component to multipolarity.

In the Russian vision of multipolarity, multilateral and international organizations, such as the OSCE and the United Nations also occupy important places because within such institutions Russia can exert influence and check American unilateralism. Even if it cannot prevent unilateral U.S. operations, it can at least work to reduce their international legitimacy.

*Limits of the Multipolar Strategy and Putin's Foreign
Policy Vision*

For the best part of his first two years as president, Vladimir Putin continued to pursue the foreign policy line developed by Primakov. On trips to places including Cuba, China, India, and Venezuela, he continued to emphasize the theme of multipolarity.[85] He also took concrete steps, most important, the signing of the Sino-Russian Treaty of Friendship in July 2001. Some Western commentators interpreted this agreement as intended to send a message to the United States that if it continued to pursue global supremacy, it would compel "closer Chinese-Russian security cooperation."[86]

While on the surface multipolarity seemed to dominate Russian foreign policy, in reality. by the time of Putin's presidency, its limits had already become apparent, and many Russian experts and ex-officials were criticizing its usefulness in formulating and securing Russian interests. Sergei Karaganov suggested:

> The concept of multipolarity presupposes an active foreign policy on all fronts. On the whole this approach is largely consistent with Russia's interests, but it

also has some serious flaws. It is not economical, it strains Russia's very meager diplomatic and other resources and it compels our country to pursue the policies of a global power at a time when it remains a declining regional power. Was it really necessary for us to become involved in the Yugoslav conflict with the resources we had at that time? What did we gain from our maneuvering over Iraq?[87]

Some sources claim that these criticisms were inspired by Putin himself: while talking the language of multipolarity, he was developing a new concept of Russia's foreign policy. According to Georgy Kunadze:

There is a group of self-styled political scientists in Russia whose main ambition is to always say whatever government wants to hear and whose main talent is the capacity to anticipate forthcoming policy changes by getting advance notice from government sources. At the start of the Yeltsin era they vigorously promoted the idea of Russia's convergence with the West. In former Prime Minister Yevgeny Primakov's heyday they strongly advocated multipolarity as an instrument to restore Russia's world status. With the same zeal and conviction they now criticize multipolarity, favoring austerity and selective engagement instead. So the new foreign policy as envisaged by Putin must be real.[88]

Limitations of the Multipolar Paradigm

Two major limitations of the multipolar paradigm were its cost and its ineffectiveness. During the period of Primakov's stewardship of Russia's foreign policy (January 1996 through September 1999), Russia did not reap any tangible benefits from the pursuit of multipolarity, although there may have been some temporary psychological gratification from the outward activism of Russian diplomacy and verbal sparring with the United States.[89] For example, Russia's strenuous objections to NATO's expansion yielded no results, and in July 1997, Poland, Hungary, and the Czech Republic were invited to join the alliance. Nor did Russia succeed in shaping events in the former Yugoslavia or the direction of Western policy there. Russia's activities in the Middle East also yielded meager results. Its decision in 1999 to provide Cyprus with an S-300 antimissile system caused a serious crisis between Turkey and Cyprus, leading Turkey to threaten that it would attack the missiles if they were installed. Under U.S. and European pressure, Cyprus abandoned this policy, embarrassing itself and Russia.[90]

Russian activities in pursuit of a multipolar world were interpreted as signs of neoimperial behavior or the resurrection of Cold War mentality and rhetoric. For example, an American analyst observed that the "Joint Russian-Chinese Declaration on a Multipolar World and the Formation of a New International Order," signed in Moscow on 23 April 1997, had "a hint of the old anti-imperialist rhetoric."[91]

Systemic Factors: Discrepancy in Economic and Military Power

The unrealistic character and ineffectiveness of the multipolar strategy derived from two sets of factors: the nature of the post–Cold War international system and the asymmetrical and often contradictory nature of interests among those countries that wanted to create a new world order in which political power is more evenly distributed. Today's international system is characterized by an overwhelming discrepancy between the combined economic and military power of the West and that of the rest of the world. Within the Western bloc, both because of the size of its economy and because of its ability to project its military power to nearly every corner of the world, unilaterally if need be, the United States occupies a special place.

This situation imposes significant costs on nations that want to defy the United States. For example, despite its many differences with the United States, China has been eager to avoid all-out confrontation. To a large extent, China depends on U.S. markets and investments. In 2001, Chinese exports to the United States amounted to $94.87 billion, while the United States exported only $17.32 billion to China.[92] In 2001, U.S. direct investment in China equaled $4.43 billion.[93] By contrast, in October 2001, the volume of Sino-Russian trade was only $10.67 billion. Moreover, Russia has virtually no investment in China; indeed, Russia is a competitor for such funds.[94] The United States has a large military presence in the Pacific region and close military and political relations with such countries as Taiwan, Japan, and South Korea, with which China has difficulties and rivalries. Thus China is limited in pressing for a multipolar world if this meant confrontation with the United States.

India is in similar circumstances. Although the volume of U.S.-Indian trade is still relatively small, the United States is an important export market. In 2000, India's total exports to the United States amounted to $9.1 billion.[95] However, the level of U.S. direct investment in India is small and in 2000 was only $336 million.[96]

By contrast, nonarms trade between Russia and India in 2000 was only $1.5 billion. In 1999, total Russian investment in India was only $32 million and Indian investment in Russia a mere $10 million.[97] Nor is the trend toward rapid increase, although there has been some Indian investment in the Russian oil and gas sectors.[98] India, too, has to be mindful of America's military might, notably its presence in the Indian Ocean/Persian Gulf region. More important, since the late 1990s, there has been considerable warming of U.S.-Indian ties, leading some Indian commentators to argue that India should form a strategic alliance with the United States, for both economic and strategic reasons. According to Satish Kumar, "There is also a growing convergence of American national security objectives with those of India in what New Delhi calls its 'extended neighborhood'—the Persian Gulf, Central Asia and South East Asia."[99]

Europe, meanwhile, has extensive economic and trade ties with the United States that argue against ambitions to help create a multipolar world. Europe and the United States are also strategic partners within NATO. No doubt, the EU would like to have some increased foreign policy and defense latitude, expressed through its Common Foreign and Security Policy (CFSP) and European Security and Defense Policy (ESDP), but European reliance on U.S. political and strategic capacities, beyond Europe as well as within it, will continue for the foreseeable future.[100]

In short, all these countries and groups have much more to lose than to gain from confrontation or geopolitical competition with the United States This does not mean that Washington can dictate to them or that they lack any means of influencing U.S. policies. It does mean that they are unlikely to jeopardize concrete interests for the sake of trying to alter a skewed international balance of power. Vladimir Lukin, a former Russian ambassador and a member of the State Duma, graphically explained this hesitance on the part of potential partners when he stated that the multipolar strategy failed because there were "no fools to follow us."[101]

Contradictory Interests and Deep-Rooted Misgivings

The constraining impact of systemic factors on implementing a multipolar strategy is compounded by conflicting interests, mutual misgivings, and animosities among the three countries required to construct a multipolar system. Influential groups and personalities in Russia have either negative feelings toward China or see it more as a threat or at least a competitor than as a strategic ally.[102]

Within the Russian political spectrum, the Westernizing Atlanticists and the ultranationalists are the most opposed to a Russian-Chinese alliance. The Westernizers' opposition derives from China's still economically underdeveloped and nondemocratic state. According to Yegor Gaidar, Russia finds itself between the "democratic" West and "poor, nondemocratic" countries of the East. He believes that China will not become a stable and prosperous country in the foreseeable future. Therefore, Russia's chosen Asian partner should be Japan.[103] Andrei Kozyrev objects to the idea because in many areas, especially in attracting Western investments, China is a main competitor for Russia and has played the Russian card to obtain concessions from the West.[104]

The ultranationalists' opposition is based on their belief that China is bound to pursue expansionist policies, especially toward the Russian Far East.[105] They are also concerned about China's demographic challenge.

Other Russian officials who do not fall within either category have also identified China as a major threat to Russia. Russian defense minister Igor Rodionov, in a speech in December 1996, included China among major threats to Russian security, an assessment for which Primakov rebuked him.[106]

In view of the imbalance of power with China, Russia's principal attraction for Beijing—its sophisticated arms and military technology—is a double-edged sword that can be used against Russia. Georgy Kunadze argues that Russia would be unwise to provide China with weapons and technology that could be potentially dangerous to Russia.[107]

These feelings of ambivalence are not surprising, as demonstrated by the fact that following the Sino-Soviet split in 1958, Russia and China were sworn enemies for more than thirty years. The pre-Soviet history of Sino-Russian relations was also deeply troubled. China has resented Russia's territorial expansion at its expense through what it characterizes as "unequal treaties," similar to concessions China was earlier forced to make to Western powers.

Indian-Chinese Suspicions

A further complicating factor in building the strategic triangle of Russia, China, and India is continued mutual suspicions between China and India and their rivalry for influence in Asia. The long-standing border dispute between the two countries continues, and India is concerned that "a significant increase in its [China's] economic and military might may lead to China throwing its weight around in its bid to seek an advantageous position and settlement of disputed issues in its favour."[108] China's close relations with Pakistan present a further obstacle to partnership between India and China, and they are also potential rivals for Central Asia's resources and markets.

Islamic Threat

The only issue on which there seems to be a meeting of minds among Russia, China, and India is the threat of Islamic extremism in South and Central Asia and the need for collaboration to defeat it. This has played a key role in enhancing both Sino-Russian and Indo-Russian collaboration. However, with the elimination of the Taliban regime in Afghanistan in the aftermath of the 11 September 2001 terrorist attacks in the United States, the Islamic threat as a unifying factor in building a multipolar world may be a wasting asset.[109] In fact, the U.S. military intervention in Afghanistan has altered many of the strategic dynamics of the multipolar strategy, especially its Russian component, by fostering a U.S-Russian rapprochement.

Putin's Vision: A More Pragmatic and Multifaceted Strategy

The official basis of Russia's foreign policy is "The Foreign Policy Concept of the Russian Federation," developed by the Foreign Ministry in June 2000. As could be expected from such a document, it has a general tone. Nevertheless, because of the issues and areas emphasized, it does indicate elements both of continuity and change in Russian foreign policy under Vladimir Putin.[110] Changes have become more pronounced since the concept was adopted and reflect Putin's personality and priorities, external events, and basic constraints of Russian diplomacy. An important underpinning of Putin's foreign policy philosophy is pragmatism. Russia's foreign policy should not be guided by any particular ideology nor be influenced by "emotional and historical sympathies and antipathies."[111] This aspect of Putin's philosophy may be attributed to Russia's experience during the Yugoslav crisis, as the Afghan experience had contributed to the New Thinking.

Multipolarity Out, Globalization In

Early in his presidency, although President Putin continued to use the language of multipolarity, he was never ideologically committed to it. By the time he assumed office, the strategy's limits had become evident. Aleksei Pushkov summed up the strategy's failure:

> By the end of the Kosovo Conflict, it was clear that pursuing a policy of coun-
> terbalancing excessive American power, as justified as that policy may have been,
> was by no means fully within our capability. . . . By the late 1990s, it was also
> clear that we had nothing substantial with which to counter NATO's steady move-
> ment Eastwards. The notion of a Moscow–New Delhi–Beijing triangle expired
> *in utero.*[112]

Nevertheless, until the events of 11 September 2001 and the ensuing changes, Russia continued to talk about creating a new international order, as developed in its official foreign policy documents, but it dropped the term "multipolarity." In November 2001, the Council on Foreign and Defense Policy issued a document signed by Yevgenii Primakov, the architect of multipolarity, and others advising that Russia should drop this strategy and instead focus on globalization and what it means for Russia.[113] In practice, however, Russia would need to follow a variant of the multipolar strategy by making ad hoc alliances with key players such as China whenever this would be both necessary and possible to advance Russian interests.[114]

President Putin seems more interested in the process of globalization at various levels, especially the economic one, and its implications for Russia. Putin seems to have learned that Russia must become part of the global economy and its major institutions, especially the World Trade Organization (WTO). Thus, as Vyacheslav Nikomov has described, "integrationism" is a major part of Putin's foreign policy thinking.[115]

Primacy of Economic Issues

Putin is fully aware that none of Russia's other ambitions can be achieved without reviving its economy. Thus a major purpose of Russian diplomacy must be to attract foreign investment and create lucrative business opportunities for Russia. Some Russian analysts, notably Sergei Markov, have noted that the preoccupation with economic concerns sometimes becomes excessive. According to Markov, making economic "rentability" a primary objective of foreign policy at times "assumes an outwardly grotesque appearance. Witness Vladimir Putin traveling all over the world and offering everyone Russian weapons systems in exchange for debts. Quite saliently this has transpired in relations with post-Soviet countries. What is required of them now is not support for Russian initiative but debt repayments."[116]

Russian Independence and Delinking Diplomatic Relations and Domestic Policies

Vladimir Putin does promote the traditional concept of independence and "noninterference in internal affairs," which is embodied in the United Nations Charter.

Thus he does not accept the idea that "any country can or should dictate to Russia how to build its policy and relations with other countries."[117] Of course, in Putin's parlance, this principle relates primarily to the United States, which has often chided Russia for its relations with such so-called rogue states as Iran, Iraq, Cuba, and North Korea. Even more important, Putin "wants to limit foreign 'interference' in domestic affairs. Putin considers the criticism of Russia's military involvement in Chechnya and of the state of the press in Russia to be groundless and unjust."[118]

Centrality of Europe

Despite official—most likely opportunistic—bows to Russia's historic and unique traditions in elaborating his notion of Russia's national identity, Putin sees Russia as first and foremost a European country and wants it to become more integrated with Europe. This is partly explained by the fact that Putin grew up in St. Petersburg, the great symbol of Russia's drive to become European. His professional experience was also in Europe (East Germany). But there are also pragmatic economic and political reasons for his orientation. Economically, Europe is a major trading partner for Russia and the largest source of financial assistance and foreign investment. Germany is the single largest investor in Russia. Meanwhile, Europe has become an increasingly important market for Russian oil and gas. Already, Germany's imports of Russian oil are higher than its imports from Organization of Petroleum-Exporting Countries (OPEC) members.[119]

Further, viewed in a realistic light, Europe is the only "pole" of international economic and political power that could accommodate Russia. As Jury Sigor has put it, "With proper assistance Russia will find its new identity if it fully integrates into a 'Big Europe.' There is no reason or chance that Moscow could ever be incorporated into a 'Big China' or a 'Big United States.' "[120] Moreover, since no single country dominates Europe and the EU is still in the process of political construction, Russia would not have to be concerned about being the junior partner in any relationship with Europe.

There are, however, certain characteristics of the EU and Russia that may make a complete integration difficult. Paramount among these are Russia's geography and European requirements on human and minority rights. Europe is unlikely to relish having common borders with China, and European human rights instruments may prove intrusive for Russian tastes. Moreover, better relations with the United States may reduce Europe's attraction, at least in the short term. Some U.S. and Russian analysts have suggested that in the post–11 September world, growing tensions between the United States and Europe, combined with more cooperative U.S.-Russian ties, could form the basis of a long-term and broad Russian-American partnership.[121] U.S.-Russian disagreement over the Iraq War dampened these expectations.

Ambivalence toward the United States or Renewed Partnership after 11 September?

By the time Putin assumed office, Russian-American relations had cooled considerably. This trend continued after January 2001, when the new Republican administration adopted a less compromising attitude toward Russia. It appeared that the two countries could face a difficult period in their relations. These anxieties were somewhat eased when Vladimir Putin and George W. Bush met in Slovenia in June 2001. But it was the 11 September 2001 terrorist attacks on the World Trade Center in New York and the Pentagon in Washington that provided Putin with a sudden opportunity to improve relations. Some in Russia viewed this event as providing a "second chance . . . to change our [Russian-U.S.] relations and the way we see each other."[122]

Three factors—the sympathy created for the United States following the September 2001 tragedy; the U.S. need to gain collaboration of as many countries as possible in its war against Osama bin Laden, Al-Qaeda, and the Taliban regime; and Russia's considerable influence with Central Asian countries and the Afghan Northern Alliance—prompted the United States to change its attitude toward relations with Russia. Meanwhile, the Russians felt that the 11 September attacks vindicated their warnings about "Islamic terrorism" and the activities of the Taliban and the bin Laden terrorists in Central Asia, the Caucasus, and other Muslim-inhabited regions of Russia.[123]

However, the Russians have been disappointed by the limited gains produced by cooperation with the United States, although the United States has recognized Russia as a market economy, which meets a key requirement of its joining the World Trade Organization. Further, the dominant U.S. position in post-Taliban Afghanistan and bilateral arrangements with individual Central Asian countries, including the stationing of U.S. military personnel, have significantly eroded Russia's influence in Central Asia.[124] The U.S. decision to help Georgia militarily to dislodge Chechen rebels and possibly foreign Muslim militants from the Pankisi Gorge has also increased the U.S. presence in Russia's immediate neighborhood. Some Russian analysts decried the loss of Russian influence in Central Asia and the Caucasus and accused the United States of pursuing a strategy of driving Russia out of the region.[125]

Yet because of "structural constraints" of Russia's diplomacy, it can do little to reverse the situation.[126] Meanwhile, after successful operations in Afghanistan, the U.S. need for Russian support has declined, which means that Russia's expectations of large gains from supporting the United States are unlikely to materialize. By early 2002, the United States had resumed criticizing Russia's actions in Chechnya, albeit in milder form.[127]

Foreseeing such developments, from the beginning of the crisis, some Russians feared that they might be used "as a kind of diplomatic Kleenex, to be used and thrown away."[128] Consequently, Russia has been trying to shift the conduct of the war on terrorism to multilateral institutions, notably the United Nations. Vladimir

Putin made statements to this effect,[129] and Russian foreign minister Igor Ivanov wrote in the *New York Times* that "one of the most urgent tasks is the strengthening of the world antiterrorist coalition, [but] common sense suggests that work in this direction would be better conducted under the auspices of the United Nations on the basis of strengthening international law."[130] In effect, by trying to enhance the role of the United Nations, Russia is trying to limit American unilateralism and increase Russia's role in setting policies as a permanent member of the United Nations Security Council, rather than having either to follow America's lead or to pay the price of opposing its policies. Some U.S. analysts have argued that this is because Putin believes that "a unilateralist approach on the part of the United States could prove disastrous for Russia" because of its vulnerability to the unintended consequences of U.S. actions.[131]

Meanwhile, Putin has been playing down the impact that the increased U.S. presence in Central Asia and the Caucasus has on Russia's ability to influence events there. Indeed, both Putin and Ivanov have stressed that the U.S. presence in Central Asia serves Russia's interests because it helps prevent the spread of Islamic extremism. Nevertheless, Russia is still uncomfortable about an open-ended U.S. presence in Central Asia and the former Soviet Union.[132] This sentiment has remained strong even after President George W. Bush's visit to Moscow (23–25 May 2002) and the conclusion of the "Joint Declaration on a New U.S.-Russia Relationship."[133] This new partnership is not the idealized Kozyrev vision, but is based on realities of power. Putin's foreign policy vision, however, is not shared by significant segments of Russia's population and influential elements of the Russian government, a fact reflecting the ongoing debate about Russian identity between the Westernizers and others.[134]

Coping with the Arc of Instability: The Islamic Challenge

Putin certainly sees Islamic extremism in an area stretching from Southeast Asia to the Balkans as a major threat to Russia and its domestic and foreign interests. In a speech to the Indian Parliament on 4 October 2000, Putin said:

> I would like to share with you the absolutely verifiable information according to which I can tell you that the same faces appear in the same extremist and terrorist organizations, and these entities take direct part in organization, planning and implementation of terrorist acts starting from Philippines and extending all the way to Kosovo, invariably including Kashmir, Afghanistan, and North Caucasus of Russia.[135]

Putin repeated similar themes in an interview with the French magazine *Paris Match* in July 2000. He stated that an Islamic terror network led by Osama bin Laden is "trying to create an Islamic Caliphate, the United States of Islam, in which a wide range of Islamic governments would join as well as some from the Central Asian states of the former USSR and parts of the present day territory of the

Russian Federation. . . . I call them fascists because he [bin Laden] calls for the creation of a united struggle against Europeans and 'crusaders' as they call us."[136] While visiting Tashkent in May 2000, Putin said that "an arc of instability has emerged in the republics on Russia's doorstep."[137] Other Russian officials, notably Sergei Yastrzhembsky, assistant to the Russian president on Chechnya, have also referred to this "arc of instability."[138]

Until 11 September 2001, Russia had to deal with this issue alone and, at times, in disagreement with the West. Indeed, the Russians felt bitter that instead of being grateful to Russia, the West was critical of the war in Chechnya, which Russia saw as a war against international terrorism. Expressing his anger at Western criticism, Vladimir Putin in the *Paris Match* interview said, "Russia finds herself on the edge of the fight with this international terrorism. And for the most part Europe should be grateful and should kneel before us since we are fighting now, unfortunately, on our own."[139] The events of 11 September demonstrated the existence of a common Islamist threat to Russia and the West and thus became the single most important factor in changing the nature and course of Russian-Western (especially Russian-U.S.) relations.

Systemic Consequences of 11 September and Russian Foreign Policy

The long-term systemic consequences of post–11 September developments did not become clear for some time because of two imponderables: the evolution of the U.S. antiterrorism strategy, especially whether U.S. goals would expand beyond eliminating terrorist networks to changing regimes it finds unsavory, and the response of other countries to such a development. With the war against Iraq in March 2003, it became clear that the U.S. anti-terrorism strategy included regime change. In fact, the basic U.S. defense doctrine became that of prevention and even preemption.[140] What remained unclear as of December 2003 was whether the United States would try to effect regime change in countries such as Iran and North Korea through the use of direct military force or by other means.[141]

Clearly, however, like the 1991 Persian Gulf War, which led to a permanent U.S. military presence in that region, post–11 September developments, notably U.S. military operations in Afghanistan and Iraq, have enhanced U.S. military, strategic, and political weight in the Middle East, South and Central Asia, and the Caucasus. This situation need not be threatening to Russia's basic security interests, but it will reduce Russia's ability to shape these regions' political map, further distance Central Asia and the Caucasus from Russia, and render the CIS an even more hollow institution than it is today.

Russia will be forced to reassess the basic framework and objectives of its foreign policy. Given its limited and declining resources—notwithstanding a temporary economic recovery beginning in 1999 driven largely by oil exports—and its acute need for external economic and financial assistance, Russia will tend to set more modest and achievable goals and pursue cooperation or at least accommodation with the West, rather than confrontation. In July 2002, President Putin stated, "Russia has completely left the confrontational period in international relations."[142] Certainly, the U.S. decision to remove the regime of Saddam Hussein in Iraq by the use of military force created serious tensions in Russia's relations with the United States, leading to near confrontation between the two. However, this episode was short-lived and, because of factors noted earlier, after the end of the more intense phase of the war, Russia moved quickly to ease tensions with the United States.

Relations with the West, however, will not be at the expense of ties with partners, most notably China. Thus after President Bush's visit to Moscow, Russian leaders were quick to reassure China that improved relations with the United States would not be at the expense of good Russian-Chinese ties.[143] In an interview with Chinese reporters, Putin said, "Russia is a European-Asian country, cooperating with both the East and the West; in the future, we will continue to develop ties with the West and the East, particularly the Russia-China relationship."[144] Putin added, "Russia-China cooperation stands above the Russia-U.S. relationship in various aspects." However, other commentators have indicated a lessening of interest in ties with China because of the aforementioned limitations.[145] For Russia, any strategy of countering U.S. influence would be both costly and counterproductive and is thus unlikely, although frictions with the United States will continue on a wide range of particular issues, including Chechnya.

Russia may become engaged in joint activities with the United States and NATO against Islamic extremism or in other regional schemes in order to avoid becoming irrelevant. Either way, Russia's ability to play the Islamic card, either positively (forging alliances with certain Muslim countries) or negatively (using the threat of Islamic extremism to enhance its influence), will be eroded. If a partnership with the United States the second time around proves more lasting than it did during the Yeltsin era, Russia's role would be that of a junior partner.

Conclusion

The evolution of Russia's post-Soviet foreign policy doctrines and resulting strategies has gone through various stages, reflecting both the impact of the debate on national identity and external developments, notably the concrete results of each strategy. The first, short-lived period was that of an excessively West-centered foreign and domestic policy. The short lifespan of this period was natural because the policy ignored certain geographic, historic, demographic, and psychological facts. It was also naïve, not because, as its critics have put it, it ignored sharp and irreconcilable differences between Russia and the West, but rather because it expected that embracing the West would immediately transform Russia into a modern and prosperous country on a par with the United States or Europe. Finally, it had a narrow base of support, represented the proclivities of ardent Westernizers, and ignored other trends within Russia.

The second period was marked by the lack of geopolitical, economic, and cultural realism. The Eurasianists who tried to re-create the former empire, albeit in a new form, ignored the geopolitical changes triggered by the USSR's disintegration, including the greater engagement of outside actors in the Soviet successor states, which limited Russia's ability to shape events. They also overlooked Russia's new economic priorities, which distanced the country from other members of the CIS, and its economic and financial constraints, which limited its ability to assist them. The combined effect of these factors was Russia's inability to retain the former Soviet space as its exclusive zone of influence.

The Eurasianists were also culturally naïve, a trait deriving from misreading the history of Russia's interaction with the empire's Muslims. Sergei Stankevich saw Russia as the great synthesizer and reconciliator of Christianity and Islam, East and West, but his views, like those of other Eurasianists, do not correspond to the historic memory of Muslims and their myth-symbol complex.

The third period of post-Soviet foreign policy strategy, the search for multipolarity, was also characterized by misreading of global economic, strategic, and cultural realities. Hence it yielded no results and may even have caused some damage. As a former U.S. ambassador to Moscow put it, ultimately the Russians realized that they would not become the center of any future "pole" if they antagonized the West.[146]

The fourth period of Russian foreign policy began with Russia's decision to join the United States and Europe in the war against international terrorism, commencing with operations in Afghanistan against the Taliban regime and the Al-Qaeda terrorist network. The long-term consequences for Russia of this policy are not yet clear. Most likely, because of the dynamics set in motion by U.S. operations in Afghanistan and elsewhere, Russia's influence with the CIS member states will be further diluted. Yet Russia would have suffered more if it had been obstructive. The Afghan operations and Russia's support for them, even though it took no direct part in military operations, discredited any notion of a Russian-Muslim coalition against the West.

Faced with a stark choice, even the anti-Western Russians discovered that culturally and in terms of interests, they have more in common with the Christian West than with the Muslim East. Contributing to this discovery were experiences of the last decade, which showed both the unreality of visions of Russia as the conciliator and harmonizer of Islamic and Western cultures and the strength of Russia's imperial legacy in the Muslim world. Russia and the West will continue both to compete and to cooperate in the Islamic world and may not always see eye to eye. On some issues, Russia at times may side with some Muslim states as it did during the U.S.-Iraq war of March 2003. But after the Afghan operation, the notion of Russian-Muslim cooperation against the West has been irrevocably discredited. The only remaining question is, Toward which one of the major poles of power in the West—Europe or the United States—will Russia gravitate? As of the end of 2003, it seemed that Russia wanted to remain on good terms with both Europe and the United States. The U.S. global reach, as demonstrated by the Iraq War, and Europe's economic power and proximity made such a choice compelling.

7

The Role of Islam in Shaping Russia's Post-Soviet External Relations

The Islamic factor, both as a geopolitical variable and a domestic factor, has influenced the evolution of post-Soviet Russia's visions of its interests, the nature of threats to these interests, and the strategies best suited to protect and advance them. It has also influenced the evolution of Russia's relations with key Muslim countries, the West, and other central players, such as China. Understandably, the strongest impact of this factor has been felt in Russia's relations with Muslim countries, especially those on Russia's immediate periphery. However, because of Islam's rising political profile on the international scene and, in particular, the emergence of militant and extremist strains of Islam determined to challenge both the West and Russia, albeit to different degrees at different times, the Islamic factor has significantly influenced Russian-Western relations. The Islamic variable has also been quite strong in shaping Russia's approach in the Balkans.

This influence is neither surprising nor a novel phenomenon. Rather, Islam has been a factor in Russia's external relations since the sixteenth century. In fact, Russia has a long history of involvement in the Islamic world that still influences the perceptions and policies of both Russia and the Muslim countries toward each other. Therefore, a brief survey of the role of the Islamic factor in shaping and rationalizing the foreign policy of tsarist and Soviet Russia, especially toward the Muslim world, should precede the discussion of the impact of the Islamic factor in shaping the pattern of post-Soviet Russia's relations with various international and regional actors. This historical background will provide a yardstick with which to measure the relative influence of this factor in the development of Russia's post-Soviet foreign policy and to establish patterns of continuity and change.

Russia and the Muslim World before 1917

Historically, Islam has impacted Russia's external relations in essentially two ways: by providing a "missionary" dimension to Russia's imperial expansion and by serving as a policy instrument for internal consolidation and in rivalries with other imperial powers. In their essentials, these functions of Islam were the same during the tsarist and Soviet periods.

From the very beginning of Russia's imperial expansion, heralded by the conquest of Kazan in 1552, worldly motives of security and territorial gains were intermingled with religious and messianic goals. For example, Russia's steady expansion into Muslim lands was to culminate in the conquest of Constantinople and its liberation from the Muslim yoke, which had begun with Byzantium's defeat by the Ottoman sultan Muhammad II (the Conqueror) on 29 May 1453. Russia had to abandon this goal after its defeat in the Crimean War (1853–56).[1] But the idea that Constantinople must belong to Russia not merely on strategic, but also religious, grounds and for the fulfillment of Russia's mission survived. Fyodor Dostoevsky best described this sentiment when he wrote in 1887:

> Yes, the Golden Horn and Constantinople—all this will be ours . . . not from the standpoint of the long-conceived necessity for a tremendous giant like Russia to emerge at last from its locked room . . . into the open spaces where he may breathe the free air of the seas and oceans. . . . Our task is deeper, immeasurably deeper. We, Russia, are really indispensable and inevitable both to all Eastern Christianity and to the whole future of Orthodoxy on earth, in order to achieve this unity. . . . In a word, no matter what may be the outcome of the present . . . sooner or later, *Constantinople must be ours,* even if it should take another century.[2]

Russian ambitions, however, were frustrated by the counterclaims of other major European powers because, in addition to the religious mission, the Russians felt that they had a "civilizing" role to play in the East and were bitter about the barriers that European powers, notably Britain, put in the way of Russian aspirations. Nikolai Danilevsky, a Russian nationalist and the originator of scientific Slavophilism, noted that Russia's efforts in Turkey and Persia and even China were frustrated by the British, despite the fact that Europe had assigned to the Russians, "her adopted children," the task of being the bearers and propagators of her civilization in the East. In an ironic tone, he asked the Europeans, "For mercy's sake where is our [Russia's] East, the East which it is our sacred mission to civilize?" to which he imagines the British replying, "Central Asia, that's the place for you, do not forget it. We could not get there anyhow. There lies your sacred historical mission."[3]

Yet whenever circumstances permitted, Russia and other imperial powers were willing to divide Muslim lands into spheres of influence or recognize special privileges for each other, as exemplified by the Russian-British agreement of 1907. The Anglo-Russian Entente settled the two empires' disputes in Central Asia, Iran, and Afghanistan.[4] While the two major protagonists for the domination of the Muslim world were reaching a mutually beneficial accommodation, social and political convulsions in Russia, the Islamic world, and Europe fundamentally altered the nature of international politics and the balance of power.

Revolutions in the East: Consequences for Posttsarist Russian-Muslim Relations

In the first decade of the twentieth century, reformist social and political movements emerged in key Muslim states, notably Turkey and Iran, to promote modernization and the establishment of constitutional governments. The roots of the Iranian constitutional movement date to the so-called Tobacco Rebellion of 1890–91, which opposed the granting of sweeping concessions to Britain. Two other events, both related to Russia, contributed to Iran's Constitutional Revolution of 1905–6: Russia's defeat in the Russo-Japanese War of 1904 and the Russian Revolution of 1905–7. The former punctured the myth of European powers' invincibility and fostered the belief that Eastern peoples could acquire the knowledge and skills needed to resist European encroachment. The latter exerted a significant influence on sociopolitical developments in some Muslim countries, including Iran. The political leadership of the revolution represented primarily the emerging Russian bourgeoisie, despite the Bolsheviks' claim that the Revolution of 1905 was the "starting point for all the national liberation movements in Asia and the pivot around which all of them revolved."[5] Nevertheless, many of the principles and goals adopted by the revolutionaries, especially during the worker strikes in Moscow and St. Petersburg and the peasant uprisings in the countryside, were influenced by socialist ideas. These ideas found a certain degree of popular support in some Muslim countries.[6]

Therefore, when the Bolshevik Revolution occurred in Russia in 1917, its leaders saw an opportunity to expand both revolutionary ideas and Russian influence in the East. To this purpose, they exploited the Muslims' yearning for independence and freedom from colonial rule. In their joint appeal to Muslims of Russia and to Muslims of the East, Lenin and Stalin fully exploited the theme of European colonialism. The Bolsheviks even claimed that the main goal of the revolution was "the liberation of the Orient, in particular the Muslim Orient."[7]

The Bolsheviks' efforts were not limited to anti-European propaganda, but offered real concessions to Muslim countries. The "Appeal to the Muslims of Russia and the East" declared:

> The treaty for the partition of Persia is null and void. As soon as the military operations cease the armed forces will be withdrawn from Persia and the Persians will be guaranteed the right of free determination of their own destiny. . . . We declare that the treaty for the partition . . . of Turkey is null and void.[8]

Another important step to attract Muslims was the holding of the Baku Conference on 15 August 1920, to which, in the words of the Executive Committee of the Communist International, "the enslaved peoples of Persia, Armenia, and Turkey" were invited. During verbal attacks on "English imperialism—Grigory Zinoviev [president of the comintern] even summoned the Muslims to a holy war (jihad) against the British—Muslim delegates applauded."[9]

Many of these gains were squandered by attacks against Muslim clergy and institutionalized Islam. At the meeting over which Zinoviev presided, the delegate A. Skatchko labeled the Muslim clergy "parasites" and accused them of having "seized enormous areas of land," declaring them to "belong to God," and added that this was even against the Shari'a.[10] Such statements betrayed a misreading of Muslim psychology and ignored Lenin's caution that the Muslim religious establishment could not be treated like the church in Russia because Muslims "are entirely under the domination of their mullah."[11] This lack of sensitivity to the Muslims' religious feelings caused them to view the Bolsheviks' atheistic creed as more threatening than British colonialism.

The Baku Conference pointed to a fundamental dichotomy between communism and Islam, two systems, one built around dialectical materialism and the other on divine law. This dichotomy complicated and ultimately defeated the Bolsheviks' efforts to use Islam to advance their strategic and ideological goals. Muslims were willing to accept the Bolshevik regime's assistance when challenging colonial powers, provided that ideology played a small role. Soviet-Muslim collaboration was further limited by Soviet ambitions to dominate Muslim lands. In short, the Soviets saw Islam merely as a potential instrument in their global competition for power. Post-Soviet theories of Russian-Muslim collaboration against the West's hegemony betray the same instrumentalist approach to Islam.

Moreover, both in the Soviet and the post-Soviet periods, Islam has been a double-edged sword in the sense that it has been used by others against Russia. Zinoviev's call for "jihad" against Britain went unheeded, but Western support for an Afghan "jihad" in 1979 was instrumental in forcing the withdrawal of Soviet troops from Afghanistan. In the last decade, the concept of "jihad" has been used in Chechnya against Russia.

Stages of Soviet-Muslim Relations and Their Legacy for Russia

Revolution and Expansion, 1917–1921

Following the Bolsheviks' failure to generate popular uprisings in the East, the Soviet Union adopted a two-pronged policy toward the Muslim world that continued until the Soviet Union's collapse. This strategy was based on an assessment of the relative role of Islam in either helping or hindering Soviet aspirations and on the conduct of relations at two levels: state to state and party to party.

Because of the Ottoman Empire's domination of Arab lands and the Sultan's pretension to be "caliph," the spiritual leader of Muslims, most Russian revolutionaries considered Turkey the key to their penetration of the Islamic world. But it was Iran that offered them the best opportunity to test their revolutionary ideas. Some Russian thinkers, notably Konstantin Troyanovsky, had always thought that Iran was more important than Turkey because of its proximity to the Indian subcontinent. In his book *Vostok i Revolutsiya*, published in 1918, he wrote:

The Persian Revolution may become the key to the revolution of the whole Orient, just as Egypt and the Suez Canal are the key to English domination in the Orient. . . . The political conquest of Persia . . . is what we must accomplish first of all. This precious key to all other revolutions in the Orient must be in our hands, come what may. Persia must be ours. Persia must belong to the revolution.[12]

For a short period, it appeared that Troyanovsky's declaration could prove prophetic. Socialist ideas had already spread in Iran, and a socialist party called Adalat (Justice) had been established.[13] The first congress of the party was held in the Iranian port of Enzeli in July 1920, during which the party changed its name to the Communist Party of Iran.

The main center of socialist activity in Iran was the northern province of Gilan, where a revolutionary movement under the leadership of Mirza Kuchek Khan Jangali was under way.[14] The Gilan Republic, or Persian Soviet Socialist Republic, was the first and the last such republic to be created in the Muslim world beyond the Muslim-inhabited lands of the Russian empire.[15] Initially recognizing the strong nationalist and middle class dimensions of the movement, the Bolsheviks did not insist on the immediate implementation of a socialist program in Gilan because they feared that this might exacerbate class antagonism and reduce the chances of uniting Persian Communists and democrats against the British.[16] However, other extremist elements, such as Muhammad Ja'afer Pishevari, and some Russian advisers opted for the implementation of a full-fledged socialist program in Gilan.[17] This proved a fatal mistake as it alerted the peasantry and the middle class to the antireligious and antinationalist dimensions of the Bolshevik program. According to Sepehr Zabih, "In the first few weeks of its rule the regime reportedly closed nineteen mosques, prohibited religious instruction, and decreed forcible unveiling of women. The Moslem clergy, who vigorously opposed these measures, were ridiculed publicly."[18]

This behavior, coupled with the conviction that the "Third International wished to use him only as a tool for the ultimate Bolshevization of Iran," led Mirza Kuchek Khan to break with the Bolsheviks.[19] According to Louis Fischer, the Bolsheviks abandoned Kuchek Khan because of a shift in their priorities from revolutionary activism to state-to-state relations.[20] However, whatever its real cause, the breach between Kuchek Khan and the Bolsheviks facilitated the Iranian government's recapture of Gilan.

The Gilan events dampened the earlier enthusiasm generated in Iran for the Bolshevik government because of its abandonment of tsarist claims against Iran, although underground Communist activities continued. Between 1921 and 1941, a common fear of communism forged an alliance between secular nationalists and the Muslim establishment that acted as a barrier to a Soviet advance in Iran.

The situation in Turkey was much less propitious to the establishment of socialist-ruled pockets because it had no equivalent to the Jangali movement, although segments of the Turkish peasantry entertained Bolshevik sympathies.[21]

Nevertheless, the Bolsheviks hoped that the Kemalist movement in Turkey would be transformed into a socialist revolution, helping Russia to achieve its long-cherished strategic goals, such as the control of the Dardanelles.[22] These expectations were frustrated when the Kemalist regime cracked down on Turkish Communists. Among those killed was Mustapha Subhi, who had organized Turkish Communist prisoners of war for the Central Bureau of the Eastern Peoples.[23] But the Bolsheviks did not permit the suppression of the Communists to prevent the normalization of relations with the Kemalist regime. In sum, despite early hopes, Islam proved to be the main obstacle to a Soviet advance in Turkey. Russian experts at the time recognized this fact. M. Pavlovich wrote, "The Turkish people, due to the historical reasons of adherence to religion, cannot at this moment entirely accept the Communist program: It will require a long and stubborn struggle to push them in that direction."[24]

Afghanistan was the next country where the Bolshevik Revolution had a direct impact, although the extent of Russian influence, especially ideological, in the unfolding of Afghan events is hard to assess. As with Iran and Turkey, the new Soviet regime's main attraction was its support for the anticolonial movements and opposition to the British presence.[25] After seizing power in 1918, Amir Amanullah Khan declared independence in April 1919, denounced Afghanistan's treaty obligations with Britain, and asked the new Bolshevik government for help.[26] The Afghans thus used the Russian card in their struggle with Britain. However, Bolshevik efforts to retain Muslim regions of the tsar's empire within the new state, combined with their antireligious campaigns and local resistance to Bolshevik activities, best represented by the Basmachi revolt, created doubts in the minds of Afghans and other Muslims about the Bolsheviks' commitment to the liberation of Muslims.[27]

Because of geographic remoteness and the lack of a long history of direct Russian interaction with the Arab world, during the revolution's early years, the Arab world was not a foreign policy priority for the Bolsheviks. Nevertheless, during the 1919 nationalist uprisings in Egypt, the Bolsheviks offered to provide Sa'ad Zaghlul, the Egyptian nationalist and proindependence leader, with arms.[28] Lenin and Stalin's famous appeal to peoples of the East, especially Muslims, also found echoes in the Arab world and was later used by Arab Communists to create an image of the Soviet Union as an early supporter of the Arab struggle for independence. The ideas of the Muslim nationalist Sultan-Galiev also influenced later Arab socialists.[29] Consequently, during the 1920s, Communist parties were established in Arab lands.[30]

The Good Neighbor Policy and Reduced Activism, 1927–1941

By 1921, the Bolshevik regime had decided to delay the goal of fomenting revolutions in the Muslim world and had opted for a strategy of establishing state-to-state relations. An important feature of this strategy was the signing of treaties of friendship and nonaggression.[31] The first such treaty was signed between Iran and the Soviet Union on 26 February 1921. It granted Iran several concessions and restored many properties taken previously by the tsarist government. The treaty also granted Iran the right of free navigation on the Caspian Sea. The two parties agreed to refrain from interfering in each other's internal affairs and to prevent the operation of hostile groups and movements in each other's territory.

One provision embodied in Article VI of the treaty has haunted Iran. It allowed the Soviet Union—and now presumably the Russian Federation—to introduce troops inside Iran if a third power should try to use Iranian territory for attacks against the Soviet Union or Russia and the Iranian government was unable to prevent this.[32] Despite the treaty, some Soviet advisers and elements from the new Soviet republic of Azerbaijan helped Mirza Kuchek Khan, the leader of the Jangali movement, to march toward Tehran in May 1921. When this effort failed, the Soviets denied any connection with it and in September 1921 withdrew their forces from Iran.[33]

On 16 March 1921, the first treaty between Russia and Mustafa Kemal's government in Turkey settled border disputes between the new regimes. This agreement was followed by the 13 October 1921 Treaty of Kars between Turkey and the sovietized Transcaucasian republics and the December 1925 Soviet-Turkish Treaty on Neutrality and Non-Aggression.[34] The Bolsheviks' new strategy contributed to Kemal's success in preventing Turkey's partition and obtaining a better deal from the European powers.

The first treaty with Afghanistan, signed on 28 February 1921, reaffirmed Afghanistan's independence. It was followed in August 1926 by the Treaty of Neutrality and Non-Aggression.

Several factors prompted the Bolsheviks' pragmatic approach. First, the new regime's economic difficulties and the introduction of the New Economic Policy weakened the Bolsheviks' position. According to one author, "The prevalence of famine made peace abroad a virtual necessity." Second, Communist propaganda had limited success in recruiting members; the 1923 yearbook of the Comintern stated that in 1922 "there were only 2,000 communists and socialists in Iran, only one communist newspaper, and altogether only 20,000 Iranians connected with trade union organizations."[35] Third, nationalist feelings and religious sentiments remained strong in the Muslim world. Fourth, the necessity of consolidating power in Russia and implementing the process of sovietization limited the Bolsheviks' willingness to become deeply involved in the internal affairs of neighboring states. Finally, the rise of fascism in Europe brought new challenges. This period also marked the beginning of a dual-track strategy of subordinating ideological goals to Soviet state interests while maintaining contacts with foreign Communist parties.

New Surge of Soviet Activism and the Muslim Backlash, 1941–1958

In a move similar to the 1907 Anglo-Russian Entente, the 1941 Molotov-Ribbentrop agreement delineated the respective spheres of influence of Germany and the USSR. Moscow demanded the right to establish a base for naval and land forces in the Dardanelles and the Bosphorus by means of a long-term lease and claimed an indefinite Soviet sphere of influence in the south of Baku and Batumi toward the Persian Gulf.

The Allied invasion of Iran in August 1941 provided the USSR with an opportunity to occupy northern Iran and revitalize its Communist movement. The Soviets, in a pattern that later became more pronounced, used their Muslim subjects to influence the Iranian population and encouraged cultural contacts between Iranian intellectuals and Soviet Muslim republics. The Soviet embassy in Tehran included Muslim personnel from Central Asia and the Caucasus fluent in Persian and minority dialects.[36]

The most ambitious Soviet activities took place in Azerbaijan and Kurdistan, where the Soviet Union tried to dismember Iran by creating Soviet-style republics, but these efforts failed as a result of skillful maneuvering by Iran's central government, the strength of nationalist sentiments, and international pressures.[37] The Islamic factor contributed to this failure, as it had in Gilan. The clerical establishment opposed the Soviet-sponsored government, and many people who would have benefited from the economic and social reforms of the puppet government remained wary of its atheistic and antireligious leanings. Ironically, greater contacts with Soviet Muslims made the Iranians aware of the USSR's anti-Islam campaigns. The support of Iran's Tudeh (Communist) Party for the Azerbaijan republic damaged its credibility, although it remained strong until the early 1960s.[38]

The Soviet Union also pressured Turkey by raising the issue of navigation in the Turkish Straits, which was regulated by the Montreux Convention of 1936. Opportunities for the sovietization of Turkey were very limited, however, because Turkish neutrality was not violated by the Allied Powers and there were no Soviet troops in Turkey.

Despite these setbacks in the postwar years, Soviet influence and the number of parties with Communist leanings—albeit to different degrees—grew in the Arab and Islamic worlds. This growth of pro-Soviet tendencies was not accompanied by the spread of communism as preached by the USSR. Rather, most of the leftist parties in the Arab world adhered to local variants of socialism, notably Arab socialism.[39] There were, however, more purist Communist parties in most Arab and Islamic countries as well.

The traditional clergy remained anti-Communist, but Arab socialists tried to demonstrate Islam's progressive and revolutionary dimensions.[40] This tendency and pro-Soviet sentiments were the strongest in Arab and other Muslim countries that had experienced Western but not Russian colonialism. The Soviet Union also exploited Arab and Muslim resentment toward the West following the creation of the state of Israel and the West's pro-Israel stand.

The Soviet Union pursued an essentially realpolitik strategy toward the Islamic world. Thus Muslim states' repression of Communist parties hardly affected their official relations with Moscow. The pattern of Soviet relations with the Muslim world in this period was uneven because the East-West competition pressured Muslim states to take sides, even if they preferred to remain neutral.[41] Those Muslim states that were geographically close to the Soviet Union and, in one form or another, had a troubled history with Russia sided with the West. Others proved more receptive to Soviet propaganda and advances.

Despite Arab and Muslim intellectuals' effort to point out similarities between communism and Islam, the latter proved more of a hindrance than a facilitator for the expansion of Soviet influence. Rather, Soviet success resulted from Muslim disappointment with Western policies.

Supremacy of Strategic and Political Interests, 1958–1978

The accentuation of pragmatism in Soviet foreign policy shifted the emphasis to securing the Soviet Union's strategic interests and rendered ideological goals secondary and, in many cases, irrelevant to the Soviet approach toward Muslim countries. The main criteria for extending support became the level of Muslim states' animosity toward the West and their willingness to embrace the USSR rather than their political philosophy or their domestic politics. In fact, this single-minded pursuit of strategic objectives resulted in the support of any Arab government "willing to pursue an anti-Western foreign policy, irrespective of its domestic program."[42] Nevertheless, many Muslim countries adopted a so-called noncapitalist—if not orthodox socialist—path of development, which created some ideological affinity with the USSR. Islam did not figure prominently in either Soviet or the Muslim states' calculations in terms of shaping their relations. This period was, at least on the surface, the era of nationalism and modernism in the Muslim world. Walter Laqueur concluded:

> The Arab countries are no more likely than most others in the world to provide a favorable breeding ground for Communism. The problem of the affinity between Islam and Communism is . . . of secondary importance at the present time. What is decisive is that *Islam has gradually ceased to be a serious competitor of Communism in the struggle for the present political elites in the countries of the Middle East.*[43]

This prognosis, while true of the elite in the 1950s and early 1960s, was premature in writing off Islam as an important social and political force, as shown by its political resurgence by the early 1970s. The 1967 Arab-Israeli War, which resulted in the fall of East Jerusalem to Israel, was a watershed in the reversal of fortunes between Islam and secular ideologies in the Arab-Islamic worlds. The Soviets grasped and exploited the psychological and political impact of this event.

Thus, once again, Soviet diplomacy extensively used the Soviet Muslim population and the government-controlled Muslim establishment in penetrating the Arab/Islamic world. In October 1967, the vice president of the Central Asian Spiritual Board toured Egypt, Syria, and Jordan to convince them of the USSR's solidarity with the Arab cause and the Soviet Muslims' support for the Arabs. He added,

"Soviet Muslims were speaking on behalf of their Arab brothers in order to facilitate the dispatch of Soviet arms to Arab countries."[44]

In the 1970s, the Soviet Union organized conferences on Islamic themes and sent delegates to such conferences held in other Muslim countries.[45] Karen Dawisha and Hélène Carrère d'Encausse note that members of the Soviet Muslim establishment "speaking a fluent Arabic and with a better knowledge of the various aspects of Islam [were] very successful emissaries for the USSR, particularly in those conservative Islamic states where the Soviet Union [had] poor or non-existent diplomatic relations."[46]

This policy had both benefits and drawbacks: Contacts with the Muslim world awakened Soviet Muslims to their secondary position. It also facilitated the penetration of new ideas, including politicized Islam, into the USSR's Muslim regions, a process that later proved disruptive. In general, the Soviet Union's use of Islam had, at best, a marginal impact in securing its strategic and political interests. It failed to bring pro-Western Muslim states into the Soviet orbit.

Dealing with Resurgent Islam, 1979–1991

In terms of the political evolution of the Middle East and South Asia, as well as East-West relations, 1978–79 was a momentous period. Islam was propelled into the forefront of regional and international politics, reasserting its importance as a potent political force. The most dramatic manifestation of Islam's revival was Iran's Islamic Revolution of 1979. Although this revolution initially posed the most serious challenge to the West, it also created new dilemmas for the Soviet Union. But it was in Afghanistan that Islam emerged as a formidable barrier to Soviet aspirations by galvanizing resistance to the Soviet invasion of the country. It was also the Soviet-Afghan War that had the most far-reaching consequences for the Soviet Union's internal evolution and its foreign policy outlook.

Afghanistan's Anti-Soviet Jihad

Afghanistan's long crisis began with the April 1978 coup d'état by the Afghan Communist Party (the People's Democratic Party of Afghanistan) that ousted the regime of General Muhammad Daoud Khan, who in 1971 had assumed power after removing his cousin, King Zahir Shah. Most Soviet sources maintain that there is no convincing evidence that the USSR was behind the coup.[47] However, by the mid-1970s, Daoud Khan, partly due to prodding by Iran and Saudi Arabia, had moved away from the USSR, leading Selig S. Harrison to blame the coup on the shah's effort to wean Afghanistan away from the USSR with the ultimate goal of creating a modern version of the ancient Persian Empire.[48] The Soviet Union had always considered a friendly Afghanistan necessary for its security and would not have welcomed such a development. Therefore, it is possible that some elements within the Soviet leadership welcomed the chance to dislodge Daoud Khan and prevent Afghanistan's drift into the Western camp.

The Communist Party of Afghanistan was divided along many lines, including ethnic ones.[49] This characteristic of the Afghan Communist Party played a significant role in the country's subsequent evolution, which finally culminated in the Soviet Union's military intervention, resulting in two decades of war and unforeseen consequences for regional and international politics, notably a worsening of East-West relations. Ultimately, it affected the fate of the Soviet Union itself.

In 1979, the Soviet civilian and military leadership was divided on the issue of sending troops to Afghanistan. A combination of practical, ideological, and even personal factors contributed to this fateful decision.[50] According to Alexei Vassiliev, Brezhnev played the decisive role. "The core of the matter pushing him in that direction was not confined to objective factors."[51]

Islam and Resistance in Afghanistan

It is ironic that "jihad" was urged against Soviet imperialism and the Afghan mujahideen (holy warriors) were received with honors in Western capitals, considering that in 1920 Zinoviev had called for jihad against British imperialism. Two factors explaining why resistance to communism took an Islamic form are important because of their contemporary relevance: (1) the ineptness of the Communist leadership and its underestimation of Islam's hold on the Afghan population, which led it to adopt anti-Islam policies, and (2) external influences, notably activities undertaken by Pakistan. Concerning the former, Alexei Vassiliev stated, "Following the naïve (even the criminally naïve) romanticism inherited from the Gilan republic and from the extremist wing of the Iranian Tudeh Party, the new government demonstrated its contempt for Islam and thus antagonized a considerable part of the Muslim clergy."[52] Similarly, according to K.M. Tsagolov, a village that had initially supported the regime joined the opposition when two radical members of the Communist Party "forbade the population to pray and brought monkeys into the mosques."[53] Realizing the negative consequences of the antireligion campaign, Babrak Karmal's regime adopted a more cooperative policy toward religion with some success, but this change in approach was not sufficient to win back the opposition to the regime's side.[54] Other policies, such as efforts to centralize a still largely tribal society and the mishandling of land reform and antismuggling efforts, further intensified opposition to the regime.

External influences further promoted Islamic-based resistance to communism. The modernization process in Afghanistan, begun in the 1930s, had created an Islamic backlash illustrated by the emergence of a successful Islamic youth movement in the 1960s and 1970s, partly with Pakistan's support. This movement organized a number of antigovernment activities. One of the student leaders who participated in an antigovernment revolt in the Panjshir Valley was Gulbuddin Hekmatyar, who fled to Pakistan after the army put down the revolt and became a major figure in the Afghan resistance.[55] The Islamization policies of General Muhammad Zia ul-Haq, who came to power in Pakistan in 1977, contributed to shaping the Afghan resistance in an Islamic direction.

The Afghan developments also reflected the trend toward Islamic revivalism throughout the Muslim world. Thus an appeal to Islam as a unifying factor for ethnically divided Afghanistan appeared natural. It was also useful in gaining the financial and moral support of the Arab states, especially Saudi Arabia.

The issue of whether resistance from the mujahideen or the change in Soviet thinking and priorities under Gorbachev led to the Soviet troop withdrawal is debatable. One analyst maintains that the military and political costs were not unbearable. Moreover, "the Soviet Union was not 'losing' the war in Afghanistan," but simply could not completely eradicate rebel groups and extend the writ of the central government throughout the country.[56]

Irrespective of the relative weight of these arguments, the Soviet withdrawal from Afghanistan was interpreted in the region and internationally as a major defeat for the USSR. Military and other assistance from the West and China played a crucial role in the Afghan resistance's victory. More important, the Afghan War led to an unprecedented level of involvement in Afghanistan by Pakistan and certain Arab states, notably Saudi Arabia, plus Iran, an involvement that continued after the withdrawal of Soviet troops in February 1989. The Soviet-Afghan War also led to the emergence of a multinational fraternity of the veterans of the Afghan War imbued with the spirit of jihad and with a strong conviction that Islam and the spirit of jihad had defeated the Soviet army. Many Russians also accepted this perspective. In short, in the Afghan context, Islam was an ideological rival and a political enemy of the Soviet Union. The mutual animosity carried over to the post-Soviet era and affected Russia's relations with Pakistan, Afghanistan, and key Arab states. The Afghan conflict also influenced these countries' approach toward post-Soviet Russia, including the conflict in Chechnya.

The Puzzle of the Iranian Revolution: Islam as Potential Ally or Rival?

Iran's Islamic Revolution posed a more difficult intellectual challenge to the Soviet Union in terms of assessing Islam's potential as a progressive force and prospective ally in its confrontation with so-called global imperialism or as a revolutionary rival. This potential challenge resulted from several fundamental characteristics of the Islamic Revolution. First, although the Islamists eventually managed to gain control of the revolutionary movement and establish an Islamic republic, the movement that brought down the monarchy was far more broad based. In particular, the left, including the Tudeh Party, played a significant role by organizing strikes in the oilfields. Second, leftist ideas had made inroads into Islamic circles, especially the medressahs, while many leftists had discovered Islam's revolutionary potential. Thus two different forms of Islamo-leftist synthesis had occurred in Iran: the Mujahidin-e-Khalq represented the Islamized traditional left, while certain elements among the Islamists, notably the group known in the 1980s as the Followers of Imam's [Ruhollah Khomeini's] Path, represented the new leftist Muslims. Third, the Iranian Revolution—except for the secular nationalists and the Islamonationalists, such as Mehdi Bazargan—was vigorously anti-Western and hence inherently progressive from the Soviet perspective. Fourth, the revolution's slogans, beneath their Islamic vocabulary, reflected traditional leftist themes and explained the international situation and class and socioeconomic divisions within Muslim societies in light of these themes. Ayatullah Khomeini's concept of "global arrogance" is the equivalent of "international imperialism." His division of the world's peoples and nations into the oppressed (Mustazafin) and the arrogant (Mustakbarin) evokes Marxist class divisions.

Thus the Soviet Union initially saw the Iranian Revolution as an important watershed in terms of Islam's progressive potential, albeit as a stage on the way to the socialist path. Yevgenii Primakov's writings reflect this perspective. He saw the emergence of Islamist movements as indicating disappointment with and rejection of the capitalist model of development. He believed that the Islamists did not offer an alternative model, which in his view provided a unique opportunity for progressive—that is, socialist—forces to determine the developmental path of any emerging Islamic type of government.[57] This is one of the reasons why, in 1978–82, the Communist Party of Iran (the Tudeh) collaborated with the Islamists against both the so-called bourgeois nationalists and the Islamo-leftists such as the Mujahidin-e-Khalq. The Tudeh and the Soviet Union lost hope that the Iranian Revolution would rapidly take a socialist turn. Therefore, the Tudeh adopted a policy of penetrating bureaucratic and military organizations with the hope of seizing power from within in cooperation with radical pro-Soviet elements. Attempted coups were foiled in 1982 as a result of information obtained from a Soviet defector and led to a large-scale purge of Tudeh sympathizers and the outlawing of the Tudeh Party.[58]

Because of the Iran-Iraq War and the ideological split within the Iranian leadership, Soviet-Iranian relations followed an uneven course until the USSR's collapse. Early Soviet expectations regarding Soviet-Iranian relations were clearly disappointed. The Soviet miscalculation in this regard resulted from the Soviet penchant for underestimating Islam's pretensions to be a cohesive spiritual, as well as socioeconomic and political, system. The Islamists' goal had always been to create an Islamic system, regardless of the affinity some of them felt for socialism. The Islamists' slogan in the 1980s, "Neither East nor West, only Islam," symbolizes their view of Islam as an alternative to the Soviet and capitalist systems.

The Soviets also underestimated the widespread suspicion regarding their objectives toward Iran prevalent among nonleftist Islamists, the legacy of the long history of Russian-Iranian interaction. Khomeini saw the Soviet Union as an imperial power that, although not as oppressive as the United States, deserved the appellation of the "lesser Satan." This jarred the Soviets and prompted some commentators to complain that the Islamic regime's struggle against the "Western devil" went together with "a struggle against the 'Eastern devil.' "[59] This revolutionary Islam was also viewed as a potentially destabilizing factor in Muslim parts of the Soviet Union. These contradictions of the Islamic Revolution, despite its anti-Western nature, contributed to heightened volatility in Soviet-Iranian relations.

Conclusion

The foregoing analysis has shown that Islam has often proved to be a barrier to the achievement of Russia's imperial goals and the Soviet Union's ideological and power ambitions. Soviet successes in making common cause with Muslims were limited to occasions when the Muslims' desire for independence and their grievances against other colonial and imperial powers, notably Britain and the United States, were manipulated.

Even many of those Muslims who tried to identify similarities between Marxism-Leninism and Islam did so in order to justify close cooperation with the Soviet Union prompted by other motives. Considerations related to the Arab-Israeli conflict and the dominant ideology of Arab leaders, especially their stand on the East-West conflict, determined Arab policies toward the USSR. In the case of other Muslims, too, it was the negative factor of opposition to the West, rather than the positive element of affinity with the Soviet Union, that shaped the pattern of their relations with the Soviet Union. Moreover, in most of the Muslim world, tsarist and Soviet policies left a negative legacy with which Russia has had to contend. On the eve of its collapse, the Soviet Union viewed Islam as more of a challenge and a barrier to its aspirations than as an ally and a facilitator of its goals.

In the post-Soviet period, too, contrary to the beliefs of certain Russian thinkers and politicians, Islam, both in the FSU and beyond, has been more of a challenge for Russia and a barrier to the advancement of its objectives than a natural ally. To the extent that Islam has served Russia's interests, it has done so in a negative sense. For instance, a common fear of extremist Islam has brought Russia and the ruling elites of some FSU countries, plus major international actors such as China and India, closer together. Until the events of 11 September 2001, Islam was a source of discord between Russia and the West, even if its impact on the character of Russian-Western relations had been limited. Since then, in a pattern similar to Russia's relations with the Central Asian states as well as China and India, the common challenge posed by extremist Islam has contributed to Russian-Western rapprochement.

8

Russian Policy toward Central Asia and the Transcaucasus

The basic objectives of Russian policy toward Central Asia and the Transcaucasus were established very early after the demise of the Soviet Union and have remained essentially constant. Russia's ability to achieve these goals, however, has evolved, thus eliciting changes in its regional strategy. The Islamic factor, especially the fear of Islamic extremism and its destabilizing potential, has played a key role in shaping Russian policies toward these regions, particularly Central Asia.

Influence of Islam on Russian Policy toward Central Asia

Until after 11 September 2001, Western analysts debated the seriousness of the extremist threat in Central Asia and the degree to which Moscow used the fear of this threat to maintain its predominant position in Central Asia, prevent the expansion of Western influence, and contain regional rivals, such as Iran and Pakistan. A substantial number of these experts believed that Russia had exaggerated the magnitude of the Islamic threat to justify its interventionist policies in Central Asia and its efforts to retain the region as its special sphere of influence, sometimes going as far as creating local conflicts. Thus some maintain that Moscow, in collaboration with Uzbekistan, contributed to the unleashing of the Tajik Civil War in 1992 in order to demonstrate the seriousness of the threat of Islamic extremism and to justify the large Russian military presence in that country. According to Sergei Gretsky, it was outside (Russian-Uzbek) interference that turned "civic strife in Tajikistan into civil war."[1] By contrast, other analysts have complained that until the late 1990s, the threat of Islamic extremism in Central Asia was underestimated in the West.[2]

Reality, however, has been more complex. Russian policy toward Central Asia since 1992 has been influenced by economic and political interests, as well as a genuine fear of the rise of Islamic extremism and its impact on Russia's security. Meanwhile, Russia has manipulated such fears to achieve its more expansionist goals.

Russian Objectives in Central Asia

During the first two years after the Soviet Union's demise, Russian foreign policy was West centered. According to Dmitri Trenin, "The main national security objective was to join NATO and the European community, rather than restore the Soviet Union."[3] This "new attitude meant that the Russian government's policy was one of benign neglect" toward most of the FSU.[4] Although this assessment of the Euro-Atlanticists' position is largely correct, Trenin fails to note that they expected that Russia's dynamism and integration with the West would attract the former Soviet republics. Therefore, the Westernizers, too, believed in regrouping former Soviet republics under Russian influence. They also saw turmoil in the south caused by Muslim extremists as the most serious threat to Russia's security. Kozyrev emphasized the seriousness of the Islamic threat during a trip to the Middle East in May 1992. Yet during this period, Central Asia did not loom large on Moscow's agenda. Russian military forces based in the region, however, were involved in local politics, especially in Tajikistan, and were promoting a policy of reestablishing Russian influence in Central Asia.[5]

Focus on the Near Abroad

By late 1992 and early 1993, for practical and philosophical reasons, the *blizhnee zarubezhie* (Near Abroad), including Central Asia, had moved up on the agenda of Russian leaders. Meanwhile, developments in Central Asia, notably the Tajik Civil War and the fall of the regime of Muhammad Najibullah in Kabul in April 1992, prompted elaboration of the "Concept of the Foreign Policy of the Russian Federation," despite Kozyrev's earlier skepticism about the necessity of such a concept. Indeed, before a final document was adopted, Russian political analysts advanced competing ideas for a new Russian foreign policy concept, and various commissions were set up to develop blueprints for such a concept.[6]

Although "the extent to which Central Asian Islam was an issue prompting the formulation of these doctrines . . . is yet to be established, . . . the doctrines contain a number of relevant provisions suggesting that Islam was seen as a threat to be reckoned with."[7] Among major threats to Russian security were noted "already existing as well as potential local conflicts, especially those fanned by 'an aggressive nationalism or religious intolerance.' "[8]

The civil war in Tajikistan intensified the fear that Islamic extremism might sweep through Central Asia and infect Russia's Muslim population. Many in Russia's security and policy circles viewed the activist and politicized or extremist brand of Central Asian Islam as inherently destabilizing because it aimed at creating Islamic states.[9]

Certain Islamist groups undoubtedly had such aspirations, but did they have any realistic prospects of realizing these goals? Moreover, a repressive policy and total exclusion of even moderate Islamic forces from the political process increased the risks that such movements would become radicalized. There was also the question of how far local elites and Russia manipulated the Islamic factor to stymie movement toward democratization and to maintain Russian influence in the region.

In the case of Tajikistan, internal and external manipulation contributed to the outbreak of the civil war. The course of the civil war and its outcome also served Russian and Uzbek purposes in Central Asia, although after 1994 their interests in Tajikistan diverged.

Causes and Consequences of the Tajik Civil War

A discussion of various factors behind the Tajik Civil War is necessary in order to assess Moscow's relative role and motives in the conflict. Paramount among the causes of the Tajik Civil War is the way the Bolsheviks created the Republic of Tajikistan. The Soviets initially had no intention of creating a separate state for Central Asia's Iranian peoples, who spoke Tajik, a language very close to Persian, plus, in some parts, other Eastern Iranian dialects. However, Stalin later found such a republic useful for controlling Central Asia and projecting influence into Afghanistan and beyond.[10] The newly created Republic of Tajikistan was deprived of the two most important centers of the region's Irano-Islamic culture, Samarkand and Bukhara, which were incorporated into the neighboring Republic of Uzbekistan. This delinkage from their historic and cultural roots made it very difficult for the Tajiks to develop a national identity transcending regional peculiarities because they "were left without two centers around which the process of nation-building was unfolding."[11] Large numbers of Tajiks living in what is now Uzbekistan were classified as Uzbek, while Uzbek-inhabited areas such as Khojand (Leninabad) were incorporated into the new Tajik republic. These policies disrupted Tajikistan's ethnic and cultural balance. Most notably, the large Uzbek minority became a hindrance to Tajik nation building. This process was further undermined by a distorted pattern of economic development favoring the Uzbek-inhabited regions and linking their industrial base to those of Uzbekistan and Russia.

Politically, too, the largely Uzbek Khojandis (Leninabadi), along with the republic's Russian population, dominated the Communist Party and hence the main levers of power. The inhabitants of Kulyab, a major center of cotton cultivation with a substantial Uzbek population, became the junior partners of the Khojandis in running the republic. A few ethnic Pamiris from the region of Gorno-Badakhshan were co-opted into this Uzbek-Russian-dominated structure. The rest of the republic remained underdeveloped and its people underrepresented.[12]

Perestroika and Its Consequences

Gorbachev's reforms reached Central Asia by 1988–89 and led to the emergence of several informal groups with a variety of cultural, environmental, and political goals. These groups were largely government orchestrated, with names like

Yavaran-e-Perestroika (Helpers of Perestroika). They later led to the formation of political groups and parties.[13] In Tajikistan, they included locally based nationalist and Islamist organizations and those favoring democratic rule.[14]

The nationalists and the Islamists generated the most fear among the Uzbek-Russian elite, who had dominated Tajikistan, as well as the Russian and Uzbek governments. Members of the traditional power structure viewed the nationalists as bent on resurrecting Tajik culture and language and the Islamists as determined to set up an Islamic state, hence challenging their rule.

Uzbekistan was deeply concerned about the revitalization of Tajik culture and identity because it feared that such activities could lead to irredentist claims toward Samarkand and Bukhara and intensify the rising ethnocultural consciousness of its Tajik minority. During this period, Uzbekistan's Tajiks started a movement to establish Tajik-language schools in the republic,[15] and Tajik nationalists attempted to establish closer links with Iran and Afghanistan.[16] Given Uzbekistan's ambition for regional leadership and its leader Islam Karimov's pan-Turkistani and, initially, even pan-Turkist tendencies, any strengthening of the Iranian element in the region was viewed with apprehension.[17] The Islamists posed an even more serious threat to the Uzbek leadership, given that their message was transethnic and that a substantial Islamist movement had arisen in Uzbekistan.

Tajikistan's Russian population was equally alarmed by the nationalist and Islamist awakening, fearing that such an awakening would challenge its privileged position. Attacks by unidentified people during riots in Dushanbe in February 1990 aggravated these fears.[18]

The manipulation of political and cultural forces and ethnic and sectarian tensions became an important part of internal power struggles in Moscow during the Ligachev-Gorbachev dispute (1987–89) and the Gorbachev-Yeltsin rivalry (1990–91). This practice extended to various republics. In Tajikistan, it exacerbated existing tensions and contributed to the civil war.

From Growing Tension to Full-Scale Civil War (1990–1992)

The tempo of political activity in Tajikistan significantly increased in 1990 and at times became violent. The wave of demonstrations and rallies that swept Dushanbe in February 1990 heralded the descent into civil war. Russian sources have blamed the nationalists and the Islamists, notably the Islamic Revival Party of Tajikistan (IRPT), for the violent turn of some of these demonstrations.[19] Certain acts committed by some Islamists, such as harassing Tajik women wearing non-Islamic attire, strengthened this perception.

However, the local leadership and warring factions in Moscow clearly manipulated rising nationalist and Islamist sentiments for a variety of political purposes. Some of the demonstrators in 1990 attacked First Secretary Kakhar Makhamov because he represented the power structure disliked by the population. But Moscow politics also had a role. Because Makhamov was Gorbachev's man, Yeltsin's supporters wanted to replace him with their man, a goal they accomplished in 1991. Following the failed August 1991 coup d'état, Makhamov was accused of supporting the coup plotters and dismissed. Rahmon Nabiev, whom Gorbachev had dismissed on charges of corruption and alcoholism in 1985, was elected president the following November.

The spread of rumors, reportedly by Azerbaijanis, in Dushanbe that large numbers of Armenian refugees were to be settled in the capital and allocated scarce housing was the immediate triggering event. Because few Armenian families were settled in Dushanbe, the question arises: Who spread the rumors and why?[20] Intranomenklatura disputes and rivalries played a role. Some analysts concluded that the regional elite instigated the riots to discredit the nationalist and Islamist opposition.[21] The declaration of independence by Tajikistan on 25 August 1990 did not calm the situation.

In September 1991, acting Tajik president Qadruddin Aslonov banned the Communist Party, as Boris Yeltsin had done in Russia. But given the Tajik Communist Party's regional and ethnic base, this decision was reversed by Aslonov's successor, Rahmon Nabiev.

During the November 1991 presidential elections, Nabiev, a Khojandi Communist, ran against Dawlat Khodanazarov, a native of Badakhshan put forward by the three main opposition parties (Rastakhiz, the IRPT, and the Democratic Party of Tajikistan). Officially, Nabiev obtained 57 percent of the votes and Khodanazarov 30 percent in what was judged to be an unfair election since the Communist Party and state controlled the media.[22]

Nabiev's victory did not stabilize the situation. Rather, it led to another series of protests and counterprotests that culminated in the civil war. Regionalism and long-standing resentment on the part of certain groups and elements contributed to the violence, but it was the Khojandis' determination to maintain their monopoly of power that played the decisive role in Tajikistan's descent into civil war.[23]

Even if the opposition was guilty of contributing to the violence, the Khojandi-Kulyab nomenklatura was responsible for its transformation into civil war. They even freed known criminals from prison to take part in the conflict and appealed to Uzbekistan president Islam Karimov for help.[24] Indeed, most impartial observers agree that without the Khojandi-Kulyab manipulation the civil strife "would never have ended with a civil war because, by early fall 1992, neither side could prevail militarily or otherwise."[25]

The Russian Role

Until early 1993, the Russian government claimed neutrality in the conflict. During the first months of 1992, Moscow apparently did not pay much attention to Central Asia, but the Russian military based in Tajikistan (the 201st Motorized Rifle Division) and in Moscow supported the Communist nomenklatura. According to Gretsky:

An overwhelming majority of the division's Russian or Russian-speaking officers were born and had lived practically all their lives in Tajikistan or other Central Asian republics. They had no chance to continue their service in Russia, which had plans to cut its armed forces and was already struggling to accommodate tens of thousands of officers brought home from Eastern Europe.[26]

Thus the Russian military, either independently or with Moscow's approval, intervened on behalf of the existing power structure. Military officials alarmed Moscow with reports of the dangers of the spread of Islamic fundamentalism and the threat it posed to Russia's interests, including the condition of ethnic Russians in Central Asia and the risk of their mass exodus. They further "convinced the Kremlin that military intervention in support of the Khujandi-PFT [Popular Front of Tajikistan] alliance was the only option to hold off the spread of Islamic fundamentalism."[27] In short, the military and the local elite manipulated the actual or perceived threat of Islamic fundamentalism to stifle movements aimed at changing the unfair and unrepresentative power structure.

Growing Role of the Military in Setting Policy toward the CIS

The Russian military in Tajikistan was helped in its goal of moving Moscow toward a policy of favoring the Communist-era power structure by the fact that by mid-1992, the Near Abroad had acquired greater importance in Moscow's foreign policy agenda. Russia's principal concerns in the Near Abroad were (1) to secure the territorial integrity of the Russian Federation by curtailing and regulating armed conflicts in its vicinity and preventing their spillover into Russia; (2) to create a "belt" of good neighbors around it; (3) to establish Russia as the legitimate guarantor of military and political stability on the territory of the former Soviet Union, thereby asserting Russia's "special security responsibilities in the FSU"; (4) to defend the Russian and Russian-speaking population of the FSU by all means, including military force; and (5) to promote the integration of the CIS and to transform it into both an effective collective security system and an economic organization similar to the European Union.[28]

Furthermore, by this time, the Russian military establishment exerted more influence in shaping Russia's policy toward Central Asia. In an article in *Segodnya*, Mastibek Davlatskayev wrote, "A paradoxical situation is developing, one in which Russia's foreign policy in the Central Asian region is beginning to be determined by the Ministries of Defense and Security."[29] Later the Foreign Ministry also backed a policy of active support to the establishment forces.

The Tajik Civil War helped Russia achieve some broader regional strategic and political goals. This was facilitated by the fall of the Russian-supported Afghan government of Najibullah in April 1992 to the forces of Tajik commander Ahmad Shah Masoud and the establishment of a new government by forces who had fought the Soviet Union. Following these events, Russia, in effect, declared that its external borders coincided with those of the CIS. Therefore, the defense of these borders was necessary for the defense of Russia. In the winter of 2003, Russian troops were still guarding the Tajik-Afghan border. According to Andrei Kortunov and Andrei Shoumikhin, it was under the impact of the Tajik Civil War that in September 1992 "a new CIS agreement on collective peacekeeping forces was adopted which modified the latter's mandate to include the functions of 'collective defense.' To support that decision, the Joint Command of CIS Peacekeeping Forces was created."[30] Kyrgyzstan, Uzbekistan, and Kazakhstan contributed troops to the peacekeeping forces in Tajikistan, which were deployed in 1997, thus giving the legitimacy of collective operations to Russia's military presence.

Uzbek-Russian Rivalry and the Tajik Peace Process

By mid-1994, the Russian-Uzbek alliance had become strained, and Russia realized that Uzbekistan was a potential rival for influence rather than a "junior partner" in the management of the region. The growing cooperation between Uzbekistan and the West, simultaneously with the cooling off of Russian-Western ties, contributed to the change of Russia's perception of Uzbekistan's role. A major watershed in U.S.-Uzbek cooperation was U.S. secretary of defense William Perry's visit to Uzbekistan in April 1995.[31] Afterwards, U.S.-Uzbek relations grew closer, while Russian-Uzbek ties became strained. Only the Taliban's capture of Kabul in September 1996 and major northern cities such as Mazar-e-Sharif in August 1998 once more brought them closer in a fight against Islamic extremism.[32]

The divergence of Russian-Uzbek interests, coupled with the Tajik government's inability to completely subdue the opposition, led to efforts to seek a negotiated settlement to the conflict, which had cost the lives of 100,000 people.[33] The most important factors in the success of the peace process, which was launched by the United Nations in 1994 and ended with the signing of the Moscow agreement of 27 June 1997, were the rise of the Taliban in Afghanistan and improved Iranian-Russian relations.[34] Concerning the former, the Taliban's capture of Kabul and the dismantling of Burhaneddin Rabbani's government increased Russian interests in a stable Tajikistan. Because the Tajiks dominated Rabbani's government, the Uzbek general Abdul Rashid Dostam, who controlled some of the northern parts of Afghanistan, had fought against the Rabbani government with the active support of both Russia and Uzbekistan, which accused the Rabbani government of helping the Tajik rebels.[35] However, the Taliban's Islamist ideology was more radical than that of either the Tajik opposition or the Rabbani faction in Afghanistan. Additionally, the Taliban were viewed as a tool of Pakistan and the West for the advancement of their strategic and economic goals in Central Asia, which conflicted with Russian interests.[36] Thus the challenge of the Taliban created common interests between Russia and Afghanistan's Tajiks.

Uzbekistan and Uzbek president Islam Karimov remained wary of collaborating with Ahmad Shah Masoud, who was now resisting the Taliban's northward advances, to help resolve the Tajik Civil War. Had the Taliban offered General Dostam and Uzbekistan an attractive deal, the latter might have actively prevented reaching a peace agreement. Indeed, even after the signing of the agreement, Uzbekistan expressed "some unhappiness with the Accords."[37] Although Uzbekistan, as one of the observers states in the inter-Tajik talks, was "supposed to be a guarantor, it initially refused to do so."[38] More seriously, Uzbekistan provided "a safe haven and operational freedom to former Prime Minister Abdul Malik Abdullojonov, leader of the Leninabadi faction, who has been campaigning against the agreement and even subtly threatening defection."[39] Since by 1996, Russia had become more serious about stabilizing Tajikistan, it pursued a resolution of the conflict.

Improved relations between Iran and Russia and between Iran and Ahmad Shah Masoud further increased prospects for a peace settlement in Tajikistan. Russian-Iranian relations had already begun to improve by late 1994, but Ahmad Shah Masoud had kept his distance from Iran with the hope of gaining U.S. support. However, the common challenge of the Taliban's new brand of Islamic extremism coupled with other strategic and political factors led the parties to accept a compromise. Iran used its influence with the Tajik opposition to facilitate the peace process.

The implementation of the peace accord's provisions has been very difficult. The allocation of some governmental posts to United Tajik Opposition (UTO) members has certainly not transformed Tajikistan's politics in the direction of a truly participatory system.[40] Nevertheless, Islamists have acquired a degree of legitimacy.

Despite the end of the Tajik Civil War, Tajikistan has continued to be Russia's front line of defense against the spread of Islamic radicalism. Tajikistan and Russia became deeply involved in the Afghan Civil War on the side of the anti-Taliban forces. In short, even after the end of the Tajik Civil War, the Islamic factor continued to play an important role in Russia's approach toward Central Asia.

Threat of Islamic Extremism: Impetus to Russian–Central Asian Cooperation, September 1996–September 2001

The fall of Kabul to the Taliban on 27 September 1996 intensified the anxiety of Russia and the Central Asian countries over the impact of this victory on their own Islamist movements and hence their security. Russia sought to use this opportunity both to revitalize the CIS collective security system and to strengthen its bonds with the Central Asian states, especially in the military sphere and in fighting Muslim militants. Because of the divergence of opinion within the CIS about the whole concept of collective security, the first goal proved unattainable. Even collective efforts limited to Central Asia proved difficult to organize, especially between 1996 and 1998 when the potential threat of the Taliban seemed fairly remote for countries such as Kazakhstan and Kyrgyzstan. Furthermore, Turkmenistan had reached a modus vivendi with the emerging Taliban forces since 1994.

There were, however, a number of meetings between Russian and Central Asian officials, including a meeting between Russian prime minister Viktor Chernomyrdin and the heads of Central Asian countries in Almaty on 5 October 1996. After the meeting, Kazakh president Nursultan Nazarbaev said, "We issue a warning. If the conflict spreads beyond the border of Afghanistan into the Commonwealth of Independent States our states will take adequate measures."[41] Nevertheless, he and his colleagues pledged to avoid interfering in the Afghan conflict, although Islam Karimov urged support for General Dostam.[42]

The Russian reaction was initially cautious, particularly regarding any active engagement in the conflict. Some officials even ruled out sending reinforcements to Tajikistan. The secretary of Russia's Defense Council, Yurii Baturin, said, "We [Russia] must act very carefully as we are dealing with the Orient."[43] However, Yevgenii Primakov, Russia's foreign minister, announced that Moscow would reinforce its troops on the Tajik-Afghan border.[44]

The only high official who supported providing aid to the anti-Taliban forces was Alexander Lebed, the chairman of the Russian Federation's Security Council, but his call was ignored.[45] Even after his removal, Lebed continued to call for active Russian support for the Afghan opposition because if Russia and Ahmad Shah Masoud failed to prevent the Taliban's advance into northern Afghanistan, "a big war might break out in Uzbekistan and Tajikistan."[46] Despite these contradictory signals from Moscow, Western media reported that Russia was sending aid to the anti-Taliban forces.[47]

However, after the capture of Kabul in September 1996 and until the fall of Mazar-e-Sharif on 8 August 1998, the rise of the Taliban did not create the kind of solidarity that Russia had expected. The Central Asian countries continued to pursue policies dictated by their peculiar conditions. Uzbekistan's main concern was to protect General Dostam and was not averse to some deal with the Taliban. Both Uzbekistan and Kazakhstan also were concerned that Russia "may use any spread in radical Islam to the former Soviet republics to strengthen its influence over the young states and their vast energy and mineral resources."[48] The circumstances, however, changed with the fall of Mazar-e-Sharif, the capture of Bamiyan on 13 September 1998, and the large-scale massacre of the Shi'as and eleven Iranian diplomats by the Taliban.

These events demonstrated that the rise of the Taliban could endanger Central Asia. Moreover, between 1996 and 1998, there was a rise in the activities of Islamist groups in Uzbekistan and Kyrgyzstan. The Uzbek government's crackdown on these groups, notably those led by Tahir Yoldash and Jumma Namangi, forced them to flee the country and find refuge in Tajikistan and Afghanistan.[49] The two united in exile to form the Islamic Movement of Uzbekistan (IMU), and in 1999 they conducted incursions into Kyrgyzstan's Batken region. The IMU also established close links with the Taliban regime in Afghanistan. Meanwhile, relations between Uzbekistan, on the one hand, and Pakistan and the Taliban regime, on the other, deteriorated. Uzbekistan accused Pakistan, or at least elements within the Pakistani intelligence community, of helping and training Uzbek Islamists.[50]

Consequently, after the Taliban's 1998 victories brought nearly 90 percent of the Afghan territory under its control, Uzbekistan showed greater willingness to cooperate with Russia and Tajikistan in preventing the Taliban's further advance. Some Western sources reported that Tajikistan was "very much the junior partner" in this tripartite collaboration. The basis of this "troika" cooperation was laid in

Moscow during a 6 May 1998 meeting between Yeltsin and Karimov to which the Tajik president was not invited. He was only contacted by telephone to agree to its terms.[51] President Karimov overcame his dislike of the Tajiks enough to meet with Ahmad Shah Masoud in Tashkent.[52]

However, even after 1998, Uzbekistan remained a reluctant partner in the Russia-directed activities designed to support the anti-Taliban forces and establish more lasting regional infrastructures to deal with radical Islamists.[53] Such regional organizations included the Shanghai Five, which was transformed first into the Shanghai Forum and later the Shanghai Cooperation Organization, the Bishkek Antiterrorism Center as part of a collective CIS antiterrorism effort, and the Rapid Reaction Force within the CIS to deal with terrorism. Uzbekistan did not join the Shanghai Five until 2001 and only in July 2000 participated in the Dushanbe Summit of the group as an observer. The absence of Uzbekistan has also made the CIS Rapid Reaction Force, which is eventually to have 3,000 men, less viable. In fact, CIS executive secretary Yurii Yarov referred to this point and noted, "The force would be more effective if Uzbekistan again acceded to the CIS Collective Security Treaty."[54]

The force's primary goal is to "fight terrorism," which essentially means extremist Islamic groups. According to President Putin's statement after the CIS Yerevan Summit on 25 May 2001, the force should eventually be transformed into a more conventional force capable of protecting the borders of Tajikistan.[55] There were other CIS-level antiterrorism activities, such as a command-and-staff exercise in the city of Osh in Kyrgyzstan code-named "South-Antiterror 2001" in which high-level representatives of intelligence and security services from nine CIS countries participated.[56] However, lingering suspicions about Russia's real motives, plus financial difficulties, have made the full and effective implementation of these measures problematic. It appears that one aspect of Russia's vision of the Bishkek Antiterrorism Center's mandate, namely, the creation of a legal framework "for the rapid deployment and operation of Russian antiterrorist units on the territories of the CIS countries," has been especially jarring to a number of CIS members.[57]

Revitalizing CIS Collective Security System

As discussed earlier, Russia always had the ambition of turning the CIS Collective Security Treaty into a multilateral regional security organization similar to NATO. But policy differences with key countries such as Uzbekistan, Azerbaijan, and Georgia made this goal impossible. Indeed, the CIS Collective Security Treaty became a rather weak mechanism for the advancement of either Russia's security interests or the maintenance of regional stability.

Notwithstanding this background, in its efforts to regain lost ground and consolidate its position in post–11 September Central Asia, Russia revived this old project and established the "Collective Security Treaty Organization" (CSTO). The decision to do so was reached at the 14 May 2002 meeting of the collective security council held in Moscow.[58] Later, on 7 October 2002, the presidents of Armenia,

Belarus, Kazakhstan, Kyrgyzstan, and Russia signed the charter and agreement on the legal status of the organization during a CIS summit in Chisinau.[59] In his answer to a question regarding the main goals of the CSTO during an April 2003 press conference in Dushanbe, President Putin said, "The purpose and meaning of the activities of the Collective Security Treaty is to ensure the security, territorial integrity and sovereignty of member countries. This is the principal task." He then specified the instruments required to realize these goals, including a unified headquarters, rapid deployment forces, and the coordination of foreign policies.[60]

The creation of the organization provides a legal and institutional framework for Russia's security-related activities in Central Asia. However, it is not certain that this effort will be more successful than previous attempts to create an effective Russia-centered collective security organization in the region.

Shanghai Cooperation Organization (SCO): Islamic Extremism as an Impetus to Broader Regional Cooperation

The Shanghai group's formation brought China into the Central Asian security equation and served as a vehicle for Sino-Russian cooperation in the region. It also facilitated the resolution of some security-related issues in China's relations with the Central Asians. The spread of Islamic extremism was a major impetus behind the group's formation, but the SCO also reflected the ascendancy of Russia's multipolar strategy. The linchpin of a new multipolar world was to be a Russian-Chinese alliance, as illustrated by Russian foreign minster Igor Ivanov's statement during the forum's 1999 summit in Bishkek: "In the world today, there is an active struggle to establish a new world order. As you know, Russia, China, and many other states want to see a multipolar world."[61] A Russian analyst explained Russia's interest in the Shanghai Forum in terms of Russia's dwindling influence:

> For Russia, the significance of the meeting in Bishkek rests, above all, on the fact that Russia is regarded less and less as a serious "player" in this region and beyond. . . . In addition, the obvious weakness of Russia revealed during the Kosovo War, which can lead to new debacles in innumerable conflicts, as in the north Caucasus, forces the Kremlin to seek alternative geopolitical alliances.[62]

The SCO came into existence as the Shanghai Five, consisting of Russia, China, Kazakhstan, Kyrgyzstan, and Tajikistan, on 26 April 1996 during a meeting in Shanghai. Its objectives range from security to economics. Some of the security-related issues concern Sino–Central Asian relations, including the delimitation of borders and the prevention of potential military tensions.[63]

Since 1998–99, the main focus of the forum's activities has shifted to fighting "religious extremism, separatism and international terrorism." The latter refers mainly to the activities of Muslim militants in the CIS. Even the politically active moderate Islamists are suspect. Moderate Muslims' call for democracy and human ‑ights is interpreted as a mere cover for more sinister objectives. According to Oleg

Zotov, "Islamic extremists and terrorists actively exploit the 'human rights' and 'democracy' slogans for already a long time."[64] Russian policy makers, including President Putin, and analysts concur that Islamic extremism in the CIS and the so-called arc of instability poses an existential threat to Russia because Islamic extremists are attempting to reclaim Central Asia, the Caucasus, the Crimea, and the Volga-Ural region and because "anti-governmental and intrinsically sectarian extremist forces are ready to turn the entire continent into a zone of chaos."[65]

Separatism is another SCO concern. Both Russia and China face separatist challenges in Chechnya and Xinjiang, where Muslim Uighurs live. In both regions, Islam strengthens autonomist tendencies even if it does not cause them. Therefore, during its first summit in 1996, the Shanghai Five signed a declaration opposing separatism aimed mainly against Muslim Uighurs.[66] It may be because of this emphasis that in May 2002, India expressed interest in joining the SCO. Iran may also be interested in the organization. This interest, according to some sources, could cause tensions between Russia and China, with China favoring and Russia objecting to Iran's membership.[67]

Western Perception of SCO and Russian Activities

Because the creation of the Shanghai Five (SCO) coincided with and was a reflection of Russia's new multipolar foreign policy, it was viewed with misgivings by Western, especially U.S., analysts and policy makers. This strategy was viewed as anti–United States and a cover for a neo-imperialist Russian policy. Western and Russian views of the nature of the Taliban regime and the actual or potential threat they posed to Central Asia differed widely.[68]

Initially, the West, especially the United States, did not view the Taliban or their ideology negatively.[69] Rather, the United States hoped that the Taliban would stabilize Afghanistan and open up new possibilities for the export of Central Asia's energy—especially Turkmen gas—to Pakistan and beyond. The United States also viewed the Taliban as useful allies in containing Iran, eliminating any possibility of Iran becoming an outlet for Central Asian energy, and checking Russian ambitions.[70]

It was only after the bombing of U.S. embassies in Nairobi, Kenya, and Dar-es-Salaam, Tanzania, on 7 August 1998 that the U.S. view began to change.[71] Osama bin Laden, an exiled Saudi, a major financial benefactor of the Taliban, and a resident of Afghanistan, was implicated. It still appeared, however, that the United States would consider recognizing the Taliban if they handed over bin Laden.[72]

Russia, by contrast, saw the emergence of the Taliban regime as part of a broader Western, especially U.S., strategy of limiting its influence in the FSU. Russia did not want an alternative southern pipeline to be built, which would have reduced the Central Asian countries' dependence on itself. Some Russian commentators saw the Taliban's emergence as part of a U.S. strategy to weaken Iran and India, both friends of Russia.[73] Moreover, from the very beginning, Russia saw direct and expanding linkages between forces in Afghanistan and their supporters in Pakistan and the Chechen rebels.[74]

Indeed, the Russians felt that in Central Asia, too, they alone were fighting to stem the tide of Islamic extremism and were bitter that the West did not appreciate their efforts or sympathize with Russia's plight. The more conspiratorial types saw Afghanistan and Chechnya as part of a broad Western plot to undermine Russia. The events of 11 September 2001 altered Western views of the SCO; some analysts began to see it as a potentially useful instrument in the fight against global terrorism.[75]

Islam, Russia, and Central Asia after 11 September 2001

The events of 11 September 2001 and ensuing developments offered both opportunities and challenges to Russia in Central Asia and globally. The Russian public and government appeared genuinely shocked and dismayed at the sight of the tragedy inflicted upon the United States, despite some discordant notes sounded by a few Communist and nationalist figures.[76] Russia also felt that its views regarding the nature of the Taliban and the interconnectedness of the Islamist terrorist network had been vindicated.[77]

The U.S. initiative to form a coalition against international terrorism provided Russia with an opportunity to recast its relations with the United States and Europe in a new framework by joining the antiterrorism coalition. The 11 September terrorist attacks and ensuing events ended the already discredited multipolar strategy, but Russia hoped that it would receive economic and other concessions from the West, as well as more sympathy for the situation in Chechnya.[78] There was also a civilizational dimension to Russia's policy. Russian officials did not refer to this factor, but analysts and commentators did. Leonid Radzikhovksy wrote in *Vremya MN*, "A clash between Islamic and Christian civilizations once seemed like science fiction, mind games. It is now a fact of life." He criticized those who still believed in Russian-Muslim cooperation to counter the West and said: "Russia will not be able to stand aside this time. This is Moscow's unique chance to become integrated into the Western world and become its real ally. Some illusions [Russian-Muslim cooperation] will have to be given up in order to do so. Let's give them up."[79]

Yet the U.S. decision to attack the Taliban-dominated regions of Afghanistan and its demand for Central Asian cooperation, including the use of their airfields, posed several dilemmas for Russia: Should Russia become militarily involved in Afghanistan? Participation could potentially have given Russia greater influence in shaping the political future of Afghanistan, including guaranteeing a more influential role for its ally, the Northern Alliance.[80] But the memories of the Afghan War argued against this option; the military, in particular, was against active involvement.[81] The Russians were also concerned about U.S. statements that the attack on Al-Qaeda and the Taliban was just the beginning of a long-term war against terrorist groups and states that sponsored them, an assertion troubling to

Russia because of its close relations with Iraq, Iran, and Syria.[82] More important, Russians were anxious that the antiterrorism campaign, after the wiping out of the Taliban, be conducted in a multilateral context.[83] Russia was concerned about the impact of the U.S.-led military operations in Afghanistan and its endorsement of them on its relations with Muslim countries. In order to protect against any negative fallout, Ahmad Kadyrov, head of the administration of the Chechen Republic, and the muftis of the North Caucasus visited Egypt, Syria, Jordan, and Iraq to explain Russia's position on terrorism.[84]

Members of the Russian leadership, at least those in the legislative branch, were also worried about the fallout of Russia's endorsememt of military operations in Afghanistan on its Muslim population. For example, Mikhail Prusak, the governor of the Novgorod region and the chairman of the Federation Council's International Committee, stated, "Russia's participation could lead to more Islamic radicalism inside the country and such a turn of events should not be disregarded. Chechnya alone is enough for us."[85] Ultimately, Russia opted for a strategy of "collaboration without military participation." After some initial hesitation, Russia acquiesced in U.S. use of the Central Asian countries' airfields.

The results of the Afghan operations on Russia's security and other interests have been mixed. On the positive side, the elimination of the Taliban regime and the change in Pakistan's approach toward its own Muslim extremist groups has weakened the position of Muslim extremists in Central Asia by drying up major sources of support. The underlying causes of extremism and hence the potential for future threats have not been eliminated, but the fall of the Taliban regime has not led to the establishment of a government under Russian influence. Rather, Afghan political leaders, notably Burhaneddin Rabbani, long supported by Russia, have been dislodged. The long-term political future of Russia's former allies in the Northern Alliance, especially the Tajiks, is also not clear, although they held influential positions within the post-Taliban government of Hamid Karzai. Having lost their charismatic leader Ahmad Shah Masoud, who was assassinated 9 September 2001, the Tajiks are internally divided and are mistrusted by the Pashtun majority, Pakistan, and the United States.[86]

In post-Taliban Afghanistan, the United States, other Western countries, and Turkey, which have assumed the leadership of an expanded international peacekeeping force, will have the most influence. In Central Asia, too, the elimination of the Taliban regime has led to the enhancement of U.S. and other Western military and political presence. The United States and its coalition partners have acquired the use of the Khanabad airbase in Uzbekistan, the Manas base near Bishkek in Kyrgyzstan, and, according to some sources, the Kulyab base in Tajikistan.[87]

During the early part of the campaign against the Taliban, the issue of the length of the U.S. military presence was left ambiguous, but with seeming understanding that it would be of limited duration. Important elements of Russia's political and military establishment oppose this presence and see it as undermining CIS collective security structures. In January 2002, *Krasnaya Zvezda*, the newspaper of Russia's armed forces, complained of "the inexorable growth" of the U.S. military presence in Central Asia despite the winding down of the military operations in Afghanistan.[88]

The U.S. and Western military presence in Central Asia is likely to be of long duration, with broader strategic objectives beyond the elimination of Al-Qaeda and the Taliban regime. During a visit to the United States in March 2002, Uzbek president Islam Karimov stated that the United States "can stay on the territory of Uzbekistan as long as it needs." This statement supports the U.S. position, which "disclaims the intent to establish 'permanent bases' in Central Asia but seeks the use of bases or stations without setting a time limit."[89] Karimov also attacked "Iranian intrigues and the power grab by the Panjshir Valley Tajik factions."[90] Some Western sources have accused the Panjshiris of "seeking to establish a new Afghan army under its own control with Russian weaponry."[91] Ironically, without the resistance of the Panjshir Tajiks and Russian and Iranian assistance, the Taliban might have reached Uzbekistan's borders.

The Kyrgyz foreign minister in early April 2002 objected "to permanent military bases in the country."[92] However, Kyrgyzstan, too, has not put any specific time limit on the Western presence. Meanwhile, the international development institutions and European countries have been showing greater interest in Central Asia, as illustrated by the April 2002 visit by the president of the World Bank, James Wolfensohn.[93]

None of these developments is necessarily against Russia's security interests. If Western involvement became large enough and stabilized the region, it would reduce Russia's fear of threats emanating from its southern frontiers. Some Russian analysts like Sergei Karaganov have seen the post–11 September conditions as providing an opportunity for Russia and the United States to strike a "grand bargain" where "Russia would join with the United States in a new coalition, stop arms trade with Iran and other countries accused of sponsoring terrorism, and reduce nuclear weapons arsenals." However, Karaganov added, "But for that, we would have to get something." That something could include "non-expansion of NATO to the borders of Russia, [and] solution of the problem of Soviet debt."[94]

It is highly unlikely that the West would be willing to make such concessions. In fact, during a November 2002 NATO summit held in Prague, seven new countries, including the three Baltic states, were invited to join the Atlantic alliance. Meanwhile, although a Western presence would reduce threats from the south, it would also limit Russia's freedom of action. It is for this reason that both President Putin and Foreign Minister Igor Ivanov, while emphasizing the point that the Central Asian countries are sovereign states and can decide their own policies, expect that the U.S. military presence will be of limited duration. This dual approach is reflected in an interview of Igor Ivanov with *Izvestia* in July 2002 in which he said:

> American presence in Central Asia would be justifiable if it were in accordance with the time frame defined by the UN Security Council for Peacemaking Operations in Afghanistan. The Afghan government expects 18 months to be enough

to form its own security and military forces. As for bilateral relations, the Central Asian countries will regulate these matters based on their own interests.[95]

Nevertheless, on other occasions, Ivanov has said that Russia is not "indifferent to how long the U.S. stays" and that it will ask the United States "for maximum transparency in their military activities in the region and time limitations for their presence."[96] Meanwhile, Russia has been bolstering its own military presence in the region, as illustrated by the establishment of a military base in Kant, Kyrgyzstan, near Bishkek, in the context of the CIS collective security system.[97] Russian analysts have interpreted this act as an attempt by Russia to recover its "lost position in Central Asia."[98]

In sum, if Russia viewed being the major player in Central Asia and establishing its claim to great power status as basic interests, the post–11 September developments have not been beneficial. The war against Iraq, which has led to a large-scale United States and British military presence in that country, and the assumption of a stronger role by NATO in Afghanistan through its support for the International Security Assistance Force (ISAF) in April 2003 intensified the adverse consequences of post–11 September developments for Russia in terms of its influence in Central Asia.[99] For a decade, Russia used the threat of Islamic radicalism to maintain its position in Central Asia. Ironically, the reduction of this threat has eroded its regional position. The magnitude of this erosion, however, depends on the extent to which the West is able and willing to assume extensive and long-term responsibility for the region's security and economic development, and how effectively Moscow strengthens its regional ties. In turn, Moscow's ability to strengthen its regional ties, to a great extent, depends on the state of its economy. This fact is illustrated by a statement made by Uzbek president Islam Karimov at a November 2001 CIS summit. Recognizing that the pace of integration within the CIS depends on Russia's economic power, Karimov stated that "if the ruble and the Russian economy continue to strengthen, none of us [CIS members] will be able to escape its influence."[100] However, with a growing Western presence, it is unlikely that Russia will ever regain its influence as the sole dominating power in Central Asia, even if its economy improves.

Russia and the Transcaucasus: The Impact of the Islamic Factor

Some of the same factors that have determined Russia's approach toward Central Asia have also influenced its policy toward the Caucasus. In this case, too, Russia's main goal has been to prevent developments in the Caucasus from adversely affecting its security. In fact, in view of Russia's problems in the North Caucasus, especially in Chechnya, the security dimensions of the Caucasus are of greater importance than those of Central Asia. The Transcaucasus region is also important to Russia from an economic perspective because of Azerbaijani oil and gas and the question of pipelines to carry these resources to world markets through Georgia and the Turkish port of Ceyhan, which would reduce the importance of the Russian export terminal of Novorossiisk. Thus the interaction of these security and economic interests and concerns has shaped Russia's policy toward the region throughout various stages of its development. The competition between Russia's powerful interests groups has been another influential variable.

Interestingly, the Islamic factor has had a lesser impact on Russian policy toward the Transcaucasus than toward Central Asia. To the extent that the Islamic factor has played a role, it has been through its connection with the Chechen conflict. Two factors account for this situation. First, although Azerbaijan's Muslims outnumber the followers of other faiths, two of the region's three countries—Georgia and Armenia—are Christian, while Islam is the predominant religion in Central Asia. Second, unlike Central Asia, which has principally been subjected to influences emanating from Afghanistan and Pakistan, where militant Islamic groups and tendencies have been strong for the last twenty-five years, the two Muslim countries in the Transcaucasus's vicinity, Iran and Turkey, for different reasons have played down the Islamic factor, especially its extremist versions, in their approach to the region.

In Turkey's case, this has been due to its desire to represent itself as a modern, secular, and Western-oriented country that could be a gateway to Europe and an alternative model of development for the Transcaucasian states. Moreover, given the predominance of Shi'ism in Azerbaijan, predominantly Sunni Turkey has found the argument of Turkic brotherhood a more useful tool of influence.

Because of its preoccupation with domestic reconstruction, concern over its southern and eastern frontiers, a lessening of the ideological dimension of its foreign policy, a determination not to antagonize Russia, and a desire to alleviate the anxiety of the Transcaucasian countries regarding its objectives, Iran has also been circumspect in using the Islamic card. Nevertheless, both Iran and Turkey have used religious affinity as an instrument of their policy. Thus, although most Azerbaijanis are Shi'a, Turkey and some Arab states have built more mosques in Azerbaijan than Iran. According to some sources, in 2000, only 10 percent of mosques in Azerbaijan were built with Iran's help.[101] This has been motivated by a desire on the part of Turkey and Arab states to spread Sunnism in Azerbaijan in order to check Iranian influence.[102] The Azerbaijani government, too, has encouraged this trend in order to undermine Iran's influence while accusing Iran of fomenting Islamic radicalism, including its Wahhabi variety, despite its strong anti-Iran and anti-Shi'a proclivities.[103]

This Turkish-Azerbaijani policy backfired. Turkey inadvertently facilitated the penetration of extremist ideas into Azerbaijan by undermining Azerbaijanis' traditional faith and enhancing Azerbaijanis' susceptibility to Wahhabi and other Islamist ideologies. It thus created opportunities for Hizb-ul-Tahrir and Osama bin Laden's followers to establish footholds in the country.[104] Since a substantial number of Azerbaijan's minorities in the north of the country bordering Dagestan are Sunnis, religious extremism has become intertwined with ethnic resentment.[105]

The Chechen conflict affected these developments, but it is hard to measure the extent of its influence. Clearly, the North Caucasus has been a conduit for the infiltration of nontraditional and radical versions of Islam into the Transcaucasus and has particularly impacted the evolution of Azerbaijani Islam.

The growth of Muslim extremist movements has introduced an Islamic dimension to Russia's relations with Azerbaijan, creating a linkage between such groups and Chechen rebels and leading Russia, at one point, to accuse Azerbaijan of having become a "hotbed of Islamic radicalism."[106] The willingness of some South Caucasian countries to allow Chechen separatists to use their territories, or their inability to prevent such linkages, has affected Russia's approach toward them.

In sum, Russia's policy toward the Caucasus has been primarily determined by economic and geostrategic considerations, plus rivalry among its interest groups. Nevertheless, the Islamic factor has also had some influence, especially through the Chechen connection. Moreover, the relative influence of these factors has varied during different stages of the evolution of Russian policy toward the region.

Evolution of Russian Policy, 1991–1993

Russian policy toward the Caucasus has gone through several stages since 1991, reflecting the evolution of the Russian debate on fundamental issues of identity and foreign policy. The last years of the Soviet Union also affected this process. During this period, intraleadership rivalries in Moscow determined policy. In Azerbaijan's case, the pro-Yeltsin factions sympathized with nationalist forces that opposed President Ayaz Mutalibov, although these forces, best represented by the Azerbaijan Popular Front (APF), had strong pro-Turkish and anti-Russian leanings.[107]

Mutalibov was a Gorbachev man and had come to power under the shadow of Russian military intervention following the introduction of Russian troops into Baku in January 1990. Ideologically, Mutalibov was not acceptable to pro-Yeltsin forces because he was a "flexible communist."[108] These attributes, plus allegations that he supported the failed August 1991 coup d'état, led to Mutalibov's fall from power in March 1992.[109] In May 1992, an effort to bring Mutalibov back to power failed, thus ushering in the era of the APF and the presidency of Abulfazl Aliev (Elçibey) from June 1992 to June 1993.[110]

Elçibey's presidency was short lived, but many of the themes he promoted in foreign and domestic policies continued after his ouster and Heidar Aliev's assumption of power. After a brief effort to conduct a more balanced foreign policy aimed at having equally good relations with Russia, Iran, and Turkey, Aliev reverted to the pro-Turkish and anti-Iran posture of the Elçibey era, but he never espoused Elçibey's intense anti-Russian sentiments and position.[111] Elçibey's ouster was linked to the shift in Russia's regional and international outlook from an optimistic vision of Russian-Western partnership to one that emphasized the necessity for Russia to reassert its influence in its former territories.

Russia's treatment of Georgia reflected a similar pattern, albeit with differences deriving from local characteristics and dynamics. Thus there was an effort to dislodge the sitting Georgian president, Zviad Gamsakurdia, following the Soviet

Union's disintegration, although he was not exactly a Gorbachev man, as Mutalibov had been.[112] But neither was Gamsakurdia a Yeltsin man, and he, too, was accused of supporting the 1991 coup d'état. Finally, Eduard Shevardnadze emerged as the best man to lead Georgia. The fact that Yeltsin owed a debt of gratitude to Shevardnadze, who in 1991 abandoned Mikhail Gorbachev and sided with the Russian president, may have also helped his assumption of power.

Shevardnadze's coming to power in March 1992 did not usher in smooth Russian-Georgian relations. Despite his alleged partiality, President Yeltsin refused to support Shevardnadze in the face of the military's opposition.[113] Although the Russian military finally reached the conclusion that Shevardnadze was the best partner it could hope for in Georgia, it humbled him first by helping the Abkhaz separatists.[114] Georgia is not a Muslim country, notwithstanding the large number of Muslim minorities in Ajaria and in the Marneuli region. Nevertheless, the Chechen factor has played an important role in shaping Russian-Georgian relations. During the second Chechen war, as Chechen combatants increasingly took refuge on Georgian territory, Russian-Georgian relations deteriorated.

Armenia escaped the process of changing governments. The perestroika-era nationalist and pro-Yeltsin leader Levon Ter-Petrossian remained in power as Armenia's president from September 1991 to February 1998. Armenia has been Russia's staunchest ally in the region, at times at great cost in terms of its relations with the West. However, these close relations do not necessarily imply total and permanent convergence of Russian-Armenian interests. Rather, they are partly the consequence of specific economic and geopolitical factors, especially the nature of the West's relations with Turkey and Iran, plus its oil-related interests, which have led it to pursue a pro-Azerbaijan policy.

Balancing Economic and Strategic Interests, 1994–2003

During the period 1994–2003, Russian policy toward the Transcaucasus was a balancing act between competing economic and strategic interests and their constituencies in Russia. Russian policy was also shaped by the actions of other regional and international actors and in response to them. Finally, Russia had to adapt its goals and ambitions to its dwindling military and economic power. Consequently, Russia increasingly tried to utilize a mix of instruments in its approach to the countries of the South Caucasus, including manipulation of their internal weaknesses. The latter tactic, however, is a double-edged sword. Given the overlapping of many of the South and North Caucasian ethnic groups, interethnic conflicts in this region affect the Russian Federation's southern areas. Thus Russia's contradictory and inconsistent policies toward the region have reflected the existing tensions among competing interests and adaptation of ends to means.

In addition to the basic security interests noted earlier, Russia has been concerned about the emergence of a "power vacuum" that could be filled by other countries, notably Turkey.[115] This has led Russia to try to maintain a substantial military presence in the region through a variety of means, including the CIS collective security system, bilateral agreements for the stationing of Russian troops and/or establishment of military bases, and the joint patrol of external borders of the Transcaucasian countries.

Some Russian analysts have maintained that this desire derived from Russia's anxiety over instability in the region, since from the beginning of perestroika, the Transcaucasus has been bedeviled by interethnic tensions and wars with the potential to invite external intervention by Russia's regional rivals. For example, Turkey might have been tempted to intervene militarily in the Armenian-Azerbaijani conflict. Certainly, Russia feared such a possibility. In order to "prevent any potential Turkish opportunism at the time of the Soviet Union's disintegration," Marshal Yevgenii Shaposhnikov, commander in chief of the Joint Armed Forces of the CIS, warned of a "Third World War" if Turkey were to interfere militarily in the Armenian-Azerbaijani conflict.[116] Also, a segment of Russia's military and political leadership viewed having a large number of military bases as an effective means of maintaining Russian influence.[117]

Russia's success in achieving these strategic objectives has been mixed. It has failed to obtain Azerbaijan's agreement for joint patrolling of the border with Iran or for the establishment of Russian bases on its territory. Later, Azerbaijan even objected to the stationing of Russian peacekeepers as part of the CSCE (now OSCE) force in Nagorno-Karabakh.[118] Russia's only military installation in Azerbaijan is the Gabalino radar station. Until Heidar Aliev's January 2002 visit to Moscow, when an agreement on the long-term leasing of the station to Russia was reached, Azerbaijan threatened to close the station on several occasions. The excuse was Russia's military support to Armenia. Despite initial expectations of a major improvement in Russian-Azerbaijani relations following Heidar Aliev's assumption of power, because of a combination of internal and external factors, both geographic and economic, Azerbaijan reverted to a policy of close cooperation with the West and Turkey, including cooperation in the military sphere. When NATO's Partnership for Peace (PFP) program was created during the NATO Brussels summit of 1994, Azerbaijan was one of the first post-Soviet countries to join. Later, Vafa Gulizade, a presidential adviser, proposed that Azerbaijan allow the establishment of U.S., NATO, or Turkish military bases in the Apsheron Peninsula, ostensibly in response to the growing Russian-Armenian military alliance.[119] However, Russian policy may have prevented any other regional state, notably Turkey, from filling the regional power vacuum.

Russian-Georgian military and strategic relations are more complex and have evolved since 1991.[120] Following the end of armed hostilities in Abkhazia and the Russian-brokered cease-fire agreement of 12 May 1994, Russian-Georgian relations seemed to improve. A major step in this regard was President Boris Yeltsin's visit to Tbilisi on 3 February 1994.[121] A main topic of discussion was the future of Russian military bases in Georgia, since Georgia had been a major center of the Russian military during the Soviet period. After independence, Georgia inherited four military bases: Vaziani (near Tbilisi), Gudauta (in the secessionist republic of

Abkhazia), Batumi (the capital of the autonomous and partly Muslim republic of Ajaria), and Akhalkalaki (in the region of Samtskhe Javakheti with a predominantly Armenian population).

The first step in the establishment of a Russian military presence in Georgia was the signing of the Framework Treaty of Friendship and Good Neighborliness.[122] Russian defense minister Pavel Grachev's visit to Georgia followed, and an agreement on long-term cooperation in the military field was signed. Georgia agreed to lease four military bases to Russia for twenty-five years.[123] The Georgian parliament never ratified either of these agreements.[124] In the following years, Georgia grew more uneasy about the Russian military presence, and Russian-Georgian relations steadily deteriorated as Georgia drew closer to Turkey and the West,[125] as illustrated by Turkey's participation in training Georgian border troops.[126]

The OSCE summit in Istanbul in November 1999 marked an important turning point in the process of the gradual withdrawal of Russian military forces from Georgia. Western countries, especially the United States, and Turkey persuaded Russia to agree to a schedule of withdrawal of its forces from Georgia. The United States pledged $10 million to help Russia cover part of the removal cost.[127] The process of the closure of bases and removal of troops has proceeded more or less according to the schedule. However, the closure of the base in Batumi may pose difficulties because the leader of the Autonomous Republic of Ajaria, Aslan Abashidze, opposes it.[128]

Armenia, meanwhile, remains Russia's main ally and partner in the South Caucasus and houses Russian military bases and personnel. However, Russian-Armenian relations have not always been without strain due to Russia's unwillingness to overly antagonize Azerbaijan, a stand criticized by some Russian analysts.[129]

Oil and Politics

The existence of substantial oil and gas reserves in Azerbaijan and the keen interest of Western energy companies and governments in their development have further complicated the task of formulating Russia's policy toward the region. Russia faced a dilemma: either prevent the development of Azerbaijan's oil and gas resources, if need be by military means, or become directly involved in this inevitable process.

When Azerbaijan on 24 September 1994 reached agreement with several major Western and a few non-Western energy companies, Russia's Foreign Ministry was not pleased.[130] Russian disapproval was not expressed merely because the Russian oil giant LUKOIL obtained only a 10 percent share in the Azerbaijan International Operating Company (AIOC).[131] Rather, it was derived from the fact that, as Alexy Gromyko has stated, "the power distribution among the parties to the contract, which underwent changes in the period from 1994 to 1998, is indicative of more meaningful interrelations. The positions of the leading states of the world are reflected in the Caspian, as an ultimate mirror of world geopolitics."[132] The military was also against the contract because its views are determined by geopolitical and not economic considerations.

The energy sector's main concern was to make money, "including money from the development of oil resources of the Caspian Sea, and even in the sector of sea claimed by Azerbaijan."[133] The attitude of LUKOIL was supported by Prime Minister Viktor Chernomyrdin, who unequivocally saw "no problem in connection with the signing of the contract."[134] Chernomyrdin's position indicates the often diverging interests of Russia's old geopolitical and new economic elites.

Ultimately, however, to confront the West in Azerbaijan would have been too great a risk for Russia. Thus Russia accepted the inevitable and tried to make the best of it, as reflected in Primakov's response to a question about Azerbaijan's drift toward the West and the growing penetration of Western oil companies: "It's perfectly natural for the Azerbaijanis to develop relations with other countries. . . . We [Russia] are attracting foreign capital in Sakhalin and Siberia."[135]

Transporting Caspian Oil: The Geopolitics of Pipeline Routes

The debate about the best route for the transport of Azeri and other Caspian energy resources became another factor affecting the evolution of Russia's relations with the Transcaucasian states. Put briefly, Russia wanted to maintain its monopoly over the export of Caspian oil through its Black Sea terminal of Novorossisk. Meanwhile, for practical geopolitical reasons, especially capacity overload at Novorossisk and the desire to reduce reliance on Russia, Western countries and energy companies felt that at least one other pipeline was necessary for the export of Caspian energy. The question of which direction—south through Iran and the Persian Gulf or west through Turkey and the Mediterranean—was ultimately settled in favor of the so-called Baku-Ceyhan line, or the Turkish alternative.[136] Russia nevertheless obtained a concession in that it was agreed that the early oil would be exported via Novorossisk. Georgia also became entangled in the pipeline politics as a rival of Russia. A pipeline carrying Azeri oil to the Georgian port of Supsa was built and became operational in 2000.

Rivalry over pipeline routes intensified Russia's desire to retain a military presence in the region and acted as a complicating factor in Russia's relations with Azerbaijan and, even more so, Georgia. It also prompted these countries to exacerbate Russia's problems in the North Caucasus in order to render Novorossisk less attractive as an export outlet.

Chechen War, Islam, and Russian-Transcaucasian Relations

The outbreak of the Chechen War on 11 December 1994 added a new source of discord to the already deteriorating relations between Russia and the Transcaucasian states, with the exception of Armenia. The Chechen conflict created opportunities for Azerbaijan and Georgia and their regional allies, such as Turkey, to limit Russian influence in the South Caucasus. The extent of these countries' active support for Chechen independence is hard to establish, but many groups in Azerbaijan and in Georgia were undoubtedly sympathetic to the Chechen cause and provided help.

During the first Chechen War, the Islamic factor was not an important motivation for helping the Chechens for Muslim Azerbaijan. A more important reason was to weaken Russia. Russian sources, however, referred to all those who helped the Chechens as "Muslim mercenaries." Among the groups suspected of helping the Chechens were the Grey Wolves, an extremist faction of the Turkish National Action Party (MHP), whose late leader, Alpaslan Turkeş, harbored pan-Turkist ideas and had a considerable following in Azerbaijan and Central Asia.[137] Andrei Nikolayev, director of the Russian Federal Border Service, accused the Grey Wolves of acting as mercenaries in Chechnya.[138] To prevent such infiltrations, Russia closed its borders with Azerbaijan immediately after the start of the war. Azerbaijan denied helping Chechen nationalists, and President Aliev argued that Azerbaijan itself was "suffering from separatism and terrorism."[139]

However, it is very likely that Azerbaijan allowed the flow of arms and men to Chechnya. During a visit to Azerbaijan in July 1997, Chechen president Aslan Maskhadov held talks with Aliev, thanked Azerbaijan for its support during the war, and offered to help Azerbaijan with its problem in Nagorno-Karabakh.[140] During this trip, the Chechen vice president Vakha Arsanov stated, "We are ready to render Azerbaijan all possible assistance and bring whomsoever to their knees."[141] This is not surprising since during Elçibey's presidency in 1992–93, a number of Chechens had fought for the Azerbaijanis.[142] There is also evidence that some Pakistanis and other Muslims, including Afghans and Arab Afghans, fought on Azerbaijan's side. Aliev thanked Pakistan for its support in the Karabakh conflict. Some Russian sources claimed that Baku first established links with the Afghan mujahideen during the war in Nagorno-Karabakh. Allegedly, hundreds of mercenaries were flown in from Afghanistan, and the Azerbaijani government arranged for Chechen guerrillas to be flown to Afghan training bases in Kunduz and Taleghan.[143]

The rising influence of Sunni extremist groups in Azerbaijan between 1994 and 1999 alarmed Azerbaijani authorities, leading them to crack down on their activities.[144] With the eruption of fighting in Dagestan and the resumption of the Russian-Chechen conflict in 1999, Azerbaijan became more concerned about the risks of antagonizing Russia, especially since Russia's second campaign in Chechnya appeared more organized and promised success. Therefore, by late 1999, Russian-Azerbaijani relations began to improve, albeit unevenly. Azerbaijan's continued desire to join NATO, talk about a possible military pact among Azerbaijan, Turkey, and Georgia, and persisting allegations that Azerbaijan was allowing Chechen rebels to enter its territory slowed the pace of progress.[145] Nevertheless, certain statements by Azerbaijani president Heidar Aliev, such as his assertion that "the military operation by Russian forces against religious extremists in the North Caucasus is Russia's internal affair, and Russia has a right to restore order on its territory," helped ease tensions.[146] The growing profile of Sunni extremism in Azerbaijan also encouraged cooperation with Russia "to effectively combat that [Islamic extremist] evil."[147]

A major breakthrough in Russian-Azerbaijani relations occurred when President

Vladimir Putin visited Baku in January 2001. Economic considerations were principally behind this improvement. Russia changed its position on the issue of the exploitation of Caspian resources, bringing it closer to Azerbaijan's position of dividing the seabed along national lines. During this trip, LUKOIL and Azerbaijan's state oil company signed an agreement on the rehabilitation, exploration, and development of the Zykh and Gosany oil fields.[148] In short, because of Azerbaijan's economic significance, Moscow has been willing to overlook some of its offenses, including its (at least) passive assistance to the Chechen rebels. Meanwhile, because of the importance of the remittances of Azerbaijan's diaspora in Russia, Azerbaijan has stopped short of total alienation of Russia. In the summer of 2002, Russian-Azerbaijani relations took a turn for the better when they signed an agreement on the delineation of their respective zones in the Caspian Sea, and Azerbaijan declared that it was clamping down on Chechen guerrillas.[149]

In Georgia's case, the conflict in Chechnya and allegations of active Georgian assistance to the Chechen rebels, especially during the second Chechen War, adversely affected bilateral Russian-Georgian relations. Russia has consistently accused Georgia of assisting Chechen rebels.[150] Evidence indicates that many Chechen refugees who arrived in Georgia during the second Chechen War were active combatants, and some were treated in Georgia's hospitals.[151] Various reports cite the number of Chechen refugees in the Pankisi Gorge as being anywhere from 1,800 to 8,000, plus 500 to 800 Chechen militants led by Ruslan Gelaev. For a long time, the Georgian government either denied the existence of Chechen rebels in the Pankisi Gorge or claimed that they might have slipped through with refugees. After the events of 11 September 2001, Georgian authorities seemed more willing to admit that the government, "fearful of a mini–Chechen War on Georgian soil made an informal pact with the Chechen rebels, allowing them to camp out as long as there was no violence on Georgian soil."[152]

In view of the deteriorating state of Russian-Georgian relations,[153] it is conceivable that Georgia also tried to use the Chechen card as a bargaining chip in its relations with Moscow, notably reducing the incentive for Russia to militarily support Abkhaz separatism or allow Abkhazia to join the Russian Federation on the basis of a law passed by the Duma in June 2001.[154] For example, according to some media reports, Ruslan Gelaev and his Chechen fighters joined forces with Georgian partisans in the Kodori Gorge during operations in fall 2001.[155]

The most serious bone of contention has been the presence of Chechens and even Arabs in Georgia's Pankisi Gorge. The attraction of the Pankisi Gorge for Chechens, Arab missionaries, and Islamist activists is its proximity to Chechnya, its ethnic and religious composition, and its difficult terrain, which hinders any efforts by Georgia (or Russia) to control the region. Since the seventeenth century, the population has consisted mainly of Kistins who belong to the Vainakh ethnic group and have a strong kinship with the Chechens. A majority of them also adhere to Islam. In view of these ethnic and religious connections, it is not surprising that Chechens took refuge there. However, non-Chechen Muslims—notably Arabs with the goal of spreading a more puritanical and perhaps extremist Islam—made more concerted efforts to infiltrate the region.[156] Some local reports after 11 September 2001 pointed to newly built mosques in some of the villages, such as Duisi, and a more conservative religious atmosphere created by Arabs who reportedly came from Chechnya.[157]

The Georgian government apparently considered the risk of tolerating Chechen militants and the potential spread of Islamic extremism less important than its difficult relations with Russia. If the Chechen War limited Russia's ability to influence events in the south and made it difficult to apply pressure on Georgia, tolerance of Chechen rebel activity on Georgian territory could, at least in the short term, serve Georgia's interests. However, the risk of complacency toward Chechen infiltrators proved higher as tensions once more rose between Russia and Georgia in the summer of 2002, when a force of 100 to 300 Chechen rebels, purportedly based in the Pankisi Gorge, entered Ingushetia in an attempt to reach neighboring Chechnya. Russian officials accused Georgian security forces of being complicit in the incursion; unidentified Russian security officials went so far as to claim that the Chechen fighters had been flown to North Ossetia on Georgian military helicopters.[158] The incursion resulted in a three-day battle that left dozens of Russian soldiers and insurgents dead and raised the threat of Russian military intervention in Georgia to halt further rebel infiltration into Russia from Georgian territory.[159]

Islam, Russia, and the Transcaucasus after 11 September

As in Central Asia, post–11 September developments were initially advantageous for Russia. They vindicated its long-held position that the Chechen rebels were receiving help from Afghanistan, Pakistan, and the Arab world and were closely connected with both the Taliban and Al-Qaeda. Russia also legitimized war in Chechnya as part of fighting international terrorism. Indeed, since late 2001, Russia has referred to its war in Chechnya as an antiterrorism campaign. However, U.S. efforts to eradicate Al-Qaeda members or sympathizers in Georgia's Pankisi Gorge, plus the expanding security and military links between the United States and the Transcaucasian states, have undermined Russia's position in the region.

President Putin has tried to minimize the adverse effects of a growing U.S.— and potentially NATO—presence on Russia's influence in the South Caucasus by putting U.S. activities in the framework of the coalition to fight international terrorism. During the March 2002 CIS summit in Kazakhstan, he stated, "If we today are speaking about a fight against terrorism in the Pankisi Gorge, we support this fight no matter who takes part in it, American or European partners or Georgian colleagues directly."[160]

However, not everyone in Russia has agreed with this position. The Russian military has been especially bitter about the expanding U.S. military and political presence within the post-Soviet space. A letter published in the 26 February 2002 issue of *Sovetskaya Rossia* signed by twenty-three high-ranking military officials, including the onetime defense minister Igor Rodionov, criticized Russia's overall policy from Gorbachev to Putin and stated, "It is precisely with your [Putin's] support that the United States acquired the military bases in Uzbekistan, Tajikistan, Kyrgyzstan, and possibly Kazakhstan as well. . . . These are not bases for delivering strikes against Osama bin Laden, but against the interests of Russia."[161]

This letter might be dismissed as the complaint of a disgruntled military man with lingering nostalgia for the Soviet era. However, more mainstream politicians and analysts, including Russian defense minister Sergei Ivanov, have also voiced criticism. After reports that U.S. and British forces were preparing to attack suspected Al-Qaeda members hiding in the Pankisi Gorge, Ivanov said, "We [Russia] just can't put up with this," and added that Georgia must act "quickly and effectively to establish control" over an area he described as a "mini-Chechnya or mini-Afghanistan."[162]

Meanwhile, Russia's chief of staff General Anatolii Kvashnin, stated, "Russia and Georgia should jointly eradicate this terrorist center in the Pankisi Gorge."[163] There was also opposition in the State Duma, where Chairman of the International Affairs Committee Dmitri Rogozin has been the most vocal opponent.[164] Key Russian leaders and the Russian media claimed that the region's problems could not be solved without Russia and that external involvement could complicate matters. Other Russian commentators wrote that Washington's main goal was not to help Shevardnadze with his problems, but to implement its earlier plans to eliminate Russian influence by, among other means, discrediting the Russian military.[165] Russian foreign minister Igor Ivanov stated that the deployment of American antiterrorism advisers and special forces "could further aggravate the situation in the region, which is difficult as it is. . . . That is our position and Washington is well aware of it."[166] Finally, President Putin himself declared that the problem of the Pankisi Gorge could not be solved "independent from cooperation with Russia. Nobody—not the American forces or the special forces of Georgia—is going to solve the problem of terrorism in Pankisi Gorge without direct and active involvement of Russian special forces, of the Russian army."[167]

President Shevardnadze, however, said that he was open to a dialogue on "future joint action with U.S. special forces in the Pankisi Gorge."[168] Later, Georgia's president more candidly expressed his happiness over the arrival of the first twenty American advisers: "We have waited for a long time, eight years, for the United States to activate cooperation with Georgia in the military sphere."[169] Approximately 200 U.S. military advisers began training between 1,200 and 2,000 Georgian troops to deal with antiterrorism missions. Some Georgian officials expressed the hope that this collaboration would facilitate Georgia's membership in NATO.[170]

In addition to being supplanted by the United States in areas of Russia's historical influence, Russia's unease derives from some fundamental differences in U.S. and Russian objectives. The main purpose of the United States was to cleanse the area of Al-Qaeda members and other extremist groups, but not to conduct an all-out campaign against all Chechens in the Pankisi Gorge. By contrast, "Russia sees the entire Chechen separatist movement as indistinguishable from Al-Qaeda."[171] Meanwhile, Georgia hopes to create a linkage between international terrorism and the Abkhaz situation and to use its newly forged ties with the United

States and newly trained forces against separatists in Abkhazia and South Ossetia.[172] Should such a linkage develop, it would reduce Russia's leverage over Georgia, since Russia presently operates with relative freedom in Abkhazia. Russia's freedom of action in the region was demonstrated when Russian defense minister Sergei Ivanov ordered the cutting off of all connecting roads between Abkhazia and Georgia in March 2002 following the kidnapping of three Russian peacekeepers.[173]

However, in the summer of 2002, Russia took advantage of the post–11 September international environment to pressure Georgia to take action against Chechen rebels in the Pankisi Gorge. After warnings from Russian foreign minister Igor Ivanov that terrorists and foreign mercenaries were continuing to use Georgian territory as a base of operations, Russia conducted a series of air strikes against targets in Georgia near the Chechen border.[174] On 28 August 2002, Putin, while not confirming the air strikes, made the case for taking action against Chechen forces in the Pankisi Gorge:

> The Taliban regime sheltered al-Qaeda, and it prepared criminal acts throughout the world, prepared and carried out the terrible terrorist act whose anniversary we will commemorate on September 11. Is the situation in Georgia any better for us, Russians? The same sort of terrorists are there, including, I repeat, foreign nationals, and they carry out attacks on our territory and make no bones about it.[175]

Putin applied further pressure on Georgia in a letter to United Nations secretary general Kofi Annan in which he again accused Georgia of harboring terrorists. The letter, delivered to the United Nations on 12 September 2002, one day before U.S. president George W. Bush was due to present his case for preemptive military action against Iraq to the United Nations General Assembly, cited the right of self-defense recognized in the United Nations Charter as justification for taking military action against rebel forces in Georgia.[176]

Under growing Russian pressure, Georgia launched military operations in the Pankisi Gorge to clear the region of Chechen rebels and Islamist elements.[177] This attempt to demonstrate that no outside (i.e., Russian) intervention was needed, however, was undermined by continued infiltration of rebels into Russia, possibly fleeing the Georgian security crackdown in the Pankisi Gorge. Not until early October 2002 did Georgian-Russian tensions began to abate, as Georgia agreed to extradite several suspected Chechen rebels to Russia and, at a CIS summit in the Moldovan capital of Chisinau, Putin and Shevardnadze agreed to begin joint border patrols to secure the Georgian-Russian border.[178] This agreement advanced Russian interests in Georgia by securing Georgian cooperation in preventing further rebel infiltration into Russia and by demonstrating to Georgia that it could not ignore Russian concerns with impunity. However, the ratification by the Georgian Parliament of a security cooperation agreement between the United States and Georgia on 21 March 2003 further intensified Russian anxieties.[179] The Russian officials were particularly concerned that the U.S.-Georgian agreement extended privileges to U.S. military personnel not enjoyed by Russian troops present in the country.[180] Nevertheless, Russia continued its efforts to balance the growing U.S. presence in Georgia. For example, Russian media reported that, in May 2003, Russia and Georgia had resumed talks to draft a framework treaty with the goal of resolving outstanding problems between them.[181] However, the extent to which Russia can reassert its position in the region on a more permanent basis remains contingent on several regional and international factors, notably the evolution of U.S. policy toward the region and the nature of Russian-American relations, as well as the Georgian presidential succession. However, with the growing U.S. presence in the Caucasus, it appeared unlikely that Russia could regain its predominant position in the region, although it would undoubtedly remain a significant player for the foreseeable future.

Post–11 September events provided the United States with opportunities to expand its security and military cooperation with Azerbaijan. Even Armenia, realizing the fundamental changes in the post–11 September international strategic equation, has been trying to expand its relations with the United States and NATO. President Bush's decision to waive U.S. congressional Resolution 907, which had prevented the United States from providing economic and military assistance to Azerbaijan and Armenia, opened the way for military cooperation between the United States and Azerbaijan.[182] Some reports have indicated that most of the $50 million in aid for 2002 would "be used largely for border security, particularly Azerbaijan's border with Iran."[183] Other analysts have expressed the opinion that the main goal of the U.S. military presence is to counter the "Iranian threat."[184] Although U.S. defense secretary Donald Rumsfeld put the emphasis on the war against terrorism during his visit to the republic in December 2001, other U.S. officials made reference to the Iranian threat.[185] Such cooperation will involve joint naval activities in the Caspian Sea. Be that as it may, such a presence will erode Russia's claim to be the major player in the Caucasus.

Conclusion

The impact of the Islamic factor on Russia's relations with Central Asia and the Caucasus has differed considerably. On balance, the Islamic factor, in the form of a common threat of Islamic extremism, has helped Russia consolidate its position in Central Asia and develop a network of security cooperation with the Central Asian states. It has also facilitated the continued presence of Russian military force in the region, notably in Tajikistan. By contrast, in the South Caucasus, the Islamic factor has been a negative variable in Russia's interaction with the region, partly because of Russia's problems with its Muslim citizens in the North Caucasus. Because of the close connection between Islam and ethnic identity, Islam has tended to strengthen particularist and proindependence tendencies, as best exemplified by Chechnya. This has worked against what Russia sees as its major security interests. This connection between Islam and ethnic identity has also offered opportunities for outsiders to influence events in the Caucasus. Moreover, despite some romantic visions of the Russian Empire as a harmonious gathering of diverse peoples, the historic memory of Caucasian Muslims of Russia is that of a conqueror and colonial power. This historic memory has colored their approach to relations with Russia in the post-Soviet era.

Even in relations with non-Muslim countries in the Caucasus, notably Georgia, the Islamic variable has been a complicating factor because of its link with the Chechen conflict. However, Islam has not been responsible for Russia's difficulties and setbacks in the Caucasus. Rather, these difficulties have derived from the peculiarities of the USSR's collapse, the growing divergence of views and interests among Russia's old and emerging elites, the haphazard and contradictory policies pursued by Russia toward the region, and the overall economic and military decline of Russia, which has made it a less attractive partner or feared enemy. The West's greater and more sustained interest in the Caucasus has also contributed to the erosion of Russian influence.

9

Russia's Relations with the Northern Tier Countries

Because of their proximity to the former Soviet republics in Central Asia and the Transcaucasus, plus their historic, ethnic, linguistic, and religious links with these regions, the four countries known as the Northern Tier during the post–Second World War era—Iran, Turkey, Afghanistan, and Pakistan—have enjoyed a high priority in Russia's post-Soviet diplomacy. However, despite some similarities among these countries, the character of their relations with Russia has been quite different, ranging from seriously strained and even hostile, as in the cases of Pakistan and Taliban-ruled Afghanistan, to pseudopartnership, as with Iran, while Turkey has occupied a more ambiguous position. The impact of the Islamic factor in shaping these relations has also vastly differed in the case of each country. In some cases, it has been a determining factor and a negative influence, as with Pakistan and Afghanistan. In other instances, its impact has been either negligible or derivative, as with Iran and Turkey.

Pakistan and Afghanistan

The Islamic factor has had a determining and adverse effect on Russia's relations with Pakistan and Afghanistan. In view of the legacy of the Soviet-Afghan War and Pakistan's policies in Afghanistan following the Soviet withdrawal, especially its role in the creation of the Taliban, this is not surprising. The Taliban's aspirations to expand their brand of extremist and obscurantist Islam into other Central Asian countries were viewed with apprehension by Russia. The frontline state in this context was Tajikistan. Some Tajik Islamists received assistance from groups in Pakistan and Afghanistan, notably the Taliban. This assistance included the training of Tajik Islamists in the medressahs (Islamic schools) and military camps in Pakistan and Afghanistan, especially after the takeover of Kabul by the Taliban forces on 26 September 1996.[1] Pakistani missionaries also became active in the Russian Federation.

On a broader level, Pakistan emerged as a potential geopolitical rival for Russia by providing an alternative for the export of some of Central Asia's oil and gas.[2]

Pakistan and Russia also competed for shaping Afghanistan's political future. Their rivalry became intense after the rise of the Taliban.

Because Russian and Pakistani political, economic, and strategic interests diverged, some level of tension between the two was inevitable, but these tensions were exacerbated because of the Islamic factor, especially through linkage with Chechnya as a triangular relationship emerged among the Taliban, Chechen rebels, and Pakistan, particularly after the first Chechen War. The Taliban and Pakistan both manipulated Russia's problems in Chechnya in order to discourage the Russian government from supporting the anti-Taliban forces in Afghanistan.

It is undeniable that close connections existed between the Taliban and the Chechen forces, predating the Taliban's emergence as the dominant political force in Afghanistan. As early as January 1995, several rallies were held in Herat (captured by the Taliban on 5 September 1995) calling on all true Muslims to join "the sacred war on the Chechen and Tajik fronts."[3] It was also reported that Afghan mercenaries were leaving for Chechnya.[4] Some officials in the Russian Defense Ministry alleged that the Taliban were planning to send financial aid ($4 million) and twenty-four Stinger antiaircraft missiles to Chechnya.[5]

Official relations between the Taliban and Chechnya expanded after the 1996 cease-fire in Chechnya and the Taliban's capture of Kabul. The Taliban did not gain international recognition, but they behaved as Afghanistan's legitimate government.[6] Under Aslan Maskhadov's presidency, Chechens also behaved as an independent state. Thus just after the start of the second Chechen War, Taliban leader Mullah Muhammad Omar and foreign minister Wakil Ahmad Mutawakkil recognized the Chechen republic during a visit by Chechen envoy Zelimkhan Yanderbiev to Kandahar.[7] According to Leonid Gonkin, Mullah Omar's decision to recognize the Republic of Ichkeria and establish "comprehensive diplomatic relations" between the two was based on a feeling of "Islamic solidarity."[8] Gonkin also speculates that the Taliban's recognition of the Chechen government was partly in retaliation for Russia's support for the anti-Taliban coalition.[9]

This act of establishing official diplomatic relations between two entities that themselves lacked international recognition did not help either party. The Chechen cause suffered, given the intimate and close relations that had developed between the Taliban and Osama bin Laden and his terrorist network, and gave credence to long-standing Russian claims that the Chechen rebels were part of an international network of Muslim extremists implicated in terrorist acts.[10] Thus the Russian Foreign Ministry responded to the Taliban's recognition of Chechnya by characterizing it as an attempt to set up "a kind of 'gangster international.' "[11] In January 2000, Sergei Yastrzhembsky, the Kremlin's official spokesman and aide to President Putin, said that a representative of Aslan Maskhadov had signed a protocol of cooperation with bin Laden. (Maskhadov denied this claim.)[12] Yastrzhembsky also talked about the possibility of launching "preventive strikes against the Taliban camps should they pose a threat to the national security of Russia or states friendly to it."[13]

Russian defense minister Sergei Ivanov graphically explained that Chechnya and

Afghanistan were "branches of one tree [terrorism], whose roots are in Afghanistan."[14] The discovery following the U.S. attacks on the Taliban that a possibly significant number of Chechens were fighting on the side of the Taliban further strengthened the Russian position.[15] However, Western observers and analysts have not always shared Russia's position regarding the dangerous nature of the Taliban or the Taliban's connection to Chechnya and international terrorism.[16]

The Pakistan Link

The Chechen-Taliban connection could not have been established without the active assistance of Pakistan, or at least influential elements within the Pakistani political and military leadership. The role of influential Islamist groups such as the Jama'at-i-Islami also should not be underestimated. The Jama'at-i-Islami sponsored Zelimkhan Yanderbiev's visit to Pakistan before his trip to Kandahar. Several anti-Russian demonstrations were held, and donations totalling $100,000 were gathered during his visit. The more extremist Jama'at-i-Ulama-i-Islam also contributed to these efforts.[17] According to Russian sources, Yanderbiev met with Pakistani officials, including a member of the National Security Council, Mahmud Ghazi.[18]

When questioned about the visit, Pakistan's ambassador to Moscow, Mansur Alam, commented: "Mr. Yanderbiev is no longer in Pakistan, it is likely that he went to Afghanistan, which is an independent sovereign country and has the right to decide independently its own problems and bear consequences for its actions." He then added that the issue related to "relations between Kabul and Moscow should be regulated by these two capitals."[19] Regarding Jama'at-i-Islami, he replied: "I would like to note that the aforementioned party [Jama'at-i-Islami] is one of the most influential parties in the country and it is independent from the government. Therefore, it independently determines its priorities and activities."[20] He explained that many other parties and peoples sympathize with Chechnya's leadership because they feel obliged to defend the interests of fellow Muslims. The ambassador drew parallels between the sympathy felt by Muslims for the Chechens with that felt by the Russians for the Serbs and said, "Such phenomenon is widely accepted in the framework of ethnic and confessional affinity."[21]

According to Russian sources, Yanderbiev was not the only Chechen leader to visit Pakistan. In July 1999, prominent Chechen rebel commander Ruslan Gelaev reportedly traveled to Pakistan and met with Pakistani intelligence officials and Taliban representatives.[22] This visit occurred just before the armed incursion of the Chechen militants into Dagestan, raising the possibility of Pakistan's and the Taliban's involvement in this event.[23]

During the first Chechen War, the Russian government and military talked about Pakistani nationals' involvement in Chechnya. In October 1996, the spokesman of the Command of the Russian Federal Army Group in Khankala announced that 200 well-armed missionaries had arrived in Chechnya from Pakistan.[24] More seriously, President Boris Yeltsin stated that Pakistani nationals were involved in hostage-taking operations by Chechen rebels under the command of Salman

Raduev in the Dagestani city of Kizlyar and the village of Pervomaiskoe, a claim rejected by Pakistan.[25] While it is difficult to assess the extent of the Pakistani nationals' involvement in Chechnya, there is no doubt that a Pakistani-Chechen link existed.

Preventing Official Rupture

Despite problems caused by the Taliban-Chechen connection, Pakistan's close links with the Taliban, and the involvement of Pakistani nationals in Chechnya and as missionaries in other parts of the Russian Federation, both Pakistan and Russia avoided a complete rupture in relations. While criticizing Russia's handling of the Chechen crisis, the Pakistani government supported the principle of Russia's territorial integrity and characterized the Chechen conflict as "Russia's internal affair."[26] It also tried to use the lure of arms purchases from Russia to improve relations.[27] Pakistan further attempted to channel humanitarian assistance to the Chechens through the federal authorities. In July 1997, the Russian and Pakistani foreign ministers held consultations in Moscow. According to Pakistani sources, Pakistani foreign minister Gauhar Ayub was able to "strike a genuine rapport with Primakov."[28]

Despite continued contacts and occasional signs of improved relations, Pakistan's and Russia's diverging geopolitical interests, especially regarding Afghanistan and the Taliban, prevented any real improvement.[29] Russia made a serious amelioration in its relations with Pakistan contingent on the latter's withdrawal of support for the Taliban.[30] Pakistan, however, rebuffed such statements, and in May 2001 Pakistan's leader Pervez Musharraf bluntly stated, "Whether anybody wants it or not the Taliban is a reality, it has come to stay in Afghanistan and those who hope that it will step down soon are hoping in vain."[31]

Post–11 September Developments

The end of the Taliban regime affected Russia's relations with both Afghanistan and Pakistan. In the case of Afghanistan, the ousting of the Taliban regime offered Russia an opportunity to reestablish its lost influence. Initially, Russia's preference was for the reestablishment of the Rabbani government, which still represented Afghanistan in the United Nations.[32] However, this was not acceptable to the United States. Consequently, Russia agreed to the formation of a new government headed by Hamid Karzai. Nevertheless, Russia has continued to support his former Northern Alliance allies who agreed to serve in the new Afghan government, most notably Muhammad Fahim, the Afghan defense minister. Part of this support is the providing of military equipment, but Russia hopes to go beyond this and help train a new national army in Afghanistan.[33] At the same time, Russia has courted Hamid Karzai, who visited Moscow in March 2002.[34] This Russian activism has caused anxieties for the United States and Pakistan.[35] The Islamic factor in the post–11 September period has acted as an impetus to Afghan-Russian cooperation in the

360 RUSSIA AND ISLAM

form of a struggle against the remnants of extremist forces in Afghanistan and a fight against international terrorism.[36] Thus the main challenge for Moscow in asserting its presence in Afghanistan is U.S. competition and financial limitations, not Islam.

In Pakistan's case, too, the fall of the Taliban opened new opportunities for improved relations by eliminating a major irritant in Russian-Pakistani relations. Pakistan's weakened regional position and serious internal problems, meanwhile, prompted its government to seek a rapprochement with Moscow. Again, Pakistan used the lure of economic gains to elicit a more positive and accommodating response from Russia. President Musharraf even delinked Russian-Pakistani relations from the Kashmir issue and Russia's close partnership with India. During a Russian parliamentary delegation's visit to Islamabad in April 2002, Musharraf said, "Relations between India and Pakistan have their own value and shall not be linked to the relations between Russia and India."[37]

Consequently, there was a flurry of Pakistani-Russian contacts at various levels, including a visit by the representative of Gazprom to discuss the possibility for Russia's participation in various Pakistani and regional energy development schemes.[38] On 4 February 2003, Musharraf arrived in Moscow for three days of talks on improving Pakistani-Russian relations. At the conclusion of his visit, Musharraf told reporters that Pakistan "speaks in recognition of the territorial integrity of Russia and regards Chechnya as an internal part [of the country]." He further guaranteed that "Pakistani territory will not be used for terrorist actions against other countries, including Russia."[39]

However, three factors have prevented significant improvement in Russian-Pakistani relations: (1) the continued Russian mistrust of Pakistan's regional intentions, notably in Afghanistan; (2) Russia's uncertainty regarding both Pakistan's willingness and ability to rein in and eventually eliminate militant Islamist groups, including those active in Kashmir; and (3) close Indian-Russian relations, such as Russia's unequivocal support for India's position regarding Kashmir and their military cooperation. India and Russia both expressed "apprehension at Pakistani interference in the post-Taliban political process in Afghanistan."[40] Regarding the latter, Russian Foreign Ministry spokesman Alexander Yakovenko stated, "The perspectives of development of Russia-Pakistan relationship directly depends on the degree of Islamabad's participation in fighting terrorist bases in cooperation with the international community."[41] He added that Pakistan should pay special attention to the "closure of the channels of material and financial supply to terrorists and announcing [the] outlaw [of] all the organizations that are practicing Jihad against any nations or government."[42] He added, "There is a definite link between the defeated terrorists in Afghanistan and their branches in Pakistan and many other regions including Chechnya and Central Asia."[43] On 22 November 2002, during a meeting with President George W. Bush, Vladimir Putin questioned whether the Pakistani government had done enough to stabilize Pakistan and the surrounding areas or to curb terrorist activities.[44]

However, the most formidable barriers remain Russia's pro-India posture on Kashmir, its strategic partnership with India, and its military and technological assistance to India. During a visit to New Delhi in February 2002, Russia's deputy prime minister Ilya Klebanov endorsed India's position on cross-border terrorism.[45] Moreover, Klebanov said, "Russia totally concurred with India's stand on Kashmir and appreciated the restraint shown by New Delhi."[46] Only a week earlier, Russian foreign minister Igor Ivanov had asked Pakistan to collaborate with India in checking cross-border infiltration into Jammu and Kashmir.[47] Russia and India have expressed support for each other's position on Kashmir and Chechnya. Ivanov further stated that the connection between terrorists in Chechnya and Kashmir was obvious to him and the Indian defense minister.[48]

Russia called Pakistan's missile testing in June 2002 "in the circumstances of extreme tension and suspicion, . . . provocative."[49] Moreover, Russian deputy foreign minister Alexander Losyukov stated, "Pakistan must take the first step in calming the situation surrounding its relations with India."[50] Pakistan had earlier condemned India's successful test firing of a supersonic cruise missile and had criticized Russia for helping India develop the missile and carry out the test.[51] Russia is also concerned about the safety of Pakistan's nuclear weapons. In December 2002, Vladimir Putin expressed his fear that Pakistan's weapons of mass destruction could fall into the hands of "bandits and terrorists."[52] This statement elicited a sharp response from Pakistan.[53]

In short, even in the post–11 September era, there are limits to Russian-Pakistani reconciliation. However, within the new geopolitical context, Russia is in a stronger position to gain a foothold in Pakistan and a more prominent profile in South Asia without jeopardizing its close ties with India. This new Russian role was evident in President Putin's declared willingness to mediate between India and Pakistan during the meeting of the Conference on Interaction and Confidence Building Measures in Asia (CICA) in Almaty in June 2002.[54] Although unsuccessful, the exercise was evidence of Russia's new regional activism. Another sign of Russia's enhanced regional position was Pakistani president Pervez Musharraf's visit to Moscow in early February 2003.

Russian-Turkish Relations: Exercise in Ambiguity?

Since the collapse of both the tsarist and the Ottoman empires, Russian-Turkish relations have had an ambiguous or, according to Dmitri Trenin, "schizophrenic character."[55] During the Soviet period, this duality was reflected in the fact that despite their political differences, including the fact that Turkey was a NATO member, Turkey and the Soviet Union maintained extensive trade and economic relations even while the USSR supported the leftist forces in Turkey. This dual aspect of Russian-Turkish relations has been accentuated in the post-Soviet era. It has also acquired new dimensions because of the fundamental changes in the broader international and regional context of Russian-Turkish relations.

The New Context of Russian-Turkish Relations

In the post-Soviet era, the context of Russian-Turkish relations and the equation of power between the two have been significantly altered in Turkey's favor. As a NATO member and a close U.S. ally, Turkey has been a major beneficiary of the systemic changes caused by the USSR's collapse and the ensuing U.S. global ascendancy. The United States promoted Turkey as the model to be emulated by the newly independent Muslim republics of the FSU and as its main partner in Central Asia and the South Caucasus.

This new context has had two consequences for Russian-Turkish relations: (1) increased linkage between the state of Russian-Western and Russian-Turkish relations and (2) intensified Russian-Turkish competition in the post-Soviet space, albeit to varying degrees since 1991. Russian views of this competition and its potential risks for Russia have varied and fluctuated over time depending on changing international and regional conditions. The main division has been between the pro-Western thinkers and politicians who see Russia's future in partnership with the West and those who favor a more independent posture for Russia and the maintenance of its influence in the FSU.

Russian-Turkish relations have also been influenced by the competing interests of Russia's economic, financial, political, and military elites. In this context, most of Russia's oligarchs have favored good ties with Turkey, whereas the military has tended to see Turkey more as a rival. These different Russian views regarding Turkey partly explain the ambiguous nature of their relations. Meanwhile, the Soviet Union's collapse and the reestablishment of extensive contacts between Turkey and the FSU, including the Russian Federation's Turkic and Muslim peoples, have altered the Turkish context of Russian-Turkish ties. Most important, they have led to a reappraisal of aspects of Turkey's Kemalist ideology, generating new interest in the Ottoman past and resulting in growing links between Turkish citizens of Caucasian and Turkic descent and their ancestral homelands in Russia. The latter factor has deeply influenced Turkey's approach to the Caucasus, especially Chechnya, and hence the character of Russian-Turkish relations.

Turkey and the USSR's Turkic and Caucasian Peoples: Contemporary Implications

The Kemalist regime, with its Westernizing vocation, delinked modern Turkey from its Ottoman Islamic past.[56] The official elimination of historical realities, however, did not eradicate their human and intellectual legacy. Modern Turkey could not rid itself of the large Turkic and Caucasian diasporas that had sought refuge in the Ottoman Empire. Many of these immigrants have become assimilated because of the Kemalist regime's culturally homogenizing policies. Others still retain emotional and, in some cases, linguistic and cultural ties to their ancestral homelands. The sense of ethnic consciousness among Turkey's North Caucasian diaspora has become stronger since the Soviet Union's disintegration and the reestablishment of contacts between the people of the diaspora and their original homelands.

There are no exact statistics about the number of people of Caucasian origin in Turkey, largely because "Turkish law reserves the status of national minority to non-Muslim peoples only."[57] Moreover, "pressure to register as a Turkish speaker" has skewed available data because state functionaries allegedly have falsified information in order to increase the ratio of Turkish speakers.[58] Consequently, estimates on the number of Turkey's North Caucasus diaspora range from 1 million to 6 million. Statistics on the ethnic breakdown of this population are even scarcer. Most of them are generally referred to as "Cherkess" (Circassian).[59] The Cherkess constitute a majority within Turkey's North Caucasian population, but there are other groups too, notably Abkhaz and Chechens.[60]

This diaspora has influenced Russian-Turkish relations, especially in the context of the Chechen conflict by encouraging Turkey in a pro-Chechen direction. Thus when the first Chechen War broke out, Turkey's Caucasian citizens held meetings, formed solidarity committees, and collected money for the Chechen side. In 1996, it was reported that "Chechen flags and portraits of Dzokhar Dudaev can be seen all over Turkey, and money is collected at every bus station."[61]

Reassessing Kemalism and Turkism in the Post-Soviet Era

David Kushner has pointed out that few peoples submerged their ethnic identity in their faith, as the Ottoman Turks immersed their identity in Islam.[62] This situation began to change by the late nineteenth century as Ottoman power continued to retrench from Europe. By the early twentieth century, Turkism had acquired greater importance as the basis of the Ottoman state's identity and had elicited new interest in other Turkic peoples. This awakening was largely due to the influence of European nationalism, the works of European scholars on the origins of the Turks, and increasing contacts with the Turks of the Russian Empire, including Central Asia.[63]

Under the Kemalist regime, Turkism became the cornerstone of the state's ideology, best illustrated by Mustafa Kemal's famous dictum "citizen speak Turkish." However, during the first two decades of the republic, Turkey's main preoccupation was internal consolidation. Hence the government did not support pan-Turkist ideas that sought the unification of all Turks, although such sentiments existed in Turkey and abroad. Many early pan-Turkist writers and intellectuals were so-called Outer Turks, especially Tatars.[64] A prominent representative of this trend was Reha Oguz Turkkan, who founded the Bozkurt (Grey Wolf or Wolf of the Steppes) *Review*. The movement that he founded is influential today.[65]

In the 1960s, Alpaslan Turkeş formed the National Action Party (Milliyetçi Haraket Partisi, NAP [MHP]), which represents the nationalist and pan-Turkist strand in Turkish politics.[66] In the 1970s, the party was engaged in fierce competition with leftist forces, a situation that contributed to the coup d'état of 1980.

Until the late 1980s, despite its behind-the-scenes influence, the NAP (MHP) was not considered a viable partner for other political parties. The party's fortunes changed following developments in the Soviet Union in the late 1980s.[67] Suddenly, the party and its ideology appeared useful as an instrument of expanding Turkish influence in the FSU. This new perception resulted from the reassessment of the Kemalist foundations of Turkey's foreign policy of "peace at home, peace abroad." Most important, the idea of an "Eastern" dimension to Turkey's foreign policy was introduced into the debate. This "Eastern" dimension became very important for a time, especially after the European Community in 1987 refused to consider Turkey's application for membership in the European Union.[68] Thus by the late 1980s, the term "pan-Turkism" acquired a new legitimacy and currency. In 1992, Professor Aydin Yalcin wrote that pan-Turkism was an idea whose time had arrived. The collapse of the Soviet Union and the discrediting of communism had "finally given a public expression and support to pan-Turkism."[69] More important for Russian-Turkish relations was the emergence of a "Turkish version" of Eurasianism that challenged Russia's claim to be the sole Eurasianist power. Turgut Ozal, Turkey's prime minister (1983–89) and later president (1989–93), saw Turkey as the hub of the Eurasian entity and the main link between the Islamic and Western worlds.

The combined effects of these developments led to a geopolitical and cultural rivalry between Turkey and Russia not dissimilar to the one that had existed between the tsarist and Ottoman empires. Duygu Bazoglu Sezer explains these diverging and competing concepts of Eurasianism in the following way:

> Russia, still the pre-eminent power in Eurasia, strongly resists a greater regional role for external actors. . . . Trans-Atlantic powers are especially not welcome. . . . Russia entertains a Russia-centered vision of Eurasia. . . . This Russian vision, this impulse, introduces an element of systemic tensions into Turkish-Russian bilateral relations. . . . In the case of Turkey, it is the country's continuing membership of the Trans-Atlantic system at the southwestern doorsteps of Eurasia, coupled with its aspiration to connect it with an open system, which exerts similar tensions in bilateral relations.[70]

Dmitri Trenin refers to a similar trend in the post-Soviet period based on the idea that the future of Russian-Turkish relations would be "a revival of the 400 year old competition, and even an advent of something which heretofore had been a marginal factor, namely a clash of civilization, Christian Orthodox and Moslem with Russia and Turkey more or less assigned the mission of Chefs de file for the respective sides."[71] In short, the end of communism also ended traditional Kemalism, thus changing the ethnocultural parameters of Russian-Turkish relations just as the collapse of the Soviet Union had altered their geopolitical context.

Islam and Russian-Turkish Relations

The weakening of Islam's position in the Turkish society, another important objective of the Kemalist project, proved hard to achieve. By the mid-1940s, Islam began to make a comeback both in Turkish society and in politics.[72] By the 1970s, the Islamic factor had become so strong in Turkey that it led to the foundation of the political party Milli Nizam Partisi (Party for National Order) by Necmettin Erbakan. Because the Turkish constitution prohibited religion-based parties, this party was not overtly Islamic. Nevertheless, the party was banned in 1971, although it later reappeared under different names: the National Salvation Party (NSP) and Refah.[73] In 1995, Erbakan became prime minister for a short period. He was forced to resign in 1997 by the military and was banned from politics in 1998. Refah reconstructed itself in the form of Fasilat (Virtue), but on 22 June 2001, Fasilat was also banned, leading Turkey's Islamic movement to divide into two factions.[74]

Along with the deep roots of Islam in Turkey, the Turkish government's policies are responsible for the political vitality of Turkish Islam. Turkey often used Islamic forces to counter the left. In the 1980s, partly in response to the Iranian Revolution, the Turkish state promoted Islam's social and political role in the country.[75] In particular, Turgut Ozal did much to legitimize a role for Islam in Turkish society and politics.[76] Thus Turkish Islam was an important political force when developments in the Soviet Union created possibilities for greater interaction between Turkish and Soviet Muslims.

Islam as an Instrument of Turkish Policy in the Post-Soviet Space

The West's view of Turkey's role in the post-Soviet space is that of the promoter of a progressive and secular model of governance in a Muslim country. Turkey has tried to export its secular system to the post-Soviet states, but it has also used the Islamic factor and its extensive Islamic infrastructure to penetrate Muslim parts of Russia and the CIS. According to Ramazan Jabarov, "Turkish Islamic organizations, which have never concealed their support for the 'Muslim movement' in the Caucasus, also got actively engaged in the region."[77] Particularly active has been Fatuhllah Gullen's movement rooted in the Nurcular tradition of Saidi Nursi, which has established a large network of schools throughout Central Asia and the Muslim parts of the Russian Federation.[78] Other followers of Saidi Nursi are also active in the post-Soviet space, including parts of the Russian Federation, notably Bashkortostan Tatarstan.[79] Private Turkish citizens have built mosques in the Russian Federation, from Makhachkala to Ufa. The Turkish government, while suppressing Islamic groups in Turkey itself, has supported these activities.

In short, the interests of the Turkish government and the interests of nationalist, pan-Turkist, and Islamist forces in gaining influence in the post-Soviet space have converged. Many Russians have been concerned about the activities of the Turkish Islamists and nationalists. Some Russian intellectuals and politicians see Turkish Islam as more dangerous because of its modern facade and softer image. Some have felt that Turkey was trying to surround Russia with a belt of Turko-Muslim states extending, as Turkish president Suleiman Demirel once claimed, from the Adriatic Sea to the Great Wall of China.[80] These fears were revived when, in June

2003, Russia's republic of Bashkortostan expelled ten Turkish nationals for allegedly conducting illegal religious and nationalist activities. Those expelled belonged to the Serhat religious and nationalist organization affiliated with Nurcular (Followers of Saidi Nursi) movement.[81] An article in *Pravda* claimed that these people were part of broader activities of the Turkish intelligence services operating in the Russian Federation, and reflected Turkey's "ambition to create a community of Turk countries under Ankara's aegis."[82] Although other considerations have led the Russian government to overlook these aspects of Turkish behavior, ethnic and religious factors have affected Russian-Turkish relations negatively, especially by influencing Turkey's policy toward Chechnya and the Russian-Chechen conflict.

Turkey's Strategic and Economic Importance

Despite Turkey's pro-Chechen policy, Russia has treated Turkey more cautiously than other states because of its strategic position on the Black Sea and its status as a NATO member. According to Alexei Vassiliev, Turkey is the third most important country for Russia, after Ukraine and Germany, because of the Turkish Straits.[83] A hostile Turkey could cause considerable trouble for Russia's access to the Black Sea. Turkey's membership in NATO also means that Russian-Turkish relations cannot be divorced from Russia's relations with the West. Therefore, in the post-Soviet era, Russia's relations with Turkey have reflected Russia's foreign policy perspective, particularly its view of the West.

Thus during the "Russian-Western honeymoon" (1992–94), Russia viewed Turkey and its regional role favorably. A Treaty of Friendship and Cooperation was initialed when Kozyrev traveled to Ankara in February 1992.[84] The foundations of this agreement were laid during Turkish president Turgut Ozal's visit to Moscow in March 1991. An important aspect of the Ten-Year Treaty of Friendship and Cooperation signed by Ozal was the stipulation that "if either of the two parties to the treaty faced aggression from a third country or a group of countries, the other will not directly or indirectly provide help to, or support the aggressor or aggressors."[85] Furthermore, the two countries agreed not to "allow their territory to be used as a staging ground for any separatist or aggressive designs on the territory, sovereignty and independence of the other."[86] While visiting Turkey a year later, Kozyrev noted, "Relations between Turkey and Russia will flourish on the basis of relations that existed between Turkey and the former Soviet Union."[87]

Economic considerations also mitigated geopolitical and ethnocultural competition. Turkey is an important market for Russia, especially for its natural gas. Russia's success in securing the agreement to provide Turkey with 16 billion cubic meters of Russian gas during the first year through the Blue Stream Pipeline was a major achievement, considering the competition from Iran, Turkmenistan, and Azerbaijan.[88] According to some Russian sources, this figure will rise to 93 billion in 2005 and 82 billion in 2020. However, such predictions are not always reliable because of the uncertainties of the Turkish economy. The agreement to build the pipeline was reached in mid-December 1997 between Russian prime minister Viktor Chernomyrdin and Turkish prime minister Mesut Yilmaz at a time when Russian-Turkish relations were strained because of Chechnya and other differences.[89] This illustrates both the contradictory nature of Russian-Turkish relations and the impact of diverging interest groups within Russia's foreign policy–making apparatus in shaping the character of Russian-Turkish relations. However, as of late June 2003, because of disagreements over the price, no Russian gas had been delivered to Turkey via the "Blue Stream" pipeline.[90]

Even without the massive gas exports envisaged in the Blue Stream Project, Russia was Turkey's fourth-largest trade partner. In 2000, Russian exports to Turkey stood at $3.887 billion.[91] Meanwhile, Turkey exported $650 million worth of goods to Russia.[92] In the first ten months of 2002, the value of Turkish exports to Russia reached $972 million and the value of Russian exports to Turkey reached $2.95 billion.[93] In addition, Turkish companies have significantly invested in Russia. In particular, Turkish construction companies have been very active in Russia.[94]

Notwithstanding serious bilateral tensions, Russia was even willing to sell arms to Turkey. In February 1996, Russian minister for foreign economic relations Oleg Davydov stated that Russia had exported $25.7 million in arms to Turkey in 1994, $70 million in 1995, and $121 million during the first two months of 1996.[95] Russian exports included helicopters and armored personnel carriers, which were used in the fight against the Kurdish Workers Party (PKK). According to some reports, Turkey intends to import $150 billion worth of arms over thirty years, thus increasing its importance as an arms market.[96] Turkey is also interested in the coproduction of arms since it wants to expand its indigenous arms industry. Reportedly, Turkey and Rosvooruzhenie (the Russian Arms Export Agency) are jointly producing Russian KA-50-2 attack helicopters.[97]

Russian-Turkish Rivalry for the Control of Eurasia and the Chechen Conflict

As Russian optimism regarding its rapid integration into the Western world and the post-Soviet states' natural gravitation toward Russia receded, a reaction set in. The position of those who advocated a less cooperative approach to relations with the West was strengthened and resulted in a more interventionist Russian policy in the post-Soviet space. This was the case especially in the South Caucasus, where Turkey had made considerable gains.

These developments negatively affected Russian-Turkish relations, leading Russia to see Turkey more as a rival than as a partner.[98] Some even saw Turkey and the so-called Turkic-Islamic factor as "the big threat over Russia."[99] Similarly, Turkey viewed Russia as a potential enemy. The ouster of Abulfazl Elçibey's pro-Turkish government in Azerbaijan in June 1993 led General Dozan Gures, chief of the general staff of the Turkish armed forces, to declare, "Russia represents a more serious threat than the Soviet Union."[100] Additionally, Turkey emerged as a major competitor to Russia as a transit route for the export of Caspian oil and gas.

All these competing interests—geopolitical, ethnocultural, and even religious—

came together during the Chechen conflict, prompting Turkey to support the Chechens' quest for independence, though such support predated the outbreak of the Russian-Chechen War. Russia subsequently began improving ties with Iran as a counterweight to Turkey. This caused more "discomfort" in Ankara, especially since Armenia and Greece were to be part of a group led by Russia to prevent the spread of Turkish influence.[101]

Strategically, the loss of Chechnya, which might have led to the loss of Dagestan, would have drastically eroded Russia's access to the South Caucasus and the Caspian Sea, allowing Turkey to expand its influence. Turkey's role as a hub for energy exports from Central Asia and the Caucasus would have also been greatly enhanced at Russia's expense. Both Turkish nationalist and Islamist groupings shared this vision. Dudaev was a frequent visitor to Turkey and participated in events sponsored by nationalist groups. Nevertheless, the Islamic factor was less important than strategic or nationalist considerations. Furthermore, the North Caucasian diaspora in Turkey and its organizations, numbering between 47 and 100, supported the Chechens and engaged in anti-Russian activities. How far the Turkish government encouraged such activities or merely abstained from preventing them remains unclear.

Turkey's Dual Policy toward Chechnya

Like many other Muslim countries, Turkey pursued a dual policy toward Chechnya. Unofficially, Turkey was far more supportive of the Chechen cause than its official stand indicated. However, between 1994 and 1996, the official and unofficial aspects of Turkey's Chechnya policy converged. Thus when the Russian Foreign Ministry called the ambassadors of Afghanistan, Iran, Jordan, Pakistan, and Saudi Arabia and the Turkish chargé d'affaires in January 1995 and asked their governments to halt the unofficial recruitment of mercenaries to fight in Chechnya, the Turkish representative was the only envoy not to characterize the Chechen War as Russia's internal affair. Instead, Turkey called for an immediate cease-fire and denounced Russia's military intervention.[102]

Turkish help for Chechnya went beyond verbal support. According to Russian sources, Dudaev had aircraft based at the Bitlis airfield, allegedly to carry weapons, drugs, counterfeit money, and wounded men for treatment in Turkish hospitals.[103] There were rumors that Prime Minister Tansu Çiller had used secret slush funds to buy and send weapons to the Chechens. These allegations were made by the secretary general of the Leftist Workers Party, Dogu Perincek, and, therefore, may not be reliable.[104]

Clearly, the Turkish government did not effectively control Turkish and Caucasian groups that were helping the Chechens. When a group of nine Turkish nationals of Caucasian origin, including Muhammad Emin Tokcan, hijacked a ferryboat on 16 January 1996 en route between Trabzon in Turkey and Sochi in Russia, President Yeltsin accused Turkey of "dragging out the situation" to give Chechens more positive international exposure.[105] The hijackers were allegedly linked to the MHP and Nizam-i-Alem, a small Islamo-nationalist party that had split from the Grey Wolves because of their insufficient commitment to Islam.[106] Other sources have alleged that Turkey allowed the training of Chechens on its territory and permitted the transit of Chechens seeking training in Afghanistan or that of foreign mercenaries going to Chechnya.[107] Islamic sentiments were certainly exploited to garner support for the Chechens, even by nationalists. According to one report, "The Grey Wolves run the mosques and commercial activities in some parts of Istanbul. It is in these mosques . . . that offerings are collected after daily prayers for the Chechens. . . . At the Faith mosque, . . . the pro-Chechen network daily enlists men to send to the front."[108]

Russian complaints of Turkish laxity in restraining support for Chechen rebels continued well into 2001. In late April 2001, the Russian Foreign Ministry criticized Turkey for failing to crack down on supporters of the rebel Chechen cause, suggesting that the Turkish government could have prevented incidents such as the seizure of an Istanbul hotel by pro-Chechen gunmen in April 2001.[109]

Meanwhile, Russia tried to exploit Turkey's problems with the PKK in order to dissuade Turkey from interfering in Chechnya. An event particularly jarring to Turkey was the meeting of the Kurdish Parliament in Exile (KPE) in Moscow on 30 October–1 November 1995 under the sponsorship of the Russian State Duma's Geopolitical Affairs Committee. The Turks claimed that the conference could not have taken place if the Foreign Ministry had not tacitly endorsed it.[110] Yet Russia, unwilling to overly antagonize Turkey, refused to grant PKK leader Abdullah Ocalan political asylum in 1999.[111]

In line with the dual character of their relations, and despite tension caused by the Chechen conflict and other rivalries, contacts between Turkey and Russia continued.[112] Russia and Turkey signed several agreements on combating terrorism. In December 1996, Turkish and Russian foreign ministers Tansu Çiller and Yevgenii Primakov met and signed yet another Protocol of Cooperation against Terrorism.[113] In 1999, the Prime Minister of Turkey, Bulent Ecevit, and Vladimir Putin met and signed a joint Declaration of Cooperation in the Struggle against Terrorism.[114] Even when in early 2001 Russia was complaining of Turkish groups' support for Chechen rebels and Turkey was expressing its disapproval of "the heavy retaliation of Russia against Chechens," Turkish foreign minster Ismail Cem visited Moscow in April, and Igor Ivanov paid a return visit in June, stating, "Turkey is an important partner for Russia."[115]

After 11 September

In view of the close linkage between the state of Russian-Western relations and the character of Russian-Turkish ties, the post–11 September Russian-American rapprochement had a positive effect on Turkey's ties with Russia. Reflecting this new mood, at the NATO-Russia Summit in Rome on 28 May 2002, the Turkish president Ahmet Necdet Sezer said, "Among the priority goals of the Turkish foreign policy is to strengthen the bilateral cooperation with our friend and neighbor

Russia and to elevate it to an advanced level of partnership to our mutual benefit. We know that Russia shares the same determination."[116] Earlier, an agreement on "military cooperation framework and military personnel training cooperation" was signed when General Anatolii Kvashnin, chief of the General Staff of the Russian Armed Forces, visited Ankara in January 2002.[117]

Another factor that, under certain circumstances, could encourage closer Russian-Turkish relations is the Turkish military's doubts about the wisdom of Turkey's attempts to join the EU, which would require significant changes in Turkey's policy toward ethnic minorities and a strengthening of civilian control over the military, prospects viewed unfavorably by the military. The Turkish military seems to favor the tripartite alliance of Turkey, Israel, and the United States to membership in the European Union. Growing U.S.-EU tensions no doubt would create a dilemma for Turkey. Therefore, some Turkish generals have talked about closer cooperation with Russia.[118]

However, Russian-Turkish relations retain their competitive dimensions. Turkey is opposed to the presence of Russian troops in Azerbaijan around the Azeri missile-tracking station.[119] It also disapproves of Russian bases in Georgia and Armenia, although it no longer sees bases in Georgia as a threat to its security.[120] With U.S. ascendancy in areas of traditional Russian influence, Turkey's position in the post–11 September period has been strengthened vis-à-vis Russia. Natalya Airapetova's article "Turetskii Marsh na Prostorakh SNG" (Turkish march in the expanses of the CIS) in *Nezavisimaya Gazeta* shows at least one strand of Russian opinion on Turkish gains in the region.[121] Other analysts, by contrast, emphasize the positive dimensions of Russian-Turkish relations. Meanwhile, Turkish and Russian officials increasingly refer to their respective countries as two great Eurasian powers, indicating that Turkish and Russian versions of Eurasianism need not be competitive. Rather, they can be complementary.[122]

The October 2002 hostage-taking operation by Chechen rebels in Moscow caused new tensions in these relations. Russia demanded that Turkey prevent the flow of arms and money to Chechens and close down Chechen organizations operating in Turkey, most notably the Caucasus-Chechnya Solidarity Association.[123] Turkey denied that such organizations existed, but to placate Moscow, it expelled Badroudine Zelimkhan Arsangereev, who claimed to be a representative of Chechnya in Istanbul.[124] Turkey also banned the holding of a Chechen congress in Turkey.[125] However, the activities of pro-Chechen organizations continue to be a source of contention between Russia and Turkey. The change of government in Turkey in November 2002 and the coming to power of the Justice and Development Party (Adalet ve Kalkilma Partisi) with its Islamic roots did not affect the basic pattern of Russian-Turkish relations. These relations continued to be characterized by strategic and cultural competition, especially in the Caucasus, and by economic cooperation. Despite some efforts by the Turkish government to curb the activities of pro-Chechen groups in Turkey, in June 2003 the Russian deputy prosecutor general listed Turkey among those countries that continued to send help to the

Chechen rebels.[126] In short, even in the post–11 September and post–Iraq War eras, Chechnya remained a source of strain in Russian-Turkish relations.

Russia and Iran: An Unequal Partnership

Despite Iran's theocratic government and its position as the vanguard of Islamic revolution in the 1980s, since early 1994 Russia and Iran have formed close and essentially friendly relations. The document outlining the Russian concept of foreign policy published in 2000 cites the expansion of relations between Russia and Iran as a principal goal of the Russian Federation's foreign policy.[127] Some Russian and Western observers and Iranian officials have termed Russian-Iranian relations as a "partnership." This partnership consists of Russia's arms supply to Iran and assistance in rebuilding the Iranian nuclear power plant in Bushehr. Western, especially U.S., sources claim that Russian scientists have helped Iran develop its missile technology, a claim denied by Russia.[128]

Yet since 1992, Russia's approach toward Iran has been neither consistent nor in the spirit of true partnership wherein there is a balance of benefits between the partners. Rather, Russia has been the main beneficiary, making the Russian-Iranian partnership highly unequal. Russia has used Iran to advance its geopolitical agenda in Central Asia (notably in Tajikistan), in the Caucasus (to balance Turkish-Azerbaijani influence), and in Afghanistan. It has used Iran as a bargaining chip in its dealings with the West and other countries to Iran's disadvantage whenever it has suited Russian interests. Iran has also been helpful to Russia by calling the Chechen crisis an internal Russian affair and, while Iran held the presidency of the Organization of the Islamic Conference (OIC) in 1997–98, moderating that organization's response to Russian policy toward Chechnya. This approach has had minimal benefits for Iran and, in fact, has entailed substantial costs: it has damaged Iran's position within the OIC and has eroded Iran's Islamic credentials and overall image in the Muslim world.[129]

The ineptness of Iranian diplomacy, especially its inability or unwillingness to improve its relations with the United States, is the main reason for this situation, because the U.S. hostility has put Iran in an extremely weak bargaining position vis-à-vis international and regional actors, including Russia.[130] Nevertheless, certain basic incompatibilities in Russia and Iran's geopolitical and economic interests, the diverging interests of Russia's economic and political elites (notably evident in the strong anti-Iran sentiments of powerful Russian lobbies), the new character of the international political system (especially U.S. predominance), and Russia's economic and military weakness have further impeded a real Russian-Iranian partnership.

The Islamic factor has played a relatively limited role in shaping Russian-Iranian relations. Its impact has been somewhat contradictory, but on the whole, positive. (This is, in fact, a distinguishing feature of Russian-Iranian relations, as opposed to Russia's ties with most other Muslim countries.) Both Iran and Russia have been the object of animosity of various Sunni extremist groups, notably the Taliban and followers of various shades of Wahhabism who consider the Shi'as to be unbelievers and are active in Russia, especially Chechnya. This fact has led some Russian Eurasianists to characterize Iran's brand of Islam as "Eurasianist Islam" because of its opposition to the global system based on Euro-Atlanticist supremacy, but others still view "Khomeinism" as equally or perhaps even more dangerous.[131]

Areas of Convergence and Divergence between Russian and Iranian Interests

Russian views regarding the extent of commonality of interest between Russia and Iran have also varied, depending on shifts in its overall worldview and foreign policy priorities and its ability to realize them. Between 1992 and 1994, key Russian foreign policy makers, notably Foreign Minister Andrei Kozyrev, saw no common strategic interests between Iran and Russia; Kozyrev considered Iran a source of instability in Russia's southern rim.[132] The Euro-Atlanticists, advocating a close partnership with the West, also supported Western positions on Middle East issues, favoring close Russian ties with Israel and supporting sanctions against Iraq.[133] U.S.-Iranian hostility and the declared U.S. policy of containing Iranian influence in Central Asia and the Caucasus further reduced Russia's interest in close relations with Iran.

Yet even in this period of coolness, Russia did not want relations with Iran to deteriorate beyond a certain point. Thus it kept its 1991 agreement to reconstruct the Bushehr power plant and continued to supply military hardware on the basis of an agreement reached in 1989 during Ayatullah Ali-Akbar Hashemi Rafsanjani's visit to Moscow.[134]

Nevertheless, Russia's attitude toward Iran remained reticent, and Russia made it clear that good Russian-Iranian relations would be on Moscow's terms. A Moscow radio broadcast to Iran in December 1993 warned Tehran that prospects for expanded relations would be harmed "if Iran proposes political conditions, for example, concerning Tajikistan or Russia's military, technical cooperation with the Arab countries of the Persian Gulf."[135]

By early 1994, the shift in Russia's foreign policy outlook, notably the growing fear of expanding Turkish influence in Russia's southern rim, increased Iran's strategic importance for Russia as a counterweight and barrier to an emerging Turkic bloc. Andranik Migranyan warned against the risks of the emergence of a "greater Turan" and even "an enormous, homogeneous ethno-religious space gravitating toward Turkey." Considering Western support for a greater Turkish role, Migranyan concluded, "Providing military and political support to Iran and Armenia is in Russia's interests, even if it is not drawn into geopolitical confrontation."[136]

This new Russian view provided one of the principal points of convergence between Iran and Russia's geopolitical interests because ideas propagated by pan-Turkists in Azerbaijan and Turkey potentially also threatened Iran's territorial integrity since the realization of pan-Turkist schemes required Iran's dismemberment in order to link Turkey to Central Asia.[137] However, this convergence of interest could disappear depending on the dynamics of either Russian-Turkish or Turkish-Iranian relations. A closer Russian-Turkish partnership and Turkey's abandonment of plans to replace Russia as the major player in the traditional areas of Russian influence would reduce Iran's strategic significance. Better Turkish-Iranian relations and the abandonment of Turkish support for Azerbaijani irredenta toward Iran would lessen Iran's fear and reduce Russia's importance. While most Russians fear the emergence of a Turkic bloc, Iran's expanding presence in the Caucasus and Central Asia is not favored either.

Fear of Separatism and Commitment to Territorial Status Quo

The rise of centrifugal tendencies in Russia, especially Chechnya's bid for independence, combined with Iran's concern over some of its own minorities' autonomist aspirations and its fear of encirclement by hostile forces, created another point of convergence, namely, opposition to separatism, especially by force. Consequently, Iran consistently and openly supported Russia's territorial integrity, even in the case of Chechnya. Yet it was only in 2001, on the eve of President Muhammad Khatami's visit to Russia, that some Russian analysts recognized the value of Iran's support. Vladimir Sazhin wrote, "For Russia, the support of Moscow's Chechen policy and its anti-terrorist campaign from such an authoritative Muslim state as Iran is extremely valuable."[138]

Economic Necessities

Iran's need to reconstruct its war-damaged economy and defenses, coupled with Russia's growing economic difficulties and disappointing results from economic reform, made Iran an attractive market and economic partner for Russia. Beyond the rebuilding of the Bushehr power plant and providing arms, Russia became involved in a number of other industrial projects in Iran.[139]

Yet Russia did not take full advantage of opportunities presented to it by Iran for most of the 1990s. The main reasons were U.S. opposition and the hostility of certain powerful interest groups in Russia, including some key financial oligarchs. Israel also lobbied hard against Russia's collaboration with Iran, warning of the risks involved in closer contacts between Iranian students and scientists and their Russian counterparts.[140] The impact of U.S. opposition was felt in 1995 when, following an agreement between U.S. vice president Al Gore and Russian prime minister Viktor Chernomyrdin, Russia stopped arms deliveries to Iran.

Iran's Good Behavior and the Emergence of New Threats

Iran's "good behavior," that is, its pragmatic and nonideological approach toward the post-Soviet states and its patience vis-à-vis Russia, contributed to a change in Russia's view of Iran. As political analyst Dmitri Simes put it, "Iran has been the good kid on the block," and Dmitri Trenin noted that Russia views Iran as "a good citizen of the region."[141] In particular, Iran's help in settling the Tajik Civil War and its stand on the Armenia-Azerbaijan conflict were noticed, although Russia has been reluctant to publicly acknowledge Iran's positive contributions. Only in 2001 did Yevgenii Primakov, former Russian foreign and prime minister, acknowledge that the "Iran-Russia alliance has been instrumental in the Caucasian region and in bringing peace to Tajikistan."[142] Iran also supported Russia's position in opposition to NATO's eastward expansion.

Most important, Iran has been very helpful to Russia on the Chechen issue, especially in the context of the OIC. True, Iran initially condemned the Russian invasion of Chechnya. On 26 December 1994, the Speaker of the Iranian parliament, Ali-Akbar Nateq-Nuri, criticized Russia for killing Chechens and destroying their homes, saying that Russia's policies were "reminiscent of the Stalin era, when terror and intimidation reigned."[143] Iran's president Ali-Akbar Hashemi Rafsanjani also expressed "regret over Russia's resort to military action" and characterized it as a "mistake."[144] A few members of the parliament used even stronger language.[145] Yet compared to other Muslim countries, Iran's reaction was muted and was accompanied by offers of mediation. It is conceivable that Iran used Russia's Chechen problems to show that it could either help Russia or cause problems for it. However, the evolution of the Chechen political scene and the growing influence of Saudi, Pakistani, and Turkish elements led Iran to view events in Chechnya as potentially threatening to its own security.[146]

Russia, meanwhile, used accusations of Iranian assistance to the Chechen rebels to force Iran into a more cooperative posture. In March 1995, Russian parliamentary deputy Mikhail Burlakov told the Russian State Duma that Dudaev had received arms from Iran.[147] Iran strongly objected to these accusations. When Primakov became foreign minister, a shift in Russia's overall foreign policy toward a multipolar strategy improved Russian-Iranian relations.

The visit of Iranian foreign minister Ali-Akbar Velayati to Moscow in March 1996 marked the beginning of an active and, from the Russian perspective, positive Iranian involvement in the Chechen issue.[148] Iran was particularly helpful to Russia within the OIC. During the OIC's 1997 summit in Tehran, Iran kept the Chechen question off its agenda. Russian minister of interior Anatolii Kulikov expressed gratitude to Tehran for its "circumspect position on the Chechen issue" and also acknowledged that it was Iran's stance that prevented Turkey from putting Chechnya on the agenda of the OIC summit.[149] Iran further created a Special Committee for Chechnya within the OIC for regular consultation with Russia to help resolve the Chechen problem. Consequently, in 1999–2000, several delegations from the OIC visited Moscow.[150] After one visit to Moscow in January 2000, the OIC issued a press release that set out the principles for resolving the Chechen conflict. Among these principles was "freedom to practice Islamic Sharia, already promised by Russian authorities."[151]

The parallel processes of reform within Iranian society and leadership, along with movement toward a more liberal interpretation of Islam in Iran and the rise of more dangerous versions of Islamic extremism in Afghanistan and Pakistan, facilitated Russian-Iranian rapprochement. Both Russia and Iran felt threatened by the rise of the Taliban in Afghanistan, especially as the Taliban threatened to gain total control of Afghanistan and began actively cooperating with extremist movements in Central Asia. After a brief effort in 1997 to reach an understanding with the Taliban, Russia joined Iran in supporting the anti-Taliban forces led by Ahmad Shah Masoud.

Impediment to Real Partnership

Yet until 1999, Russia did not seriously strengthen its ties with Iran. According to A.I. Gousher, "There was a time when the Russian side simply ignored many invitations offering the official visit to Tehran, which were directed to the former high-ranking Russian officials (former Minister of Defense Pavel Grachev, former Chairman of Security Council Ivan Rybkin, and others). Only Yevgenii Primakov, while he was Russia's minister of foreign affairs, visited Teheran."[152] The following factors impeded closer Russian-Iranian ties: (1) American opposition; (2) Russian ambivalence about strengthening Iran economically and militarily; (3) energy competition; and (4) Russia's lingering suspicion of Iran's Islamic system.

American Opposition

The single most important impediment to Russian-Iranian partnership has been strong and persistent U.S. opposition. Although the Gore-Chernomyrdin agreement of 1995 was limited to the military sphere, it affected all aspects of cooperation. U.S. opposition was a major brake on Russian-Iranian cooperation.[153]

It was only after Russia withdrew from the Gore-Chernomyrdin agreement in 1999 that it tried to revitalize relations with Iran. Interestingly, in a pattern reminiscent of the past use of its Muslim population as instruments of its diplomacy, in the fall of 1999, Russia sent two Muslim deputies of the State Duma's Refakh political movement, Abdul Vahid Niazov and Kurban Ali Amirov, to Tehran. In addition to meeting President Mohammed Khatami, the two met with the supreme leader Ayatullah Khamenei. During this meeting, Niazov stated, "The development of Russian-Iranian relations can no longer be contingent on the view of a third party, a view that was imposed on us."[154] However, opposition from the United States continues to be the most serious obstacle in Russian-Iranian relations, and there have been disagreements within the Russian leadership on how far Russia can safely go in promoting relations with Iran without jeopardizing ties with the United States.

Russian Ambivalence about Strengthening Iran

Given its more favorable geographical location, a stable and reasonably strong Iran was useful to Russia as a counterweight to Turkey, but a truly strong Iran could potentially be a formidable competitor for Russia in Central Asia and the Caucasus because, from an economic and geographic perspective, Iran is the most logical route for the export of the energy resources of the Caspian region. Yet Iran can also be a valuable partner for Russia in Central and South Asia, linking Russia with the Indian subcontinent, especially since the West has been promoting an East-West corridor linking Uzbekistan to Moldova and Ukraine. This corridor even has a security dimension in the context of the regional organization (GUUAM) whose members are Georgia, Uzbekistan, Ukraine, Azerbaijan, and Moldova.[155] To counter the East-West corridor, since 2002 Russia has been working to create a North-South corridor. This corridor, which is supposed to link Mumbai in India with St. Petersburg in Russia via Iran's Persian Gulf ports and territory, involves a large network of sea, rail, and land transportation.[156] Potentially, the network could extend to Southeast Asia. The basic agreement on the creation of the network has been reached; however, its realization is far from certain. Whether Russia sees Iran as a partner or competitor in the coming years will depend on developments in Iran, including a potential change of direction in its regime and hence its foreign policy outlook and the availability of other options for Russia.

Energy Competition

Russia and Iran possess 50 and 13 percent, respectively, of global reserves of natural gas. Since proximity to consumer markets is an important factor in natural-gas trade, Iran has an edge in Turkey, southern Europe, and the Indian subcontinent. When the Islam-oriented party Refah led the Turkish government and its leader, Necmettin Erbakan, was prime minister, Turkey signed an agreement with Iran for the delivery of Iranian gas.[157] Turkey had to build a 1,000-kilometer pipeline to transport the gas to Ankara from the Iranian border. With Erbakan's removal, Turkey changed its policy and supported Russia's Blue Stream Project. Consequently, the completion of the Turkish part of the pipeline took longer than anticipated.[158]

Russian-Iranian competition extended to the Caspian region, including the division of its resources. Initially, Russia and Iran shared similar views on the legal status of the Caspian Sea and the division of seabed resources.[159] However, because of the energy lobby's influence, Russia changed its position and signed bilateral agreements with Azerbaijan, Kazakhstan, and Turkmenistan on the exploitation of energy resources.[160] This Russian attitude undermined Iran's position and could ultimately leave it with the least share of Caspian resources.[161]

Iran has bitterly resented Russia's change of position, which it sees as symbolic of its cavalier attitude toward relations with Iran, including disregarding and refusing to implement agreements reached. A.I. Gousher pointed out, "Iran's trust is often undermined by the irresponsibilities of our [Russian] representatives, who do not honor the agreements."[162] According to some reports, Russia's deputy foreign minister signed an agreement with an Iranian counterpart in 1998 in which he affirmed Moscow's readiness to take into account Tehran's insistence on a 20 percent share of the Caspian Sea.[163] In the summer of 2000, Iran reportedly reminded

Viktor Kalyuzhny, Russia's deputy foreign minister and presidential envoy to the Caspian Sea region, of this agreement and said, "Pastukhov [Kalyuzhny's predecessor] gave us guarantees, but where is he now? Now you are making different proposals, but what will become of them if you go, too?"[164]

By mid-2002, Russia was growing increasingly impatient with Iran's position.[165] Competition over the Caspian Sea is acquiring a military dimension as well, and Russia is determined to show that it is the most powerful military power in the region. After the failed Ashgabat Summit of Caspian littoral states in April 2002, Vladimir Putin called for massive military exercises in the region involving the Caspian fleet and stated that a strong naval force was critical for achieving Russia's economic and political interests.[166] Iran sees this as a direct effort to intimidate it.[167]

Lingering Suspicion of Iran's Islamic System

Despite Iran's decade-long accommodation and friendly posture toward Russia, certain powerful interest groups remain suspicious of Iran's Islamic regime. The Russians are also still rankled by the memory of Iran's characterization of the USSR as the "Shaitan [Satan] number two," or "small Shaitan [Satan]," denouncing its policy as "red imperialism."[168]

To sum up, Russia's pursuit of partnership with Iran has been halfhearted and motivated largely by negative factors. Russia has used Iran as a bargaining chip in relations with the United States and regional countries. Meanwhile, it has reaped economic benefits from its ties with Iran, although not to the extent it could have.[169] Even at the height of Russian-Iranian rapprochement, symbolized by President Khatami's visit to Moscow in March 2001, the main Russian motivations were derivative and inspired by fear rather than by a vision of common strategic interest.

First, Russian-American relations were at a low ebb following the inauguration of George W. Bush as U.S. president in January 2001. The two countries were at odds over a number of issues, notably the Anti-Ballistic Missile (ABM) Treaty and U.S. plans to build a National Missile Defense (NMD) system. Moreover, the Bush administration generally downgraded the importance of relations with Russia.[170] Russia's insecurity regarding the future of its relations with the West is reflected in Vladimir Kucherenko's comment, "Today, whatever people in the West might say, no one is in any hurry to admit Russia to the circle of developed countries, allotting to us the fate of being suppliers of raw materials, with a dying high-tech industry."[171]

Second, following the coming to power of President Khatami, the emergence of a strong reformist movement in Iran, which swept parliamentary elections in 2000, and a relative thaw in U.S.-Iranian relations, the Russians became concerned about the normalization of U.S.-Iranian ties.[172] Were this to happen, given the long history of Iran's military and economic ties to the United States, the superior quality of U.S. products, and a large Iranian-American diaspora, the United States would drive Russia out of the Iranian market. Russian commentators have long attributed U.S. opposition to Russia's arms sales and involvement in other projects in Iran to the U.S. desire to develop Iran as a market for American companies.[173] According to Mikhail Chernov, "The historical reaction of Washington to the Russian-Iranian military rapprochement is determined not only by the fact of the Russian entry into Iran, but also by the fact that by doing so Russia is finally pushing the United States out of this country."[174] Even Russian foreign minister Igor Ivanov has intimated that America's insistence that Russia forgo economic relations with countries whose behavior it dislikes is motivated by long-term economic interests.[175]

Russian-Iranian Relations after 11 September

The terrorist attacks of 11 September 2001 dramatically altered the context and dynamics of Russian-American relations, leading to a much more cooperative relationship. Russian-Iranian ties will not be unaffected, depending on how deep and lasting Russian-American partnership becomes. If Russia views the United States as completely replacing it in its southern rim, its relations with Iran will remain important. If Russian-American partnership deepens without an improvement in U.S.-Iranian ties, Russian-Iranian relations will suffer. By January 2002, the United States had abandoned the idea of reaching an accommodation with Iranian reformists and had opted for an eventual change of regime.[176]

By early 2003, although there was no dramatic shift in Russia's approach toward relations with Iran, the enthusiasm generated by Khatami's visit had disappeared. Relations were characterized by contradictory signals and a creeping chill. During his meeting with President Bush in May 2002, President Putin defended Russia's role in building the Bushehr plant.[177] Other Russian officials denied that Russia was helping Iran with military uses of nuclear energy and dismissed the idea that Iran posed a threat either to Russia or the United States.[178] However, there were reports that Russia might stop work on the Bushehr plant and other cooperative plans. The Iranian press also raised the issue of whether Russia would be able to resist U.S. pressures.[179] Russia's change of position on the Caspian, illustrated by the Russian-Kazakh agreement to divide the northern part of the sea and the fortification of the Caspian fleet, added to the cooling of relations and prompted the *Tehran Times* to characterize Putin as politically immature.

Meanwhile, it was reported in the Russian press that Vladimir Putin would visit Iran before the end of 2002, without, however, giving an exact date. A Russian-Iranian presidential summit might signal a more lasting partnership.[180] However, by the winter of 2003, Putin had not yet visited Tehran. But other contacts continued to support Russia's ties with Iran. During the visit of an Iranian delegation to Moscow in January 2003, Russian deputy foreign minister Vyacheslav Trubnikov stated, "Russia regards Iran as an important regional partner.... [Iran] not only condemns international terrorism, but has also proved this by concrete action, especially in Afghanistan."[181]

Russia's approval of the draft of a long-term program (extending to 2012) for enhancing trade, economic, industrial, and technical scientific ties between Russia and Iran further indicates that despite better ties with Washington, Russia does not want to burn the bridge with Iran. The conflicting signals are also a sign of a power struggle between pro-Iran and anti-Iran lobbies.[182] The latter appeared to be gaining the upper hand when Russia signed the agreement on the delineation of respective Russian and Azeri zones in the Caspian Sea, disregarding Iranian concerns.[183] The crisis over Iraq, culminating in the Anglo-American war against Iraq, increased Iran's strategic value to Russia and led to a warming of their bilateral relations. As indication of this warming trend, Russian foreign minister Igor Ivanov visited Tehran in March 2003.[184] A number of economic and security issues were addressed during this meeting. Among security-related issues, in addition to the Iraq crisis, were those concerning the Caucasus region. According to a report in *Online Pravda*, Iranian foreign minister Kamal Kharazi expressed Iran's readiness to collaborate with Russia to establish stability in the North Caucasus, including Chechnya.[185] However, the hardening of the U.S. position toward Iran—first indicated in President George W. Bush's "Axis of Evil" speech on 29 January 2002, followed by accusations by other U.S. officials, including Secretary of Defense Donald Rumsfeld, that Iran was sheltering Al-Qaeda members—and renewed tensions in 2003 over Iran's nuclear activities exacerbated Russia's dilemmas in dealing with Iran.

As in the past, Russia tried to balance its interests in keeping its presence in Iran and remaining on good terms with the United States. This balancing act was best illustrated by Russia's decision to pressure Iran to abandon any ambitions of developing a nuclear weapon capability while simultaneously insisting that Russia would continue the work on the Bushehr plant and provide it with fuel, provided proper legal and other arrangements were made for the return of the spent fuel to Russia. Illustrative of this balancing act was the statement of Georgy Mamedov. During a meeting with the Iranian ambassador to Moscow, he expressed concern over the existence of "serious, unclarified issues in connection with nuclear research in Iran."[186] He also urged Iran to sign the additional protocol to the Non-Proliferation Treaty (NPT), which allows for more intrusive IAEA inspections.[187]

Meanwhile, Russia did not end its cooperation with Iran on the building of the Bushehr plant. Following the visit of Gholam Reza Aqazadeh, Iranian vice president and head of Iran's Atomic Energy Organization (IEAO), to Moscow on 30 June 2003, the two sides seemed to be on the point of finalizing legal arrangements for the disposal of spent fuel at Bushehr.[188] During this visit, Igor Ivanov also urged Iran to sign the additional protocol, and said doing so would "be another sign of the peaceful nature of the Iranian nuclear program as well as of the close cooperation of Iran and the IAEA."[189] Other economic and trade delegations from Iran and Russia paid visits to Tehran and Moscow in the course of spring of the 2003.[190]

However, despite this warming trend, at the end of 2003 the basic barriers for a significant upgrading of Moscow-Tehran relations remained. The most significant of these barriers continued to be U.S. opposition to Russian-Iranian cooperation and U.S. pressures on Russia to curtail its relations with Iran.

Conclusion

The Islamic factor has had a significant impact on Russia's relations with the Northern Tier countries. Its effects, however, have been different among the individual countries, depending on three factors: (1) the importance of Islam in determining the policies of individual states toward Russia and toward issues and regions of vital interest to Russia, most notably the Chechen conflict; (2) the relative strategic and economic importance of these countries to Russia; and (3) the position of other great powers, notably the United States, toward these states. Therefore, the strongest impact of the Islamic factor has been felt on Russia's relations with Afghanistan and Pakistan because of their support for the Chechen rebels, including extremist elements, and for Islamist groups in other parts of the Russian Federation and in Central Asia.

In Iran's case, despite the Iranian government's accommodating posture toward Russia, including its position on the Chechen conflict, the Islamic factor has exerted a negative influence in the form of lingering suspicions of a regime that bases its entire political system on Islam, even if its external polices are increasingly determined by pragmatic considerations. However, the most significant limiting factor in the expansion of Russian-Iranian relations has been the U.S. policy of isolating Iran.

In Turkey's case, the Islamic factor has had a greater role than is generally admitted. This is due to Turkey's support of Chechen separatists, the extensive involvement of private Turkish organizations in rebuilding Russia's Muslim infrastructure, and Turkey's extensive cultural and educational networks in the Russian Federation, Central Asia, and the Caucasus. However, because of Turkey's economic and strategic importance, especially its position as a favored and vital Western ally, Russia has overlooked the other dimensions of its policy.

10

Russia's Relations with the Arab World and the Balkans

President Vladimir Putin has often spoken of an "arc of instability" stretching from Kosovo to the Philippines and passing through the Caucasus, Central Asia, and Afghanistan, a vast area he describes as threatened by extremist Islam and its adherents bent on spreading their ideology and changing the political landscape of this vast territory. The inspiration and more tangible help for these extremists are seen as coming primarily from the Arab and Muslim worlds, although the extent of direct involvement of governments in these countries is subject to debate. Similarly, it is not easy to measure the nongovernmental assistance to these extremist groups because there has been a tendency on the part of Russia and other countries facing the challenge of Islamic extremism to consider any aid to Muslim populations and institutions as potentially abetting the extremists. Nevertheless, it is clear that areas with substantial Muslim populations in both the former Soviet space and the Balkans have developed networks of relations with external Arab and Muslim countries and groups, some of which have been linked to extremist movements. The growth of these networks was prompted by the fragmentation of the Soviet Union and Yugoslavia, which led to a crisis of identity and state and resulted in armed conflicts in Chechnya and in Bosnia and Kosovo. In these conflicts, the Islamic factor played and continues to play a role by intensifying a separate sense of identity and by serving as an instrument for achieving independence.

In Russia's relations with the Arab world, the Islamic factor has played an important role largely though the involvement of certain Arab states and their nongovernmental organizations in the Chechen War and the civil war in Afghanistan. By contrast, the conflict in Bosnia, although it was an irritant for Russia, did not significantly affect Russia's relations with the Arab world. In determining Russia's approach to the Bosnian crisis, the Islamic factor also had a secondary role, although later in the conflict Russia did become worried about the potential impact of its support for the Serbian side on its own Muslim populations and regions. However, the Islamic factor played an important role in Russia's approach to the conflict in Kosovo, partly because Russia's Muslim population became more involved with the issue and partly because of the linkages that Russia perceived between the Chechen conflict and the events in Kosovo.

Post-Soviet Russia and the Arab World

Even prior to the breakup of the Soviet Union, Russian policy toward the Arab world had undergone considerable change. During the Soviet era, Russia had established the closest relations with the anti-Western Arab states, such as Iraq, Syria, Libya, and Egypt under Gamal Abdul Nasser. These countries were attracted to the Soviet Union because it acted as a counterweight to the United States, particularly in the context of the Arab-Israeli conflict. The Soviet Union supported the Arab position and severed diplomatic relations with Israel after the 1967 Arab-Israeli War. Under the influence of Gorbachev's "New Thinking," the Soviet attitude in this regard changed fundamentally because the underlying principle of New Thinking demanded that the USSR unburden itself of "useless" Third World allies "whose interests were purely mercenary."[1] In 1987, Gorbachev told Syrian president Hafiz al-Assad that the lack of diplomatic relations between Tel Aviv and Moscow was "not normal." In 1988, he told Yasser Arafat that Israel, too, had legitimate security concerns.[2] In short, the Soviet Union was no longer willing to lend unconditional support to the Arab cause, and certainly not to the maximalist position of radical states.

Gorbachev, meanwhile, improved relations with the pro-Western and traditionally anti-Soviet states, such as Saudi Arabia.[3] The Soviet Union's withdrawal from Afghanistan and support for U.S.-led military operations against Iraq in 1991 opened new possibilities for its diplomacy. Despite these efforts, the Soviet Union not only failed to replace the United States as the moderate Arabs' principal security ally and economic partner, but by downgrading relations with its traditional allies, it undermined its overall presence in the Arab world.

The Soviet Union's policy change was also prompted by its economic difficulties. The USSR could no longer afford to provide military and economic assistance to countries such as Syria and Iraq, which by the late 1980s had accumulated large debts owed to the Soviet Union.[4] Hence the desire arose to expand ties with those Arab states, such as Saudi Arabia, that could be viable economic and trading partners.

This posture initially paid off. After the Soviet Union supported military action against Iraq, Saudi Arabia and the USSR resumed diplomatic relations on 17 September 1990, and the Saudis offered the Soviet Union $1.5 billion in aid.[5] After the USSR's demise, Russia continued this approach until 1994, despite policy differences regarding Bosnia and Chechnya. Both Andrei Kozyrev and Viktor Chernomyrdin visited Saudi Arabia in 1992 and 1994 as part of a larger tour of the Gulf Cooperation Council (GCC) states.[6] Russia hoped to gain a share of the arms market in the Gulf, as illustrated by Kozyrev's statement:

> Our visit is part of a drive for markets, including arms markets. . . . In the past
> our country relied on just a handful of states in the region—Iran, Iraq, Libya,
> etc. But that was an extremely unfortunate choice. Now we prefer to deal with
> stable, moderate regimes, and these are the ones with which we are trying to
> develop military cooperation.[7]

However, the close association with and dependence on the United States for their
security limited the ability of Saudi Arabia, the Gulf states, and other moderate
Middle East countries to expand ties with Russia. The United States made it clear
that it was determined that neither Russia nor any other country would be allowed
to reduce its influence in the Gulf.[8]

The U.S. factor influenced Russia's relations with the Arab world in another
way: namely, the state of Russian-American relations affected the willingness of
moderate Arabs to cooperate with Moscow. Therefore, good relations between the
United States and Russia until 1994 had a positive effect on Russia's relations with
pro-Western Arab countries. By contrast, when Russian-American relations deteriorated in 1995–2001, Russia's relations with pro-Western Arab states also suffered, leading Russia to refocus on its old allies, such as Iraq and Syria. At the
same time, regional developments—especially the rise of the Taliban, who enjoyed
the support of Saudi Arabia and the United Arab Emirates, combined with their
connections to extremist movements in the Caucasus—not only made early expectations for economic and political gains unrealistic, they also caused a serious
deterioration of Russia's relations with the key Arab states, notably Saudi Arabia.

The Chechen Conflict: A Source of Tension in
Russian-Arab Relations

A number of regional conflicts involving Muslim populations adversely affected
Russia's relations with several important Arab states. One such conflict was the
war between the Serbs and Bosnian Muslims, during which Russia supported the
Serbs. But the conflict that has had the most adverse and long-lasting impact on
Russian-Arab relations has been the Chechen conflict. For several reasons, the most
damaging impact of the Chechen conflict has been on Russia's relations with Saudi
Arabia. First, Saudi Arabia has been the most vocal among Muslim states in con-
demning Russia's actions in Chechnya. Notwithstanding King Fahd's comment to
Kozyrev in 1992 about safeguarding Russia's territorial integrity, Saudi Arabia
showed concern about the fate of Chechen Muslims even before the start of the
Chechen-Russian military confrontation. As military hostilities began in December
1994, Saudi Arabia took the lead in bringing the Chechens' plight to the attention
of the Muslim world. In January 1995, the Saudi government appealed to the United
Nations Security Council, urging it to halt the wars in Bosnia and Chechnya.[9] Saudi
Arabia was even more vocal about the Chechen problem within the OIC. Given
Saudi Arabia's influence within the organization, its attitude largely determined the
OIC's approach toward the Russian-Chechen conflict. During an OIC meeting on
27–30 June 2000 in Kuala Lumpur, Malaysia, the Saudi representative called Rus-

sia's military operations "an inhumane act against the Muslim people of Chechnya," and referred to terms such as the "right of self-determination," which could be interpreted as support for Chechen independence.[10]

Second, Saudi Arabia, while giving verbal support for Russia's territorial integrity, provided a great deal of material and moral assistance to the Chechens. In 1997, Aslan Maskhadov visited Saudi Arabia and met with Saudi and other Muslim leaders. Appearing on television in Chechnya, he called his visit successful.[11] Relations between Maskhadov and Riyadh, however, were not always smooth, especially when extremist Muslim groups began to undermine the Chechen government. For example, Apte Batalov, an aide to the Chechen leader, accused Saudi Arabia of financing the spread of Wahhabism in Chechnya, including its "military ingredient."[12] However, despite these differences, Saudi Arabia continued its support for proindependence forces, including Maskhadov. In March 2001, when Chechen militants hijacked a Russian plane and forced it to land in Saudi Arabia, Saudi interior minister Prince Nayef bin Abdul Aziz condemned terrorism, stating, "The Saudi Kingdom rejects terrorism in all its forms, particularly the hijacking of airplanes . . . in virtue of Islamic law which forbids such practices and forbids the killing of innocents." He added, however, that "we are with the Chechens in all domains, and, personally, I chair a committee that assists Chechens."[13]

Third, the flow of private financial assistance from Saudi Arabia to Chechnya caused discord in Russian-Saudi relations. It is difficult to assess the magnitude of Saudi assistance to the Chechens, especially since most of the information on this subject is based on Russian sources, which tend to exaggerate the extent of Saudi help to the Chechens. Nevertheless, assistance from official and private Saudi sources has clearly been channeled to the Chechens. Some of this assistance can legitimately be characterized as humanitarian aid, and the official part has mostly been channeled through the federal government in Moscow, but it is quite likely that some of the private assistance has been diverted to other operations. The most widely noted Saudi organizations providing assistance to the Chechens are Al-Haramein al-Sharifein and Al-Iqra'a. According to Russian sources, Al-Haramein was set up during the 1980s to support the Afghan mujahedin and later extended its support to Chechen rebels and extremist groups in Dagestan.[14] Al-Iqra'a has reportedly been very active in Dagestan.[15] Other private charitable organizations listed are the International Islamic Organization of Survival (Al-Igasa) and Al-Khairiya (Benevolence International Foundation.) The World League of Islamic Youth is also active in Russia, especially in the North Caucasus, and is allegedly devoted to the recruitment of youth and their military training.[16] Similarly, the Ibragim Bin Ibragim foundation is suspected of spreading extremist ideas by organizing "summer camps of Islamic youth" in various parts of Russia, even though it is officially registered with the Russian Ministry of Justice.[17]

Fourth, certain personalities with alleged links to Saudi Arabia have been involved in conflicts in Chechnya and Dagestan. The most prominent of these personalities are the notorious Khattab and Osama bin Laden, although the Saudi origins of Khattab have not been reliably established and Saudi relations with bin Laden have been strained since the end of the Soviet-Afghan War. The Russian linking of Saudi Arabia with bin Laden, therefore, derives from the connection between him and the Taliban regime and the latter's support for the Chechen rebels.[18] These Russian tendencies to see Saudi Arabia as the cause of "all their problems within or near their borders" has been frustrating to the Saudis.[19] By the same token, Saudi Arabia's insistence that Russia provide proof that Saudi money has gone to the Chechen rebels and/or militant Islamic groups has irritated Russia. The Russians claim, "The money is provided to these groups in such a way that there is no proof where it came from. . . . Merely because Moscow cannot provide proof that Riyadh is providing money to Chechen and other Muslim opposition movements does not mean that this is not occurring."[20]

Other Sources of Saudi-Russian Tensions

In addition to the Chechen conflict, with its Islamic dimensions, and other sources of Saudi-Russian discord that have an Islamic component, a number of economic and political issues have tended to strain Russia's relations with Saudi Arabia, notably (1) oil and energy competition; (2) diverging perceptions of regional players; and (3) closer Russian-Israeli relations. Concerning oil and energy resources, Saudi Arabia and Russia are the two largest oil producers in the world, with differing demographic and economic profiles and financial needs. Saudi Arabia has the ability to drastically increase or lower the level of its production and thus remains the only "swing" producer in the world. Russia lacks such flexibility, but it is capable of disrupting the oil markets and undermining OPEC's influence in setting oil prices.[21] Russian-OPEC relations have become even more complex in the aftermath of 11 September 2001 because many analysts and policy makers have increasingly talked of using Russian energy, which could reduce Saudi and OPEC influence, as an instrument of forging a Russian-Western strategic partnership.[22] However, the United States control of Iraqi oil following Iraq's occupation by American and British troops, which potentially would give the United States tremendous influence over both OPEC's future and that of world oil markets, inevitably undermines Russia's position unless Iraq's stabilization and the revitalization of its oil industry takes longer than anticipated. At the end of 2003, it appeared that the revitalization of Iraq's oil industry would be a lengthy and expensive process.

Regarding differing perceptions of regional players, since 1994, the patterns of Russian and Saudi alliances have diverged both in the Middle East and South Asia. Russia has had good relations with Iran and Iraq, while Saudi Arabia mistrusts them.[23] In Afghanistan, Saudi Arabia supported the Taliban, while Russia helped Tajik commander Ahmad Shah Masoud and the Northern Alliance. Since the restoration of Soviet-Israeli diplomatic relations in October 1991, there has been a drastic improvement in Russian-Israeli relations, thus causing a major shift in Russia's position on the Arab-Israeli conflict. The Chechen War has helped cement these relations by creating a mutually held sentiment of victimization at the hands of Muslim extremists.[24] The Chechen rebels were also accused of helping the Palestinians.[25] Thus parallels were drawn between Russia's fight against terrorism in Chechnya and Israel's fight in Palestine.

International and regional changes after 11 September 2001 have helped improve Saudi-Russian relations by eliminating some areas of dispute, such as Saudi support for the Taliban. The winding down of hostilities in Chechnya has reduced the impact of the Chechen factor. Meanwhile, tense Saudi-American relations have prompted the Saudis to seek better ties with Russia.[26] The exacerbation of the Arab-Israeli conflict and Saudi efforts to revitalize a moribund peace process, combined with Russia's desire to become engaged in the Arab-Israeli peace negotiations as a way of enhancing its international role, have contributed to this improvement. This was illustrated by the visit of Saudi foreign minister Prince Saud bin Faisal bin Abdul Aziz to Moscow in April 2002 and his meeting with President Vladimir Putin.[27] Russia has also supported the Saudi peace plan, which was endorsed by the Arab League in March 2002.

Nevertheless, as of early 2003, the specter of Chechnya continued to cast a shadow over Saudi-Russian relations.[28] Tensions became evident on 31 July 2002, when the Saudi Shari'a court gave what the Russians considered mild sentences to two Chechen militants who had hijacked a Russian airliner and forced it to land in Saudi Arabia. Expressing Russian displeasure, the Russian general prosecutor's office affirmed, "We consider this verdict too soft. It does not reflect the seriousness of the crime."[29] Russian officials added that Russia was considering a formal request that Saudi Arabia extradite the hijackers. Alexei Volin, deputy head of the government administration, went so far as to state, "This ruling might represent Saudi Arabia as a breeding ground for potential terrorists."[30] The October 2002 hostage-taking operation in Moscow rekindled Russian resentment of Saudi Arabia. This led President Putin in his meeting with U.S. president George W. Bush, in an allusion to Saudi Arabia, to assert, "We [the United States, Russia, and the international community] should not forget those who finance terrorism." He also drew attention to the fact that fifteen of the terrorists who carried out the attacks on the World Trade Center and the Pentagon were Saudi citizens.[31] Yet by early 2003, Saudi-Russian tensions seemed to have subsided, and there were reports that Saudi crown prince Abdullah would visit Moscow in April 2003.[32] On 8 May 2003, Prince Saud Ibn Faisal, Saudi Arabia's foreign minister, visited Moscow and met with Foreign Minister Igor Ivanov. Prince Saud and Igor Ivanov discussed the arrangements for Prince Abdullah's visit at a date to be agreed upon later.[33] During the meeting with Ivanov, Prince Saud said that Russia had an important role to play in solving various problems in the Middle East, notably the Arab-Israeli conflict.[34] Crown Prince Abdullah's visit finally took place in September 2003 and was viewed as an important watershed in Russia's relations with the Arab and Islamic worlds. Principal issues discussed were Chechnya, energy, and the expansion of Russian-Saudi economic relations—especially in the energy field.

The Gulf and Other Arab States

The Islamic factor as played out in Chechnya also adversely affected Russia's relations with the Gulf Arab states and Jordan. Among the Gulf States, relations with the United Arab Emirates (UAE) suffered most because of UAE-based financial institutions' support and official sympathy for the Chechen cause. After a meeting with the leaders of the UAE in June 1995, Russian deputy foreign minister Viktor Pasuvalyuk noted that the UAE had a "somewhat different understanding" of the conflict.[35] Reports regarding anti-Russian propaganda by Chechen elements based in the UAE and other Gulf states appeared in the Russian media.[36] It is difficult to ascertain the veracity of such reports. What is known, however, is that both Movladi Udogov and Zelimkhan Yanderbiev visited the UAE in January 2000.[37] The UAE's close connection with the Taliban and the latter's links with the Chechen rebels also contributed to strained Russian-UAE relations.[38]

Chechnya has also been a source of tension in Russia's relations with Qatar. Following his trip to Pakistan, Zelimkhan Yanderbiev met with the emir of Qatar and was given refuge there, despite Russian efforts to extradite him, until his assassination in Doha in February 2004. This prompted Alexander Yakovenko, a representative of the Foreign Ministry, to say that "the reception of the Chechen terrorists' envoy on such a high level is an unfriendly act and can negatively influence bilateral ties."[39] Russian newspapers had charged that "Qatar supports Islamic extremists throughout the world. . . . Financial aid for the Wahhabites is not a private initiative but part of the policy of the State of Qatar."[40] These accusations were rebutted by the Qatari paper *Al Watan*.[41]

There were no official visits by Chechen leaders to Kuwait, but Kuwaiti citizens fought in the Chechen War, and Kuwaiti Islamists supported the Chechen cause. Thus when a Kuwaiti volunteer, Salem al-Ajmi, was killed in Chechnya, an Islamist member of the Kuwaiti parliament called him "a hero who sacrificed his life on the fields of jihad."[42] Nevertheless, Russia maintained diplomatic ties with the UAE and other Gulf states, notably Kuwait, which had been the only Gulf state with ties to the Soviet Union.

Because of the existence of a large Chechen and other Caucasian diaspora in Jordan, there have been strong pro-Chechen and anti-Russian feelings in the country.[43] Some of Jordan's Chechens hold high positions in the army and at court.[44] Khalid Fakhrid-Din Dagestani, head of the Chechen-Ingush Friendship Society of Jordan, which was created in 1989, appealed to the king of Jordan, the United Nations, and the OIC to denounce the war in Chechnya. He also called on the International Monetary Fund (IMF) to "stop providing Russia with funds, which are used for waging war."[45] A number of wounded Chechens were treated in Jordanian hospitals, but according to Dagestani, "These patients are not militants, but peaceful citizens who came here independently, and then the Chechen diaspora and the government of Jordan assisted them."[46] The Jordanian diaspora's financial assistance to Chechnya has been mainly directed through relatives or family connections. During the first Chechen campaign, the society tried to deliver medical aid through the Red Cross, but most of the supplies were taken by Russian officials.[47]

Officially, Jordan has avoided confrontation with Russia over Chechnya by characterizing Chechen events as Russia's internal affair and upholding Russia's territorial integrity.[48] The two countries also maintained official contacts. In June 1995, King Hussein received a Russian presidential envoy to discuss developments in the Arab-Israeli conflict and bilateral relations.[49] In June 1996, Jordanian crown prince

Hassan Bin Talal met visiting Russian deputy foreign minister Viktor Pasuvalyuk.[50] In 1996, Jordan imposed a ban on pro-Dudaev propaganda and refused to accept a group of wounded Chechen rebels into the country.[51] For the rest of the 1990s, Russian-Jordanian relations remained stable. In August 2001, relations significantly improved with new Jordanian king Abdullah's visit to Moscow.[52] The issue of Jordan's purchase of Russian weapons was raised at the time.

The Chechen conflict has hardly impacted Russia's friendly relations with Egypt because President Hosni Mubarak opposes Egypt's own Islamists. According to Alexander Shumilin, "Egypt never officially denounced Moscow's policies because it did not want to be seen as giving support to those who want an Islamic Republic in Egypt itself."[53]

Because the Islamic factor is not an important determinant of Egypt's overall foreign policy, the fate of Chechnya had little impact on Egypt's approach toward Russia. Instead, Russia's potential role in resolving the Arab-Israeli conflict has been more important. Thus only four months after the start of the first Chechen War, Russian foreign minister Kozyrev visited Egypt.[54] In 1996, President Yeltsin participated in the antiterrorism summit held in Sharm-ul-Shaikh, hoping to justify the Chechen War as part of the struggle against terrorism.[55] Egyptian foreign minister Amr Musa's high-level visit in July 1996 was the first from a major Muslim country to Russia after the beginning of the Chechen War. Amr Musa expressed Egypt's belief that the Chechen problem should be resolved by peaceful means and noted that any peace settlement should safeguard Russia's territorial integrity.[56] President Mubarak visited Russia twice, in 1997 and in 2001.[57] Additionally, there were other visits by high-level Russian and Egyptian officials to Cairo and Moscow.

On the other hand, Egypt's general population, especially Islamic groups, has been very critical of Russian policies in Chechnya. The Muslim Brotherhood called Russian operations in Chechnya "deviant savagery." Mufti Sheikh Wassel appealed to Islamic countries to boycott Russia "politically and economically."[58] Individual Egyptians fought on the side of the Chechens.[59]

Meanwhile, Iraq remained Russia's staunch ally and did not allow the Chechen issue to interfere in its relations with Moscow. Moscow reciprocated by criticizing sanctions or any military attack on Iraq. Irina Zviagelskaya noted that Iraq remained "an acceptable partner for Russia, despite the ambiguous character of Saddam Hussein."[60] After the Gulf War, Baghdad remained generally loyal to Russia. It was the only Islamic country that showed indifference toward the conflict in Chechnya, with the Iraqi media covering it "in a neutral, or even pro-Russian way."[61]

Post–11 September Developments

Developments in the Middle East, notably the continuation of the Arab-Israeli conflict and the growing possibility of a U.S.-led military operation against Iraq due to Iraqi leader Saddam Hussein's refusal to fully cooperate with United Nations weapons inspectors, presented opportunities for Russia to reassert its presence in the region.[62] A number of key Arab states, including Saudi Arabia, the GCC members, Egypt, and Jordan, sought Russia's assistance to restart the Arab-Israeli peace process and to find a nonmilitary solution to the Iraq crisis. Thus beginning in late 2001, Moscow witnessed the arrival of a steady stream of high-ranking Arab officials and even heads of state. In November 2001, Jordan's King Abdullah visited Moscow to discuss the Arab-Israeli conflict and Russia's role "in putting an end to the cycle of violence between Palestinians and Israelis."[63] They also discussed military and economic cooperation. During a visit by the king in July 2002, he and President Putin encouraged their private sectors to increase investment and trade.[64] King Abdullah again visited Moscow in November 2002. Meanwhile, Jordan's Chechen community indicated that it was distancing itself from the conflict in Chechnya.[65]

Other high-level visitors from the Middle East included Moroccan king Muhammad VI, Yemeni president Ali Abdullah Saleh, and secretary general of the Arab League Amr Musa.[66] During the Yemeni president's visit to Moscow in December 2002, a Russian-Yemeni declaration on friendly relations and cooperation was signed. President Putin emphasized Yemen's strategic position and said that "Russia views Yemen as a reliable partner with which it has much in common."[67] Contacts at the level of foreign minister were even more frequent.[68] There was more talk of Russian-Arab economic cooperation. Nearly all Arab states applauded Russia's positive role in seeking a settlement to the Arab-Israeli conflict and in averting a war with Iraq.[69]

However, despite its continued support for nonmilitary solutions, Russia's attitude toward Iraq grew more ambiguous. In January 2003, Russian authorities announced that they still believed that a military strike against Iraq was not the best way to deal with Saddam Hussein. During a press conference with the German and Russian mass media, President Putin stated that there was no evidence linking Iraq to Al-Qaeda or weapons of mass destruction (WMD). He added:

> Our common task is to convince Iraq to return international observers back into the country. There are many means that will allow us to reach that goal. They are not all finished yet. And it seems to me that it is politically incorrect to talk about the use of force while not all means have been used fully.[70]

Nevertheless, some American observers expressed the opinion that if the United States satisfied Russia's economic interests in Iraq and reached an understanding on Iraq's post-Saddam political structure, Russia might not actively oppose U.S. military intervention in Iraq. Ariel Cohen believed that the United States could even make Russia a full partner in the anti-Saddam coalition if it offered to (1) support the repayment of Iraq's Soviet-era debt by a future pro-Western government or alternatively broker a deal in which the $100 billion Soviet-era debt to the Paris Club would be reduced by the amount of Iraq's debt to Russia; (2) support Russian companies' contractual rights to Iraqi oil fields; (3) begin an exchange of data on black-market oil sales and arms and military technology transfers from Russia, including WMD procurements; and (4) appoint a senior official to negotiate a U.S.-Russian understanding on a post-Saddam Iraq. President Putin should appoint an equally high-ranking and qualified official to conduct these talks.[71]

These measures were deemed necessary to overcome "the lingering pro-Iraqi sentiment in the Foreign Ministry, military-industrial complex, and oil lobby"[72] and to demonstrate that "Russia's cooperation in the coalition would benefit Russia."[73] The Russian strategy, however, until the last few weeks before the start of the war was one of balancing its interest in consolidating its partnership with the United States and revitalizing its ties with the Arab and Islamic world. Consequently, Russia pursued a more nuanced diplomacy in regard to the Iraq issue than that just suggested. Rather, it tried to keep its options open so as to be able to adjust its policy to evolving conditions. In January 2003, President Putin and other Russian officials indicated that if there were evidence of Iraq's connection with international terrorism, and especially with Chechen rebels, Russia would support military action against Iraq.[74] By mid-February, however, Russia had reverted to a less cooperative posture on the use of force and was advocating the resolution of the crisis through political means. On 17 February 2003, ITAR-TASS reported that Igor Ivanov had stated, "There is a political way to the settlement of the situation in Iraq and it is necessary to stick to it."[75] President Putin went even further and, during an interview on French television, indicated that Russia might use its veto power to block United Nations approval for military intervention in Iraq.[76] Ultimately, however, Russia decided to join France and Germany and the majority of the UN members in opposing United States and British military action against Iraq. However, since no new Security Council resolution on this issue was put forward, Russia did not have to face the dilemma of whether to exercise its veto power. As of the winter of 2003, Russia's position on the handling of post-war Iraq remained at odds with those of the U.S.; Russia favored a greater role for the United Nations and a more swift transfer of power to the Iraqis.

Reconciliation with the OIC

Improved Arab-Russian relations also led to efforts to establish better ties with the OIC. A watershed event in this process was the visit of OIC secretary general Abdelouahed Belkeziz to Moscow in January 2003.[77] The tone of this visit was different from those of other OIC secretaries general in 1994 and 1997. The former visits had been prompted by the Chechen crisis and had taken place at a time when Russia's relations with key Arab and Muslim countries were strained. Moreover, in those times, because of its strained relations with the West, notably the United States, Russia had been in a weaker and more defensive position vis-à-vis the OIC and its members. By contrast, in the post–11 September international environment, especially in light of closer U.S.-Russian ties, the OIC became eager to mend fences with Russia. This was evidenced by the statement of the OIC secretary general that the organization considered the Chechen problem "exclusively an internal matter of the Russian Federation."[78] The OIC secretary general further promised that "the

OIC will do everything possible to curb aid to the Chechen rebels." However, he added that he had "no information confirming Arab financial aid to the Chechen rebels" and indicated that the OIC "could help rehabilitate Chechnya after the conflict is settled."[79] Other issues discussed during this visit included conditions of Russian Muslims, the Arab-Israeli conflict, and the Iraq crisis.

Russian foreign minister Igor Ivanov stated that the Russian leadership "attaches great importance to the strengthening of ties with the Islamic world and with such a representative and authoritative international organization as the OIC."[80] Ivanov also announced that the Ministry of Foreign Affairs had created a "position of ambassador at large, who will especially deal with all issues concerned with Islam."[81] On 20 February 2003, Veniamin Popov, former Soviet ambassador to the United Arab Emirates, was named to fill this post.[82] In addition to gaining the support and collaboration of the OIC for its policy in Chechnya, according to Foreign Ministry spokesman Alexander Yakovenko, Russia's desire to have better ties with the OIC derived from the fact that its "Islamic population exceeds 20 million."[83] In advancing this goal, the Kremlin, following a long tradition of Soviet/Russian diplomacy, used its Muslim citizens and leadership. Thus the OIC secretary general met Mufti Talgat Tadzhuddin and members of the Russian Council of Muftis under the leadership of Sheikh Ravil Gainutdin.[84] He also visited Kazan, where he was reportedly impressed by the large number of mosques.[85] The improving Russian-OIC relation culminated in President Vladimir Putin's statement that Russia wanted to join the OIC, although at first as an observer. He made this statement at a meeting with Malaysian prime minister Mahathir Muhammad during a visit to Malaysia in August 2003. Should this happen, Russia's relation with the Muslim world would acquire a whole new character.

Russia and the Balkans

Historically, Russia's relations with the Balkans region, especially its Orthodox Christian population, have always had a religious dimension. A large part of the Balkans had come under Ottoman/Muslim rule by the sixteenth century, and Russia often cloaked its imperial policies toward the region in religious garb, justifying them in terms of liberating enslaved Christians. Yet in reality, the interests of the Balkan Slavs were subordinated to other Russian national interests.[86]

The first of the Balkan wars began in 1991 as a result of the breakup of the Socialist Federal Republic of Yugoslavia and the determination of several constituent parts of the Yugoslav federation to obtain independence. When the Bosnian Muslims attempted to form an independent state, the religious dimension was inevitably introduced as an important variable in the conflict. This factor significantly influenced the approach of different actors toward the conflict. In the Muslim world, the plight of Bosnian Muslims galvanized widespread sympathy for their cause and led many Muslim governments—most notably Turkey, the Western ally and NATO member with the closest historic links to Bosnia—to speak on behalf of the Bosnian Muslims and push for Western military intervention to protect them.[87] The OIC, at a June 1993 meeting of its members, including Bosnia, offered to send 7,600 troops and affirmed its willingness to send more if requested by the United Nations in order to help protect six designated "safe areas" of Bosnia inhabited primarily by Muslims.[88]

It is difficult to assess the extent to which lobbying by Muslim states contributed to the West's decision to intervene militarily (through NATO) in the conflict and to broker a peace accord at Dayton in 1995. Clearly, the fear that Western inaction could ignite Muslim anger had some influence on Western policies;[89] but other strategic factors played more important roles. In particular, the West feared the expansion of the conflict to other parts of southeastern Europe, potentially resulting in a large influx of Bosnian refugees to Western Europe. Another major concern was the future viability of NATO and the European Union.[90]

The Evolution of Russia's Balkan Policy and Its Main Determinants

Russia's policy toward the conflicts that broke out in Yugoslavia underwent several phases reflecting Russia's domestic developments and the evolution of its foreign policy doctrine. In the case of Kosovo, the cool state of Russian-Western relations influenced its approach toward the conflict. In the case of the Bosnian conflict, an important determinant of policy was Russia's perceptions of the West and its assessment of the impact of its Bosnian policy on its broader relations with the West. Andrei Edemskii identifies four phases in Russia's policy toward the Yugoslav conflicts, notably in Bosnia, between 1991 and 1994.[91] A fifth phase must be added to update Edemskii's analysis: the four-year period from the start of NATO operations in Bosnia in August 1995, when Russia was no longer in a position to prevent NATO intervention, until the end of the Kosovo crisis in the summer of 1999.

First Phase: Last Days of the Soviet Union

Because the Yugoslav conflicts erupted in 1991, the first phase of Russian policy should be characterized as that of the Soviet Union. During the summer and autumn of 1991, when Mikhail Gorbachev was still endeavoring to prevent the unraveling of the Soviet Union, Russia tried hard to preserve Yugoslavia's unity. In this endeavor, Moscow had the backing of Washington, which shared Moscow's fear about "the precedent that the breakup of Yugoslavia might set for the Soviet Union, the preservation of which was central not only to Gorbachev's policies but to those of the Bush [I] Administration."[92]

The attitude of Boris Yeltsin and his supporters was different because "they drew parallels between Moscow's keeping the Baltic republic in the USSR and Belgrade's attitude to the secession of Slovenia and Croatia."[93] They interpreted Belgrade's silence during the failed August 1991 coup as "anti-Yeltsin." The Yeltsin camp also viewed the Belgrade leadership as antidemocratic or, in Kozyrev's words, "commun-nationalist."[94]

Second Phase: Russian-Western Honeymoon, 1992–1993

The second phase of the Bosnian crisis corresponds to a sensitive period in Russia's domestic politics when drastic economic reforms were initiated. In foreign policy, this was the height of the Russian-Western honeymoon. During this phase, two factors dominated Russia's policy: (1) domestic concerns about the effects of shock therapy on the population and (2) Russia's desire to become part of the West—this was still the period of Euro-Atlanticist ascendancy—while establishing Russia as a major international player and a presence throughout Yugoslavia. Thus Russia established full diplomatic relations with Slovenia and Croatia, although it called the necessity to do so "unfortunate."[95]

During the early phase of the Bosnian crisis, religious and ethnocultural factors, namely, Orthodox and Slavic solidarity, played relatively small roles in Moscow's official policy toward the conflict.[96] Paul Goble's observation that although the influence of historical and cultural factors "is the one mentioned most often, [it] is probably the most overrated and the least understood as a factor in Russian concerns and calculations," is correct.[97] Popular sentiments in Russia, however, were supportive of the Serbs, and there were Russian volunteers fighting on the Serbian side.[98]

This popular sympathy did have some impact on Russian policy. With growing domestic support for the Serbs and increasingly frequent accusations that Russia's foreign policy was too subservient to the West, Russia's policy toward Yugoslavia became a balancing act between safeguarding relations with the West and domestic pressures. These criticisms became more strident after Russia voted for United Nations Resolution 757 on 30 May 1992 to impose sanctions on all parties to the conflict.[99] Some commentators indicated that Russia at least could have abstained. Such an act, they explained, "would have weakened the message the resolution is intended to send to Belgrade and might have undermined the support of developing countries such as India for sanctions."[100]

Two reasons seem to have been behind this Russian decision: (1) the lack of response of the Yugoslav government to Russia's peacemaking efforts, which was highly embarrassing to the Russian leadership, and (2) Russia's domestic economic concerns and the need for Western, including IMF, assistance. Andrei Kozyrev expressed Russia's frustrations when he wrote:

> We saw with our own eyes, that, despite the large measure of responsibility for the conflict that is borne by various forces—Bosnian Serbs, Croats, and Moslems—Belgrade had the strongest economic, political and military levers for influencing the situation in Bosnia and Herzegovina. And when despite the advice, in the words of the Yugoslav press itself, of "friendly great Russia", the "Russian peace"—i.e., the plan we had coordinated—was wrecked by the vigorous actions of armed forces controlled by or dependent on Belgrade, the President of the Russian Federation decided to support the UN sanctions.[101]

Be that as it may, the Russian vote gave new ammunition to the opponents of Yeltsin's foreign policy, some of whom called for Kozyrev's resignation.[102]

Phase Three: Cracks in the Russian-Western Partnership

Phase three lasted throughout 1993. During this period, Russia still continued the strategy of partnership with the West. However, because of domestic opposition, plus disenchantment with the West and the gradual ascendancy of non-Atlanticist trends, Russia was moving toward a more assertive foreign policy, trying to show its independence from the West, which at times meant using some anti-American rhetoric.[103]

In terms of the Balkan policy, this meant greater Russian activism and reiteration of its basic interest in the region. In this period, Russia tried to prevent NATO from playing a decisive role in the conflict and promoted the role of the United Nations.[104] It also worked against lifting the embargo as a way of preventing the arming of the Bosnian Muslims because that would have both undercut Moscow's ties to Belgrade, including the religious subtext of those ties, and played into NATO's hands in what Moscow perceived was an effort to extend its influence toward areas that have historically been in at least the penumbra of the Russian/Soviet sphere of influence. Therefore, Russia intensified its diplomatic efforts and became an important player in efforts to solve the Yugoslav crisis.[105] However, it was not prepared to embrace Western positions.

Phase Four: Russia's Nostalgia for Great-Power Status

During phase four, which began in 1994, domestic developments forced Yeltsin to pursue a foreign policy more independent from the West and to reassert Russia's great-power status. Some analysts believed that the West's effort to involve Russia in a Western-engineered scheme for Yugoslavia was intended "to reach a subsequent surrender of Russia's political will and the destruction of its influence in the Balkans."[106] Yugoslavia became one of the areas to test Yeltsin's new approach. This was translated into stronger support for the Serbs and strenuous efforts to prevent any military action by NATO.

Phase Five: Harsh Rhetoric and Pragmatic Policy

Phase five began with the NATO air strikes on 30 August 1995 and, later, the signing of the Dayton Peace Accord on 21 November 1995. Russian policy in this period was characterized by rhetorical harshness and pragmatic behavior in order to secure for Russia a role in the management of post-Dayton Bosnia. Thus while President Yeltsin characterized the NATO bombing as "genocide," Russia agreed to assign 1,400 Russian troops to take part in the NATO-led Implementation Force (IFOR) and, later, the Stabilization Force (SFOR) in Bosnia.[107] It appears that this decision was taken by Pavel Grachev to show the Russian military that it had a useful role to play, and to deal Russia into key Western/NATO diplomacy.[108]

Assessing the Impact of Religious Factors on Russia's Bosnian Policy

For most of the Bosnian crisis, religious factors played a relatively small role in Russia's policy. However, these factors were influential in determining popular attitudes. The Russian Orthodox Church especially was willing to show its support for the Serbs. Thus during a visit to Serbia in May 1994 to attend the celebration of the 500th anniversary of the publication of the first Slav book, Russian Orthodox Patriarch Alexii II, "in an implicit plea on behalf of the Serbs," said, "It is necessary to lift all unilateral sanctions because, as experience has shown, they are not productive."[109]

The patriarch's entrance into the policy debate came as the religious factor began exerting more influence on Russian policy.[110] Russian diplomacy emphasized the Slavonic and Orthodox bonds of the Russian and Serb peoples, and Russia demanded that the West put more pressure on the Bosnian Muslims. During this period, however, the Islamic factor did not seem to play a significant role in shaping Russia's policies. Clearly Russia did not want to see a truly viable Muslim state emerge in the heart of the Balkans, but neither did the West. Nor was Russia overly preoccupied with the impact of the Bosnian War and its position toward the war on its own Muslim population. This was partly because Russia's Muslim citizens were relatively passive during the Bosnian War. Even Russia's Muslim religious establishment was quiescent in this regard. Whatever activities they conducted were in the context of efforts for interfaith understanding. For example, Mufti Ravil Gainutdin participated in a conference in Istanbul in February 1994 organized by the Turkish government titled "The World and Religious Tolerance." The main focus of the conference was to be the problems faced by the Muslim communities of Albania and Bosnia-Herzegovina.[111]

However, Moscow was not totally unaware of the impact of Serbia's actions against the Bosnian Muslims, especially later in the conflict when large-scale massacres of Bosnian Muslims took place, and its own pro-Serb attitude both on its Muslim populations and on its relations with the Muslim world. This concern prompted Russian deputy foreign minister Sergei Shakhrai, who earlier had been in charge of Russia's policies toward its national minorities, to accuse parts of the Russian media of depicting Russia "as an anti-Muslim country due to its tilt towards the Bosnian Serbs who share a common Orthodox faith," and of "deliberately overlooking the fact that there are nearly [15] million Russian Muslims."[112]

The Party of Russian Unity and Accord (PRES), to which Shakhrai belonged, in a press statement added, "There is an impression that somebody wants to transform the local Bosnian conflict into a global confrontation between the Muslim and Orthodox civilizations."[113] The statement criticized the "anti-Muslim mood" being spread in the country and added, "They [the sections of the media] want us to clash with the Muslim states of the Commonwealth of Independent States [and] with our traditional partners in the Arab world."[114]

These considerations, plus the worsening of the Chechen crisis and the outbreak of the first Chechen War in December 1994, led Russia to attempt to appear less one sided in the Yugoslav conflict. Thus when Bosnian prime minister Haris Silajdzic visited Moscow in February 1995, he noted that a large number of Muslims lived in Russia. He added, "In the light of the Bosnian experience we [the Bosnians] are very sensitive to civilian victims in Chechnya. . . . The way in which certain problems, such as Chechnya, are being resolved—and this is Russia's internal matter—could channel in Moscow's direction the dissatisfaction of Muslims throughout the world."[115]

Church leaders also made some positive gestures toward the Bosnian Muslims. During his visit to Serbia in May 1995, Patriarch Alexii II met with Bosnian Muslim leader Mustafa Ceric when visiting Sarajevo. Cardinal Franjo Kuharic of Croatia and Serb Patriarch Pavel were also present.[116] According to Metropolitan Kirill, this was to show that the Yugoslav conflict was not "fueled by religious passions."[117]

Notwithstanding these developments, the Islamic factor had little impact on Russia's foreign policy toward the Bosnian conflict. The situation proved to be different in the case of Kosovo.

Influence of Islam on Russian Policy during the Kosovo Crisis

Compared to the earlier Yugoslav events, Russia reacted far more strongly and rapidly to the crisis in Kosovo and, in particular, to the NATO bombing of Serbia, including Belgrade, in March 1999.[118] Its engagement in the Kosovo crisis combined competing themes, as it had during the earlier Yugoslav conflicts. Russia did not want to be isolated from key diplomacy in a consequential period for determining the future shape of Europe, and thus it joined the renewed Contact Group for Kosovo diplomacy.[119] Thus Russian policy was partly propelled by its concern that the West would go to war with Serbia over Kosovo. Coming at almost the same time that three Central European countries were admitted to the alliance, such an event would have signaled a further NATO advance and symbolized Russia's diplomatic defeat. By joining the Contact Group, Russia wanted to exert some influence over Western actions. The cool state of U.S.-Russian relations was another reason for Russia's swift response. More important, Russia was concerned that Kosovo would set a bad precedent for Chechnya, namely, secession of a rebellious Muslim province from a multiethnic state. An added concern was that the potential separation of Kosovo could lead to the creation of a greater Albania. Moscow saw this prospect as disquieting because such an entity would change the Slav/non-Slav equation in the Balkans and could join other Muslim states in a larger alliance. Furthermore, close Turkish-Albanian ties would contribute to the emergence of the kind of Islamic belt that Russia fears.[120]

In the case of Kosovo, unlike Bosnia, the Islamic factor played a more significant role in determining Russia's approach. Russian Muslims also became far more active during the Kosovo conflict. For example, in the Republic of Tatarstan, a small number of young men volunteered to fight in Kosovo.[121] However, the government of Tatarstan and the official Muslim establishment did not sanction such acts, although they sympathized with Kosovo Muslims, especially as a Muslim minority in a largely Christian country. The deputy head of the Muslim Religious Board of Tatarstan said, "As we are Muslims from an autonomous region in Russia, it would be the same tragedy for us if someone began to persecute us."[122] President Shaimiev spoke against any volunteers—Muslim or Christian—becoming involved in the Yugoslav quagmire:

> In this half Christian, half Muslim region volunteers could go to join both the Serbian and Kosovo Albanian sides in the conflict. . . . Just imagine people going to Yugoslavia from a land of peace and ethnic harmony and starting to shoot each other, then coffins start arriving from both sides. Where do you think this may lead? I am not talking only about Tatarstan but about the whole of Russia, where Christians and Moslems live together.[123]

However, there were reports that the Tatar nationalists were recruiting volunteers to fight in Kosovo. The All-Tatar Public Center (ATPC) was considered the main organization engaged in this activity. The ATPC reportedly also supported NATO actions "to rein in [Slobodan] Milosevic's bloody regime, efforts that are aimed at protecting the rights of all ethnic minorities," and called on the Tatars to provide "to the best of their ability, moral and other support for the Kosovo Albanians' struggle for independence and a dignified existence."[124]

There were even claims that close links existed between the Kosovars and the Chechens. It was reported that official Chechen elements had been recruiting volunteers for the Kosovo Liberation Front (KLA) to fight against the Serbs in a "Muslim peoples" Holy War in Kosovo.[125] Later, Russian security officials claimed that Chechen fighters were hiding out in Kosovo. One media report quoted an FSB official as saying, "Chechen fighters have established contact with Albanian separatists, on the side of Kosovo, on which many mercenaries from Chechnya have fought."[126] However, there has been no firm evidence of Chechen participation in the Kosovo conflict, although the existence of some form of connection between the two is not beyond the realm of possibility. Later, Prime Minister and then President Putin would often refer to the arc of instability running from Kosovo to the Philippines and passing through the Caucasus and Afghanistan. Speculation about Yugoslavia joining the Russia-Belarus Union elicited a negative reaction on the part of the leaders of Russia's Muslim republics, as well as many ordinary people. Some reacted with counterproposals of creating a union of Turkic peoples. The Moscow-based daily *Nezavisimaya Gazeta* reported that the news of the union had generated fears among Russia's Muslims that the country "has embarked on the path of openly encouraging the ideology of Slav chauvinism."[127] In response, the nationalist All-Tatar Public Center called for the creation of a Union of Turkic Peoples and suggested that "the Assembly of Turkic peoples" could become the basis for this union. The ATPC also sent a statement to this effect to the United Nations secretary general, the NATO secretary general, and EU leaders.[128]

Referring to this issue, Mufti Ravil Gainutdin asked, "What steps will be taken next with regard to the non-Slav and non-Orthodox peoples?"[129] Murtaza Rakhi-mov, president of Bashkortostan, expressed his opposition to the idea of a three-nation union. Rakhimov believed that Milosevic was responsible for the tragedy in the Balkans and that the Kosovo problem could be solved only by giving the people there the right to self-determination, which he interpreted as meaning autonomy.[130] Meanwhile, Ruslan Aushev, the president of Ingushetia, suggested that should Yugoslavia join the union, Tatarstan and Ingushetia also should be made members of the Union rather than mere subjects of the Russian Federation.[131] These statements reportedly reflected the view of the president of Tatarstan, Mintimir Shaimiev, although he did not comment publicly on the subject.[132] However, it should be noted that concerns about the prerogatives of Russia's ethnic republics, rather than Muslim religious feelings, were principally behind these statements.

Meanwhile, differences of opinion within Russian policy-making circles made for contradictory policies. As a member of the Contact Group, Russia tried to prevent war. After receiving promises of substantial economic assistance at the June 1999 meeting of the Group of Eight in Cologne, Viktor Chernomyrdin, former Russian prime minister, paired with Finnish president Martti Ahtisaari to convince Serbian president Slobodan Milosevic to end the war, to the evident surprise of the West.[133] Yet almost simultaneously, Russian troops went into Pristina in June 1999, causing consternation among some NATO commanders.[134] However, it is not clear whether this action was taken merely on the initiative of the local commander of Russian forces in Bosnia, which were participants in the NATO-led peacekeeping mission, without the approval of President Yeltsin and the Russian defense and foreign ministries or with the approval of the Russian minister of defense but without the knowledge or approval of President Yeltsin. The statement by Russian foreign minister Igor Ivanov that "the movement of the troops into Kosovo was a colossal mistake" suggests that the move was made by the military.[135]

However, it should be remembered that this was a period of growing Russian fears about U.S. global hegemony and of Russia's efforts to create a multipolar world. For many Russians, NATO was increasingly seen as symbolizing a unipolar world.[136] Thus the Russian move may have been prompted to show that Russia was still a player in the Balkans.[137] Eventually, Russia joined the NATO-led Kosovo peacekeeping force (Kosovo Force, or KFOR), thus securing a place for itself in the region's future.

Conclusion

The Islamic factor has had a mixed impact on Russian-Arab relations, especially regarding the Chechen conflict. In some cases—Saudi Arabia and the UAE—it has had a strongly negative influence. In other cases—Egypt and Jordan—it has been of marginal importance. Even in Saudi Arabia's case, other issues such as differences over Afghanistan and competition in the energy sector have played important roles. By the beginning of 2003, with Afghanistan out of the picture as a source of conflict, diminished Arab assistance to the Chechens, and increased tensions in

U.S.-Arab relations, Russia had found new opportunities in the Arab world. In the case of the Iraq War, the Islamic factor, in the form of large scale aversion of Russia's Muslims to the war, played a significant, albeit not primary, role in deciding Russia's approach. Since Russia's opposition to the war contributed to the warming of its relations with the Arab world, it can be said that, in this context, the Islamic factor exerted a positive influence in shaping the pattern of Russia's relations with the Arab world. In the case of the Balkan crisis, Russian policy was determined by the interplay of domestic and external factors, including the dominant ideology and worldview of Russia at various phases of the crisis. The Islamic factor played a relatively small role, although it was more significant in the case of the Kosovo crisis because of the Chechen connection and Russia's growing fears of an Islamist threat to its security and territorial integrity.

11

Russian-Western Relations

Since the Bolshevik Revolution and the Communists' appeal to the Muslims to rise up against Western (British) imperialism, Islam has played a large role in shaping Russia's relations with the West. Both have used Islam to undermine each other's position and win the Muslims to their side.

The best example of using Islam as an ally to fight communism and the Soviet Union occurred in Afghanistan during the 1980s, where the West supported a call to jihad against the Soviet Union and succeeded. During the Afghan War, the West and some of its regional allies also came to see the Soviet Union's Muslim population and Soviet Islam's remarkable ability for survival as a potentially strong instrument to undermine the USSR.

Yet Islam was not an insurmountable barrier for the expansion of Soviet influence into Muslim lands. Notwithstanding the atheistic character of Soviet Communist ideology, some Muslims saw certain affinities between their religion's egalitarian aspects and socialism, which at times facilitated Soviet inroads in certain countries. Additionally, pragmatic considerations led some Muslim states to side with the Soviets in the East-West competition.

However, by the early 1980s, an Islamic movement had emerged that had strong political-ideological dimensions and that pretended to offer an alternative model both to socialist and Western systems. The Iranian Revolution during its first decade was the embodiment of this new Islam. This politicized Islam posed a challenge both to the Soviet Union and to the West, albeit to varying degrees. It also challenged the status quo or establishment Islam that, in the past, had been the West's ally against the Soviet Union. The Soviet Union's collapse not only caused a deep identity crisis within Russia, but also created a paradigmatic vacuum in the international system, which for fifty years had been dominated by and organized around the concept of East-West conflict.

Clash of Civilizations as the New Paradigm: The Threat of Islam

In the post-Soviet period, the most influential effort to offer an overarching paradigm capable of explaining the dynamics of the emerging international system, including the lines along which alliances and counteralliances will be formed, has been the "clash of civilizations" thesis. This theory is identified with Samuel Huntington, but its real originator is Bernard Lewis, who introduced the idea in his article "The Roots of Muslim Rage" in 1990.[1]

This paradigmatic debate has become enmeshed with the more narrow issue of the nature of Russia's post-Soviet identity, the direction of its internal politics, and its foreign policy. For two reasons, the clash of civilizations paradigm has special significance for Russia: (1) according to this theory, the "Orthodox" civilization is inherently incompatible with Western liberal civilization, much like Islam and Confucianism, and (2) since the eighteenth century, there has been an ongoing civilizational battle within Russia between the Westernizers and "Russian authenticists," often wrongly lumped together under the rubric of Slavophiles, which was only superficially buried during the Communist era and has reemerged.

According to Samuel Huntington's thesis, some or even all non-Western civilizations will make common cause against the West, the so-called West against the Rest scenario. Yet since the introduction of his theory, international events have unfolded along the two following lines: (1) pragmatic or even opportunistic alliances across civilizational divides, as illustrated by U.S. support for the Taliban in the first years of the Taliban's rule in Afghanistan and by the engagement of some U.S. allies on the side of the Chechen extremists, and (2) cross-cultural alliances against the extremist or even activist brand of Islam. In other words, the reverse of Huntington's theory has to some degree materialized as the Rest have coalesced against Islam. This latter trend is best illustrated by the international coalition against terrorism inspired and perpetrated by Muslim extremists following the events of 11 September 2001. It is in the framework of these two cross-cutting contexts, one international and one related to Russia's internal identity debate, that the role of the Islamic factor in shaping Russian-Western relations should be analyzed and assessed.

Islam as a Source of Discord and Cooperation

The nature of the role played by Islam has been closely linked to Russia's internal debate, including that over its foreign policy, and the impact of external events. Thus during the first two years of the post-Soviet era, when pro-Western Euro-Atlanticists were ascendant, the concept of a threat from the "South," a euphemism for Russia's Muslim periphery, acted as a unifying force in Russian-Western relations. The Euro-Atlanticists believed that Russia should cooperate with the West in dealing with threats from the South. The West, meanwhile, was essentially willing to allow Russia a relatively free hand in dealing with its southern rim provided that it behaved well in the Western front or regions of concern to the West, such as the Middle East.

Michael Mandelbaum, commenting on what the United States should do about Chechnya, stated, "Russia will, in the best case, pursue the slow, difficult work of constructing a market economy and a democratic government with occasional ugly departures such as Chechnya," and recommended that the U.S. policy should be guided "by two precepts. . . . One is distinction between Russia's relations with the peoples and countries to its south, in Central Asia and the Caucasus, and those to its west, in Ukraine, Estonia, Latvia, and Lithuania. Chechnya is part of the south. It is, to be sure, officially part of the south . . . of the Russian Federation."[2]

Before the Chechen War, as Russia embarked on a more assertive and interventionist policy in the South Caucasus in 1993, Jim Hoagland wrote:

> The Russians are asking the West to join their efforts in the south or at least to extend understanding and support for what they are doing. This has led to debate in Western capitals among those who fear a rebirth of Russian imperialism and those who would give Mr. Yeltsin a relatively free hand in his own neighborhood if that is what is needed to save his government in Moscow. The latter approach is the right one.[3]

It is safe to assume that Hoagland, too, does not consider Ukraine or Latvia, despite Russian-speaking populations, its "neighborhood."

In short, during this period, a perceived common threat of Islam helped cement Russian-Western relations and led the United States to act leniently toward Russia despite its obvious transgressions against its own Muslim population and its Muslim and non-Muslim southern neighbors. This complacency began to change with the rise of nationalist movements in Russia, coupled with a general mood of disappointment with the West and increasing pressures on President Yeltsin to act more assertively in the so-called Near Abroad. However, the intensity of reaction to these developments in Russia differed within the Western, most notably the U.S., policymaking community. Jim Hoagland, who in 1993 had advocated allowing Russia a free hand in the South, wrote in 1994:

> The West, accustomed to seeing the Soviet empire as a monolith, risks not seeing the Central Asian trees for the Russian forest. The United States and its European allies risk depriving the new States of the vital room to maneuver by seeing events in the [States] of Central Asia through the prism of Russian expansionism.[4]

According to Anatol Lieven, during the crucial years of 1994–2000, the often contradictory policies that the United States pursued toward Russia were the result of a process of accommodation between diverging perceptions of what he characterizes as "Russophiles" and "Russophobes," both within the U.S. administration and outside.[5] Whether or not those who feared a resurgence of Russian expansionism were, as Lieven states, motivated by "a deep underlying hostility to Russia [that] . . . may well be considered implacable," their influence was felt in the mix of policies applied toward Russia.[6] As late as May 2001, Fiona Hill, not known as a Russophobe, argued that the West should not join Russia in fighting Islamic extremism nor support Putin in his goal to become "the gendarme of Eurasia."[7] In at least two instances, Afghanistan and Chechnya, the West used Islam to check Russian influence and advance its and its regional allies' goals and the interests of Western energy companies at Russia's expense. Whether this is a fair assessment of Western policies may be debatable. What is important is that many Russians believed it to be so.[8]

Some Russian commentators have also alluded to U.S. acquiescence, if not active support, for the Taliban. An article in the Russian press claimed that "many experts attribute the very idea of the creation of the Taliban to the efforts spearheaded by the United States."[9] The article attributes part of the U.S. motive to a desire to build a southern pipeline through Afghanistan that would undermine Russia's monopoly as the sole export outlet for Caspian energy.

In addition to Chechnya and Afghanistan, in three other cases the Islamic factor came to play a divisive role in the evolution of Russian-Western relations, although its significance was secondary. These were (1) Bosnia, (2) Kosovo, and (3) Russia's relations with Iran and Iraq, especially Iran, since the Iraqi Ba'athist regime, despite Saddam Hussein's manipulation of Islam, was a secular state.

Chechnya

Considering the brutality of the two Chechen wars, the official Western response in both cases was essentially muted. Despite the supposed influence of the Russophobes, no serious pressures were brought to bear upon Russia. There were some verbal criticisms, at times harsh, of Russia's policy toward Chechnya, but these were not backed by strong action.[10] Indeed, Western policy on Chechnya was a clear example of realpolitik. A quote from an unnamed European diplomat in the *Irish Times* sums up the West's Chechnya policy: "The political reality dictates that, if we're smart, we'll keep fairly quiet while making the right noises of concern. But that means we put aside the moral questions as the price."[11]

There were, however, certain symbolic acts aimed at showing that the Russian actions in Chechnya would not leave relations with the West unaffected. In January 1995, President Clinton declined an invitation from Boris Yeltsin to visit Moscow in May.[12] However, a senior U.S. official "took pains to declare that scheduling a summit is not hostage to a satisfactory finish to the attack on Chechnya,"[13] and Clinton subsequently decided to travel to Moscow in May to participate in celebrations of the fiftieth anniversary of the Allies' victory over Germany in the Second World War. German defense minister Volker Rühe withdrew his invitation to Pavel Grachev in May 1995, the Russian defense minister. This decision was partly prompted by Grachev's harsh attack on two of the most trenchant critics of the war in Chechnya, Sergei A. Kovalev, Yeltsin's estranged human rights commissioner, and Sergei Yushenko, the head of the Duma's Defense Committee.[14] These acts were accompanied by some mild threats of curtailing aid to Russia. German foreign minister Klaus Kinkel warned, "If things continue in Chechnya as they appear at the moment then investment, and of course economic support as well, will be automatically withheld."[15] German minister of the economy Günter Rexrodt added, "Russia risked 'gambling away' Western aid and investment if it continued to pursue the war."[16] In March 1995, the European Union froze a wide-ranging trade agreement with Russia because of Moscow's military tactics in Chechnya, including aerial bombing and extensive artillery attacks on a largely defenseless city, Grozny, the Chechen capital.[17]

Yet neither the United States nor Europe was prepared to pressure Russia too much on the Chechen conflict. It was Russia's domestic dynamics, namely, the unpopularity of the first Chechen War with the Russian population and Russia's electoral calendar, that forced a change in Russian policy.

In fact, despite all the verbal threats, there was no real change in the Western approach to Russia. On the contrary, at the height of the Chechen crisis, Russia was accepted into the Group of Seven in June 1995.[18] Moreover, Moscow received a $6.8-billion loan from the IMF and another $106 million from the World Bank.[19] Meanwhile, the groundwork was being laid for a new framework for NATO-Russian relations.[20] In January 1996, the Council of Europe voted to admit Russia into the group by a vote of 164–35, although Europe had been more critical of Russian operations in Chechnya than the United States.[21]

Reasons for Western Complacency and the Russian Response

Several reasons account for Western nations' disregard of the Chechen War in deciding their policy toward Russia. Most prominent was the "Yeltsin factor." Notwithstanding a U.S. official's statement that American policy toward Russia was not "Yeltsin-centric," the fact is that from the West's point of view he was the best person they could hope for to lead Russia at that time in a pro-Western direction.[22] By early 1995, the United States did try to distance itself from Yeltsin and to put relations with Russia within a long-term framework.[23] Nevertheless, the U.S. administration attacked efforts by some members of Congress to "condition or cut aid to Russia because of Chechnya and Iran."[24] In a speech delivered at Indiana University, Secretary of State Warren Christopher commented that such cuts "would undermine moves to a market economy and the dismantling of Russia's nuclear arsenal."[25]

Second, by the time the Chechen War broke out, Russian-Western relations had already become strained over issues ranging from Bosnia to the planned eastward expansion of NATO and disagreements over Iraq and Iran. Under these circumstances, it was feared that too strong a Western reaction to the Chechen problem could seriously endanger relations.

Third, following Russia's October 1993 parliamentary elections, nationalist and Communist forces had made gains in the State Duma. Thus it was feared that Western overreaction on Chechnya could further strengthen these forces and perhaps even jeopardize Boris Yeltsin's reelection.

Russian responses to Western reactions were also a mixture of defiance and the pursuit of "business as usual." Most of the defiant speeches and calls for counter-measures were from Duma members. Responding to a statement issued by the Estonian parliament in support of Chechnya, Vladimir Lukin said that it was a "gross interference in Russia's domestic affairs."[26] The State Duma also responded negatively to the European Parliament's resolution regarding Chechnya, explaining that it "does not contain a clause about the European Parliament's respect for territorial integrity of the Russian Federation." The lower house of the Russian parliament claimed that the resolution was an attempt to "interfere into the internal affairs of Russia."[27] For this reason, the Duma refused to issue visas to a European Parliament mission to Chechnya. The Speaker of the Duma, Ivan Rybkin, further justified the Duma's stance, explaining that "Russia was profoundly misunderstood by the West over the Chechnya conflict. . . . The Chechens—and particularly their 'adventurer' leader—were closely aligned with Libya's Colonel Gadaffi."[28] The reference to Libyan leader Muammar Gadaffi was clearly an appeal to the West's fear of extremist Islam, even though Libya was never a major player in the Chechen drama.

Certain statements of the Russian Foreign Ministry were also harshly critical of the West's attitude toward Chechnya. In January 1995, the Foreign Ministry issued a statement attacking what it termed the West's "inappropriate and hasty" criticism of its military actions in Chechnya.[29] Foreign Ministry spokesman Grigory Karasin claimed that Russia's failure to "counteract the separatist and criminal regime [in Chechnya] could lead to a repetition of the Yugoslav scenario in Russia."[30] He also warned that the recently forged partnership between the West and Russia was being tested by events in Chechnya and said that "the West should ask itself whether it is right to so hastily and categorically destroy the accumulated positive experience of interaction with Russia."[31]

Meanwhile, although Russia had refused entry to human rights observers in January 1995, President Yeltsin granted permission for an OSCE delegation to visit Russia the following March.[32] In 1996, when campaigning for the presidency, Yeltsin indicated that the West had been more supportive of Moscow's war in Chechnya than the Russians. Yeltsin attributed this to the fact that the West understood that Chechnya is a "stronghold of international terrorism," whereas "some of our compatriots have failed to comprehend this as yet."[33]

To sum up, by and large, the West was unwilling to seriously challenge Russia in Chechnya. In addition to the factors already discussed, the fact that Chechnya was part of the Russian Federation and its separation could have led to greater instability in Russia played a role. Moreover, unlike the case of Bosnia, there was no sustained and concerted effort on the part of the West's Muslim allies to pressure it into adopting a firmer position on Chechnya. But even if they had, it would have been to no avail because, unlike Bosnia, Chechnya was not located in the heart of Europe.

Western Response to the Second Chechen War

Valerii Tishkov has argued that between August 1996 and September 1999, Chechnya was moving toward a new war as though following the advice of a Russian "ultra-radical activist," Valeria Novodvorskaya.[34] Reportedly, in an interview with Chechen television, she had said, "A peace treaty is a good thing, of course. But knowing how unpredictable Russia is, I would advise the Chechens to trust Allah, but to keep the camel tied up. As long as the Chechens have arms, the peace will be observed."[35]

Tishkov seems to believe that the West and some of its allies saw a resumption of the Chechen War as a prelude to "Russia's disintegration," an outcome Tishkov believed many in the West desired. According to him, "In the geopolitical sense the 'international community' (—argot [slang]—for Western countries and their allies) began to see that idea [Russian disintegration] as preferable even in the face of other global risk factors: the 'Islamic threat,' international drug traffic, uncontrolled nuclear weapons, and others."[36] Tishkov maintained that, following the signing of the Khasavyurt accord in 1996 and the Yeltsin-Maskhadov agreement in 1997, the de facto independence of Chechnya was considered a foregone conclusion.[37] He believes, however, that this view in the West suffered a blow when the Chechens transferred their "allegiance from the West to the Islamic world. That was due both to changes in the political positions of the leading Western countries (limiting their attention and moral support for Chechnya) and Chechnya's growing reliance on the ideological and military resources of the Muslim Arab allies."[38]

This view of Chechen estrangement from the West does not seem quite convincing—at least as far as the Maskhadov government is concerned—if one only takes into account the number of visits that Maskhadov made to Western capitals and his efforts to entice Western investors into Chechnya. It was reported that in November 1997, a Caucasus Investment Fund was formed by, among others, Khorh-Akhmed Nukhayev, a former deputy prime minister of Chechnya.[39] Moreover, Maskhadov paid private visits to the United States, Britain, where he met with Margaret Thatcher, and Warsaw.[40] It appears more credible that while Maskhadov was trying to build official ties with Western and Muslim countries, more extremist groups were developing ties with other extremists, such as the Taliban. Some Russian conspiratorial theories see collusion between Western and Islamic centers, even the extremist elements.

Irrespective of the validity of any of these theories, the fact is that the West's reaction to the second Chechen War was more negative, although still cautious. Certainly there was little willingness in the West to go beyond symbolic gestures such as postponing an IMF loan or suspending Russia's membership in the Council of Europe.[41] Western criticism was also slow in coming. Thus during the first two months of the war, little criticism was voiced against Russia by the United States.[42] As reported in the *Christian Science Monitor*, it was only after fighting "drove more than 170,000 residents from their homes, and a rocket attack on the market killed more than 100 people," that U.S. officials called the offensive "deplorable and ominous."[43]

By December 1999, however, the exchanges between Western capitals and Moscow had become extremely acrimonious.[44] President Yeltsin walked out of the OSCE summit in Istanbul held in November 1999. During a visit to China, Yeltsin wondered "whether Mr. Clinton had forgotten that Russia has a 'full arsenal' of nuclear weapons."[45]

Other Russian officials pointed out that considering NATO-led operations in Kosovo, the West had no moral authority to criticize Russia.[46] Vladimir Putin, first as Russia's prime minister and later as president, accused the Europeans of not supporting Russia's war in Chechnya "because they are afraid of a reaction among the Muslim inhabitants of Europe, but that is the wrong conclusion." He added, "That should not be their conclusion. . . . Western Europe could pay heavily for this."[47] Putin made these comments during a visit to Britain after his election to the presidency. As he had done in the past, Putin suggested that "the West should be grateful for the bloody invasion he had unleashed seven months ago" because this was to stem the tide of Islamic terrorism, which could engulf the West if it were unchecked in the North Caucasus.[48]

Reasons for Harsh Rhetoric and the Lack of Real Pressure

The harsher Western rhetoric toward Russia reflected differences that had been deepening between the two sides since 1996, when Primakov became Russia's foreign minister. Primakov advocated a less West-centric policy for Russia and promoted the strategy of multipolarity. Primakov's elevation to prime minister in 1998 signaled a further widening of the rift between Russia and the West. This led Russia to strengthen ties with China and to help Iraq in its confrontation with the United Nations over the issue of weapons inspectors, actions that were viewed as potentially hostile to the West.[49] Meanwhile, the war in Kosovo had seriously strained Russian-Western ties, hence the harsh rhetoric. Yet practical factors that had prevented strong Western pressure on Russia during the first Chechen War, notably the risk of isolating Russia and encouraging nationalist and anti-Western forces, were still important. As a result, the threats of cutting aid to Russia never went beyond words.[50]

In addition, during the second Chechen War, three factors made the adoption of a harsher attitude toward Russia more difficult. First, the Russians justified their activities in Chechnya in terms of fighting Islamic extremists who they claimed received help from some U.S. allies. By August 1998, the Taliban adventure had gone wrong and Osama bin Laden, the Saudi-born extremist with links to the Taliban, had launched terrorist attacks against the U.S. embassies in Kenya and Tanzania and had become a major problem for the United States. Thus U.S. inhibitions had "been strengthened by the Russian claim to be fighting Islamic terrorism, always a popular enemy in Washington, particularly when the Islamists in the

Caucasus may [have been] getting financial support from America's chief hate figure of the moment, Saudi-born terrorist Osama Bin Laden."[51]

Second, the Kosovo War, as the Russians never tired of saying, had weakened the West's moral authority. Regardless of whether this Russian claim is justified, with Russian-Western tensions over Kosovo, the West was hesitant to come to blows over Chechnya.

Third, the question of the Chechen War and U.S. policy toward Russia became inextricably linked with U.S. domestic politics, especially during the 2000 presidential election in the United States. The Republicans were questioning the Clinton administration's long-term strategy toward Russia based on the principle of "strategic patience." This concept was identified with Strobe Talbott and was embraced by Democratic presidential candidate Al Gore, who "credited the policy with having minimized the risk of Communist resurgence in Russia and having helped contain the threat from Russia's vast nuclear arsenal."[52] The Republicans were also "charging that United States and international aid [had] been sucked down the plughole of the Yeltsin government's massive corruption and incompetence."[53] The Republicans favored a tougher stand toward Russia in general, and especially with respect to Chechnya.[54] Under these circumstances, the Clinton administration could not have pressured Russia too much without discrediting its entire strategy. However, when the Republicans assumed power, and despite the initial frostiness in Russian-American relations, which only began to thaw after the meeting between Presidents Putin and Bush in Slovenia on 16 June 2001, there was no change in the U.S. policy toward Chechnya.

The events of 11 September 2001 vindicated both Russia's claim that there were links between the Chechen rebels, the Taliban, bin Laden, and their supporters and Russia's position that these groups posed a threat to the West as well as Russia.[55] This further reduced both European and U.S. willingness to pressure Russia on Chechnya, despite continued reports of widespread human rights abuses by Russian forces in Chechnya and despite Russia's decision to close the OSCE mission in Chechnya at the end of 2002.[56] On the contrary, the United States confirmed the involvement of Al-Qaeda in Chechnya and Georgia's Pankisi Gorge. The United States also indicated in February 2003 that it would soon formally include some Chechen groups on its list of terrorist organizations.[57] Russia's positive response to President Bush's call to form an international coalition against terrorism opened a new page in Russian-American relations. In short, the Islamic factor as it was played out in Chechnya had both a divisive and a unifying impact on Russian-Western, especially Russian-American, relations.

Afghanistan

Following the collapse of the Soviet Union, the Yeltsin government did not pay much attention to developments in Afghanistan even when the Moscow-supported government of President Muhammad Najibullah was removed by Afghan mujahideen forces led by Ahmad Shah Masoud in April 1992. Until 1994 and the emergence of the Taliban, Afghanistan as a policy issue disappeared from Russian-Western relations.

As the Taliban grew more powerful and ideologically more extremist, the Russians began supporting their opponents, notably the forces of the Tajik commander Ahmad Shah Masoud. Meanwhile, until August 1998, the West looked favorably toward the Taliban, and ultimately it was disagreement over bin Laden that caused a change in the Western assessment of the Taliban.[58] Thus from 1994 to 1996, Afghanistan and its new breed of Muslim leaders became a cause for disagreement between Russia and the West. But in December 2000, Russia and the United States collaborated in the United Nations to impose economic sanctions on the Taliban regime.[59]

Before the events of 11 September 2001, Western countries refused to openly acknowledge any links between the Taliban and their supporters and rebel groups in Chechnya. But after 11 September, Afghanistan became a factor in improved Western-Russian relations, although entirely on Western terms. The Russians would have liked to see the Rabbani government, which they had long supported, confirmed as the country's legitimate government. Vladimir Putin expressed support for the internationally recognized government of Afghanistan during a meeting with the president of Afghanistan, Burhaneddin Rabbani, in Dushanbe, the capital of Tajikistan.[60] But U.S. opposition to Rabbani, Pakistan's opposition to any government dominated by the Northern Alliance, and divisions within the alliance itself between pro- and anti-Rabbani elements made this scheme impossible. Iran, too, despite its preference for Rabbani, did not press for his continuation in power, partly in hopes of propitiating the United States and improving relations with America. Consequently, Russia declined to challenge the United States and insist on keeping the Rabbani government.

The Balkans

The primary causes of Russian-Western tensions in the Balkans were Russia's concern over its dwindling influence, NATO's eastward expansion, and Russia's general unease over the emerging international system, which it characterized as "unipolar." The fact that the longest-lasting conflict, in Bosnia and Kosovo, involved Muslim populations was of secondary importance. This was certainly true of the Russian leadership. But other political forces and a large segment of the Russian population saw the West's intervention—albeit belated for Bosnia—as proof of its inherently anti–Russian/Orthodox feelings. According to Dimitri Danilov, director of the European Security Institution in Moscow, many Russians saw NATO operations in Yugoslavia as a forerunner of what could happen to Russia. This sentiment was reflected in the slogan "Today Yugoslavia—tomorrow Russia."[61]

The Kosovo crisis and NATO military strikes on Belgrade were especially shocking to Russia and brought relations to their lowest ebb. From the Russian perspective, this was because, in the words of Anatolii Torkunov, NATO actions were "a graphic manifestation of a regional defense organization's ambition that tried to usurp the UN responsibilities and appoint itself a rival of 'global respon-sibility' in the European Atlantic area and beyond it."[62] Since Russia is not a NATO member, while it has a permanent seat on the United Nations Security Council and veto power, it clearly saw such a perceived development as undercutting Russia's role.

In short, Russian-Western tension in the Balkans was about the changing global balance of power. The fact that the most serious crisis involved Muslims was only incidental. Nevertheless, to the extent that Balkan events strengthened Russian fears of a potential Western-Muslim alliance against Russia, the Islamic factor did play a role.

Iran and Iraq

Moscow's and Washington's diverging views of Iraq and Iran have been a major source of tension in U.S.-Russian relations, even at the time of their honeymoon. Until the eruption of the dispute between the United States and Britain, on one side, and the overwhelming majority of United Nations members, on the other, over the decision to initiate military action against Iraq, disagreement on Iran was the greatest cause of discord in U.S.-Russian relations. Major U.S. complaints against Russia were the sale of Russia military equipment and the building of a nuclear plant in the southern Iranian city of Bushehr. The issue of arms supply seemed to have been eliminated by the Gore-Chernomyrdin agreement of 30 June 1995, in which Russia agreed to stop arms sales to Iran. But soon after the signing of this agreement, Russia decided to help Iran rebuild the Bushehr plant. The United States objected to this cooperation on the basis that it would enable Iran to build nuclear weapons. Newt Gingrich, Speaker of the U.S. House of Representatives, declared that the United States would cut off all aid to Russia if it helped Iran to build weapons of mass destruction.[63] The Clinton administration also made it clear that such a deal would damage relations with the United States and would not be "cost free."[64] The involvement of Russia's gas giant Gazprom was another source of irritation.[65]

In early 2003, U.S. concern over Iran's nuclear ambitions intensified when it was discovered that Iran had built a heavy water production plant at Arak and a uranium enrichment facility at Natanz,[66] and, later, that Iran had failed to inform the International Atomic Energy Agency (IAEA) about the importation of small amounts of enriched uranium from China in the early 1990s.[67]

This increased concern, in turn, led the United States to press the Russian gov-ernment to end its nuclear cooperation with Iran and to pressure the Iranian gov-ernment to abandon its nuclear ambitions.[68] According to Russian sources, one senior Bush Administration official, Undersecretary of State for Arms Control John Bolton, "practically accused Russia of conniving in the supply of weapons of mass destruction technology to Iran."[69] Officials at the Russian Ministry of Internal Af-fairs characterized Bolton's statements as "empty words."[70] Moreover, these alleged statements raised the following question in official circles in Moscow: "Is this senior official expressing his personal opinion—'extravagant' as usual—or is he simply expressing the views of those groups in Washington that are opposed to the strategic choice in favor of partnership and cooperation confirmed by the presidents of Russia and the United States?"[71]

Throughout 2003, Russia endeavored to balance its desire to remain on good terms with the United States and to maintain its ties with Iran. Thus, while Russian officials, including President Vladimir Putin, expressed their commitment to preventing the spread of weapons of mass destruction, Russia insisted that it would fulfill its commitments to Iran regarding the Bushehr plant, including the supply of fuel for the reactor.[72] However, the spokesman of the Russian Foreign Ministry, Alexander Yakovenko, said that the provision of the fuel was contingent on "securing a separate bilateral deal with Iran to send spent fuel back to Russia for reprocessing."[73]

In addition to the nuclear issue, Iran remained a potential source of greater disagreement between Moscow and Washington in case the United States opted for military action, even if short of full-scale invasion, to deal with Iran's nuclear challenge or to bring about a change of regime in Teheran.

The Islamic factor definitely influenced Russia's decision to cooperate with Iran and contributed to U.S. opposition to such cooperation. The United States still viewed Iran as a country whose foreign policy was driven by Islamic ideology hostile to the United States and its closest allies, especially Israel. The most serious irritant was Iran's links with the Shi'a militant group Hizb-ul-Allah in Lebanon, but also with various Palestinian Islamist groups, most notably Hamas. Iran was also suspected by some of having been involved in terrorist acts against the United States, most notably the bombing of the Khobar Towers in Saudi Arabia, which housed U.S. marines.[74] In short, the Islamic nature of the Iranian regime and its lingering revolutionary ideology, which influenced Iran's ties with extremist Islamic groups in the Middle East, adversely affected U.S. interests and those of its allies and caused serious tensions in Iran's relations with the West, especially the United States.

By contrast, Iran pursued an essentially nonideological policy toward Russia and the post-Soviet states. Moreover, Iran used its influence with certain Muslim groups in Tajikistan and Afghanistan in ways that helped Russia. Iran's support for Russia's Chechnya policy, especially within the OIC, was also helpful to Russia. Thus the Islamic factor was a consideration in Russia's approach to Iran: Russia has attempted to co-opt Iranian Islam.

However, as the ebb and flow of Russian-Iranian relations has illustrated, Russia's decision to initiate a rapprochement with Iran was determined by broader geostrategic and economic considerations and its shifting worldview. For example, Primakov's objection to the United States unilaterally branding countries such as Iran and Iraq as rogue states was a reflection of Russian unease over an international system dominated by the United States. The same considerations were behind Russia's resistance to U.S. pressures to end its relatively close ties with Iran. In fact, the Islamic character of the Iranian regime limited the scope of Russian-Iranian cooperation.

Until the U.S. decision to topple Saddam Hussein's regime, Iraq was an irritant, but not a principal source of tension in Russia's relations with the West. Nor did the Islamic factor play a significant role in this regard because, despite its efforts to wrap itself in the Islamic flag, the Iraqi regime was fundamentally secular. The Islamic factor also had little role in shaping the character of Russia's ties with Iraq, largely because of Saddam Hussein's limited credibility in the Muslim world, including among Russian Muslims, and hence its inability to be either of significant help to Russia or to cause it problems, either in the larger Islamic world or within Russia's own Muslim communities. Rather, the main factors behind Russian-Iraqi friendship were the long history of Soviet collaboration and alliance with Iraq, the lure of Iraq's oil riches and trade opportunities once UN sanctions were lifted, and Iraq's potential role in the context of Russia's multipolar strategy. However, the intensification of the international crisis over Iraq during the winter of 2002–2003, culminating in the U.S.-British war on Iraq, caused serious tensions in Russia's relations with the United States and the United Kingdom, as Russia sided with France and Germany in opposing the invasion.

Once military operations began, Russia called for an early end to the war. Together with France and Germany, it also called for an important role to be played by the UN in rebuilding post-War Iraq.[75] Russia's position caused strained relations with the United States—though, at least on the surface, far less severe than strains between Washington and both Berlin and Paris. There were negative comments about Russia from U.S. officials throughout the crisis. For example, Richard Perle, until March 2003 the chairman of the Pentagon's Defense Policy Board, said, "We work closely with our friends but friends don't . . . let me just say that there was nothing friendly about the Russian policy in Iraq."[76] On 24 March, pressures escalated to the point that President Bush himself telephoned President Putin to discuss "the United States' concerns . . . involving prohibited hardware that has been transferred from Russian companies to Iraq."[77] (The hardware reportedly included antitank missiles, night vision goggles and jamming gear.)[78] Such a step at that level was clearly meant to send a message of disapproval regarding Russia's overall stance on Iraq. The connection between Russian behavior and post-war benefits was made clear by the U.S. ambassador in Moscow, Alexander Vershbow, on 26 March, when he indicated that the United States could not guarantee Russia's access to Iraqi oil.[79]

The Islamic factor also acquired greater importance as Russia's Muslim establishment, including political leaders, notably President Mintimer Shamiev of Tatarstan, and largely Muslim-inhabited republics expressed strong opposition to the war. President Shamiev said that the war with Iraq "will be accumulating negative energy in the whole Moslem world, and that this moment will be joined by neutral Arab countries, which previously were not part of the anti-American coalition."[80]

It is difficult to assess the extent to which such opposition determined Russia's position and to what extent it was used by the Russian authorities to justify a position adopted on other grounds, such as economic and strategic. For example, the Russian ambassador to the United States, in an article published in the *Washington Post* on 3 April 2003, said: "Americans should understand and accept that many Russians and other Europeans are opposed to war in Iraq. *This view is especially strong among the many millions of Muslims living in Russia.*[81] By April, however, both Russia and the United States had reached the conclusion that their broader economic and strategic interests required that they put their differences over Iraq behind them. This realization led to intensified contacts among key U.S. and Russian policy makers, including visits to Moscow by Secretary of State Colin Powell and National Security Adviser Condoleezza Rice in May, culminating in President Bush's visit to St. Petersburg for ceremonies marking the 300th anniversary of the city's founding.[82]

The meeting between Presidents Bush and Putin vastly improved the atmosphere of Russian-American relations. During their meeting, Bush said, "I think this experience [disagreeing on Iraq] will make our relationship stronger, not weaker. . . . We will show the world that friends can disagree, move beyond disagreement and work in a very constructive and important way to maintain the peace."[83] But according to key Russian analysts, relations still remained fragile and lacked substance.[84]

Britain, meanwhile, took the first step to reach out to Russia when Prime Minister Tony Blair visited Moscow in late April 2003. Putin's reception of Blair was rather cool. According to some reports, Blair "was humiliatingly mocked by Vladimir Putin . . . over the failure to find Saddam Hussein or his deadly weapons."[85] This initially cool reception did not discourage the British government form pursuing the path of reconciliation. This policy culminated in Putin's state visit to Britain in June 2003, the first time since 1874 that a Russian leader was so honored, during which a number of important economic agreements were signed.[86]

Conclusion

This analysis of the influence of the Islamic factor on post-Soviet Russian-Western relations leads to three main conclusions. First, until 11 September 2001, the Islamic factor played a limited role in Russian-Western relations. To the extent that this factor has had an effect, it has been at regional levels and in the context of specific regional conflicts or issues. However, since 11 September the Islamic factor has also had an impact on the overall character of Russian-Western relations. Second, Islam has been used more successfully by the West than by Russia as a tool of its influence and an instrument for advancing its objectives. Third, Islam has been both a divisive and a unifying factor in Russian-Western relations, although its unifying potential may be more significant as long as both Russia and the West remain targets of Muslim grievances.

Conclusion: Russia's Encounter with Islam

The foregoing analysis of nearly a thousand years of Russia's interaction with Islam and the Muslim world, plus the more recent dynamics of this interaction within the post-Soviet Russian Federation, has yielded a number of important conclusions. These include observations about the challenges Russia has faced in the transition from a totalitarian system with a colonial and imperial past to a more democratic society and in relating to the outside world within a fundamentally changed international system. It has also provided partial answers to the questions posed at the beginning of the study, particularly those related to the challenges a posttotalitarian state in transition faces in developing a new identity and reconciling imperatives of democratic pluralism and demands for ethnic, religious, cultural, and political self-determination with the requirements of state security and territorial integrity. Some of these conclusions challenge many long-established views regarding the process of Russia's identity formation, the evolution of its sense of statehood, nationhood, and system of values, and its perception of its place and role in the world. Others, especially those relating to Russia's Muslim minorities, conform to a large extent to well-established historic patterns of interaction between them and the Russian society and state. Still others point to the ongoing process of transition in Russia, the difficulties it faces in reconciling many contradictory objectives, and the risks of a slowing and perhaps a reversal of democratic trends and its consequences both for Russia's overall evolution and the fate of its Muslim minorities.

The most important conclusions are the following: (1) Islam has played a much more significant role in the process of Russia's identity formation, state building, worldview, and hence the nature of its interaction with the outside world than is generally assumed. (2) The dynamics of the evolution of the cultural, national, and political identity of Russian Muslims have been deeply influenced by the fact of their incorporation through conquest into the Russian and Soviet empires and the contradictory pressures of assimilation, resistance to the loss of their identity, and periodic efforts at acquiring greater self-determination. Similar dynamics have been at work in the post-Soviet Russian Federation as the liberalizing trends of the last years of the Soviet Union and the immediate post-Soviet years resulted in an upsurge, at times excessive, in the Muslim quest for self-determination and the Russian government's efforts to curb such demands, including by forceful means, as in the case of Chechnya. (3) In the post-Soviet era, Islam and the Russian Federation's Muslim population have remained important variables in the processes just noted. Developments in Russia's Muslim regions, especially Muslims' drive for greater cultural, administrative, and even political self-determination, have had a considerable impact on the evolution of Russia's post-Soviet identity, its governmental system, and its external relations. (4) This process of interaction between Russia's Muslims and the rest of society has highlighted the difficulties involved in the transition from a totalitarian to a democratic system, especially in terms of forging a new and more inclusive ethnic-cultural-religious identity reconciling competing demands of self-determination and state security and integrity. (5) Islam has affected the evolution of post-Soviet Russia's foreign policy and security perspectives and the character of its relations with key international and regional actors in conjunction with other important factors such as adjusting from an imperial to a national mode of thinking in foreign policy, adjusting Russia's external goals and ambitions to its dwindling means, both economic and military, and adapting policy to new domestic and international contexts.

Impact on Identity Formation and Worldview

Russia's historic evolution as a nation and an empire, the process of the formation of its collective identity, and its worldview, including its perception of its own role in the world, have been almost exclusively analyzed and explained in terms of its interaction with the West. This interaction has either taken the form of opposition to the West or emulation of it. No doubt, encounter with the West has had a formative impact on all the previously noted areas and processes. Russia's separation for a long period of time from the Western Christian world consequent to its choice of Eastern Orthodoxy and Byzantine traditions and its later periodic efforts to emulate the West especially stand out. Even more important, encounter with the West, either as a model to be emulated or as a rival and threat, has led to a still ongoing debate between the Russian Westernizers, on the one hand, and a wide range of Russian authenticists, notably the Slavophiles, on the other. This debate extends to all aspects of Russian life, from the patterns of intellectual development to the conduct of its external relations and the values and principles underpinning them.

By contrast, the role that Islam and Islamic civilization have played in these processes has received little or no attention except in the very narrow context of the Mongol invasion and domination. Yet for a millennium, Russia has interacted with Islam, and its gradual but inexorable expansion into Muslim lands over nearly five centuries has made Islamic civilization an important, albeit unrecognized, part of Russia's cultural landscape despite some nods made in this direction in the post-Soviet era. Attention has been focused on the Mongol invasion and the "Mongol-Tatar yoke" and its devastating physical and intellectual consequences for Russia.

No doubt, this episode had a traumatic and formative impact on Russia and has given rise to some deeply rooted, widespread, and mostly negative feelings. The period of the Mongol-Tatar yoke has been considered the main culprit for Russia's separation from the West, thus depriving it of the first fruits of Western progress, and for the worst aspects of its political culture, notably a tendency toward authoritarianism. This period has given Russia a sense of victimhood vis-à-vis the Western Europeans by generating the belief that Russia protected Europe from the Mongol onslaught without receiving recognition and appreciation for its sacrifice. Meanwhile, the Islamic factor has been omitted from this context. This feeling of not being appreciated for its contributions to European and Western civilization and interests has carried over to the present day and is an important factor in the present context of Russian-Western interaction.

Yet following the Mongol invasion, Islam became the second and, for the duration of Mongol-Tatar rule, the main hostile "other" in juxtaposition to which Russia defined itself. It also acted as a catalyst for the creation of the post-Kievan Russian state. The Islamic factor further contributed to the consolidation of the Russian belief in its role as the guardian of true Christianity and its defensive flank on the eastern front. This belief, which has been revived in the post-Soviet period because of the Chechen War and the infiltration of Muslim extremist ideas and groups into Russia, has been articulated by Russian leaders who have said that in Chechnya, Russia is defending Europe and the West, again without receiving any recognition for its sacrifice. This belief in Russia's role as the defender of Christianity has nurtured its messianism, including its long-cherished desire to liberate the citadel of true Christianity and the capital of Byzantium, Constantinople, from Muslim control. This Russian messianism later was translated into socialist utopianism, with Muslim lands as a major field of experimentation. In sum, the encounter with Islam has been a major contributing factor to the development of Russia's messianic streak and has also partly shaped its view of the West as basically unconscious of Russia's service to Christians and Christian civilization. This sentiment, in turn, has intensified a sense of Russia's cultural uniqueness and belief in its own distinct civilization in juxtaposition to both Western and Islamic civilizations.

Russian mobilization to overthrow Tatar/Muslim rule also marks the beginning of its imperial expansion and the development of a strong imperial impulse. The conquest of Kazan symbolizes both an ethnic and a religious victory, namely, that of Orthodox Russians against Muslim Tatars. It also heralds the dawning of Russia's imperial age. Russia's imperial expansion was not limited to Muslim-inhabited lands. Nevertheless, it was in this direction that it found its most extensive and long-lasting realization. Similarly, it was in the Muslim lands that Russia would find space to satisfy its colonial and civilizing mission. Even after the creation of the Soviet Union, the essentially colonial nature of relations between the Russians and Muslim peoples did not change, although some aspects of it were mitigated, at least superficially.

It was also Russia's expansion into Muslim lands and its victories over Muslim powers that consolidated Russia's belief in its inherent right to great-power status, as well as making it a major player on the European and global scene. Of course, Russia's expansion was not limited to Muslim lands. In particular, after 1945, Russia extended its sphere of influence in Eastern Europe and the Baltic region. Nevertheless, Russia's colonial experience and imperial expansion flourished in Muslim lands. In short, the Islamic factor played a central role in developing many of the key characteristics of Russian nationhood and statehood.

Islam, Russia, and the World

In addition to contributing considerably to the shaping of Russia's worldview and thus influencing its external behavior, since the early eighteenth century, Islam has been an important factor in Russia's foreign policy. This has resulted from the empire's expansion, which was initiated by Ivan the Terrible and took a southward direction, as recommended by Peter the Great in his famous Testament, in quest of warm waters. In this process, Islam acted mostly as a barrier to Russia's imperial ambitions. This was nowhere more true than in the northern Caucasus. However, because the blossoming of Russia's imperial impulse coincided with the decline of Iran and the Ottoman Empire, the two most important Muslim powers at the time, Muslim resistance to Russia took more localized forms, although Iran fought two series of wars with Russia in the early nineteenth century (1804–13 and 1824–38), and the Ottomans were engaged in military conflict with Russia for a much longer period and over a much larger geographic space. In most of these battles, Russia was victorious unless a Western power became engaged, as was the case in the Crimean War (1854–56), when Britain intervened on behalf of the Ottomans.

The stirring of anticolonial movements in the Muslim world offered the Bolsheviks an opportunity to make an ally of Islam, but the atheist nature of the Communist ideology and the harsh treatment of Muslims in the Soviet Union made these efforts fruitless. In the 1950s, 1960s, and 1970s, the USSR did make inroads in the Muslim world—Egypt, Syria, Iraq, Libya—but this was due to some Muslim countries' disillusionment with and resentment toward the West rather than to a special affinity between Islam and the USSR. On the contrary, the majority of key Muslim countries sided with the West during the Cold War. Indeed, the West was more successful in harnessing Islam as a barrier to Soviet expansion, as best exemplified by the Soviet-Afghan War, than the Russians were in using it to thwart Western policies.

In the post-Soviet era, too, Islam has been an important variable in shaping the pattern of Russia's external relations, albeit in a contradictory fashion. On balance, Islam has continued to be more of a challenge than an ally to Russia, despite the expectations of certain schools of Russian political thought that Islam and the Muslim world could serve as allies for Russia in countering Western, especially U.S., predominance. Ironically, Islam, especially its politicized and extremist versions, has brought Russia and the West together in the wake of the September 2001 terrorist attacks on the United States, but this is not surprising since Russia is a majority Christian country and has more in common with the Western Christian world, notwithstanding the historic rift between the Eastern and Western churches and the long history of Russia's conflicted relations with the West. After all, as noted by Dostoevsky, a major proponent of Russian authenticity, the quarrel between Russia and the West was essentially a family dispute, while Russia's problems with the Muslim world, including its own Muslim-inhabited lands, have deeper cultural and religious roots. Russia's treatment of its immediate Muslim neighbors in the so-called Near Abroad has retained more of an imperial tinge than that toward its Christian neighbors in the West, including those that once formed part of the Soviet Union. This has been the case because the West has been more willing to accept such behavior toward Muslims, confirming the point made earlier. Meanwhile, Russia has maintained workable and, in some cases, close relations with Muslim countries whenever its interests have required this. It has also not been above exploiting the West's problems with the Muslim countries with the goal of regaining its lost or diminished influence in the Islamic world.

Russia's Impact on Muslim Identity and Aspirations

As the encounter with Islam has marked the Russians' collective identity and their sense of mission and purpose, the encounter with Russia has had an even deeper impact on Muslims' self-identity and their aspirations. In the last 500 years, the Muslim experience with Russia has been that of conquered with conqueror. Thus the main dynamics that have shaped Muslim identity have been those of struggle for survival and quest for self-determination. This experience has also marked the collective identity of Muslims and their self-perceptions. Russia's treatment of its Muslim population has fluctuated over a long period of domination. Nevertheless, a prominent feature of these relations has been that of suppression of the Muslims' cultural, religious, and political self-determination, at times reaching levels that jeopardized the very survival of Islam in Russia. However, the resilience of the Muslim peoples and their culture, plus periods of a more tolerant Russian attitude toward Muslims or a position of benign neglect, prevented such an outcome. Nevertheless, for nearly 500 years, the most important challenge for Russia's Muslims was cultural and in some cases, such as for the Cherkess and Chechens, physical survival.

The challenge of cultural survival did not result merely from suppression, but also from active efforts of assimilation at times embraced by many Muslims, either because of belief in the superiority of Russian/Soviet culture or for reasons of expediency, such as social and economic mobility. As Russians view the period of Tatar-Mongol rule as responsible for their deficiencies, Muslims see isolation from the rest of the Islamic world as responsible for their intellectual and institutional underdevelopment. This situation became particularly acute under Communist rule, during which periodic antireligion campaigns were carried out with special rigor against Muslims. The negative consequences of this intellectual and institutional weakness became palpable in the post-Soviet era when outsiders tried to fill the vacuum created by this weakness.

Meanwhile, with few exceptions, Russia's Muslim peoples and regions remained economically, socially, and educationally underdeveloped compared with other parts of the country. Thus the loss of indigenous cultural capital was not compensated by acquiring new skills and knowledge on a par with the ethnic Russians and other Slavs. In regard to socioeconomic and educational indicators, the Muslims of the former Soviet Union fared better than many of their neighboring Muslim kin. Nevertheless, a disproportionate number of Russia's Muslims remained rural and enjoyed a lower standard of living than the Slavic population, a situation that also generated interethnic tensions and resentment. The perpetuation of large economic, social, educational, and other disparities between the Muslims and ethnic Russians and other Slavs contributed to the consolidation of Muslims' separate sense of identity. It also made them view their position more as that of colonial subjects than as that of full-fledged citizens. This meant that ideas of autonomy and even independence remained present among Russian Muslims and came to the fore whenever conditions permitted it. This was facilitated by the fact that despite the all-consuming challenge of survival and a large measure of isolation from major trends in the rest of the Islamic world and the West, Russia's Muslims gained some access to a wide spectrum of ideas ranging from secular nationalism to modernization and Islamic reformism. The impact of these ideas by the turn of the twentieth century led to a Muslim reawakening, at least at the elite level. When broader conditions in Russia permitted, as was the case during 1905–07, when there was a limited liberalization, Russia's Muslims agitated for greater cultural self-determination and political representation within Russia's governmental institutions, notably the short-lived first Duma. A similar, but stronger movement arose following the February and October Revolutions of 1917. Yet until 1918, separatist tendencies within Russia's Muslim regions were not strong. Most Russian Muslims wanted a greater degree of self-determination, but within a Russian state preferably based on a federal model. Even during the period of Gorbachev's reforms, Muslim aspirations were largely limited to greater self-determination within a reformed Soviet federal system. It was only after the strengthening of proindependence movements in the Baltic republics and the Russian heartland itself that similar tendencies became stronger in the Muslim regions.

In sum, Russian/Soviet treatment of Muslims contributed greatly to the survival of a separate sense of identity within significant segments of Russia's Muslim population. Meanwhile, the mostly harsh treatment of Muslims resulted in a low feeling of loyalty to the Russian/Soviet state and a weak notion of citizenship. Thus the desire for greater self-determination—religious, cultural, and even political—remained strong among Russia's Muslims and carried over to the post-Soviet era.

Impact of the Islamic Factor on Russia's Internal Evolution

The Islamic factor has had a considerable impact on the process of the formation of Russia's post-Soviet identity, culture, and system of values, as well as its governmental structure. The very revival of Islam, both as a religion and culture, has been viewed as threatening to Russia's cultural integrity and authenticity. Alarmists in Russia even see a threat in higher Muslim birth rates to the very survival of Russia as a Russian Orthodox entity. These demographic trends, plus Muslim cultural assertiveness and demands for self-determination, have elicited demands for the protection of ethnic Russians, Russian culture, Orthodox Christianity, or, in a nutshell, the "Russianness" of Russia. But more consequential in this context have been the emergence of separatist movements in parts of Russia and the rise of Islamic extremism. It is regrettable that the Muslim quest for self-determination did not always take a peaceful form and in some cases deteriorated into outright separatism, as in Chechnya. The verdict of history on the causes of the Chechen War and whether its occurrence was inevitable has yet to be pronounced. What is clear so far is that the Chechen conflict created an environment in which Islamic militancy could flourish. It also kindled fears of the potential disintegration of the Russian Federation, thus pitting the principle of self-determination against the maintenance of the territorial integrity of the state. Most damaging, the Chechen conflict greatly contributed to the strengthening of the centralizing tendencies in Russia that are deeply rooted in the country's history. The result has been the actual or potential loss of many of the gains made by Muslims in terms of administrative and, to some degree, political self-determination as Russia since 1999 has gradually moved in the direction of a narrow and restrictive interpretation of federalism.

Islamic extremism in Chechnya and other parts of the North Caucasus, meanwhile, reinforced anti-Muslim feelings and strengthened demands for the establishment and nurturing of a more Russocentric national culture. The result was the passage of new legislation restricting the establishment and activities of religious organizations and political parties, with adverse consequences for Muslims' ability to participate in the political process and to achieve a good measure of cultural self-determination. In fact, while developments in Muslim regions of Russia have had a wide-ranging impact on many aspects of Russia's evolution, Russia's Muslims have had very little influence in shaping national policies, even those that affect them directly. This is evidenced by the way Muslim political groups are used as vehicles for obtaining Muslim votes and then, after elections, rapidly disbanded. Indeed, some of these groups are formed for this purpose rather than with a goal of creating responsible, mainstream Muslim politicians capable of representing the interests of their communities. Meanwhile, developments such as the emergence of religious extremism in some Muslim regions have contributed to the resurrection of another tendency with deep roots in Russia, namely, greater government control of Muslim religious establishments and Muslim life in general. Admittedly, some of the measures to exert more government control over religious establishments were not solely aimed at Muslims and reflected broader political and cultural factors; however, growing popular and elite suspicion of Islam and Russia's Muslims provided much of the underlying support for their implementation, and the Muslims and their organizations bore the brunt of these measures. Inevitably, the growth of anti-Muslim sentiments among the ethnic Russians strengthened the Muslims' feeling of distinctiveness and sense of cultural particularism. Thus developments within Russia's Muslim community, most important, the rise of highly politicized and extremist Islam, hindered the development of a less ethnocentric and religion-based sense of identity and a concept of Russianness based on citizenship and loyalty to a Russian state that is ruled on the basis of democratic principles and equal rights for all citizens and equal treatment of its main cultures.

To these factors must be added the existence of a great deal of disarray within Russia's Muslim community and authoritarian tendencies of Muslim political leaders. In fact, Russian Muslims' inability to achieve a greater measure of self-determination and become more fully engaged in post-Soviet Russia's social, political, and cultural life has also been due to divisions within the Russian *ummah* along ethnic, sectarian, and ideological lines. These divisions had historically prevented Russia's Muslims from taking advantage of occasional political openings to enlarge their margin of self-determination and consolidate their scattered members, even among ethnically close groups, while becoming active and engaged citizens of Russia. These intra-Muslim divisions helped the Bolsheviks in their incorporation of the tsar's colonies into the new Soviet state. In the post-Soviet era, too, these factors have impeded the achievement of the Muslims' aspirations and have limited their impact on broader developments in the Russian Federation related to the character of the country's national identity, dominant culture, and system of governance. More disturbing, within their own republics and regions, Muslims have failed to create more modern, lasting, and broad-based establishments—religious, social, and political.

Part of this inability has been due to broader developments in Russia, but part of it has been the result of the authoritarian tendencies of Muslim republican leaders, many of whom are leftovers from the Communist era. In one case, Chechnya, unwise leadership and deep internal divisions coupled with exogenous ideological influences in the form of militant and politicized Islam contributed to the republic's plunge into chaos and war, with far-reaching and adverse consequences for the entire Muslim community in Russia. Even more damaging has been periodic manipulation by republican leaders of Islam and ethnic nationalism for their own purposes. These actions have done little to increase the margin of Muslim self-determination, but they have intensified Russian fears of a potential Muslim challenge to the country's political stability and even its territorial integrity. Russian authorities have exploited these fears to curtail Muslims' autonomy in a variety of areas and to conduct a long and costly—in human and material terms, both for Russians and Muslims—war in Chechnya.

Difficulties of Democratic Transition in Multiethnic Posttotalitarian States

Any process of transition from a closed social and political system ruled by a narrow elite is highly difficult. However, such a process becomes even more difficult in the case of totalitarian—as opposed to authoritarian—societies. The problems are compounded if the posttotalitarian state in transition is also ethnically and religiously diverse, especially if its diversity is the result of past imperial and colonial expansion. Several reasons account for this difficulty.

First, unlike the authoritarian state, in which the main goals are the perpetuation of the power of the ruling elite and the silencing of dissent and suppression of challenges to the existing power structure, a totalitarian state is ideologically motivated and aims at controlling the minds as well as the actions of its citizens. While few totalitarian regimes fully achieve this objective, the impact of state ideology is pervasive within the society irrespective of whether the population fully subscribes to it. The Soviet Union, with Russia at its apex, falls into this category, although long before its demise, the number of true believers in the Communist ideology had dwindled. Moreover, although a totalitarian system is incapable of eliminating preexisting cultural elements, it superimposes its ideology on them, giving rise to new interpretations of old symbols, myths, and beliefs. In short, in totalitarian societies, state ideology has a central role in determining "collective identity," at least officially and as a legitimizing instrument for the existing power structure and social and political order. Thus the collapse of a totalitarian system raises issues of identity that are not encountered in postauthoritarian systems.

This question of "identity" and its foundations becomes more acute in the case of multiethnic and multireligious societies, especially if the existence of ethnic and religious minorities within the state has been the consequence of a history of imperial expansion. Consequently, posttotalitarian states immediately face the question of what is or should be their national identity and its core constituents. This applies both to the majority population and to minorities. As the superimposed and ideologically generated notions of identity crumble, the more primordialist, exclusionary, and suppressed elements of identity come to the surface. This is what has happened in post-Soviet Russia.

Under these circumstances, there is a natural drive for the reassertion of long-suppressed minority identities, together with demands for self-determination. This dual and contradictory process of identity destruction and reconstruction in posttotalitarian states often leads to conflicts between the majority and minority perceptions regarding the core components of the collective identity. In cases where the cultural reassertion is accompanied by demands for political autonomy and/or independence, the majority's tolerance for minority cultures diminishes. This tendency is even stronger in cases where the transition to a posttotalitarian system has been accompanied by loss of territory, power, and international standing, as has been the case in Russia. Thus the primary dynamic of identity formation becomes the struggle between the minorities' efforts at cultural self-assertion and the majority's determination to forge a national identity based on its own ethnic, religious, and cultural traditions and to prevent any further loss of territory and power. As gleaned throughout this study, this dynamic has been at work in Russia. So far, Russia has not been successful in developing a sense of identity that can overcome these divides. However, at least at the official level, there is a greater recognition of the legitimacy of minority religions and cultures, which under the right circumstances could evolve into a more inclusive national identity. But the requirements of state cohesion—challenged by separatist demands of some Muslims, notably the Chechens—have overridden concerns about forging a more inclusive national identity. Rather, state rebuilding and the requirement of harnessing popular support to subdue the Chechen separatists have led to an emphasis on the core Russian ethnic and Orthodox Christian elements as the building blocks of Russia's post-Soviet identity.

Second, in totalitarian systems, such as that of the Soviet Union, the power of the state is more pervasive than in authoritarian systems. In particular, there is a complete fusion of economic and political spheres and a large bureaucracy to regulate society.

Third, in totalitarian states, civil society is weak. This was particularly the case in the prereform Soviet Union. Consequently, the collapse of such systems, as happened in post-Soviet Russia, leads to economic and social crisis and a decline of living standards for the majority of the people. While the democratic transition in authoritarian societies of southern Europe—Greece, Portugal, and Spain—was accompanied by rapid industrialization, in Russia the reverse has been true.[1] This situation has created general discontent, a sense of national humiliation, and a search for scapegoats.

Muslims have been victims of this process in two ways. As economically and socially vulnerable segments of society, they have suffered more from the economic downturn, especially in economically depressed and war-torn regions such as the North Caucasus. Meanwhile, some Muslims working as small tradesmen in cities such as Moscow have become scapegoats for justified frustrations of people at their worsening economic conditions. The theory of a causal relationship between the level of economic well-being and democracy is not unchallenged. Nevertheless, there is agreement that prosperous societies have a better chance of becoming and remaining democratic.[2] It should be added that shared prosperity can mitigate other sources of interethnic and sectarian tensions and make reaching mutually acceptable compromises easier. Thus Russia's economic problems, which are not unusual in a posttotalitarian transition, have hampered the process of forging an identity that transcends ethnicity and religion while securing the state's integrity and cohesion. These problems have also strengthened the security-driven concerns at the expense of democratization, especially as it applies to the case of Muslim self-determination.

In addition to the factors already mentioned, theories of democratic transition emphasize the importance of the external environment for the success of such transitions. Certainly, in the case of the three southern European countries, membership in the European Community (European Union) greatly facilitated their process of democratization by, among other things, speeding their economic development and revival through large amounts of aid and investment as well as contributing to their security and political stability. The collapse of the Soviet Union resulted in the emergence of a belt of unstable countries that once formed part of the USSR, many of which harbor historic grievances toward Russia. Meanwhile, the former Soviet space, especially its southern belt, became an area of international and regional competition, with external intervention sometimes aimed at undermining Russian influence and interests. Given the Islamic nature of this southern periphery, linkages with Russia's Muslim regions and peoples emerged, some of which were detrimental to Russia.

Furthermore, Russia's relations with the West were not always harmonious. Rather, suspicions of renewed Russian ambitions continued to linger in the West, although the necessity of helping the Russian transition to succeed was recognized. In short, the unhospitable external environment complicated the task of Russia's internal transformation, thus making the achievement of the goal of creating a pluralistic and democratic society more difficult. Meanwhile, some of Russia's responses to these external challenges, both in the post-Soviet space and internationally, worsened its external environment by reviving and/or strengthening suspicions of its intentions. This led certain international actors to pursue polices toward Russia's internal problems, including the problem of separatism in Chechnya, that made the achievement of other goals more difficult.

To sum up, Russia, Islam, and Russia's Muslim peoples have influenced one another for nearly a thousand years. For the last five centuries, Russia has closely interacted with the Muslim world and played a significant role in defining the destiny of a large portion of its peoples. This centuries-long relationship has been characterized more by conflict, or at least silent resentment, than cooperation, with the Muslims being subdued for most of the last five centuries despite periodic efforts at cultural self-assertion and even political independence. However, periods of peaceful coexistence and relative tolerance have not been lacking in the history of the two peoples and civilizations. In the post-Soviet period, Russia's Muslims have striven for greater self-determination. In most cases, such efforts have been limited to attempts to gain a greater recognition for Islam as an integral part of Russia's cultural and political landscape and a measure of religious and cultural autonomy; they have rarely been aimed at outright independence or secession from the Russian Federation. This record of moderation indicates that Muslim self-determination need not be at the expense of the Russian state's integrity. Initially, Muslims made some gains, but some of these advances are now at risk.

Although Muslims today enjoy more freedom, Islam still is not fully accepted as an integral part of Russia's cultural fabric, and Russia's dominant social and political institutions do not reflect fully the society's multiethnic and multicultural nature. Muslims certainly remain at the margins of Russia's economic and political life beyond the confines of their own regions. The future of Russia's Muslim peoples thus remains unclear. Their future status depends largely on Russia's cultural and political evolution, especially whether the trend toward political centralism and cultural uniformity intensifies or a more reasonable equilibrium can be achieved between, on one hand, excessive devolution and the dilution of Russia's core culture and, on the other hand, centralization and cultural homogenization. The overall economic and social progress of Russia, especially in its Muslim regions, and the consolidation of civil institutions, including viable political parties, are also important determinants. Last, but not least, an end to the Chechen conflict that satisfies the requirements of Russian territorial integrity and Chechen aspirations for self-determination is vital for Russia's successful transition to democracy, the healing of cultural wounds of the last decade, and the nurturing of cooperative Muslim-Russian relations within a unified and democratic Russia.

Russia's experience since the end of the Soviet Union has fully demonstrated the difficulties involved in a totalitarian multinational state's transition to a democratic system. Russia has not been spared serious crises, including two devastating wars in Chechnya, nor has it been successful in developing an inclusive civic national identity. Moreover, the process of Russia's democratization is far from complete. Yet Russia's success in meeting all these challenges is necessary for the future stability of a vast Eurasian region encompassing the energy-rich Caspian basin, the Black and Baltic Seas, much of Eastern Europe, and thousands of miles of border with a rapidly changing and increasingly tumultuous China.

Appendix
Maps

All of the following maps are from the Central Intelligence Agency and are available through the Perry-Castañeda Library Map Collection of the University of Texas at Austin at <http://www.lib.utexas.edu/maps/commonwealth.html#R>.

428

Map 1. Commonwealth of Independent States, 1994 (Armenia, Azerbaijan, Belarus, Georgia, Kazakhstan, Kyrgyzstan, Moldova, Russia, Tajikistan, Turkmenistan, Ukraine, Uzbekistan)

430

Map 2. Russia: Administrative Divisions, 1994

Arctic Ocean

SEVERNAYA
ZEMLYA

NEW
SIBERIAN
ISLANDS

East
Siberian Sea

Wrangel
Island

U.S.

Bering Sea

Chukotka [b]
(AOk)

Koryakia
(AOk)

U.S.

Laptev Sea

Taymyria
(AOk)

Magadan

Kamchatka

Petropavlovsk-
Kamchatskiy

North
Pacific
Ocean

Yakutia
[Sakha]

Sea
of
Okhotsk

KURIL
ISLANDS

Evenkia
(AOk)

Sakhalin

occupied by
Soviet Union in 1945,
administered by Russia,
claimed by Japan

asnoyarsk

Khabarovsk

Amur

Blagovesh-
chensk

Birobijan
(Yevrey AO)

Yuzhno-
Sakhalinsk

Lake
Baikal

Aga
(Aginskiy
Buryat
AOk)

Primorskiy
[Maritime]

Ust'-Orda
(AOk)

Buryatia

Chita

Irkutsk

vo

akassia

Sea
of
Japan

JAPAN

Tuva

CHINA

MONGOLIA

NORTH
KOREA

SOUTH
KOREA

1	Krasnodar	7	Ingushetia [a]
2	Stavropol'	8	Chechenia [a]
3	Adygea	9	Mordovia
4	Karachay-Cherkessia	10	Chuvashia
5	Kabardino-Balkaria	11	Mari El
6	North Ossetia	12	Udmurtia

[a] Boundary between Chechenia and Ingushetia has not been established.
[b] Chukotka may be independent of Magadan Oblast.

0   750 Kilometers

0   750 Miles

432

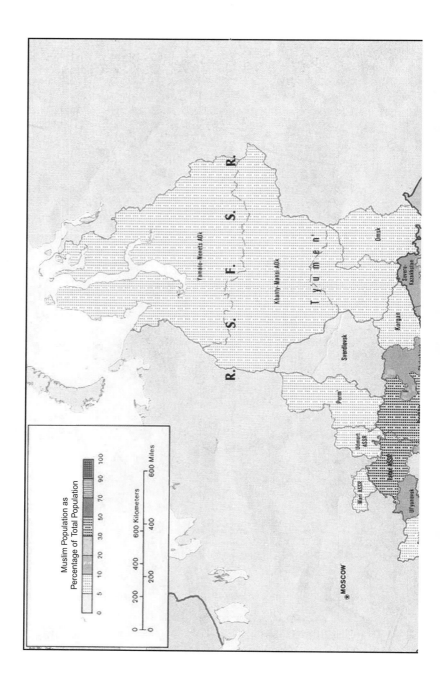

Muslim Population as
Percentage of Total Population

0   5   10   20   30   50   70   90   100

0   200   400   600 Kilometers
0   200   400   600 Miles

433

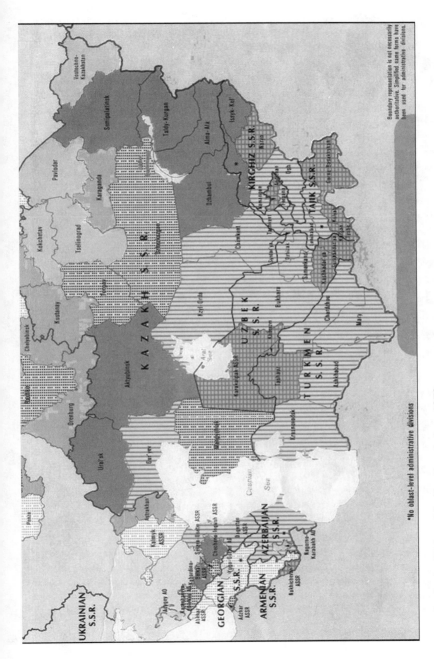

Map 3. Soviet Union: Muslim Population, 1979

*No oblast-level administrative divisions

434

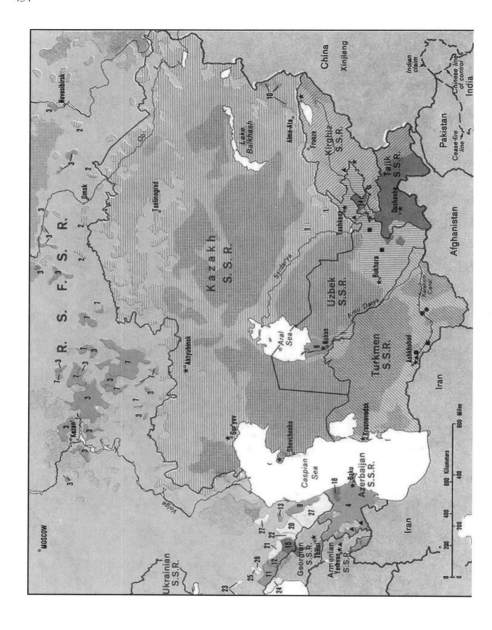

Turkic Peoples

#		1979 Population (in thousands)
1	Uzbeks	12,456
2	Kazakhs	6,556
3	Tatars	6,317
4	Azerbaijanis	5,477
5	Turkmens	2,028
6	Kirghiz	1,906
7	Bashkirs	1,371
8	Karakalpaks	303
9	Kumyks	228
10	Uighurs	211
11	Karachays	131
12	Balkars	66
13	Nogays	60

Iranian Peoples

#		1979 Population (in thousands)
14	Tajiks	2,898
15	Osetins	542
16	Kurds	116
17	Iranians	31
18	Tats	22
19	Baluchis	19

Peoples of the Caucasus

#		1979 Population (in thousands)
20	Chechens	756
21	Kabardians	322
22	Ingush	186
23	Adgeys	109
24	Abkhaz	91
25	Cherkess	46
26	Abazins	29
27	Dagestani peoples:	
	Avars	483
	Lezgins	383
	Dargins	287
	Laks	100
	Tabasarans	75
	Rutuls	15
	Tsakhurs	14
	Aguls	12

★ Slavic peoples (primarily Russian and Ukrainian)

Other non-Muslim peoples

Sparsely populated area

Map 4. Muslim Peoples in the Soviet Union, 1979

436

Map 5. Distribution of Muslim Population in the Russian Federation, 1994

Notes

Notes to Introduction

1. For the ethnic composition of the Soviet Union's population, see Rachel Denber, ed., *The Soviet Nationality Reader: The Disintegration in Context* (Boulder, CO: Westview Press, 1992). For the religious makeup of the Soviet population, see Igor Troyanovsky, ed., *Religion in the Soviet Republics: A Guide to Christianity, Judaism, Islam, Buddhism, and Other Religions* (San Francisco, CA: HarperSanFrancisco, 1991).
2. The preliminary results of the Russian census of 2002 show that the population of Russia is at least 145 million. "Russian Census Sets Population at More than 145 Million: Putin," Agence France-Presse, 19 December 2002.
3. "Schools Get Orthodoxy Course," *St. Petersburg Times*, no. 821, 19 November 2002 <http://www.times.spb.ru/>.
4. According to Father Gennadii, archpriest of the Kazan Cathedral in Moscow's Red Square, the church has "lots of historical documents that the Tsar or the Emperor at least paid heed to the opinions of the Patriarch and the Church when making up his mind on the most crucial aspects of Russia's foreign and domestic policy." See *International Affairs* (Moscow), no. 2 (March 1996): p. 15; and C. Cem Oguz, "Orthodoxy and the Reemergence of the Church in Russian Politics," *Perceptions: Journal of International Affairs* vol 4, no. 4 (December 1999–February 2000) (available at www.mfa.gov.tr/grupa/percept/IV=4/oguz.htm.).
5. Based on an interview with a Moscow-based U.S. diplomat, May 2002.
6. The Russocentric nationalists who believe in the centrality of the Russian ethnic and cultural element in the reinvigoration of Russia—politically, economically, and culturally—fall into this category. A good representative of this school is Russian philosopher Viktor Vladimirovich Aksiuchits. According to him, for the Russians, "the first act of national self-consciousness was 'baptism into Orthodoxy.' . . . It was after the baptism that we see the different neighboring tribes begin to crystallize into one people." See James Billington and Kathleen Parthé, eds., *The Final Report of the Third Colloquium on Russian National Identity* (Washington, DC: Library of Congress, December 2000), p. 15.
7. There are more than 100 ethnic groups in Russia, some numbering only a few hundred people.
8. Quoted in Marie Broxup, "Islam in Central Asia since Gorbachev," *Asian Affairs* 18, no. 3 (October 1987): p. 283.
9. Alexei Malashenko, "Russian Nationalism and Islam," in *Conflicting Loyalties and the*

State in Post-Soviet Russia and Eurasia, ed. Michael Waller, Bruno Coppieters, and Alexei Malashenko (London: Frank Cass, 1998), p. 189.

10. Russian philosopher Viktor Vladimirovich Aksiuchits is one representative of this view. See Billington and Parthé, *Final Report of Third Colloquium on Russian National Identity,* p. 16). Hunter's interview with Aksiuchits in June 2001 confirmed this analysis. Sergei Kortunov also holds similar views. See Sergei Kortunov, *Russia's National Identity in a New Era,* Strengthening Democratic Institutions Project (Cambridge, MA: John F. Kennedy School of Government, Harvard University, 1998), p. 11.

Notes to Chapter 1

1. The collapse of the Sassanid Empire is generally dated to 642 A.D.
2. See Allen J. Frank, *Islamic Historiography and "Bulghar" Identity among the Tatars and Bashkirs of Russia* (Leiden: Brill Academic Publishers, 1998); and Aislu Yunusova, "Islam Between the Volga River and the Ural Mountains," in *Political Islam and Conflicts in Russia and Central Asia,* ed. Lena Jonson and Murad Esenov (Luleå, Sweden: Central Asia and the Caucasus Information and Analytical Center, 1999).
3. For a comprehensive examination of the Islamization of the Bulghars, see Frank, *Islamic Historiography and "Bulghar" Identity among the Tatars and Bashkirs of Russia*; also R. A. Nabiev, ed., *Islam in Tatarstan: Experience of Tolerance and Culture of Co-existence,* Culture, Religion, and Society, no. 9 (Kazan: Master One, 2002).
4. Quoted in Azade-Ayse Rorlich, *The Volga Tatars: A Profile in National Resilience* (Stanford, CA: Hoover Institution Press, 1986), p. 16; and Sergei M. Soloviev, *Istoriia Rossii s drevneishikh vremen* (History of Russia from the earliest times), 50 vols. (Gulf Breeze, FL: Academic International Press, 1976–2000).
5. See Alexandre A. Bennigsen and Marie Broxup, *The Islamic Threat to the Soviet State* (New York: St. Martin's Press, 1983), p. 6.
6. See Elizabeth Gleick, "Russia's High Spirit," *Time* 154, no. 5 (1999) <http://www.time.com/time/magazine/intl/article/0,9171,1107990802-29599,00.html>.
7. Bennigsen and Broxup, *The Islamic Threat to the Soviet State,* p. 5.
8. Ibid.
9. On the impact of Mongol rule on Russian culture, see Paul Harrison Silfen, *The Influence of the Mongols on Russia: A Dimensional History* (Hicksville, NY: Exposition Press, 1974). Also see Charles J. Halperin, *Russia and the Golden Horde: The Mongol Impact on Medieval Russian History* (Bloomington: Indiana University Press, 1985).
10. On the brutality of the conquest of Kazan by Tsar Ivan IV (the Terrible), see Yahya G. Abdullin, "Islam in the History of the Volga Kama Bulgars and Tatars," *Central Asian Survey* 9, no. 2 (1990): p. 6.
11. On the causes of the Battle of Kulikovo, see Janet Martin, "From Kiev to Muscovy: The Beginnings to 1450," in *Russia: A History,* ed. Gregory L. Freeze (Oxford: Oxford University Press, 1997), pp. 20–21.
12. The president of Tatarstan, Mintimer Shaimiev, sent a letter to President Vladimir Putin in March 2001 in which he requested that the day celebrating the Battle of Kulikovo be excluded from the official list of federal holidays commemorating the "days of military glory," but he received a stiff refusal from the Kremlin. At a 20 July 2001 press conference, the chairman of the National-Democratic Party Vatan, Magomed Minachev, demanded that the celebration of the Battle of Kulikovo be abolished nationwide. He was backed by the deputy plenipotentiary permanent representative of the Republic of Tatarstan in the Russian Federation, Shamil Shamsutdinov. See "Prazdnovat li Kulikovskuiyu bitvu?" (Should we celebrate the Battle of Kulikovo?), *Peterburgskii Chas pik ezhenedelnik* (St. Petersburg peak hour weekly), 24 July 2001 <http://lenta.chaspik.spb.ru/cgi-bin/index.cgi?date=24&month=07&year=2001&rub

=9&stat=0> and "Tatari protiv" (Tatars are against), *Ogonyok*, no. 25(4700) (June 2001) <http://www.ropnet.ru/ogonyok/win/welcome.html>.
13. According to the first statewide census of the Russian Empire in 1897, 14–15 million of the empire's population were of predominantly Muslim origins. However, the methodology used in the census was based on the native language and seems to have been deficient. The 1926 Soviet national census revealed that 6.5 million non-Russian citizens considered Russian to be their native tongue, indicating possible underestimation of Muslims. Richard Pipes, *The Formation of the Soviet Union: Communism and Nationalism, 1917–1923* (Cambridge, MA: Harvard University Press, 1997), p. 2.
14. Most important among Russia's cultural rivals were the Catholic Poles and other Catholic Slavs and, later, Protestant Swedes, Germans, and other Western European powers.
15. According to John Thompson, a Soviet history professor asked him the following rhetorical question, "How does the United States fear us? The Russians saved Western civilization in the thirteenth century by taking the brunt of the Mongol onslaught. And look what it cost us!" John M. Thompson, *Russia and the Soviet Union: An Historical Introduction from the Kievan State to the Present*, 3rd ed. (Boulder, CO: Westview Press, 1994), pp. 33–34.
16. Quoted in Abdullin, "Islam in the History of the Volga Kama Bulgars and Tatars," p. 6.
17. Ibid.
18. Bennigsen and Broxup, *The Islamic Threat to the Soviet State*, p. 9.
19. Paul B. Henze, "Circassian Resistance to Russia," in *The North Caucasus Barrier: The Russian Advance Towards the Muslim World*, ed. Marie Bennigsen Broxup (New York: St. Martin's Press, 1992), pp. 62–111. Also see Stephen D. Shenfield, "The Circassians: A Forgotten Genocide?" in *The Massacre in History*, ed. Mark Levine and Penny Roberts (New York: Berghahn Books, 1999), pp. 149–62.
20. According to the last Soviet census of 1989, out of a total of 5.5 million Tatars in the Russian Federation, only 1.8 million lived in the Republic of Tatarstan. Tatars constituted 48.5 percent of the population of Tatarstan, while Russians were 43.3 percent. According to the latest population statistics available at the official Web site of the Republic of Tatarstan, Tatars constitute 51 percent of the population <http://www.tatar.ru/english/00000031.html>. These figures may be subject to revision depending on the final results of the 2002 Russian census.
21. Alan Fisher, *The Crimean Tatars* (Stanford, CA: Hoover Institution Press, 1978), pp. 78–79.
22. Bennigsen and Broxup, *The Islamic Threat to the Soviet State*, p. 16.
23. Fisher, *The Crimean Tatars*, p. 70; also see Chantal Lemercier-Quelquejay, "Les missions Orthodoxes en pays Musulman," *Cahiers du Monde Russe* 8, no. 3 (1967): pp. 369–403.
24. Fisher, *The Crimean Tatars*, p. 70.
25. Abdullin, "Islam in the History of the Volga Kama Bulgars and Tatars," p. 7.
26. Bennigsen and Broxup, *The Islamic Threat to the Soviet State*, p. 16.
27. Ibid., p. 18. Also see John T. Alexander, *Catherine the Great: Life and Legend* (New York: Oxford University Press, 1989); and Isabel De Madariaga, *Russia in the Age of Catherine the Great* (New Haven, CT: Yale University Press, 1981).
28. Quoted in Fisher, *The Crimean Tatars*, p. 71.
29. Ibid.
30. Ibid.
31. Nabiev, *Islam in Tatarstan*, p. 59.
32. R.A. Utyabai-Karimi and D.D. Azamatov, "The Central Spiritual Board of Muslims of Russia and the European countries of CIS" [in Russian], *The Muslim Dictionary of the Bashkir State University* <http://www.bdxc.ru/encikl/c/centr_du.htm>.
33. The Russian Orthodox Church was opposed to many of Peter's reforms.

34. Serge A. Zenkovsky, *Pan-Turkism and Islam in Russia*, Russian Research Center Studies, no. 36 (Cambridge, MA: Harvard University Press, 1960), p. 49.
35. On the Russian-Ottoman agreement to divide Iran's northern provinces, see R.K. Ramazani, *The Foreign Policy of Iran: A Developing Nation in World Affairs, 1500–1941* (Charlottesville: University Press of Virginia, 1966), p. 21.
36. Edward Lazzerini, "The Crimea under Russian Rule, 1783 to the Great Reforms," in *Russian Colonial Expansion to 1917*, ed. Michael Rywkin (London: Mansell, 1988); also Alan Fisher, *The Russian Annexation of the Crimea, 1772–1783* (Cambridge: Cambridge University Press, 1970).
37. Anna Zelkina, *In Quest for God and Freedom: The Sufi Response to the Russian Advance in the North Caucasus* (New York: New York University Press, 2000).
38. John Dunlop, *Russia Confronts Chechnya: Roots of a Separatist Conflict* (Cambridge and New York: Cambridge University Press, 1998); also Moshe Gammer, *Muslim Resistance to the Tsar: Shamil and the Conquest of Chechnia and Daghestan* (London: Frank Cass, 1994).
39. Dunlop, *Russia Confronts Chechnya*; Gammer, *Muslim Resistance to the Tsar*.
40. This rapid deterioration of the Naqshbandi orders was due to the fact that the brotherhoods had not yet established deep roots among the population at the time of Sheikh Mansur's death.
41. M.N. Chichagova, *Shamil' na Kavkaze i v Rossii* (Shamil in Caucasus and Russia) (Moscow: Adir Publishing House, 1991); and Gammer, *Muslim Resistance to the Tsar*.
42. See Marie Bennigsen-Broxup, "The Last Ghazavat: The 1920–21 Uprising," in *The North Caucasus Barrier: The Russian Advance towards the Muslim World*, ed. Marie Bennigsen Broxup (New York: St. Martin's Press, 1992), pp. 112–45.
43. Dunlop, *Russia Confronts Chechnya*, p. 43. On conflicting Russian views of Chechen and other North Caucasian peoples, see Harsha Ram, "Prisoners of the Caucasus: Literary Myths and Media Representations of the Chechen Conflict," Working Paper Series, Berkeley Program in Soviet and Post-Soviet Studies, Berkeley, CA., summer 1999 <http://ist-socrates.berkeley.edu/~bsp/publications/1999_01-ram.pdf>.
44. See Ramazani, *The Foreign Policy of Iran*, pp. 43–47.
45. Alexandre A. Bennigsen and Chantal Lemercier-Quelquejay, *Islam in the Soviet Union* (New York: Praeger, 1967); and Mehrdad Haghayeghi, *Islam and Politics in Central Asia* (New York: St. Martin's Press, 1995), pp. 1–10.
46. See Haghayeghi, *Islam and Politics in Central Asia*, pp. 2–6.
47. A.N. Grigoriev, "Khristianizatsia nerusskikh narodnostei kak odin iz metodov natsionalno-kolonialnoi politiki tsarizma v Tatarii s polovini 16 veka do fevralia 1917 g." (Christianization of non-Russian peoples as one of the methods of tsarist national-colonial policies in Tatarstan from the middle of the sixteenth century to February 1917), *Materiali po istorii Tatarii* (The documents on the history of Tatarstan), no. 1 (Kazan, 1948): pp. 226–85.
48. Paul W. Werth, "From 'Pagan' Muslims to 'Baptized Communists': Religious Conversion and Ethnic Particularity in Russia's Eastern Provinces," *Comparative Studies in Society and History* 42, no. 4 (2000): pp. 497–523.
49. Haghayeghi, *Islam and Politics in Central Asia*, pp. 7–9. Also see Daniel R. Brower and Edward J. Lazzerini, eds., *Russia's Orient: Imperial Borderlands and Peoples, 1700–1917* (Bloomington: Indiana University Press, 1997).
50. Bennigsen and Broxup, *The Islamic Threat to the Soviet State*, pp. 21–22.
51. Alexander Chubarov, *The Fragile Empire: A History of Imperial Russia* (New York: Continuum, 1999).
52. Quoted in Richard A. Pierce, *Russian Central Asia, 1867–1917* (Berkeley: University of California Press, 1960), p. 214.
53. Bennigsen and Broxup, *The Islamic Threat to the Soviet State*, p. 21.
54. Bennigsen and Lemercier-Quelquejay, *Islam in the Soviet Union*, p. 14.

55. Bennigsen and Broxup, *The Islamic Threat to the Soviet State*, p. 22.
56. Haghayeghi, *Islam and Politics in Central Asia*, p. 8.
57. Adeeb Khalid, *The Politics of Muslim Cultural Reform: Jadidism in Central Asia* (Berkeley: University of California Press, 1998).
58. Bennigsen and Broxup, *The Islamic Threat to the Soviet State*, p. 23.
59. Haghayeghi, *Islam and Politics in Central Asia*, p. 9.
60. Evgenii Glushchenko, *Geroi Imperii: Portrety rossiiskikh kolonial'nykh deiatelei* (A Hero of Empire: Portraits of Russian colonial functionaries) (Moscow: XXI vek–Soglasie, 2001).
61. Bennigsen and Broxup, *The Islamic Threat to the Soviet State*, pp. 24–25.
62. Ibid.
63. Ibid.
64. On the events of 1905–07, see Abraham Ascher, *The Revolution of 1905*, 2 vols. (Stanford, CA: Stanford University Press, 1988–1992); and Solomon M. Schwarz, *The Russian Revolution of 1905: The Workers' Movement and the Formation of Bolshevism and Menshevism* (Chicago: University of Chicago Press, 1967). On the Soviet account of the Revolution of 1905–07, see Anna M. Pankratova, *Pervaia russkaia revolutsiia 1905–1907 g.g.* (The First Russian Revolution of 1905–1907) (Moscow: Gosudarstvennoe Izdatelstvo Politicheskoi Literatury, 1951).
65. Particularly noteworthy were the activities of Reshid Ibragimov, Yusuf Akchurin, and Ismail bey Gasprinsky, among many others. Zenkovsky, *Pan-Turkism and Islam in Russia*, pp. 37–54.
66. See L.M. Maksimova, "Ittifaq-al-Muslimin" [in Russian], *The Muslim Dictionary of the Bashkir State University* <http://www.bdxc.ru/encikl/iii/ittifak.htm>.
67. According to Serge A. Zenkovsky, the number of delegates to the first congress exceeded 150. Zenkovsky, *Pan-Turkism and Islam in Russia*, p. 41; Maksimova, "Ittifaq-al-Muslimin."
68. Maksimova, "Ittifaq-al-Muslimin."
69. In this context, we should assume that the word "convention" probably stands for the freedom to form associations and assemblies.
70. Zenkovsky, *Pan-Turkism and Islam in Russia*, p. 41.
71. Maksimova, "Ittifaq-al-Muslimin."
72. The first and second congresses were held secretly. See Maksimova, "Ittifaq-al-Muslimin." Serge A. Zenkovsky refers to the Union of Russian Muslims by its Turkish title, Russiia musulmanlarin ittifaki. Zenkovsky, *Pan-Turkism and Islam in Russia*, p. 41.
73. The Kadets stood for the Party of Constitutional Democrats (which in Russian abbreviation is represented by the letters K and D of the Russian alphabet). Zenkovsky, *Pan-Turkism and Islam in Russia*, p. 42.
74. Ibid. The most active Muslim politicians at the time, Yusuf Akchurin and Reshid Ibragimov, were elected to the central committee of the Kadet party, where they were supposed to represent the interests of Muslim minorities. Moreover, for the sake of maintaining the alliance with the Muslims, the Kadet party agreed to amend certain articles of its political platform, including the following demands: the complete autonomy of the Spiritual Board of Muslims from government control; the recognition that Islamic law should be taken into account in developing civil and criminal legislation; and that education in predominantly non-Russian regions be in local languages.
75. Ibid., pp. 37–38. This was the same Reshid Ibragimov who in 1895, while in temporary exile in Turkey, published the pamphlet *Chulpan Ildizi* (Northern star), in which, in incendiary tones, he accused the Russian government of forcing Tatars to convert to Christianity and appealed to the Tatars and other Muslims to unite in opposition to such attempts.
76. The delegates elected Ali Mardan bey Topchibashev, an oil industrialist from Baku, as

the chairman and Yusuf Akchurin as first secretary of the presidium. Other members of the presidium included Ismail bey Gasprinsky, Reshid Ibragimov, Shahaidar Syrtlanov, and Galimjan Barudi. Eleven of fifteen members of the central committee of Ittifaq were Tatars from the Ural-Volga region, which demonstrated the preponderance of Tatars in Ittifaq leadership. See *1906 sano 16–21 Augustosda ictimag Rusya Musulmanlarynin nadvesi* (The proceedings of the third All-Russia Congress of Muslims, 16–21 August 1906) (Kazan: 1906): pp. 9, 169–70.

77. As part of educational reforms, Ittifaq demanded the introduction of compulsory primary education in native languages. Zenkovsky, *Pan-Turkism and Islam in Russia*, pp. 47–48.

78. Ibid., p. 51.

79. Ibid., p. 49. The head of the suggested central administration of Muslim affairs was to be called *ramsul ulama*—a spiritual leader of the Islamic community of Russia (probably *ramsul ulama* is an incorrect transcription of the Arabic *rais ul-ulama* or *ra's ul-ulama*, meaning "the head of the clergy"). The commission envisioned that he would hold the rank of a minister, which would allow him to have the right of private audience with the monarch.

80. This group was mostly preoccupied with the Russian colonization policy and bitterly opposed the expropriation of the Bashkir lands and their subsequent transfer to Russian colonists. Hence the group's agenda was explicitly nationalist, and, therefore, it was at odds with Ittifaq, which it accused of being too bourgeois dominated. Maksimova, "Ittifaq-al-Muslimin"; Zenkovsky, *Pan-Turkism and Islam in Russia*, p. 52.

81. According to the modern Gregorian calendar, the first Russian revolution of 1917 took place in March, but according to the Julian calendar in use in Russia at the time, the revolution occurred on 24–28 February 1917.

82. A.B. Yunusova and M.G. Valeeva, "The All-Russia Congresses of Muslims," [in Russian], *The Muslim Dictionary of the Bashkir State University* <http://www.bdxc.ru/encikl/s/siezd_mus.htm>.

83. According to Serge A. Zenkovsky, the "centralists" were mainly comprised of Tatars with a pan-Turkist orientation. The "territorial autonomists" were represented by the Muslims from the borderlands of Russian Empire—Caucasus, Crimea, and Central Asia—envisioned a federated Russian republic wherein Muslim peoples would form autonomous national entities. This debate significantly contributed to intra-Muslim tensions and divisions. Zenkovsky, *Pan-Turkism and Islam in Russia*, pp. 141–42.

84. Shafiga Daulet, "The First All Muslim Congress of Russia, Moscow, 1–11 May 1917," *Central Asian Survey* 8, no. 1 (1989): pp. 34–35. Rasulzade's views also stem from the fact that he was a pan-Turkist and wished to see the cultural and ultimately political unification of all Turkic peoples under Ottoman influence. On Rasulzade and the evolution of his political views, see Alexandre A. Bennigsen, "Pan-Turkism and Pan-Islamism: History and Today," *Central Asian Survey* 3, no. 3 (1985). The dichotomy between nationalists and proponents of Muslim unity was pervasive in other parts of the Muslim world at the time.

85. Yunusova and Valeeva, "The All-Russia Congresses of Muslims."

86. Ibid. Two All-Russia Muslim Military Congresses were held in Kazan—on 17–26 July 1917 and on 8 January–18 February 1918. The 200 delegates to the first congress voted for the creation of the Harbi Shuro (All-Russia Muslim Military Council). The main resolution passed at the first congress stated that if the army were to be preserved, it should be based on the nationality principle. Also, it was noted that eventually the army should be replaced by a popular militia.

87. Ibid. For more details, see S.G. Rybakov, *Ustroistvo i nuzhdi upravlenia dukhovnimi delami musul'man Rossii* (The structure and needs of the administration of spiritual affairs of Muslims of Russia) (Petrograd: 1917); and S.M. Iskhakov, "First and Second

All-Russia Congresses of Muslims" and "First and Second All-Russia Muslim Military Congresses," in S.M. Iskhakov, *Politicheskie Deiateli Rossii 1917: Biograficheskii Slovar'* (Political figures of Russia in 1917: Biographical dictionary) (Moscow: 1993).

88. S.M. Iskhakov, "Milliat Mejlisi" [in Russian], *The Muslim Dictionary of the Bashkir State University* <http://bdxc.ru/encikl/mmmm/milliyat_m.htm>.

89. According to the old-style Julian calendar, the Bolshevik seizure of power occurred in October 1917, hence the appellation the October Revolution.

90. The full official title of this territorial entity was the Ural-Volga Autonomous Territorial State (Republic). The Ural-Volga State was supposed to incorporate the entire Ufa *gubernia* and parts of the Kazan, Samara, Simbirsk, Orenburg, Perm and Viatka *gubernias*. Furthermore, upon inception of the Ural-Volga State, it was envisioned that it would be divided into two *okrugs* (a unit of administrative division equivalent to "district") based on the predominant ethnic group residing in each area. For instance, the eastern *okrug* would cover Bashkiria. See S.M. Iskhakov, "The Ural-Volga State" [in Russian], *The Muslim Dictionary of the Bashkir State University* <http://bdxc.ru/encikl/u/ural_v.htm>. Also see B.Kh. Yuldashbaev, *Natsional'ni vopros v Bashkirii nakanune i v period Oktyabrskoi revolutsii* (The nationality question in Bashkiria on the eve of and during the October revolution) (Ufa: 1984).

91. Iskhakov, "The Ural-Volga State." This document was published on 16 January 1918.

92. The fate of the second All-Russia Muslim Military Congress reflects the Soviet suppression of the nascent Muslim political activism and the endemic factionalism among Muslim political forces. The proposition advanced by the Kollegia (Council) of the Milliat Mejlisi advocated the creation of separate autonomous republics for the peoples of Tatarstan and Bashkortostan based on the Soviet model. This idea divided the congress into two factions. The leftist faction supported the Soviet model, whereas the rightist faction favored the federation. As a result of the standoff, the leftist faction withdrew from the congress proceedings and joined the growing ranks of the Bolshevik sympathizers. On 15 February 1918, the Kazan Soviet of Representatives of Workers, Soldiers, and Peasants introduced martial law in the city of Kazan and arrested the leadership of the congress. See Iskhakov, "Ural-Volga State." On 28 February 1918, the Kazan Soviet arrested the most active participants of the second Muslim Military Congress, and on 24 March 1918, the Soviet issued a decree on the liquidation of the Harbi Shuro. See Yunusova and Valeeva, "All-Russia Congresses of Muslims."

93. David Marples, *Lenin's Revolution: Russia, 1917–1921* (Longman, 2000), p. 118.

94. Cited in Pipes, *The Formation of the Soviet Union*, p. 155.

95. Muhammed Salyahetdinov, "Unification under the State Roof. The History of Muslims of Russia Demonstrates That They Have Never Been 'the Masters of Their Own Fates,'" [in Russian], *Nezavisimaya Gazeta*, no. 74(2384) (25 April 2001) <http://religion.ng.ru/islam/2001-04-25/6_unification.html>.

96. In describing the composition of the Fifth Red Army, Serge A. Zenkovsky quotes Mirsaid Sultan-Galiev. See Zenkovsky, *Pan-Turkism and Islam in Russia*, p. 189.

97. The choice of the name Azerbaijan was controversial since the areas that comprised the region historically were not called by that name. Because the republic was established with the help of Ottoman troops, it caused anxieties in Iran. The Iranian government objected to naming the republic Azerbaijan, fearing that it would be a prelude to the annexation of the Iranian province. On the question of Iranian anxieties, see Ahmad Kasravi, *Tarikh-e-Hedjdah Saleh-e-Azerbaijan* (The eighteen-year history of Azerbaijan) (Tehran: Entesharat-e-Amir Kabir, 1353 [1974]). On the origins of the name Azerbaijan and its geographic confines, see Shireen T. Hunter, "Greater Azerbaijan: Myth or Reality?" in *Le Caucase Post-Sovietique: La Transition dans le Conflict* (The post-Soviet Caucasus: Transition in conflict), ed. M.R. Djalili (Paris: Librairie Generale de Droit et de Jurisprudence [Bruyant-Bruxelles], 1994), pp. 115–22.

98. Haghayeghi, *Islam and Politics in Central Asia*, p. 17.

99. Pipes, *The Formation of the Soviet Union*, pp. 79, 81.
100. Alexander Garland Park, *Bolshevism in Turkestan, 1917–1927* (New York: Columbia University Press, 1957).
101. Haghayeghi, *Islam and Politics in Central Asia*, p. 17.
102. Marie Broxup, "The Basmachi," *Central Asian Survey* 2, no. 1 (1983): 57–83; Park, *Bolshevism in Turkestan*. Opinions diverge on the duration of the Basmachi uprising due to the sporadic nature of the insurgency, especially toward its end. See H.B. Paksoy, " 'Basmachi': Turkestan National Liberation Movement 1916–1930s," in *Modern Encyclopedia of Religions in Russia and the Soviet Union* (Gulf Breeze, FL: Academic International Press, 1991), 4: pp. 5–20 <http://www.ku.edu/~ibetext/texts/paksoy-6/cae12.html>.
103. Edward Walker, *The Dog That Didn't Bark: Tatarstan and Asymmetrical Federalism in Russia* (Berkeley: University of California at Berkeley, 1996), p. 8.
104. See Iskhakov, "Ural-Volga State." Also see Yuldashbaev, *Natsionalni vopros v Bashkirii nakanune i v period Oktyabrskoi revolutsii*.
105. In 1922, the battle against the Red Army was still raging, and an estimated 18,000 rebels were engaged in the struggle, but they were no match for the 160,000-strong Soviet military force.
106. Quoted in Patrick Karam, "La Russie et l'Islam: Entre alliance et rejet" (Russia and Islam: Between alliance and rejection), *Les Cahiers de l'Orient* 41 (Spring 1999): p. 31.
107. Bennigsen and Broxup, *Islamic Threat to the Soviet State*, p. 26.
108. Karl Marx, "Contribution to the Critique of Hegel's Philosophy of Law," in Karl Marx and Frederick Engels, *Collected Works*, vol. 3 (Moscow: Progress Publishers, 1975).
109. Frederick Engels, *Anti-Dühring* (Moscow: Progress Publishers, 1978), p. 382.
110. Marx and Engels, *Collected Works*, vol. 3, p. 175.
111. V.I. Lenin, "Socialism and Religion," in *Collected Works*, 4th English ed., vol. 10 (Moscow: Progress Publishers, 1972), pp. 83–87.
112. Ibid, pp. 83–87.
113. Bennigsen and Broxup, *Islamic Threat to the Soviet State*, p. 37.
114. Ibid.
115. Ibid., p. 38.
116. Ibid., p. 40.
117. Ibid., p. 47.
118. Article II, paragraph 13 of the Constitution allowed propaganda. The full text of the Constitution of the RSFSR adopted by the Fifth All-Russia Congress of Soviets is available at <http://www.marxists.org/history/ussr/constitution/1918/index.htm>.
119. V.I. Lenin, "On the Significance of Militant Materialism," in *Collected Works*, vol. 33 (Moscow: Progress Publishers, 1972), pp. 361–63.
120. Meaning "Godless" and "without religion."
121. Bennigsen and Broxup, *The Islamic Threat to the Soviet State*, pp. 46–47.
122. Quoted in Haghayeghi, *Islam and Politics in Central Asia*, p. 22.
123. Joshua Rothenberg, "The Legal Status of Religions in the Soviet Union," in *Aspects of Religion in the Soviet Union, 1917–1967*, ed. Richard H. Marshall, Jr. (Chicago: University of Chicago Press, 1971), pp. 72–82.
124. Alexandre A. Bennigsen and S. Enders Wimbush, *Muslim National Communism in the Soviet Union: A Revolutionary Strategy for the Colonial World* (Chicago: University of Chicago Press, 1979).
125. Bennigsen and Broxup, *The Islamic Threat to the Soviet State*, pp. 51–52.
126. As early as the 1930s, the Soviets used their Muslim subjects to gain influence in other Muslim states, notably Iran.
127. Haghayeghi, *Islam and Politics in Central Asia*, p. 33; Michael Bourdeaux, "Reform and Schism," *Problems of Communism* 16 (September–October 1967): pp. 108–18.

128. See Leonid Medvedko, "Islam and Liberal Revolution," *New Times*, no. 43 (October 1979): pp. 18–21.

129. Ibid.

130. The first conference in 1979 celebrated the tenth anniversary of the publication of "Muslims of the Soviet East." The second conference, also held in 1979, commemorated the "contribution of the Muslims of Central Asia, of the Volga, and of the Caucasus to the development of Islamic thought, to the cause of peace, and social progress." The 1980 conference celebrated "the fifteenth century of Hijra." See Haghayeghi, *Islam and Politics in Central Asia*, pp. 35–36.

131. Jan Åke Dellenbrant, "Soviet Decision-Making on Regional Stability under Brezhnev and Gorbachev," *Journal of Communist Studies* 4, no. 1 (March 1988).

132. According to Igor Ermakov and Dmitri Mikulski, in 1979, on the territory of the then Chechen-Ingush Republic, which was part of the RSFSR, the number of nonregistered mosques was almost sixty times higher than that of the registered mosques. Igor Ermakov and Dmitri Mikulski, *Islam in Russia and Central Asia* [in Russian], (International Lotus Foundation for the Cultures of the Orient, Lotus Book Series no. 1-1993 (Moscow: Lotus Foundation/Detskaya Literatura, 1994), p. 18.

133. Quoted in Marie Broxup, "Islam in Central Asia since Gorbachev," *Asian Affairs* 18, no. 3 (October 1987): pp. 287–288.

134. Ibid.

135. On these self-appointed religious leaders, see Bess Brown, "The Phenomenon of Self-Appointed Mullah," *Radio Liberty Research*, no. 220 (May 1981).

136. Ibid.

137. Broxup, "Islam in Central Asia since Gorbachev," p. 283.

138. S. Muslimov, "In Search of Persuasiveness—Some Pressing Problems of Atheistic Propaganda," [in Russian], *Sovetskiy Dagestan*, no. 6 (Makhachkala, 1983): pp. 38–39.

139. Quoted in Alexandre A. Bennigsen, "Mullahs, Mujahidin, and Soviet Muslims," *Problems of Communism* 33 (November–December 1984): p. 31.

140. See Allaberid Khayyidov and Amanmazar Ashyrov, "The Writer, Islam, and Atheism," *Adabiyat Vasungat* (Ashkhabad), 22 April 1983, trans. Foreign Broadcasting Information Service (FBIS), 23 August 1983, p. 23.

141. See I.A. Makatov, "Ateisti v Nastuplenii" (Atheists on the offensive), *Sovetskaya Rossiya*, 1978, pp. 16–17.

142. Ibid.

143. Alexandre A. Bennigsen, "Soviet Islam since the Invasion of Afghanistan," *Central Asian Survey* 1, no. 2 (July 1982): pp. 65–78.

144. See I. Dzhabbarov, "Religious Propaganda Aimed at Muslims in USSR: 'Ideological Subversion' " [in Uzbek], *Soviet Uzbekistani*, 17 February 1985, in *BBC Summary of World Broadcasts*, 23 April 1985 <www.lexis.com>.

145. Quoted in Bennigsen, "Mullahs, Mujahidin, and Soviet Muslims," p. 32. Also on the need to improve atheistic propaganda, see "Azerbaijan Conference Calls for Better Atheistic Education" [in Azeri], *Kommunist*, 22 October 1986, in *BBC Summary of World Broadcasts*, 6 December 1986, <www.lexis.com>.

146. On the evolution of Soviet-Iranian relations see Shireen T. Hunter, *Iran and the World: Continuity in a Revolutionary Decade* (Bloomington: Indiana University Press, 1990), pp. 79–97.

147. Bennigsen, "Mullahs, Mujahidin, and Soviet Muslims," p. 34.

148. See Ahmed Rashid, "Islam in Central Asia: Afghanistan and Pakistan," in *Islam and Central Asia: An Enduring Legacy or an Evolving Threat?* ed. Roald Sagdeev and Susan Eisenhower (Washington, DC: Center for Political and Strategic Studies, 2000), pp. 213–236.

149. See I. Dzhabbarov, "Use of Religious Subversion and 'Islamic Factor' by Imperialism"

[in Russian], *Pravda Vostoka*, 17 April 1986, in *BBC Summary of World Broadcasts*, 14 June 1986 <www.lexis.com>.

150. See Michael Bourdeaux, *Gorbachev, Glasnost, and the Gospel* (London: Hodder and Stoughton, 1990), p. 36.

151. Martha Brill Olcott, ed., *The Soviet Multinational State: Readings and Documents* (Armonk, NY: M.E. Sharpe, 1990), p. 375.

152. In April 1987, Patriarch Pimen appealed to Gorbachev. See Bourdeaux, *Gorbachev, Glasnost, and the Gospel*, p. 42.

153. Yevgeny Yevtushenko, "The Source of Morality Is Culture" [in Russian], *Komsomolskaya Pravda*, 10 December 1987, p. 2, in *Current Digest of the Soviet Press* 38, no. 52 (28 January 1988): p. 1.

154. Rafik Mukhametshin, *Islam v obshchestvenno-politicheskoi zhizni Tatarstana v kontse XX veka* (Kazan: Iman, 2000), p. 56.

155. Ibid., p. 57.

156. Ibid., p. 97.

157. On the founding of IRP from a Russian perspective, see I.P. Dobaev, *Islamskii radikalizm v mezhdunarodnoi politike: Na primere regionov Blizhnego, Srednego Vostoka, i Severnogo Kavkaza* (Islamic radicalism in international politics: Examples of Near and Middle East and North Caucasus) (Rostov-on-Don: Rostizdat, 2000).

158. See Dmitri Mikulski, "Muslims and Their Organizations in Russia," in George Fox University's *Religions in Eastern Europe* program, 16 December 1998 <http://cis.georgefox.edu/ree/html_articles/MIKULSKI.ISL.html>.

Notes to Chapter 2

1. See F.M. Mukhametshin and A.A. Dubkov, "Musulmanskie Organizatsii v Rossiiskoi federatsii" (Muslim Organizations in the Russian Federation), Institut gosudarstvenno-konfessionalnikh otnoshenii i prava (Institute of relations between the state and religious denominations and law), 3 July 2001 <http://www.state-religion.ru/cgi/run.cgi?action=show&obj=1304>.

2. Alexander Ignatenko, "The Choice of Muslims of Russia: They Will Vote for Stability, Not for Parties or Governments with the Word 'Islam' in Their Name" [in Russian], *Nezavisimaya gazeta*, no. 163(1979) (3 September 1999) <http://www.ng.ru/ideas/1999-09-03/vybor.html>.

3. Quoted in Alexei Malashenko, "Russian Nationalism and Islam," in *Conflicting Loyalties and the State in Post-Soviet Russia and Eurasia*, ed. Michael Waller, Bruno Coppieters, and Alexei Malashenko (London: Frank Cass, 1998), p. 187.

4. A 1995 Russian television show on the effects of the high birthrate in Muslim families in Kiev claimed, "There is a danger of Russia being transformed into an Islamic state." Quoted in Malashenko, "Russian Nationalism and Islam," p. 191. The claim of Geidar Jemal, the chairman of the Islamic Committee of Russia, that Russia's Muslims number 30 million is clearly intended to exaggerate Muslims' political significance.

5. Mikhail Tulskiy, "Are Wahhabites Defeating the Moderate Muslims in Russia?" [in Russian], *Nezavisimaya gazeta*, no. 108(2418) (19 June 2000) <http://www.ng.ru/printed/ideas/2001-06-19/8_vakhabit.html>.

6. Aleksei Maximov, "The Leaders of Muslim Schism: Ravil Ganutdin" [in Russian], *Nezavisimaya gazeta*, no. 12(75) (28 June 2001) <http://faces.ng.ru/printed/dossier/2001-06-28/7_split.html>.

7. Tulskiy, "Are Wahhabites Defeating the Moderate Muslims in Russia?"

8. R. Silantiev, "Kratkii obzor sovremennogo polozheniia nekhristianskikh traditsionnikh religii Rossii" (A brief survey of present conditions of non-Christian traditional religions of Russia), Institut gosudarstvenno-konfessionalnikh otnoshenii i prava (Institute

of relations between the state and religious denominations and law) <http://www
.state-religion.ru/cgi/run.cgi?action=show&obj=1164>.

9. Sergei Ivanenko and Alexander Shegortsov, "Islam in Russia" [in Russian], *Russian
Federation Today*, no. 10 (2001) <http://www.russia-today.ru/no_10/10_dossier
.htm>.

10. Quoted in Tulskiy, "Are Wahhabites Defeating the Moderate Muslims in Russia?"
DUMER is also referred to as the Moscow Muftiyat. In this volume, DUMER and
Moscow Muftiyat will be used interchangeably.

11. Mukhametshin and Dubkov, "Musulmanskie Organizatsii v Rossiiskoi Federatsii."

12. The Saudi ambassador also added that Russia did not fully utilize its quota. "What
Does Hajj Mean for Hijaz?" [in Russian], *Nezavisimaya gazeta*, no. 36(2346) (28
February 2001) <http://religion.ng.ru/printed/islam/2001-02-28/1_hadzh.html>. More
than 80 percent of Russian pilgrims are from Dagestan. See Gaji Magomedov, "What
Is Worse than Wahhabism? Dagestan Might Change the Secular Authority to a Reli-
gious One" [in Russian], *Nezavisimaya gazeta*, no. 143(2453) (7 August 2001)
<http://www.ng.ru/regions/2001-08-07/1_vahhabism.html>.

13. Ministry of Foreign Affairs of the Russian Federation, "RIA NOVOSTI Interview with
Russian Foreign Ministry Official Spokesman Alexander Yakovenko on the Eve of
Russian Visit by Secretary General of the Organization of the Islamic Conference
Abdelouahed Belkeziz on January 27–29," *Daily News Bulletin*, 27 January 2003
<www.mid.ru>.

14. Ivanenko and Shegortsov, "Islam in Russia."

15. See Murray Feshbach, "Russia's Population Meltdown," *Wilson Quarterly* 25, no. 1
(winter 2001): pp. 12–21. Valerii Tishkov, the director of the Institute of Ethnology
and Anthropology of the Russian Academy of Sciences, has a less pessimistic view
and believes that loss of population can be compensated for by in-migration of Russians living outside the Russian Federation. Valerii Tishkov, conversation with Hunter,
Moscow, May 2002.

16. The alarming decrease in the birthrate in Russia was one of the main leitmotifs of
President Putin's Annual State-of-the-Nation Address to the Federal Assembly of the
Russian Federation on 8 July 2000. President Putin noted, "We, the citizens of Russia,
are becoming fewer and fewer year by year. For several years already the size of the
population of our country has been decreasing by an annual average of 750,000. And
if we trust the demographic forecasts, and these forecasts are based on the real work,
real work of people, who are confident in their expertise, and who have devoted their
lives to this end, then in approximately 15 years the number of Russian citizens will
decrease by 22 million people." President Vladimir Putin, Annual State-of-the-Nation
Address to the Federal Assembly of the Russian Federation [in Russian], 8 July 2000
<http://www.kremlin.ru/events/42.html>.

17. According to Yelena Pobedonostseva, a researcher at the Institute of General Genetics,
a population group must have a birthrate of at least 2.2 to avoid extinction. Nabi
Abdullaev, "Moscow's Face Is Getting Darker," *Moscow Times*, 29 January 2003
<http://www.themoscowtimes.com/stories/2003/01/29/002-print.html>.

18. Ibid.

19. According to Usman Usmanov, chairman of the Union of Muslims of Kamchatka,
Muslims of Kamchatka consist of fifteen ethnic groups, including Tatars and Bashkirs
(10,000), Azeris (7,000), local Turkic peoples, and peoples from Central Asia and the
North Caucasus. Interview with Usman Guseinovich Usmanov for the newspaper *As-
salam*, which is issued by the Spiritual Board of Muslims of Dagestan [in Russian],
Assalam, no. 14 (November 2000) <http://assalam.dgu.ru/html14/a14-6.html>.

20. Silantiev, "Kratkii obzor sovremennogo polozheniia nekhristianskikh traditsionnikh religii Rossii."

21. Maksim Yusin, "Skol'ko u nas Musulman?" (How many muslims do we have?), *Izvestia* 16 October 2001 <http://izvestia.ru/community/article7771>.
22. The Mir Arab Medressah is more than 850 years old. The Islamic Institute of Al-Bukhari was established in 1971.
23. Ignatenko, "Choice of Muslims of Russia."
24. See Mukhametshin and Dubkov, "Musulmanskie Organizatsii v Rossiiskoi Federatsii."
25. F.A. Asadullin, *Muslim Spiritual Organizations and Unions of the Russian Federation* [in Russian] (Moscow: Russian Council of Muftis, 1999), p. 28.
26. According to Ignatenko, because a significant number of Muslim organizations do not register with Russian authorities, the number of functioning organizations is likely double the number of those officially registered, raising the number to between 6,000 and 7,000 (Ignatenko, "Choice of Muslims of Russia").
27. This total includes the registered and nonregistered organizations as well as those that were undergoing registration at the time of the survey. Mukhametshin and Dubkov, "Musulmanskie organizatsii v Rossiiskoi Federatsii."
28. For purposes of clarity and simplification, the distribution of Muslim organizations in Table 2.2 is organized according to the seven administrative districts created by President Putin in 2000.
29. R.A. Silantiev, "Etnicheskii aspekt raskola islamskogo soobshchestva Rossii" (The ethnic aspect of the division in the Islamic community of Russia), *Seriia "Issledovaniia po prikladnoi i neotlozhnoi etnologii"* (The series "Studies in applied and urgent ethnology"), no. 149, Institute of Ethnology and Anthropology of the Russian Academy of Sciences, 25 December 2001.
30. Ibid., p. 3.
31. Article 7 of the law defines a religious group as "a voluntary association of citizens formed for the joint profession and dissemination of a faith and pursuing its activity without official registration and the acquisition of the status of legal entity." Article 8 defines a religious organization as a "voluntary association of citizens of the Russian Federation and other persons residing permanently and on a legitimate basis on the territory of the Russian Federation formed for the joint profession and dissemination of a faith and registered as a legal entity." "Russian Federation Federal Law on Freedom of Conscience and Religious Associations" [in Russian], *Rossiiskaya Gazeta*, 9 October 1997, pp. 3–4, trans. Foreign Broadcast Information Service, FBIS-SOV-97-282, 10 October 1997 <http://wnc.fedworld.gov>.
32. Russian Federation Federal Law on Freedom of Conscience and Religious Associations, Articles 16–20.
33. Ibid., Article 9.
34. Evgeny Strelchik, "The Constitutional Court Forgave the 'Jehovists' Their Sins, But Did Not Grant an Indulgence" [in Russian], *Nezavisimaya gazeta*, 8 December 1999, reproduced by Russia Intercessory Prayer Network <http://www.ripnet.org/law/decisionpositive>.
35. For discussion of the controversial provisions of the law, see U.S. Department of State, *2000 Annual Report on International Religious Freedom*, 5 September 2000 <http://www.state.gov/www/global/human_rights/irf/irf_rpt/irf_russia.html>.
36. This amendment, enacted as part of the Putin-sponsored Law on Counteracting Extremist Activity, changed the wording of the 1997 Law on Freedom of Conscience and Religious Associations, which now states, "The activity of a religious association may be terminated, a religious organization may be liquidated, and the activity of a religious association that is not a religious organization [i.e., an unregistered informal religious group] may be prohibited in accordance with the Law on Counteracting Extremist Activity." Andrei Krasnov, "President Signs Law on Struggle with Extremism" [in Russian]. *Kommersant-Daily*, 29 July 2002, trans. in Stetson University, *Russia Religious News* <http://www.stetson.edu>.

37. Dinara Mukhametshina, "Ummah of Russia before Elections" [in Russian], *Nezavisi-maya Gazeta*, no. 4(51) (23 February 2000) <http://religion.ng.ru/islam/2000-02-23/3 _umma.html>.
38. See Ignatenko, "Choice of Muslims of Russia."
39. R.A. Utyabai-Karimi and D.D. Azamatov, "The Central Spiritual Board of Muslims of Russia and the European Countries of CIS" [in Russian], *The Muslim Dictionary of the Bashkir State University* <http://www.bdxc.ru/encikl/c/centr_du.htm>.
40. See A.B. Yunusova and M.G. Valeeva, "The All-Russia Congresses of Muslims" [in Russian], *The Muslim Dictionary of the Bashkir State University* <http://www.bdxc .ru/encikl/s/siezd_mus.htm>.
41. Ibid.
42. Official server of the Central Spiritual Board of Muslims of Russia and the European Countries of the CIS (CSBM) [in Russian] <http://www.muslim-board.narod.ru/>.
43. Ibid.
44. Utyabai-Karimi and Azamatov, "Central Spiritual Board of Muslims of Russia and the European Countries of CIS."
45. Maximov, "Leaders of Muslim Schism: Ravil Gainutdin."
46. The official website of the CSBM: <http://www.muslim-board.narod.ru>.
47. RTR-Vesti.ru, "Tsentralnoe dukhovnoe upravlenie musulman Rossii pomenialo naz-vanie" (Central spiritual board of Muslims of Russia changed its name), 31 March 2003 <http://www.rtr-vesti.ru>; Information agency Rosbalt, "TsDUM Rossii mozhet bit pereimenovan v Islamskoe tsentralnoe dukhovnoe upravlenie musulman Sviatoi Rusi" (CSBM of Russia can be renamed into Islamic central spiritual board of Muslims of Holy Rus), 1 April 2003 <http://www.rosbalt.ru/2003/04/01/91761.html>.
48. Islamic Information Channel IslamInfo.ru, "Administratsia Prezidenta Rossii soglasna s pozitsiei Soveta muftiev Rossii o nevozmozhnosti vzaimodeistvia s t.n. Verkhovnym muftiem TsDUM pokornykh Bogu Sviatoi Rusi, Talgatom Tadzhuddinom" (The administration of the president of Russia agrees with the Russian Council of Muftis on impossibility of interaction with the so-called Supreme Mufti of the central spiritual board of Muslims obedient to God of Holy Rus, Talgat Tadzhuddin), 18 April 2003 <http://www.islaminfo.ru>.
49. RTR-Vesti.ru, "Tsentralnoe dukhovnoe upravlenie musulman Rossii pomenialo naz-vanie"; Information agency Rosbalt, "TsDUM Rossii mozhet bit pereimenovan v Is-lamskoe tsentralnoe dukhovnoe upravlenie musulman Sviatoi Rusi."
50. Ibid.
51. Mukhametshina, "Ummah of Russia before Elections."
52. Ignatenko, "Choice of Muslims of Russia."
53. See Tulskiy, "Are Wahhabites Defeating the Moderate Muslims in Russia?"
54. Official Web site of the RSBM of Permskaya Oblast or Muftiyat of Permskaya Oblast [in Russian] <http://www.raid.ru/customers/mufti/>.
55. Mukhametshin and Dubkov, "Musulmanskie Organizatsii v Rossiiskoi Federatsii."
56. Mukhametshina, "Ummah of Russia before Elections." According to F.M. Mukhamet-shin and A.A. Dubkov, the law on freedom of conscience of the Republic of Tatarstan explicitly stipulates that there can be only one centralized religious entity in the re-public—the Spiritual Board of Muslims of the Republic of Tatarstan. Mukhametshin and Dubkov, "Musulmanskie Organizatsii v Rossiiskoi Federatsii."
57. Silantiyev, "Kratkii Obzor Sovremennogo Polozhenia Nekhristianskikh Traditsionnikh Religii Rossii."
58. Official Web site of the RSBM of Permskaya Oblast.
59. Mukhametshina, "Ummah of Russia before Elections."
60. See Silantiyev, "Kratkii Obzor Sovremennogo Polozhenia Nekhristianskikh Traditsion-nikh Religii Rossii."
61. Ibid.

62. For an unflattering portrait of Mufti Ravil Gainutdin, see Maximov, "Leaders of Muslim Schism: Ravil Gainutdin."
63. See Maximov, "Leaders of Muslim Schism: Ravil Gainutdin."
64. Farid Asadullin, "Ummah and the Center" [in Russian], *Nezavisimaya Gazeta* no. 51 (2113), (22 March 2000) <http://religion.ng.ru/printed/islam/2000-03-22/4_umma .html>.
65. See Mukhametshina, "Ummah of Russia before Elections."
66. Ibid.
67. Asadullin, "Ummah and the Center."
68. Mukhametshina, "Ummah of Russia before Elections," and Tulskiy, "Are Wahhabites Defeating the Moderate Muslims in Russia?"
69. See Mukhametshina, "Ummah of Russia before Elections."
70. Asadullin, "Ummah and the Center."
71. Maximov, "Leaders of Muslim Schism: Ravil Gainutdin."
72. Official Web site of the Russian Council of Muftis (RCM) [in Russian] <http://www .muslim.ru>.
73. Dinara Mukhametshina seems to confirm this official aggregate figure provided by DUMER itself in "Ummah of Russia before Elections."
74. See Mukhametshina, "Ummah of Russia before Elections," and Silantiyev, "Kratkii Obzor Sovremennogo Polozhenia Nekhristianskikh Traditsionnikh Religii Rossii."
75. Official Web site of the RCM.
76. *Halal* refers to food prepared according to Muslim rules of slaughter. Ibid.
77. Ignatenko, "Choice of Muslims of Russia," and Mukhametshina, "Ummah of Russia before Elections."
78. Mikhail Tulskiy observes that most likely, only five of its members can be considered as substantial and well-organized congregations. Tulskiy, "Are Wahhabites Defeating the Moderate Muslims in Russia?"
79. Mukhametshina, "Ummah of Russia before Elections."
80. Ibid.
81. In this case, the word "Kaziyat" denotes the regional association of religious councils.
82. Mukhametshin and Dubkov, "Musulmanskie Organizatsii v Rossiiskoi Federatsii."
83. The chairman and founder of the Association of the Mosques of Russia is Sheikh Ismail Shangareev. He is also the mufti of Orenburg Oblast and, surprisingly, a co-chairman (on the rotating basis) of the RCM. Ibid.
84. Ignatenko, "The Choice of Muslims of Russia."
85. Mukhametshin and Dubkov, "Musulmanskie Organizatsii v Rossiiskoi Federatsii."
86. Independent Islamic Information Channel Islam.ru, "I.Berdieva pozdravili s naznach-eniem na dolzhnost glavy KTsM SK" (I.Berdiev is congratulated with the appointment on the position of the head of CCSBMNC), 13 May 2003 <http://www.islam.ru>.
87. Ilyas Tahirov, "Koordinatsionnii tsentr musulman Severnogo Kavkaza vnov nastupil na grabli" (The coordinating center of Muslims of North Caucasus stepped on a rake again), 15 May 2003 <http://www.pravda.ru>.
88. Independent Islamic Information Channel Islam.ru, "I.Berdieva pozdravili s naznach-eniem na dolzhnost glavy KTsM SK."
89. "The Coordinating Center of Spiritual Boards of Muslims of North Caucasus Is Established" [in Russian], *Agency of Religious Information "Blagovest Info,"* no. 177 (25 February 1999) <http://www.blagovest-media.com/177_2502.html>.
90. See Silantiyev, "Kratkii Obzor Sovremennogo Polozhenia Nekhristianskikh Traditsionnikh Religii Rossii."
91. See Mukhametshin and Dubkov, "Musulmanskie Organizatsii v Rossiiskoi Federatsii."
92. "Dagestan zanimaet pervoe mesto po religioznosti" (Dagestan occupies the first place in terms of religiosity), *Assalam* no. 18 (January 2001) <http://www.assalam.dgu.ru/ html18/assalam.html>.

93. Mukhametshina, "Ummah of Russia before Elections."
94. Maximov, "Leaders of Muslim Schism: Ravil Gainutdin."
95. Ignatenko, "Choice of Muslims of Russia."
96. G. Murklinskaya, "The Clowns in 'Islamic' Masks on the Stages of Russian Politics" [in Russian], Agentstvo Analiticheskoi Informatsii "Kavkaz XXI vek" (The agency of analytical information "Caucasus XXI century"), 22 June 2001 <http://www.kavkaz21ru/2001/06/22/analitik11.htm>.
97. Dmitriy Starostin, "The Sheikh Does Not Want Jihad with the Kremlin" [in Russian], *Vesti*, 6 March 2001 <http://www.vesti.ru/2001/03/06/983896954.html>.
98. See Ivanenko and Shegortsov, "Islam in Russia."
99. Mukhametshin and Dubkov note that the commission uses the aggregate term "Muslim devotional buildings" (*Musulmanskie kul'tovie zdania*) to describe various buildings used for religious purposes by Muslims. Therefore, the figures given here include purpose-built mosques, prayer houses, temporary devotional buildings, and properties rented for religious practices. See Mukhametshin and Dubkov, "Musulmanskie Organizatsii v Rossiiskoi Federatsii."
100. Ibid.
101. President Boris Yeltsin signed Executive Order no. 281, "On the Transfer of the Devotional Buildings and Other Property to the Religious Organizations," on 23 April 1993. The corresponding law of the Russian Federation no. 248 was enacted on 14 March 1995.
102. Mukhametshin and Dubkov, "Musulmanskie Organizatsii v Rossiiskoi Federatsii."
103. Hunter's interview with Maksim Shevchenko, Moscow, 28 May 2002.
104. Mukhametshin and Dubkov, "Musulmanskie Organizatsii v Rossiiskoi Federatsii."
105. Ibid.
106. Ibid.
107. Ibid.
108. Hunter visited the mosque in September 2000.
109. Independent Islamic Information Channel Islam.ru (English mirror site), "The Kshkar mosque—a historical monument—is restored," 19 September 2002 <http://eng.islam.ru/>.
110. The official Web site of the Perm-based fund "Mosque" [in Russian] <http://mechet.perm.ru>.
111. Independent Islamic Information Channel Islam.ru (English mirror site), "The 'Mausilya' mosque is restored in Bashkortostan," 11 May 2002 <http://eng.islam.ru/>.
112. "Murmansk Residents Protest Mosque Restoration," Radio Free Europe/Radio Liberty (RFE/RL) *Russian Federation Report* 2, no. 42 (15 November 2000).
113. Russell Working and Norma Chernyakova, "[Russian] Mosque's Construction Is Met with Hostility," *San Jose Mercury News*, 6 August 2000.
114. Ibid.
115. "Local Community Divided over Mosque Restoration," RFE/RL *Russian Federation Report* 2, no. 42 (15 November 2000).
116. Ibid.
117. Ibid.
118. Related to Hunter in a personal interview in Rostov, June 2000.
119. Independent Islamic Information Channel Islam.ru (English mirror site), "A new mosque to be opened on the Don," 5 December 2002 <http://eng.islam.ru/>.
120. Independent Islamic Information Channel Islam.ru (English mirror site), "Krasnodar authorities are against a mosque in Sochi," 28 May 2003 <http://eng.islam.ru/>.
121. The Muslim community of Petrozavodsk numbers some 6,000 members. Official Web site of the Muslim community of the Republic of Karelia [in Russian] <http://www.murm.ru/islam/activ.html>.
122. Geraldine Fagan, "Russia: Karelian Authorities Alarmed by Growth of Islam," Kes-

ton News Service, 1 May 2001 <http://www.ripnet.org/strategies/religions/rkaabgoi.htm>.

123. "Karelian Officials Concerned about Alleged Muslim Extremists," RFE/RL *Newsline*, 2 May 2001.

124. The Muslim community of Vologda unites some 300 members. "Vlast' Vologdi Protiv . . ." (The authorities of Vologda are against . . .), *Vse ob Islame* ('Everything about Islam'), no. 3 (June 2002); official Web site of the RCM <http://www.muslim.ru/razde.cgi?id=333&rid0=178&rid1=333&rid2>.

125. Quoted in Igor Rotar, "Russia: Mosque Demolition Case to Go to Supreme Court," Keston News Service, 11 May 2001, Russia Intercessory Prayer Network <http://www.ripnet.org/strategies/religions/rmdctgtsc.htm>; "Vologda: Construction of City's First Mosque Draws Protests," RFE/RL *Russian Federation Report* 2, no. 7 (16 February 2000).

126. Ibid.

127. Ibid.

128. "Vlast' Vologdi Protiv . . . ."

129. According to Andrei Ivanov, after meeting Sheikh Gainutdin, President Putin instructed his chief of staff, Alexander Voloshin, "to interfere immediately in this conflict and to communicate to certain government structures the unlawfulness of their actions." Andrei Ivanov, "Vologodskie Musul'mane pishut pis'ma prezidentu" (The Vologda Muslims write letters to the President), *Kommersant-SPb* no. 20 (6 February 2002) <http://spb.kommersant.ru/print.htm?year=2002&issue=020&id=10088&section=45>.

130. "A Mosque on the Motorway Is to Be Opened in Russia for the First Time," Independent Islamic Information Channel Islam.ru, 20 September 2002 <http://eng.islam.ru/press/rus/2002-09-20/?single=314>.

131. "V moskovskom aeroportu 'Domodedovo' otkrilas' mechet' " (The mosque opened at Moscow Domodedovo airport), Islam.ru, 25 December 2002 <http://www.islam.ru/press/rus/2002-12-25/?single=1701>.

132. *Islam and Muslims in Russia* (Moscow: Russian Council of Muftis, Moscow Islamic University [in Russian] (College), 1999), p. 176.

133. According to some sources, Saitakov was born in Uzbekistan and moved to Tatarstan in 1996. Dmitriy Mikhailin, "Wahhabism Is Not Just an Evil, It Is a Deadly Evil" [in Russian], *Rossiiskaya Gazeta*, 28 September 1999 <http://www.rg.ru/anons/arc_1999/0928/2.htm>.

134. Elmira Yakovleva, "Dennis Saitakov Is No Longer Alive" [in Russian], *Vechernie Chelny* no. 52(216) (13 December 2000) <http://vechorka.chelny.ru/view.php3?viewyear=2000&viewart=5>.

135. "Medressah Yolduz Is Closed Because of the Accusations of Wahhabi Indoctrination" [in Russian], Islam.ru, 24 February 2001 <http://www.islam.ru/php/print.php?id=100&cat=mod&action=printable>.

136. Hunter's discussions with officials at the Muhammadiyya Higher Muslim Medressah, September 2000.

137. The Spiritual Board of Muslims (SBM) of Tatarstan has established guidelines for the duration of religious education in the republic. The Russian Islamic University offers the following: bachelor's degree, four years; master's degree, six years; the equivalent of the doctoral degree (*aspirantura*), eight years. Official Web site of the Spiritual Board of Muslims of the Republic of Tatarstan [in Russian] <http://www.e-islam.ru/education>.

138. This institution existed in Naberezhnie Chelny during Hunter's visit in September 2000. However, the official Web site of the Tatarstan SBM does not include it in its list of the republic's religious schools.

139. Asadullin, *Muslim Spiritual Organizations and Unions of the Russian Federation*, pp. 87–103.

140. Independent Islamic Information Channel Islam.ru (English mirror site), "The Nizhny Novgorod Madrassah Medina' announced the enlistment of students," 10 April 2003 <http://eng.islam.ru/>.

141. "Religioznoe Obrazovanie v Dagestane (Statistika)" (The religious education in Dagestan [statistics]), *Novoe Delo*, no. 49 (12 July 2001) <http://www.ndelo.ru/4901/religija.html>.

142. "Dagestan zanimaet pervoe mesto po religioznosti."

143. Independent Islamic Information Channel Islam.ru (English mirror site), "A females department is opened in the Northern Caucasus Islamic University," 30 September 2002 <http://eng.islam.ru/>.

144. Asadullin, *Muslim Spiritual Organizations and Unions of the Russian Federation*, p. 44.

145. Ibid., p. 45.

146. Independent Islamic Information Channel Islam.ru, "V Astrakhani ozhidaetsia pervii za 100 let vipusk imamov" (The first graduation of imams in 100 years is expected in Astrakhan), 16 May 2003 <http://www.islam.ru>; Information Agency Integrum Techno, VolgaInform, "Astrakhanskaya oblast. Gubernator pozdravil musulman s prazdnikom Kurban-bairam" (Astrakhan oblast. The governor congratulated Muslims with the holiday of Kurban-bairam), 11 February 2003; <http://www.integrum.ru/webpush/regions/w0067496.htm>.

147. "SBM of Dagestan Does Not Recommend Muslims to Study Abroad without Receiving Education at Islamic Universities in Dagestan" [in Russian], Islam.ru, 9 July 2001 <http://www.islam.ru/pressclub/pressclub.htm?id=825&cat=rus>.

148. "The Russian Talibs" [in Russian], Islam.ru, 5 January 2002 <http://www.islam.ru/epressclub/modern.htm?id=2455&cat=emod>.

149. Ibid.

150. Ibid.

151. See Sergei Gradirovsky, "Russkiy Islam kak yavlenie i kak predmet issledovaniya" (Russian Islam as a phenomenon and as a subject of study), Information Portal "Religiya i SMI" (Religion and media), 27 May 2003 <http://www.religare.ru/>.

152. See Kirill Frolov, "Totalnyi Khasavyurt" (Total Khasavyurt), Network of Russian Political Experts, 19 November 2002 <http://www.kreml.org/experts/1037698896>. In the name of the article the author refers to the Dagestani village of Khasavyurt, where the then Russian Security Council secretary Alexander Lebed and the Chechen army chief of staff Alsan Maskhadov signed the ceasefire agreement ending the first Chechen war (1994–1996). According to Frolov, the "single system of Muslim education in Russia" does not mean the legal realization of Muslims' educational rights in a regional framework but a factual Islamization of Russia; Andrei Nikolaevich Savelyev (writing under nom de plume A. Kolyev), "Islamizatsiya Rossii: 'Russkiy Islam' zaduvaet s Povolzhya" (Islamization of Russia: 'Russian Islam' blows winds from Povolzhye), Author's website, 15 May 2002 <www.kolev3.narod.ru/news/islam3.htm>.

153. On Muslim concerns regarding the project, see the letter of Mufti Farid Salman, the deputy chairman of the Central Spiritual Board of Muslims of Russia (CSBM) for public relations to the Director of the Federal Security Service of the Russian Federation, N.P. Patrushev dated 27 February 2003, posted on the website "Gosudarstvo i Religiya v Rossii" (State and religion in Russia) on 4 March 2003 <http://www.state-religion.ru/cgi/run.cgi?action-show&obj-1690>.

154. Nikolai Konstantinov, "Operedit' drug druga v dobrikh delakh" (Competing with each other in good deeds), *Nezavisimaya Gazeta*, 19 June 2002 <http://religion.ng.ru/printed/facts/2002-06-19/1_gaynutdin.html>.

155. "Tirazh gazeti 'Muslima' dostig 5 tisiach" (The circulation of the newspaper "Muslima" reached 5 thousand), Islam.ru, 29 January 2003 <http://www.islam.ru/press/rus/2003-01-29/?single=1829>.

156. Asadullin, *Muslim Spiritual Organizations and Unions of the Russian Federation*, pp. 104–116.
157. "V Severnoi Osetii teper' vikhodit gazeta o zhizni musul'man" (Newspaper about the life of Muslims is published now in North Ossetia), Islam.ru, 20 December 2002 <http://www.islam.ru/press/rus/2002-12-20/?single=1669>.
158. "New Muslim Paper Is Published in Kazan," RFE/RL *Tatar-Bashkir Report*, 5 August 2002 <http://www.rferl.org/bd/tb/reports/archives/2002/08/0-050802.html>.
159. Pravda.ru, "Pravovernie sozdali Soyuz musulmanskikh zhurnalistov" (The faithful created the Union of Muslim journalists), 23 May 2003 <http://society.pravda.ru/society/2003/8/26/321/10711_soyuz.html>; Islamic Information Portal IslamInfo.ru, "Vpervie v istorii Rossii Soyuz musulmanskikh zhurnalistov"(For the first time in the history of Russia the Union of Muslim journalists is created), the official release by the press-service of the Russian Council of Muftis, 22 May 2003 <http://www.islaminfo.ru/news/?id=1155>.
160. Ibid
161. Ibid
162. On the Chechen press during the period between the two Chechen wars (August 1996–September 1999), see Timur Muzaev, "Chechen Crisis '99: The Press" [in Russian], Political News Channel Polit.ru, 10 June 1999 <http://polit.ru/documents/113389.html>.
163. Ibid.
164. Yuri Akboshev, "Scare-Mongering Film Causes Outrage," Institute for War and Peace Reporting (IWPR) *Caucasus Reporting Service*, no. 55 (27 October 2000) <http://www.iwpr.net/index.pl?archive/cau/cau2000105504eng.txt>.
165. Zarina Kanukova, "Adygea Hits Back: Ethnic Leaders in Adygea Say They Are Being Demonized by the Russian Media," IWPR *Caucasus Reporting Service*, no. 57 (10 November 2000) <http://www.iwpr.net/index.pl?archive/cau/cau_200011_57_01_eng.txt>.
166. Marat Murtazin, "Muslims and Russia: War or Peace?" *Central Asia and the Caucasus* (Center for Social and Political Studies, Luleå, Sweden), no. 1 (2000) <http://www.ca-c.org/journal/eng01_2000/17.murtazin.shtml>.
167. Asadullin, *Muslim Spiritual Organizations and Unions of the Russian Federation*, p. 60.
168. See chapter 5 for details.
169. Imam Abu Hanifa admonishes Muslims to be patient (*sabr*) in the face of adversity rather than revolt. Brannon M. Wheeler, *Applying the Canon in Islam: The Authorization and Maintenance of Interpretive Reasoning in Hanafi Scholarship* (Albany: State University of New York Press, 1996).
170. Based on Hunter's conversations on Islam with Bakhtiar Babadjanov, the Uzbek expert on Islam, Bishkek, Kyrgyzstan, August 1999.
171. See V.V. Chernous, "Islam v etnokonfessionalnoi situatsii na Severnom Kavkaze" (Islam in the ethno-confessional situation in North Caucasus); I.P. Dobaev, "Traditsionalizm i radikalizm v sovremennom islame na Severnom Kavkaze" (Traditionalism and radicalism in contemporary Islam in the North Caucasus); and K.M.Khanbabaev, "Sufizm v Dagestane" (Sufism in Dagestan); all in *Yuzhnorossiiskoe Obozrenie* (South Russia Survey), no. 1, 2001, issued by Institute for Retraining and Improving Qualifications of Instructors in Humanitarian and Social Sciences at the Rostov State University, <http://ippk.ru/htmldocs/csrip/elibrary/uro/vl/vol%201_main.html>.
172. Based on Hunter's conversations with Farid Asadullin, September 2000 and May 2002.
173. See Tulskiy, "Are Wahhabites Defeating the Moderate Muslims in Russia?"
174. Ibid. In November 1999, the agents of the Russian Federal Security Service (Federalnaya Sluzhba Bezopasnosty, FSB) broke into Ashirov's apartment under the pretext

of searching for weapons and explosives. Aleksei Bichurin, "Strannie Aktsii s Ney-asnimi Posledstviami" (Strange actions with unclear consequences), *Nezavisimaya Gazeta*, 22 December 1999 <http://religion.ng.ru/facts/1999-12-22/2_actions.html>. Ashirov recounted this incident in the summer of 2000 to Hunter.

175. Alexandre Bennigsen and S. Enders Wimbush, *Mystics and Commissars: Sufism in the Soviet Union* (Berkeley: University of California Press, 1985).

176. For an example of the alarmist view on the growing influence of Sufi sheikhs on Dagestani politics, see Magomedov, "What Is Worse than Wahhabism?"

177. Based on Hunter's interviews.

178. Interview with Geidar Jemal in M. Bagirov, "The Russian Islamic Committee Proposes the Ideology of Russia's Rebirth" [in Russian], *Aina*, 9 July 1999, National News Service (electronic archive of Russian articles) <http://www.nns.ru/press-file/dagestan/jemal_int1.html>.

179. The Jihadists do not believe that holy war is only justified in self-defense. Rather, they see it as a major instrument for change. According to the Jihadists, jihad can be conducted against domestic and foreign enemies.

180. Johannes J.G Jansen, *The Neglected Duty: The Creed of Sadat's Assassins and Islamic Resurgence in the Middle East* (New York: Macmillan, 1986).

181. For details, see chapter 9.

182. "Chechen Warlord Warns of Attacks on Russia," Reuters, *New York Times*, 23 November 2002; Michael Wines, "Suicide Bombers Kill at Least 46 at Chechen Government Offices," *New York Times*, 28 December 2002, p. A1.

183. Yuri Bagrov, "Truck explodes near government compound, killing at least 41 in northern Chechnya," Associated Press, 12 May 2003 <http://lexis-nexis.com>.

184. "Suicide bomb attack kills 8, injures 12 in Ilaskhan-Yurt," ITAR-TASS, 14 May 2003 <http://lexis-nexis.com>.

185. Susan B. Glasser, "Attack Kills at Least 17 Near Chechnya," *Washington Post*, 6 June 2003, p. A20.

186. Susan B. Glasser, "16 Die in Explosions At Russian Concert," *Washington Post*, 6 July 2003, p. A01.

187. "Chechen Blast Death Toll Rises To 80—Russian TV" [in Russian], Channel One TV, 30 December 2002, trans. *BBC Monitoring*, 30 December 2002 <http://lexis-nexis .com>; "Putin alleges Saudi, Chechen suicide attacks linked," Agence France Presse, 13 May 2003 <http://lexis-nexis.com>.

188. Susan B. Glasser, "Attack Kills at Least 17 Near Chechnya"; Susan B. Glasser, "16 Die in Explosions At Russian Concert."

189. The group of Chechen rebels who organized the hostage-taking operation in Moscow's Dubrovka Theater was a part of the Reconnaissance and Sabotage Battalion "Riyadh as-Salihin" (The Gardens of the Righteous), according to Shamil Basaev, who later praised the group's actions in a public statement released in November 2002; "Chechen Warlord Warns of Attacks on Russia," Reuters, 23 November 2002.

190. In a separate statement Shamil Basaev claimed responsibility for the two suicide attacks that occurred in May 2003. "Chechen warlord Basayev claims for last week's suicide blasts," Agence France Presse, 19 May 2003 <http://lexiis-nexis.com>.

191. "Radical Chechen warlord has trained over 30 female suicide bombers: official," Agence France Presse, 15 May 2003 <http://lexis-nexis.com>.

192. Murtazin, "Muslims and Russia: War or Peace?"

193. Anatoly Savateev, "The Sources of Fundamentalism are in Poverty" [in Russian], *Nezavisimaya Gazeta*, no. 144(2454) (8 August 2001) <http://religion.ng.ru/printed/islam/2001-08-08/6_efflux.html>.

194. Ibid.

195. U.S. Committee for Refugees, *2002 Country Report: Russian Federation* <http://www.refugees.org/world/countryrpt/europe/russian_federation.htm>.
196. Savateev, "Sources of Fundamentalism Are in Poverty."
197. Ibid.
198. See Alexei Malashenko, "Islam in Russia: Notes of a Political Scientist," *Russian Social Science Review* 41, no. 6 (November–December 2000): pp. 58–59.
199. Ravil Gainutdin, quoted in Konstantinov, "Operedit' drug druga v dobrikh delakh."
200. Maskhadov's address was aired on Chechen television on 15 July 1998. *Al Qaf* [in Russian], October 1998, Chechnya.ru <http://www.chechnya.ru:8080/query.asp?page=8&archive=12/8/2000&lang=r&part=library&id_news=232>.
201. Ibid. Maskhadov referred to the armed clashes between the forces of National Guards on one side and the Islamic Battalion and Shari'a Guards on the other. This incident took place on 13–15 July 1998 in Gudermes, the second-largest city of Chechnya. In April 2002, Khattab was killed by a poisoned letter that was given to him by a trusted aide who apparently had been recruited by Russia's Federal Security Service (FSB). See "Obituary: Chechen Rebel Khattab," BBC News, 26 April 2002 <http://news.bbc.co.uk/1/hi/world/europe/1952053.stm>.
202. D.V. Makarov, *Ofitsialni i neofitsialni Islam v Dagestane* (Official and unofficial Islam in Dagestan) (Moscow: Institute of Oriental Studies of Russian Academy of Sciences and International Center for Strategic and Political Studies, 2000) Makarov's book is also available in several parts on-line <http://www.ansar.ru/arhives/arch/left09.06.html>. As of October 2002, in accordance with Aslan Maskhadov's order, Shamil Basaev assumed responsibility for coordinating all military operations of the Chechen resistance forces. Amina Azimova, "Aslan Maskhadov Personally Discredited the Rumors about His Death in a Televised Address" [in Russian], Radio Svoboda RFE/RL Russian Service, 19 September 2002 at <http://www.svoboda.org/ll/caucasus/0902/ll.091902-1.asp>.
203. It is likely that the name of this group is derived from the title of the book *Riyadh as-Salihin* (Gardens of the righteous) written by a renowned Shafei scholar, Imam Muhyiaddin Abu Zakariyya' Yahya bin Sharaf an-Nawawi (1233–1278).
204. "Chechen Warlord Basaev's Statement on Moscow Siege," [in Russian], Kavkaz-Tsentr news agency, 1 November 2002, trans. in *BBC Monitoring; Johnson's Russia List*, no. 6528 (2 November 2002) <http://www.cdi.org/russia/johnson/6528-3.cfm>.
205. Makarov, *Ofitsialni i neofitsialni Islam v Dagestane* <http://www.ansar.ru/arhives/arch/left09.06.html>.
206. Ibid.; and D.V. Makarov, "Radical Islamism in the North Caucasus: Dagestan and Chechnya" [in Russian], *Bulletin Conflict-Dialogue-Cooperation*, International Center for Strategic and Political Studies (Moscow), no. 1 (September–November 1999) <http://icsps-project.arcon.ru/buleten1/4.htm>.
207. "Dagestan's Wahhabis Plan to Create 'Separate Islamic Territory,' " Interfax *Daily News Bulletin* (Moscow), 16 August 1998; and "Dagestani Government Placates Two Local Muslim Villages," Interfax *Daily News Bulletin* (Moscow), 6 August 1998.
208. "A Turning Point in Dagestan," RFE/RL *Caucasus Report*, 8 September 1998.
209. Makarov, "Official and Unofficial Islam in Dagestan."
210. Ibid.
211. Ibid.
212. "There Is No 'Chechen Connection' in the Explosion at the Manezhnaya Square" [in Russian], Lenta.ru, 3 September 1999 <http://www.lenta.ru/russia/1999sh09/03/dagestan/hasbulat.htm_Printed.htm>.
213. See Makarov, "Official and Unofficial Islam in Dagestan."
214. On 28 December 2001, the Dagestani Supreme Court sentenced Salman Raduev to life imprisonment for organizing the attack and for taking hostages in the city of Kizlyar,

Dagestan, in January 1996. See "Chechen Field Commander Sentenced to Life Imprisonment," RFE/RL *Newsline*, 28 December 2001.

215. "Muslim Extremists Suspected in Vladikavkaz Blast," Jamestown Foundation *Monitor*, vol. 5, no. 58 (24 March 1999).

216. Anna Matveeva, *The North Caucasus: Russia's Fragile Borderland* (London: Royal Institute of International Affairs, 1999), p. 37.

217. "Islamic Groups Active in Adygeya," East-West Institute *Russian Regional Report* 6, no. 37 (24 October 2001).

218. Dmitri Nepomnyashy, "Coup Rumors Rattle North Caucasus," IWPR *Caucasus Report Service*, no. 96 (31 August 2001) <http://www.iwpr.net/index.pl?archive/cau/cau_200108_96_2_eng.txt>.

219. On the Tatar reform movement and its various stages, see Azade-Ayse Rorlich, *The Volga Tatars: A Profile in National Resilience* (Stanford, CA: Hoover Institution Press, 1986), pp. 48–83.

220. On motivations and other dynamics of Jadidism, see Adeeb Khalid, *The Politics of Muslim Cultural Reform: Jadidism in Central Asia* (Berkeley: University of California Press, 1998).

221. Rafael Khakimov, "Euro-Islam in a Dialogue between Civilizations," Tatar.ru, the official Web site of the government of the Republic of Tatarstan <www.tatar.ru/hakimov/euroislam_e.doc>.

222. Ibid.

223. Rafael Khakimov, "Russia and Tatarstan at a Crossroad of History," *Anthropology and Archeology of Eurasia* 37, no. 1 (Summer 1998): p. 70.

224. Ibid.

225. Rafael Khakimov, "Gde nasha Mekka? (Manifest Evro-Islama)" (Where is our Mecca? [Manifesto of Euro-Islam]), working paper given to Hunter by the author, February 2003.

226. Ibid.

227. Ibid.

228. Ibid.

229. Khakimov, "Euro-Islam in a Dialogue between Civilizations."

230. The document "Osnovnie Polozhenia Sotsial'noi Programmi Rossiiskikh Musul'man" (The fundamental principles of the social program of Russian Muslims) was developed by the rector of Moscow Islamic University, Marat Murtazin, the chairman of the RCM, Mufti Ravil Gainutdin, and Viyacheslav Ali Polosin, Ph.D., and was presented on 25 May 2001 at the DUMER headquarters in Moscow. It is divided into eight parts: "Foundations of Religious Teaching of Islam," "The Rights and Freedoms of People," "Islam and Social Problems," "Science, Culture, Education," "Islam and Nations," "The Attitude of Muslims toward the Representatives of Other Religions," "Muslims and the State," and "Muslims in the Russian State." "Muslims Adopted Social Program" [in Russian], *Nezavisimaya Gazeta*, no. 95(2405) (30 May 2001) <http://religion.ng.ru/style/2001-05-30/10-2.html>; and "Russian Muslims Now Have Their Own Social Program" [in Russian], Islam.ru, 25 May 2001 <http://www.islam.ru/pressclub/pressclub.htm?id=512&time+989006400>.

231. "Osnovnie Polozhenia Sotsial'noi Programmi Rossiiskikh Musul'man" (The fundamental principles of the social program of Russian Muslims, MSP), Introduction, official Web site of the RCM <http://www.muslim.ru/razde.cgi?id=219&rid0=156&rid1=219&rid2>.

232. MSP, Introduction.

233. MSP, Section 1, Subsection 1.5, "The Traditional Russian Muslim Movements and Schools of Islam."

234. Ibid.

235. Ibid.

236. MSP, Section 6, Subsection 6.2, "The Attitude toward Pseudo-Muslim Extremist Organizations."
237. Ibid.
238. Ibid. Wahhabism and other radical forms of Islam are characterized by the following three features: (1) rejection of basic traditions of Islam, including four historically developed *mazhabs* and Shiism; (2) the idea of exclusive righteousness that enables adherents to declare others "non-Muslims," including Muslims who disagree with such interpretation; and (3) arbitrary infringement of others' rights, including killing "infidels" and Muslims who do not share this viewpoint.
239. MSP, Section 7, Subsection 7.1, "The Role of an Accord in Islam."
240. Ibid.
241. Ibid.
242. Ibid.
243. Ibid.
244. Ibid.
245. Ibid.
246. MSP, Section 7, Subsection 7.2, "The Attitude toward Authority and Law."
247. Ibid.
248. Ibid.
249. MSP, Section 7, Subsection 7.3, "The Attitude toward the Problems of War and Peace: The Concept of 'Jihad.' "
250. Ibid.
251. Ibid.
252. MSP, Section 8, Subsection 8.1, "The Formation of the Unified Russian *Ummah.*"
253. Ibid.
254. Ibid.
255. MSP, Section 8, Subsection 8.2, "The Muslims and Legal Relations in Russia."
256. MSP, Section 8, Subsection 8.3, "The Attitude toward Army and Law-Enforcement Agencies."
257. MSP, Section 8, Subsection 8.4, "The International Connections of Russian Muslims."
258. Ibid.
259. MSP, Section 8, Subsection 8.5, "The Russian Council of Muftis."
260. Ibid.
261. V.I. Bushkov and S.P. Polyakov, *Sotsialno-ekonomicheskaya situatsia v Severo-Kavkazskom regione* (Socioeconomic situation in the North Caucasus region), Issledovania po prikladnoi i neotlozhnoi etnologii (Studies in applied and urgent ethnology), no. 108 (Moscow: Institute of Ethnology and Archeology of Russian Academy of Sciences, 1997) <http://www.iea.ras.ru/lib/neotl/07112002061822.htm>.
262. Ibid.
263. See I.G. Kosikov and L.G. Kosikova, *Severny Kavkaz: Sotsial'no-Ekonomicheskii Spravochnik* (The Northern Caucasus: a socioeconomic guide) (Moscow: Mikron-Print, 1999), pp. 35–36.
264. Ibid., p. 36.
265. Ibid., p. 35.
266. See *Sotsial'no-Ekonomicheskoe Polozhenie Rossii 2001 god* (Socioeconomic situation in Russia in 2001) (Moscow: State Committee of Russian Federation on Statistics [Goskomstat], 2001), p. 396.
267. See *Informatsionni Biulleten Ministerstva Truda i Sotsial'nogo Razvitia Rossii* (Information Bulletin of the Ministry of Labor and Social Development of the Russian Federation) no. 6 (2–9 December 1999), Ak&M Analytical Information Agency <http://www.akm.ru/rus/gosinfo/mintrud/mintrud.htm>.
268. Ibid.

269. *North Caucasus: Islam in Politics or Politics in Islam?* [in Russian] (Moscow: Carnegie Center, 23 August 1999) <http://www.carnegie.ru/russian/Pr/1999/pr99-0823.htm>.
270. See Kosikov and Kosikova, *Severny Kavkaz: Sotsial'no-Ekonomicheskii Spravochnik*, p. 37.
271. Ibid.
272. See "Employment in the North Caucasus Acquires State Importance, Says Russian Minister of Labor and Social Development" [in Russian], *RIA Novosti*, 19 November 1999, <http://www.lexis-nexis.com>.
273. See *Informatsionni Biulleten Ministerstva Truda i Sotsial'nogo Razvitia Rossii*.
274. See Polina Sanaeva, "Sotsialnaya Sfera Vosstanavlivaetsia s Nulia" (The social sphere is being rebuilt from nothing), *Nezavisimaya Gazeta* no. 215(2031) (17 November 1999) <http://www.ng.ru/events/1999-11-17/2_area.html>.
275. "The Tatars in Mordovia," *Tatar Gazette* <http://www.peoples.org.ru/tatar/eng_tatary.html>.
276. From Sergei Kirienko's speech addressing the participants of the roundtable "The Islamic Factor in Russian Politics." See Aleksei Lampsi, "A Step toward Unity of Muslims of Russia" [in Russian], *Nezavisimaya Gazeta*, no. 124(2434) (11 July 2001) <http://religion.ng.ru/facts/2001-07-11/1_muftij.html>.
277. The *2000 Annual Report on International Religious Freedom,* issued by the U.S. Department of State, notes that "in Russian context, 'Wahhabism,' the name of a strict branch of Sunni Islam that originated in Saudi Arabia, has become a pejorative term because of persistent allegations that 'Wahhabi extremism' is to blame for terrorist attacks linked to Chechnya." U.S. Department of State, *2000 Annual Report on International Religious Freedom*, 5 September 2000 <http://www.state.gov/www/global/human_rights/irf/irf_rpt/irf_russia.html>.
278. Maximov, "Leaders of Muslim Schism: Ravil Gainutdin."
279. Tulskiy, "Are Wahhabites Defeating the Moderate Muslims in Russia?" and Maximov, "Leaders of Muslim Schism: Ravil Gainutdin."
280. Starostin, "Sheikh Does Not Want Jihad with the Kremlin."
281. "The Chasm among Muslims of Russia" [in Russian], *Nezavisimaya Gazeta*, no. 220(2036) (24 November 1999) <http://religion.ng.ru/facts/1999-11-24/1_vesti.html>.
282. For more information on this event, see Andrei Kovalev and Sergei Mikhailov, "The Islamic Scandal in the Synagogue" [in Russian], *Nezavisimaya Gazeta*, no. 66(2128) (12 April 2000) <http://religion.ng.ru/facts/2000-04-12/2_scandal.html>.
283. See Mikhail Tulskiy, "The Leaders of Muslim Schism: Talgat Tadzhuddin" [in Russian], *Nezavisimaya Gazeta*, no. 12(75) (28 June 2001) <http://faces.ng.ru/dossier/2001-06-28/4_split_2.html>.
284. Interview with Mufti Ravil Gainutdin, "On Necessity of Precise Definitions" [in Russian], *Nezavisimaya Gazeta*, no. 226(2288) (29 November 2000) <http://religion.ng.ru/islam/2000-11-29/4_vahhab.html>.
285. Ibid.
286. Mikhail Tulskiy, "Another Schism in Russia: This time It's Islamic" [in Russian], *Russian Journal*, 4 July 2001 <http://www.russ.ru/politics/20010704-tul-pr.html> and Tulskiy, "Are Wahhabites Defeating the Moderate Muslims in Russia?"
287. Tulskiy, "Are Wahhabites Defeating the Moderate Muslims in Russia?"
288. Interview with Mufti Talgat Tadzhuddin, "On Importance of Struggle against Extremism" [in Russian], *Nezavisimaya Gazeta* no. 226(2288) (29 November 2000) <http://religion.ng.ru/printed/islam/2000-11-29/4_islam.html>.
289. Vasilii Mikhailov, "The OSCE Announces Jihad to Russia" [in Russian], *Kommersant Daily* 18 November 1999, National News Service (electronic archive of Russian articles) <http://www.nns.ru/press-file/dagestan/expert/dag306.html>.
290. Quoted in Starostin, "Sheikh Does Not Want Jihad with the Kremlin."

291. Ibid.
292. Interview with Mufti Ravil Gainutdin, "On Necessity of Precise Definitions."
293. Geraldine Fagan and Lawrence Uzzell, "Church-State Relations in Putin's Russia: What's Next?" Keston Institute, 13 April 2000, Orthodox Christian News Service <http://www.orthodoxnews.com/doodad.fcgi?tcode=98&story=KES4242000135853 .shtml>.
294. Interview with Mufti Ravil Gainutdin, "On Necessity of Precise Definitions."
295. Ibid.
296. "The Chairman of Council of Muftis of Russia on the Problem of Prohibition of Wahhabism" [in Russian], Islam.ru, 27 July 2001 <http://www.islam.ru/php/print.php ?id=934&cat=&action=printable>. Ravil Gainutdin and Ahmad Kadyrov were classmates at the Medressah Mir Arab.
297. Starostin, "Sheikh Does Not Want Jihad with the Kremlin."
298. Ignatenko, "Choice of Muslims of Russia."
299. Vera Postnova, "Yet Another Assault: The Muslims of Tatarstan Cannot Divide the Mosque of Bulgari" [in Russian], Nezavisimaya Gazeta no. 188(2498) (9 October 2001) <http://www.ng.ru/printed/regions/2001-10-09/6-attack.html>.
300. In an interview with Nezavisimaya Gazeta, Tadzhuddin bitterly complained about the loss of the mosque of Bulgar to the Tatar SBM. Nikolai Konstantinov, "Eshche raz o nabolevshem" (Once again regarding the familiar problems), Nezavisimaya Gazeta no. 5(100) (17 July 2002) <http://religion.ng.ru/facts/2002-07-17/1_tadjuddin.html>.
301. See Mufti Magomedgali Khuzin's autobiography at the official Web site of the Perm-based fund "Mosque" [in Russian] <http://mechet.perm.ru/Hyzin.htm>. Magomedgali Khuzin became the chairman of the Regional Spiritual Board of Muslims of Permsk Oblast and received the religious title of Mufti by the order of Supreme mufti Talgat Tadzhuddin on 15 December 1997. Officially he assumed his responsibilities on 26 December 1997. He is an active participant in Russia's Inter-Religious Council.
302. "The Conflict among Muslims of Perm" [in Russian], Russian Line/Radonezh (the newsline of the Moscow Patriarchate/Orthodox Christian Botherhood), 5 September 1999 <http://www.radrad.ru/nw/arh/ar4/n55.htm>.
303. Ibid.
304. See Nikolai Ivanov, "The Schism among Muslims of Perm. No End Is in Sight for Conflict in Islamic Community of Western Ural" [in Russian], Nezavisimaya Gazeta, no. 6(2316) (17 January 2001) <http://religion.ng.ru/printed/facts/2001-01-17/2 _raskol.html>.
305. See the interview with Khuzin at the official server of the CSBM [in Russian] <http://muslim-board.narod.ru/interview-khusin.htm>.
306. Nikolai Ivanov maintains that in legal terms the Perm city mosque is a municipal property. Therefore, in order to register the congregation of the mosque, it is necessary to receive permission from the mayor's office. So far, the city authorities have refused to give such permission to either the representatives of DUMER or Mufti Khuzin and his followers. This approach of the municipal bureaucrats may be because of reluctance to take sides in the ongoing dispute between the two rival Muslim establishments. Ivanov, "Schism among Muslims of Perm."
307. Vadim Biserov, "The Employees of Muftiyat Seal the Mosque: Perm Has Ceased to Be the Oasis of Confessional Tranquility" [in Russian], Nezavisimaya Gazeta, no. 54(2364) (28 March 2001) <http://religion.ng.ru/printed/islam/2001-03-28/5_mosque .html>.
308. Dadan Upadhyay, "Russia's Muslim Head Supports Putin on Chechen Campaign," Indian Express, 17 March 2000 <http://www.indian-express.com/ie/daily/20000317// iin17024.html>.
309. "The End of Ramadan in Moscow" [in Russian], Nezavisimaya Gazeta, no. 3(2313), (12 January 2001) <http://religion.ng.ru/printed/facts/2000-01-12/1_vesti.html>.

310. Aislu Yunusova, "Islam Between the Volga River and the Ural Mountains," in *Political Islam and Conflicts in Russia and Central Asia*, ed. Lena Jonson and Murad Esenov (Luleå, Sweden: Central Asia and the Caucasus Information and Analytical Center, 1999).

311. Asadullin, "Ummah and the Center." Also based on Hunter's conversations with Asadullin.

312. See Maximov, "Leaders of Muslim Schism: Ravil Gainutdin."

313. Ibid.

314. Among the officials and dignitaries attending the opening ceremony of the new mosque were the plenipotentiary representative of the president in Volga Federal Okrug, Sergei Kirienko; the mayor of Nizhny Novgorod, Yuri Lebedev; the governor of Nizhny Novgorod Oblast, Ivan Skliarov; Mufti Talgat Tadzhuddin, the mufti of Nizhny Novgorod, Umar Idrisov; and the mufti of Tatarstan, Gusman Iskhakov. It is noteworthy that Mufti Gainutdin, as well as his ally Mufti Nafigulla Ashirov, were absent from this ceremony, even though administratively Nizhny Novgorod falls under the jurisdiction of DUMER. See "New Mosque for Regional Capital," RFE/RL *Russian Federation Report*, vol. 1, no. 15 (9 June 1999) <http://www.rferl.org/russianreport/1999/06/15-090699.html>.

315. Aleksei Lampsi, "A Step toward Unity of Muslims of Russia" [in Russian], *Nezavisimaya Gazeta*, no. 124(2434) (11 July 2001) <http://religion.ng.ru/facts/2001-07-11/1_muftij.html>.

316. Ibid.

317. "Idei pan-Turkizma Zhivi" (The ideas of pan-Turkism Are alive) *Severny Kavkaz*, no. 5(511) (February 2001), p. 5.

318. Kovalev and Mikhailov, "Islamic Scandal in the Synagogue." The Council of Interactions with Religious Organizations is the government structure responsible for communicating and coordinating the official policy on religion, religious practices, and religious organizations in the Russian Federation. This is done mostly through the Inter-Religious Council of Russia.

319. "Tadzhuddin Is Elected into the Central Council of Eurasia" [in Russian], Islam.ru, 24 April 2001 <http://www.islam.ru/php/print.php?id=374&cat=&action=printable>.

320. Vitaliy Khliupin, "Islam in Russia: In the Vise Grip of Politics and Politicking" [in Russian], *Kazakh Internet Magazine "Continent,"* no. 8(21) (19 April–2 May 2000) <http://www.continent.kz/2000/08/15.html>.

321. Aleksei Krymin and Georgi Engelgardt, "The Influence of September 11 on Russia's Islam" [Russian] Scientific Research Institute of Social Systems of the M.V. Lomonosov Moscow State University <http://www.niiss.ru/nb/News/krym_engel.htm>.

322. Ibid.

323. For more on this meeting, see ibid.

324. Based on interview with Hunter on 28 May 2002. Maksim Shevchenko was the chief editor of *NG Religii*, which is a printed supplement to the newspaper *Nezavisimaya Gazeta* that focuses on religion.

325. Leaders present at this meeting included five from the North Caucasus, three from the RCM (Muftis Ravil Gainutdin, Mukaddas Bibarsov, and Gusman Iskhakov), and three from the CSBM (including Mufti Talgat Tadzhuddin). See Krymin and Engelgardt, "The Influence of September 11 on Russia's Islam." Also see "Putin Reports on His Meeting with Russian Muslim Leaders," RFE/RL *Newsline*, 25 September 2001.

326. The full text of the interview with Talgat Tadzhuddin, published on 28 May 2002 in *Gazeta*, is available at the official Web site of the All-Russia Political and Social Movement "Eurasia" [in Russian] <http://eurasia.com.ru/tadjuddin2805.html>.

327. See "The Statement of the Russian Council of Muftis on the Provocative Publication of 'Gazeta' of 28 May 2002" [in Russian], official Web site of the RCM <http://www.muslim.ru/razde.cgi?id=209&rid0=8&rid1=209&rid2>.

328. The official justification for Iskhakov's absence, according to the press center of SBM

462 NOTES TO PAGES 113–115

of Tatarstan, was that the format of the conference differed significantly from what was originally planned. Gamil Gabidullin, "Mufti of Tatarstan Gusman Hazrat Iskhakov did not take part in the conference 'Islam against terrorism' " [in Russian], 31 May 2002, official Web site of the SBM of Tatarstan <http://www.e-islam.ru/news/?ID=16>.

329. Gainutdin denies that CCSBMNC participated in the conference, whereas Tadzhuddin states the opposite. For Gainutdin's version, see Konstantinov, "Operedit' drug druga v dobrikh delakh." (Competing with each other in good deeds). For Tadzhuddin's version, see Konstantinov, "Eshche raz o nabolevshem." (Once again regarding the familiar problems).

330. Ali Vagabov, "Tretiya Kavakzskaya Voina" (The Third Caucasian War), *Russian Journal—Religion*, 9 July 2002 <http://religion.russ.ru/expert/20020709-pr.html>.

331. See "Muslim Leaders Urge Putin to Clear Russia of Wahhabites," Interfax *Daily News Bulletin* (Moscow), 29 May 2002; "Russian Islamic Leader Asks Putin to Cleanse Country of Wahhabism," RFE/RL *Newsline*, 30 May 2002.

332. In the interview with Nikolai Konstantinov of *Nezavisimaya Gazeta*, Tadzhuddin voiced his opposition to this idea when he stated, "We are not ready yet for the creation of the High Islamic Council, which would unite all major Spiritual Boards of Russia's Muslims." See Konstantinov, "Eshche raz o nabolevshem." (Once again regarding the familiar problems).

333. Based on Hunter's conversations with Maksim Shevchenko.

334. The interviews with Tadzhuddin and Gainutdin reveal the importance that both Muslim leaders assign to relationships with the CCSBMNC. For these interviews, see the notes 326 and 332.

335. According to one observer, "It is hard to imagine that the head of the CSBM would have sabotaged the conference without receiving prior approval from the Kremlin. This supposition becomes even more plausible if we take into account the fact that the organization of the conference was a personal initiative of the president." See Alexander Shtalman, "Noviy konflkt na staroi pochve" (A new conflict on the old ground), *Nezavisimaya Gazeta*, 5 June 2002 <http://religion.ng.ru/printed/facts/2002-06-05/4_conflict.html>.

336. Channel One Russia, "Delegatsiya predstaviteley musulmanskoy i pravoslavnoy konfessii Rossii vyletela v Iraq" (Delegation of the representative of Muslim and Orthodox confessions left Russia for Iraq), 17 March 2003 <http://www.ltv.ru/>.

337. Ministry of Foreign Affairs of the Russian Federation, Information and Press Department, "Russian council of Muftis. Communication Statement by the Russian Council of Muftis Regarding the Start of the US Military Attack on Iraq," *Daily News Bulletin*, 21 March 2003 <http://www.mid.ru>.

338. Information Agency Rosbalt, "Islamiskiy Komitet Rossii gotov vystupit' posrednikom na peregovarah mezhdu islamskim mirom i pravitel'stvom Rossii" (The Islamic committee of Russia is ready to be an intermediary at the talks between the Islamic world and the leadership of Russia), 2 April 2003 <www.rosbalt.ru/2003/04/02/92070.html>.

339. Anton Klyuev, Elena Rotkevich, Irina Serbina, Larisa Sheremet, and Yurii Nikolaev, "Oruzhie—Molitva. Rossiiskie musulmane ugrozhayut Amerike dzhikhadom" (Prayer is a weapon. Russian Muslims threaten American with jihad), Izvestia.ru, 25 March 2003 <http://www.izvestia.ru/community/article31704>.

340. Ibid.

341. "Russian Muslim leader says Jihad against U.S. could have 'results' in 2–3 days," Foreign Broadcast Information Service, FBIS/SOV _2003_0403, 3 April 2003. For the full text of Tadzhuddin's speech, see "Talgat Tadzhuddin: uzhe dve nedeli antikhrist mira voyuet, podnya golovu, zaraza" (Talgat Tadzhuddin: It has been two weeks since

anti-Christ of the world started the war), *Konservator*, 11 April 2003 <www.egk
.ru>.

342. See "Russian Justice Ministry reacts to Muslim's declaration of jihad against US,"
Foreign Broadcast Information Service, FBIS/SOV_2003_0403,3 April 2003.

343. Nikolai Petrov, "Holy Russian Jihad," *Moscow Times*, 15 May 2003 <http://www
.themoscowtimes.com/>.

344. Artyom Puhov, "Talgat Tadzhuddin v detskom sadu. Chem zanimayutsya religioznye
lidery, oltuchyonnie ot vlasti" (Talgat Tadzhuddin in a nursery school. What do religious leaders who have been removed from power do?), *Nezavisimaya Gazeta*, 21 May
2003 <http://ng.ru/>.

345. "Russia prosecutors say Muslim leader's call to Jihad against U.S. illegal," Foreign
Broadcast Information Service, FBIS/SOV_2003_0404, 4 April 2003; "Russian prosecutors say Muslim Council may be disbanded for jihad against U.S.," Foreign Broadcast Information Service, FBIS/SOV_2003_0404, 4 April 2003.

346. "Russia's Council of Muftis reject jihad declaration," Foreign Broadcast Information
Service, FBIS/SOV_2003_0430, 3 April 2003.

347. Mikhail Tulskiy, "Skandal v islamskom semeistve. Talgat Tadzhuddina smeschayut s
posta uzhe v pyatyi raz" (Scandal in the Islamic family. Talgat Tadzhuddin is being
dismissed for the fifth time), *Konservator*, 25 April 2003 <http://www.egk.ru/>.

348. Artyom Puhov, "Talgat Tadzhuddin v detskom sadu. Chem zanimayutsya religioznye
lidery, oltuchyonnie ot vlasti."

349. The Law on Freedom of Conscience and Religious Associations, Preamble, "Russian
Federation Federal Law on Freedom of Conscience and Religious Associations."

350. Angela Charlton, "Russian Church Gets Closer to State," Associated Press, 21 January
2000.

351. See Inna Naletova, "Religion, the State, and Civil Society," *Perspective* 12, no. 3 (January–February 2002) <http://www.bu.edu/iscip/vol12/Naletova.html>.

352. From an interview of Metropolitan Kirill commenting on the Sixth World Russian
People's Council (Vsemirniy Russkii Sobor), which was held in Moscow's Church of
Christ the Savior on 14 December 2001. See Stetson University, *Russia Religion News*,
19 December 2001 <http://www.stetson.edu/~psteeves/relnews/0112b.html#15>.

353. See Charlton, "Russian Church Gets Closer to State."

354. The interview of the chief editor of *NG Religii*, Maksim Shevchenko, with Metropolitan Kirill, "How the Relations between Orthodoxy and Islam Are Built in Russia" [in
Russian] *Nezavisimaya Gazeta*, no. 75(2385) (24 April 2001) <http://religion.ng.ru/
facts/2000-04-26/1_relations.html>.

355. The excommunication of Father Gleb Iakunin is one example of the application of this
rule. See Naletova, "Religion, the State, and Civil Society."

356. On the concept of "active neutrality," see Vsevolod Chaplin, "Active Neutrality" [in
Russian] *Nezavisimaya Gazeta*, no. 21(44) (10 November 1999) <http://religion.ng
.ru/pravoslav/1999-11-10/3_neutral.html>.

357. For an example, see the church's official statement on the seizure of the property of
the Russian Orthodox Church by Israeli soldiers in Bethlehem, official Web site of the
Moscow Patriarchate [in Russian] <http://www.russian-orthodox-church.org.ru/
ne204022.htm>. On the humanitarian assistance to Afghan refugees on 23–25 May
2002, see the official Web site of the Moscow Patriarchate [in Russian] <http://www
.russian-orthodox-church.org.ru/ne205293.htm>.

358. "Duma Approves Amendment to Law on Freedom of Religions," Interfax *Daily News
Bulletin* (Moscow), 10 July 1996, trans. *BBC Summary of World Broadcasts*, 12 July
1996.

359. John O'Mahony, "Orthodoxy Regains Its 'Special Role,' " *Russia Today*, 2 February
2000 <http://www.russiatoday.com/features.php3?id=131052>.

360. Yelena Lebedeva, "A Black Stone with Red Paint" [in Russian], *Moskovskiye Novoste*, no. 32 (7–14 August 1994), trans. in *Current Digest of the Post-Soviet Press* 46, no. 32 (7 September 1994).

361. Church officials implicitly favor Mufti Talgat Tadzhuddin over Mufti Ravil Gainutdin because the former is characterized by a malleable style of leadership and explicit willingness to accept a subordinate position in the country's hierarchy of traditional religions, whereas Gainutdin favors the establishment of a more equal relationship between Islam and Orthodox Christianity.

362. Donna E. Arzt, "Historical Heritage or Ethno-National Threat? Proselytizing and the Muslim Umma of Russia," Emory University Law and Religion Program, 1998 <http://www.law.emory.edu/EILR/special/artz.html>.

363. The controversy surrounding the ownership of Suzdal Monastery and churches between the Russian Orthodox Church and its unrecognized offshoot the Free Orthodox Church is a good illustration of this. Michael R. Gordon, "Chafing Faiths in Russia's Onion Dome," *New York Times*, 12 October 1997, p. 1.

364. Consider the case of Father Georgi Kochetkov, who has had problems with the patriarchate over his proposals to amend prayer books in order to make them more understandable for the people. The church leadership also opposed Father Kochetkov's experiment with inviting Catholic and Protestant priests to deliver lectures at the Orthodox theological seminary, where he still teaches. See Naletova, "Religion, the State, and Civil Society."

365. For more information on the IRCR, see the organization's official website [in Russian] <http;//www.m-s-r.ru>.

366. Andrei Kovalev and Sergei Mikhailov, "The Islamic Scandal in the Synagogue" [in Russian], *Nezavisimaya Gazeta*, no. 66(2128), 12 April 2000 <http://religion.ng.ru/facts/2000-04-12/2_scandal.html>.

367. Malashenko, "Islam in Russia: Notes of a Political Scientist," p. 61.

368. Ibid., p. 60.

369. Charlton, "Russian Church Gets Closer to State."

370. Ibid.

371. "Russian Orthodox Patriarch Backs Chechen War," Reuters, 30 January 2000.

372. Arzt, "Historical Heritage or Ethno-National Threat?"

373. Frank Brown, "Forging a Bond Over Chechnya," 3 May 2000, Religion News Serivce (RNS) <http://www.beliefnet.com/story/23/story_2320_1.html>.

374. Sabirzyan Badretdin, "Is Ethnic Assimilation Reversible?" *Tatar Gazette*, nos. 1–2 (2000) <http://www.peoples.org.ru/tatar/eng_052.html>.

375. Ibid.

376. Ibid.

377. Malashenko, "Islam in Russia: Notes of a Political Scientist."

378. "Press Conference on the Results of the First Congress of the Union of Muslims of Russia" [in Russian] *Official Kremlin International News Broadcast*, 6 September 1995, trans. <http://www.lexis-nexis.com>.

379. See the interview of the Dagestani journalist E. Emirov with the chairman of the Islamic Party of Russia Muhammad Rajabov. E. Emirov, "Mi privnesem v politiku Islamskie tsennosti" (We shall bring the Islamic values into politics), *Novoe Delo*, no. 2 (11 January 2002) <http://www.ndelo.ru/0202/politika.htm>.

380. Notes from Hunter's interview with Leonid Sukiyainen, Moscow, May 2002.

381. Ibid.

382. "Russia's Foreign Ministry Is Considering a Proposal by a Russian Muslim Group for Russia to Join the Organization of the Islamic Conference (OIC)," Interfax *Daily News Bulletin* (Moscow), 2 November 2000, reproduced by FBIS-SOV-2000-1102, <http://wnc.fedworld.gov>.

Notes to Chapter 3

1. Bronwyn McLaren, "Big Brains Bog Down in Hunt for the Russian Idea," *St. Petersburg Times*, 18–24 August 1997.
2. Sergei Kortunov, *Russia's National Identity in a New Era*, Strengthening Democratic Institutions Project (Cambridge, MA: John F. Kennedy School of Government, Harvard University, 1998), p. 6.
3. Ekaterina Larina, "National Idea Back on Russia's Agenda: Putin Seeks Theme for Nation," *Russia Journal* (Moscow), no. 40 (29 November 1999) <http://www .russiajournal.com/weekly/article.shtml?ad=1887>.
4. Kortunov, *Russia's National Identity in a New Era*, p. 6.
5. The Muslim members of the last Politburo of the Central Committee of the Communist Party of the USSR (1990–91) were A.S. Dzasokhov, I. Karimov, K. Makhamov, A.M. Masaliev, A.N. Mutalibov, N.A. Nazarbaev, and S.A. Niazov. "Soviet Union: Leadership of the Communist Party," National Politics Web Guide <http://lego70.tripod .com/ussr/heads_of_party.htm>.
6. Yuri Shevtsov suggests that "if the Soviet Union did not fall apart in 1991, then today half of the Politburo would likely be represented by Muslims." Yuri V. Shevtsov, "Oni priidut s Yuga pod zelionim znamenem Islama" (They will come from the South under the green banner of Islam), in *Rossiia: Put' na Sever: Geopoliticheskie tendentsii, v sfere deistvia kotorikh nakhoditsa Rossiia* (Russia: The way to the North: The geopolitical tendencies that define Russia's international environment), (Minsk: Beliy Svet and Geopolitika, 2001) <http://europa.ehu.by/geopolitics/4.htm>.
7. A case in point is Kyrgyzstan, where newly elected president Askar Akaev had to practice speaking Kyrgyz before delivering his inaugural speech in 1990 in the Kyrgyz language.
8. These policies erected what Alexandre Bennigsen has identified as an "Islamic Iron Curtain" separating Soviet Muslims from the rest of the Islamic world.
9. Teresa Rakowska-Harmstone, "The Study of Ethnic Politics in the USSR," in *Nationalism in the USSR and Eastern Europe in the Era of Brezhnev and Kosygin*, ed. George Simmonds (Detroit: University of Detroit Press, 1977), p. 22.
10. John Dunlop, *The Faces of Contemporary Russian Nationalism* (Princeton, NJ: Princeton University Press, 1983), pp. 34–35.
11. Quoted in Robert Conquest, *The Nation Killers: The Soviet Deportation of Nationalities* (London: Macmillan, 1970), p. 85.
12. Dunlop, *Faces of Contemporary Russian Nationalism*, p. 38.
13. Conquest, *Nation Killers*, pp. 90–91.
14. S. Enders Wimbush, *Contemporary Russian Nationalist Responses to Non-Russians in the USSR* (Santa Monica, CA: RAND, 1978), p. 13.
15. Wayne Allensworth, *The Russian Question: Nationalism, Modernization, and Post-Communist Russia* (Lanham, MD: Rowman and Littlefield, 1998), p. 147.
16. Ibid.
17. Quoted in John Dunlop, *The Rise of Russia and the Fall of the Soviet Empire* (Princeton, NJ: Princeton University Press, 1993), p. 3.
18. Ibid., p. 55.
19. Hunter's conversation in Kazan, September 2001.
20. Tensions arising from the introduction and implementation of strict language laws have been especially serious in the Baltic states.
21. Fred Hiatt, "Moscow Warns West on Criticism over Chechnya," *Washington Post*, 13 January 1995.
22. Wendy Sloane, "The War in Chechnya as Seen from a Kremlin Perspective," *Christian Science Monitor*, 18 January 1995.

23. See Vladimir Shlapentokh, Munir Sendich, and Emil Payin, *The New Russian Diaspora: Russian Minorities in the Former Soviet Republics* (Armonk, NY: M.E. Sharpe, 1994).
24. Richard Sakwa, *Russian Politics and Society* (London and New York: Routledge, 1993), p. 284.
25. Ibid.
26. Some Russian thinkers distinguished between communism, which they saw as alien, and Bolshevism, which they considered a modern expression of Russia's old communal tradition. See Dunlop, *Faces of Contemporary Russian Nationalism.*
27. Dunlop, *Rise of Russia*, p. 55.
28. Dunlop, *Faces of Contemporary Russian Nationalism*, p. 11.
29. Ibid., pp. 7, 108. These historians include Dimitry Pospielovsky and Alexander Nekrich.
30. General Alexander Lebed often referred to this term, which means "the flourishing economy set in motion by former high party bureaucrats who simply robbed state funds under their control and privatized them for their own gain." Benjamin S. Lambeth, *The Warrior Who Would Rule Russia* (Santa Monica, CA: RAND, 1996), p. 70.
31. Quoted in Tim McDaniel, *The Agony of the Russian Idea* (Princeton, NJ: Princeton University Press, 1996), p. 179.
32. Quoted ibid.
33. Ibid.
34. Quoted in Ariel Cohen, "General Alexander Lebed: Russia's Rising Political Star," Heritage Foundation, 26 September 1995 <http://www.heritage.org/library/categories/forfal/fyig5.html>.
35. Quoted in Phil Reeves, "Moscow Is Ignoring Advice from the West and Confusing Its Currency Presses," *Independent*, 6 September 1998.
36. McDaniel, *Agony of the Russian Idea*, pp. 176–77.
37. Ibid., pp. 176–77.
38. Ibid., p. 177.
39. Quoted in Lambeth, *Warrior Who Would Rule Russia*, pp. 71–72.
40. Kortunov, *Russia's National Identity in a New Era*, p. 21.
41. According to Oleg Volkov, as the meaning of the USSR recedes, so does nostalgia for it, especially among the younger generation. Oleg Volkov, "Decade of Regret: Most Russians Still Wish for the Soviet Union," [in Russian] *Vremya Novostei*, 7 December 2001, reproduced by the WPS Monitoring Agency [Moscow] <http://www.wps.ru:8101>.
42. Quoted in Steven Erlanger, "Five Years Later: Eastern Europe, Post-Communism—A Special Report; East Europe Watches the Bear, Warily," *New York Times*, 21 October 1994.
43. Ibid.
44. Andrei Kozyrev, "The Lagging Partnership," *Foreign Affairs* 73, no. 3 (May–June 1994): p. 62.
45. Some Western commentators also warned about statements by General Lebed to the effect that "Russia must not only be recognized as a great power, it must also be feared." Quoted in Josef Joffe, "Embr..cing Mr. Wonderful," *Time International* 148, no. 3 (15 July 1996) <http://www.time.com/time/international/1996/960715/viewpoint.html>.
46. See Oxana Shevel, "Fenomen natsionalnogo prynyzhennia v postimperskoi Rossii" (The phenomenon of national humiliation in postimperial Russia), *Moloda Natsia*, no. 8 (August 1998): pp. 89–120.
47. Allensworth, *Russian Question,* pp. 16–17.
48. Anthony D. Smith, *The Ethnic Origins of Nations* (Oxford: Basil Blackwell, 1986), p. 12.

49. See Adam Roberts, "Beyond the Flawed Principle of National Self-Determination," in *People, Nation, and State: The Meaning of Ethnicity and Nationalism*, ed. Edward Mortimer (London: I.B. Tauris, 1999), pp. 77–103.
50. Allensworth, *Russian Question*, p. 1.
51. Smith, *Ethnic Origins of Nations*, p. 12.
52. Ibid., p. 11.
53. On Gellner's views, see Ernest Gellner, *Nations and Nationalism* (Oxford: Blackwell, 1990).
54. Smith, *Ethnic Origins of Nations*, p. 14.
55. Benedict Anderson, *Imagined Communities*, rev. ed. (London: Verso, 1991). According to Anderson, the nation is imagined because "the members of even the smallest nations will never know most of their fellow members. . . . It is limited because even the largest of them, encompassing perhaps a billion living human beings, has finite, if elastic, boundaries beyond which lie other nations. . . . It is imagined as sovereign because the concept was born in an age in which enlightenment and revolution were destroying the legitimacy of the divinely ordained, hierarchical dynastic realm. . . . It is imagined as a community because, regardless of the actual inequality and exploitation that may prevail in each, the nation is always conceived as a deep horizontal comradeship" (pp. 6–7).
56. See Walker Connor, *Ethnonationalism: The Quest for Understanding* (Princeton, NJ: Princeton University Press, 1994).
57. Anthony Smith, "The Nation: Real or Imagined?" in *People, Nation, and State; The Meaning of Ethnicity and Nationalism* ed. Edward Mortimer (London: I.B. Tauris, 1999), p. 37.
58. Smith, *Ethnic Origins of Nations,* p. 212.
59. Smith, "Nation: Real or Imagined," p. 41.
60. Ibid.
61. Michael Ignatief, "Benign Nationalism? The Possibilities of the Civic Ideal," in *People, Nation, and State; The Meaning of Ethnicity and Nationalism,* ed. Edward Mortimer (London: I.B. Tauris, 1999), p. 144.
62. Ibid., p. 145. As examples, he cites British and American nationalism.
63. See Uri Ra'anan, "The Nation-State Fallacy," in *Conflict and Peacemaking in Multiethnic Societies,* ed. Joseph V. Montville (Lexington, MA: Lexington Books, 1991), pp. 5–20.
64. Ignatief, "Benign Nationalism?" p. 145.
65. Ibid.
66. Smith, "Nation: Real or Imagined," p. 41.
67. John M. Thompson, *Russia and the Soviet Union: An Historical Introduction from the Kievan State to the Present*, 3rd ed. (Boulder, CO: Westview Press, 1994), pp. 10–11.
68. "Many historians in Russia . . . would prefer to have the role of the Vikings downgraded and the contributions of Slavs highlighted. . . . Russian writers are unhappy with the theory that the word Rus is of Scandinavian origin." Ibid., p. 11.
69. "We do not know Vladimir's reasons for choosing Eastern Christianity, but can surmise fairly safely that the close commercial and political ties with Byzantium were an important factor" Ibid., p. 17.
70. See Alexandre A. Bennigsen and Marie Broxup, *The Islamic Threat to the Soviet State* (New York: St. Martin's Press, 1983), p. 50.
71. Thompson, *Russia and the Soviet Union*, p. 20.
72. Samuel P. Huntington, *The Clash of Civilizations and the Remaking of World Order* (New York: Simon and Schuster, 1996), p. 21. For a more detailed and analytical concept of the "other" and its manifold ramifications, see Vilho Harle, *The Enemy with a Thousand Faces* (Westport, CT: Praeger, 2000).
73. Furio Cerutti, "Political Identity and Conflict: A Comparison of Definitions," in *Iden-*

tities and Conflicts: The Mediterranean, eds. Furio Cerutti and Rodolfo Ragionieri (Basingstoke, England: Palgrave, 2001), pp. 15–16.

74. As examples, Smith mentions the Greeks and the Persians, and the French and the Germans.

75. Harle, *Enemy with a Thousand Faces*, p. 11.

76. Ibid.

77. Thompson, *Russia and the Soviet Union*, p. 37.

78. Benningsen and Broxup, *Islamic Threat to the Soviet State*, p. 7.

79. See Paul Harrison Silfen, *The Influence of the Mongols on Russia: A Dimensional History* (Hicksville, NY: Exposition Press, 1974); Donald G. Ostrowski, *Muscovy and the Mongols: Cross-Cultural Influences on the Steppe Frontier, 1304–1589* (Cambridge and New York: Cambridge University Press, 1998); Leo de Hartog, *Russia and the Mongol Yoke: The History of the Russian Principalities and the Golden Horde, 1221– 1502* (London and New York: British Academic Press, 1996); Charles J. Halperin, *The Tatar Yoke* (Columbus, OH: Slavica Publishers, 1986); and George Vernadsky, *The Mongols and Russia* (New Haven, CT: Yale University Press, 1953).

80. Nicholas V. Riasanovsky, *A History of Russia*, 5th ed. (New York: Oxford University Press, 1993), p. 75.

81. Ibid., p. 74.

82. Ibid.

83. Ibid.

84. See Rafael Khakimov, "Russia and Tatarstan at a Crossroad of History," *Anthropology and Archeology of Eurasia* 37, no. 1 (Summer 1998); pp. 30–71, available through the Kazan Institute of Federalism <www.kazanfed.ru/authors/khakimov/pub3>.

85. Ibid <www.kazanfed.ru/authors/khakimov/pub3>.

86. For a more extensive treatment of Russian-Mongol interaction, see the sources cited in note 79.

87. Thomson, *Russia and the Soviet Union*, p. 39.

88. Ibid.

89. Turgut Ozal, the former prime minister of Turkey, had a vision of Eurasia with Turkey as the critical link. See Shireen T. Hunter, Turkey at the Crossroads: Islamic Past or European Future, CEPS Paper no. 66 (Brussels: Centre for European Policy Studies, 1995). On Russian fears of Turkish replacing Russian in the Turkic-speaking part of Russia and the CIS, see Yelena Kostyuk and Nadezhda Kozhukhova, "Linguistic War Rages On in the CIS Countries," *Moscow News*, 13 February 2002. Kostyuk and Kozhukhova quote Alexander Baksakov of the Russian Academy of Sciences Institute of Linguistics as saying that Turkey is "obsessed with the idea of language hegemony, whereby Turkish is proposed as the main instrument of communication of all Turkic peoples."

90. Quoted in Eric G.E. Zuelow, "Nationalism in a Global Age: The Case of Scotland's Three Nationalisms" (bachelor's thesis in political science, University of Washington, Seattle, 1995) <http://www.sit.wisc.edu/~egzuelow/eZ_Pages/Acad/titlepage.htm>.

91. Ibid.

92. Boris Kipkeyev, "N. Ossetian Head, Russian Commander on 'Unstable' Caucasus," ITAR-TASS, 17 July 1998, reproduced by the Foreign Broadcast Information Service, FBIS-TOT-98-198 <http://wnc.fedworld.gov>.

93. Ian Traynor, "Chechnya Fuels Russian-Turkish Tension," *Guardian*, 26 April 2001.

94. Paul Goble, "Idel-Ural and the Future of Russia," Radio Free Europe/Radio Liberty (RFE/RL) *Weekday Magazine*, 3 May 2000 <http://www.rferl.org/nca/features>. Non-governmental activists held a conference in Ioshkar-Ola, the capital of Marii-El, supporting the idea of setting up an Idel-Ural fund to propagate these goals.

95. "Ideia Osmanskoi imperii zhivet. I uzhe pobezhdaet v Rossii?" (The idea of Ottoman

Empire lives on. And is already winning?), *Komsomolskaya Pravda*, 24 April 2001 <http://213.248.5.99/articles/issue22539/print3657.html>.

96. Ibid.
97. Alexei Malashenko, "Russian Nationalism and Islam," in *Conflicting Loyalties and the State in Post-Soviet Russia and Eurasia*, eds. Michael Waller, Bruno Coppieters, and Alexei Malashenko (London: Frank Cass, 1998), p. 190.
98. On 15 September 1999, the State Council of Tatarstan passed a law requiring a transition to the Latin alphabet in Tatarstan by 2011. "Moscow Conference Warns against Change of Alphabet in Tatarstan" [in Russian], Mayak Radio, broadcast on 18 September 2001, reproduced by the Foreign Broadcast Information Service, FBIS-SOV-2001-0918, <http://wnc.fedworld.gov>. However, the implementation of the law faces difficulties arising from local and federal opposition.
99. "Idei pan-Turkizma zhivi" (The ideas of pan-Turkism are alive), *Severny Kavkaz*, no. 5(511) (February 2001); p. 5.
100. Ibid.
101. Ibid.
102. See Zuelow, "Nationalism in a Global Age," p. 5.
103. Based on Hunter's conversations with Iranian scholars.
104. See Alexandre A. Bennigsen and Chantal Lemercier-Quelquejay, *Islam in the Soviet Union* (New York: Praeger, 1967), p. 17. Bennigsen and Lemercier-Quelquejay state, "The Russians were convinced of their cultural superiority and on this point remained quite intractable."
105. Among Russian literary figures who were critical of Yermolov's tactics were Alexander Turgenev and Mikhail Lermontov. Susan Layton, *Russian Literature and Empire: Conquest of the Caucasus from Pushkin to Tolstoy* (Cambridge: Cambridge University Press, 1994).
106. On the impact of rivalries within the central leadership in Moscow and on the handling of the Chechen situation, see Emil Pain and Arkady Popov, "Chechnya," in *U.S. and Russian Policymaking with Respect to the Use of Force*, ed. Jeremy Azrael and Emil Payin (Santa Monica, CA: RAND, 1996); and Andrei Grachev, *Final Days: The Inside Story of the Collapse of the Soviet Union* (Boulder, CO: Westview Press, 1995).
107. John Dunlop, *Russia Confronts Chechnya: Roots of a Separatist Conflict* (Cambridge and New York: Cambridge University Press, 1998) pp. 165–67; and Pyotor Yudin, "Source of Chechen Arms Sparks Rift," *Moscow Times*, 25 December 1994. According to one anti-Dudaev Chechen, Yusup Soslambekov, "A significant part of firearms and auto transport of the Russian [military] command (ranging in rank from division commander, to company commander, to battalion commander) was sold in advance to the local populace." Quoted in Dunlop, *Russia Confronts Chechnya*, p. 167.
108. On Dudaev's shortcomings, see Vitaliy Cherkasov, "Crime World Allegedly behind Dudayev's Rise to Power" [in Russian], *Rossiiskaya Gazeta*, 14 January 1995, reproduced by the Foreign Broadcast Information Service, FBIS-SOV-95-017-S <http://wnc.fedworld.gov>.
109. According to Emil Pain and Arkady Popov, the 1992 Chechen constitution officially made the parliament responsible for deciding the republic's domestic and foreign policies. Therefore, negotiating a treaty with Russia was the parliament's responsibility. But in late 1992 and early 1993, the Chechen president and the parliament were locked in a row that resembled the rising confrontation between President Yeltsin and the Russian parliament, led by Ruslan Khasbulatov. Pain and Popov, "Chechnya," p. 182; and Dunlop, *Rise of Russia*, pp. 262–69, 294–95.
110. Dunlop, *Russia Confronts Chechnya*, p. 184. Academics and Russian officials involved in Chechen affairs at the time are divided on the question of whether a meeting between Yeltsin and Dudaev would have averted a war. Valerii Tishkov, Yeltsin's minister of

nationalities at the time, believes that Yeltsin should have met with Dudaev to avoid war. But Emil Pain and Arkady Popov believe that such a meeting with Dudaev, whom they view as someone "completely without principle," would not have achieved much. Pain and Popov, "Chechnya"; Emil Pain and Arkady Popov, "Rossiiskaya politika v Chechne" (Russian policy in Chechnya), *Izvestia*, 9 February 1995.

111. Allensworth, *Russian Question*, p. 292.

112. According to Valerii Tishkov, abuse of alcohol was a major reason for many mistakes. Valerii Tishkov, *Understanding Violence for Post-Conflict Reconstruction in Chechnya* (Geneva: Center for Applied Studies in International Negotiations, 2001), p. 20.

113. According to a variety of opinion polls, by the spring of 1996, more than 60 percent of Russians thought that ending the war in Chechnya should be President Yeltsin's top priority. Alesandra Stanly, "Yeltsin Tells Russia Peace Is at Hand," *New York Times*, 7 April 1996; "Anniversary of Dispatch of Federal Troops: Poll Shows Mounting Opposition to Handling of Chechen Conflict," *BBC Summary of World Broadcasts*, 12 December 1995.

114. The first step toward a cease-fire agreement was taken on 31 March 1996 by President Yeltsin when he issued an order to the Russian military to cease offensive military operations. This was followed by a meeting between Zelimkhan Yanderbaev and Russian prime minister Viktor Chernomyrdin during which they signed a cease-fire agreement that provided for an exchange of prisoners and a Russian troop withdrawal. This agreement contributed to Yeltsin's victory in July, but since this was a very vaguely worded document, intense fighting between Moscow and Grozny resumed soon afterwards. Edward W. Walker, "No Peace, No War in the Caucasus: Secessionist Conflicts in Chechnya, Abkhazia, and Nagorno-Karabakh," Strengthening Democratic Institutions Project, Harvard University, 1998, p. 3.

115. On constitutional hurdles, see ibid., pp. 5–10.

116. Cited in Francis Boyle, "Independent Chechnya: Treaty of Peace with Russia of 12 May 1997," Chechen Republic Online <http://www.amina.com/article/peace_tret .html>.

117. On internal developments in Chechnya in the interwar period, see Isabelle Astigarraga, "Chechnya, Three Years of Chaos" [in French], *Le Monde Diplomatique*, 1 March 2000, reproduced by the Foreign Broadcast Information Service, FBIS-WEU-2000-0322 <http://wnc.fedworld.gov>.

118. See Alexander Prasolov, "Kontrazvedka v Chechne" (Counterintelligence in Chechnya), *Argumenty i Fakty*, no. 5 (1995).

119. John Dunlop notes that once Dudaev became the head of the Chechen state, he "was careful to project himself as an observant and respectful Muslim." Dunlop, *Russia Confronts Chechnya*, p. 98.

120. Ibid., p. 95.

121. During this early period, Dudaev preferred to gain support by promising to "guarantee every citizen the development of their culture, faith, language, and national traditions." (Anatol Lieven, *Chechnya: Tombstone of Russian Power* (New Haven, CT: Yale University Press, 1998), p. 363.

122. Quoted in Alexei Malashenko, "Does Islamic Fundamentalism Exist in Russia?" in *Muslim Eurasia: Conflicting Legacies*, ed. Yaacov Roi (London: Frank Cass, 1995), p. 46.

123. Chechen Constitution, Article IV, 1992, quoted in Paul Henze, *Islam in the North Caucasus: The Example of Chechnya* (Santa Monica, CA: RAND, 1995), p. 35.

124. "Details of Mobilization Edict," Interfax News Agency's *Daily News Bulletin* (Moscow), 11 August 1994.

125. Dunlop, *Russia Confronts Chechnya*, p. 149.

126. Galina Yemelianova, "Islam and Nation Building in Tatarstan and Dagestan of the Russian Federation," *Nationalities Papers* 27, no. 4 (1999): p. 613. Among Russia's

Muslim peoples, the Chechens are among the most observant. Susan Goodrich Lehman, "Islam Commands Intense Devotion among the Chechens," *Opinion Analysis: USIA*, U.S. Information Agency, m-112-95, 27 July 1995.

127. David Hearst, "Chechen Leader Pledges Holy War," *Guardian*, 16 April 1996.

128. Vakhid Akaev, "Religious-Political Conflict in the Chechen Republic of Ichkeria," in *Political Islam and Conflicts in Russia and Central Asia*, ed. Lena Jonson and Murad Esenov (Luleå, Sweden: Center for Social and Political Studies, 1999) <http://www.ca-c.org/dataeng/m_akaev.shtml>.

129. "Civil and Political Rights in Post-War Chechnya," Human Rights Watch <htttp://ww.hrw/reports/1997/russia2/russia-07.htm>.

130. Edward Walker, "Islam in Chechnya," *Contemporary Caucasus Newsletter*, University of California at Berkeley, Issue 9 (fall 1998).

131. "Chechnya Puts Final Touches on Islamic Constitution," Jamestown Foundation *Monitor* 5, no. 91 (11 May 1999); and "Chechnya Adopts Islamic Constitution," *Russian Regional Report* 4, no. 18 (12 May 1999).

132. Quoted in Yossef Bodensky, "Chechnya: The Mujahedin Factor," January 1998, Armenia Network <http://www.armenia.com/article/muj-fact.html>.

133. Russian-Turkish rivalry over the pipeline routes and Russia's fears of Turkish influence in an independent Chechnya seem to have contributed to the decision to invade. Anatol Lieven relates a comment by a Russian official who claimed that if Chechnya gained independence, the Turks would open an embassy in Grozny and turn Chechnya into "a base behind our [Russian] lines." Lieven, *Chechnya: Tombstone of Russian Power*, p. 314.

134. The contagion effect of the Chechen conflict beyond the North Caucasus was less than what many predicted. Nevertheless, certain Islamic institutions and political groups in Tatarstan were said to help train and recruit volunteers to fight in Chechnya. "Tatar Volunteers Arrive in Chechnya to Aid Dudayev" [in Russian], *Komsomolskaya Pravda*, 21 December 1994, reproduced in *BBC Summary of World Broadcasts*, 23 December 1994; and "Tatarstan Muslims Said Recruited by Chechen Rebels" [in Russian], ORT [Russian Public Television], in *BBC Summary of World Broadcasts*, 20 September 1999.

135. See chapter 2 for a description of various Islamist groups that arose in Dagestan and Chechnya.

136. See Nabi Abdullaev, "Dagestan's True Believers," *Transitions* 6, no. 3 (March 1999): pp. 53–57.

137. Anna Matveeva, *The North Caucasus: Russia's Fragile Borderland* (London: Royal Institute of International Affairs, 1999), pp. 30–31. Matveeva uses the title "Fighting Squads of Jamiat of Dagestan" to describe the Dagestani mujahideen.

138. Ibid., p. 36.

139. "Over 50 Said Killed in Clashes between Wahhabi Fighters and National Guards," ITAR-TASS, 16 July 1998, in *BBC Summary of World Broadcasts*, 18 July 1998.

140. See "Chechen President Bans Wahhabism," RFE/RL *Newsline*, 16 July 1998.

141. Ilia Maksakov and Maksim Sevchenko, "Musulmanskii konflikt v Dagestane: Vlasti dostigli peremirya" ("Muslim Conflict in Dagestan: Authorities Achieve Armistice"), *Nezavisimaya Gazeta*, 15 May 1997.

142. Matveeva, *North Caucasus*, p. 35.

143. "Mujahedeen Plan to Make Dagestan an Independent Islamic State—Basayev," Interfax *Daily News Bulletin*, (Moscow), 16 August 1999.

144. John Dunlop, "Two Incursions into Dagestan and Their Extraordinary Consequences," *Contemporary Caucasus Newsletter*, Berkeley Program in Soviet and Post-Soviet Studies, University of California at Berkeley, Issue 9 (Spring 2000): pp. 21–22.

145. "Shura Statements on the Web," *BBC News*, 10 August 1999 <http://news.bbc.co.uk>.

146. The real causes of the second Chechen War are not clear. For an examination of the oil factor as one of the causes of the second Chechen campaign, see Shamsuddin Mamaev, "Caucasus," in *The Oil Geopolitics of Caucasus and Chechen Terrorism*, Information-Analytical Agency, 13 August 1999 <http://www.nns.ru/press-file/dagestan/expert/dag10.html>. On the alleged sponsorship by Russian oligarchs of the incursion into Dagestan, see "FSB Chief Accuses Berezovsky of Financing Chechen Rebels," Jamestown Foundation *Monitor* 8, no. 18 (25 January 2002).

147. "Justice Minister to Tackle Extremism by Compiling Database," ITAR-TASS, 10 February 1998, in *BBC Summary of World Broadcasts*, 12 February 1998.

148. Anna Dolgova, "Islamic Group Claims Moscow Bombing," Associated Press, 2 September 1999.

149. Ibid.

150. "Shopping Center Blast May Be Linked to Caucasus, Extremists," Interfax *Daily News Bulletin* (Moscow), 1 September 1999. The flyer expressed "complete solidarity with those comrades who, like a squadron of Icaruses, are putting out the false sun of a consumer way of life. . . . Messrs Consumers! We do not like your way of life and it is not safe for you."

151. David Hoffman, "Violence Resumes in Dagestan: Bomb Kills 30 at Russian Army Residence; Chechen Guerrillas Seize Villages," *Washington Post*, 6 September 1999. The casualty figure cited in Hoffman's article was later raised to 58 dead and 150 injured. "Russian Supreme Court Upholds Verdict in Apartment Building Bombing," RFE/RL *Newsline*, 22 January 2001.

152. Michael Gordon, "Another Bombing Kills 18 in Russia," *New York Times*, 17 September 1999.

153. "Putin Says Moscow Apartment Bombers Were Trained in Urus-Martan," Jamestown Foundation *Monitor* 6, no. 7 (11 January 2000).

154. Patrick Tyler, "6 Convicted in Russia Bombing That Killed 68," *New York Times*, 20 March 2001.

155. "FSB Close to Detaining Key Organizers of Apartment Building Bombing in Moscow, Volgodonsk," Interfax *Daily News Bulletin* (Moscow), 21 July 2002. Officials at the FSB also accused Achemez Gochiyaev, a native of Karachaevo-Cherkessia and a staunch Wahhabi, of organizing the attacks at the instruction of Khattab. Some reports claimed that Gochiyaev was trained in terrorist camps in Chechnya and was paid $500,000 for his work. Simon Saradzhyan, "FSB Says Moscow Bomber Paid $500,000 by Chechens," *Moscow Times*, 27 June 2000.

156. "FSB behind Moscow Apartment Blasts in 1999, New Book Says," RFE/RL *Newsline*, 28 August 2001.

157. Natalia Gevorkyan and Vladimir Kara-Murza, "Boris Berezovsky Stages 'An Assault on Russia' " [in Russian], *Kommersant Daily*, 6 March 2002, reproduced by the WPS Monitoring Agency (Moscow) <http://www.wps.ru/e_index.html>.

158. Peter Baker and Susan Glazer, "Rebels Hold Hundreds Hostage in Moscow, Chechen Gunmen Take Over Theater," *Washington Post*, 24 October 2002; and Dan Eggen, "Concerns Arise over Type of Gas Used by Moscow," *Washington Post*, 27 October 2002.

159. On Maskhadov's role, see "Maskhadov Denies Backing the Attack," *Moscow Times*, 28 October 2002; and Thomas de Waal, "Chechen Fury, not al-Qaeda Agitators, May be to Blame," *The Times* (London), 28 October 2002. The Arabic name of the group is wrongly translated. The correct translation is Gardens of the Righteous (see Preface).

160. Baker and Glazer, "Rebels Hold Hundreds Hostage."

161. Peter Baker and Susan Glazer, "Chechen Rebels Issue Threats, Officials Say Guerrillas Set to Release Foreigners," *Washington Post*, 25 October 2002.

162. Michael Wines, "Russia Links Arab Militants to Bombing in Chechnya," *New York Times*, 29 December 2002.

163. Michael Gordon, "New on the Russian Frontlines: Army Chaplains," *New York Times*, 15 January 2000.
164. Ibid.
165. Amelia Gentleman, "Moscow Backlash of Faith Shakes Atheists: Non-Believers Fight for Rights as Power of Church Grows in Russia," *Observer*, 7 January 2001.
166. Gordon, "New on the Russian Frontlines."
167. "Moscow Police to Go Ahead with Expulsion Plan," MSNBC, 22 September 1998, During a raid on the Veshnyaki market in Moscow, where most of the trade is in fruits and vegetables and the vendors are from the Caucasus region, one policeman belonging to a special security force said, "Blacks, blacks, blacks. Do you see any Russians here? That is what is wrong with this city. That's what's wrong with this country. Nothing but blacks. We ought to round them up and deport them all." David Filipov, "Eyeing Chechnya, Moscow Police Wage Racist War," *Boston Globe*, 6 October 1999.
168. See Valerii Solovei, "Dragon's Teeth: A Look at Right-Wing Extremism among Russian Youth" [in Russian], *Vek*, no. 17 (April 2001), reproduced by the WPS Monitoring Agency (Moscow) <www.wps.ru/e_index.html>. Reports indicate that the number of neo-Nazis has been on the increase, and their membership could be as high as 30,000. "Ranks of Neo-Nazis Swell to 30,000," RFE/RL *Newsline,* 30 April 2001.
169. See "Russian Skinheads Attack People from Caucasus in Moscow," RFE/RL *Newsline,* 23 April 2001. On the rise of xenophobia in Russia, see Yuri Zarakhovich, "From Russia, with Hate," *Time* (European edition), 22 April 2002 <http://www.time.com/time/europe/magazine/article/0,12005,901020422-230458,00.html>.
170. Cherkes Bek, "Racist Violence Plagues Russian Army," *Caucasus Reporting Service* (Institute for War and Peace Reporting), no. 49 (15 September 2000) <http://www.iwpr.net>.
171. Ibid.
172. Quoted in Sophie Lambroschini, "Russia: Racism Freely Expressed," RFE/RL *Weekday Magazine*, 29 September 1999 <http://www.rferl.org/nca/feature>.
173. Ibid.
174. See Peter Baker, "Attacks on Foreigners Rising in Russia: Frequency of Violence by Fascist Groups Alarms Kremlin," *Washington Post*, 11 August 2002.
175. Alexander Tarasov, "Russian Skinheads: A Social Portrait" [in Russian], *Kontinent-Daily*, no. 32 (August 2002), reproduced by the WPS Monitoring Agency (Moscow) <www.wps.ru/e_index.html>.
176. Ibid.
177. Alexei Malashenko, "Xenophobia in Post-Soviet Society," in *Lack of Acceptance in Russia*, ed. Galina Vitkovskaya and Alexei Malashenko (Moscow: Carnegie Center, 1999), p. 2.
178. Quoted in Lambroschini, "Russia: Racism Freely Expressed."
179. Malashenko, "Xenophobia in Post-Soviet Society," p. 5.
180. Ibid.
181. M. Zakiev, "Is There Any Need of Paleontology?" Obtained by Hunter at a conference on Islamic civilization in the Volga-Ural region held in Kazan, Republic of Tatarstan, June 2001.
182. Ibid.
183. See Khakimov, "Russia and Tatarstan at a Crossroad of History," p. 37.
184. Ibid., p. 38.
185. Ibid., p. 56.
186. Ibid.
187. "Tatar Nationalist Groups Face Criminal Prosecution for Gathering," RFE/RL *Newsline*, 31 October 2001.
188. John P. LeDonne, *The Russian Empire and the World, 1700–1917: The Geopolitics of Expansion and Containment* (Oxford: Oxford University Press, 1997), p. 309.

189. This paradox is depicted in a statement of a prominent Russian scholar of political philosophy and history, Alexei Kara-Murza, who notes, "Russia is both 'Europe in Asia' and 'Asia in Europe.'" Alexei Kara-Murza, "Dualizm rossiiskoi identichnosti: Tsivilizatsionnoe zapadnichestvo versus geopoliticheskoe evraziistvo" ("The duality of Russian identity: The civilizational Westernization versus geopolitical Eurasianism"), *Russkii Zhurnal*, 26 October 1998 <http://www.russ.ru/journal/98-10-26/k_murz.htm>.
190. LeDonne, *Russian Empire and the World*, pp. 308–22.
191. John Alexander, "The Petrine Era and After," in *Russia: A History*, ed. Gregory Freeze (Oxford: Oxford University Press, 1997), pp. 101–3; and Riasanovsky, *History of Russia*, pp. 227–38.
192. Riasanovsky, *History of Russia*, p. 230.
193. Ibid.
194. Ibid. The tsar had a religious function as the defender of the Holy Orthodox Church, but the emperor did not have any such responsibilities.
195. Allensworth, *Russian Question*, p. 35.
196. Ibid.
197. Gary Marker, "The Age of Enlightenment, 1740–1801," in *Russia: A History*, ed. Gregory Freeze (Oxford: Oxford University Press, 1997), p. 116.
198. Ibid.
199. Ibid., pp. 138–40.
200. Ibid., p. 138. Catherine's views on the combination of principles of the Enlightenment and reform with absolutist monarchy are elaborated in her *Instruction to the Legislative Commission of 1767*.
201. Allensworth, *Russian Question*, p. 35.
202. Nicholas Berdyaev, *The Origin of Russian Communism* (London: Geoffrey Bles, 1955), p. 12.
203. Ibid., pp. 12–13.
204. Ibid.
205. Ibid., p. 13.
206. Ibid.
207. Ibid.
208. Ibid., p. 14.
209. Ibid., pp. 14–15.
210. Allensworth, *Russian Question*, p. 54.
211. Pyotr Yakovlevich Chaadaev, "Letters on the Philosophy of History: Letter 1," in *A Documentary History of Russian Thought*, ed. and trans. W.J. Leatherborrow and D.C. Offord (Ann Arbor, MI: Ardis Publishers, 1987), pp. 72–73.
212. Leatherborrow and Offord, *Documentary History of Russian Thought*, p. 73.
213. According to historian Andrzej Walicki, "The term Slavophilism was originally used as a gibe to underline a certain narrow tribal particularism that was felt to be typical of the opponents of Russian Westernism." Andrzej Walicki, *A History of Russian Thought From the Enlightenment to Marxism* (Stanford, CA: Stanford University Press, 1979), p. 92.
214. For more on Shcherbatov's views, see Andrzej Walicki, *The Slavophile Controversy*, trans. Hilda Andrews-Rusiecka (Oxford: Clarendon Press, 1975).
215. Ibid., pp. 32–44.
216. Ibid.
217. Quoted in Ibid.
218. The Slavophiles believed that once "Russia rediscovered her *narodnost'* and the principles that were 'organically' correct for her growth," it would be able to bring the world a new culture. Stephen Lukashevich, *Ivan Aksakov, 1823–1886: A Study in*

Russian Thought and Politics (Cambridge, MA: Harvard University Press, 1965), pp. 3–5.

219. Ibid., p. 5.
220. Walicki, *History of Russian Thought*, p. 113.
221. Ibid.
222. Ibid., p. 114.
223. See Nazih N. Ayubi, *Political Islam: Religion and Politics in the Arab World* (New York: Routledge, 1991).
224. Berdyaev, *Origin of Russian Communism*, p. 15.
225. Quoted in Walicki, *History of Russian Thought*, pp. 324–25.
226. Berdyaev, *Origin of Russian Communism*, p. 113.
227. Peter J.S. Duncan, "Changing Landmarks? Anti-Westernism in National Bolshevik and Russian Revolutionary Thought," in *Russian Nationalism, Past and Present*, ed. Geoffrey Hosking and Robert Service (London: Macmillan, 1998), p. 60.
228. See Nicholas V. Riasanovsky, "The Emergence of Eurasianism," *California Slavic Studies* 4 (1967): p. 51.
229. Alexander Blok, "Scythians" <http://social.chass.ncsu.edu/~vladimir/295/blok.html>.
230. Duncan, "Changing Landmarks?" p. 60.
231. Ibid.
232. Ibid.
233. Ibid.
234. Riasanovsky, "Emergence of Eurasianism," p. 57.
235. Ibid.
236. Ibid.
237. Ibid.
238. Ibid.
239. Ibid.
240. Ibid., p. 67. This was true of Russian symbolists and futurists, such as Vasily Kemensky, Elena Guro, Velimir Khlebnikov, David Burliuk, Vladimir Mayakovsky, and Nataliya Goncharova, and even artists such as Kazimir Malevich and Vasily Kandinsky.
241. Ibid., p. 70.
242. Harle, *Enemy with a Thousand Faces*, p. 131.
243. Quoted in Dunlop, *Faces of Contemporary Russian Nationalism*, p. 26. Dunlop reports that according to some church leaders, such as Father Gleb Yakunin, Patriarch Alexii I and his entourage believed in such a vision that saw Stalin as a new Constantine.
244. Ibid., p. 24.
245. Ibid., p. 28.
246. An anonymous author writing in the Russian nationalist publication *Veche*, quoted Ibid., p. 141.
247. Alexander Solzhenitsyn, quoted ibid., p. 157.
248. Ibid., p. 162.
249. Alexander Solzhenitsyn, quoted in Dunlop, *Faces of Contemporary Russian Nationalism*, p. 275.
250. Robert Strayer, *Why Did the Soviet Union Collapse? Understanding Historical Change* (Armonk, NY: M.E. Sharpe, 1998), p. 175.
251. Ibid. However, some union republics boycotted the referendum.
252. On the Tatar nationalist movement, see Sergei Kondrashov, *Nationalism and the Drive for Sovereignty in Tatarstan, 1988–92: Origins and Development* (New York: St. Martin's Press, 2000).
253. This opinion was expressed by Russia's minister in charge of nationalities, Vladimir Zorin, during a presentation at the Brookings Institution in Washington, DC, in November 2001.

254. Allensworth, *Russian Question*, p. 57.
255. This aspect of Solzhenitsyn's views is best developed in his *From under the Rubble* (New York: Bantam Books, 1975), p. 195.
256. Alexander Solzhenitsyn, *Rebuilding Russia* (New York: Farrar, Straus, and Giroux, 1991), pp. 60–61.
257. Alexander Solzhenitsyn, *The Russian Question at the End of the Twentieth Century*, trans. Yermolai Solzhenitsyn (New York: Farrar, Straus, and Giroux, 1995), p. 108.
258. Ibid., p. 174.
259. Malashenko, "Russian Nationalism and Islam," p. 189.
260. Solzhenitsyn advocated granting independence to the North Caucasian republics, but not to Tatarstan because Tatarstan lacked external borders and nearly half of its population was ethnic Russian.
261. "Solzhenitsyn Wants Death Penalty for Chechens," RFE/RL *Newsline*, 30 April 2000.
262. Allensworth, *Russian Question*, p. 99.
263. James Billington and Kathleen Parthé, *The Final Report of the Third Colloquium on Russian National Identity* (Washington, DC: Library of Congress, 2000), p. 15.
264. Walter Laqueur, *Black Hundred* (New York: Harper Collins, 1993).
265. Allensworth, *Russian Question*, pp. 105–106.
266. Maria Nikiforova, "Advances and Debts," [in Russian], *Vremya Novostei*, 16 July 2002, reproduced by the WPS Monitoring Agency (Moscow), 19 July 2002 <http://www.wps.ru/e_index.html>.
267. Based on Hunter's conversations with Aksiuchits.
268. The Circassian peoples of Russia are today divided into the three ethnic designations Cherkess, Kabard, and Adygei. According to some ethnographers, the Abazin of the North Caucasus and the Abkhaz of Georgia are also linked ethnically to the Circassians. Stephen Shenfield, "The Circassians: A Forgotten Genocide?" in *The Massacre in History*, ed. Mark Levine and Penny Roberts (New York: Berghahn Books, 1999), pp. 149–62).
269. Mehrdad Haghayeghi, *Islam and Politics in Central Asia* (New York: St. Martin's Press, 1995), p. 5.
270. Allensworth, *Russian Question*, p. 114.
271. Ibid.
272. In conversations with Hunter, Aksiuchits characterized himself as an enlightened patriot.
273. Allensworth, *Russian Question*, p. 118.
274. "Penza Muslim Community Objects to Religious Symbol on Local Flag," RFE/RL *Newsline*, 21 February 2003.
275. See Vladimir Malyavin, "Rossia mezhdu Vostokom i Zapadom: Tretii put'?" (Russia between East and West: The third Way?), in *Inoe* (part of the four-volume *Chrestomathy of New Russian Consciousness*) (Moscow: S.B. Chernyshev, 1995) <http://www.russ.ru/antolog/inoe/maljav.htm>.
276. Ibid.
277. For example, Zyuganov is reported to have said that Christ was the first communist.
278. Quoted in Allensworth, *Russian Question*, p. 165.
279. Quoted ibid., pp. 165–66.
280. Ibid.
281. Ibid., p. 167.
282. Ibid., p. 168. For more details on the Communist Party leader's views, see Gennady Zyuganov, *Derzhava* (Moscow: Informpechat', 1994).
283. Quoted in David Hoffman, "Gennady Zyuganov: Zyuganov's Goal Is Russia's Glory; Presidential Front-Runner Blames West for Decline," *Washington Post*, 13 May 1996.
284. Quoted in the Keston Institute News Service [in Russian], 5 February 2000 <http://www.radiotserkov.ru/news/archive/00021.html>.

285. Quoted in Hoffman, "Gennady Zyug012020anav: Zyuganov's Goal Is Russia's Glory."
286. "Zyuganov Appeals for Support from Russia's Muslims" [in Russian], *Sovetskaya Ros-siya*, 13 June 1996, in *BBC Summary of World Broadcasts*, 19 June 1996. According to this report, Zyuganov said, "We condemn the past repressions against Muslim clergy and the restrictions on the rights of the faithful. We realize that this led to the destruction of many monuments of the people's national culture."
287. Ibid.
288. "Zyuganov Publishes Communist Election Appeal" [in Russian], *Rossiiskaya Gazeta*, 14 March 2001, in *BBC Summary of World Broadcasts*, 21 March 2001.
289. Ibid.
290. Ibid. The article states, "At the same time, a crusade on the Russian language and Russian culture as a whole has begun, a crusade against Orthodoxy and Islam. Foreign terrorists have, incidentally, come to Chechnya as part of this crusade."
291. Quoted in Graham Frazer and George Lancelle, *Absolute Zhirinovsky* (London: Penguin Books, 1999), p. 94.
292. Quoted in Allensworth, *Russian Question*, p. 197.
293. Ibid.
294. Malashenko, "Russian Nationalism and Islam," p. 190.
295. Ibid.
296. Allensworth, *Russian Question*, p. 298.
297. Ibid.
298. Ibid., p. 259.
299. Ibid.
300. Ibid. According to Dugin, the ancient prototype of the Atlantic power was Carthage, and the Eurasian prototype was the Roman Empire.
301. Ibid., p. 250.
302. Alexander Dugin, "Eurasia above All: Manifesto of the Eurasist Movement," 17 December 2001 <http://eurasia.com.ru/english.html>.
303. Ibid.
304. Ibid.
305. The manifesto states, "Without the revival of the Russian nation, the Eurasist project has no chance to become a reality." Ibid.
306. Ibid.
307. Ibid.
308. Ibid.
309. Ibid.
310. Ibid.
311. Alexander Dugin, "Islam protiv Islama" ("Islam against Islam"), 15 February 2000 <http://www.arctogaia.com/public/dug7.htm>.
312. Presentation by Alexander Dugin at the conference "Islamic Threat or Threat to Islam," Moscow, 28 June 2001 <www.utenti.tripod.it/ArchivEurasia/islconf_dugin.html>.
313. Ibid.
314. Ibid.
315. Ibid.
316. Dugin, "Islam protiv Islama."
317. Ibid.
318. Ibid.
319. Khakimov, "Russia and Tatarstan at a Crossroad of History," p. 59.
320. Ibid., p. 60. Quoting D.V. Dragunskii regarding the ethnic situation in the Orenburg corridor, Khakimov says that the author "is not concerned about the unification of Slavic and Turkic peoples; he fears Turkic ascendancy and expansion beyond their previously confined boundaries within previous empires."
321. At the beginning of the Iranian Revolution, some Soviet commentators stated that the

revolution was progressive in nature because of Islam's, especially Shiism's, emphasis on justice and equality. Leonid Medvedko, "Islam and Liberation Revolution," *New Times*, no. 43 (October 1979): pp. 13–21.

322. See Kara-Murza, "Dualizm rossiiskoi identichnosti."

323. Ibid.

324. Ibid.

325. For an analysis of the beginnings of the RNU, see Allensworth, *Russian Question*, pp. 215–34; and Alexander Barkashov, *Azbuka Russkogo natsionalista* (The alphabet of a Russian nationalist) (Moscow: RNU, 1999).

326. Ibid. By the early 1960s, there was a neopagan revival spearheaded by Valerii Skurlatov, who played the role of philosopher-priest in Russian neopagan circles into the 1990s. Laqueur, *Black Hundred*, pp. 112–18.

327. The RNU supported Croatia because the party saw the Croats, who lived under a Nazi puppet regime during the Second World War, as the best upholders of the Aryan ideal. Allensworth, *Russian Question*, p. 230.

328. For a list of right-wing groups in Russia, see Vladimir Pribylovsky, "A Survey of Radical Right-Wing Groups in Russia," *RFE/RL Research Reports*, vol 3, no. 16 (22 April 1994): pp. 28–37. For an extensive list of extremist nationalists, see Vladimir Pribylovsky, "National Patriots within the Framework of the Election for the Third Duma" <http://www.panorama.ru:8100/works/patr/bp/1eng.html>; and Alexander Verihovsky, "Ultra-Nationalists in Russia at the Beginning of the Year 2000," (paper presented at the University of California, Davis, 23 February 2000) <http://www.panorama.ru:8101/works/patr/bp/finre.html>.

329. See the interview with Boris Mironov in Yuri Vasilyev, "Party Game's On," *Moskovskiye Novosti*, no. 48 (2002) <http://www.mn.ru/english/printer.php?2002_48_4>.

330. Information and Expert Group "Panorama" <http://www.panorama.ru/works/pots/govpol/gov/02/10/003.html>.

331. Boris Mironov served as the head of the Committee for the Press and Information in the Chernomyrdin cabinet. Vasilyev, "Party Game's On."

332. Ibid.

333. Malashenko, "Russian Nationalism and Islam," p. 191.

334. Allensworth, *Russian Question*, p. 229.

335. See Matt Taibbi, "Pogroms Return to Russia," *Nation*, 14 November 2000 <www.thenation.com>. Yabloko party member and State Duma deputy Sergei Mitrokhin stated, "It is very convenient for an authoritarian government to have at its disposal these crowds of willing young violent youths who will do just about anything you tell them to do." Quoted ibid.).

336. Solovei, "Dragon's Teeth."

337. Ibid.

338. Ibid.

339. From an interview published in *Zavtra*, 3 August 1995, and quoted in Allensworth, *Russian Question*, p. 300. Also see Wayne Allensworth, "Derzhavnost: Alexander Lebed's Vision of Russia," *Problems of Post-Communism* 45, no. 2 (March–April 1998): pp. 51–60.

340. Allensworth, *Russian Question*, p. 300.

341. Ibid.

342. Ibid., p. 302.

343. For example, at times, Lebed seems to favor a Pinochet style of government combining political authoritarianism with economic liberalism. Ibid.

344. Ibid.

345. Ibid., p. 304. Also see Benjamin Lambeth, *The Warrior Who Would Rule Russia* (Santa Monica, CA: RAND, 1996).

346. This was mentioned in the Yabloko party's founding statement. For the founding documents of Yabloko see <http://www.yabloko.ru>.

347. Lukin's views are elaborated in Vladimir Lukin and Anatoly Utlin, *Rossiya i Zapad: Obshchnost' ili Otchuzhdeniye* (Russia and the West: Community or estrangement) (Moscow: Sampo, 1995).

348. Ajay Goyal, "Democracy Irreversible, Putin Says," *Russia Journal*, no. 38 (30 September 2000) <http://www.2.russiajournal.com/weekly/article.shtml?ad=3650>.

349. Ibid.

350. "Russia's Putin Reaffirms His Determination to Boost State Power," *Izvestia*, 19 July 2000, English translation in BBC World Monitoring.

351. Ibid.

352. John Thornhill, "Chechnya War Is a 'Signal to Region,' " *Financial Times*, 20 October 1999.

353. Ibid.

354. John Dunlop, "Russia under Putin: Reintegrating the Post-Soviet Space," *Journal of Democracy* 11, no. 3 (2000): pp. 39–47. Other political figures are more enthusiastic about this project of reintegration than Putin. Some go as far as claiming that the union would be open to other Slavic or Orthodox countries.

355. Vladimir Putin, "Russia at the Turn of the Millennium" <http://www.government .gov.ru/english/statVP_engl_1.html>. In most of his speeches, Putin used phrases such as "reinforcement of the state," "strong state," and "revival of state power." For an analysis of Putin's philosophy based on his word choice, see Ekaterina Mikhailov-skaya, "Putin's Speaking Address of the Acting President to the Citizens" <http:// www.panorama.ru/works/pats/bp/6eng.html>.

356. Goyal, "Democracy Irreversible, Putin Says."

357. Astrid Tuminez, *Russian Nationalism and Vladimir Putin's Russia*, PONARS Policy Memo no. 151 (April 2000) <www.csis.org/ruseura/ponars/policymemos/pm_015/ .pdf>.

358. John Thornhill, "Russia's Right Seeks Tsar Appeal," *Financial Times*, 15–16 January 2000.

359. Michael McFaul, "Putin Shows His Colors," *Hoover Digest*, no. 3 (2001) <www .hoover.stanford.edu/publications/digest—mcfaul.html>; see also Nikolai Petrov, "Consolidating the Centralized State, Weakening Democracy and the Federal System," *Russian Regional Report* 6, no. 23 (19 June 2000).

360. Putin, "Russia at the Turn of the Millennium."

361. Goyal, "Democracy Irreversible, Putin Says."

362. Putin, "Russia at the Turn of the Millennium."

363. Denis Petrov, "News from Russia," <www.fordinstitute.org/news/petrov/newsdp 012601.htm>.

364. Ibid.

365. Ibid.

366. Ibid.

367. Angela Charlton, "Russian Church Gets Closer to State," Associated Press, 21 January 2000 <www.river.org/~chuck/byline/2000/01/RussianChurchGetsClosertoState .html>.

368. "Moscow Patriarch Holds Festive Service for Putin," ITAR-TASS, 7 May 2000, reproduced by the Foreign Broadcast Information Service, FBIS/SOV-2000-0507 <http:// wnc.fedworld.gov>.

369. Ibid.

370. Ibid.

371. Quoted in Alexander Morozov, "Politicheskii konservatizm i opyt tserkvi" ("Political conservatism and church experience") *Nezavisimaya Gazeta*, 18 October 2000 <www .ng.ru/printed/idea/2000.10-18-8-conserv.html>.

372. Putin, "Russia at the Turn of the Millennium."

373. Ibid.

374. Quoted in Morozov, "Political Conservatism and Church Experience."

375. Lilia Shevtsova, "From Yeltsin to Putin: The Evolution of Presidential Power," in *Gorbachev, Yeltsin, and Putin: Political Leadership in Russia's Transition*, ed. Archie Brown and Lilia Shevtsova (Washington, DC: Carnegie Endowment for International Peace, 2001), p. 99.

376. Ibid.

377. At times, he has spoken in language not becoming a president. For Putin's colorful language on Chechen rebels, see Johanna Mcgeary, "The Spy Who Came In from the Crowd," *Time*, 3 April 2000.

378. Dmitry Solovyov, "Russians' Worries Clash with Putin's TV Optimism," Reuters, 24 December 2001.

379. Ibid.

380. Sabirzyan Badretdin, "Pan-Turkism: Past, Present, and Future," *Tatar Gazette*, nos. 3–4 (18 April 2000) <http://peoples.org.ru/tatar/eng_099.html>.

381. On the basic ideas and principal ideologues of Tengrism see Rafik Mukhametshin, *Islam v obshchestvenno-politicheskoi zhizni Tatarstan v Kontse XX veka* (Islam in the Sociopolitical Life of Tatarstan at the End of the Twentieth Century) (Kazan: Iman, 2000), pp. 88–90.

382. Ibid., p. 89.

383. Ibid.

384. Aislu Yunusova, "Islam between the Volga River and the Ural Mountains," in *Political Islam and Conflicts in Russia and Central Asia*, ed. Lena Jonson and Murad Isenov (Luleå, Sweden: Central Asia and the Caucasus Information and Analytical Center, 1999).

385. Ibid.

386. Quoted in Mukhametshin, *Islam in the Sociopolitical Life of Tatarstan*, p. 81.

387. Ibid., p. 81.

388. Ibid.

389. Andrei Zolotov, Jr., "Schools to Teach Orthodox Culture," *Moscow Times*, 18 November 2002.

390. Valerii Tishkov, "Posle mnogonatsional' nosti" ("After multinationalism") *Znamya*, no. 3(2003) <www.magazines.russ.ru/znamia/2003/3/TishkPr/html>.

391. For a discussion of the project see Chapter 2.

Notes to Chapter 4

1. "Putin Edict on District Representatives" [in Russian], *Rossiiskaya Gazeta*, 16 May 2000, reproduced by the Foreign Broadcast Information Service, FBIS-SOV-2000-0516 <http://wnc.fedworld.gov>.

2. The term "federation subject" refers to the Russian Federation's territorial divisions, which consist of thirty-two national territories (or homelands) for non-Russian ethnic groups and fifty-seven geographically defined regions with predominantly ethnic Russian populations.

3. Sergei Khrushchev has pointed out that economically driven "regionalization," as opposed to nationalist-based secession, was a driving force behind Russia's rapid decentralization in the early 1990s. Sergei Khrushchev, "The Political Economy of Russia's Regional Fragmentation," in *Russia's Future: Consolidation or Disintegration?* ed. Douglas Blum (Boulder, CO: Westview Press, 1994), pp. 91–107.

4. The Bolsheviks also faced military intervention by several foreign powers, including forces from Japan, Britain, and the United States.

5. Alexandre A. Benningsen and Chantal Lemercier-Quelquejay, *Islam in the Soviet Union* (New York: Praeger, 1967), p. 82.

6. The original signatories of the 1922 Union Treaty were the newly created soviet so-

cialist republics of Russia, Belarus, Ukraine, and Transcaucasia. The Soviet leadership soon afterwards divided the Transcaucasian Republic into the separate republics of Azerbaijan, Armenia, and Georgia.

7. F.J.M. Feldbrugge, ed., *The Constitutions of the USSR and the Union Republics: Analysis, Texts, Reports* (Germantown, MD: Sijthoff & Noordhoff, 1979), RSFSR Constitution, Article II, 1918.
8. Feldbrugge, *The Constitutions of the USSR and the Union Republics*, USSR Constitution, Articles IV and VI, 1924.
9. Feldbrugge, *The Constitutions of the USSR and the Union Republics*, pp. 112–14.
10. USSR Constitution, Article VI, 1977.
11. Darrell Hammer, *The USSR: The Politics of Oligarchy*, 2nd ed. (Boulder, CO: Westview Press, 1986), pp. 80–81.
12. Cited in Richard Pipes, *The Formation of the Soviet Union: Communism and Nationalism 1917–1923* (Cambridge, MA: Harvard University Press, 1997), p. 245.
13. Robert Kaiser, *The Geography of Nationalism in Russia and the USSR* (Princeton, NJ: Princeton University Press, 1994), p. 331.
14. Robert Strayer, *Why Did the Soviet Union Collapse? Understanding Historical Change* (Armonk, NY: M.E. Sharpe, 1998), p. 75.
15. By the early 1930s, the Soviet regime had assigned Latin-based alphabets to seventy languages spoken by a total of 36 million people. Gerhard Simon, *Nationalism and Policy toward the Nationalities in the Soviet Union* (Boulder, CO: Westview Press, 1991), p. 44.
16. Ibid., p. 45.
17. By 1989, 18.7 million non-Russians in the Soviet Union claimed Russian as their first language, and approximately 62 percent of non-Russian citizens were fluent in Russian. Ann Sheehy, "The Ethnodemographic Dimension," in *Soviet Federalism: Nationalism and Economic Decentralisation*, ed. Alastair McAuley (New York: St. Martin's Press, 1991), p. 82.
18. Ronald Suny, *The Revenge of the Past: Nationalism, Revolution, and the Collapse of the Soviet Union* (Stanford, CA: Stanford University Press, 1993), p. 108.
19. See chapters 1 and 2 for details.
20. Suny, *Revenge of the Past*, pp. 122–23.
21. John Dunlop, *The Rise of Russia and the Fall of the Soviet Empire* (Princeton, NJ: Princeton University Press, 1993), p. 4.
22. Mikhail Gorbachev, *Perestroika: New Thinking for Our Country and the World* (New York: Harper and Row, 1987), p. 19.
23. John M. Thompson, *Russia and the Soviet Union: An Historical Introduction from the Kievan State to the Present*, 3rd ed. (Boulder, CO: Westview Press, 1994), p. 283.
24. On Gorbachev's approach toward ethnic conflicts, see Ludmilla Alexeyeva, "Unrest in the Soviet Union," *Washington Quarterly* 13, no. 1 (winter 1990): pp. 63–77.
25. Dunlop, *Rise of Russia*, pp. 27, 30, 59–62.
26. Although the law recognized a right of secession, it mandated a series of difficult and lengthy steps necessary to secede, including gaining approval from the USSR Supreme Soviet and consenting to a five-year transition period. Hélène Carrère d'Encausse, *The End of the Soviet Empire: The Triumph of the Nations*, trans. Franklin Philip (New York: BasicBooks, 1992), pp. 212–13.
27. For the text of the founding treaty of the CIS, see the Web site of the Executive Committee of the Commonwealth of Independent States <www.cis.minsk.by/russian/cis_doc4.htm>.
28. Cited in Edward Walker, "The Dog That Didn't Bark: Tatarstan and Asymmetrical Federalism in Russia," Kazan State University, November 1996 <http://www.kcn.ru/tat_en/politics/dfa/f_media/tatar.htm>.
29. Cited in Alexei Zverev, "Qualified Sovereignty: The Tatarstan Model for Resolving

Conflicts," in *Conflicting Loyalties and the State in Post-Soviet Russia and Eurasia*, ed. Michael Waller, Bruno Coppieters, and Alexei Malashenko (London: Frank Cass, 1998), p. 122.

30. Prior to this administrative change, the RSFSR contained sixteen autonomous republics, five autonomous oblasts, and ten autonomous okrugs. Afterwards, the RSFSR contained twenty republics, one autonomous oblast, and ten autonomous okrugs. In 1992, the Russian parliament recognized the division of Chechnya-Ingushetia into two separate republics, raising the number of republics to twenty-one.

31. Gail Lapidus, "Asymmetrical Federalism and State Breakdown in Russia," *Post-Soviet Affairs* 15, no. 1 (January–March 1999): p. 84.

32. Such proclamations came from the oblasts of Astrakhan, Amur, Chelyabinsk, Chita, Kaliningrad, Perm, Orenburg, Kurgan, Sverdlovsk, and Vologda, Primorsky Krai, and the federal city of St. Petersburg. Gail Lapidus and Edward Walker, "Nationalism, Regionalism, and Federalism: Center-Periphery Relations in Post-Communist Russia," in *The New Russia: Troubled Transformation*, ed. Gail Lapidus (Boulder, CO: Westview Press, 1995), p. 98.

33. Khrushchev, "Political Economy," p. 93; Kathryn Stoner-Weiss, "Central Weakness and Provincial Autonomy: Observations on the Devolution Process in Russia," *Post-Soviet Affairs* 15, no. 1 (January–March 1999): p. 93.

34. "Kaliningrad Region Declares State of Emergency," Interfax *Daily News Bulletin* (Moscow), 8 September 1998, reproduced by the Foreign Broadcast Information Service, FBIS-SOV-98-251 <http://wnc.fedworld.gov>.

35. Eugene Huskey, "Political Leadership and the Center-Periphery Struggle: Putin's Administrative Reforms," in *Gorbachev, Yeltsin, and Putin: Political Leadership in Russia's Transition,* ed. Archie Brown and Lilia Shevtsova (Washington, DC: Carnegie Endowment for International Peace, 2001), pp. 115, 134.

36. "Ingush Parliament Adopts Law Legalizing Polygamy," Interfax *Daily News Bulletin* (Moscow), 2 August 1999; "Ingush President Backs Down over Referendum," Radio Free Europe/Radio Liberty (RFE/RL) *Newsline*, 19 February 1999.

37. "Adygeya's Slav Majority Protests Discrimination," RFE/RL *Caucasus Report* 4, no. 12 (23 March 2001) <http://www.rferl.org/caucasus-report>.

38. Iver Neumann, *Uses of the Other: The East in European Identity Formation* (Minneapolis: University of Minnesota Press, 1999), pp. 187–89.

39. Alfred Stepan, "Russian Federalism in Comparative Perspective," *Post-Soviet Affairs* 16, no. 2 (April–June 2000): p. 155.

40. A. Uglanov, "Is Russia Breaking Up?" [in Russian], *Argumenty i Fakty* no. 2 (1993), in *Russian Press Digest* (Moscow), 15 January 1993.

41. Sergei Kudryashov, "The Bashkirization of Bashkiria" [in Russian], *Izvestia*, 20 July 1993, in *Current Digest of the Post-Soviet Press* 45, no. 29 (18 August 1993): p. 27.

42. While most ethnic Ossets are Orthodox Christian, a large percentage of Ossets in North Ossetia are Muslim.

43. Sergei Kondrashov, *Nationalism and the Drive for Sovereignty in Tatarstan, 1988–92: Origins and Development* (New York: St. Martin's Press, 2000), pp. 120–21, 127.

44. Cited in Zverev, "Qualified Sovereignty," p. 126.

45. Ravid Bukharaev, *The Model of Tatarstan* (New York: St. Martin's Press, 1999), p. 101.

46. Sabirzyan Badretdin, "Fauzia Bayramova: Tatarstan's Iron Lady," *Tatar Gazette* (Mordovia, Russian Federation), 18 April 2000 <www.peoples.org.ru/tatar/eng_100 .html>.

47. Bukharaev, *Model of Tatarstan*, p. 102.

48. Cited in Rafik Mukhametshin, *Islam v obshchestvenno-politicheskoi zhizni Tatarstana v Kontse XX veka* (Islam in the sociopolitical life of Tatarstan at the end of the twentieth century) (Kazan: Iman, 2000), pp. 8, 62–63.

49. Quoted ibid., p. 57.
50. Quoted ibid., p. 73.
51. Quoted in Aislu Yunusova, "Islam between the Volga River and the Ural Mountains," in *Political Islam and Conflicts in Russia and Central Asia*, ed. Lena Jonson and Murad Esenov (Luleå, Sweden: Central Asia and the Caucasus Information and Analytical Center, 1999).
52. Mukhametshin, *Islam v obschestvenno-politicheskoi zhini Tatarstona v Kontse XX reka*, pp. 24, 65.
53. Walker, "Dog That Didn't Bark" <http://www.ken.ru/tat_en/politics/dfa/_media/tatar.htm>.
54. Ibid.; Kondrashov, *Nationalism and the Drive for Sovereignty*, p. 178.
55. Zverev, "Qualified Sovereignty," p. 129.
56. Alexander Krolikov and Nikolai Sorokin, "Preliminary Results of Referendum in Tatarstan," ITAR-TASS, 22 March 1992; Deborah Seward, "Yeltsin Urges Tatarstan to Cancel Independence Referendum," Associated Press, 19 March 1992.
57. Nail Midkhatovich Moukhariamov, "The Tatarstan Model: A Situation Dynamic," in *Beyond the Monolith: The Emergence of Regionalism in Post-Soviet Russia*, ed. Peter J. Stavrakis, Larry Black, and Joan DeBardeleben (Washington, DC: Woodrow Wilson International Center for Scholars, 1997), p. 219.
58. Walker, "Dog That Didn't Bark" <http://www.ken.ru/tat_en/politics/dfa/_media/tatar.htm>.
59. Anatol Lieven, *Chechnya: Tombstone of Russian Power* (New Haven, CT: Yale University Press, 1998), p. 58.
60. John Dunlop, *Russia Confronts Chechnya: Roots of a Separatist Conflict* (Cambridge and New York: Cambridge University Press, 1998), pp. 95, 105, 108.
61. Sharip Asyuev and Alexander Kharchenko, "Dudayev Elected Chechen President," ITAR-TASS, 30 October 1991. The elections took place on territory designated by Dudaev as belonging to the Republic of Chechnya and excluded six (out of fourteen) districts that were inhabited largely by Ingush or Cossack populations. Stasys Knezys and Romanas Sedlickas, *The War in Chechnya* (College Station: Texas A&M University Press, 1999), p. 19.
62. Quoted in Lyoma Usmanov, "Documents on Russo-Chechen Relations" (Washington, DC: Woodrow Wilson International Center for Scholars, 2000), document 271.
63. Dunlop, *Russia Confronts Chechnya*, p. 147; "Muslim Clergy in Chechnia Support President Dudayev," Interfax *Daily News Bulletin* (Moscow), 30 May 1993, in *BBC Summary of World Broadcasts*, 1 June 1993.
64. Knezys and Sedlickas, *War in Chechnya*, p. 20.
65. Pavel Felgenhauer, "The Chechen Campaign," in *War in Chechnya: Implications for Russian Security Policy*, ed. Mikhail Tsypkin (Monterey, CA: U.S. Naval Postgraduate School, 1995) <http://www.mis.nps.navy.mil/nsa/fel.html>.
66. Stoner-Weiss, "Central Weakness and Provincial Autonomy," p. 101.
67. Vladimir Shlapentokh, Roman Levita, and Mikhail Loiberg, *From Submission to Rebellion: The Provinces versus the Center in Russia* (Boulder, CO: Westview Press, 1997), pp. 98–99.
68. Huskey, "Political Leadership," p. 115.
69. Nikolai Petrov, "The Presidential Representatives: Moscow's Men in the Regions," *Prism* 4, no. 7 (April 1998) <www.jamestown.org/pubs/view/pri_004_007_002.htm>.
70. For the text of the Federation Treaty, see "Treaty on Demarcating Objects of Jurisdiction and Powers between the Federal Bodies of State Power of the Russian Federation and the Bodies of Power of the Republics within the Russian Federation" [in Russian], *Rossiiskaya gazeta*, 18 March 1992, in *Current Digest of the Post-Soviet Press* 44, no. 13 (29 April 1992): p. 15.

484 NOTES TO PAGES 223–226

71. Thompson, *Russia and the Soviet Union*, pp. 196–98.
72. For the text of the 1993 Russian constitution, see the Russian embassy Web site <http://www.russianembassy.org>.
73. In the first two years of Russian independence, Russia's national income in real (inflation-adjusted) terms declined 32 percent, while the annual inflation rate reached a high of more than 2,500 percent. Richard Ericson, "The Russian Economy since Independence," in *The New Russia: Troubled Transformation*, ed. Gail Lapidus (Boulder, CO: Westview Press, 1995), pp. 45, 48.
74. Joan DeBardeleben, "The Development of Federalism in Russia,"in *Beyond the Monolith: The Emergence of Federalism in Post-Soviet Russia*, ed. Peter J. Stavrakis, Larry Black and Joan DeBardeleben (Washington, DC: Woodrow Wilson International Center for Scholars, 1997), pp. 44–45.
75. Zverev, "Qualified Sovereignty," p. 132.
76. Moukhariamov, "Tatarstan Model," p. 221.
77. "Russia, Tatarstan Sign Agreement on Mutual Delegation of Powers," ITAR-TASS, 15 February 1994.
78. Department of Foreign Affairs to the President of the Republic of Tatarstan, "Treaty on the Delimitation of Jurisdictional Subjects and Mutual Delegation of Authority between the State Bodies of the Russian Federation and the State Bodies of the Republic of Tatarstan," 1994 <http://www.tatar.ru/>.
79. Tatarstan Constitution, Article LXI, 1992, cited in Edward Walker, "Dog That Didn't Bark" <www.ken.ru/tat_en/politics/dfa/f_media/tatar.htm>.
80. Department of Foreign Affairs to the President of the Republic of Tatarstan, "Treaty on the Delimitation of Jurisdictional Subjects and Mutual Delegation of Authority between the State Bodies of the Russian Federation and the State Bodies of the Republic of Tatarstan."
81. According to some estimates, by early 2002, demographic changes (primarily due to higher Tatar birth rates) had left Tatars with more than half (about 52 percent) of the republic's population. "Deputy from Bashkortostan Wants to Postpone Census," RFE/RL *Newsline*, 12 February 2002.
82. Stoner-Weiss, "Central Weakness and Provincial Autonomy," pp. 89–90.
83. Jeff Kahn, "The Parade of Sovereignties: Establishing the Vocabulary of the New Russian Federalism," *Post-Soviet Affairs* 16, no. 1 (January–March 2000): p. 83.
84. Federation Council chairman Yegor Stroev denounced the power-sharing treaties as "primitive agreements" and claimed that they had abetted "disintegration within the framework of the country." "Federal Government Examines Federalism," *Russian Regional Report* 4, no. 3 (28 January 1999).
85. Leokadia Drobizheva, "Power Sharing in the Russian Federation: The View from the Center and from the Republics," in *Preventing Deadly Conflict: Strategies and Institutions*, ed. Gail Lapidus and Svetlana Tsalik (Washington, DC: Carnegie Commission on Preventing Deadly Conflict, 1996) <http://wwics.si.edu/subsites/ccpdc/pubs/moscow/6.htm>.
86. Stoner-Weiss, "Central Weakness and Provincial Autonomy," p. 93.
87. For extensive surveys of resistance to Russian rule in the North Caucasus, see Marie Bennigsen Broxup, ed., *The North Caucasus Barrier: The Russian Advance towards the Muslim World* (New York: St. Martin's Press, 1992); and Moshe Gammer, *Muslim Resistance to the Tsar: Shamil and the Conquest of Chechnia and Daghestan* (London: Frank Cass, 1994).
88. For a detailed account of the deportation of the Chechen people, see William Flemming, "The Deportation of the Chechen and Ingush Peoples: A Critical Examination," in *Russia and Chechnia: The Permanent Crisis*, ed. Ben Fowkes (New York: St. Martin's Press, 1998), pp. 65–86.
89. Vladimir Zhirinovsky's nationalist Liberal Democratic Party won more votes than any

other party (23 percent), while Gennady Zyuganov's Communist Party of the Russian Federation and its ally, the Agrarian Party, won a combined total of just over 20 percent. Norwegian Institute of International Affairs, "1993 State Duma Elections," 1995 <http://www.nupi.no/russland/elections/1993_state_duma_elections_Russia.htm>.

90. Advocates of a military solution in Chechnya included Minister for Nationalities and Regional Affairs Nikolai Yegorov, Defense Minister Pavel Grachev, Minister of Internal Affairs Anatolii Kulikov, FSB Director Sergei Stepashin, and Security Council Secretary Oleg Lobov. Lobov reportedly assured Yeltsin of a "short, but victorious war" in Chechnya. Gail Lapidus, "Contested Sovereignty: The Tragedy of Chechnya," *International Security* 23, no. 1 (summer 1998): p. 20.

91. Quoted in Dunlop, *Russia Confronts Chechnya*, p. 140.

92. In 2000, Russia completed a pipeline running through Dagestan, allowing the Baku-Novorossisk oil pipeline (which links Azerbaijan's Caspian Sea port in Baku to the Russian Black Sea port of Novorossisk) to bypass Chechen territory. "Russia Completed Chechnya Bypass Pipeline," Interfax *Daily News Bulletin* (Moscow), 27 March 2000.

93. For a review of Russian allegations of Turkish assistance to Dudaev, see Ernest Andrews, "Russias Counterintelligence Service Takes Aim at Turkey," *Prism*, vol. 1, no. 20 (September 1995) <www.jamestown.org/pubs/view/pri_001_020_003.htm>.

94. Emil A. Payin and Arkady A. Popov, "Chechnya: From Past to Present," Chechen Republic Online, 1998 <www.amina.com/article/history.html>.

95. Carlotta Gall and Thomas de Waal, *Chechnya: A Small Victorious War* (London: Pan Books, 1997), p. 152.

96. Dunlop, *Russia Confronts Chechnya*, pp. 188–89.

97. Vladimir Bobrovnikov, "Post-Socialist Forms of Islam: Caucasian Wahhabis," *ISIM Newsletter*, International Institute for the Study of Islam in the Modern World (Leiden, the Netherlands), no. 7 (March 2001) <www.isim.nl/newsletter/7/regional/18.html>.

98. Sophie Lambroschini, "Russia: Racism Freely Expressed," RFE/RL *Weekday Magazine*, 29 September 1999 <http://www.rferl.org/nca/feature>.

99. Emil Payin, "From the First Chechen War towards the Second," *Brown Journal of World Affairs* 8, no. 1 (winter–spring 2001), p. 8. For a discussion of the change in Russian popular opinion toward Chechnya and the Chechens, see John Russell, "Mujahedeen, Mafia, Madmen: Russian Perceptions of Chechens during the Wars in Chechnya, 1994–96 and 1999–2001," *Journal of Communist Studies and Transition Politics*, vol. 18, no. 1 (March 2002), pp. 73–96.

100. "Federal Forces Have Killed over 2000 Terrorists in Dagestan," Interfax *Daily News Bulletin* (Moscow), 16 September 1999.

101. "281 Russian Soldiers Killed in Dagestani Crisis," Interfax *Daily News Bulletin* (Moscow), 23 September 1999.

102. "UNHCR: 22,000 Have Fled Fighting in Dagestan," Agence France-Presse, 7 September 1999.

103. "Chechen Operation Was Planned in March 1999," Interfax *Daily News Bulletin* (Moscow), 27 January 2000.

104. "Government Has to Work!—Television Address by the Russian President to the Country's Citizens" [in Russian], *Rossiiskaya gazeta*, 19 May 2000, in *Current Digest of the Post-Soviet Press* 52, no. 20 (14 June 2000): p. 5.

105. "Putin Names Presidential Representatives to the Security Council," *Russian Regional Report* 5, no. 21 (31 May 2000).

106. "Prime Minister Kasyanov Signs Resolution on Presidential Envoys," ITAR-TASS, 16 August 2000, reproduced by the Foreign Broadcast Information Service, FBIS-SOV-2000-0816 <http://wnc.fedworld.gov>.

107. The legislation allows the Russian president to dismiss regional chief executives if they

are charged with a federal crime and to disband regional legislatures if they pass laws that violate federal norms. Sophie Lambroschini, "Federation Council Approves Putin-Led Reforms," RFE/RL *Newsline*, 27 July 2000.

108. Katherine Graney, "Ten Years of Sovereignty in Tatarstan: End of the Beginning or Beginning of the End?" *Problems of Post-Communism* 48, no. 5 (September–October 2001): p. 37; Lev Makarevich, "Regions Cut Off from World Capital Market: Having Failed with Corporations, Putin Sets Off on Quest against Regions" [in Russian], *Vremya MN*, 16 September 2000, reproduced by the Foreign Broadcast Information Service, FBIS-SOV-2000-0919 <http://wnc.fedworld.gov>.

109. "Rakhimov to Fight Law on Police," RFE/RL *Russian Federation Report* 3, no. 24 (8 August 2001) <http://www.rferl.org/russianreport>.

110. "Putin Cracks Down on Regional Laws," *Russian Regional Report* 5, no. 19 (17 May 2000); ". . . And Putin Overturns More Governors' Decrees," RFE/RL *Russian Federation Report*. 2, no. 22 (14 June 2000) <http://www.rferl.org/russianreport>; and "Putin Stays Governor's Resolution on Scrap Metal," ITAR-TASS, 14 August 2000.

111. "Kozak to Regions: We'll See You in Court," RFE/RL *Newsline*, 17 October 2001.

112. "Full Text of Putin Annual State-of-the-Nation Address to Russian Parliament" [in Russian], RTV (Moscow), 18 April 2002, reproduced by BBC Monitoring <http://www.monitor.bbc.co.uk>.

113. For a discussion of Khakimov's views of Russian federalism, see Raphael Khakimov, "Prospects of Federalism in Russia: A View from Tatarstan," *Security Dialogue* 27, no. 1 (1996) pp. 69–80.

114. Emil Pain, "Republics Resist Centralization," *Perspective* (Institute for the Study of Conflict, Ideology, and Policy, Boston) 11, no. 4 (March–April 2001), pp. 69–80, <www.bu.edu.iscidp/vol1/pain>.

115. Sergei Shakhrai, presentation at the conference "Federalism at the Dawn of the XXI Century: Russia and International Factors" (Kazan State University, 2001) <http://federalmcart.ksu.ru/conference/konfer2/index/htm>.

116. Vitaly Golovachov, "Order at All Costs?—Most Citizens Support the President's Proposals to Strengthen the Vertical Chain of Authority" [in Russian], *Trud,* 15 June 2000, in *Current Digest of the Post-Soviet Press* 52, no. 24 (12 July 2000): p. 16.

117. Boris Lagutenko, "Kak obustroit 'Asymmetrichnuyu' Rossiiu?" (How to right an "asymmetric" Russia?), *Nezavisimaya gazeta*, 24 October 2000 <www.ng.ru/printed/ideas/2000-10-24/8_assim.html>.

118. "Four Regions Renounce Power-Sharing Treaties," *Russian Regional Report* 6, no. 26 (9 July 2001).

119. Svetlana Babayeva, "Dmitriy Kozak: I Am Not Afraid to Go to Putin" [in Russian], *Izvestia*, 4 June 2002, reproduced by the Foreign Broadcast Information Service, FBIS-SOV-2002-0605 <http://wnc.fedworld.gov>.

120. "Another Governor Calls for Making Office Appointed," RFE/RL *Russian Federation Report* 2, no. 26 (19 July 2000) <http://www.rferl.org/russianreport>.

121. "Yedinstvo Introduces Bill to Allow President to Appoint Governors," *Russian Regional Report* 5, no. 45 (6 December 2000).

122. "More Equal than Others?" Jamestown Foundation *Monitor* 7, no. 11 (17 January 2001).

123. "Rossel Bends to Federal Pressure," RFE/RL *Newsline*, 16 October 2001.

124. Ana Uzelac, "Primorye Governor Resigns," *Moscow Times*, 6 February 2001.

125. Quoted in "Constitutional Court Overturns Sovereignty of Republics," *Russian Regional Report* 5, no. 25 (28 June 2000).

126. Svetlana Mikhailova, "More about Sovereignty" [in Russian], *Vremya Novostei*, 10 July 2000, in *Current Digest of the Post-Soviet Press* 52, no. 28 (9 August 2000): p. 12.

127. Ibid.
128. Quoted in "Moscow-Based Officials Discuss Inevitability of Reduction of Regions," *Russian Federation Report* 3, no. 14 (18 April 2001) <http://www.rferl.org/russian report/>.
129. Paul Goble, "An End to Russia's Ethnic Federalism?" RFE/RL *Newsline*, 30 August 2001.
130. According to the 1989 census, titular nationalities constitute majorities in the republics of Chechnya, Chuvashia, North Ossetia, Tyva, and Ingushetia. Pending results of the 2002 census, Tatars may comprise more than half of Tatarstan's population.
131. Maria Tsvetkova, "Zhirinovsky Calls for Abolition of Federation," Gazeta.Ru, 21 May 2001 <http://www.gazeta.ru/2001/05/14/ZhirinovskyC.shtml>.
132. For details on the acquiescence of many national territories to the receding of ethnic-based autonomy, see the following reports: "Buryatia Gives Up Sovereignty Declaration," RFE/RL *Newsline*, 16 April 2002; "Mari-El Amends Republican Election Laws," *Russian Regional Report* 5, no. 25 (14 June 2000); "Komi Republic Repudiates Sovereignty Declaration," RFE/RL *Newsline*, 27 September 2001; "New Constitution Limits Sovereignty," RFE/RL *Russian Federation Report* 3, no. 17 (9 May 2001) <http://www.rferl.org/russianreport/>; "Siberian Region Alters Ethnic Requirement," RFE/RL *Newsline*, 15 February 2001; and "Udmurt Referendum: Synchronizing Local and Federal Law," Jamestown Foundation *Monitor* 6, no. 68 (5 April 2000).
133. "Putin Could Start Combining Regions with Autonomous Okrugs," *Russian Regional Report* 5, no. 29 (26 July 2000).
134. Vladimir Nikolayev, "This Ruling Will Keep Some of Them from Getting into Mischief: Constitutional Court Upholds President's Vertical Chain of Command" [in Russian], *Kommersant*, 5 April 2002, in *Current Digest of the Post-Soviet Press* 54, no. 14 (1 May 2002).
135. "Adygea Brings Some Laws into Line with Federal Legislation," RFE/RL *Caucasus Report* 4, no. 21 (8 June 2001) <http://www.rferl.org/caucasus-report/>.
136. "Kabardino-Balkaria Adopts New Constitution," RFE/RL *Newsline*, 24 July 2001.
137. Natalia Yefimova, "Aushev Says Kremlin Didn't Push Him Out," *Moscow Times*, 25 January 2002.
138. "Chechnya after the Duma By-Election," RFE/RL *Caucasus Report* 3, no. 36 (7 September 2000) <http://www.rferl.org/caucasus-report/>.
139. In October 2001, Aslakhanov accused Russian forces of fostering genocide of the Chechen people. "Duma Deputy from Chechnya Calls on Duma to Stop Genocide of the Chechen People," Interfax *Daily News Bulletin* (Moscow), 19 October 2001). Kadyrov joined Aslakhanov's criticism, stating, "The cases of groundless use of firearms against villages . . . are not rare." Andrei Shukshin, "Pro-Moscow Chechnya Chief Condemns Troops' Actions," Reuters, 16 September 2001.
140. Quoted in Valeria Korechagina, "February 23 Is Not a Holiday for This General," *Moscow Times*, 25 February 2002.
141. "Moscow Pays High Price for Dagestan's Stability," *Russian Regional Report* 7, no. 3 (23 January 2002).
142. For a discussion of Dagestan's ethnic-based political system and its impact on inter-ethnic relations, see Enver Kisriev and Robert Bruce Ware, "Political Stability in Dagestan: Ethnic Parity and Religious Polarization," *Problems of Post-Communism* 47, no. 2 (March/April 2000): pp. 23–33.
143. Enver Kisriev, "Resistance of Dagestan's Political Institutions System to the Creation of a 'Unified Legal Environment' in Russia," in *Federalism in Russia*, ed. Rafael Khakimov (Kazan: Tatarstan Academy of Sciences and Kazan Institute of Federalism, 2002), p. 131.
144. Dagestan's system of ethnically designated electoral districts was challenged in federal

court in 2000, but delays in court proceedings allowed Dagestani authorities to address the legal complaint through cosmetic changes that preserved the principle of proportional ethnic representation. See ibid., pp. 123–24.

145. The Dagestani government's loyalty to Putin may have gone as far as massive fraud during Russia's 2000 presidential election. According to an investigation conducted by the *Moscow Times*, as many as 88,000 votes in Dagestan may have been stolen from the Communist candidate Gennady Zyuganov and transferred to Putin. Yevgenia Borisova, "And the Winner Is?" *Moscow Times*, 9 September 2000.

146. Kisriev, "Resistance of Dagestan's Political Institutions Systems," pp. 125–28.

147. "Tatarstan, Bashkortostan Resolve Passport Dispute with Moscow," RFE/RL *Newsline*, 19 December 2000; and "Shaimiev Plays Nationalist Card Again," Jamestown Foundation *Monitor* 7, no. 113, 12 June 2001.

148. "Procurator Protests New Bashkortostan Constitution," *Russian Regional Report* 6, no. 1 (10 January 2001).

149. "List of Moscow's Objections Is Long despite Passage of Amended Constitution," RFE/RL *Tatar-Bashkir Weekly Review*, 5 April 2002 <http://www.rferl.org/bd/tb/reports/weekly>.

150. "Possible Showdown over Tatarstan Constitution Looms," RFE/RL *Newsline*, 2 July 2002.

151. Igor Rotar, "Chechen Spark, Caucasian Powderkeg," *Perspective* (Institute for the Study of Conflict, Ideology, and Policy, Boston) 10, no. 2 (November–December 1999).

152. Ingush-Osset clashes culminated in a four-day anti-Ingush pogrom that left more than 600 dead and induced 70,000 Ingush to flee across the border to Ingushetia. Alexei Zverev, "Ethnic Conflicts in the Caucasus, 1988–1994," in *Contested Borders in the Caucasus*, ed. Bruno Coppieters (Brussels: VUBPRESS, 1996) <http://www.vub.ac.be/pol/publi/ContBorders/eng/homepage.htm>.

153. See chapter 3 for details.

154. "Government Releases Chechnya Casualty Figures," RFE/RL *Newsline*, 23 December 2002.

155. "Indictment Confirmed for Assailants Involved in Attack on Perm Policemen," Interfax *Daily News Bulletin* (Moscow), 14 March 2001.

156. "Prosecutor General's Office Passes to Court the Case of Terrorist Acts in Mineralnye Vody, Karachayevo-Cherkessia," Interfax *Daily News Bulletin* (Moscow), 25 March 2002.

157. Timofey Borisov, "The Coup Was Prepared by the Amirs" [in Russian], *Rossiiskaya Gazeta*, 18 August 2001, in *Russian Press Digest* (Moscow), 20 August 2001; and "Wahhabite Leader Convicted in Karachayevo-Cherkessia," Interfax *Daily News Bulletin* (Moscow), 19 September 2001.

158. "Tatar Nationalists Burn New Federation Map," RFE/RL *Newsline*, 13 June 2000.

159. Eleonora Rylova, "Ivan the Terrible Burned in Effigy in Kazan" [in Russian], *Rossiiskaya gazeta*, 16 October 2001, in *Current Digest of the Post-Soviet Press* 53, no. 42 (14 November 2001).

160. Quoted in "Milli Mejlis Pledges to Defend Tatarstan's Statehood," RFE/RL *Tatar-Bashkir Report*, 24 October 2001 <http://www.rferl.org/bd/tb/reports/today.html>.

161. "Popular Front Opposes Revision of Tatarstan Constitution," RFE/RL *Tatar-Bashkir Report*, 4 March 2002 <http://www.rferl.org/bd/tb/reports/today.html>.

162. Yuri Vasilyev, "Tatarstan, Moscow's Next Can of Worms?" *Moscow News*, 21–27 February 2001.

163. See chapter 2, pp. 138–39.

164. "Mufti Supports Muslim Women in Passport Debate," RFE/RL *Tatar-Bashkir Report*, 13 September 2002 <http://www.rferl.org/bd/tb/reports/today.html>; "Tadzhuddin Backs Demands of Muslim Women," *Tatar-Bashkir Weekly Review*, 26 July 2002 <http://www.rferl.org/bd/tb/reports/weekly>; and "Tatar Legislature Chair Wants Mus-

lim Women to Be Allowed Shawls in Passport Photos," Interfax *Daily News Bulletin* (Moscow), 3 August 2002.

165. Cited in "Muslim Organization Supports Protest over Passport Photos," RFE/RL *Tatar-Bashkir Report*, 30 July 2002 <http://www.rferl.org/bd/tb/reports/today.html>.
166. Cited in Fred Weir, "A New Terror-War Front: The Caucasus," *Christian Science Monitor*, 26 February 2002.
167. "Has a Process of 'Chechenization' of the Conflict Begun?" Jamestown Foundation *Chechnya Weekly* 2, no. 37 (16 October 2001) <http://chechnya.jamestown.org/pub-chweekly.htm>.
168. Chechen Constitution, Article I, Paragraph 2. The text of the 2003 Chechen constitution is available through the Voice of Russia broadcasting company at <www.chechnyafree.ru>.
169. Chechen Constitution, Article XI, Paragraph 1 <www.chechnyafree.ru>.
170. Chechen Constitution, Article I, Paragraph 1 <www.chechnyafree.ru>.
171. "Opinion Poll Shows Chechens Blame Moscow, Not Separatists for Troubles," Interfax *Daily News Bulletin* (Moscow), 18 February 2003, reproduced by BBC Monitoring <http://www.monitor.bbc.co.uk>.
172. "Over 95 percent of Votes support Chechen Constitution," ITAR-TASS, 26 March 2003 <www.itar-tass.ru>.
173. Gregory Feifer, "Chechnya: Russian Officials Say Chechen Referendum Broadly Approves Constitution," RFE/RL *Weekday Magazine*, 24 March 2003 <www.rferl.org/nca/features>.
174. Mikhail Petov, "Russia, Chechnya Should Draw Power-Sharing Agreement," ITAR-TASS, 27 March 2003 <www.itar-tass.ru>.
175. "Vladimir Putin Signs Order Aimed at Strengthening Public Accord in Chechnya," RIA Novosti, 12 May 2003 <www.rian.ru>.
176. "Amnesty Plan Gets Duma Nod," *St. Petersburg Times*, 6 June 2003.
177. Michael Wines, "Suicide Bomber Kills at Least 17 on Bus Near Chechnya," *New York Times*, 5 June 2003.
178. "Chechen Rebel President Says Russian Amnesty Will not Stop War" [in Russian], Kavkaz-Tsentr News Agency, 18 June 2003, reproduced by *BBC Monitoring* <http://www.monitor.bbc.co.uk>.
179. Simon Ostrovsky and Oksana Yablokova, "Suicide Bombers Strike Rock Concert," *Moscow Times,* 7 July 2003.
180. "Putin Urges Security Chiefs to 'Destroy the Terrorists,'" REF/RL *Newsline*, 8 July 2003.
181. Igor Barinovich, "Court Rules Federal Government Can Move against Tatarstan, Bashkortostan," *Russian Regional Report* 6, no. 19 (23 May 2001).
182. "Russian Supreme Court Annuls 37 Articles of Bashkir Constitution," RFE/RL *Tatar-Bashkir Report*, 20 June 2002 <http://www.rferl.org/bd/tb/reports/today.html>.
183. Igor Rabinovich, "Bashkortostan Adopts New Constitution under Federal Pressure," *Russian Regional Report* 8, no. 1 (January 2003).
184. "Kazan: Moscow Seeks to Reduce the Number of Tatars in 2002 Census," *Russian Regional Report* 6, no. 44 (12 December 2001).
185. Mufti Ravil Gainutdin, head of the Russian Council of Muftis, denounced this policy as an attempt to artificially divide a single nation. Ravil Gainutdin, "Appeal of Mufti Council of Russia in Connection with the All-Russian Census," Muslim.Ru, Russian Council of Muftis (Moscow), 2 February 2002 <www.muslim.ru/razde.cgi?id=rid0=8&rid1=60&rid2>.
186. "Deputy Says Rejection of Republican Citizenship Violates International Law," RFE/RL *Tatar-Bashkir Weekly Review*, 4 March 2002 <http://www.rferl.org/bd/tb/reports/weekly>.

187. "Duma Seeks to Prohibit Use of Non-Cyrillic Scripts," RFE/RL *Tatar-Bashkir Report*, 18 February 2002 <http://www.rferl.org/bd/tb/reports/today.html>.

Notes to Chapter 5

1. On various arguments on the compatibility of Islam and democracy, see John Esposito and John Voll, *Islam and Democracy* (New York: Oxford University Press, 1996); and Shireen T. Hunter, *The Future of Islam and the West: Clash of Civilizations or Peaceful Coexistence?* (Westport, CT: Praeger, 1998).
2. Quoted in Bernard Lewis, *The Crisis of Islam: Holy War and Unholy Terror* (Modern Library, 2003), p. 7.
3. Quoted in John Dunlop, *The Faces of Contemporary Russian Nationalism* (Princeton, NJ: Princeton University Press, 1983), p. 211.
4. Tim McDaniel, *The Agony of the Russian Idea* (Princeton, NJ: Princeton University Press, 1996), p. 35.
5. Quoted in Andrzej Walicki, *A History of Russian Thought from the Enlightenment to Marxism*, trans. Hilda Andrews-Rusiecka (Stanford, CA: Stanford University Press, 1979), p. 55.
6. Robert Byrnes, "Pobedonostsev on the Instruments of Russian Government," in *Continuity and Change in Russian and Soviet Thought*, ed. Ernest Simmons (Cambridge, MA: Harvard University Press, 1955), p. 118.
7. Quoted in Walicki, *History of Russian Thought*, p. 299.
8. Sergei Utechin, *Russian Political Thought* (New York: Praeger, 1963), pp. 78–79.
9. Walicki, *History of Russian Thought*, pp. 82, 248.
10. See V.I. Lenin, *Essential Works of Lenin: "What Is to Be Done?" and Other Writings*, ed. Henry M. Christman (New York: Dover Publications, 1987).
11. *Vadim tsymburskii, Rossiia—zemlia za velikim limitrofo: tsivilizatsia i ee geopolitika* (Russia—The land behind the great frontier: Civilization and geopolitics) (Moscow: URSS Editorial, 2000), Vladimir Malyavin, *"Rossia mezhdu Vostokom in Zapadom: Tretii put'?"* (Russia between the East and the West: A third way?), in *Inoe* (part of the four-volume *Chrestomathy of New Russian Consciousness*) (Moscow: S.B. Chernyshev, 1995) <http://www.russ/ru/antolog/inoe/maljav.htm>.
12. Stephen White, *Russia's New Politics: The Management of a Postcommunist Society* (Cambridge: Cambridge University Press, 2000), p. 256.
13. John M. Thompson, *Russia and the Soviet Union: An Historical Introduction from the Kievan State to the Present*, 3rd ed. (Boulder, CO: Westview Press, 1994), pp. 175–76. On Muslim political activism, see chapter 1.
14. Nicholas V. Riasanovsky, *A History of Russia*, 5th ed. (New York: Oxford University Press, 1993), p. 456.
15. The Bolsheviks permitted elections for deputies to the Constituent Assembly in November 1917, which had been scheduled before the Communists seized power. However, upon receiving unfavorable results (the Bolsheviks won just 25 percent of the body's seats), they disbanded the assembly on the day of its first meeting in January 1918. David Marples, *Lenin's Revolution: Russia, 1917–1921* (Pearson Education Limited, 2000), pp. 49, 51.
16. *Samizdat* began as a loose association of authors dedicated to distributing officially banned writings. In the 1960s, it expanded into an explicitly politicized movement, producing such works as the human rights chronicle *Journal of Current Events* and Andrei Sakharov's *Reflections on Progress, Peaceful Coexistence, and Intellectual Freedom*. By 1979, the *samizdat* movement claimed nearly 300,000 activists and had distributed about 4,000 volumes. Gregory Freeze, "From Stalinism to Stagnation,

1953–1985," in *Russia: A History*, ed. Gregory Freeze (Oxford: Oxford University Press, 1997), p. 379.

17. Throughout the 1990s, political parties consistently ranked last among twelve public institutions trusted by the Russian public. Only 5 percent of the population expressed complete confidence in political parties as late as 1998. Stephen White, *Russia's New Politics*, p. 270. These data are corroborated by other surveys indicating that out of sixteen public institutions, the Russian public trusts political parties the least. Edwin Bacon, "Russia: Party Formation and the Legacy of the One-Party State," in *Political Parties and the Collapse of the Old Orders*, ed. John Kenneth White and Philip John Davies (Albany: State University of New York Press, 1998), p. 206.

18. Michael McFaul, "Party Formation and Non-Formation in Russia," working paper, Carnegie Endowment for International Peace, Washington, DC, May 2000 <www .ceip.org/files/publications/pdf/partyform.pdf>.

19. For a discussion of the rise of civil society under Gorbachev, see Anne White, *Democratization in Russia under Gorbachev, 1985–91: The Birth of a Voluntary Sector* (New York: St. Martin's Press, 1999); and Judith Sedaitis and Jim Butterfield, eds. *Perestroika from Below: Social Movements in the Soviet Union* (Boulder, CO: Westview Press, 1991).

20. Marcia Weigle, *Russia's Liberal Project: State-Society Relations in the Transition from Communism* (University Park: Pennsylvania State University Press, 2000), p. 80.

21. Richard Sakwa, *Russian Politics and Society* (London and New York: Routledge, 1993), p. 138.

22. Michael Urban, Vyacheslav Igrunov, and Sergei Mitrokhin, *The Rebirth of Politics in Russia* (Cambridge: Cambridge University Press, 1997), pp. 205, 208–9.

23. Sakwa, *Russian Politics and Society*, pp. 151–54.

24. Weigle, *Russia's Liberal Project*, p. 142.

25. Until 1990, the RSFSR was the only union republic without a Communist party organization to represent it in the CPSU. Sakwa, *Russian Politics and Society*, p. 133.

26. Urban, Igrunov, and Mitrokhin, *Rebirth of Politics*, p. 211.

27. Among the most prominent parties to emerge from these CPSU factions were (1) from the Democratic Platform: the Democratic Party of Russia, the Republican Party of Russia, and Aleksandr Rutskoi's People's Party of Free Russia; (2) from the Marxist Platform: the Socialist Party and the Labor Party; and (3) from the Movement for Communist Initiative: the Communist Workers' Party led by Albert Makashov and Victor Anpiolov. Michael Urban and Vladimir Gelman, "The Development of Political Parties in Russia," in *Democratic Changes and Authoritarian Reactions in Russia, Ukraine, Belarus, and Moldova*, ed. Karen Dawisha and Bruce Parrot (Cambridge and New York: Cambridge University Press, 1997), pp. 181–82, 213.

28. Peter Duncan, "The Rebirth of Politics in Russia," in *The Road to Post-Communism: Independent Political Movements in the Soviet Union, 1985–1991*, by Geoffrey Hosking, Jonathan Aves, and Peter Duncan (London and New York: Pinter, 1992), p. 104.

29. Sakwa, *Russian Politics and Society*, p. 156.

30. Urban and Gelman, "Development of Political Parties," p. 182.

31. Stephen White, *Russia's New Politics*, pp. 38, 58, 60.

32. See McFaul, "Party Formation."

33. Bacon, "Russia: Party Formation," p. 212.

34. The threat of dissolving parliament deterred the State Duma from adopting a no-confidence motion against the Yeltsin administration for its policies in Chechnya in the summer of 1995 and enabled Yeltsin to place Sergei Kirienko in the post of prime minister in 1997 despite strong objections from a majority in parliament.

35. Of those participating in the 1993 referendum, 58 percent expressed confidence in Yeltsin as president, and 53 percent approved of his policies. Christopher Marsh, *Rus-*

sia at the Polls: Voters, Elections, and Democratization (Washington, DC: CQ Press, 2002), pp. 52–53.

36. Thompson, *Russia and the Soviet Union*, pp. 298–300.
37. McFaul, "Party Formation" <www.ceip.org/files/publicatons>.
38. Quoted in Sergei Sossinsky, "First Steps toward a Multiparty State," *Perspective* 8, no. 1 (September–October 1997) <http://www.bu.edu/iscip/vol8/Sossinsky.html>.
39. Darrell Slider, "Russia's Governors and Party Formation," in *Contemporary Russian Politics: A Reader*, ed. Archie Brown (Oxford: Oxford University Press, 2000), p. 233.
40. Bartek Cichocki, with the Center for Eastern Studies in Warsaw, during a presentation at the Center for Strategic and International Studies in Washington, DC, on 27 November 2001.
41. "Majority of Russians Do Not Identify with a Political Party," Radio Free Europe/Radio Liberty (RFE/RL) *Newsline*, 9 October 2001 <http://www.rferl.org/newsline>.
42. James L. Gibson, "The Russian Dance with Democracy," *Post-Soviet Affairs* 17, no. 2 (April–June 2001), pp. 101–28.
43. Ana Uzelac, "Bill Would Wipe Out 90% of Parties," *Moscow Times*, 14 December 2000.
44. Central Election Commission of the Russian Federation <www.fci.ru/zakon/zakon95/95fz.htm>.
45. Law on Freedom of Conscience and Religious Associations, Article 4, in "Russian Federation Federal Law on Freedom of Conscience and 'Religious Associations' [in Russian], *Rossiiskaya Gazeta*, 9 October 1997, reproduced by the Foreign Broadcast Information Service, FBIS-SOV-97-282 <http://wnc.fedworld.gov>.
46. Maria Nikiforova, "Advances and Debts" [in Russian], *Vremya Novostei*, 16 July 2002, reproduced by the WPS Monitoring Agency (Moscow) <http://www.wps.ru:8101>.
47. "Justice Ministry Reveals Drawbacks in Party Law," *Russian Issues*, National News Service (Moscow), 29 October 2001 <http://www.strana.ru>.
48. "Duma Adopts Law on Extremism," Interfax *Daily News Bulletin* (Moscow), 27 June 2002; and Andrei Krasnov, "President Signs Law on Combating Extremism" [in Russian], *Kommersant* (Moscow), 29 July 2002, in *Current Digest of the Post-Soviet Press* 54, no. 30 (21 August 2002).
49. Fred Weir, "Russian Bill Pits Free Speech against National Security," *Christian Science Monitor*, 21 June 2002.
50. John Daniszewski, "Russia Targets Racist Groups," *Los Angeles Times*, 28 June 2002.
51. Ibid.
52. "Chechen President's Envoy Expelled from Party," RFE/RL *Newsline*, 25 February 2003.
53. For an economic profile of the Muslim regions of Russia, see chapter 2.
54. See Shireen T. Hunter, *Central Asia since Independence* (Westport, CT: Praeger, 1996), pp. 49–52.
55. See Vladimir Bobrovnikiv, "Muslim Nationalism in the Post-Soviet Caucasus: The Dagestani Case," *Caucasian Regional Studies* 4, no. 1 (1999) <http://poli.vub.ac.be/publi/crs>.
56. Marie Broxup, "Political Trends in Soviet Islam after the Afghanistan War," in *Muslim Communities Reemerge: Historical Perspectives on Nationality, Politics, and Opposition in the Former Soviet Union and Yugoslavia*, ed. Edward Allworth (Durham, NC: Duke University Press, 1994), p. 311. Also see chapter 1, pp. 74–75.
57. Quoted Broxup, "Political Trends in Soviet Islam," p. 315.
58. Quoted ibid., p. 310.
59. Mark Saroyan, *Minorities, Mullahs, and Modernity: Reshaping Community in the Former Soviet Union*, ed. Edward Walker (Berkeley: University of California, 1997), pp. 93–94, <http://repositories.cdlib.org/uciaspubs/research/95>.
60. Saroyan, *Minorities, Mullahs, and Modernity*, pp. 100–101.

61. Galina Yemelianova, "Islam and Nation Building in Tatarstan and Dagestan of the Russian Federation," *Nationalities Papers* 27, no. 4 (1999): p. 616.

62. Dimitri Mikulski, "Muslims and Their Organizations in Russia" (Moscow: Russian Academy of Sciences, 1998) <http://cis.georgefox.edu.ree/html_articles/mikulski.isi .html>.

63. John Anderson, *Religion, State, and Politics in the Soviet Union and Successor States* (Cambridge and New York: Cambridge University Press, 1994), p. 200. On the origins and program of the IRP, see Dimitri Mikulski, "Central Asian Alternatives: The Islamic Revival Party of Tajikistan," *Vostok*, no. 6 (November–December 1994): pp. 47–58, in *FBIS Daily Report*, FBIS-SOV-95-067-S, 7 April 1995.

64. "A New Tatar Party Launched," ITAR-TASS, 14 October 1990.

65. Amri Shikhsaidov, "Islam in Dagestan," in *Political Islam and Conflicts in Russia and Central Asia*, ed. Lena Jonson and Murad Esenov (Luleå, Sweden: Central Asia and the Caucasus Information and Analytical Center, 1999) <www.ca-c.org/dataeng/00 .political_islam_and_conflicts.shtml>.

66. Alexei Malashenko, *Islamic Rebirth in Contemporary Russia* (Moscow: Carnegie Moscow Center, 1998), pp. 135–36.

67. "Islamic Committee," National News Service (Moscow), 2 September 1999 <www .nns.ru/Person/jemal/jemal_2.html>.

68. "Congress of Russian Muslims: For a Socially Oriented Economy in Russia's Muslim Regions" [in Russian], *Kommersant*, 5 September 1995, in *Current Digest of the Post-Soviet Press* 47, no. 38 (18 October 1995): p. 8.

69. Broadcast by Khalit Yakhin on Russian Public Television (Moscow), 23 November 1995, in *BBC Summary of World Broadcasts*, 24 November 1995.

70. "Central Electoral Commission Registers Two More Blocs, Rejects Two," Interfax *Daily News Bulletin* (Moscow), 9 November 1995, in *BBC Summary of World Broadcasts*, 10 November 1995.

71. Report from Ren TV (Moscow), 15 January 2002, reproduced by BBC Monitoring <http://www.monitor.bbc.co.uk>.

72. Quoted in Amara Shkel, "Elections Will Be Party-Based" [in Russian], *Rossiiskaya Gazeta*, 29 May 2002, reproduced by the Foreign Broadcast Information Service, FBIS-SOV-2002-0529 <http://wne.fedworld.gov>.

73. Bacon, "Russia: Party Formation," p. 217.

74. Alexander Ignatenko, "The Choice of *Muslims of Russia*: They Will Vote for Stability, Not for Parties or Governments with the word 'Islam' in Their Names" [in Russian], *Nezavisimaya gazeta* no. 163(1979) (3 September 1999) <http://www.ng.ru/ideas/ 1999=90=03/vybor.html>.

75. Marsh, *Russia at the Polls*, p. 83.

76. "Union of Muslims Elects New Leader, Adopts Programme," Interfax *Daily News Bulletin* (Moscow), 3 September 1995, in *BBC Summary of World Broadcasts*, 3 September 1995.

77. Zhirinovsky's willingness to infiltrate both movements is not surprising, given his utilitarian approach to Islam and Russia's Muslims. Although he has spoken of an "Islamic peril" and proposed civilizing the Muslim peoples in lands to the south of Russia by incorporating them into a revived Russian Empire (see Vladimir Zhirinovsky, *Posledniy Brosok na Yug* [Last dash to the south] [Moscow: 1993]), he has also demonstrated flexibility in his views on Islam when this is politically advantageous, as he did in 1998 when he visited Iraq to encourage Arab-Russian cooperation against U.S. influence in the Middle East.

78. Bakhtiyar Akhmedkhanov, "There Should Be Mujahadin in the Government of Russia" [in Russian], *Obshchaya gazeta*, no. 2 (25 January 1999), reproduced by the Foreign Broadcast Information Service, FBIS-SOV-99-025 <http://wnc.fedworld.gov>.

79. Igor Rotar, "Muslims of Russia Hold Congress, but Haven't Yet Decided Whom to

Vote For" [in Russian], *Izvestia*, 16 April 1996, in *Current Digest of the Post-Soviet Press* 48, no. 15 (8 May 1996): p. 1.

80. Sergei Nuriyev, "Islam in Russian Politics Today," *Moscow News*, 21 August 1997.

81. Quoted in Rotar, "Muslims of Russia Hold Congress."

82. Anna Paretskaya, "Russian Muslims Unite," OMRI *Daily Digest*, no. 86, part 1 (2 May 1996); and "Two Main Russian Muslim Organizations Unite," Interfax *Daily News Bulletin*, 1 May 1996.

83. Nabi Abdullaev, "Nadir Khachilaev: Building Power through Ethnic Conflict," *Russian Regional Report* vol. 3, no. 23 (11 June 1998).

84. Nabi Abdullaev, "Nadir and Magomed Khachilaev: Politicians for the New Russia," *Prism*, no. 18 (October 1999); and Guria Murlinskaya, "Dagestani Leaders Stand Trial," Institute for War and Peace Reporting (London) *Caucasus Reporting Service*, no. 36 (16 June 2000) <http://www.iwpr.net>.

85. "Dagestan Riot Leaders Sentenced, Amnestied," RFE/RL *Newsline*, 14 June 2000 <http://www.rferl.org/newsline>.

86. Ignatenko, "The Choice of *Muslims of Russia*."

87. Tamara Ivanova, "Russian Muslim Movement NUR Banned from Election Race," ITAR-TASS, 27 October 1999.

88. "Moslem Party Rejected," *Moscow Times*, 28 October 1999.

89. "Biography of State Duma Deputy from Chechnya Aslanbek Aslakhanov," ITAR-TASS, 22 August 2000, reproduced by BBC Monitoring <http://www.monitor.bbc.co.uk>.

90. Dmitri Glinski-Vassiliev, "Islam in Russian Society and Politics: Survival and Expansion," PONARS *Policy Memo* 198 (May 2001).

91. A.W. Niyazov, A.B. Rudakov, and D.O. Serazhetdinov, *Summary of the Fourth Congress of the Socio-Political Movement Refah* (Moscow: Insan, 2000). Also based on interviews with Niazov at Refakh headquarters in 2000 and 2001.

92. Ibid.

93. "Muslims Found Bloc ahead of Duma Elections," RFE/RL *Newsline*, 8 July 1999.

94. "Russian Moslems Form Party to Make Run on Parliament," Agence France-Presse, 7 July 1999.

95. Quoted in Leonid Berrs, "Wahhabis Are Ready to Make an Alliance with Makashov and Ilyukhin" [in Russian], *Kommersant*, 24 July 1999, reproduced by the WPS Monitoring Agency (Moscow) <http://www.wps.ru:8101>.

96. M. Bagirov, "The Russian Islamic Committee Proposes the Ideology of Russia's Rebirth," *Aima*, 9 July 1999, reproduced by the National News Service (Moscow), 19 June 2002 <www.nns.ru/press-file/dagestan/jemal_int.html>.

97. "Election Broadcast by Movement in Support of the Army," Russian Public Television (Moscow), 1 December 1999, reproduced by BBC Monitoring <http://www.monitor.bbc.co.uk>.

98. Marsh, *Russia at the Polls*, p. 92.

99. Glinski-Vassiliev, "Islam in Russian Society and Politics."

100. Marsh, *Russia at the Polls*, p. 92.

101. Simon Saradzhyan, "Aslakhanov Declared Winner of Duma Poll," *Moscow Times*, 26 August 2000.

102. "Two Russian Muslim Parties Agree to Merge," ITAR-TASS, 20 October 2000.

103. Alla Barakhova, "Moslems of All Russia Are Uniting in a Single Party" [in Russian], *Kommersant*, 13 November 2000, in *Russian Press Digest* (Moscow), 15 November 2000; and "Eurasians Meet to Form Party," RFE/RL *Newsline*, 20 June 2001.

104. "Abdul-Wahed Niyazov Looks for Non-Islamic Support," *Islam.Ru*, 26 June 2001 <www.islam.ru/epressclub/pressclub.htm>.

105. Anna Zakatnova, "Eurasianism Is Not a Kremlin Project" [in Russian], *Nezavisimaya*

gazeta, 31 July 2001, in *Current Digest of the Post-Soviet Press* 53, no. 31 (29 August 2001).

106. Paul Goble, "Duma Deputy from Chechnya Joins OVR," RFE/RL *Newsline*, 11 October 2001.
107. Quoted in Larisa Reznikova, "Refakh Urges All Religions to Vote for Putin," ITAR-TASS, 26 January 2000, reproduced by the Foreign Broadcast Information Service, FBIS-SOV-2000-0126 <http://wnc.fedworld.gov>.
108. "Pro-Putin Unity Bloc Expels Two Members for Misrepresentation," ITAR-TASS, 20 March 2001, reproduced by the Foreign Broadcast Information Service, FBIS-SOV-2001-0320 <http://wnc.fedworld.gov>.
109. Natalia Panshina, "Eurasian Party to Join in Election Marathon," ITAR-TASS, 15 December 2002.
110. "Eurasian Party Head Declares Ambitious Election Goals," RFE/RL *Newsline*, 15 January 2003.
111. Natalia Panshina, "Eurasian Party Contemplates Election Alliance with Glaziev," ITAR-TASS, 22 May 2003.
112. "Party Platform of the Islamic Party of Russia," International Center for Strategic and Political Studies (Moscow), July–August 2001 <http://icsps-project.arcon.ru/document/RussiaListDoc/jul_aug2001.htm>.
113. "Russian Islamic Organization Becomes Party," RIA News Agency (Moscow), 27 April 2002, reproduced by BBC Monitoring <http://www.monitor.bbc.co.uk>.
114. "New Islamic Party Founded," RFE/RL *Newsline*, 17 September 2002; and Nelyogkaya partiynaya zhizn! Do vyborov v gosudarstvennuyu dumu ostalsya god" (Difficult party life! One year left before elections to the state duma), Vremya Novostei, no. 232 (18 December 2002).
115. For a discussion of the merging of political and business elites in Russian provinces, see *Politika v regionakh: Gubernatory i gruppy vliianiia* (Politics in the regions: Governors and influence groups) (Moscow: Center for Political Technologies, 2002) <http://cpt.aznet.org/cpt>.
116. Cameron Ross, "Political Parties and Regional Democracy in Russia," *Fiftieth Annual Conference of the Political Studies Association* (London), 10–13 April 2000 <http://www.psa.ac.uk/cps/2000/Ross%20Cameron.pdf>.
117. Vladimir Ryzhkov, "A New Era of Stagnation," *Moscow Times*, 25 January 2002.
118. Kathryn Stoner-Weiss, "The Limited Reach of Russia's Party System: Under-Institutionalization in the Provinces," PONARS *Policy Memo* 123, April 2000.
119. Cameron Ross, "Political Parties and Regional Democracy," in *Regional Politics in Russia*, ed. Cameron Ross (Manchester and New York: Manchester University Press, 2002), pp. 39, 53.
120. Jorn Gravingholt, "Bashkortostan: A Case of Regional Authoritarianism," in *Regional Politics in Russia*, ed. Cameron Ross (Manchester and New York: Manchester University Press, 2002), pp. 180–85.
121. In an anonymous interview, an official in the Magomedov administration confided that the State Council chairman's only competitor was placed on the ballot "just to make sure the outcome of the vote would not be challenged in court." Nabi Abdullayev, "Dagestan Leader Gets Third Term," Institute for War and Peace Reporting (London) *Caucasus Reporting Service*, no. 135 (27 June 2002) <http://www.iwpr.net>. According to Russian federal law, uncontested elections can be challenged in court.
122. Yemelianova, "Islam and Nation Building," p. 616.
123. "Dagestani Leader Announces Plans to Seek Another Term," *Russian Regional Report* 6, no. 24 (27 June 2001).
124. "Kabardino-Balkaria Almost Unanimous in Support of Kokov," *Chronology of Events* (Oslo: Norwegian Institute for International Affairs), 15 January 1997 <http://www.nupi.no>.

125. "Incumbent Re-Elected in Kabardino-Balkaria," RFE/RL *Newsline*, 14 January 2002.
126. Fatima Chekunova, "Political Violence Flares in Karachai-Cherkessia," Institute for War and Peace Reporting (London) *Caucasus Reporting Service*, no. 146 (12 September 2002) <http://www.iwpr.net>.
127. Tatyana Polyakova, "Adygea: Gold Magnate Makes His Mark," Institute for War and Peace Reporting (London) *Caucasus Reporting Service*, no. 138 (19 July 2002) <http://www.iwpr.net>.
128. "Kremlin Candidate Elected President in Ingushetia," RFE/RL *Caucasus Report* 5, no. 15 (3 May 2002) <http://www.rferl.org/caucasus-report>.
129. Sergei Kondrashov, *Nationalism and the Drive for Sovereignty in Tatarstan, 1988–92: Origins and Development* (New York: St. Martin's Press, 2000), pp. 120, 125.
130. Ibid., p. 165.
131. Ibid., p. 173.
132. Ibid., p. 178.
133. Sabirzyan Badretdin, "Fauzia Bayramova: Tatarstan's Iron Lady," *Tatar Gazette*, 18 April 2000 <www.peoples.org.ru/tatar/eng_100.html>.
134. Andrei Zolotov, "Keeping Islam in Line," *Moscow Times*, 16 May 1998.
135. For information on the Muslims of Tatarstan movement, see the official Web site of the Republic of Tatarstan <http://www.tatar.ru/musultat.html>.
136. "New Political Movement Formed," RFE/RL *Tatar-Bashkir Report*, 1 December 1998 <http://www.rferl.org/bd/tb/reports/today.html>.
137. Midkhat Farukhshin, "Tatarstan: Syndrome of Authoritarianism," in *Regional Politics in Russia*, ed. Cameron Ross (Manchester and New York: Manchester University Press, 2002), p. 196.
138. "Civil Servants on Edge as Shaimiev Starts Third Term," *Russian Regional Report* 6, no. 16 (2 May 2001).
139. Farukhshin, "Tatarstan: Syndrome of Authoritarianism," p. 196; and Ross, "Political Parties and Regional Democracy," p. 48.
140. For a description of regional parties and movements operating in Tatarstan and Bashkortostan, see the official Web site of the Volga Federal District <http://pfo.metod.ru>.
141. Alexander Sadchikov, "President to Sign New Law on Elections" [in Russian], *Izvestia*, 1 June 2002, reproduced by the WPS Monitoring Agency (Moscow) <http://www.wps.ru:8101>.
142. Quoted in Shkel, "Elections Will Be Party-Based."

Notes to Chapter 6

1. Henry Trofimenko, *Russian National Interests and the Current Crisis in Russia* (Aldershot, Hampshire, England: Ashgate Publishing, 1999), p. 287. Stalin did not try to get a separate seat for Russia in the United Nations, although he did so for Belorussia and Ukraine.
2. George Kennan thought that Stalin's policies were more influenced by traditional tsarist objectives than by imperatives of the Communist International.
3. See Michael Mandelbaum, ed., *The New Russian Foreign Policy* (New York: Council on Foreign Relations, 1998), pp. 1–3.
4. Britain created the Commonwealth, while France assumed major responsibilities in French-speaking Africa.
5. See Sergei Medvedev, "Power, Space and Russian Foreign Policy," in *Understandings of Russian Foreign Policy*, ed. Ted Hopf (University Park: Pennsylvania State University Press, 1999), pp. 17–95.
6. Ibid., p. 17.

7. Ibid.
8. See Geoffrey Roberts, *The Soviet Union in World Politics: Coexistence, Revolution, and Cold War, 1945–1991* (London and New York: Routledge, 1999), pp. 7–9.
9. See Samuel P. Huntington, *The Clash of Civilizations and the Remaking of World Order* (New York: Simon and Schuster, 1996).
10. Value and belief systems and ideologies are instruments of legitimation and delegitimation of power. They make sense, in a systematic and at least superficially coherent manner, of seemingly unintelligible conditions, thus providing psychological comfort. They also provide scapegoats and identifiable objects of hostility to serve as agents responsible for various ills, thus easing the pain of individuals and states, reconciling them to their conditions. In short, they bridge the "emotional gap between things as they are and as one would have them be, thus ensuring the performance of roles that might otherwise be abandoned in despair and apathy." Clifford Geertz, *The Interpretation of Cultures* (New York: Basic Books, 1973), p. 205.
11. See Shireen T. Hunter, *The Future of Islam and the West: Clash of Civilizations or Peaceful Coexistence?* (Westport, CT: Praeger, 1998).
12. F.S. Northedge, "The Nature of Foreign Policy," in *The Foreign Policies of the Powers*, ed. F.S. Northedge (London: Faber and Faber, 1968), p. 10; and James Rosenau, *Linkage Politics: Essays on the Convergence of National and International Systems* (New York: Free Press, 1969).
13. Alexei A. Kara-Murza, "Seasonal Cooling or New Ice Age?" *Russia Watch*, no. 5 (March 2001): p. 23.
14. See Donald N. Jensen, "The Politics of Policy Making," Radio Free Europe/Radio Liberty (RFE/RL), 1998 <http://www.rferl.org/aca/special/ruwhorules/policy_6 .html>.
15. Iurii Fedorov, "Interest Groups and Russia's Foreign Policy," *International Affairs* (Moscow) 44, no. 6 (1998): pp. 173–82.
16. Ibid., p. 174; and Hunter's personal conversations with Russian and other experts.
17. See Kimberly Marten Zisk, "The Foreign Policy Preferences of Russian Defense Industrialists," in *The Sources of Russian Foreign Policy after the Cold War*, ed. Celeste Wallander (Boulder, CO: Westview Press, 1996), pp. 95–120.
18. Quoted in Seweryn Bialer, *Stalin's Successors: Leadership, Stability, and Change in the Soviet Union* (New York: Cambridge University Press, 1980), p. 270.
19. Mandelbaum, *New Russian Foreign Policy*, p. 1.
20. Although Yevgenii Primakov was a champion of creating a multipolar world and opposed to unipolarity (in the form of U.S. supremacy), he declared the end of the era of superpowers. Yevgenii Primakov, "Segodnyashasi mǐr v epokhn post-superdezluw" ("Today's World in the Post Superpower Epoch"), *Rossiiskaya Gazeta*, 12 January 2003.
21. Robert Donaldson and Joseph Nogee, *The Foreign Policy of Russia: Changing Systems, Enduring Interests* (Armonk, NY: M.E. Sharpe, 1998), p. 94.
22. Alexander Dallin, "New Thinking on Foreign Policy," in *New Thinking in Soviet Politics*, ed. Archie Brown (New York: St. Martin's Press, 1992), p. 75.
23. Sarah Mendelson, *Changing Course: Ideas, Politics, and the Soviet Withdrawal from Afghanistan* (Princeton, NJ: Princeton University Press, 1998), pp. 23–25.
24. Donaldson and Nogee, *Foreign Policy of Russia*, p. 94.
25. Dallin, "New Thinking on Foreign Policy," p. 72.
26. Gorbachev also warned Iran not to spread fundamentalism in the Caucasus, despite the fact that the Iranian government had declared events in Azerbaijan "internal affairs" of the USSR.
27. Quoted in Suzanne Crow, "Competing Blueprints for Russian Foreign Policy," RFE/RL *Research Report* 1, no. 50 (18 December 1992): p. 45.

28. Alexander Rahr, " 'Atlanticists' versus 'Eurasians' in Russian Foreign Policy," RFE/
    RL *Research Report* 1, no. 22 (29 May 1992): p. 19.
29. Ibid.
30. Ibid.
31. Ibid.
32. Ibid., and "B.N. Yeltsin's Press Conference at the UN" [in Russian], *Rossiiskaya gaz-
    eta*, 3 February 1992, in *Current Digest of the Post-Soviet Press* 44, no. 5 (February
    1992): p. 12.
33. Mohiaddin Mesbahi, "Russian Foreign Policy and Security in Central Asia and the
    Caucasus," *Central Asian Survey* 12, no. 2 (1993): p. 184.
34. Vasiliy Mikhailov, "OBSE ob'iavit Rossii dzhikhad" (OSCE will declare jihad against
    Russia), *Kommersant Daily*, 18 November 1999, reproduced by the National News
    Service (Moscow) <http://www.nns.ru/press-file/dagestan/expert/dag306.html>.
35. Vladimir Putin, "Why We Must Act," *New York Times*, 14 November 1999.
36. Henry Kissinger, "What to Do with the New Russia," *Washington Post*, 14 August
    2001.
37. Ibid.
38. In an interview with *Le Monde*, Kozyrev, recalling General Charles de Gaulle's com-
    ment that the principal objective of France's foreign policy was to make every French-
    woman coming home from the market happy and smiling, said, "The Russian Foreign
    Ministry will feel that it has been useful, when Russian women no longer wait in line
    for hours thinking of how to feed their families." *Le Monde*, 8 June 1992.
39. Yevgeniy Gusarov, "Toward a Europe of Democracy and Unity," *Rossiiskaya gazeta*,
    5 March 1992.
40. For more details, see Kozyrev's interview with *TASS*, reproduced by the Foreign Broad-
    cast Information Service, FBIS-SOV 92-060, 27 March 1992.
41. Gusarov, "Towards a Europe of Democracy and Unity."
42. Mesbahi, "Russian Foreign Policy and Security," pp. 183–84.
43. For the full text of the charter, see *FBIS Daily Report*, FBIS-SOV-92-118, 18 June
    1992.
44. Andranik Mingranyan, "Russia and the Near Abroad" [in Russian], *Nezavisimaya Gaz-
    eta,* 12 January 1994, in *Current Digest of the Post-Soviet Press* 46, no. 6 (9 March
    1994).
45. Ednan Agayev, "Rossiia prevyshe vsego" (Russia above all else), *Moskovskiye novosti*,
    no. 18 (3 May 1992).
46. Mingranyan, "Russia and the Near Abroad."
47. Sergei Stankevich, "Russia in Search of Itself," *National Interest*, summer 1992, p. 47.
48. Ibid.
49. Quoted in Donaldson and Nogee, *Foreign Policy of Russia*, p. 21.
50. Stankevich, "Russia in Search of Itself," p. 57.
51. Sergei Goncharov, "The Special Interests of Russia—What Are They?" *Izvestia*, 25
    February 1992. This view is flawed because southern Europe borders on the Middle
    East, and Europe has a large Muslim population. See Shireen T. Hunter, ed., *Islam,
    Europe's Second Religion: The New Social, Cultural, and Political Landscape* (West-
    port, CT: Praeger, 2002).
52. Stankevich, "Russia in Search of Itself," p. 48.
53. See Neil Malcolm, Alex Pavda, Roy Allison, and Margo Light, *Internal Factors in
    Russian Foreign Policy* (Oxford: Oxford University Press, 1996), pp. 54–56.
54. The Eurasianists reject economic shock therapy and social Darwinism in favor of eco-
    nomic reforms with a social conscience.
55. Stankevich, "Russia in Search of Itself," p. 47.
56. Quoted in Mesbahi, "Russian Foreign Policy and Security," p. 187.
57. According to Primakov, "Russia cannot be great, it cannot play the positive role it is

destined to in the absence of such a wide geopolitical scope. In promoting relations with all these countries, we must remember that history never mollifies geopolitical values." Ibid.

58. Igor Torbakov, "The 'Statists' and the Ideology of Russian Imperial Nationalism," RFE/RL *Research Paper* 1, no. 11 (December 1992): pp. 10–16.

59. Andranik Mingranyan, "Real and Illusory Guidelines in Foreign Policy" [in Russian], *Rossiiskaya gazeta*, 4 August 1992, in *Current Digest of the Post-Soviet Press* 4, no. 32 (9 September 1992): pp. 1–4.

60. On Ambartsumov's views, see Suzanne Crow, "Ambartsumov's Influence on Russian Foreign Policy," RFE/RL *Research Report* 2, no. 19 (7 May 1993): pp. 32–90.

61. See "Interview by Russia's Foreign Minister Igor Ivanov to the Itogi Weekly," Ministry of Foreign Affairs of the Russian Federation, Information and Press Department, 29 January 2003 <www.mid.ru>.

62. Alexei Malashenko, "Rossiia i Islam" (Russia and Islam), *Nezavisimaya gazeta*, 22 February 1992. "The Muslim East represents the region that Russia cannot afford to lose, especially given the connections accumulated throughout the centuries." Ibid.

63. Ibid.

64. Alexei Vassiliev, "Assessing Russia's Ties with the Moslem World" [in Russian], *Izvestia*, 10 March 1992, in *Current Digest of the Post-Soviet Press* 44, no. 10 (8 April 1992).

65. Malashenko, "Rossiia i Islam."

66. Mesbahi, "Russian Foreign Policy and Security," p. 189.

67. Therese Raphael, "Kozyrev's Doctrine: The CIS Is Our Turf," *Wall Street Journal* (Europe), 20 June 1994.

68. Quoted in Mesbahi, "Russian Foreign Policy and Security," p. 187.

69. Ibid.

70. Suzanne Crow, "Russia Promotes CIS as an International Organization," RFE/RL *Research Report* 3, no. 11 (13 March 1994): pp. 33–38. On CIS failures, see Ann Sheehy, "The CIS: A Shaky Edifice," RFE/RL *Research Report* 2, no. 1 (January 1993); and Elizabeth Teague, "The CIS: An Unpredictable Future," RFE/RL *Research Report* 3, no. 1 (7 January 1994).

71. Primakov became foreign minister in 1996 and prime minister in 1999. For a critical view of the concept of "multipolarity," see Ariel Cohen, "The 'Primakov Doctrine': Russia's Zero-Sum Game with the United States," *Heritage Foundation*, no. 167 (15 December 1997).

72. For the text and the list of those who endorsed the new strategy, see the official website of the Council on Foreign and Defense Policy <http://www.svop.ru>.

73. Peter W. Rodman, "The World's Resentment: Anti-Americanism as a Global Phenomenon," *National Interest*, no. 60 (Summer 2000): p. 33.

74. "China, France Sign Joint Declaration," *Beijing Review* 40, no. 22 (2–8 June 1997) <www.dawning.iist.unu.edu/china/bjreview/95Jun/97-22-7.html>.

75. For the text of Primakov's speech, see <http://www.unip.org/missions/russianfed/rus_mis/press/1997/prb97efl.htm>.

76. "Text of PRC-Russia Statement Released" (in Chinese), Xinhua Domestic Service (Beijing), 25 April 1996, reproduced by the Foreign Broadcast Information Service, FBIS-CHI-96-081 <http://wnc.fedworld.gov>. Some Western observers have seen this call as a sign of "deep enmity toward the liberal-democratic order." Chandler Rosenberger, "Russian Roulette," *National Review*, 26 January 1998.

77. "Yeltsin Champions 'Multipolar' World," Interfax *Daily News Bulletin* (Moscow), 7 February 1998, reproduced by the Foreign Broadcast Information Service, FBIS-SOV-98-038 <http://wnc.fedworld.gov>.

78. Primakov's speech to the United Nations <http://www.unip.org/missions/russianfed/rus_mis/press/1997/prb97efl.htm>.

79. Julie M. Rahm, "Russia, China, India: A New Strategic Triangle for a New Cold War?" *Parameters* (U.S. Army War College Quarterly) 31, no. 4 (Winter 2001): pp. 87–96.
80. Reportedly, at a Council of Europe meeting in October 1997, Yeltsin criticized U.S. objections to French investment in Iran's oil industry and said, "We do not need an uncle from elsewhere. . . . We in Europe can unite ourselves." Quoted in Chandler Rosenberger, "Moscow's Multipolar Mission," *Perspective* 8, no. 2 (November–December 1997) <http://www.bu.edu/iscip/vol8/Rosenberger.html>.
81. Cohen, " 'Primakov Doctrine,' " p. 3.
82. Aleksey Chichkin, "An 'Asian Entente' Could Become a Reality" [in Russian], *Rossiiskaya gazeta*, 12 May 1997, reproduced by the Foreign Broadcast Information Service, FBIS-SOV-97-091 <http://wnc.fedworld.gov>. Chichkin stated: "Elements of a new world order are starting to take shape in Asia. They are being created in relations among three great powers—Russia, China, and Iran."
83. Shireen T. Hunter, *Iran between the Gulf and the Caspian Basin: Strategic and Economic Implications* (Abu Dhabi: Emirates Center for Strategic Studies and Research, 2000).
84. Primakov visited Iran when he was foreign minister.
85. Dimitry Gornastayev, "Putin visits Beijing, Pyongyang" [in Russian], *Nezavisimaya gazeta*, 19 July 2000, in *Current Digest of the Post-Soviet Press* 52, no. 29 (6 September 2000); Lyudmila Yerumkova, "Venezuela, Russia Have Same Concept of Multipolar World," ITAR-TASS, 15 May 2000; Dimitry Gornastayev, "In Cuba, Putin, Castro Find Much Common Ground" [in Russian], *Nezavisimaya gazeta*, 16 December 2000, in *Current Digest of the Post-Soviet Press* 52, no. 50 (10 January 2001). In their joint statement in July 2001 dealing with the Anti-Ballistic Missile Treaty and the United States plans to develop a national missile defense, system, Putin and and French President Jacques Chirac noted, "In order to take the strategic context and, in particular, the formation of multipolarity into account more freely, it is essential that they are not supplanted by a less binding system that would pave the way for a new rivalry." Ksenia Fokina, "Chirac Visit Yields Modest Results" [in Russian], *Nezavisimaya gazeta*, 3 July 2001, in *Current Digest of the Post-Soviet Press* 53, no. 27 (1 August 2001).
86. Nicholas Berry, "Treaty Sends a Message," *Financial Times*, 20 July 2001.
87. Quoted in Roy Medvedev, "Vladimir Putin: New Emphasis in Russian Foreign Policy" [in Russian], *Rossiiskaya gazeta*, 8 August 2000, in *Current Digest of the Post-Soviet Press* 52, no. 32 (6 September 2000).
88. Georgy Kunadze, "Russia Pursues New Foreign Policy," *Daily Yomiuri*, 14 March 2000.
89. Russian journalist Anna Perfilyeva, commenting on Primakov's performance at the meeting of the Association of Southeast Asian Nations (ASEAN), applauded his "brilliant maneuvering" and the "wonderful way" he had of "giving vent to the irritation about the unceremoniousness of American foreign policy which has been building up deep inside ASEAN." Anna Perfilyeva, "Not Everything Is All Right with Mrs. Albright. The Ball Thrown by Yevgeniy Primakov at the ASEAN Forum Hits the Target" [in Russian], *Obshchaya gazeta*, no. 30 (1 August 1997), reproduced by the Foreign Broadcast Information Service, FBIS-SOV-97-217 <http://wnc.fedworld.gov>.
90. On the missile crisis, see Yuriy Glotyuk, "Missiles for Cyprus," *Izvestia*, 1 December 1999, reproduced in *Defense and Security*, 3 December 1999.
91. Rosenberger, "Moscow's Multipolar Mission."
92. "U.S. Trade Balance with China," U.S. Census Bureau, Foreign Trade Division <http://www.census.gov/foreign-trade/balance/c5700.htm>.
93. "China Statistical Data," China.Org <http://www.china.org.cn/e-company/02-04-11/web020217.htm>.
94. "Russian Minister Hopes Trade with China Will Continue Expanding," *BBC Monitoring International Reports*, 29 November 2002.
95. Figures based on information provided by the embassy of India, Washington, DC.

96. "U.S. 'Worried' over Indian Trade Ties," *Business Day* (Johannesburg), 30 January 2002 <http://www.bday.co.za>.

97. Quoted in A. Azimov, "Moscow and Delhi in a Multipolar World," *International Affairs* (Moscow) 46, no. 5 (2000): p. 92.

98. Vladimir Radyukin, "India's Trade with Russia Declining," *Hindu,* 4 November 2001 <http://www.hinduonnet.com/thehindu/2001/11/04/stories/03040009.htm>.

99. Satish Kumar, "India between America and Russia: Need to Tilt towards U.S." *Journal of World Affairs,* 16 January 2001 <http://www/ipcs.org/issues/articles/449_ifp_satish .html>.

100. The crisis over Iraq and the war that ensued caused serious tensions in the United States' relations with some of its key European allies, notably France and Germany, throughout the winter and spring of 2002–2003. By July 2003, relations had been somewhat mended, but trans-Atlantic relations remained fragile, especially in light of a potential crisis looming over Iran and possibly Syria because of United States efforts to effect a change of regime in these countries, particularly Iran.

101. Recorded by Hunter during a speech by Lukin at a conference in Moscow on 28 May 2002.

102. See Dmitri Trenin, "The China Factor: Challenge and Chance for Russia," in *Rapprochement or Rivalry? Russia-China Relations in a Changing Asia,* ed. Sherman W. Garnett (Washington, DC.: Carnegie Endowment for International Peace, 2000).

103. Yegor Gaidar, "Rossiya XXI veka: Ne mirovoi zhandarm, a forpost demokratii v Evrazii" ('Russia in the twenty-first Century: Not a world policeman, but an outpost of democracy in Eurasia'), *Izvestia,* 18 May 1995.

104. Andrei Kozyrev, "Riski svoi i Chuzhie" ("Risks of our own and of others"), *Moskovskiye Novosti,* no. 30 (1 August 2000). Regarding diverging Russian views on China, see Alexei D. Voskressenski, "Russia's Evolving Grand Strategy towards China," in *Rapprochement or Rivalry? Russia-China Relations in a Changing Asia,* ed. Sherman W. Garnett (Washington, DC:).

105. See Alexander Lukin, "Russia's Images of China and Russian-Chinese Relations," *East Asia* 17, no. 1 (Spring 1999): pp. 5–39.

106. See Rajan Menon, "The Strategic Convergence between Russia and China," *Survival* 39, no. 2 (summer 1997): pp. 101–25.

107. Georgy Kunadze, "Sindrome Kuzkinoy matery" (An "I'll teach you a lesson" syndrome), *Novoe vremya,* no. 37 (19 September 1999).

108. Jyotsna Bakshi, "Russia-China Military-Technical Cooperation: Implications for India," *Strategic Analysis* 24, no. 4 (July 2000), <http://www.idsa_india.org>.

109. Jyotsna Bakshi, "Sino-Russian Strategic Partnership in Central Asia: Implications for India," *Strategic Analysis* 25, no. 2 (May 2001), <http://www.idsa_india.org>.

110. Russia's foreign minister discussed the new concept and its implications for Russia's external relations in Igor Ivanov, "The New Russian Identity: Innovation and Continuity in Russian Foreign Policy," *Washington Quarterly* 24, no. 3 (summer 2001): pp. 7–13.

111. Vyacheslav Nikomov, "Russian Gaullism: Putin's Foreign Policy Doctrine," *Russia Watch,* no. 5 (March 2001): p. 18.

112. Aleksei Pushkov, "From Dreams of Harmony to Tough-Minded Realism—The Evolution of Our Foreign Policy Concept from Early Yeltsin to Early Putin" [in Russian], *Nezavisimaya gazeta,* 18 July 2000, in *Current Digest of the Post-Soviet Press* 52, no. 29 (16 August 2000): p. 7.

113. Yevgeniy Verlin, "Experts' Mandate to the President" [in Russian], Vremya MN, 2 November 2001, reproduced by the Foreign Broadcast Information Service, FBIS-SOV-2001-1102 <http://wnc.fedworld.gov>.

114. Igor S. Ivanov, *The New Russian Diplomacy* (Washington, DC: Nixon Center and Brookings Institution Press, 2002), p. 122.

115. Nikomov, "Russian Gaullism," p. 18.

116. Sergei Markov, "Russia Revamps Its Foreign Policy," *Russia Watch*, no. 5 (March 2001), p. 20.
117. Nikomov, "Russian Gaullism," p. 18. Putin is not consistent in this policy, however, or at least he has a broad interpretation, as in his challenge in 2002 to Georgia and occasionally to the Baltic states.
118. Ibid.
119. Vladimir Smelov, "Russia—Biggest Oil Supplier to Germany," ITAR-TASS (Moscow), 30 July 2001.
120. Jury Sigor, "Why Putin Wants Russia to Become More European," *European Affairs* 2, no. 4 (fall 2001): p. 112.
121. Lilia Shevtsova and Angela Stent, "America, Russia, and Europe: A Realignment," *Survival* 44, no. 4 (winter 2002–2003): pp. 121–34.
122. Statement by Mikhail Margelov, member of the Russian Federation Council, quoted in Alan Sipress, "U.S., Russia Recast Their Relationship," *Washington Post*, 4 October 2001.
123. Oksana Antonenko, "Putin's Gamble," *Survival* 43, no. 4 (winter 2001–2002), pp. 51–53.
124. Fedor Sukhov, "The Great Silk Road Leads to the United States: Asian Frontiers Are Becoming an Outpost of the West" [in Russian], *Obshchaya gazeta*, no. 49 (6–12 December 2001), reproduced by the Foreign Broadcast Information Service, FBIS-NES-2001-1212 <http://wnc.fedworld.gov>.
125. Tatyana Rubleva, "Proschai, Kavkaz! USA nachinaiut operatsiiu po vitesneniiu Rossii" (Good-bye Caucasus! USA starts operation to drive Russia out), *Nezavisimaya gazeta*, 23 January 2003 <http://www.ng.cis.2002-08-27/1_caucasus.html>.
126. Rajan Menon, "Structural Constraints on Russian Diplomacy," *Orbis*, fall 2001 <http://www.findarticles.com/cb_dlstm0365414_45/79379266/print.shtml>.
127. Peter Baker, "U.S.-Russia Ties Suffer a Renewal of Tension," *Washington Post*, 15 January 2002. Baker writes, "U.S. officials recently have spoken out against the crackdown on the independent media in Russia, espionage trials . . . and the use of force against civilians in the breakaway southern region of Chechnya."
128. Nina Bachkatov, "Russia: Winning without Fighting" [in French], *Le Monde Diplomatique*, November 2001 <http://mondediplo.com/2001/11/03russia>.
129. "Russian President's Televised Address to the Nation" [in Russian], *Kommersant*, 25 September 2001, reproduced by the WPS Monitoring Agency (Moscow) <http://www.wps.ru>.
130. Igor Ivanov, "Organizing the World to Fight Terror," *New York Times*, 27 January 2002.
131. Clifford Giddy and Fiona Hill, "Putin's Agenda, America's Choice: Russia's Search for Strategic Stability," *Brookings Institution Policy Brief* no. 99 (May 2002).
132. Irina Chumakova, "Russia Will Strive to Limit U.S. Military Presence in Central Asia," ITAR-TASS, 11 June 2002.
133. United States Embassy, Moscow, 14 May 2002 <http://www.usembassy.ru/policy/new.htm>.
134. Sharon LaFraniere, "Anti-Western Sentiment Grows in Russia," *Washington Post*, 19 January 2003.
135. Speech of the President of the Russian Federation, V.V. Putin <http://www.kremlin.ru/events/77.html>.
136. Marek Halter, "We Will Seek to Come to an Agreement with Chechens," [in Russian], *Nezavisimaya Gazeta*, 8 July 2000, in *Russian Press Digest* (Moscow), 10 July 2000. For more on Russian views of bin Laden and the Islamic terror network, see Vladimir Lapskiy, "Octopus Tentacles" [in Russian], *Rossiiskaya Gazeta*, 24 October 2000, reproduced by the Foreign Broadcast Information Service, FBIS-SOV-2000-1024 <http://wnc.fedworld.gov>.
137. "Putin Notes Extremist, Terror Threats to Republics," Interfax *Daily News Bulletin*

(Moscow), 19 May 2000, reproduced by the Foreign Broadcast Information Service, FBIS-SOV-2000-0519 <http://wnc.fedworld.gov>.

138. "Yastrzhembsky Points Out the Increasing Coordination of Actions of Terrorists in a Zone of 'Arc of Instability,'" Associated Press, 16 October 2000.

139. "Putin Notes Extremists, Terror Threats to Republics."

140. "Defending the United States requires prevention and sometimes preemption. It is not possible to defend against every threat, in every place, at every conceivable time. Defending against terrorism and other emerging threats requires that we take the war to the enemy." See Donald H. Rumsfeld, "Transforming the Military," *Foreign Affairs* 81, no. 3 (May–June 2002): p. 31; "[Sweeping new ideas in the Bush administration] call for American unilateral and preemptive, even preventive, use of force, facilitated if possible by coalitions of the willing—but ultimately unconstrained by the rules and norms of the international community." See G. John Ikenberry, "America's Imperial Ambition," *Foreign Affairs* 81, no. 5 (September–October 2002): p. 44.

141. "In an interview on Friday, Mr. Powell said the publicity over the doctrine of preemption, enshrined in the administration's National Security Strategy published last year, overlooked the fact that preemption was only one tool among many. A victory in Iraq did not mean that military action would be used against other countries, he said." See Steven R. Weisman, "Pre-emption: Idea with a Lineage Whose Time Has Come," *New York Times*, 23 March 2003.

142. "Putin Says Russia Completely Abandons Confrontation in International Relations," Interfax *Daily News Bulletin* (Moscow), 25 July 2002, reproduced by the Foreign Broadcast Information Service, FBIS-SOV-2002-0725 <http://wnc.fedworld.gov>.

143. See Putin's interview in Jing Xianfa and Ma Jian, "In an Exclusive Interview with Renmin Ribao, Putin Stresses That Russia and China Should Strengthen Their Bilateral Ties" (in Chinese), *Renmin Ribao* (Beijing), 31 May 2002, reproduced by the Foreign Broadcast Information Service, FBIS-CHI-2002-0531 <http://wnc.fedworld.gov>.

144. Ibid.

145. Andrei Savitski and Igor Korotchenki, "Provalnii visit Ivanov v Pekin" (Sergei Ivanov's failed visit to Beijing), *Nezavisimaya Gazeta*, 3 June 2002, <http://ng.ru/world/2002 -06-03/1_ivanov.html>.

146. Attributed to Ambassador James Collins.

Notes to Chapter 7

1. On Catherine the Great's ambitions to conquer Constantinople, India, and Persia, see Ivar Spector, *The Soviet Union and the Muslim World, 1917–1958* (Seattle: University of Washington Press, 1959), pp. 6–7.

2. Quoted ibid., pp. 16–17 (emphasis added). Dostoevsky's writings have echoes of Zhirinovsky's talk about a last drive south where Russians can relax in the soft breezes of the Indian Ocean.

3. Quoted ibid. pp. 17–18. Danilevsky wrote these passages in his book *Russia and Europe*, published in 1869.

4. David Gillard, *The Struggle for Asia, 1828–1914: A Study in British and Russian Imperialism* (New York: Holmes and Meier, 1977).

5. Spector, *Soviet Union and the Muslim World*.

6. For example, the socialist movement from the early 1900s was strong in parts of northern Iran, which had close interaction with Muslim parts of the tsarist empire, notably Baku.

7. Spector, *Soviet Union and the Muslim World*, p. 37. The Bolsheviks, for a time, made their own Muslims believe that it was the hand of Providence that had brought about the Bolshevik Revolution. Some ignorant Soviet Muslims spread propaganda to the

effect that the new regime would be established on the basis of the Qu'ran and the Shari'a.

8. Ibid., p. 34.
9. Ibid., pp. 48–49, 53.
10. Ibid., p. 57.
11. Ibid.
12. Quoted in ibid., p. 85.
13. This was a branch of the party by the same name that had been created in Baku in 1917.
14. This movement was very complex and had many dimensions, including religious/ Islamic ones. There were also divisions within the movement's leadership between those who were Iranian nationalists and those who were dedicated Bolsheviks.
15. For a discussion of the Jangali movement, see Sepehr Zabih, *The Communist Movement in Iran* (Berkeley: University of California Press, 1966), pp. 16–19. For a recent Russian view of this episode and Russia's role in it, see Moisei Persits, *A Shamefaced Intervention: The Soviet Intervention in Iran, 1920–21* (Moscow: Russian Center for Strategic Research and International Studies, 1999). During Stalin's rule, Soviet troops occupied much of predominantly Muslim Eastern Turkestan (currently the Xinjiang Province of China) and helped establish the short-lived Eastern Turkestan Republic in 1944. However, the Soviet Union never created a formal Communist government in the region and surrendered control of the territory to Mao Zedong's forces shortly after the establishment of the People's Republic of China.
16. In a cable to General Fedor Fedorovich Roskolnikov, commander of the Soviet military and naval detachments that had landed in the Iranian port of Enzelik, L.M. Morakhan said, "I fear any haste in establishing Soviet principles there could result in class antagonism and weaken the struggle in Persia." Quoted in Zabih, *Communist Movement in Iran*, p. 18.
17. Spector, *Soviet Union and the Muslim World*, p. 90.
18. Zabih, *Communist Movement in Iran*, p. 21.
19. Spector, *Soviet Union and the Muslim World*, p. 90.
20. Louis Fischer, *The Soviets in World Affairs* (Princeton, NJ: Princeton University Press, 1951), pp. i, xvi.
21. Spector, *Soviet Union and the Muslim World*, pp. 65–68.
22. Yu. Steklov, in an article published on 23 April 1917 in *Izvestia*, after recalling imperial rivalries over the Dardanelles, said that "the Turkish Revolution is returning the Dardanelles to the Turkish masses and through them to the world proletariat, which includes also the Russian." Quoted in Spector, *Soviet Union and the Muslim World*, p. 65.
23. The Central Bureau of the Eastern Peoples was an organization whose purpose was to spread Communist ideals among people of the east. Spector, *Soviet Union and the Muslim World*, p. 79.
24. Quoted ibid., p. 80.
25. In his letter to Lenin written in December 1920, Amanullah Khan acknowledged that he was acquainted with "the high ideals of the Soviet government in connection with the national liberation struggle of the peoples of the East." Ibid., p. 99.
26. Ibid., p. 97.
27. Turkey and Afghanistan provided assistance to the Basmachi movement.
28. Alexei Vassiliev, *Russian Policy in the Middle East: From Messianism to Pragmatism* (Reading, England: Ithaca Press, 1993), p. 3.
29. Jaan Pennar, *The USSR and the Arabs: The Ideological Dimension* (New York: Crane, Russak and Company, 1973), pp. 30–31.
30. Spector, *Soviet Union and the Muslim World*, pp. 127–72. On the Egyptian Communist Party, see Rami Ginat, *The Soviet Union and Egypt, 1945–1955* (London: Frank Cass, 1993).

31. A.A. Gromyko and B.N. Ponomarev, eds., *Soviet Foreign Policy, 1917–1980, vol. 1, 1917–1945* (Moscow: Progress Publishers, 1980), pp. 133–52.
32. Following the Soviet Union's disintegration, the Iranian government declared Article VI of the 1921 treaty null and void, but its status remains unclear, and it thus still poses a potential problem for Iran.
33. Spector, *Soviet Union and the Muslim World*, pp. 92–93.
34. Ibid., pp. 75–76.
35. Ibid., p. 95.
36. Ibid., p. 196.
37. Alvin Z. Rubinstein, *Soviet Policy toward Turkey, Iran, and Afghanistan: The Dynamics of Influence* (New York: Praeger, 1982), pp. 63–65.
38. See Zabih, *Communist Movement in Iran*, pp. 124–141.
39. See Tareq Y. Ismael, *The Arab Left* (Syracuse, NY: Syracuse University Press, 1976); and A.M. Said Salama, *Arab Socialism* (New York: Barnes and Noble, 1972).
40. Michel Aflaq, the father of Arab socialism, especially its Ba'athist variant, although a Christian, "attempted to integrate Islamic spiritual-religious elements as an essential component of Arab socialism." Ginat, *Soviet Union and Egypt*, pp. 58–60. Meanwhile, certain ulema and intellectuals, notably Mustafa as-Sibai in Syria, tried to demonstrate that Islam contained all the positive elements of socialism. Hamid Enayat, *Modern Islamic Political Thought* (Austin: University of Texas Press, 1982), pp. 148–52.
41. A good example is Iran, where the majority preferred a neutral position, or what the nationalist Iranian prime minister Muhammad Mossadegh called the strategy of "negative equilibrium." But Mossadegh was ousted as a result of an Anglo-American coup d'état, after which Iran joined the Western camp.
42. Karen Dawisha and Hélène Carrère d'Encausse, "Islam in the Foreign Policy of the Soviet Union: A Double-Edged Sword," in *Islam in Foreign Policy*, ed. Adeed Dawisha (Cambridge: Cambridge University Press, 1983), p. 163.
43. Walter Laqueur, *Communism and Nationalism in the Middle East* (London: Routledge and Kegan Paul, 1956), p. 6 (emphasis added).
44. Dawisha and Carrère d'Encausse, "Islam in the Foreign Policy of the Soviet Union," p. 166.
45. Ibid.
46. Ibid., pp. 166–67. Between 1970 and 1976, four major conferences were organized in Tashkent in which representatives of more than twenty Muslim countries participated. Also, between 1972 and 1978, Soviet Muslim delegations traveled to Islamic countries, from Saudi Arabia to Mali and Senegal, to take part in conferences. For details, see ibid.
47. According to Alexei Vassiliev, "There was no evidence that the USSR was behind the coup and no such charges were even made by serious Western sources even at the height of the anti-Soviet propaganda campaign." Vassiliev also repeats a conversation with Professor Y.V. Gonkovski, an expert on Afghanistan and Pakistan, to the effect that "when the poet and writer [Nar Muhammad] Taraki came to Moscow as a guest of the Writers Congress, he was not received by anyone at the top level. Moreover, an official of the International Department of the Central Committee told him that Afghanistan was not ripe for a 'socialist revolution.' " Vassiliev, *Russian Policy in the Middle East*, p. 249.
48. Selig S. Harrison, "The Shah, Not Kremlin, Touched Off Afghan Coup," *Washington Post*, 13 May 1978.
49. The Parcham was composed mostly of the upper middle class, especially Tajiks, and was more westernized. The Khalq was mostly Pashtun.
50. According to Vassiliev, "The propaganda cliché of 'international duty,' with which the Soviet army was entrusted, was not entirely insincere." Because the Afghan Communist Party "was a 'fraternal party' that had taken power under the banner of Marxism-

Leninism—it was ours." Vassiliev, *Russian Policy in the Middle East*, pp. 251–52. See ibid., pp. 246–67.

51. Ibid., p. 257. Brezhnev had been upset and insulted by Taraki's murder. There were also rumors that Hafizullah Amin (the president of Afghanistan from September to December, 1979) had connections with the CIA, which could have tipped the balance in favor of intervention.

52. Ibid., p. 249.

53. Quoted in Antonio Giustozzi, *War, Politics, and Society in Afghanistan, 1978–1992* (Washington, DC: Georgetown University Press, 2000), p. 5.

54. Ibid., pp. 57–64.

55. See Barnett Rubin, *The Fragmentation of Afghanistan* (New Haven, CT: Yale University Press, 1995).

56. Tad Daley, "Afghanistan and Gorbachev's Global Foreign Policy," *Asian Survey* 29, no. 5 (May 1989): pp. 496–97.

57. Ye.M. Primakov, "Islam i protsessy obshchestvemovo razvitiia stran zarubezhnova vostoka" (Islam and the processes of social development in the countries of the foreign East), *Voprosi Filosofii* (Questions of philosophy), no. 8 (1980): pp. 60–63.

58. Shireen T. Hunter, *Iran and the World: Continuity in a Revolutionary Decade* (Bloomington: Indiana University Press, 1990), pp. 81–89. The Soviet defector was Vladimir Andreyevich Kuzichkin, ex–vice consul in Tehran and a senior KGB official. Among those executed was Captain Bahram Afzali, commander of the Iranian navy and a special adviser to the Speaker of the Iranian parliament, Ali-Akbar Hashemi Rafsanjani. "Iran Tries Ex-Navy Chief," *Washington Post*, 7 December 1983.

59. One such commentator was Alexander Bovin. On general Soviet disillusionment, see Muriel Atkin, "Moscow's Disenchantment with Iran," *Survey* (autumn/winter 1983): pp. 247–60.

Notes to Chapter 8

1. Sergei Gretsky, "Civil War in Tajikistan: Causes, Developments, and Prospects for Peace," in *Central Asia: Conflict, Resolution, and Change*, ed. Roald Z. Sagdeev and Susan Eisenhower (Washington, DC: Center for Political and Strategic Studies, 1995) <http://www.cpss.org/casiabk/chap16.txt>; and Monika Shepherd, "The Effects of Russian and Uzbek Intervention in the Tajik Civil War," *Soviet and Post-Soviet Review* 23, no. 3 (1996): pp. 28–32.

2. Allen Hetmanek, "Islamic Revolution and Jihad Come to the Former Central Asia," *Central Asian Survey* 12, no. 3 (1993): pp. 365–78.

3. Dmitri Trenin, "Russia's Security Interests and Policies in the Caucasus Region," in *Contested Borders in the Caucasus*, ed. Bruno Coppieters (Brussels: VUPRESS, 1996) <http://poli.vub.ac.be/publ/ContBorders/eng/ch0301.htm>.

4. Ibid.

5. Following the failure of the August 1991 coup d'état, the 201st Division of the Russian army became involved in the Tajik civil strife. President Yeltsin sent Yegor Gaidar to restrain the military, but to no avail. Sergei Gretsky, "Russia's Policy toward Central Asia," in *Central Asia and the Caucasus* (Luleå, Sweden Center for Social and Political Studies: May, 1997) <http://www.ca-c.org/dataeng/GRETSKY.shtml>.

6. Suzanne Crow, "Competing Blueprints for Russian Foreign Policy," Radio Free Europe/Radio Liberty (RFE/RL) *Research Report* 1, no. 50 (18 December 1992): pp. 45–50.

7. Fleming Splidsboel-Hansen, "The Official Russian Concept of Contemporary Central Asian Islam: The Security Dimension," *Europe-Asia Studies* 49, no. 8 (1997), p. 1501.

8. Quoted ibid., p. 1502.

9. Ibid., p. 1503.
10. See Teresa Rakowska-Harmstone, *Russia and Nationalism in Central Asia: The Case of Tadzhikistan* (Baltimore: Johns Hopkins Press, 1970), pp. 71–74.
11. Gretsky, "Civil War in Tajikistan."
12. See Aziz Niyazi, "Tajikistan I: The Regional Dimension of Conflict," in *Conflicting Loyalties and the State in Post-Soviet Russia and Eurasia*, ed. Michael Waller, Bruno Coppieters, and Alexei Malashenko (London: Frank Cass, 1998).
13. Shireen T. Hunter, "Nationalist Movements in Soviet Asia," *Current History* 89, no. 549 (October 1990): p. 327.
14. Shahrbanou Tadjbakhsh, "The Tajik Spring of 1992," *Central Asia Monitor*, no. 2 (1993): pp. 10–14.
15. The most important organization pursuing this goal was the Samarkand Movement. See Shireen T. Hunter, *Central Asia since Independence* (Westport, CT: Praeger, 1996), pp. 51–52. Uzbekistan's Tajik minority became more willing to identify themselves as such on their internal passports. Monika Shepherd, "Intervention in Central Asia," *Perspective* vol 7, no. 3 (January–February 1997) <http://www.bu.edu/iscip/vol.7/shepherd.h>.
16. Hunter, *Central Asia since Independence*, p. 32.
17. In an interview in a Turkish newspaper, Karimov, after referring to the establishment of a Slavic union, said, "Why should the people in Central Asia not be able to do the same and why should this unity not include Turkey and Azerbaijan? I believe it will." "President Karimov Interviewed on Turkish Ties," *Cumhuriyet*, 27 December 1991, reproduced by the Foreign Broadcast Information Service, FBIS-SOV-91-249 <http://www.wnc.fedworld.gov>.
18. Some Russian authors characterized these attacks as "pogroms whose victims were Russians." Irina Zviagelskaya, "The Tajik Conflict," *Central Asia and the Caucasus*, May 1997, http://www.ca_mc.org/dataeng/st_oq_zvjag_3.sh>.
19. Viktor Ponomarev, "The Bells of Hope," *Pravda*, 10 May 1990. The author claimed that teahouses were turned into prayer houses for the establishment of an Islamic state. He also claimed, "Groups of militants, galvanized by local mullahs, were already hastening to the capital from outlying areas shouting demands for the establishment of an Islamic republic."
20. David Remnick, "Up to 37 Said to Die in Soviet Asian Riots; Protests Spread to Another Republic," *Washington Post*, 13 February 1990. Considering the harsh economic conditions of the country, the high rate of unemployment, and the severe shortage of housing, "any rumor that outsiders—especially Christian outsiders—would be 'taking away' precious housing from the local Moslem community was bound to be explosive." Ibid.
21. Zviagelskaya, "Conflict Dynamics." Zviagelskaya notes that those who tended to agree with the opposition's views believed that the main reason was to discredit the opposition.
22. Barnett Rubin, "The Fragmentation of Tajikistan," *Survival* 35, no. 4 (winter 1993–94): p. 77. What is disputed is whether the elections were totally rigged.
23. According to Sergei Gretsky, "Since independence, the opposition [has] articulated its desire to work together with President Rahmon Nabiev and his government in building a truly independent Tajikistan. Yet the Khujandis have been more interested in preserving their own power than addressing challenges of post-Soviet existence." Gretsky, "Civil War in Tajikistan."
24. Michael Collins Dunn, "Uzbek Role in Tajik Civil War Is Ominous Portent for Central Asia," *Washington Report on Middle East Affairs*, March 1993 <http://www.washington.report.org/backissues/0393/9303020.1>. Dunn writes, "If reports in the West and the Muslim World are to be believed, in the final rounds of fighting in

November and December [1992] Uzbekistan sent helicopter gunships, tanks and ground troops into Tajikistan in support of the ex-communist side."

25. Gretsky, "Civil War in Tajikistan."

26. Ibid.

27. Ibid. The PFT is the Popular Front of Tajikistan, and is made up mostly of Uzbeks and Kulyabis.

28. Maxim Shashenkov, "Russia in Central Asia: Emerging Security Links," in *From the Gulf to Central Asia: Players in the New Great Game*, ed. Anoushiravan Ehteshami (Exeter, England: University of Exeter Press, 1994), pp. 168–87. On Kozyrev's view of Russia's special role in the post-Soviet space, see "Kozyrev's Doctrine: The CIS Is Our Turf," *Wall Street Journal* (Europe), 20 June 1994; and Suzanne Crow, "Russia Promotes the CIS as an International Organization," RFE/RL *Research Report* 3, no. 11 (18 March 1994): pp. 33–38.

29. Mastibek Davlatskayev, "The Russian Foreign Ministry Distances Itself from the Tajik-Afghan Conflict" [in Russian], *Segodnya*, 23 July 1993, in *Current Digest of the Post-Soviet Press* 45, no. 29 (18–19 August 1993).

30. Andrei Kortunov and Andrei Shoumikhin, "Russia and Central Asia: Evolution of Mutual Perceptions, Policies, and Interdependence," in *Ethnic Challenges beyond Borders: Chinese and Russian Perspectives of the Central Asian Conundrum*, ed. Yongjin Zhang and Rouben Azizian (London: Macmillan P, 1998), p. 22.

31. "Central Asia: Awkward Friends," *Economist*, April 8, 1995; and "Perry in Tashkent, Karimov on Russia," *Omri Daily Digest*, 7 April 1995.

32. Ahmed Rashid, *Taliban: Militant Islam, Oil, and Fundamentalism in Central Asia* (New Haven, CT: Yale University Press, 2001).

33. The large number of Tajik casualties was due to the fact that the fighting was mostly in the south. The large Uzbek-inhabited region of Khujand was left unscathed, and the Uzbeks were protected by government forces. Barnett Rubin reports that several houses in the Vakhsh Raion of Kurghan Teppa "bore inscriptions such as 'This is an Uzbek house; do not touch' " (Rubin, "Fragmentation of Tajikistan," p. 81).

34. The Moscow Agreement and its annexes are incorporated in United Nations document A/52/219S/1997/5170 of 2 July 1997.

35. Ahmed Rashid, "Proxy State," *Far Eastern Economic Review*, 15 September 1994. Rashid writes that "the Russians and the Uzbeks have showered support on General Rashid Dostam, the Uzbek warlord who is fighting Rabbani."

36. This conflict of interest was partly related to the energy issue and pipeline routes exporting Central Asian energy. See Shireen T. Hunter, "The Afghan Civil War: Implications for Central Asian Stability," in *Energy and Conflict in Central Asia and the Caucasus*, ed. Robert Ebel and Rajan Menon (Lanham, MD: Rowman and Littlefield, 2000), pp. 198–99.

37. Barnett R. Rubin, "Introduction: The Tajikistan Peace Agreement," 2000 <http://www.eurasianet.org/resource/regional/rubinintro.html>.

38. Ibid.

39. Ibid.

40. The presidential elections on 6 November 1999 indicated that the inclusion of opposition figures in the government has not led to democratic politics in Tajikistan. Davlat Usmon of the Islamic Revival Party, the only opposition candidate to run against incumbent President Emomali Rakhmonov, pulled out of the presidential elections. Rakhmonov, as the sole candidate, won a "landslide victory," with 96 percent of the vote and with more than 96 percent of registered voters turning out. "Tajikistan Vote Challenged," *Houston Chronicle*, 8 November 1999; and "Tajikistan: Vote Goes Ahead," *Gazette* (Montreal), 6 November 1999.

41. Sander Thoenes, "CIS Presidents Warn Taliban," *Financial Times*, 5 October 1996.

42. Ibid.

43. "Defense Council Secretary: No Aid for Anti-Taleban Groups," Interfax *Diplomatic Panorama*, 7 October 1996, reproduced by the Foreign Broadcast Information Service, FBIS-SOV-96-196 <http://wnc.fedworld.gov>.
44. Ibid.
45. Sander Thoenes, "Central Asia Eyes Taliban," *Financial Times*, 7 October 1996.
46. "Lebed Urges Support to Anti-Taleban Forces in Afghanistan," Interfax *Presidential Bulletin* (Moscow), 3 March 1997, reproduced by the Foreign Broadcast Information Service, FBIS-SOV-97-062 <http://wnc.fedworld.gov>; and Marcia Kunstel and Joseph Albright, "Focus on Afghanistan," *Atlanta Constitution*, 8 October 1996.
47. Kunstel and Albright, "Focus on Afghanistan."
48. Chris Bird, "Afghan Turmoil Rattles Central Asia," *Guardian* (London), 5 October 1996.
49. Ahmed Rashid, *Jihad: The Rise of Militant Islam in Central Asia* (New Haven, CT: Yale University Press, 2002), pp. 137–86.
50. In 1998, the Uzbek foreign minister stated that recruits from the Ferghana Valley were being indoctrinated and trained by groups based in Peshawar. "Uzbek Says Pakistan Islamist Groups Train Fighters," Reuters, 16 February 1998.
51. Pavel Kuznetsov and Viktor Troyanovskiy, "Yeltsin: Russia, Tajikistan, Uzbekistan Can Hold Taleban," ITAR-TASS, 14 August 1998, reproduced by the Foreign Broadcast Information Service, FBIS-SOV-98-226 <http://wnc.fedworld.gov>; and "Russian-Uzbek-Tajik Troika Apt to Complicate Pacification Efforts," Jamestown Foundation *Monitor* 4, no. 91 (12 May 1998).
52. Ahmad Shah Masoud visited Uzbekistan in the context of United Nations–sponsored Afghan peace talks in Tashkent. "Masud Hails Importance of Tashkent Meeting," Interfax *Daily News Bulletin* (Moscow), 22 July 1999, reproduced by the Foreign Broadcast Information Service, FBIS-SOV-1999-0722 <http://wnc.fedworld.gov>.
53. Igor Torbakov, "Putin's Threats to Bomb the Taliban Meant for Central Asians," *Eurasian Insight*, 13 June 2000 <http://www.eurasianet.org>.
54. "CIS Collective Force Gets Green Light," RFE/RL *Newsline*, 29 May 2001. Uzbekistan withdrew from the CIS Collective Security Pact in 1999. Georgia and Azerbaijan also did not renew their membership, and Turkmenistan never joined.
55. "Collective Anti-Terrorism Troops for Central Asia," Jamestown Foundation *Monitor* 7, no. 104 (30 May 2001).
56. "Nine Countries' Intelligence Services Hold 'Antiterrorism Exercises,' " Jamestown Foundation *Monitor* 7, no. 82 (27 April 2001).
57. Moscow's goals for the center were first outlined during the June 2000 CIS summit and later developed by the center's head, Lieutenant General Boris Melnikov, then Federal Security Services Director Nikolai Patrushev, and Security Council Secretary Sergei Ivanov. "Anti-Terrorism Center Remains Elusive," Jamestown Foundation *Monitor* 6, no. 129 (3 July 2000).
58. "Alexander Yakovenko, the Official Spokesman of Russia's Ministry of Foreign Affairs, Answers Russian Media Questions Regarding the Collective Security Council Session Held in Dushanbe on April 27–28 2003," Ministry of Foreign Affairs of the Russian Federation, Information and Press Department, 30 April 2003 <www.mid.ru>.
59. "Six CIS States Finalize Collective Security Treaty Organization," *Asia Africa Intelligence Wire*, 7 October 2002 <http://web2.infotrac.galegroup.com/itw/infomark/911/71/38565140w2/purl=rc1_GRGM_0_A92571282&dyn=7!xrn_2_0_A92571282?sw_aep=rock21695r>.
60. "Russian President Vladimir Putin Replies to Questions at Press Conference of Heads of States of Collective Security Treaty Member States, Dushanbe, April 28, 2003," Ministry of Foreign Affairs of the Russian Federation, Information and Press Department, 29 April 2003 <www.mid.ru>.
61. Jeremy Bransten, "Kyrgyzstan: Shanghai Five Summit Focuses on Separatism, Re-

gional Ties," RFE/RL *Weekday Magazine*, 25 August 1999 <http://www.rferl.org/nca/features>.

62. Vladimir Volkov, "Meeting of the 'Shanghai Group' in Bishkek: China Moves toward Moscow to Strengthen Its Influence in Central Asia," 2 September 1999 <http://www.wsws.org>.

63. In fact, the first agreement reached among the five countries on 26 April 1996 at Shanghai was titled "Moscow Agreement on the Reduction of Military Forces along Border Regions" and called for a "minimum militarized zone" where only border troops would be stationed within the 100-kilometer radius or buffer zone if signatory countries shared borders.

64. Oleg Zotov, "Outlooks of the Bishkek Treaty in the Light of Timur's Geopolitics and Political Development Trends of Late XX–Beginning of XXI Century," 20 September 2000 <www.trans-caspian.ru>.

65. Ibid.

66. The question of separatism was discussed in later summit meetings. Bruce Pannier, "Tajikistan: Shanghai Five Discuss Separatist Threats, Trade," RFE/RL *Weekday Magazine*, 5 July 2000 <http://www.rferl.org/nca/features>.

67. Valeri Agarkov, "India Ready to Enter Shanghai Cooperation Organization," ITAR-TASS, 7 June 2002, reproduced by the Foreign Broadcast Information Service, FBIS-SOV-2002-0607 <http://wnc.fedworld.gov>.

68. Viktoria Panfilova and Armen Khanbabjan, "Iran Accuses Putin of Being 'Politically Immature' " [in Russian], *Nezavisimaya gazeta*, 23 May 2002, reproduced by the WPS Monitoring Agency (Moscow) <http://www.wps.ru:8101>.

69. Richard Mackenzie, "The United States and the Taliban," in *Fundamentalism Reborn? Afghanistan and the Taliban*, ed. William Maley (New York: New York University Press, 1998), p. 95. Ahmed Rashid also talks about the favorable attitude of the United States toward the Taliban until late 1998. See Ahmed Rashid, *Taliban: Militant Islam, Oil and Fundamentalism in Central Asia* (New Haven, CT: Yale University Press, 2000).

70. Mackenzie, "United States and the Taliban," p. 96; and Thomas Lippman, "U.S. Plans More Active S. Asia Role; Albright's Trip Signals New Interest in Region," *Washington Post*, 19 November 1997.

71. By late 1997, however, the Taliban's treatment of women had aroused the anger of U.S. women's organizations, forcing U.S. secretary of state Madeleine Albright to criticize the Taliban regime during a visit to Pakistan in November 1997. Steven Erlanger, "In Afghan Refugee Camp, Albright Hammers Taliban," *New York Times*, 19 November 1999. Albright based U.S. nonrecognition of the Taliban regime on its violations of human rights, especially its treatment of women and children.

72. According to some press reports, U.S. officials hinted that if the Taliban expelled bin Laden and cooperated with the United States, "There would be economic rewards." Suzanne Goldberg and Ian Black, "America Tells Taliban to Dump Bin Laden," *Guardian*, 4 February 1999. Also see "The Taliban's Strategy for Recognition," *Economist*, 6 February 1999.

73. On the Russian perception of the Taliban and the West's role in its emergence, see *Dvizhenie "Taliban"* (The Taliban movement), Grani.Ru <http://txt.grani.ru/antiterror/facts/Taliban/print.html>; and Vakhtang Shelia, "Kogdato Pakistan i SShA sovmestno sozdali proekt 'Taleban' " (Once upon a time Pakistan and the United States jointly engineered the Taliban project), *Novaya Gazeta*, 15 October 2001.

74. "Russia Responds to Taleban Statement on Chechnya," Interfax *Daily News Bulletin* (Moscow), 17 January 2000, reproduced by the Foreign Broadcast Information Service, FBIS-SOV-2000-0117 <http://wnc.fedworld.gov>; "On Islamic Assistance, Mercenaries," ITAR-TASS, 6 January 2000, reproduced by the Foreign Broadcast Information Service, FBIS-SOV-95-005, <http://wnc.fedworld.gov>; and "Afghan Taleban to Send

Stingers to Chechen Rebels," Interfax *Daily News Bulletin* (Moscow), 1 November 1999, reproduced by the Foreign Broadcast Information Service, FBIS-SOV-1999-1101 <http://wnc.fedworld.gov>.

75. Stent and Shevtsova, "America, Russia and Europe: A Realignment?" *Survival* 44, no. 4 (winter 2002–2003), p. 130.

76. See "Zhirinovskiy Backs Taleban as Duma Debates US Terror Attacks," ITAR-TASS, 19 September 2001, reproduced by the Foreign Broadcast Information Service, FBIS-SOV-2001-0919 <http://wnc.fedworld.gov>; and "Communist Leader Says Putin Letting US Drag Russia into War with Muslim World," Interfax *Daily News Bulletin* (Moscow), reproduced by the Foreign Broadcast Information Service, 20 November 2001, FBIS-SOV-2001-1120 <http://wnc.fedworld.gov>.

77. Sergei Lebedev, the head of the Foreign Intelligence Service, said that the attacks had proved "the global nature of the threat of international terrorism." Ana Uzelac, "Terror May Be the Tie That Binds," *Moscow Times*, 13 September 2001.

78. Susan B. Glasser, "Russia May Seek U.S. Concessions," *Washington Post*, 23 September 2001. According to Alexander Olson, a pollster who works for the Kremlin, the cooperation with the United States would be "unprecedented, of a level unseen ever before.... But without doubt, Russia will put its conditions on this cooperation." Quoted *ibid.*

79. Leonid Radzikhovsky, "The 21st Century Begins" [in Russian], *Vremya MN*, 14 September 2001, reproduced by the WPS Monitoring Agency (Moscow) <http://www.wps.ru>. Radzikhovsky further claimed that the Arabs (and presumably other Muslims) and even Third World countries had been fighting the West for a long time. He wrote, "When a U.N. Conference denounces Zionism as a form of racism, when billions are demanded from the West as compensation for the Third World, it is also war: the War merely shifted to a new form on September 11. The form changed, but not the ultimate objective: the destruction of Christian civilization."

80. See "Russia Struggles to Define Terrorism Policy," Jamestown Foundation *Monitor* 7, no. 17 (18 September 2001).

81. Sergei Blagov, "Russia-Central Asia: Lessons of Afghanistan Make Moscow Wary," Interpress Service, 20 September 2001.

82. "Afghanistan is just the beginning. If anyone harbors a terrorist, they're terrorists. If they fund a terrorist, they're terrorists. If they house terrorists, they're terrorists." "Remarks by President George W. Bush," Federal News Service, 26 November 2001.

83. During a telephone conversation, Russian foreign minister Igor Ivanov and his Iranian counterpart, Kamal Kharazi, stressed that "anti-terrorist actions should be taken in accordance with generally recognized international norms, preserving the leading role of the United Nations." "Russian, Iranian Foreign Ministers Support Fight against Terrorism," Interfax *Daily News Bulletin* (Moscow), 19 September 2001, reproduced by the Foreign Broadcast Information Service, FBIS-SOV-2001-0919 <http://wnc.fedworld.gov>.

84. "Pro-Moscow Chechnya Chief to Visit Mideast," Agence France-Presse, 18 September 2001.

85. "Politician Warns against Russia's Participation in US Retaliation," Interfax *Daily News Bulletin* (Moscow), 14 September 2001, reproduced by the Foreign Broadcast Information Service, FBIS-SOV-2001-0914 <http://wnc.fedworld.gov>.

86. Ahmad Shah Masoud was assassinated on 9 September 2001 by two Moroccans posing as journalists and suspected of having links to the Taliban. Fredrick Starr, a prominent U.S. expert on Central Asia, called the Northern Alliance "full subsidiaries of Russia and Iran." Sebastian Junger, "Massoud's Last Stand," *Vanity Fair*, February 2002.

87. In April 2002, the total number of forces at the Manas airbase was estimated at 1,700. In February, the number of forces was estimated at 1,200, of which 700 were American and 460 French. "French Fighter Planes Arrive in Kyrgyzstan," *Kyrgyzstan Daily Di-*

gest, 28 February 2002 <http://www.eurasianet.org>; and Bruce Panmier and Antoine Blua, "Central Asia Six Months After: Alliances Shift with West, Russia," RFE/RL *Weekday Magazine*, 12 March 2002 <http://www.rferl.org/nca/features>.

88. Ian Traynor, "Russia Edgy at Spread of U.S. Bases in Its Backyard," *Guardian*, 10 January 2002. Traynor notes that Gennady Seleznev, the Speaker of the Russian State Duma, asserted during a visit to Kazakhstan that "Russia would not approve of the appearance of permanent U.S. military bases in Central Asia."

89. "America and Uzbekistan Seal Strategic Partnership," Jamestown Foundation *Monitor* 8, no. 55 (19 March 2002).

90. Ibid.

91. Ibid.

92. "Foreign Minister Says No Permanent Foreign Bases in Kyrgyzstan," Interfax *Daily News Bulletin* (Moscow), 1 April 2002, reproduced by the Foreign Broadcast Information Service, FBIS-SOV-2002-0401 <http://wnc.fedworld.gov>.

93. On the World Bank president's visit to Central Asia, see "Tajikistani, World Bank Presidents Discuss Hydropower Plant Projects," ITAR-TASS, 10 April 2002, reproduced by the Foreign Broadcast Information Service, FBIS-SOV-2002-0410 <http://wnc.fedworld.gov>; and "World Bank, Turkmenistan to Sign Strategic Partnership," *Financial Times*, 12 April 2002.

94. Glasser, "Russia May Seek U.S. Concessions."

95. Svetlana Babayeva, "Igor Ivanov, Ministr Inostrannyh Del: 'Glovnoye chtoby vneshniaia politika ne privodila k Rasklay Vnutri Strany' " (Igor Ivanov, minister of foreign affairs: Main objective—A foreign policy that does not cause divisions within the country), *Izvestia*, 9 July 2002 <http://izvestia/ru/politic/article20780>.

96. Viktoria Panfilova, "Kyrgiziia stanovitsia bolshim voyennym aerodrom" (Kyrgyzstan Becomes a big military airfield), *Nezavisimaya gazeta*, 4 July 2002 <http://ng.ru/cis/2002_07_04/s_Kirghizia.html>.

97. Ibid.

98. Ibid.; and Igor Torbakov, "Russia Moves to Reassert Influence in Central Asia, Caucasus," *Eurasia Insight*, 16 December 2002 <http://www.eurasianet.org>.

99. "NATO to Enhance Peacekeeping Role in Afghanistan," U.S. Department of State, International Information Programs <http://usinfo.state.gov/regional/nea/sasia/afghan/text2003/0416nato.htm>.

100. Igor Torbakov, "Economic Clout Gives Russia Growing Power in CIS," *Eurasia Insight*, 5 December 2001 <http://www.eurasianet.org>.

101. Igor Rotar, "Islamic Fundamentalism in Azerbaijan: Myth or Reality?" *Prism*, vol. 6, no. 8 (31 August 2001).

102. See Alexander Kuznetsov, "Islam v Strannakh SNG" (Islam in the Countries of the CIS), *Evraziiskoe obozrenie* (Eurasian review), no. 2 <http://eurasia.com.ru/eo/207 .html>. Kuznetsov states, "The religious illiteracy of the population is exploited by certain Turkish circles, which recently initiated the construction of two Sunni mosques in Baku."

103. Among the major mosques financed by Arab countries is the Cuma or Abu-Bekr mosque in Baku, built by a Kuwaiti foundation. In 1998, it was announced that an Islamic university would be constructed in Baku with Kuwaiti funds. Liz Fuller, "Could 'Alternative Islam' Become a Force in Azerbaijani politics?" RFE/RL *Caucasus Report*, 14 March 2002; and "Azerbaijani Authorities Make Cautious Overtures to Islam," Jamestown Foundation *Monitor* vol 4, no. 148 (3 August 1998). On accusations against Iran, see "Azerbaijani Security Official Accuses Iran," RFE/RL *Newsline*, 2 May 2001.

104. According to Azerbaijan's deputy national security minister, Tofiq Babaev, as of 1 May 2001, 7,000 people in Azerbaijan had converted to Wahhabism. Fuller, "Cold 'Alternative Islam' Become a Force in Azerbaijani politics?" See also Samir Razimov, "Bin

Laden's Azeri Connections," Institute for War and Peace Reporting (IWPR) *Caucasus Reporting Service*, no. 100 (5 October 2001) <http://www.iwpr.net>.

105. The center of Wahhabi activity is in Azerbaijan's Zakatala region, which has a substantial Avar minority. Mamed Suleimanov, "Baku Alarmed over 'Wahhabi Menace,' " IWPR *Caucasus Reporting Service*, no. 97 (7 September 2001) <http://www.iwpr.net>.

106. "Azerbaijan Says It Has Arrested Activists Working to Promote an Islamist State," RFE/RL *Newsline*, 31 August 2001. Many of the activists belonged to the Hizb-ul-Tahrir. Liz Fuller, "Azerbaijan Moves to Impose Tighter Control over Religious Organizations," RFE/RL *Newsline*, 24 August 2001.

107. Shireen T. Hunter, *The Transcaucasus in Transition: Nation-Building and Conflict* (Washington, DC: Center for Strategic and International Studies, 1994), pp. 70–73.

108. On Mutalibov's views and their evolution, see Elizabeth Fuller, "The Azerbaijani Presidential Elections: A One Horse Race," RFE/RL *Report on the USSR*, 13 September 1991, p. 14.

109. During the coup, Mutalibov was visiting Iran and reportedly expressed happiness over his ouster. Hunter, *Transcaucasus in Transition*, p. 71).

110. For an assessment of Aliev's presidency, see ibid., pp. 75–85.

111. Whether Heidar Aliev was indeed Moscow's choice or managed to parlay himself into power against Russia's wishes is unclear. Most likely, opinion in Moscow was divided, with some supporting Aliev and others supporting the reinstatement of Mutalibov. Daniel Sneider, "Turkey and Russia Back Rivals in Azerbaijan Power Struggle," *Christian Science Monitor*, 30 June 1993. Sneider refers to an article titled "Why Not Gaidar Alievz" in the Russian Ministry of Defense daily *Krasnaya zvezda*. Also see Shireen T. Hunter, "Unwilling Partners: Gaidar Aliev and the Moscow Connection," *Armenian International Magazine* 5, no. 7 (August 1994).

112. Gamsakurdia claimed that the plot to dislodge him was hatched during the last months of the Gorbachev period to punish him for refusing to sign the Union Treaty proposed by Gorbachev in March 1991. When he refused to attend the 21 December 1991 meeting in Alma Ata, where the leaders of various republics were to sign the treaty establishing the CIS, Moscow began actively to implement the plan to dislodge him. *Soviet Analyst* 21, nos. 9 and 10 (April 1993).

113. On many occasions, Shevardnadze told Western visitors that Yeltsin went back on his promises to him. Based on Hunter's interviews with Western officials and academics.

114. Hunter, *Transcaucasus in Transition*, pp. 128–33.

115. Trenin, "Russia's Security Interests and Policies"; and Pavel K. Baev, "Russia Refocuses Its Policies in the Southern Caucasus," Caspian Studies Program, Harvard University, 2001 <http://ksgnotes1.harvard.edu/BCSIA/Library.nsf/pubs/PavelBaev>.

116. Ibid.

117. In April 1994, Defense Minister Pavel Grachev talked about the necessity of having twenty-eight military bases abroad. Viktor Litovkin, "Grachev Talks of 28 Foreign Bases, but So Far Only Georgia, Armenia Have Any" [in Russian], *Izvestia*, 8 April 1994, in *Current Digest of the Post-Soviet Press* 46, no. 14 (4 May 1994).

118. Boris Vinogradov, "3,000 Peacekeepers Are Supposed to Create Conditions for Settlement in Karabakh" [in Russian], *Izvestia*, 9 December 1994, in *Current Digest of the Post-Soviet Press* 46, no. 49 (4 January 1995). Such a force was never created.

119. Arif Useinov, "Azerbaijan Doesn't Want to Be Russia's Ears" [in Russian], *Vremya MN*, 5 February 1999, in *Current Digest of the Post-Soviet Press* 51, no. 5 (3 March 1999).

120. Part of the complexity derives from the fact that Russian military forces in Georgia became enmeshed in the implementation of the Conventional Forces in Europe (CFE) Treaty, which is designed to reduce conventional military forces in Europe.

121. Yevgeny Krutikov, "Russia Signs a Friendship Treaty with Georgia," *Megapolis-Ekspress*, no. 6 (9 February 1994): p. 15, in *Current Digest of the Post-Soviet Press* 46, no. 5 (2 March 1994): p. 10.
122. Ibid.
123. Pavel Felgengauer, "The Russian Army in Transcaucasus" [in Russian], *Segodnya*, 25 March 1995, in *Current Digest of the Post-Soviet Press* 47, no. 12 (19 April 1995).
124. Ibid.
125. Vera Tsereteli, "Where Does the Sun Rise for Georgia?" [in Russian], *Obshchaya gazeta*, 4 June 1997, reproduced by the Foreign Broadcast Information Service, FBIS-SOV-97-111 <http://wnc.fedworld.gov>.
126. Ibid.
127. Russia agreed to close its bases in Vaziani and Gudauta by 1 July 2001 and agreed to discuss the closure of the bases at Batumi and Akhalkalaki by 2003–4. Ivlian Khaindrava, "Last Post for Russians in Georgia," IWPR *Caucasus Reporting Service*, no. 48 (8 September 2000) <http://www.iwpr.net>.
128. Abashidze feels that the Russian military presence allows him to remain largely independent from Tbilisi. "Russian Military Presence Remains Strong in Former Soviet Union," *Russia Journal*, no. 11 (12 April 1999) <http://www.russiajournal.com/weekly/articleshtml?ad=876>.
129. Andranik Migranyan and Konstantin Zatulin, "Russia's Policies Said to Imperil CIS Integration" [in Russian], *Godruzhestvo NG* (monthly supplement to *Nezavisimaya gazeta*), no. 1 (December 1997), reprinted in *Current Digest of the Post-Soviet Press* 49, no. 50 (15 January 1998). Migranyan and Zatulin write, "While concluding a strategic partnership treaty with Armenia, Russia calls Azerbaijan the same sort of strategic partner in the region. Thus, by sending contradictory signals to the region, Russia, while not strengthening its relations with Azerbaijan in any real way and not neutralizing the Western and Turkish intrusion into the region, is at the same time making the Armenian side wary and suspicious of its reliability as a partner."
130. On Kozyrev's disapproval, see Dmitriy Gorokhov and Andrey Serov, "Kozyrev on Mutual Exploitation of Oil," ITAR-TASS, 22 September 1994, reproduced by the Foreign Broadcast Information Service, FBIS-SOV-94-184 <http://wnc.fedworld.gov>; and "Russian Official on Caspian Status," ITAR-TASS, 21 September 1994, reproduced by the Foreign Broadcast Information Service, FBIS-SOV-94-184 <http://wnc.fedworld.gov>.
131. AIOC members are BP (British Petroleum) (34.1 percent operator), Unocal (10.2 percent), LUKOIL (10 percent), Exxon Mobil (8 percent), TPAO (Türkiye Petrolleri Amonim Ortakligi) (6.8 percent), Devon Energy (5.6 percent), Itochu (3.9 percent), Amerada Hess (1 percent), and Delta (1.7 percent). Other companies having shares include STATOIL (Norway). The shares are often traded and therefore percentages change. This was an eight year $30 billion contract to develop three oil fields: Azeri, Chirag, and the deepwater portions of Gunashli. "Azerbaijan Country Analysis Brief," U.S. Energy Information Administration, May 2001 <http://www.eia.doe.gov/emeu/cabs/azerproj.html>; and "Moscow Wants Increased Share in Oil Contract," Interfax *Daily News Bulletin* (Moscow), 21 September 1994, reproduced by the Foreign Broadcast Information Service, FBIS-SOV-94-184 <http://wnc.fedworld.gov>.
132. Alexy Gromyko, "Novaya 'Velikaya Igra': Kaspii Stal sredotechiem geopoliticheskikh interesov gosudarstv regionov" (The "new great game": The Caspian became the focal point of geopolitical interests of the countries of the region), *Nezavisimaya Gazeta*, 20 August 1998 <http://www.Gromyko.ru/Russian/CPE/alex3.html>.
133. Robert Freedman, "Russia and Azerbaijan: Are Relations Beginning to Improve?"

Caspian Crossroads 2, no. 4 (Spring 1997) <http://ourworld.compuserve.com/home
pages/usazerb/241.htm>.

134. Quoted in John Roberts, *Caspian Pipelines* (London: Royal Institute of International
Affairs, 1996), p. 51.

135. Stanislav Kondrashov, "Primakov Gives Year-End Foreign Policy Review" [in Rus-
sian], *Izvestia*, 23 December 1997, in *Current Digest of the Post-Soviet Press* 59, no.
1 (4 February 1998).

136. "Ankara and Washington Reaffirm Support for Baku-Ceyhan Oil Route," Deutsche
Presse-Agentur, 28 October 1998.

137. Grey Wolf (Bozkurt) is the totem of the Turkic peoples. Jacob M. Landau, *Radical
Politics in Modern Turkey* (Leiden: E.J. Brill, 1974), pp. 205–42. On Turkeş's popularity, see Sami Kohen, "Contacts with Central Asian States: A Foundation for Pan-
Turkism," *Washington Report on Middle East Affairs* 11, no. 3 (August/September
1992): pp. 17–18.

138. "Reportage: Commentary on Conflict in Chechnya—Nikolayev Cited on Muslim Mercenaries," ITAR-TASS, 3 February 1995, reproduced by the Foreign Broadcast Information Service, FBIS-SOV-95-024 <http://wnc.fedworld.gov>.

139. "Aliev Denies Chechen Rebels, Weapons Present in Azerbaijan," Interfax *Daily News
Bulletin* (Moscow), 26 January 1996, reproduced by the Foreign Broadcast Information
Service, FBIS-SOV-96-019 <http://wnc.fedworld.gov>.

140. "Aliyev Holds Talks with Chechen Leader Maskhadov," Interfax *Daily News Bulletin*
(Moscow), 26 September 1996, reproduced by the Foreign Broadcast Information Ser-
vice, FBIS-SOV-96-189 <http://wnc.fedworld.gov>; and "Russia: Chechnya Appoints
'Ambassador' to Azerbaijan," *Turan* (Baku), 23 April 1998, reproduced by the Foreign
Broadcast Information Service, FBIS-SOV-98-113 <http://wnc.fedworld.gov>.

141. "Azerbaijan: Chechnya Ready to Assist Azerbaijan Militarily in Karabakh," *Turan*
(Baku), 27 August 1997, reproduced by the Foreign Broadcast Information Service,
FBIS-SOV-97-239 <http://wnc.fedworld.gov>.

142. Mehman Gafarly, "Does Azerbaijan Need Chechen Militants?" [in Russian], *Nezavisimaya Gazeta*, 31 August 2000, reproduced by the WPS Monitoring Agency (Moscow) <http://www.wps.ru:8101>.

143. Sanobar Shermatova, "Khattab and Central Asia," *Moscow News*, 13 September 2000.

144. Mamed Suleimanov, "Baku Crushes 'Wahhabi' Gang," IWPR *Caucasus Reporting Service*, no. 50 (22 September 2000) <http://www.iwpr.net>.

145. On a potential military pact among Baku, Tbilisi, and Ankara, see Arman Dzhilavyan,
"Axis and Counter-Axis in the Caucasus" [in Russian], *Nezavisimaya gazeta*, 2 February 2000, in *Current Digest of the Post-Soviet Press* 52, no. 5 (1 March 2000).

146. Georgy Dvali and Nikolai Gulko, "Caucasus Tangle Becomes More Complicated,"
Kommersant [in Russian], 11 November 1999, in *Current Digest of the Post-Soviet
Press* 51, no. 45 (8 December 1999).

147. Mehman Gafarly, "There's No Friend like an Old Friend," *Nezavisimaya gazeta* [in
Russian], 16 October 1999, in *Current Digest of the Post-Soviet Press* 51, no. 42 (17
November 1999).

148. "Oil Giant Signs Deal on Azeri Fields," Interfax *Daily News Bulletin* (Moscow), 19
January 2001, reproduced by BBC Monitoring <http://www.monitor.bbc.co.uk>.

149. Namik Ibrahimov, "Baku Sides with Moscow over Chechnya," IWPR *Caucasus Reporting Service*, no. 149 (4 October 2002) <http://www.iwpr.net>.

150. On the Russian accusations, see Daniel Williams, "Georgia Walks Tightrope in Tense
Caucasus; Former Soviet State Trying to Avoid Angering Moscow over Chechen War,"
Washington Post, 28 December 1999.

151. "Russia Accuses Georgia of Helping Chechen Separatists," Interfax *Daily News Bulletin*, 22 December 1999.

152. Sharon LaFraniere, "Pressed by U.S., Georgia Gets Tough with Outsiders," *Washington Post*, 28 April 2002.
153. The Chechen-Georgian amity, which began after the end of the first Chechen War, is rather ironic because Chechen forces, notably Shamil Basaev's battalion, fought on the side of Abkhaz separatists in 1992–93. Tsereteli, "Where Does the Sun Rise for Georgia?"; and "Chechnya's Basayev Denies Involvement in Abkhazia Conflict," ITAR-TASS, 29 July 1997, reproduced by the Foreign Broadcast Information Service, FBIS-SOV-97-210 <http://wnc.fedworld.gov>. By 1997, Chechen president Aslan Maskhadov, wanting to repair ties with Georgia, offered to help resolve the Abkhaz problem. "Chechnya Prepared to Mediate in Abkhazian Conflict," ITAR-TASS, 31 July 1997, reproduced by the Foreign Broadcast Information Service, FBIS-SOV-97-212 <http://wnc.fedworld.gov>. Internal divisions in Chechnya and the conflict between Maskhadov and the militant Islamists made this difficult.
154. In June 2001, the Duma passed a law to allow republics in the South Caucasus to join the Russian Federation. Mikhail Vignansky, "Russian Imperialism Threatens," IWPR *Caucasus Reporting Service*, no. 90 (17 July 2001) <www.iwpr.net>. On the basis of this law, the Georgian breakaway regions of Abkhazia and South Ossetia, as well as the separatist regions of Nagorno-Karabakh in Azerbaijan and Transniester in Moldova, could join Russia. Earlier, in September 2000, Speaker of the Russian State Duma Gennady Seleznev had called for introducing automatic citizenship for all former Soviet citizens, thus raising anxieties in the Transcaucasus. Kornely Kakacia, "Citizenship to All Former Soviets Would Jeopardize Transcaucasus," *Central Asia/Caucasus Analyst*, 25 October 2000 <http://www.cacianalyst.org/October_25/citizenship .htm>.
155. Alan Kasaev and Ekaterina Tsemnikova, "Abkhazskii Front Afghanskoi Voini" (The Abkhaz front of the Afghan War), *Nezavisimaya gazeta*, 10 October 2001 <http://ng .ru/cis/2001-10-10/1_front.html>.
156. LaFraniere, "Pressed by U.S."
157. Paul Quinn-Judge, "The Forbidden Valley," *Time Magazine* (Europe), 1 April 2002 <http://www.time.com/time/eu>.
158. Jean-Christophe Peuch, "Caucusus: Heaviest Clashes Reported in Ingushetia since Beginning of Chechen Campaign," RFE/RL *Weekday Magazine*, 27 September 2002 <http://www.rferl.org/nca/features>.
159. Steven Lee Myers, "Russians Battle Chechen Force in Ingushetia for 3rd Day," *New York Times*, 29 September 2002.
160. Patrick E. Tyler, "Russia's Leader Says He Supports American Military Aid for Georgia," *New York Times*, 2 March 2002.
161. "Kto otvetit za razval?" (Who will answer for the breakdown?), *Sovetskaya Rossiia*, 26 February 2002.
162. Ian Traynor, "Russia Angry at U.S. War Plan for Georgia," *Guardian*, 22 February 2002.
163. Ibid.
164. "Duma Likely to Raise Issue of Recognizing Abkhazia's Independence—Rogozin," Interfax *Daily News Bulletin*, 27 February 2002.
165. Tatyana Rubleva, "Dosvidanye Kavkaz" (Goodbye Caucasus), *Nezavisimaya gazeta*, 27 August 2002 <http://www.ng.ru/cis/2002-08-27/caucasus.html>.
166. Tony Karon, "Why U.S. Arrival in Georgia Has Moscow Hopping Mad," *Time* (online edition), 27 February 2002 <http://www.time.com/time/world/article/0,8599,213413, 00.html>.
167. "Press Conference of Vladimir Putin, President of the Russian Federation," Moscow, 24 June 2002 <http://President.Kremlin.ru/text/APPTEmplAppearId16748.shtml>.
168. Ian Traynor, "Russia Angry at U.S. War Plan."

169. "Week in Review: 26 February–4 March 2002," *Transitions Online* <http://www.tol
     .cz>.
170. Shalva Pichkhadze, Georgian presidential adviser, expressed such speculation. "Presi-
     dent Downplays Possibility of Georgia Hosting U.S. Military Base," RFE/RL *Newsline*,
     8 March 2002.
171. Ibid.
172. "Week in Review: 26 February–4 March 2002," *Transitions Online* <http://www.tol
     .cz>.
173. Armen Khanbabjan and Anatoly Gordiyenko, "Russia Takes Abkhazia Away from
     Georgia," *Nezavisimaya gazeta*, 20 March 2002 <http://www.therussiannews.com/
     topics/53/02/03/20/13765.html>.
174. Russia denied violating Georgian air space, but a subsequent investigation by the OSCE
     confirmed that Georgia had been bombed by unidentified aircraft. Georgy Dvali and
     Gennady Sysoyev, "OSCE Confirms Georgia Was Bombed" [in Russian], *Kommersant*,
     9 August 2002, in *Current Digest of the Post-Soviet Press* 54, no. 32 (4 September
     2002).
175. Giorgy Kupatadze, "Pankisi in Uproar at Bombing Raids," IWPR *Caucasus Reporting
     Service*, no. 144 (30 August 2002) <http://www.iwpr.net>.
176. Jaba Devdariani, "Putin Ultimatum Raises Stakes in Georgia," *Eurasia Insight*, 11
     October 2002 <http://www.eurasianet.org/>.
177. Georgy Dvali, "Georgia Wages War on Terrorism" [in Russian], *Kommersant*, 26 Au-
     gust 2002, *Current Digest of the Post-Soviet Press* 54, no. 35 (25 September 2002).
178. "Russia, Georgia Soften Georgia-Russia Discrepancies," RFE/RL *Newsline*, 7 October
     2002.
179. Sergei Blagov, "U.S.-Georgian Security Cooperation Agreement Provokes Outcry in
     Russia," *Eurasia Insight*, 16 April 2003 <www.eurasianet.org>.
180. Ibid.
181. "Russia and Georgia Preparing a "Major Treaty," WPS Monitoring Agency's *Media
     Highlights of the Day* (Moscow), 28 May 2003 <http://wps.wm.ru.8101/chitalka/
     media_politic/en/20030528-txt.shtml>.
182. Antoine Blua, "Azerbaijan: U.S. Lifts Restrictions on Aid," RFE/RL *Weekday Maga-
     zine*, 29 January 2002 <http://www.rferl.org/nca/features>.
183. Ibid.
184. Stephen Blank, "U.S. Military in Azerbaijan, to Counter Iranian Threat," *Central Asia/
     Caucasus Analyst*, 10 April 2002 <http://www.cacianalyst.org/2002-04-10/20020410
     _US_Azerbaijan_Iran>.
185. U.S. assistant secretary of state Richard Armitage said that the United States would
     not allow Iran to exert pressure on Azerbaijan. "USA to stop Iran from Exerting Pres-
     sure on Azerbaijan, U.S. Official," *Global News Wire*, 8 March 2002, reproduced by
     BBC Monitoring <http://www.monitor.bbc.co.uk>.

Notes to Chapter 9

1. On Pakistan's connection with the Tajik Islamists, see Dietrich Reetz, "Islamic Activism in Central Asia and the Pakistan Factor," *Journal of South Asian and Middle
   Eastern Affairs* 23, no. 1 (fall 1999): pp. 1–37.
2. Shireen T. Hunter, "The Afghan Civil War: Implications for Central Asian Stability,"
   in *Energy and Conflict in Central Asia and the Caucasus*, ed. Robert Ebel and Rajan
   Menon (Lanham, MD: Rowman and Littlefield, 2000), pp. 201–2.
3. "On Islamic Assistance, Mercenaries," ITAR-TASS, 17 January 2000, reproduced by

the Foreign Broadcast Information Service, FBIS-SOV-2000-0117 <http://wnc.fedworld.gov>.

4. Ibid.

5. "Afghan Taleban to Send Stingers to Chechen Rebels," Interfax *Daily News Bulletin* (Moscow), 1 November 1999, reproduced by the Foreign Broadcast Information Service, FBIS-SOV-1999-1101 <http://wnc.fedworld.gov>; see also Elena Ovcharenko, "The Talibs Will Help Militants with Money and Stingers" [in Russian], *Komsomolskaya Pravda*, 19 February 2000, reproduced by the National News Service (Moscow) <http://www.nns.ru/press_file/dagestan/expert/dag4180.html>.

6. Only three countries recognized the Taliban regime: Pakistan, Saudi Arabia, and the United Arab Emirates.

7. "Taleban Government May Recognize Chechen Independence," Interfax *Daily News Bulletin* (Moscow), 30 May 1997, reproduced by the Foreign Broadcast Information Service, FBIS-SOV-97-150 <http://wnc.fedworld.gov>. Prior to his visit to Pakistan, Yanderbiev served as Chechnya's acting president from Dzhokar Dudaev's assassination in April 1996 until the inauguration of Aslan Maskhadov as Chechnya's elected president in January 1997.

8. Leonid Gonkin, "Talibi priznali nezavisimost Chechni" (The Talibs recognized the independence of Chechnya), *Kommersant*, 18 January 2000, reproduced by the National News Service (Moscow) <http://www.nns.ru/press-file/dagestan/expert/dag450.html>.

9. Ibid.

10. On the Russian view of bin Laden's connection with Chechnya, see Vladimir Yanchenkov, "Khattab upovaet na Ben Ladena" (Khattab relies on bin Laden), *Trud*, 6 September 2000, reproduced by the National News Service (Moscow) <http://www.nns.ru/press-file/dagestan/expert/dag908.html>.

11. "Russia Responds to Taleban Statement on Chechnya," Interfax *Daily News Bulletin* (Moscow), 17 January 2000, reproduced by the Foreign Broadcast Information Service, FBIS-SOV-2000-0117 <http://wnc.fedworld.gov>.

12. "Chechnya Sets Up 'Fundamentalist Axis with Taleban,'" ITAR-TASS, 21 January 2000, reproduced by the Foreign Broadcast Information Service, FBIS-SOV-2000-0121 <http://wnc.fedworld.gov>.

13. Ibid.

14. "Russia: Ivanov Says Chechnya, Afghanistan 'Branches of One Tree,'" Interfax *Daily News Bulletin* (Moscow), 24 September 2001, reproduced by the Foreign Broadcast Information Service, FBIS-SOV-2001-0924 <http://wnc.fedworld.gov>.

15. "Hundreds of Chechens Fighting for Taliban Reported Killed in Afghanistan," ITAR-TASS, 23 November 2001, reproduced by the Foreign Broadcast Information Service, FBIS-SOV-2001-1123 <http://wnc.fedworld.gov>; Ann Scott Tyson, "Taliban Holdouts Keep U.S. on Edge," *Christian Science Monitor*, 26 November 2001; and Rory Carroll, "Pakistanis Reinforce Taliban Tranches," *Guardian*, 7 November 2001. Several Russian citizens, most of whom were from Bashkortostan and Kabardino-Balkaria, were captured by American forces and held in Guantanamo Bay: "U.S. Expedites Extradition of Russian Guantanamo Detainees," Radio Free Europe/Radio Liberty (RFE/RL) *Newsline*, 12 June 2002.

16. Vladimir Terekhov, "Talibanim to varishch" (Taliban' is their friend) *Vek*, 26 May 2000, reproduced by the National News Service (Moscow) <http://www.nns.ru>.

17. Ibid.

18. Ibid.

19. Yurii Tyssovsky, "Interview with Pakistan's Ambassador to the Russian Federation, Mansur Alam," [in Russian], *Vek*, 11 February 2000, reproduced by the National News Service (Moscow) <http://www.nns.ru>.

20. Ibid.

21. Ibid.
22. Terekhov, " 'Taliban' Is Their Friend."
23. "Pakistan Denies Knowledge of Its Mercenaries Fighting in Pervomayskoye," Interfax *Daily News Bulletin* (Moscow), 17 January 1996, in *BBC Summary of World Broadcasts*, 17 January 1996.
24. "200 Well-Armed 'Missionaries' in Chechnya Arrive from Pakistan," ITAR-TASS, 9 October 1996, reproduced by the Foreign Broadcast Information Service, FBIS-SOV-96-97 <http://wnc.fedworld.gov>.
25. "Moscow Will Take 'Seriously' Mercenaries among Gunmen—Pakistan Denies Pervomaiskoe Involvement," Interfax *Daily News Bulletin* (Moscow), 16 January 1996, reproduced by the Foreign Broadcast Information Service, FBIS-SOV-96-016 <http://wnc.fedworld.gov>. Some Russian sources have claimed that the Kizlyar raid was planned by a Pakistani citizen. "Pakistani Citizen Reportedly Prepared Kizlyar Raid— Pakistani Involvement Not Confirmed," Interfax *Daily News Bulletin* (Moscow), 11 January 1996, reproduced by the Foreign Broadcast Information Service, FBIS-SOV-96-008 <http://wnc.fedworld.gov>.
26. In July 1997, Pakistan's ambassador to Moscow, Tanvir Ahmad Khan, said, "As for the problem of Chechnya, it is entirely an inner affair of the Russian Federation. So we are not in a position to interfere here." "Ambassador on Possible Purchase of Arms from Russia," *Nation* (Islamabad), 21 July 1997, reproduced by the Foreign Broadcast Information Service, FBIS-NES-97-202 <http://wnc.fedworld.gov>.
27. Ibid.
28. In the interview with Yurii Tyssovsky noted earlier, Pakistan's ambassador said, "Pakistan was negotiating with the Russian authorities regarding the transfer of humanitarian assistance to the Chechens."
29. "Tanvir Ahmad Khan, a Gentle Thaw in Moscow," *News* (Islamabad), 21 July 1997, reproduced by the Foreign Broadcast Information Service, FBIS-SOV-97-202 <http://wnc.fedworld.gov>.
30. "Russia Wants Pakistan to Stop Backing Afghan Taliban," Voice of the Islamic Republic of Iran (Mashad), 25 December 2000, reproduced by the Foreign Broadcast Information Service, FBIS-NES-2000-1226 <http://wnc.fedworld.gov>.
31. "Pakistani Leader Urges Russian Mediation in Kashmir, Recognition of Taleban," Interfax *Daily News Bulletin* (Moscow), 31 May 2001, reproduced by the Foreign Broadcast Information Service, FBIS-SOV-2001-0531 <http://wnc.fedworld.gov>.
32. Some Russian experts disagreed with this strategy because the Rabbani government did not enjoy Pashtun support. Igor Torbakov, "Russia's Growing Presence in Afghanistan Hints at Regional Rivalry with Western Powers," *Eurasian Insight*, 4 December 2001 <http://www.eurasianet.org>.
33. Sergei Blagov, "Russia Strives to Maintain Political Clout in Afghanistan," *Eurasian Insight*, 2 December 2001 <http://www.eurasianet.org>.
34. "Afghan Premier Seeks Russian Aid," Afghan News Network, 12 March 2002 <http://www.myafghan.com/news2.asp?id=430527145&search=3/12/2002>.
35. Ahmed Rashid, "Jockeying for Influence, Neighbors Undermine Afghan Pact," *Eurasian Insight*, 15 January 2003 <http://www.eurasianet.org>.
36. Galina Gridneva and Valery Zhukov, "Russia, Afghanistan Set to Cooperate in Fighting Terrorism," ITAR-TASS, 18 October 2002.
37. "Pakistani Leader Tells Russian MPs Cooperation Not Conditional on India Issues," BBC Monitoring *International Reports*, 16 April 2002.
38. On various Russian-Pakistani contacts, see Sergei Artemyev, "Pakistan and Russia for Broader Economic Cooperation," ITAR-TASS, 16 April 2002; "Russian Gas Giant in Pakistan to Promote Cooperation," RIA News Agency (Moscow), 25 May 2002, reproduced by BBC Monitoring <http://www.monitor.bbc.co.uk>; Vladimir Radhuyin, "Russia to Upgrade ties with Pakistan," *The Hindu*, 15 April 2002. According to ITAR-

TASS Dmitri Rogozin visiting Islamabad in April 2002 said, "The Pakistanis expect the Russian side will take an active part in the development of the country's economic sector, especially of enterprises that were built with the participation of the former USSR;" "Russia: MP Says Pakistan Seeking Closer Relations." ITAR-TASS, 24 April 2002, reproduced by the Foreign Broadcast Information Service, FBIS/SOV-2002-0423 <http://fedworld.gov>.

39. "Musharraf Guarantees Pakistan Territory Will Not Be Used for Terrorist Activities," ITAR-TASS, 6 February 2003, reproduced by the Foreign Broadcast Information Service, FBIS-SOV-2003-0206 <http://wnc.fedworld.gov>.

40. "India, Russia Wary of Pakistan Interference in Afghanistan," PTI News Agency (New Delhi), 17 February 2002, reproduced by BBC Monitoring <http://www.monitor.bbc .co.uk>.

41. "Russia-Pakistan Relationships Depend on Islamabad's Position towards Terrorists," RBC Network (Moscow), 7 March 2002.

42. Ibid.

43. Ibid.; and "Russia Urges Pakistan to Continue Fight against Terrorism," Interfax *Daily News Bulletin*, 6 March 2002, reproduced by BBC Monitoring <http://www.monitor .bbc.co.uk>.

44. Ron Fournier, "Putin Questions Terrorism Efforts," Associated Press, 22 November 2002.

45. "Pakistan Must Act on India's Request: Russia," *Hindu* (New Delhi), 8 February 2002.

46. Ibid.

47. Ibid.

48. "Russia, India Voice Support for Each Other on Chechnya, Kashmir," ITAR-TASS, 11 April 2002, reproduced by BBC Monitoring <http://www.monitor.bbc.co.uk>.

49. "Sergei Ivanov Considers Pakistan's Missile Tests a Provocation," Interfax *Daily News Bulletin* (Moscow), 3 June 2002.

50. "Russia Calls on Pakistan to Take First Step in India Standoff," Agence France Presse, 30 May 2002.

51. "Pakistan Condemns India-Russia Cooperation on Missile," *Middle East News Online*, 30 April 2002 <http://www.middleeastwire.com>.

52. "Pakistani Weapons Could Fall into the Hands of 'Bandits and Terrorists': Putin," Agence France-Presse, 1 December 2002.

53. "Pakistan Rejects Putin's Fears, Says Its Nukes in 'Safe Hands,' " *IndoLINK* (San Ramon, California), 21 December 2002 <http://www.indolink.com>.

54. Pierre Celerier, "Russia Seizes India-Pakistan Chance to Boost Regional Role," Agence France-Presse, 11 June 2002.

55. Dmitri Trenin, "Russia and Turkey: A Cure for Schizophrenia," *Perceptions: Journal of International Affairs* 2, no. 2 (June–August 1997) <http://www.mfa.gov.tr/grupa/ perceptII2/default.htm>.

56. The best example of this policy of delinking was the change in alphabet from Arabic to Latin.

57. Egbert Wesselink, "The North Caucasian Diaspora in Turkey," UN High Commissioner for Refugees REFWorld, May 1996 <http://www.unhcr.ch/refworld/country/writenet/ writur.htm>.

58. Ibid.

59. Circassians often refer to themselves as Adygei.

60. Estimates for the Abkhaz population in Turkey range from 30,000 to 300,000. There are no reliable estimates for Chechens.

61. "Trabzon Hijackers State Their Case on Turkish TV" [in Turkish], Kanal-D Television (Istanbul), 17 January 1996, in *BBC Summary of World Broadcasts*, 18 January 1996.

62. David Kushner, *The Rise of Turkish Nationalism, 1876–1908* (London: Frank Cass, 1977), p. 1.

63. Ibid., pp. 7–14.
64. Kushner, *The Rise of Turkish Nationalism, 1876–1908*; and Jacob M. Landau, *Pan-Turkism in Turkey: A Study of Irredentism* (Hamden, CT: Anchon Books, 1981).
65. Ibid., p. 87.
66. On the origins and ideology of NAP and Turkei, see Jacob M. Landau, *Radical Politics in Modern Turkey* (Leiden: E. J. Brill 1974), pp. 205–32.
67. Until July 2002, the MHP was part of the coalition ruling Turkey.
68. On the EU's refusal, see Sami Kohen, "Turks Feel Growing Disillusionment with West," *Christian Science Monitor*, 29 June 1987; and Edward Mortimer, "A Culture Shock for Europe," *Financial Times*, 14 July 1987.
69. Quoted in Sami Kohen, "Contacts with Central Asian States: A Foundation for 'Pan-Turkism,' " *Washington Report on Middle East Affairs*, 7 May 1993, p. 17.
70. Duygu Bazoglu Sezar, "Turkish-Russian Relations a Decade Later: From Adversity to Managed Competition," *Perceptions: Journal of International Affairs* 6, no. 1 (March–May 2001) <http://ww.mfa.gov.tr/grupa/percept/v1-1/default.htm>.
71. Trenin, "Russia and Turkey."
72. See Binnaz Toprak, *Islam and Political Development in Turkey* (Leiden: Brill, 1981); and Feroz Ahmad, *The Making of Modern Turkey* (London: Routledge, 1993).
73. Landau, *Radical Politics in Modern Turkey*, pp. 189–193; and Turker Alkan, "The National Salvation Party," in *Islam and Politics in the Modern Middle East*, ed. Metin Heper and Raphael Israeli (New York: St. Martin's Press, 1984), pp. 79–102.
74. Reformists grouped around the former mayor of Istanbul, Recep Tayyip Erdogan, while hard-liners supported Necmettin Erbakan. Selcan Hacaoglu, "Turkey's Islamic Movement Divides between Radicals and Moderates," Associated Press, 4 July 2001. Erdogan formed the party Adalet ve Kalkinma (Justice and Progress). Its main Islamic rival is Saadet Partisi (the Felicity Party), made up of the "old guard." Jean-Christophe Peuch, "2001 in Review: Patronage, Corruption Root Causes of Turkey's Worst Economic Crisis since WWII," RFE/RL *Weekday Magazine*, 18 December 2001 <http://www.rferl.org/nca/features/2001/12/18122001093221.asp>.
75. Sami Zubaida, "Trajectories of Political Islam: Egypt, Iran, and Turkey," *Political Quarterly* 71, no. 3 (August 2000): p. 72.
76. Ibid.; and Edward Mortimer, "A Tale of Two Funerals: Reviving Islam Challenges Ataturk's Legacy of Secularism," *Financial Times Surveys: Turkey*, 7 May 1993.
77. Ramazan Jabarov, "Ekstremisti Protiv Traditionalistov: Islamskii Faktor v Sovremennoi Chechne i Ego Zarubezhnie Sponsory" (Extremists versus traditionalists: the Islamic factor in contemporary Chechnya and its foreign sponsors), *Nezavisimaya Gazeta*, 20 October 1999 <http://www.ng.ru/ideas/1999-10-20/extremists.html>.
78. For a list of Gullen-sponsored schools in Central Asia and other parts of the post-Soviet space, including the Russian Federation, see Bülent Aras, "Turkey's Policy in the Former Soviet South: Assets and Options," *Turkish Studies* 1, no. 1 (Spring 2000): p. 50. The total number is 113.
79. During a conference on "Islamic Civilization in the Volga-Ural Region" held in Kazan in June 2001, Hunter witnessed the activities of the Nurcular movement, which included spreading their message, publications, and ideas.
80. Anatoliy Kurganov, "Gray Wolf on Hind Legs in Istanbul" [in Russian], *Rossisskaya Gazeta*, 15 May 1997, reproduced by the Foreign Broadcast Information Service, FBIS-SOV-97-136 <http://wnc.fedworld.gov>.
81. Raul Tukhvatullin, "Baskortostan Expels 10 Turks for Illegal Religious Activities," ITAR-TASS, 20 June 2003, reproduced by the Foreign Broadcast Information Service, FBIS-SOV-2003-0620 <http://wnc.dialogue.com>.
82. Vasily Bubkov "Turkey Ambitious About Turkish Community: Ankara Uses the Humanitarian Expansion Tactics for This," Pravda.Ru, 23 June 2003 <http://english.pravda.ru/world/20/91/366/1030/_turkey.html>.

83. Hunter's interview with Alexei Vassiliev, Russian expert and author on the Middle East and a member of the Russian Academy of Sciences, in Moscow on 29 April 2002.

84. "Turkey, Russia to Initial Friendship, Cooperation Pact," Xinhua News Service (Beijing), 4 February 1992.

85. Xu Wenqun, "Roundup: Turco-Soviet Relations Go into High Gear," Xinhua News Service (Beijing), 20 March 1991.

86. Ibid.

87. "Turkey, Russia to Initial Friendship, Cooperation Pact."

88. Vladimir Kuchenko, "Blue Stream Crosses Black Sea" [in Russian], *Rossiiskaya Gazeta* (Moscow), 8 August 2001, reproduced by the Foreign Broadcast Information Service, FBIS-SOV-2001-0808 <http://wnc.fedworld.gov>; and "Blue Stream Pipeline," in *Russia: Oil and Natural Gas Export Pipelines*, U.S. Department of Energy, Energy Information Administration, April 2002 <http://www.eia.docs.gov/emeu/cabs/russpip .html>.

89. Robert M. Cutler, "The 'Blue Stream' Gas Project: Not a Pipe-Dream Anymore," *Central Asia/Caucasus Analyst*, 1 August 2001 <http://www.cacianalyst.org/August_1 _2001/August_1_2001_THE_BLUE_STREAM_GAS_PROJECT.htm>.

90. "Russian-Turkish Gas Talks Fail To Produce Compromise" ITAR-TASS, 26 June 2003, reproduced by the Foreign Broadcast Information Service, FBIS-SOV-2003-0626 <http://wnc.dialogue.com>.

91. Republic of Turkey, Undersecretary of Foreign Trade <http://www.dtm.gov.tr/ead/ ticaret/trk00/dsticektab00-12.xls>.

92. Republic of Turkey, Undersecretary of Foreign Trade <http://www.dtm.gov.tr/ead/ ticaret/trk00/dstic00tablo-22.xls>.

93. Republic of Turkey, Prime Ministry, Undersecretariat of Foreign Trade <http://www .foreigntrade.gov.tr/engmenu.htm#>.

94. In December 1997, it was reported that Turkish companies were fulfilling building contracts in Russia worth $6 to $7 billion. Andrey Palaria, "Russia Concerned over Turkish-Russian Contract Imbalance," ITAR-TASS, 5 December 1997, reproduced by the Foreign Broadcast Information Service, FBIS-SOV-97-339 <http://wnc.fedworld .gov>; and Marshall Inguverson, " 'The Turks Are Coming,' Cry Russians in Their Ex-Empire," *Christian Science Monitor*, 26 September 1995.

95. "Russia Anticipates Increased Arms Exports to Turkey," Jamestown Foundation *Monitor* 2, no. 32 (14 February 1996.)

96. Umit Enginsoy, "Russia Can Meet Turkey's Arms Needs: Ambassador," Agence France-Presse, 26 February 1997.

97. Nikolay Novichkov, "Turkey Negotiates with Russian Arms Manufacturers," ITAR-TASS, 15 March 2000, reproduced by the Foreign Broadcast Information Service, FBIS-SOV-2000-0315 <http://wnc.fedworld.gov>; "Russia Reduces Helicopter Prices for Turkey," Interfax *Daily News Bulletin* (Moscow), 25 October 2000, reproduced by the Foreign Broadcast Information Service, FBIS-SOV-2000-1025 <http://wnc .fedworld.gov>. There were also reports that the Russian Kamov firm was negotiating with the Turkish Ministry of Public Health regarding the sale of KA-62 helicopters. "Russia to Sell KA-62 Helicopters to Turkey," ITAR-TASS, 29 March 2001, reproduced by the Foreign Broadcast Information Service, FBIS-SOV-2001-0329 <http:// wnc.fedworld.gov>.

98. Russia found Turkey's efforts to establish a controlling influence in Azerbaijan and to organize a Turkic group under its leadership as contrary to Russian interests. Kelly Couturier, "Discord between Russia, Turkey Growing; Nations Frustrated over Lack of Leverage in Caucasus, Ex-Soviet States of Central Asia," *Washington Post*, 4 December 1994.

99. "National Republican Leader Warns of 'Turkic-Islamic Fascism,' " Interfax *Daily News*

Bulletin (Moscow), 29 March 1995, in *BBC Summary of World Broadcasts*, 1 April 1995.

100. Radiy Fish, "War between Turkey and Russia?" *Moscow News*, 15 July 1994.
101. Sezaer, "Turkish-Russian Relations a Decade Later."
102. "Russia Protests Muslim Mercenaries," United Press International, 4 January 1995.
103. This claim was made by Anton Surikov, an expert at the Russian Defense Research Institute. Anatoliy Yurkin, "Expert Claims Dudayev Has Warplanes in Azerbaijan, Turkey," ITAR-TASS, 5 April 1996, reproduced by the Foreign Broadcast Information Service, FBIS-SOV-96-067 <http://wnc.fedworld.gov>.
104. The allegations are quoted in Robert Olson, *Turkey's Relations with Iran, Syria, Israel, and Russia, 1991–2000* (Costa Mesa, CA: Mazda Publishers, 2001), pp. 180–81. Tansu Çiller was Prime Minister from 1993–1995 and later became Foreign Minister from July 1996–June 1997.
105. John Barham and Chrystia Freeland, "Black Sea Crisis Ends as Gunmen Surrender: Russian Diplomatic Row with Turkey Worsens," *Financial Times*, 20 January 1996.
106. See Egbert Wesselink, "The North Caucasian Diaspora in Turkey," UN High Commissioner for Refugees *REFworld*, May 1996 <http://www.unhcr.ch/refworld/country/writenet/writur.htm>; and Ali Isingor, "Istanbul: Gateway to a Holy War: On the Banks of the Bosphorus the Assault on Grozny is Seen as a Family Matter," CNN.com <http://cnn.org/SPECIALS/2000/russia/story/chechnya/istanbul.connection>.
107. Wesselink, "North Caucasian Diaspora"; and Isingor, "Istanbul: Gateway to a Holy War."
108. Isingor, "Istanbul: Gateway to Holy War."
109. "The Tension Caused by Chechen Militants' Action Continues between Turkey and Russia: Russia Asks 'Serious Steps' from Turkey," *Turkish Daily News* (Ankara), 26 April 2001.
110. "Turkey Protests to Russia about Kurdish Parliament-in-Exile," Deutsche Presse-Agentur, 31 October 1995.
111. Margaret Rigillo, "Death Awaits Ocalan Because No Country Wanted to Irritate Turkey," *Herald* (Glasgow), 7 June 1999.
112. In January 1995, Turkish interior minister Nahit Mentese visited Moscow and signed a Protocol to Prevent Terrorism. On this occasion, Russian minister of internal affairs Viktor Yerin called the PKK a "terrorist" organization. Umit Erginsoy, "Interior Minister's Moscow Visit Detailed," *Turkish Daily News* (Ankara), 25 January 1995, reproduced by the Foreign Broadcast Information Service, FBIS-WEU-95-019 <http://wnc.fedworld.gov>. In February, Sergei Stepashin, director of Russia's counterintelligence service, visited Ankara and met with President Demirel. They agreed that "Turkey will not interfere in Chechen events while Russia will turn a blind eye to the suppression of the Kurdish movement by Ankara." "Russia-Turkey Collusion in Chechnya, Northern Iraq," *Turan* (Baku), 30 March 1995, reproduced by the Foreign Broadcast Information Service, FBIS-SOV-95-062 <http://wnc.fedworld.gov>.
113. "Primakov: Russia Satisfied with Turkey's Stand on Chechnya," Interfax *Daily News Bulletin* (Moscow), 18 December 1996, reproduced by the Foreign Broadcast Information Service, FBIS-SOV-96-245 <http://wnc.fedworld.gov>.
114. "Ecevit Holds News Conference after Talks in Moscow," *Anatolia* (Ankara), 5 November 1999, reproduced by the Foreign Broadcast Information Service, FBIS-SOV-1999-1105 <http://wnc.fedworld.gov>.
115. "Defense Minister Favors Peaceful Solution of Chechen Problem," *Anatolia* (Ankara), 27 August 2001, reproduced by the Foreign Broadcast Information Service, FBIS-SOV-2001-0827 <http://wnc.fedworld.gov>; "Russia Hopes for Chechnya Progress during Turkish Minister's Visit," ITAR-TASS, 27 April 2001, reproduced by the Foreign Broadcast Information Service, FBIS-SOV-2001-0427 <http://wnc.fedworld.gov>;

and "Russia's Ivanov Arrives for Talks, Says Turkey Important Partner," *Anatolia* (Ankara), 7 June 2001, reproduced by the Foreign Broadcast Information Service, FBIS-SOV-2001-0608 <http://wnc.fedworld.gov>.

116. "Turkey Deems Russia Partner—Turkish President," Xinhua News Service (Beijing), 28 May 2002.

117. Broadcast by TRT2 Television (Ankara), January 2002, reproduced by BBC Monitoring ("Turkey, Russia Sign Military Cooperation Agreement") <http://www.monitor.bbc.co.uk>.

118. Florence Biedermann, "General's Comments Shake Debate on Turkey's Bid to Join EU," Agence France-Presse, 8 March 2002.

119. "Turkey Opposes Russian Military Presence in Azerbaijan," Agence France-Presse, 8 February 2002.

120. Tengiz Pachkoria, "Russia Bases in Georgia No Threat to Turkey's Security," ITAR-TASS, 11 June 2002.

121. Natalya Airapetova, "Turetskiy Marsh na Prostorah SNG" (Turkish march in the expanses of the CIS), *Nezavisimaya Gazeta*, 13 May 2002 <http://www.ng.ru/courier/2002-05-13/7_turkish.html>.

122. Igor Torbakov, "The Turkish Factor in the Geopolitics of the Post-Soviet Space," Foreign Policy Research Institute (Philadelphia), 10 January 2003 <http://www.fpri.org/enotes/20030110.balkansturkey.torbakov.turkeypostsovietspace.html>.

123. Aleksei Slobodin, "Turks Vow to Put Pressure on Moscow's Antagonists," [in Russian] *Vremya Novostei*, 1 November 2002, in *Current Digest of the Post-Soviet Press* 54, no. 44 (27 November 2002).

124. "Turkey Expels Chechen Activist," Agence France-Presse, 16 November 2002.

125. "Russian-Turkish Talks Focus on Chechen Threat," 19 December 2002, ITAR-TASS, reproduced by BBC Monitoring <http://www.monitor.bbc.co.uk>.

126. "Russian Legal Official says Al-Qa'ida, Foreign Countries Assisting Chechen Rebels," ITAR-TASS, 16 June 2003, reproduced by the Foreign Broadcast Information Service, FBIS-SOV-2003-0616 <http://wnc.dialogue.com>.

127. Russian Ministry of Foreign Affairs, "The Foreign Policy Concept of the Russian Federation," June 2002 <http://www.great-britain.mid.ru/GreatBritain/econc.htm>.

128. "Rogue Russian Agency Gives Iran a Nuclear Boost," *Boston Globe*, 26 May 2002.

129. For example, the United Kingdom's *Al-Muhajiroun* condemned Iran for its failure to support Muslims in Chechnya. "Nobody's Happy—Iran's Stance on Chechnya," *Middle East News Items*, 18 January 2000 <www.nexis.com>. For a general criticism of the OIC, see Heshmatollah Falahat Pisheh, "The Great Tragedy" [in Persian], *Jomhuri-ye Eslami* (Tehran), 9 December 1999, reproduced by the Foreign Broadcast Information Service, FBIS-NES-2000-0110 <http://wnc.fedworld.gov>; "Is there a Rescuer?" [in Persian], *Jomhuri-ye Eslami* (Tehran), 8 December 1999, reproduced by the Foreign Broadcast Information Service, FBIS-NES-2000-0113 <http://wncfedworld.gov>; and "Chechnya and the Islamic World: An Unconvincing Excuse and a Crafty One" [in Arabic], *Al-Sharq al-Awsat* (London), 20 January 2000, reproduced by the Foreign Broadcast Information Service, FBIS-SOV-2000-0120 <http://wnc.fedworld.gov>.

130. For an analysis of the failure of Iranian diplomacy, see Shireen T. Hunter, *Iran, between the Gulf and the Caspian Basin: Strategic and Economic Implications* (Abu Dhabi: Eminates Center for Strategic Studies and Research, 2000).

131. Alexander Igatenko, "Ot Filipin do Kosovo" (From the Philippines to Kosovo), *Nezavisimaya Gazeta*, 12 October 2000.

132. "During his recent trip to Ankara, Russian Foreign Minister Andrei Kozyrev found completely mutual understanding with Turkish leaders, who share Moscow's fears of a possible 'Islamization of Central Asia.' " (Maksim Yusin, "Teheran Declares 'Great Battle' for Influence in Central Asia. Russia, the U.S., and Turkey Seek to Prevent Iran from Winning That Battle" [in Russian], *Izvestia*, 7 February 1992, in *Current*

Digest of the Post-Soviet Press 44, no. 6 (11 March 1992). Furthermore, Foreign Minister Kozyrev included Iran in the "southern belt of instability" that surrounded Russia. Sergey Strokan, "Tehran-95: Wind Southerly. Gusty," [in Russian], *Moskovskiye Novosti*, 5 May 1995, reproduced by the Foreign Broadcast Information Service, FBIS-SOV-95-087 <http://wnc.fedworld.gov>.

133. Robert Freedman, "Russian-Iranian Relations in the 1990s," *Middle East Review of International Affairs* 4, no. 2 (June 2000) <http://meria.biu.ac.il>.

134. Rafsanjani was then Speaker of the Iranian parliament and later became president. "Soviet-Iranian pact to Cost Tehran $15.1 billion; Doubled Estimate Includes Spending for Reconstruction," *Record*, 3 July 1989.

135. Quoted in Robert O. Freedman, "Yeltsin's Russia and Rafsanjani's Iran: A Tactical Alliance," *Middle East Insight* 11, no. 3 (July–August 1995): p. 90.

136. Andranik Mingranyan, "Real and Illusory Guidelines in Foreign Policy" [in Russian], *Rossiiskaya Gazeta*, 4 August 1992, in *Current Digest of the Post-Soviet Press* vol 44, no. 32 (9 September 1992).

137. The first step in this direction is the reunification of the so-called northern and southern Azerbaijan. Some Western analysts also champion this cause. See David Nissman, "The Two Azerbaijans: A Common Past and a Common Future," *Caspian Crossroads* 1, no. 2 (Spring 1995) <http://ourworld.compuserve.com/homepages/usazerb/126.htm>.

138. Vladimir Sazhin, "Kakovi Ranki Rossiisko-Iranskogo Partniorstva?" (What is the framework of Russian-Iranian partnership?) *Nezavisimaya Gazeta* (1 March 2001) <http://world.ng.ru/ozimuth/2001-03-01/2_iran.html>.

139. For only a few examples, see "Company Considers Gas Pipeline Project in Iran," Interfax *Daily News Bulletin* (Moscow), 24 October 2000, in *BBC Summary of World Broadcasts*, 3 November 2000; "Iran, Gazprom to Complete Gas Field Development Talks by March," *ITAR-TASS*, 15 February 2000; "Russian TU-334 Planes to Be Manufactured in Iran," IRNA (Tehran), 23 August 1999, in *BBC Summary of World Broadcasts*, 31 August 1999; "Russia and Iran to Build New Seaport for Caspian Trade," Interfax *Daily News Bulletin* (Moscow), 13 August 1997, in *BBC Summary of World Broadcasts*, 15 August 1997; "Russia, Iran Transport Ministers Looking at Major Projects," ITAR-TASS, 3 June 1997; and "Russia to Build Highway, Expand Trade," *Iran Brief*, 5 December 1996.

140. See A. I. Gousher, "K novomu etapu Rossiisko-Iranskikh Otnoshenii" (Toward a new stage of Russian-Iranian relations), *Evraziisky Vestnik* (Eurasian herald), no. 9 (January 2001) <http://www.e-journal.ru/p_zarub_stj-g.html>.

141. Cited in Peter Baker, "Russia Plans 5 More Nuclear Plants in Iran," *Washington Post*, 27 July 2002.

142. "Iran: Russians See Khatami's Moscow Visit as 'Big Event,' " IRNA (Tehran), 11 March 2001, reproduced by the Foreign Broadcast Information Service, FBIS-NES-2001-0311 <http://wnc.fedworld.gov>. On overall Russian-Iranian relations and their regional impact, see V. Vishniakov, "Russian-Iranian Relations and Regional Stability," *International Affairs* (Moscow) 45, no. 1 (1999): pp. 143–53.

143. "Iran Offers to Mediate in Settlement of Chechen Conflict," RIA News Agency (Moscow), 26 December 1994, in *BBC Summary of World Broadcasts*, 29 December 1994.

144. "Rafsanjani Terms Russian Military Action 'Mistake,' " Xinhua News Agency (Beijing), 4 January 1995.

145. The deputy speaker of the Parliament, Hasan Rohani, characterized the Chechen struggle for independence as "jihad." "Rohani Says Chechens Are Fighting a Jihad" [in Persian], *Vision of the Islamic Republic of Iran*, Network 2 Broadcast, 12 January 1995, in *BBC Summary of World Broadcasts,* 14 January 1995.

146. For a view of Iran's Chechnya policy as a cynical exercise in realpolitik, see A. William Samii, "Iran and Chechnya: Realpolitik at Work," *Middle East Review* 8, no. 1 (March 2001): pp. 48–57.

147. Ivan Novikov, "Duma Deputy Claims Dudayev Received Arms from Iran, Turkey," ITAR-TASS, 22 March 1995, reproduced by the Foreign Broadcast Information Service, FBIS-SOV-95-056 <http://wnc.fedworld.gov>.
148. "Iranian FM Meets Yeltsin, Primakov in Moscow," Agence France-Presse, 7 March 1996.
149. "Interior Minister Kulikov Thanks Iran for 'Circumspect Position' on Chechnya," Interfax *Daily News Bulletin* (Moscow), 20 December 1997, in *BBC Summary of World Broadcasts*, 20 December 1997.
150. On OIC visits, see "Iran, Russia," IRNA (Tehran), 8 December 1999, reproduced by the Foreign Broadcast Information Service, FBIS-NES-1999-1208 <http://wnc .fedworld.gov>. Kamal Kharazi, the Iranian foreign minister, headed an OIC delegation on a visit to Russia.
151. "Ivanov: Russia Ready to Boost Relations with OIC," IRNA (Tehran), 18 January 2000, reproduced by the Foreign Broadcast Information Service, FBIS-NES-2000-0118 <http://wnc.fedworld.gov>. During a meeting with an OIC delegation headed by Iran's deputy foreign minister, Ivanov stated that Russia attached high importance to its relations with the OIC.
152. Gousher, "K noromu etapu Rossíisko-Iranskikh Otnoshenii."
153. Maksim Gribov, "Khatami Receives Guests from Moscow—Russia Sends Muslim Deputies to Bargain with Iran," *Nezavisimaya gazeta*, 2 December 2000, in *Current Digest of the Post-Soviet Press* 52, no. 49 (2 December 2000.) According to Gribov, because of U.S. opposition for ten years, "Russia [has] curtailed practically all of its programs of cooperation with its neighbor to the south."
154. Ibid.
155. On GUUAM, see "The GUUAM Group: History and Principles," briefing paper, November 2000 <http://www.guuam.org/general/browse.html>.
156. See Sudha Ramachandran, "India, Iran, Russia Map Out Trade Route," *Asia Times*, 29 June 2002 <http://www.atimes.com/ind-pak/ind-pak.html>; and "North-South Corridor: India, Russia, and Iran to Iron Out Operational Issues," *Iran Expert*, 11 June 2002 <http://www.iranexpert.com/2002/russiannorthsouthcorridor_1june.html>.
157. "Oil Minister: Turkey's 'National Will' Guarantees Gas Deal with Iran," IRNA (Tehran), 18 August 1996, in *BBC Summary of World Broadcasts*, 20 August 1996.
158. Nevertheless, the pipeline was finally completed and inaugurated in April 2002. The pipeline was expected to supply Turkey with four billion cubic meters of gas in 2002. Iran also has an option to send some of the gas through Turkey and into Europe. Jeonni Stell, "Special Report: World Wide Construction Update," *Oil and Gas Journal*, 8 April 2002.
159. Iran's basic position, with which Russia initially agreed, was that the entire Caspian— its subsoil resources, water mass, and surface—should be used in common by all states, the so-called condominium approach. Later, when this option became impossible because others did not agree, Iran adopted the position that the Caspian should be divided into five equal portions, giving each country a 20 percent share. For a brief analysis of the Caspian Sea's legal status, see "Caspian Sea Region: Legal Issues," U.S. Department of Energy, Energy Information Administration, February 2002 <http://www .eia.doe.gov/emeu/cabs/casplaw.html>.
160. On bilateral agreements, see "Russia Finishes Division of Caspian Sea with Azerbaijan" [in Russian], *Izvestia*, 7 June, 2002, reproduced in *Russian Oil and Gas Report*, 10 June 2002. In May 2002, Kazakhstan was the first country with which Russia signed an agreement for dividing the Caspian Sea floor. A treaty with Azerbaijan was signed on 9 June 2002 with Azerbaijanis President Geidar Aliev. Since Russia borders only Kazakhstan and Azerbaijan, the treaties settle all of Russia's disputes. See also "Focus; Russia and Kazakhstan Agree on Offshore Boundary," *Petroleum Economist,* 25 June 2002.

161. On the basis of the 1921 and 1941 Soviet-Iranian treaties, Iran has only a 13 percent share of the sea. In the context of the negotiations, it has been suggested that if Iran agrees to a global settlement, its share might be increased to 15 or 16 percent.

162. Gousher, "K noromu etapu Rossiisko-Inanskikh Otnoshenii."

163. "Iran and Russia Sign Joint Communiques on Caspian Sea, Tajikistan," Voice of the Islamic Republic of Iran (Tehran), 19 July 1998, in *BBC Summary of World Broadcasts*, 20 July 1998.

164. Arkady Dubnov, "Kalyuzhny Gets Involved in Game with Iranians—and Uses America to Intimidate Them" [in Russian], *Vremya novostei*, 3 August 2000, in *Current Digest of the Post-Soviet Press* 52, no. 31 (30 August 2000).

165. On Russia's impatience and frustration, see Gordon Geller, "Fighting over the 'Slice of Caspian Sea Oil,' " *Gulf News*, 15 June 2002; and Dubnov, "Kalyuzhny Gets Involved." However, it is wrong to think that it is only Iran's opposition that prevents an agreement on the Caspian Sea. There are many differences among other littoral states, notably Azerbaijan and Turkmenistan.

166. "Putin Orders to Build Up Russian Naval Presence on Caspian Sea," ITAR-TASS, 25 April 2002.

167. Ibid. However, in view of growing U.S.-Azeri and U.S.-Georgian military cooperation, these maneuvers may also be a signal to other regional countries that Russia is still a force to be reckoned with. President Putin's statements that the problems of the Pankisi Gorge cannot be resolved without active Russian participation attest to this fact. See "Russia: Putin—U.S. Must Join Moscow to Fight Terrorism in Georgia," RFE/RL *Newsline,* 24 June 2002; and "Vladimir Putin Believes Pankisi Gorge Problem Cannot be Solved without Russia," *RIA Novosti* (Moscow), 24 June 2002.

168. Sazhin, "Kakovi Ranki Rossiisko-Iranskogo Partniorstva?" (What is the framework of Russian-Iranian partnership?).

169. According to some sources, the Bushehr plant created 20,000 jobs in Russia. Several hundred Russian military and civilian specialists have also been working in Iran.

170. One analyst remarked that the Bush administration "is in no hurry to put U.S.-Russian relations on any kind of pedestal." Martin Kettle, "Back to the Old Days?" *Guardian*, 23 March 2001. Also see Condoleezza Rice, "Campaign 2000: Promoting the National Interest," *Foreign Affairs* 79, no. 1 (January–February 2000): pp. 45–62.

171. Vladimir Kucherenko, "How Many Ideas in Iranian Field?" [in Russian], *Rossiiskaya Gazeta*, 12 March 2001, reproduced by the Foreign Broadcast Information Service, FBIS-NES-2001-0312 <http://wnc.fedworld.gov>.

172. Based on Hunter's observations during visits to Moscow. For example, a Russian journalist participating in a panel discussion on France's Antenne 2 Television clearly said that a U.S.-Iranian rapprochement would be bad news for Russia.

173. Vadim Markushin, "The Russian Opportunity in Iran Does Not Inspire the Americans" [in Russian], *Krasnaya Zvesda*, 13 April 1995, reproduced by the Foreign Broadcast Information Service, FBIS-SOV-95-071 <http://wnc.fedworld.gov>.

174. Mikhail Chernov, "Iranskaia Partiia Putina" (Putin's Iranian Party), *Caspian Ekspert* (Moscow: Caspian News Agency), 20 March 2001 <http://www.caspian.ru/cgi/article .cgi?id=858(Russia)>.

175. "A state with whom Moscow has one day been 'advised' not to maintain mutually beneficial relations because of supposed 'bad behavior' the next day joins the ranks of the United States' partners and its markets are suddenly flooded with American companies." Igor Ivanov, *The New Russian Diplomacy* (Washington: Nixon Center and Brookings Institution Press, 2002), p. 118.

176. Robin Wright, "Bush Endorses Reform in Iran; Diplomacy: President Expresses Support for Pro-Democracy Activists after Clashes with Police and a Leading Cleric's Resignation this Week," *Los Angeles Times,* 13 July 2002.

177. "Russian-Iranian Cooperation no Threat for Non-Proliferation Efforts—Putin," Interfax

Daily News Bulletin (Moscow), 24 May 2002; Dubnov, "Kalyuzhny Gets Involved." There were even reports that Russia may build a second nuclear reactor for Iran. "Russia to Build a Second Nuclear Reactor for Iran," Agence France-Presse, 26 July 2002.

178. "Russia to Continue Cooperation with Iran—Bulayevsky," Interfax *Daily News Bulletin* (Moscow), 24 May 2002; Dubnov, "Kalyuzhny Gets Involved."

179. "Will Russians Be Able to Resist Washington Pressure?" [in Persian], *Afarinesh* (Tehran), 26 May 2002, reproduced by the Foreign Broadcast Information Service, FBIS-WEU-2002-0619 <http://wnc.fedworld.gov>.

180. Georgiy Zotov, "Scheherezade's Nuclear Night" [in Russian], *Izvestia*, 11 July 2002, reproduced by the Foreign Broadcast Information Service, FBIS-NES-2002-0711 <http://wnc.fedworld.gov>.

181. "Moscow Defends Tehran Ties As Top Iranian Delegation Begins Russia Visit," Agence France-Presse, 13 January 2003; and "Russia, Iran Call for Anti-Terrorism System under UN," Associated Press, 15 January 2003.

182. According to Dmitri Trenin, "The vested interests on Iran in Russia are very powerful. Even if Putin wanted to, he might not have the capacity to stop them." Quoted in Peter Baker, "Russia Plans More Nuclear Plants in Iran; U.S. Has Sought an End to Current Construction," *Washington Post*, 27 June 2002.

183. For details of the Russian-Azerbaijani agreement, see Gregory Feifer, "Russia, Azerbaijan Sign Agreement on Sea Boundaries," RFE/RL *Weekday Magazine,* 24 September 2002 <http://www.rferl.org/nca/features>.

184. Jeremy Bransten, "Russia: Ivanov in Iran Amid Warming Bilateral Ties," RFE/RL *Weekday Magazine*, 11 March 2003 <http://www.rferl.org/nca/features>.

185. "Tehran Ready to Cooperate With Moscow in North Caucasus," *Online Pravda*, 14 March 2003 <http://english.pravda.ru/diplomatic/2003/03/14/44419.html>.

186. "Deputy Foreign Minister and Russian Political Director of the G-8 Georgy Mamedov Meets Iranian Ambassador to Moscow Gholamreza Shafei," Ministry of Foreign Affairs of The Russian Federation Information and Press Department, 27 May 2003 <http://www.In.mid.ru/bl.nsf/900b2c3ac91734634325698f002d9dcf/387c6138126f8053 43256d330048d073?OpenDocument>.

187. Ibid.

188. "Russia Says Nothing Can Hamper Nuclear Cooperation with Iran," ITAR-TASS, 1 July 2003, reproduced by BBC Monitoring <http://www.monitor.bbc.co.uk>; and "Iran 'Ready to Sing' Non Proliferation Treaty Protocol," ITAR-TASS, 1 July 2003, reproduced by BBC Monitoring <http://www.monitor.bbc.co.uk>.

189. Simion Sradzhyan, "Russia presses Iran over Nukes," *Moscow Times*, 1 July 2003.

190. "Arrival of Iranian Delegations in Russia for Oil Talks," IRNA (Tehran), 8 April 2003, reproduced by the Foreign Broadcast Information Service, FBIS-NES-2003-0408 <http://wwwnc.dialogue.com>; and "Russian Delegation in Isfahan to Discuss Industrial Cooperation," IRNA (Tehran); 24 May 2003, reproduced by the Foreign Broadcast Information Service, FBIS-NES-2003-0524 <http://.wnc.dialogue.com>.

Notes to Chapter 10

1. Viktor Kuvaldin, "From Cold War to New World Order," in *Soviet Foreign Policy, 1917–1991: A Retrospective*, ed. Gabriel Gorodetsky (London: Frank Cass, 1994), p. 193.

2. Carol R. Saivetz, *The Soviet Union and the Gulf in the 1980s* (Boulder, CO: Westview Press, 1989), p. 11.

3. Boris Pankin, the Soviet Union's last foreign minister, reports that in 1991, after the failed coup d'état, Gorbachev said, "Talk to Primakov, he has good contacts with the

Saudis. Their King is a strong supporter of our democracy. We must change priorities, get rid of prejudices. Yasser Arafat, Gaddafi—they call themselves our friends, but only because they dream of our returning to the past." Boris Pankin, *The Last Hundred Days of the Soviet Union* (London: I.B. Tauris, 1996), p. 53.

4. In 1988, Syria's debt to Russia was approximately $15 billion, while Iraq's debt reached about $8 billion due to its war with Iran. Talal Nizameddin, *Russia and the Middle East* (New York: St. Martin's Press, 1999), p. 53.

5. Ibid., p. 190.

6. Ibid., p. 191. The issue of Chechnya, however, did come up in the discussions. King Fahd reportedly told Kozyrev, "Tell your President that we will never interfere in the internal affairs of other states. No matter what the religious convictions of a person living in Russia are, for us he is first and foremost a citizen of the Russian Federation." Maksim Yusin, "Our Visit Is a Drive for Markets, Including Arms Markets" [in Russian], *Izvestia*, 5 May 1992, in *Current Digest of the Post-Soviet Press* 44, no. 18 (3 June 1992).

7. Yusin, "Our visit is a Drive for Markets, including Arms Markets."

8. Nizameddin, *Russia and the Middle East*, p. 195.

9. "Saudi Arabia Urges UN to Halt Wars in Chechnya, Bosnia," Agence France-Presse, 9 January 1995.

10. "Islamic Conference, Saudis Condemn Chechen War," *Russia Today*, November 1999; and "Moscow Officially Protests Alleged Saudi Interference in Chechnya," Jamestown Foundation *Monitor* 6, no. 129 (3 July 2000).

11. Said Isayev, "Chechen President Says Saudi Visit 'Successful,' " ITAR-TASS, 27 April 1997, reproduced by the Foreign Broadcast Information Service, FBIS-SOV-97-117 <http://wnc.fedworld.gov>.

12. "Maskhadov's Aide Says Saudi Arabia Finances Wahhabites," Interfax *Daily News Bulletin* (Moscow), 27 April 2000.

13. "Saudi Arabia Still in Solidarity with Chechnya Despite Hijacking, Said Saudi Minister," Agence France-Presse (Riyadh), March 19, 2001. The plane was diverted from Istanbul to Medina, where Saudi commandos stormed it to rescue the hostages.

14. According to the FSB, part of the money provided by the organization "proceeds to the banking accounts of some warlords, including Shamil Basayev and Khattab. . . . Al-Haramein envoys are working with Chechen warlords, including rebel leader Aslan Maskhadov. Abdul Latif Bin Abdul Karim al-Darovan dispenses advice to Maskhadov and Abu Umar al-Sayf, Bosayef, and Khattab." "Russian FSB Accuses Saudi Body of Aiding Chechen Militants," ITAR-TASS, 19 May 2000, reproduced by the Foreign Broadcast Information Service, FBIS-SOV-2000-0519 <http://wnc.fedworld.gov>. The FSB further claimed that Russian security forces had intercepted messages from the Saudi-based Islamic organization Al-Haramein to its envoy in Chechnya. One of the messages said, "The load is ready for sending—grenade launchers with ammunition, bullets for various systems, machine guns, Kalashnikov submachine guns, and sniper rifles." Grigory Dubovitsky and Boris Kipkeyev, "Arab Countries Still Sending Arms to Chechnya," ITAR-TASS, 19 May 2000, reproduced by the Foreign Broadcast Information Service, FBIS-SOV-2000-0519 <http://wnc.fedworld.gov>.

15. On Al-Iqra'a's activities in Dagestan, see Ilya Maksakov, "Islamskii missioner v Dagestane" (An Islamic missionary in Dagestan), *Nezavisimoe voennoe obozrenie* (Independent military review), no. 13 (13 April 2001) <http://nvo.ng.ru/wars/2001-04-13/2_dagestan>. According to Maksakov, the headquarters of this organization is in Jeddah, and it is headed by the former minister of information of Saudi Arabia, Muhammad Abdu Yamani. Affiliated with Al-Iqra'a's Charitable Society, Egyptian national Servah Abid-Saad became very active in Dagestan. After settling in Kizilyurt, he established contacts with the leaders of the Wahhabi insurgence in the villages of Karamakhi and Chabanmakhi. Reportedly, he also tried to acquire Russian citizenship.

16. Ibid.
17. See "O rasprostranenii idei religioznogo ekstremizma na territorii Rossiiskoi Feder- atsii" (On the spread of the ideas of religious extremism on the territory of the Russian Federation), *Spravka*, reproduced by Rosinformcenter (Russian Information Center), 2 December 1999 <http://www.infocentre.ru/win/user/index.cfm?page=5&date=1999 -10-08&startrow=1&msg_id=1814>.
18. Sanobar Shermatova, "Islamic Sword Bearer" [in Russian], *Moskovskie novosti*, 31 January 1999, reproduced by the Foreign Broadcast Information Service, FBIS-SOV- 1999-0212 <http://wnc.fedworld.gov>.
19. Mark N. Katz, "Saudi-Russian Relations in the Future Era," *Middle East Journal* 55, no. 4 (autumn 2001): p. 615. According to Katz, the Saudis believe that "if Moscow treated these Muslims respectfully instead of offensively, its problems with them would disappear."
20. Ibid., pp. 615–16. Katz further states that the Russians "insist that the money is pro- vided to these groups in such a way that there is no proof where it comes from. The Russians know this . . . because they themselves used these techniques during the So- viet era to provide support to opposition movements in other countries so that it could not be traced back to Moscow."
21. Svetlana Novaldskaya, "Russia Escapes the OPEC Embrace" [in Russian], *Vedomosti*, 27 September 2001, reproduced by the WPS Monitoring Agency (Moscow), <http:// wps.ru/e_index/html>.
22. Leon Dron, "Russian Oil and U.S. security," *New York Times*, 5 May 2002.
23. Saudi-Iranian relations have improved since 1997. However, a militarily strong Iran would be of concern for the Russians. See Shireen T. Hunter "Outlook for Iranian- Gulf Relations: Greater Cooperation or Renewed Risk of Conflict?" in *Iran, Iraq, and the Arab Gulf States*, ed. Joseph A. Kechichian (New York: Palgrave, 2001), pp. 428– 31.
24. See Dmitri Furman, "The Chechen Crisis: A Russian Liberal's Perspective" [in Rus- sian], *Obshchaya Gazeta*, no. 40 (8 October 1999), in *ASF Archive Documents*, trans. Edward Kline <http://www.wdn.com/asf>.
25. According to Dmitri Furman, "The Chechen and Palestinian terrorists not only share common traits, they are linked. They form a single network nourished by the ideology of militant Islamic fundamentalism" <http://www.wdn.com/asf>. Also see Arieh O'Sullivan, "Chechens Offered 150 Fighters for Intifadah," *Jerusalem Post*, 9 August 2001 <http://pqsab.pqarchiver.com/jpost>; and "Russia: Palestine Envoy Dismisses Claims of Chechen Rebels Aiding Palestine," Interfax *Daily News Bulletin* (Moscow), 13 October 2000.
26. Scott Lindlaw, "Tensions Loom as Bush Meets with Saudi Crown Prince," Associated Press, 25 April 2002.
27. "Russia: Putin Meets with Saudi Arabia's FM, Supports Saudi Peace Initiative," Inter- fax *Daily News Bulletin* (Moscow), 19 April 2002, reproduced by the Foreign Broad- cast Information Service, FBIS-SOV-2002-0419 <http://wnc.fedworld.gov>.
28. See Vladimir Radyuhin, "Petrodollars Fuelling Terrorism in Russia" *Hindu*, 11 October 2001.
29. "Russia Displeased by Verdict Handed Down on Chechen Hijackers," Interfax *Daily News Bulletin* (Moscow), 31 July 2002.
30. "Moscow Denounces Saudi Arabian Verdict to Plane Hijackers," Interfax *Daily News Bulletin* (Moscow), 31 July 2002.
31. Ron Fournier, "Putin Questions Terrorism Efforts," Associated Press, 23 November 2002.
32. This information was given by Vladimir Trofimov at a meeting with Arab ambassadors at the offices of *Izvestia*. Gennadii Charodeev, "Almost All Ambassadors Came to Izvestia," *Izvestia*, 30 January 2003 <http://www.izvestia.ru/world/29278>.

33. "Saudi FM in Moscow, Preparation for Crown Prince Visit, Iraq Agenda," Arabic News.com, 8 May 2003 <http://www.arabicnews.com/ansub/Daily/Day/030508/2003050802.html>.
34. "Russian, Saudi Foreign Ministers Meet," RFE/RL *Newsline*, 9 May 2003.
35. "Russian Deputy Foreign Minister Ends Tour with Talk in UAE," ITAR-TASS, 27 June 1998, in *BBC Summary of World Broadcasts*, 27 June 1998.
36. One Russian newspaper reported, "The Chechen propaganda machine has started working again. A few days ago Khattab . . . gave an interview to the Al-Jazira TV company which broadcasts in the Arab world." Vladimir Petrov and Stepan Dvornikov, "Minimal Losses" [in Russian], *Vremya MN*, 6 October 1999, reproduced by the WPS Monitoring Agency (Moscow) <http://wps.ru/e_index/html>.
37. Zelimkhan Yanderbiev was the vice-president of Chechnya before the death of President Dzhokhar Dudaev, and afterwards he served as an acting president. He was a prominent figure in Chechen resistance. Movladi Udogov is one of the radical ideologues of Chechen independence. In the Maskhadov's government, he was First Deputy Prime Minister and Minister of Foreign Affairs of the Chechen Republic. "Chechnya Sets Up 'Fundamentalist Axis' with Taliban," ITAR-TASS, 21 January 2000, reproduced by the Foreign Broadcast Information Service, FBIS-SOV-2000-0121 <http://wnc.fedworld.gov>.
38. The UAE was one of three countries to officially recognize the Taliban. "Taliban Official Holds Talks in U.A.E." Agence France-Presse, 14 January 1995; "Afghan Official Holds Talks in Dubai," *Middle East News Items*, 6 October 1998; and "U.A.E. Offers to Provide Economic Aid to Taliban If Fighting Stops," Agence France-Presse, 16 January 1998.
39. "Foreign Ministry Summons Qatari Ambassador Due to Chechen Envoy's Reception," Interfax *Daily News Bulletin* (Moscow), 21 March 2000.
40. "Qatari Daily Rejects Russian Charges over Chechnya," *Russia Today*, 17 November 1999 <http://www.russiatoday.com/news:php39id=110805>.
41. Ibid.
42. "Kuwaiti MP Salutes 'Hero' Killed Fighting alongside Chechen Rebels," *Russia Today*, 21 February 2000 <http://www.russiatoday.chechnyainfocus/news/php37id=1364247_2>. Ajmi reportedly entered Chechnya through Turkey.
43. There are approximately 15,000 Chechens living in Jordan, plus another 150,000 people of Caucasian origin. "Chechens Hold Anti-Russian Rally in Jordan," Agence France-Presse, 23 February 1995. The number of Chechens living in Jordan is hard to estimate because they are often confused with the Cherkess and other Caucasians who have settled in the area.
44. The Jordanians claim that "in the past thirty years there have been more than a dozen Chechens who have achieved the rank of a general in the Jordanian armed forces, whereas in the USSR there was only one Chechen general—Dudaev." Elena Suponina and Victor Paukov, "Brothers in Faith and Blood" [in Russian], *Vremya MN*, 22 December 1999, reproduced by the National News Service (Moscow) <http://www.nns.ru/pressfile/dagestan/expert/dag.395.html>.
45. Ibid.
46. Ibid.
47. Ibid.
48. "Senior Officials: Chechnya Part of Russian Federation," *Jordan Times*, 9 February 1995, reproduced by the Foreign Broadcast Information Service, FBIS-NES-95-027 <http://wnc.fedworld.gov>.
49. "King Receives Russian Presidential Envoy," Xinhua News Agency (Beijing), 18 June 1995.
50. "Jordanian Crown Prince Meets with Russian Envoy," Xinhua News Agency (Beijing), 12 June 1996.

51. "Paper Says Jordan Clamping Down on Support for Chechen Separatists" [in Russian], *Komsomolskaya Pravda*, 19 March 1996, in *BBC Summary of World Broadcasts,* 19 March 1996.
52. On the August visit of King Abdullah, see "King Abdullah Visits Moscow: Jordanian-Russian Politics," Arabic News.com, 23 August 2001 <http://www.arabicnews.com/arab/Daily/Day/0108231/2001082315.html>.
53. Alexander Shumilin, "A Visit of Special Importance" [in Russian], *Literaturnaya gazeta*, 17 July 1996, in *Russian Press Digest* (Moscow), 17 July 1996.
54. "Russian Foreign Minister Kozyrev Hints of New Ideas to Move Peace Forward," Middle East News Agency (Cairo), 31 March 1995, in *BBC Summary of World Broadcasts*, 31 March 1995.
55. "Against Whom Do Terrorist Fighters Make Friends?" [in Russian], *Moskovskie novosti*, 15 March 1996, reproduced by the Foreign Broadcast Information Service, FBIS-SOV-96-052 <http://wnc.fedworld.gov>.
56. "Russia: Egypt's Musa Comments on Talks with Russian Officials," Middle East News Agency (Cairo), 16 July 1996, reproduced by the Foreign Broadcast Information Service, FBIS-SOV-86-138 <http://wnc.fedworld.gov>.
57. "Mubarak Leaves Moscow after Talks," United Press International, 24 September 1997; "Mubarak's Visit to Moscow, New Horizons for Support for Egypt-Russia Cooperation," ArabicNews.com, 5 March 2001; and "Mubarak's Visit to Russia Termed as Successful and Satisfactory," *News Desk*, 29 April 2001 <http://www.presidency.gov.eg/html/29-April2001_press.html>.
58. "Egypt: MB Condemns Russian 'Savagery' in Chechnya," Agence France-Presse, 8 December 1999, reproduced by the Foreign Broadcast Information Service, FBIS-NES-1999-1208 <http://wnc.fedworld.gov>.
59. Among the most prominent figures were Abu-Ahmad and Abu-Ainan. Viktor Khlistun, "Mercenaries" [in Russian], *Trud*, 19 November 1999, reproduced by the National News Service (Moscow) <http://www.nns.ru/Press-file/dagestan/expert/dag395.html>.
60. Cited in Sergei Strokan, "Moscow Seeks to Win Friends and Influence in Iraq," Interpress Service, 20 December 1996.
61. Ibid.
62. On Russia's desire to become more engaged in Middle East peacemaking, see Irina Chumakova and Irina Shatalova, "Russia, U.S. Play Key Role in Mideast Settlement—Ivanov," ITAR-TASS, 16 March 2002; "Russian Senators Looking for More Active Role in the Middle East Settlement," *Ekho Moskvy* (Moscow), 25 January 2002, reproduced by BBC Monitoring <http://www.monitor.bbc.co.uk>; and Yevgeny Satanovsky, "Russia's Role in the Mideast," *Statesman*, 5 August 2001.
63. "King Abdullah Stresses Importance of Russia's Role in Bid to Revive Peace Process," *Jordan Times*, 22 November 2001 <http://www.jordanembassyus.org/11222001001.html>.
64. "King, Putin Discuss Bilateral Ties, Mideast," *Jordan Times*, 10 July 2002 <http://www.jordanembassyus.org/07102002001.htm>.
65. "Jordanian-Chechens Keep Distance from Conflict," *Russia Journal*, 1 February 2003.
66. Putin met with the Moroccan king in October 2002 and with the president of Yemen in December 2002. See the Kremlin Web site <http://kremlin.ru/withflash/news/200/12.shtml>. On Amr Musa's visit, see "Head of Arab League Discusses Iraq, Israel with Russian Foreign Minister," Associated Press, 10 December 2002.
67. "Putin Praised Russian-Yemeni Declaration on Friendly Relations," Interfax *Diplomatic Panorama* (Moscow), 17 December 2002, reproduced by the Foreign Broadcast Information Service, FBIS-SOV-2002-1218 <http://wnc.fedworld.gov>.
68. Most of these meetings occurred in the context of the United Nations General Assembly. See *Daily News Bulletin*, Russian Ministry of Foreign Affairs <http://www.ln.mid.ru/bl.nsf>.

69. Viktor Lebedev, "Arabian Monarchies Laud Russian Diplomat's Role in Mideast," ITAR-TASS, 21 January 2003. Lebedev reported, "Secretary General of the Gulf Cooperation Council (GCC) Abdel Rahman Al-Ateyyahhs lauded the role of Russian diplomats in the Middle East and called for the development of comprehensive cooperation with Moscow, especially in investment."

70. Transcript of the meeting of President of the Russian Federation Vladimir V. Putin with representatives of the Russian and German mass media, 4 April 2002, official Web site of President Putin <http://194.226.80.159/events/497.html>.

71. Ariel Cohen, "Bringing Russia into an Anti-Saddam Coalition," *Executive Memorandum* (Heritage Foundation) no. 812, 29 April 2002. Russian oil companies have signed lucrative oil contracts with Iraq that could amount to $30 billion over twenty years.

72. Ibid.

73. Ibid.

74. Michael Wines, "Russia Softens Opposition to Military Action in Iraq," *New York Times*, 31 January 2003.

75. "Russian Foreign Minister Willing to Discuss New UN Resolution to Help Inspectors," ITAR-TASS, 17 February 2003, reproduced by the Foreign Broadcast Information Service, FBIS-SOV-2003-0217 <http://wnc.fedworld.gov>.

76. "Putin Says Russia Ready to Use Security Council Veto," Radio Free Europe/Radio Liberty (RFE/RL) *Russian Foreign Policy and Security Watch* 4, no. 7 (19 February 2003).

77. "RIA NOVOSTI Interview with Russian Foreign Ministry Official Spokesman Alexander Yakovenko on the Eve of Russian Visit by Secretary General of the Organization of the Islamic Conference Abdelouahed Belkeziz on January 27–29," Russian Ministry of Foreign Affairs, Information and Press Department, 28 January 2003 <http://www.ln.mid.ru>.

78. "Russian Minister of Foreign Affairs Igor Ivanov Holds Talks with Organization of the Islamic Conference Secretary General Abdelouahed Belkeziz," Russian Ministry of Foreign Affairs, Information and Press Department, 28 January 2003 <http://www.ln.mid.ru>.

79. "OIC Promises to Help Curb Financial Flow to Chechen Terrorists from Arab States," Interfax *Daily News Bulletin* (Moscow), 28 January 2003.

80. "Russian Minister of Foreign Affairs Igor Ivanov Holds Talks."

81. "Transcript of RF Foreign Minister Igor Ivanov's Remarks at the Joint Press Conference with Secretary General of the Organization of the Islamic Conference Abdelouahed Belkeziz on the Results of Their Talks," Russian Ministry of Foreign Affairs, Information and Press Department, 28 January 2003 <http://www.ln.mid.ru>.

82. "New Ambassador Named for Islamic Issues," RFE/RL *Newsline*, 21 February 2003.

83. "RIA NOVOSTI Interview."

84. "Gen-Sek OIK vstretilsia s Talgatom Tadzhuddinom" (OIC general secretary met with Talgat Tadzhuddin), Religion.Ru, 29 January 2003 <http://www.religion.ru/arch/29jan2003/news/5213.html>.

85. "Gen-Sec OIK udivilsia chislu mechetei v Tatarstane" (OIC general secretary impressed by number of mosques in Tatarstan), Islam.Ru, 31 January 2003 <http://www.islam.ru/press/rus/2003-01-31#1852>.

86. Serbian agitation to gain freedom from Ottoman rule began in 1804, but the Serbs did not achieve independence until 1830 following the Russian-Turkish War of 1829–30. In the interim period, Serbia's aspirations were at the mercy of broader European politics. L.S. Stavrianos, *The Balkans since 1453* (New York: Rinehart, 1958), pp. 246–50.

87. On Turkey's policies toward the Bosnian crisis, see Hasan Unal, "Bosnia II: A Turkish Critique," *World Today* 51, no. 7 (15 July 1995) pp. 28–29; and Sami Kohen, "Heeding Its Islamic Roots, Secular Turkey Builds Ties to Balkans," *Christian Science Monitor*,

8 September 1995. In 1993, Turkish president Turgut Ozal called on the U.S. government to send arms to Bosnia and hinted that Turkey might not allow the use of the Incerlik airbase for bombing Iraq. Norman Kempster, "Angry over Bosnia, Turks May Halt Use of Airbase," *Los Angeles Times*, 28 January 1993. Turkey became more actively involved in Bosnia after the Dayton Peace Accords with the West's blessing, in part to counteract Iran's influence, which had become substantial. Turkey's interest later waned, largely under U.S. pressure. See "Ciller Visits Sarajevo," *Turkish Press Review*, 29 November 1995 <http://www.hri.org/news/Turkey/trkpr/95-11-29.trkpr>; and Tim Zimmerman, Colin Soloway, and Richard J. Newman, "An Iranian Foothold in the Balkans: A Wartime Alliance Becomes a Peacetime Threat; Sarajevo," *U.S. News and World Report*, 11 March 1996, pp. 39–40.

88. Christopher Lockwood, "Muslim Nations Offer Troops for 'Safe Areas'—War in Bosnia: Islamic Leaders Take First Real Steps to Support Sarajevo," *Daily Telegraph*, 14 July 1993. It took more than two years for NATO to take action while the Muslim offer was ignored.

89. "Fear of God (Muslim Troops to Police in Bosnia)," *Economist*, 17 June 1993.

90. Based on Shireen Hunter's conversations with various U.S. and European officials. Also see Robert E. Hunter, "NATO's Role in Bosnia and the New European Security Framework," *Oxford International Review* 7, no. 2 (Spring 1996): pp. 12–22.

91. Andrei Edemskii, "Russian Perspectives," in *International Perspectives on the Yugoslav Conflict*, ed. Alex Danchev and Thomas Halverson (London: Macmillan, 1996), p. 29.

92. Ibid.

93. Ibid.

94. Ibid., p. 32. Also see Mike Bowker, "The Wars in Yugoslavia: Russia and the International Community," *Europe-Asia Studies* 50, no. 7 (November 1998), p. 1248. Bowker states, "Boris El'tsin, the new Russian leader, declared his support for the concept of national self-determination and saw no reason to back the Serbs since Milosevic had backed his opponents at the time of the Moscow coup in August 1991."

95. Edemskii, "Russian Perspectives," p. 33.

96. On the dynamics of the Bosnian War, see Susan L. Woodward, *Balkan Tragedy: Chaos and Dissolution after the Cold War* (Washington, DC: Brookings Institution, 1995).

97. Paul Goble, "Dangerous Liaisons: Moscow, the Former Yugoslavia, and the West," in *The World and Yugoslavia's Wars*, ed. Richard H. Ullman (New York: Council on Foreign Relations, 1996).

98. For two different views of Russian volunteers in Bosnia, see Igor Nerkasov, "Here in Bosnia We Defend Russia," *Moscow News*, 26 February 1993; and Mark Almond, "Barbarians at the Gate; They Kill for Money, Power, or Their Perverted Idea of Patriotism. Forget Bosnia. A Sinister New Breed of Mercenary from Russia Is Threatening the Peace of Europe," *Daily Mail*, 11 February 1993. According to Nerkasov, most Russian volunteers were Cossacks.

99. Aleksandr Shalnev, "The U.S. Has Reasserted Its Leadership in the Balkan Crisis" [in Russian], *Izvestia*, 1 June 1992, in *Current Digest of the Post-Soviet Press* vol. 44, no. 22 (1 July 1992).

100. Ibid.

101. Andrei Kozyrev, "Whose Side Is Russia On in the Yugoslav Conflict?" [in Russian], *Izvestia*, 8 June 1992, in *Current Digest of the Post-Soviet Press* 44, no. 22 (1 July 1992).

102. N. Garifullina, "Who Betrays His Brothers" [in Russian], *Sovetskaya Rossiia*, 6 June 1992, in *Current Digest of the Post-Soviet Press* 44, no. 22 (1 July 1992). The Russian Unity Opposition bloc in a statement said, "We express solidarity with the fraternal people of the federal republic of Yugoslavia and once again call on the citizens of Russia and political and public organizations to use all constitutional means to bring

about the earliest possible resignation of the current leadership of the Russian Ministry of Foreign Affairs."

103. Yeltsin complained, "Why do they [the United States] have to dictate to us from across the Atlantic?" "Bosnia Talks Begin as Yeltsin Sounds Warning," Agence France-Presse, 8 September 1995.

104. See Edemskii, "Russian Perspectives," pp. 38–41.

105. Ibid.

106. Natalia Narochnitskaya, "Russian Foreign Policy at the Threshold of the Third Millennium," Pravoslavie.Ru <http://www.pravoslavie.ru/english/rusforeignpolicy.htm>.

107. Sergei Shargorodsky, "Russian Government Accuses NATO of Genocide against Bosnian Serbs," Associated Press, 12 September 1995.

108. Conversations with U.S. officials.

109. Rajiv Tiwari, "Bosnia-Herzegovina/Russia: Muslim Relations Hurt by Warped Media," Interpress Service, 16 May 1994.

110. For more on Patriarch Alexii's involvement in the policy debate on Bosnia, see "Press Conference with the Metropolitan Kirill on the Forthcoming Visit to the Former Yugoslavia by Patriarch Alexii II," Official Kremlin International News Broadcast, 13 May 1994; and Edemskii, "Russian Perspectives," p. 42.

111. Dmitry Zlodarev, "Central Russian Muslim Leader to Attend Istanbul Conference," ITAR-TASS, 4 February 1994. Other organizers were the Turkish Ministry for Islamic Affairs, the ecumenical patriarch, as reported, and the Turkish Orthodox Church.

112. Tiwari, "Bosnia-Herzegovina/Russia." For an example of anti-Muslim sentiments, see Ksenia Mialo, "Bosnian Plot" (Bosniiski Kotiol)," an excerpt of chapter 4 in *Russia and the Last Wars of the 20th Century: The History of the Fall of a Superpower* (Moscow: Russian National Foundation, 2002) <www.russiannational.fund.ru>. The author accuses Bosnian leader Alija Izetbegovic of a fascist background and Muslim fundamentalist tendencies.

113. Ibid.

114. Ibid.

115. "Relations with Russia: Bosnian Premier in Moscow Discusses Problems Facing Bosnian and Russian Muslims" [in Serbo-Croatian], Radio Bosnia-Hercegovina (Sarajevo), 2 February 1995, in *BBC Summary of World Broadcasts*, 4 February 1995.

116. Tiwari, "Bosnia-Herzegovina/Russia."

117. Ibid.

118. "UPI Focus: Yeltsin Warns of 'Extreme Measures,' " *United Press International*, 25 March 1999.

119. The Contact Group also included the United States, the United Kingdom, France, Germany, and Italy.

120. Ksenia Fokina, "Albanians Attempt to Break Off Part of Macedonia" [in Russian], *Nezavisimaya Gazeta*, 1 March 2001, in *Current Digest of the Post-Soviet Press* 53, no. 9 (28 March 2001): p. 19; Pavel Kandel, "How to Turn Kosovo into Chechnya" [in Russian], *Moskovskiye Novosti*, no. 30 (2–8 August 1998), in *Current Digest of the Post-Soviet Press* 50, no. 31 (2 September 1998): p. 16.

121. Judith Matloff, "Kosovo War Rallies Muslims in Russia," *Christian Science Monitor*, 20 May 1999.

122. "Tatarstan Calls for Fighters to Aid Kosovo Albanians," Agence France-Presse, 5 April 1999; and "Tatar Volunteers to Fight for Kosovo Albanians," Interfax *Daily News Bulletin*, 5 April 1999.

123. "Tatarstan Leader Opposes Serbia Volunteers," *Russia Today*, 8 April 1999 <http://www.RussiaToday.com/rtoday/news/05.html>.

124. Vera Postnova, "Albanians Find Allies" [in Russian], *Nezavisimaya gazeta*, 31 March 1999, in *Current Digest of the Post-Soviet Press* vol. 51, no. 13 (28 April 1999).

125. Graham H. Turbiville, Jr., "Chechens May Recruit Volunteers for Kosovo," *Special Warfare* (Professional Bulletin of the John F. Kennedy Special Warfare Center and School/Foreign Military Studies Office) 12, no. 1 (winter 1999): pp. 80–99 <http://call.army.mil/fmso/sof/issues/winter.99.h>.

126. Jen Tracy, "FSB Dubs Kosovo a Chechen Hideout," *Moscow Times*, 24 February 2000 <http://www.moscowtimes.ru/24_Feb_2000/stories/story6.html>.

127. "Russia's Muslims Upset by Plans for Yugoslav Membership of Russia-Belarus Union" [in Russian], *Nezavisimaya Gazeta*, 21 April 1999, reproduced by BBC Monitoring <http://www.monitor.bbc.co.uk>.

128. Ibid.

129. Ibid.

130. Pyotr Akopov, " 'Special Path'—Russian Foreign Policy in Jeopardy" [in Russian], *Nezavisimaya gazeta*, 15 April 1999, in *Current Digest of the Post-Soviet Press* 51, no. 15 (12 May 1999).

131. Ibid.

132. Ibid.

133. For a comparison of the Chernomyrdin-Ahtisaari plan with the Rambouillet Plan of February 1999, see Phyllis Bennis, "Differences between Ahtisaari-Chernomyrdin Agreement with Milosevic and the Rambouillet Text," June 1999 <http://www.zmag.org/crisescurevts/bennissettle.htm>.

134. Wesley Clark, *Waging Modern War: Bosnia, Kosovo, and the Future of Combat* (New York: Public Affairs, 2001).

135. Steven Erlanger, "Crisis in the Balkans: The Overview; Russians Enter Kosovo Early, but Moscow Calls It a Mistake; British Lead NATO's Vanguard," *New York Times*, 12 June 1999. Some experts believe that Yeltsin and the Ministry of Defense knew of the move, but not the Ministry of Foreign Affairs. Conversation with Janusz Bugajski, Balkan/Eastern Europe expert at the Center for Strategic and International Studies, Washington, DC).

136. Aleksandr Sabos, "Has Peace Ended with the War?" [in Russian], *Rossiiskaya gazeta*, 13 July 1999, reproduced by the Foreign Broadcast Information Service, FBIS-SOV-1999-0713 <http://wnc.fedworld.gov>.

137. Certainly the Yugoslavs felt this way, as reported in the Western press. Erlanger, "Crisis in the Balkans."

Notes to Chapter 11

1. See Bernard Lewis, "The Roots of Muslim Rage," *Atlantic Monthly*, September 1990, p. 47–60; and Samuel Huntington, *The Clash of Civilizations and the Remaking of World Order* (New York: Simon and Schuster, 1996).

2. Michael Mandelbaum, "Despite Chechnya, Leave Russia Alone," *Newsday*, 11 January 1995.

3. Jim Hoagland, "Crises Near Home," *Washington Post*, 26 October 1993.

4. Jim Hoagland, "Russia's Southern Strategy," *Washington Post*, 10 February 1994, also reprinted under the clever title "Central Asia: Stationing the Fox at the Chicken Coop," *International Herald Tribune*, 18 February 1994.

5. Anatol Lieven, "Ham-Fisted Hegemon: The Clinton Administration and Russia," *Current History* 98, no. 630 (October 1999): pp. 307–15.

6. Ibid., p. 308.

7. Fiona Hill, "West Shouldn't Back Russia's Crackdown on Islamic Terror," *Orlando Sentinel*, 7 May 2001 <www.orlandosentinel.com>.

8. Ramazan Jabarov claims that Khattab received financial assistance from the CIA and Saudi Arabia. Jabarov, "Extremists versus Traditionalists."

9. "Dvizhenie 'Taliban' " (The Taliban movement), Grani.Ru (Moscow) <http://txt.ru/ antiterror/facts/Taliban/print.html>. Another article published after the September 11 events refers to a *Wall Street Journal* article written in 1996 that allegedly stated, "The Taliban is, perhaps, the best that could have happened in Afghanistan in the past years. . . . The Taliban are not religious fanatics, at least to the degree that they would be considered dangerous." The author characterizes the United States as the Taliban's "Godfather." Vakhtang Shelia, "Kogda-to Pakistan i SShA sovmestno sozdali: 'Proekt Taliban' " [(Once upon a Time Pakistan and the United States jointly engineered the 'Taliban' project')], *Novaya gazeta*, no. 75 (15 October 2001) <http://2001 .novayagazeta.ru/nomer/2001/75n/n75n-s31.shtml>. On Pakistani and U.S. collaboration, see Andrei Klochkov and Vladimir Goryunov, "Avganskii uzel" (Afghan knot), National News Service (Moscow), 10 October 1996 <http://www.nns.ru/analytdoc/ ugroza5.html>.

10. For example, in December 1994, the German foreign minister, in an interview with the *Berliner Zeitung*, said, "The methods which the Russian government is using to try to resolve the conflict are the cause for utmost concern." Meanwhile, the U.S. State Department directly criticized Russia for the first time and urged an end to attacks on civilians. John Tarnhill, "West Criticizes Russia over Chechnya Assault," *Financial Times*, 31 December 1994.

11. "West Faces Dilemma over Chechnya," *Irish Times*, 4 January 1995.

12. Daniel Williams and Ann Devroy, "Clinton Declines Moscow Summit Invitation; U.S. Seeks to Address Several Problems before Setting Date: Issue Is on Geneva Agenda," *Washington Post*, 17 January 1995.

13. Ibid.

14. Reportedly, Grachev said, "This sleazebag Yushenko is slandering the army that gave him education and rank. This sleazebag defends the scoundrels who want to demolish the country." Sonni Efron, "Chechen War Drives Wedge between Russia, Germany; Europe: Moscow Defense Chief Unlikely to Be Invited to Munich Meeting after Criticizing Opponents of Fighting," *Los Angeles Times*, 23 January 1995.

15. Chrystia Freeland, "Western Criticism of War in Chechnya Grows More Strident," *Financial Times*, 24 January 1995.

16. Ibid.

17. Steven Erlanger, "Yeltsin to Allow a European Rights Mission in Chechnya," *New York Times*, 10 March 1995.

18. Olivia Ward, "Yeltsin Muscles In on Reluctant G-7 Members—Russian Press Crows of Country's New Role on World Stage," *Toronto Star*, 12 June 1995.

19. Ibid.

20. Martin Kosindord, "Expanding NATO, U.S. Offers Plan for Russia, Former East Bloc Allies to Join," *Newsday*, 7 September 1996.

21. "Europe Council Lets Russia In," *Toronto Star*, 26 January 1996.

22. Daniel Williams, "U.S. Strikes 'Pragmatic Stance' Towards Moscow; Shift in Policy Outlined by Christopher Reflects Concern about Russian Moves," *Washington Post*, 30 March 1995; and Mike Trickey, "West Considers the Best of the Worst," *Ottawa Citizen*, 21 January 1995.

23. Ibid.

24. Ibid.

25. Williams, "U.S. Strikes 'Pragmatic Stance' Toward Moscow."

26. "Russia Slams Estonia for Interference in Its Internal Affairs," Baltic News Service, 12 January 1995.

27. "Duma Blasts European Parliament's Resolution on Chechnya," ITAR-TASS, 27 January 1995.

28. "Tough Measures for EU from Douma President," *Euro-East*, 16 March 1995.

29. Fred Hiatt, "Moscow Warns West on Criticism over Chechnya," *Washington Post*, 13 January 1995.

30. Ibid.

31. Ibid.

32. Erlanger, "Yeltsin to Allow a European Rights Mission in Chechnya."

33. Lee Hockstader, "Yeltsin Cites West's Grasp of Russia's Chechnya War," *Washington Post*, 18 April 1996.

34. Valery Tishkov, *Understanding Violence for Post-Conflict Reconstruction in Chechnya* (Geneva: Center for Applied Studies in International Negotiations, January 2001), p. 31.

35. Quoted ibid from *Put Dzhokhara*, no. 9 (28 July–3 August 1997), p. 4.

36. Tishkov, *Understanding Violence*, p. 31.

37. Ibid. Tishkov relates that the French journalist Brice Fleutiaux, who was released from Chechen captivity in the summer of 2000, said that he "did not know Chechnya was part of Russia" when he was crossing its border from Georgia.

38. Ibid.

39. Igor Rotar, "Chechnya Looks to the West and to the East—Caucasus Investment Fund Established in London" [in Russian], *Nezavisimaya gazeta*, 20 November 1997, in *Current Digest of the Post-Soviet Press* 49, no. 47 (24 December 1997). Rotar states that Lord Alistair McAlpine, "a well-known politician and close friend of Margaret Thatcher," was also involved in setting up the fund.

40. On Maskhadov's trips abroad, see Yevgeny Krutilov, "President Maskadov's Secret Paths" [in Russian], *Segodnya*, in *Russian Press Digest* (Moscow), 24 November 1997, and Stanislav Tarasov, "Aslan Maskadov in the Role of 'Russian Envoy' " [in Russian], *Literaturnaya gazeta*, in *Russian Press Digest* (Moscow), 22 November 1997; Yefin Barba, "Maskadov Is Counting on Margaret Thatcher," *Moscow News*, 19 March 1998; and "Chechnya's Aslan Maskadov Arrives in Warsaw," ITAR-TASS, 13 October 1998.

41. "IMF Postpones Loan to Russia," *Seattle Times*, 4 December 1999. Reportedly, France and Germany insisted on holding back the loan, whereas the U.S. administration insisted on "keeping IMF loans separate on its criticism of the war." On the European Council's suspension of Russia's membership, see Margaret Coker, "European Council Suspends Russia," *Atlanta Constitution*, 7 April 2000.

42. David Ott, "Timid West Wary of Baiting the Bear." *The Scotsman*, 30 September 1999.

43. Justin Brown, "U.S. Toughens Chechnya Talk but Has Little Leverage," *Christian Science Monitor*, 28 October 1999.

44. At the end of October, U.S. secretary of state Madeleine Albright called the Russian attacks "deplorable and ominous." "Russia Rejects Criticism of Chechnya Offensive; Moscow Cites War in Kosovo, Accuses West of Hypocrisy," Associated Press, 26 October 1999. In December, U.S. deputy secretary of state Strobe Talbott, reported to be a "Russophile," accused Russia of breaking the "norms of international law" in its ruthless offensive in Chechnya. Ian Traynor, "U.S. Accuses Russia of Flouting International Law in Chechnya," *Guardian*, 24 December 1999. Meanwhile, Javier Solana, secretary general of the European Council, said that the EU "had to be prepared to go further" if political pressure did not work. Geoff Kitney, "Expect More Talk than Action from EU Leaders," *Sydney Morning Herald*, 11 December 1999.

45. Christopher Lockwood, "Yeltsin Stalks Off in Huff over Chechnya—Russian President Snubs West at OSCE Summit After Clinton Fails to Mollify Him," *Daily Telegraph*, 19 November 1999; and "Back to the Cold War? Yeltsin's Comments Are a Measure of Russia's Frustrations" (editorial), *Pittsburgh Post-Gazette*, 11 December 1999.

46. "Russia Rejects Criticism of Chechnya Offensive."

47. Jamie Walker, "Chechnya a War for Europe: Putin," *Australian*, 19 April 2000.

48. Ibid.

49. On Primakov's role in the question of United Nations inspections in Iraq, see "Russia: Primakov Urges Iraq to Give Up Idea of Moratorium on UNSCOM," ITAR-TASS, 28

January 1998, reproduced by the Foreign Broadcast Information Service, FBIS-SOV-98-028 <http://wnc.fedworld.gov>.

50. Moreover, most of the new IMF loans to Russia were designed to enable Russia to repay earlier debt.
51. Ott, "Timid West Wary of Baiting the Bear."
52. Ibid.
53. Ibid.
54. Condoleezza Rice, "Campaign 2000." *Foreign Affairs* 79, no. 1 (January/February 2000).
55. According to media reports in Russia and the West, a significant number of Chechens were discovered fighting alongside the Taliban during the anti-Taliban operations in Afghanistan. Farhan Bokhari and Andrew Jack, "Alliance Meets Match in Konduz: Foreign Fighters," *Financial Times*, 22 November 2001; and Dmitry Kirsanov, "Chechen Gunmen Fight on Taliban Side in Afghanistan," ITAR-TASS, 25 January 2002.
56. Declaring that the OSCE had failed to assess the altered situation in Chechnya, which was now "returning to normal," Russia placed new conditions on any extension of the OSCE mission's mandate in Chechnya beyond its December 2002 expiration date. The OSCE declined to accept the new conditions. Valentinas Mite, "Caucasus: OSCE Closes Chechnya Mission with Little Protest," Radio Free Europe/Radio Liberty *Weekday Magazine*, 2 January 2003.
57. Guy Chazan, "U.S. to Include Chechen Groups on List of Terror Organizations," *Wall Street Journal*, 10 February 2003; and Amy Knight, "At Last, the Connection between Chechnya and al-Qaeda," *Globe and Mail*, 10 February 2003.
58. The Clinton administration appears to have held out the possibility of international recognition if the Taliban handed over bin Laden to the United States. U.S. secretary of state Madeleine Albright indicated that the Taliban would enhance their chances of American recognition and acceptance by the United Nations if they handed over bin Laden. "The Taliban's Strategy for Recognition," *Economist*, February 6, 1999.
59. On U.S.-Russian cooperation on sanctions against the Taliban, see Barbara Crossette, "U.S. and Russia Ask Harsh Sanctions on Afghanistan," *New York Times*, 8 December 2000.
60. "Putin Voices His Support for Afghan President Rabbani Government," ITAR-TASS, 21 October 2001, reproduced by the Foreign Broadcast Information Service, FBIS-SOV-2001-1022 <http://wnc.fedworld.gov>; and "Russia Bolsters Northern Alliance," *BBC News*, 22 October 2001 <http://news.bbc.co.uk/hi/english/world/south_asia/newsid_1612000/1612898.stm>. By contrast, although U.S. secretary of state Colin Powell stated that the United States saw the Northern Alliance as an important component of its strategy against the Taliban, Washington withheld its wholehearted support from it. ("Putin Pledges More Military Aid to Northern Alliance," *Turkish Daily News*, 23 October 2001 <http://www.turkishdailynews.com/old_editions/10_23_01/for3.htm#f33>.
61. Dimitri Danilov, "Implications of the NATO Attack against Yugoslavia for European Security and Russian-Western Relations," *Mediterranean Quarterly* 10, no. 3 (summer 1999): p. 68.
62. Anatolii Torkunov, "International Relations in the Post-Kosovo Context," *International Affairs* (Moscow), no. 1 (2000).
63. Fred Kaplan, "Reactor Sale Adds to U.S.-Russian Strains: Moscow-Iran Deal Raises Worry of Atomic Weapons," *Boston Globe*, 26 February 1995.
64. "U.S. Warns It Will Cut Cooperation If Russia Sells Nuke Reactors to Iran," Agence France-Presse, 9 April 1995.
65. Igor Borisenko, "Group of U.S. Senators Demand Sanctions against Gazprom," ITAR-TASS, 10 May 1998.
66. Richard Boucher, "Iranian Nuclear Facilities: Arak and Natanz," U.S. State Department, Washington, DC, 9 May 2003 <http://www.state.gov/r/pa/prs/ps/2003/20439.htm>.
67. "Iran Admits Building Large UCF Facility in Esfahan," Iran Press Service (Teheran),

10 June 2003 <http://www.iran-press-service.com/articles_2003/Jun-2003/irran_nuclear_10603.htm>.

68. Ron Synovitz, "U.S./Russia: Rice Excepts Bush-Putin Summit to Address Iranian Nuclear Issues," RFE/RL *Weekday Magazine*, 29 May 2003 <http://www.rferl.org/nca/features>.

69. "Russian Interior Ministry Displeased with John Bolton," WPS Monitoring Agency *Media Highlights of the Day* (Moscow), 6 June 2003 <www.wps.ru:8100/chitalka/media_politic/en/last.php3>.

70. Ibid.

71. Ibid.

72. "Russia Insists it Will Send Nuclear Fuel to Iran," *Gazeta.Ru*, 6 June 2003 <http://www.gazeta.ru/2003/06/06Russiainsits.html>.

73. Ibid.

74. John Lancaster, "Iran Has Strong Links to Anti-West Terror; Charges Mount of Tehran-Backed Attacks on Pro-U.S. Arab Regimes," *Washington Post*, 1 November 1996.

75. In May 2003, French Foreign Minister Dominique de Villepin claimed that France, Germany and Russia had decided to back a U.S.-proposed resolution on lifting U.N. sanctions against Iraq, even though they "would have preferred a greater role for the United Nations in the reconstruction of Iraq and had failed to obtain a timetable for setting up a legitimate domestic administration in Iraq." "France, Germany, Russia to Back Iraq Resolution," RusNet *CIS Today* (Bilthoven, The Netherlands), 22 May 2003 <http://www.rusnet.nl/news/2003/05/22/politics04.shtml>. Also see "Russia Scorns U.S. Claims of 'Liberating' Iraq," *Gazeta.Ru*, 27 March 2003 <http://www.gazeta.ru/print/2003/03/27/Russiascorns.shtml>.

76. "An Interview with Richard Perle," Washington Profile News Service, 7 April 2003 <www.washprofile.org>.

77. Press Briefing by Ari Fleischer, The White House, Office of the Press Secretary, 24 March 2003. As Fleisher put it, in U.S.-Russian relations over Iraq "there are problems."

78. Andrea Koppel, "U.S. Protests Russian Arms Sales to Iraq," CNN.com, 23 March 2003 <http://www.cnn.com/2003/WORLD/meast/03/23/sprj.irq.russia.military.sales/>.

79. "Vershbow: U.S. Cannot Guarantee Russian Access to Iraq's Oil," Interfax *Daily News Bulletin* (Moscow), 26 March 2003.

80. "Russia's regional Leaders Opposed to Iraq War," ITAR-TASS, 20 March 2003, reproduced by the Foreign Broadcast Information Service, FBIS-SOV-2003-0320 <http://wnc.dialgue.com>; and "Chechen Leader Says Iraq War Offensive to Chechen Muslims," ITAR-TASS, 20 March 2003, reproduced by the Foreign Broadcast Information Service, FBIS-SOV-2003-0320 <http://wnc.dialgue.com>.

81. Uri Ushakov, "At a Critical Juncture," *Washington Post*, 3 April 2003 (emphasis added).

82. Vitaly Tseplyayev, "Russia and the United States: Powell to Name Price of Friendship," *Argumenty i Fakty*, 14 May 2003, reproduced by WPS Monitoring Agency (Moscow) <http://www.wps.ru:8101>.

83. "Press Availability with President Bush and President Putin," U.S. Embassy, Moscow, 1 June 2003 <http://www.usembassy.ru/meet/transcript16.htm>.

84. Sergei Rogov, director of the Institute for USA and Canada Studies, characterized the relationship as fragile because the personal relationship between Bush and Putin "was never institutionalized." According to Lilia Shevtsova, a political analyst at the Carnegie Moscow Center, "Definitely, there is no substance to the relationship." Susan Glazer, "Bush-Putin Sessions Seen Primarily as Fence-mending," *Washington Post*, 2 June 2003; "Press Availability with President Bush and President Putin."

85. Paul Eastham, "From Russia with Scorn," *Daily Mail*, 30 April 2003.

86. Christopher Adams and Andrew Jack, "Blair and Putin Put Differences behind Them," *Financial Times*, 27 June 2003.

Notes to Conclusion

1. See Graeme Gill, *The Dynamics of Democratization: Elites, Civil Society, and the Transition Process* (New York: St. Martin's Press, 2000).
2. Seymour Martin Lipset, "Some Social Requisites of Democracy, Economic Development, and Political Legitimacy," *American Political Science Review* 53, no. 1 (March 1959): pp. 69–105.

Selected Bibliography

BOOKS

Ahmad, Feroz. *The Making of Modern Turkey*. London: Routledge, 1993.

Alexander, John T. *Catherine the Great: Life and Legend*. New York: Oxford University Press, 1989.

Allensworth, Wayne. *The Russian Question: Nationalism, Modernization, and Post-Communist Russia*. Lanham, MD: Rowman and Littlefield, 1998.

Anderson, Benedict. *Imagined Communities*. Rev. ed. London: Verso, 1991.

Anderson, John. *Religion, State, and Politics in the Soviet Union and Successor States*. Cambridge and New York: Cambridge University Press, 1994.

Asadullin, F.A. *Muslim Spiritual Organizations and Unions of the Russian Federation* [in Russian]. Moscow: Russian Council of Muftis, 1999.

Ascher, Abraham. *The Revolution of 1905*. 2 vols. Stanford, CA: Stanford University Press, 1988–1992.

Ayubi, Nazih N. *Political Islam: Religion and Politics in the Arab World*. New York: Routledge, 1991.

Barkashov, Alexander. *Azbuka Russkogo Natsionalista* (The alphabet of a Russian nationalist). Moscow: RNU, 1999.

Bennigsen, Alexandre A., and Marie Broxup. *The Islamic Threat to the Soviet State*. New York: St. Martin's Press, 1983.

Bennigsen, Alexandre A., and Chantal Lemercier-Quelquejay. *Islam in the Soviet Union*. New York: Praeger, 1967.

Bennigsen, Alexandre A., and S. Enders Wimbush. *Muslim National Communism in the Soviet Union: A Revolutionary Strategy for the Colonial World*. Chicago: University of Chicago Press, 1979.

Bennigsen, Alexandre A., and S. Enders Wimbush. *Mystics and Commissars: Sufism in the Soviet Union*. Berkeley: University of California Press, 1985.

Bialer, Seweryn. *Stalin's Successors: Leadership, Stability, and Change in the Soviet Union*. New York: Cambridge University Press, 1980.

Blum, Douglas, ed. *Russia's Future: Consolidation or Disintegration?* Boulder, CO: Westview Press, 1994.

Bourdeaux, Michael. *Gorbachev, Glasnost, and the Gospel*. London: Hodder and Stoughton, 1990.

Brower, Daniel R., and Edward J. Lazzerini, eds. *Russia's Orient: Imperial Borderlands and Peoples, 1700–1917*. Bloomington: Indiana University Press, 1997.

Brown, Archie, ed. *Contemporary Russian Politics: A Reader.* Oxford: Oxford University Press, 2000.

Brown, Archie, ed. *New Thinking in Soviet Politics.* New York: St. Martin's Press, 1992.

Brown, Archie, and Lilia Shevtsova, eds. *Gorbachev, Yeltsin, and Putin: Political Leadership in Russia's Transition.* Washington, DC: Carnegie Endowment for International Peace, 2001.

Broxup, Marie Bennigsen, ed. *The North Caucasus Barrier: The Russian Advance towards the Muslim World.* New York: St. Martin's Press, 1992.

Carrère d'Encausse, Hélène. *The End of the Soviet Empire: The Triumph of The Nations.* Translated by Franklin Philip. New York: BasicBooks, 1992.

Chichagova, M.N. *Shamil na Karkaze ì v Rossi* (Shamil in Caucasus and Russia). Moscow: Adir Publishing House, 1991.

Chubarov, Alexander. *The Fragile Empire: A History of Imperial Russia.* New York: Continuum, 1999.

Clark, Wesley. *Waging Modern War: Bosnia, Kosovo, and the Future of Combat.* New York: Public Affairs, 2001.

Connor, Walker. *Ethnonationalism: The Quest for Understanding.* Princeton, NJ: Princeton University Press, 1994.

Conquest, Robert. *The Nation Killers: The Soviet Deportation of Nationalities.* London: Macmillan, 1970.

Dawisha, Adeed, ed. *Islam in Foreign Policy.* Cambridge: Cambridge University Press, 1983.

Dawisha, Karen, and Bruce Parrot, eds. *Democratic Changes and Authoritarian Reactions in Russia, Ukraine, Belarus, and Moldova.* Cambridge and New York: Cambridge University Press, 1997.

De Madariaga, Isabel. *Russia in the Age of Catherine the Great.* New Haven, CT: Yale University Press, 1981.

Denber, Rachel, ed. *The Soviet Nationality Reader: The Disintegration in Context.* Boulder, CO: Westview Press, 1992.

Dobaev, I.P. *Islamskii radikalizm v mezhdunarodnoi politike* (Islamic radicalism in international politics). Rostov-on-Don: Rostizdat, 2000.

Donaldson, Robert, and Joseph Nogee. *The Foreign Policy of Russia: Changing Systems, Enduring Interests.* Armonk, NY: M.E. Sharpe, 1998.

Dunlop, John. *The Faces of Contemporary Russian Nationalism.* Princeton, NJ: Princeton University Press, 1983.

Dunlop, John. *The Rise of Russia and the Fall of the Soviet Empire.* Princeton, NJ: Princeton University Press, 1993.

Dunlop, John. *Russia Confronts Chechnya: Roots of a Separatist Conflict.* Cambridge and New York: Cambridge University Press, 1998.

Ebel, Robert, and Rajan Menon, eds. *Energy and Conflict in Central Asia and the Caucasus.* Lanham, MD: Rowman and Littlefield, 2000.

Ehteshami, Anoushiravan, ed. *From the Gulf to Central Asia: Players in the New Great Game.* Exeter, England: University of Exeter Press, 1994.

Enayat, Hamid. *Modern Islamic Political Thought.* Austin: University of Texas Press, 1982.

Engels, Frederick. *Anti-Dühring.* Moscow: Progress Publishers, 1978.

Ermakov, Igor, and Dmitri Mikulski. *Islam in Russia and Central Asia* [in Russian]. International Lotus Foundation for the Cultures of the Orient, Lotus Book Series no. 1–1993. Moscow: Lotus Foundation/Detskaya Literatura, 1994.

Esposito, John, and John Voll. *Islam and Democracy.* New York: Oxford University Press, 1996.

Feldbrugge, F.J.M., ed. *The Constitutions of the USSR and the Union Republics: Analysis, Texts, Reports.* Germantown, MD: Sijthoff & Noordhoff, 1979.

Fischer, Louis. *The Soviets in World Affairs.* Princeton, NJ: Princeton University Press, 1951.

Fisher, Alan. *The Crimean Tatars*. Stanford, CA: Hoover Institution Press, 1978.
Fisher, Alan. *The Russian Annexation of the Crimea, 1772–1783*. Cambridge: Cambridge University Press, 1970.
Frank, Allen J. *Islamic Historiography and "Bulghar" Identity among the Tatars and Bashkirs of Russia*. Leiden: Brill Academic Publishers, 1998.
Frazer, Graham, and George Lancelle. *Absolute Zhirinovsky*. London: Penguin Books, 1999.
Freeze, Gregory L., ed. *Russia. A History*. Oxford: Oxford University Press, 1997.
Gall, Carlotta, and Thomas de Waal. *Chechnya: A Small Victorious War*. London: Pan Books, 1997.
Gammer, Moshe. *Muslim Resistance to the Tsar: Shamil and the Conquest of Chechnia and Daghestan*. London: Frank Cass, 1994.
Garnett, Sherman W., ed. *Rapprochement or Rivalry? Russia-China Relations in a Changing Asia*. Washington, DC: Carnegie Endowment for International Peace, 2000.
Geertz, Clifford. *The Interpretation of Cultures*. New York: Basic Books, 1973.
Gellner, Ernest. *Nations and Nationalism*. Oxford: Blackwell, 1990.
Gill, Graeme. *The Dynamics of Democratization: Elites, Civil Society, and the Transition Process*. New York: St. Martin's Press, 2000.
Gillard, David. *The Struggle for Asia, 1828–1914: A Study in British and Russian Imperialism*. New York: Holmes and Meier, 1977.
Ginat, Rami. *The Soviet Union and Egypt, 1945–1955*. London: Frank Cass, 1993.
Giustozzi, Antonio. *War, Politics, and Society in Afghanistan, 1978–1992*. Washington, DC: Georgetown University Press, 2000.
Glushchenko, Evgenii. *Geroi Imperii: Portrety rossiiskikh kolonial'nykh deiatelei* (A Hero of Empire: Portraits of Russian colonial functionaries). Moscow: XXI vek–Soglasie, 2001.
Gorodetsky, Gabriel, ed. *Soviet Foreign Policy, 1917–1991: A Retrospective*. London: Frank Cass, 1994.
Grachev, Andrei. *Final Days: The Inside Story of the Collapse of the Soviet Union*. Boulder, CO: Westview Press, 1995.
Gromyko, A.A., and B.N. Ponomarev, eds. *Soviet Foreign Policy, 1917–1980*. Vol. 1, *1917–1945*. Moscow: Progress Publishers, 1980.
Haghayeghi, Mehrdad. *Islam and Politics in Central Asia*. New York: St. Martin's Press, 1995.
Hakhimov, Raphael, ed. *Federalism in Russia*. Kazan: Tatarstan Academy of Sciences and Kazan Institute of Federalism, 2002.
Halperin, Charles J. *Russia and the Golden Horde: The Mongol Impact on Medieval Russian History*. Bloomington: Indiana University Press, 1985.
Halperin, Charles J. *The Tatar Yoke*. Columbus, OH: Slavica Publishers, 1986.
Hammer, Darrell. *The USSR: The Politics of Oligarchy*. 2nd ed, Boulder, CO: Westview Press, 1986.
Harle, Vilho. *The Enemy with a Thousand Faces*. Westport, CT: Praeger, 2000.
Hartog, Leo de. *Russia and the Mongol Yoke: The History of the Russian Principalities and the Golden Horde, 1221–1502*. London and New York: British Academic Press, 1996.
Henze, Paul. *Islam in the North Caucasus: The Example of Chechnya*. Santa Monica, CA: RAND, 1995.
Heper, Metin, and Raphael Israeli, eds. *Islam and Politics in the Modern Middle East*. New York: St. Martin's Press, 1984.
Hopf, Ted, ed. *Understandings of Russian Foreign Policy*. University Park: Pennsylvania State University Press, 1999.
Hosking, Geoffrey, Jonathan Aves, and Peter Duncan. *The Road to Post-Communism: Independent Political Movements in the Soviet Union, 1985–1991*. London and New York: Pinter, 1992.

Hosking, Geoffrey, and Robert Service, eds. *Russian Nationalism, Past and Present*. London: Macmillan, 1998.

Hunter, Shireen T. *Central Asia since Independence*. Westport, CT: Praeger, 1996.

Hunter, Shireen T. *The Future of Islam and the West: Clash of Civilizations or Peaceful Coexistence?* Westport, CT: Praeger, 1998.

Hunter, Shireen T. *Iran and the World: Continuity in a Revolutionary Decade*. Bloomington: Indiana University Press, 1990.

Hunter, Shireen T. *Iran, between the Gulf and the Caspian Basin: Strategic and Economic Implications*. Abu Dhabi: Emirates Center for Strategic Studies and Research, 2000.

Hunter, Shireen T. *The Transcaucasus in Transition: Nation-Building and Conflict*. Washington, DC: Center for Strategic and International Studies, 1994.

Hunter, Shireen T., ed. *Islam, Europe's Second Religion: The New Social, Cultural, and Political Landscape*. Westport, CT: Praeger, 2002.

Huntington, Samuel P. *The Clash of Civilizations and the Remaking of World Order*. New York: Simon and Schuster, 1996.

Iskhakov, S.M. *Politicheskie Deiateli Rossii, 1917: Biograficheskii Slovar'* (Political figures of Russia in 1917: Biographical dictionary). Moscow: 1993.

Islam and Muslims in Russia [in Russian]. Moscow: Russian Council of Muftis, Moscow Islamic University (College), 1999.

Ismael, Tareq Y. *The Arab Left*. Syracuse, NY: Syracuse University Press, 1976.

Ivanov, Igor S. *The New Russian Diplomacy*. Washington, DC: Nixon Center and Brookings Institution Press, 2002.

Jansen, Johannes J.G. *The Neglected Duty: The Creed of Sadat's Assassins and Islamic Resurgence in the Middle East*. New York: Macmillan, 1986.

Kaiser, Robert. *The Geography of Nationalism in Russia and the USSR*. Princeton, NJ: Princeton University Press, 1994.

Kasravi, Ahmad. *Tarikh-e-Hedjdah Saleh-e-Azerbaijan* (The eighteen-year history of Azerbaijan). Tehran: Entesharat-e-Amir Kabir, 1353 (1974).

Kechichian, Joseph A., ed. *Iran, Iraq, and the Arab Gulf States*. New York: Palgrave, 2001.

Khalid, Adeeb. *The Politics of Muslim Cultural Reform: Jadidism in Central Asia*. Berkeley: University of California Press, 1998.

Knezys, Stasys, and Romanas Sedlickas. *The War in Chechnya*. College Station: Texas A&M University Press, 1999.

Kondrashov, Sergei. *Nationalism and the Drive for Sovereignty in Tatarstan, 1988–92: Origins and Development*. New York: St. Martin's Press, 2000.

Kortunov, Sergei. *Russia's National Identity in a New Era*. Strengthening Democratic Institutions Project. Cambridge, MA: John F. Kennedy School of Government, Harvard University, 1998.

Kosikov, I.G., and L.G. Kosikova. *Severny Kavkaz: Sotsial'no-Ekonomicheskii Spravochnik* (The Northern Caucasus: A socioeconomic guide). Moscow: Mikron-Print, 1999.

Kushner, David. *The Rise of Turkish Nationalism, 1876–1908*. London: Frank Cass, 1977.

Lambeth, Benjamin S. *The Warrior Who Would Rule Russia*. Santa Monica, CA: RAND, 1996.

Landau, Jacob M. *Pan-Turkism in Turkey: A Study of Irredentism*. Hamden, CT: Archon Books, 1981.

Lapidus, Gail, ed. *The New Russia: Troubled Transformation*. Boulder, CO: Westview Press, 1995.

Laqueur, Walter. *Black Hundred*. New York: Harper Collins, 1993.

Laqueur, Walter. *Communism and Nationalism in the Middle East*. London: Routledge and Kegan Paul, 1956.

Layton, Susan. *Russian Literature and Empire: Conquest of the Caucasus from Pushkin to Tolstoy*. Cambridge: Cambridge University Press, 1994.

Leatherborrow, W.J., and D.C. Offord, eds. and trans. *A Documentary History of Russian Thought*. Ann Arbor, MI: Ardis Publishers, 1987.

LeDonne, John P. *The Russian Empire and the World, 1700–1917: The Geopolitics of Expansion and Containment*. Oxford: Oxford University Press, 1997.

Lenin, V.I. *Collected Works*. 4th English ed. Vols 10 and 33. Moscow: Progress Publishers, 1972.

Lenin, V.I. *Essential Works of Lenin: "What Is to Be Done?" and Other Writings*. Edited by Henry M. Christman. New York: Dover Publications, 1987.

Levine, Mark, and Penny Roberts, eds. *The Massacre in History*. New York: Berghahn Books, 1999.

Lieven, Anatol. *Chechnya: Tombstone of Russian Power*. New Haven, CT: Yale University Press, 1998.

Lukashevich, Stephen. *Ivan Aksakov, 1823–1886: A Study in Russian Thought and Politics*. Cambridge, MA: Harvard University Press, 1965.

Lukin, Vladimir, and Anatoly Utlin. *Rossiya i Zapad: Obshchnost' ili Otchuzhdeniye* (Russia and the West: Community or estrangement). Moscow: Sampo, 1995.

Malashenko, Alexei. *Islamic Rebirth in Contemporary Russia*. Moscow: Carnegie Moscow Center, 1998.

Malcolm, Neil, Alex Pavda, Roy Allison, and Margo Light. *Internal Factors in Russian Foreign Policy*. Oxford: Oxford University Press, 1996.

Maley, William, ed. *Fundamentalism Reborn? Afghanistan and the Taliban*. New York: New York University Press, 1998.

Mandelbaum, Michael, ed. *The New Russian Foreign Policy*. Washington, DC: Brookings Institution Press, 1998.

Marples, David. *Lenin's Revolution: Russia, 1917–1921*. Harlow, England: Longman 2000.

Marsh, Christopher. *Russia at the Polls: Voters, Elections, and Democratization*. Washington, DC: CQ Press, 2002.

Marshall, Richard H., Jr., ed. *Aspects of Religion in the Soviet Union, 1917–1967*. Chicago: University of Chicago Press, 1971.

Marx, Karl, and Frederick Engels. *Collected Works*. Vol. 3. Moscow: Progress Publishers, 1975.

Matveeva, Anna. *The North Caucasus: Russia's Fragile Borderland*. London: Royal Institute of International Affairs, 1999.

McAuley, Alastair, ed. *Soviet Federalism: Nationalism and Economic Decentralisation*. New York: St. Martin's Press, 1991.

McDaniel, Tim. *The Agony of the Russian Idea*. Princeton, NJ: Princeton University Press, 1996.

Mendelson, Sarah. *Changing Course: Ideas, Politics, and the Soviet Withdrawal from Afghanistan*. Princeton, NJ: Princeton University Press, 1998.

Mukhametshin, Rafik. *Islam v obshchestvenno-politicheskoi zhizni Tatarstana v kontse XX veka* (Islam in the sociopolitical life of Tatarstan at the end of the twentieth century). Kazan: Izdatel'stvo "Iman," 2000.

Nabiev, R.A., ed. *Islam in Tatarstan: Experience of Tolerance and Culture of Co-existence*. [in English and Russian] Culture, Religion, and Society, no. 9. Kazan: Master-line, 2002.

Neumann, Iver. *Uses of the Other: The East in European Identity Formation*. Minneapolis: University of Minnesota Press, 1999.

Nizameddin, Talal. *Russia and the Middle East*. New York: St. Martin's Press, 1999.

Northedge, F.S., ed. *The Foreign Policies of the Powers*. London: Faber and Faber, 1968.

Olcott, Martha Brill, ed. *The Soviet Multinational State: Readings and Documents*. Armonk, NY: M.E. Sharpe, 1990.

Olson, Robert. *Turkey's Relations with Iran, Syria, Israel, and Russia, 1991–2000*. Costa Mesa, CA: Mazda Publishers, 2001.

Ostrowski, Donald G. *Muscovy and the Mongols: Cross-Cultural Influences on the Steppe Frontier, 1304–1589*. Cambridge and New York: Cambridge University Press, 1998.

Pankin, Boris. *The Last Hundred Days of the Soviet Union*. London: I.B. Tauris, 1996.

Pankratova, Anna M. *Pervaia russkaia revolutsiia 1905–1907 g.g.* (The First Russian Revolution of 1905–1907). Moscow: Gosudarstvennoe Izdatel'stvo Politicheskoi Literaturi, 1951.

Park, Alexander Garland. *Bolshevism in Turkestan, 1917–1927.* New York: Columbia University Press, 1957.

Pennar, Jaan. *The USSR and the Arabs: The Ideological Dimension.* New York: Crane, Russak and Company, 1973.

Persits, Moisei. *A Shamefaced Intervention: The Soviet Intervention in Iran, 1920–21.* Moscow: Russian Center for Strategic Research and International Studies, 1999.

Pierce, Richard A. *Russian Central Asia, 1867–1917.* Berkeley: University of California Press, 1960.

Pipes, Richard. *The Formation of the Soviet Union: Communism and Nationalism, 1917–1923.* Cambridge, MA: Harvard University Press, 1997.

Piscatori, James P. *Islam in a World of Nation-States.* Cambridge: Cambridge University Press, 1986.

Ragsdale, Hugh, ed. *Imperial Russian Foreign Policy.* Cambridge: Cambridge University Press, 1993.

Rakowska-Harmstone, Teresa. *Russia and Nationalism in Central Asia: The Case of Tadzhikistan.* Baltimore: Johns Hopkins University Press, 1970.

Ramazani, R.K. *The Foreign Policy of Iran: A Developing Nation in World Affairs, 1500–1941.* Charlottesville, VA: University Press of Virginia, 1976.

Rashid, Ahmed. *Jihad: The Rise of Militant Islam in Central Asia.* New Haven, and London: Yale University Press, 2002.

Rashid, Ahmed. *Taliban: Militant Islam, Oil, and Fundamentalism in Central Asia.* New Haven, CT: Yale University Press, 2001.

Riasanovsky, Nicholas V. *A History of Russia.* 5th ed. New York: Oxford University Press, 1993.

Roberts, Geoffrey. *The Soviet Union in World Politics: Coexistence, Revolution, and Cold War, 1945–1991.* London and New York: Routledge, 1999.

Roi, Yaacov. *Islam in the Soviet Union: From the Second World War to Gorbachev.* New York: Columbia University Press, 2000.

Rorlich, Azade-Ayse. *The Volga Tatars: A Profile in National Resilience.* Stanford, CA: Hoover Institution Press, 1986.

Rosenau, James. *Linkage Politics: Essays on the Convergence of National and International Systems.* New York: Free Press, 1969.

Ross, Cameron, ed. *Regional Politics in Russia.* Manchester and New York: Manchester University Press, 2002.

Rubin, Barnett. *The Fragmentation of Afghanistan.* New Haven, CT: Yale University Press, 1995.

Rubinstein, Alvin Z. *Soviet Policy toward Turkey, Iran, and Afghanistan: The Dynamics of Influence.* New York: Praeger, 1982.

Rybakov, S.G. *Ustroistvo i nuzhdi upravlenia dukhovnimi delami musul'man Rossii* (The structure and needs of the administration of spiritual affairs of Muslims of Russia). Petrograd: 1917.

Rywkin, Michael, ed. *Russian Colonial Expansion to 1917.* London: Mansell, 1988.

Sagdeev, Roald Z., and Susan Eisenhower, eds. *Central Asia: Conflict, Resolution, and Change.* Washington, DC: Center for Political and Strategic Studies, 1995.

Said Salama, A.M. *Arab Socialism.* New York: Barnes and Noble, 1972.

Saivetz, Carol R. *The Soviet Union and the Gulf in the 1980s.* Boulder, CO: Westview Press, 1989.

Sakwa, Richard. *Russian Politics and Society.* London and New York: Routledge, 1993.

Schwarz, Solomon M. *The Russian Revolution of 1905: The Workers' Movement and the Formation of Bolshevism and Menshevism.* Chicago: University of Chicago Press, 1967.

Sedaitis, Judith, and Jim Butterfield, eds. *Perestroika from Below: Social Movements in the Soviet Union.* Boulder, CO: Westview Press, 1991.

Shlapentokh, Vladimir, Roman Levita, and Mikhail Loiberg. *From Submission to Rebellion: The Provinces versus the Center in Russia.* Boulder, CO: Westview Press, 1997.

Shlapentokh, Vladimir, Munir Sendich, and Emil Payin. *The New Russian Diaspora: Russian Minorities in the Former Soviet Republics.* Armonk, NY: M.E. Sharpe, 1994.

Silfen, Paul Harrison. *The Influence of the Mongols on Russia: A Dimensional History.* Hicksville, NY: Exposition Press, 1974.

Simmons, Ernest, ed. *Continuity and Change in Russian and Soviet Thought.* Cambridge, MA: Harvard University Press, 1955.

Simon, Gerhard. *Nationalism and Policy toward the Nationalities in the Soviet Union.* Boulder, CO: Westview Press, 1991.

Smith, Anthony D. *The Ethnic Origins of Nations.* Oxford: Basil Blackwell, 1986.

Soloviev, Sergei M. *Istoria Rossii s drevneishikh vremen* (History of Russia from the earliest times). 50 vols. Gulf Breeze, FL: Academic International Press, 1976–2000.

Solzhenitsyn, Alexander. *From under the Rubble.* New York: Bantam Books, 1975.

Solzhenitsyn, Alexander. *Rebuilding Russia.* New York: Farrar, Straus, and Giroux, 1991.

Sotsial'no-Ekonomicheskoe Polozhenie Rossii 2001 god (Socioeconomic situation in Russia in 2001). Moscow: State Committee of Russian Federation on Statistics (Goskomstat), 2001.

Spector, Ivar. *The Soviet Union and the Muslim World, 1917–1958.* Seattle: University of Washington Press, 1959.

Stavrakis, Peter J., et al., eds. *Beyond the Monolith: The Emergence of Regionalism in Post-Soviet Russia.* Washington, DC: Woodrow Wilson International Center for Scholars, 1997.

Strayer, Robert. *Why Did the Soviet Union Collapse? Understanding Historical Change.* Armonk, NY: M.E. Sharpe, 1998.

Suny, Ronald. *The Revenge of the Past: Nationalism, Revolution, and the Collapse of the Soviet Union.* Stanford, CA: Stanford University Press, 1993.

Thompson, John M. *Russia and the Soviet Union: An Historical Introduction from the Kievan State to the Present.* 3rd ed. Boulder, CO: Westview Press, 1994.

Tishkov, Valerii. *Understanding Violence for Post-Conflict Reconstruction in Chechnya.* Geneva: Center for Applied Studies in International Negotiations, January 2001.

Toprak, Binnaz. *Islam and Political Development in Turkey.* Leiden: Brill, 1981.

Trofimenko, Henry. *Russian National Interests and the Current Crisis in Russia.* Aldershot, Hampshire, England: Ashgate Publishing, 1999.

Troyanovsky, Igor, ed. *Religion in the Soviet Republics: A Guide to Christianity, Judaism, Islam, Buddhism, and Other Religions.* San Francisco, CA: HarperSanFrancisco, 1991.

Ullman, Richard H., ed. *The World and Yugoslavia's Wars.* New York: Council on Foreign Relations, 1996.

Usmanov, Lyoma. *Documents on Russo-Chechen Relations.* Washington, DC: Woodrow Wilson International Center for Scholars, 2000.

Utechin, Sergei. *Russian Political Thought.* New York: Praeger, 1963.

Vassiliev, Alexei. *Russian Policy in the Middle East: From Messianism to Pragmatism.* Reading, England: Ithaca Press, 1993.

Vernadsky, George. *The Mongols and Russia.* New Haven, CT: Yale University Press, 1953.

Vitkovskaya, Galina, and Alexei Malashenko, eds. *Lack of Acceptance in Russia.* Moscow: Carnegie Center, 1999.

Walicki, Andrzej. *A History of Russian Thought from the Enlightenment to Marxism.* Translated by Hilda Andrews-Rusiecka. Stanford, CA: Stanford University Press, 1979.

Walicki, Andrzej. *The Slavophile Controversy: History of a Conservative Utopia in Nineteenth-Century Russian Thought*. Translated by Hilda Andrews-Rusiecka. Oxford: Clarendon Press, 1975.

Walker, Edward. *No Peace, No War in the Caucasus: Secessionist Conflicts in Chechnya, Abkhazia, and Nagorno-Karabakh*. Strengthening Democratic Institutions Project. Cambridge, MA: Harvard University, 1998.

Wallander, Celeste, ed. *The Sources of Russian Foreign Policy after the Cold War*. Boulder, CO: Westview Press, 1996.

Waller, Michael, Bruno Coppieters, and Alexei Malashenko, eds. *Conflicting Loyalties and the State in Post-Soviet Russia and Eurasia*. London: Frank Cass, 1998.

Weigle, Marcia. *Russia's Liberal Project: State-Society Relations in the Transition from Communism*. University Park: Pennsylvania State University Press, 2000.

Wheeler, Brannon M. *Applying the Canon in Islam: The Authorization and Maintenance of Interpretive Reasoning in Hanafi Scholarship*. Albany: State University of New York Press, 1996.

White, Anne. *Democratization in Russia under Gorbachev, 1985–91: The Birth of a Voluntary Sector*. New York: St. Martin's Press, 1999.

White, John Kenneth, and Philip John Davies, eds. *Political Parties and the Collapse of the Old Orders*. Albany: State University of New York Press, 1998.

White, Stephen. *Russia's New Politics: The Management of a Postcommunist Society*. Cambridge: Cambridge University Press, 2000.

Wimbush, S. Enders. *Contemporary Russian Nationalist Responses to Non-Russians in the USSR*. Santa Monica, CA: RAND, 1978.

Woodward, Susan L. *Balkan Tragedy: Chaos and Dissolution after the Cold War*. Washington, DC: Brookings Institution, 1995.

Yuldashbaev, B.Kh. *Natsional'ni vopros v Bashkirii nakanune i v period Oktyabrskoi revolutsii* (The nationality question in Bashkiria on the eve of and during the October Revolution). Ufa: 1984.

Zabih, Sepehr. *The Communist Movement in Iran*. Berkeley: University of California Press, 1966.

Zelkina, Anna. *In Quest for God and Freedom: The Sufi Response to the Russian Advance in the North Caucasus*. New York: New York University Press, 2000.

Zenkovsky, Serge A. *Pan-Turkism and Islam in Russia*. Russian Research Center Studies, no. 36. Cambridge, MA: Harvard University Press, 1960.

Zhang, Yongjin, and Rouben Azizian, eds. *Ethnic Challenges beyond Borders: Chinese and Russian Perspectives of the Central Asian Conundrum*. London: Macmillan, 1998.

Zyuganov, Gennady. *Derzhava*. Moscow: Informpechat', 1994.

JOURNAL ARTICLES

Abdullaev, Nabi. "Dagestan's True Believers." *Transitions* 6, no. 3 (March 1999).

Abdullin, Yahya G. "Islam in the History of the Volga Kama Bulgars and Tatars." *Central Asian Survey* 9, no. 2 (1990).

Alexeyeva, Ludmilla. "Unrest in the Soviet Union." *Washington Quarterly* 13, no. 1 (winter 1990).

Antonenko, Oksana. "Putin's Gamble." *Survival* 43, no. 4 (winter 2001–2002).

Azimov, A. "Moscow and Delhi in a Multipolar World." *International Affairs* (Moscow) 46, no. 5 (2000).

Bennigsen, Alexandre. "Pan-Turkism and Pan-Islamism: History and Today." *Central Asian Survey* 3, no. 3 (1985).

Broxup, Marie. "The Basmachi." *Central Asian Survey* 2, no. 1 (1983).

Daley, Tad. "Afghanistan and Gorbachev's Global Foreign Policy." *Asian Survey* 29, no. 5 (May 1989).

Daulet, Shafiga. "The First All Muslim Congress of Russia, Moscow, 1–11 May 1917." *Central Asian Survey* 8, no. 1 (1989).

Dunlop, John. "Aleksandr Lebed and Russian Foreign Policy." *SAIS Review* 17, no. 1 (winter/ spring 1997).

Dunlop, John. "Russia under Putin: Reintegrating the Post-Soviet Space." *Journal of Democracy* 11, no. 3 (2000).

Fedorov, Iurii. "Interest Groups and Russia's Foreign Policy." *International Affairs* (Moscow) 44, no. 6 (1998).

Feshbach, Murray. "Russia's Population Meltdown." *Wilson Quarterly* 25, no. 1 (winter 2001).

Gibson, James L. "The Russian Dance with Democracy." *Post-Soviet Affairs* 17, no. 2 (April–June 2001).

Graney, Katherine. "Ten Years of Sovereignty in Tatarstan: End of the Beginning or Beginning of the End." *Problems of Post-Communism* 48, no. 5 (September–October 2001).

Hetmanek, Allen. "Islamic Revolution and Jihad Come to the Former Central Asia." *Central Asian Survey* 12, no. 3 (1993).

Hunter, Shireen T. "Nationalist Movements in Soviet Asia." *Current History* 89, no. 549 (October 1990).

Ikenberry, G. John. "America's Imperial Ambition." *Foreign Affairs* 81, no. 5 (September–October 2002).

Ivanov, Igor. "The New Russian Identity: Innovation and Continuity in Russian Foreign Policy." *Washington Quarterly* 24, no. 3 (summer 2001).

Kahn, Jeff. "The Parade of Sovereignties: Establishing the Vocabulary of the New Russian Federalism." *Post-Soviet Affairs* 16, no. 1 (January–March 2000).

Khakimov, Rafael. "Prospects of Federalism in Russia: A View from Tatarstan." *Security Dialogue* 27, no. 1 (1996).

Khakimov, Rafael. "Russia and Tatarstan at a Crossroad of History." *Anthropology and Archeology of Eurasia* 37, no. 1 (summer 1998).

Kisriev, Enver, and Robert Bruce Ware. "Political Stability in Dagestan: Ethnic Parity and Religious Polarization." *Problems of Post-Communism* 47, no. 2 (March/April 2000).

Kozyrev, Andrei. "The Lagging Partnership." *Foreign Affairs* 73, no. 3 (May–June 1994).

Lapidus, Gail. "Asymmetrical Federalism and State Breakdown in Russia." *Post-Soviet Affairs* 15, no. 1 (January–March 1999).

Lapidus, Gail. "Contested Sovereignty: The Tragedy of Chechnya." *International Security* 23, no. 1 (summer 1998).

Li, Jingjie. "Pillars of the Sino-Russian Partnership." *Orbis* 44, no. 4 (fall 2000).

Lieven, Anatol. "Ham-Fisted Hegemon: The Clinton Administration and Russia." *Current History* 98, no. 630 (October 1999).

Menon, Rajan. "The Strategic Convergence between Russia and China." *Survival* 39, no. 2 (summer 1997).

Mesbahi, Mohiaddin. "Russian Foreign Policy and Security in Central Asia and the Caucasus." *Central Asian Survey* 12, no. 2 (1993).

Pain, Emil. "From the First Chechen War towards the Second." *Brown Journal of World Affairs* 8, no. 1 (winter–spring 2001).

Rodman, Peter W. "The World's Resentment: Anti-Americanism as a Global Phenomenon." *National Interest*, no. 60 (summer 2000).

Rumsfeld, Donald H. "Transforming the Military." *Foreign Affairs* 81, no. 3 (May–June 2002).

Russell, John. "Mujahedeen, Mafia, Madmen: Russian Perceptions of Chechens during the

Wars in Chechnya, 1994–96 and 1999–2001." *Journal of Communist Studies and Transition Politics* 18, no. 1 (March 2002).

Shevtsova, Lilia, and Angela Stent. "America, Russia, and Europe: A Realignment." *Survival* 44, no. 4 (winter 2002–2003).

Sigor, Jury. "Why Putin Wants Russia to Become More European." *European Affairs* 2, no. 4 (fall 2001).

Splidsboel-Hansen, Fleming. "The Official Russian Concept of Contemporary Central Asian Islam: The Security Dimension." *Europe-Asia Studies* 49, no. 8 (1997).

Stepan, Alfred. "Russian Federalism in Comparative Perspective." *Post-Soviet Affairs* 16, no. 2 (April-June 2000).

Stoner-Weiss, Kathryn. "Central Weakness and Provincial Autonomy: Observations on the Devolution Process in Russia." *Post-Soviet Affairs* 15, no. 1 (January–March 1999).

Tadjbakhsh, Shahrbanou. "The Tajik Spring of 1992." *Central Asia Monitor*, no. 2 (1993).

Walker, Edward. "The Dog That Didn't Bark: Tatarstan and Asymmetrical Federalism in Russia." University of California at Berkeley, 1996.

Yemelianova, Galina. "Islam and Nation Building in Tatarstan and Dagestan of the Russian Federtion." *Nationalities Papers* 27, no. 4 (1999).

Index

7–10, 13, 23; population of, 224–25, 242, 439n.20, 484n.81

Tatarstan, 39, 56–57, 449n.56; educational infrastructure of, 452nn.137, 138; identity formation in, 198–200; Islamic education in, 71; Islamic print and news media in, 75; mosques in, 66–68; nationalist challenge in, 205, 217–20; political parties in, 273–75; power-sharing treaty and, 224–26; response of to recentralization, 235–36, 238, 241–42

Tengrism, 198–99

Ter-Petrossian, Levon, 345

territorial integrity of Russian Federation, 192–93

terrorist attacks in Russian cities, 155–56; Dubrovka Theater, 84–85, 156, 455n.182

Thompson, John, 439n.15

Tishkov, Valerii, 203, 406, 447n.15, 469–70n.110, 470n.112

Tkachev, Petr, 249

Topchibashev, Ali Mardan bey, 441–42n.76

Torkunov, Anatolii, 409–10

totalitarian states: democratic transitions of multiethnic, 421–27; vs. authoritarian states, 421–23

Trancaucasus (South Caucasus). See Caucasus

Traspov, Aleksander, 262

Trenin, Dmitri, 328, 364, 374, 528n.182

Troshin, Leonid, 115

Troyanovsky, Konstantin, 316

Trubetskoy, N.S., 169

Trubnikov, Vyacheslav, 378

True Patriots of Russia, 270–71

Tsagolov, K.M., 323

Tsymbursky, Vadim, 249

Tulskiy, Mikhail, 43, 56–57, 80, 116, 450n.78

Turkes, Alpaslan, 349, 363

Turkestan, 16, 22–23

Turkey: after September 11, 369–71; Chechen conflict and, 367–71; and EU, 371; Islam and, 364–66; post-Soviet Russian relations with, 343, 345–46, 362–71, 533–34n.87; relations with U.S., 362; rivalry with Russia and, 367–68, 522n.98; Soviet Russian relations with, 317–20, 361; strategic and economic importance of, 366–67; and

USSR's Turkish and Caucasian peoples, 362–63, 520n.60, 522n.98

Turkic neopaganism, 198–200

Turkish cultural influence, 146–48, 468n.89

Turkism, 363–64

Turkkan, Reha Oguz, 363

Turko-Muslim myth-symbol complex, 159–61

Udogov, Movladi, 153, 387, 531n.37

unemployment in Muslim regions, 98–102, 101t

Unified Command of Dagestani Mujahideen, 90, 154

uniformity and intolerance, in Russian culture, 248–49

Union of Muslim Journalists (UMJ), 76

Union of Muslims of Russia (UMR), 262–65

Union of Right Forces, 253, 255

Union Treaty (1922), 207–8, 480–81n.6

unipolar international system, 288, 409

United Arab Emirates, 386–87

United States: relations with Armenia, 354; relations with Azerbaijan, 354, 517n.185; relations with Georgia, 352–54; Russian relations with, 308–11, 351–52, 400–13. See also West, the

Unity, 254–55

universities and colleges, Islamic, 71–73

Ushurma, Sheikh Mansur, 11

utopian philosophy, 129–31; retrospective, 167–68

Uzbekistan, 335–36; historical background of, 14–15; and relations with U.S., 333–34, 341; in Tajik Civil War, 327, 329–30, 333–34

Uzzell, Lawrence, 106

Vagabov, Mikhail, 63

Vasetsky, Father Innokenty, 121

Vassiliev, Alexei, 298, 323, 366, 505n.47

Vatan (Homeland), 260–61, 276

Velayati, Ali-Akbar, 374

Velitov, Mahmud, 114–15

Vernadsky, G.V., 170

Vershbow, Alexander, 412

vertikal' vlasti (vertical of power), 229

Veshnyakov, Alexander, 263

Vladimir, Prince of Liev, 3–4

Volga-Ural Republic (Idel-Ural), 22, 24, 443n.90

Shireen Hunter is the director of the Islam Program at the Center for Strategic and International Studies, having earlier been deputy director of the Middle East Program at CSIS, and a visiting fellow at the Center for European Policy Studies, Brussels. She has written extensively on Iran, the Persian Gulf, Central Asia and the Transcaucasus, and Islamic Revivalism. Her publications include: *Islam, Europe's Second Religion* (2002), *Islam and the West: Clash of Civilizations or Peaceful Coexistance?* (1998), *Central Asia Since Independence* (1996), *The Transcaucasus in Transition: Nation Building and Conflict* (1994), *Iran and the World: Continuity in a Revolutionary Decade* (1990), and *The Politics of Islamic Revivalism: Diversity and Unity* (1988).

Jeffrey L. Thomas is currently a consultant to the Center for the Study of Presidency. Prior to that, he was a research associate with the Russia and Eurasia Program and the Islam Program at the Center for Strategic and International Studies.

Alexander Melikishvili is a research associate at the Center for Non-Proliferation Studies, Monterey Institute of International Studies, Washington DC. Prior to that, he was a research assistant with the Islam Program at the Center for Strategic and International Studies.